MAKE THE MOST OF YOUR TIME IN BRITAIN

500 GREAT BRITISH EXPERIENCES

ROUGH GUIDES

Publishing information

This first edition published May 2011 by **Rough Guides Ltd**

80 Strand, London WC2R 0RL

14 Local Shopping Centre, Panchsheel Park, New Delhi 110017, India

Distributed by the Penguin Group

Penguin Books Ltd, 80 Strand, London WC2R 0RL

Penguin Group (USA), 375 Hudson Street, NY 10014, USA

Penguin Group (Australia), 250 Camberwell Road, Camberwell, Victoria 3124, Australia

Represented in Canada by Tourmaline Editions Inc. 662 King Street West, Suite 304, Toronto, Ontario M5V 1M7

Penguin Group (NZ) 67 Apollo Drive, Mairangi Bay, Auckland 1310, New Zealand

Typeset in Serifa and Kievit to an original design by Diana Jarvis

Printed and bound by Star Standard PTE, Singapore

© Rough Guides 2011

368pp includes index

A catalogue record for this book is available from the British Library

ISBN: 978-1-84836-685-5

The publishers and writers have done their best to ensure the accuracy and currency of all the information in
Make the Most of Your Time in Britain. However, they can accept no responsibility
for any loss, injury, or inconvenience sustained by any traveller as a result of information or advice contained in the guide.

1   3   5   7   9   8   6   4   2

Credits and acknowledgements

Editor: Edward Aves **Managing editor**: Jo Kirby **Designer**: Diana Jarvis **Picture editor**: Mark Thomas
Additional editing: Alice Park, Samantha Cook
Cartography: Stuart James
Additional design input: Dan May, Scott Stickland
Proofreading: Karen Parker **Production**: Rebecca Short

Thanks to all our writers and photographers for their great ideas,
fine writing and beautiful pictures, which are credited at the back of the book.

CONTENTS

INTRODUCTION

For almost thirty years Rough Guides' writers and researchers have explored the world, producing inspirational guides to more than 200 destinations, from Australia to Mexico to Zanzibar. Our enthusiastic writers leapt at the chance to explore destinations around the world that had an excitement, novelty and vibrancy that Britain – Rough Guides' home turf – seemed to lack. In fact, let's be honest, thirty years ago the British holiday experience was often a rather dreary affair of staid B&Bs, lacklustre service, humdrum restaurants, outdated museums and early-closing days. Who wouldn't have wanted to escape to the sun? Well, what a transformation! Three decades later, we still can't guarantee the sun but we can show you just how much Britain has changed for the better. It's not just the obvious, more appealing manifestations – the cosmopolitan, rejuvenated cities, Michelin-starred restaurants, gourmet gastropubs, boutique hotels, eye-popping new architecture and all-singing, all-dancing attractions. There's been an injection of energy and innovation right across the domestic travel industry, which now offers more to inspire holiday-makers, families and foreign visitors than ever before. And in uncertain economic times, it's heartening to know that some of the very best things to do in the world are right here on our doorstep. We've chosen 500 of them, across England, Scotland and Wales, that we're convinced will help you "Make the Most of Your Time in Britain". Everyone knows the richness of British history, heritage, culture and landscape, and as you'd expect we cover many of Britain's world-class draws, from the Edinburgh Festival to Wimbledon to the British Museum. But our indefatigable Rough Guide writers have also gone behind the scenes, as it were, to turn up an amazing collection of in-the-know, off-beat or just plain wonderful British travel experiences – from singing sea shanties in Cornwall to wild-swimming in the Isle of Skye to foraging for food in the Welsh woods. It's a nation to be proud of, and with lots to be proud about – so come home with us at Rough Guides and discover the very best of Britain.

ESCAPE TO THE CITY

urban adventures

Where better to look for an urban adventure than Britain, the world's first urbanized nation? Ever since the Industrial Revolution sparked the shift from country to city, urban life has been firmly rooted in the British psyche. There's a glorious urban diversity here that few other countries can match, from a fabulous array of market towns, university cities and beautiful historic centres to the truly global capital. What's more, Britain's cities continue to innovate. Ever-changing, novelty-seeking London needs no introduction – though we've uncovered a few unexpected treats alongside the iconic big-hitters, so by all means take a tour of Parliament or the British Museum by day, but come night time lose yourself in the throbbing beats of dubstep, or root out some of the East End's quirkiest nights. However, you might also be surprised that places like Manchester, Newcastle and Glasgow have thrown off much of their old, industrial grime and emerged as classy, vibrant destinations in their own right – as much on the Euro city-break scene as Bilbao or Berlin. There are terrific museums, monuments and galleries, of course, but we also celebrate contemporary city escapes, whether it's cycle-speeding around Manchester's Velodrome, skiing in Sheffield or indulging in a weekend of hedonism Brighton-style. Even in the older historic towns and classic tourist centres there are different ways to get under Britain's skin, from tramping the two-thousand-year-old walls of Chester to unlocking the mysterious secrets of Georgian Bath and exploring Edinburgh's creepy past. The message is dig deeper – whether to find the very new, the very old, or the quirky and unusual experiences – there's a unique story in every corner of this rich, urban, national brew.

001 Come and have a go if you think you're fast enough

Got some trackie bottoms and a tenner? Then take them to Manchester and buy yourself the ride of your life. Just ten minutes from the city centre, opposite Man City's football ground, the Manchester Velodrome – or to give it its proper title, the National Cycling Centre – is the fastest and busiest velodrome in the world. Home of British Cycling, the sport's national governing body, and the entire GB cycling team, it's also open to anyone aged 9 and over who wants to have a go.

All new riders have to start with an introductory, hour-long taster session. You and up to fifteen others (but often fewer, especially midweek) are each kitted out with a bike and helmet, and then head out onto the track – a stunning, Olympic-standard loop of Siberian pine – with your own coach. After an initial spot of equipment checking, you're talked through the basics and start by wobbling along on the flat for a couple of laps. Then you're taught another set of skills and inch your way up onto the bank's lower slopes, and so on until, by the end of the (oh, too brief) sixty minutes, you might – if you're competent and confident enough – be whizzing along like the masters at an angle approaching 42.5°, more or less horizontal and utterly thrilling.

Once you've successfully completed a taster session, and the bug's bitten, you can follow a structured programme to enhance your track skills and fitness. Jason Queally, Olympic 1km champion in Sydney 2000, started his track-cycling career on a taster session here just four years earlier...so who knows where it could lead?

A tip: get there before your allotted time, and you might well catch the end of a GB team training session – you could find yourself cycling in the still-warm tracks of the likes of Sir Chris Hoy or Victoria Pendleton. Or come as a spectator for some top-level racing, and gasp as riders hurtle along the upper bank at an exhilarating 85km/hr. And for even more two-wheeled kicks, they're building a BMX centre next door.

Need to know The National Cycling Centre, Stuart St, Manchester ☎0161/223 2244 option 3, ⓦwww.nationalcyclingcentre.com. Daily 8am–10pm, excluding bank holidays. Taster sessions £9.90. From Piccadilly Gardens (stop D) take bus #216 to Sport City.

Map 3, C10

002 Melancholy beauty at Highgate Cemetery

Need to know Highgate Cemetery, Swain's Lane, London N6 ☎020/8340 1834, Ⓦwww. highgate-cemetery.org. East: March–Oct daily 10am–4.30pm, Nov–Feb till 3.30pm, £3; West: daily, guided tours only, check website for schedule, £7.
Map 1, F3

Follow the trail of goths and American tourists through North London's quaintest village to Highgate Cemetery East, a grand Victorian burial ground of lovingly tended graves, fresh flowers and clipped shrubs. Nip off the main path, however, to encounter something far less civilized: overgrown wooded tracks, thick with blackberry bushes and thorny wild roses, where ivy-tangled tombstones seem to grow from the earth. Thick roots thrust entire casings upwards, while rusty iron railings crumble into the damp soil. The names of those who lie beneath may not be legible, but here are endless simple eulogies to long-lost lives – babies and octogenarians; Londoners felled by war or illness or old age; the couple who after 41 years are reunited in death, "Old Pals Forever".

The cemetery's once exclusive western side is even more overgrown; strange to think that these towering ash and sycamore trees didn't exist when the place was built in 1839. Once a grand private enterprise, selling its manicured lawns and sweeping city views to London's finest, Highgate Cemetery West is being tidied to resemble more closely its original state. Trees are being lopped and paths cut through the undergrowth – but it remains a magical, wild place, and gloomily beautiful still. The otherwordly light reveals eroded tombstones, brittle as bone, scratched with the ghostly scrawl of long-gone creepers. Toppled columns have smashed neighbouring gravestones; a marble angel's lonely arm lies beside a melancholy mound of rotting crab apples.

This being Highgate, there are countless freethinkers buried here – artists, eccentrics, revolutionaries – and several oddities among the familiar Celtic crosses and Victorian draped urns. On one unmarked grave a distraught Sisyphus pushes his colossal stone; another, belonging to Thomas Sayers, Cockney pugilist and publican, is guarded by a likeness of his hulking dog. Seek out the big-hitters on the East side, of whom there are many: Karl Marx, naturally, his lumpen colossus topped with that familiarly hirsute visage; George Eliot, marked by an obelisk and surrounded by deceased friends and fans. Malcolm McLaren's gravestone is poignant in its rawness, "Malcolm Was Here" freshly carved on a rough wooden slab. Perhaps most startling, however, is Patrick Caulfield's stark, self-designed stone, spelling out the simple truth: D-E-A-D.

003 Out on the Toon

Need to know For Newcastle listings see Ⓦwww. thecrackmagazine.com, or for individual venues check: The Black Swan Ⓦwww.newcastle-arts-centre.co.uk; Trillians Rock Bar ☎0191/232 1619; and The Cluny Ⓦwww.thecluny.com.
Map 4, E15

It's time to banish the cliché: no longer is Newcastle's nightlife solely about indecently cheap drinks, indecently short skirts and indecent behaviour. Of course, if you're into that malarkey, there's still plenty of it – the city is a perennial location for riotous stag and hen parties – but there are alternative scenes to enjoy, from supping local ales in traditional boozers to shaking your hips at a salsa class, and from raucous punk rock gigs to elegant cocktail bars.

Newcastle being where it is – eight miles from the wind-whipped North Sea – means that most of the time it's a pretty chilly place. Best spend the evening by a crackling fire in a snug pub: pick of the bunch is the Crown Posada at 31 The Side, a diminutive Victorian inn, all etched glass and wood panelling. Local and loyal, the crowd knocks back guest ales from nearby breweries like Wylam near Hadrian's Wall. Another great pub is The Free Trade at St Lawrence Road, a gloriously shabby, spit-and-sawdust place with a magnificent beergarden overlooking the river. A smarter nightlife scene is also on the rise: Popolo, at 82–84 Pilgrim St, is a fun American diner-themed cocktail bar with killer mojitos, while cute wine bar, Vineyard, at 1 Grey St, is a lovely spot for a glass of wine, and Toyko at 17 Westgate Rd, with its chic roof terrace, is a stylish pre-club warm-up.

Newcastle is a honeypot for live music lovers – not just at the enormous spaces like the Metro Radio Arena and the Sage, but at more intimate locations, too. The little cellar bar The Black Swan, at the Newcastle Arts Centre, doles out folk, jazz and salsa music, while rock and punk fans should head straight for Trillians Rock Bar at Princess Square. The city's best live music venue, though, is The Cluny, nestled in the heart of the burgeoning Ouseburn Valley at 36 Lime St; gigs change nightly, showcasing anything from fledgling indie bands to rock'n'roll. That said, if all you want is a bottle of Blue WKD and a boogie to S Club 7, you're certainly in the right city.

004 Getting high in Portsmouth

Portsmouth harbour is something of a geographical marvel, a shipping motorway protected by the lobster claws of Portsea on one side and Gosport on the other. You can only really appreciate this layout, however, by rising up to the heights of the Spinnaker Tower, the UK's most beautiful viewing platform.

A sleek white structure with a steel ribbed sail that indeed resembles a billowing spinnaker, the tower rises to nearly 560ft above Gunwharf Quays. Only the top of the ribs is accessible in the form of three viewing decks.

Visitors are led into a lift, and within seconds of the doors closing (28, to be precise) – virtually before the guide has explained what's happening – you've arrived at Deck 1, unaware you've moved at all. Despite being the lowest of the three levels, this is surely the most impressive: a glass space giving awesome views across all of Portsmouth one way and over the ferries, tankers and naval ships towards the Isle of Wight to the other. But just when you think the views can't get better, you realize that a large proportion of the deck's floor is made of glass.

At this point, sufferers of vertigo should look away. The glass floor – Europe's largest – offers a vertical drop, straight down to the tourists in the plaza far below, who from this height resemble matchstick Lowry figures. Children – and the odd foolish adult – seem compelled to lie face down on the two-inch-thick glass, as if daring it to give way.

Deck 3 offers a different thrill. The top viewing point, known as The Crow's Nest, is open to the elements. Go on a windy day to really appreciate this, and be reassured by the wire mesh roof, designed to keep visitors firmly anchored.

The middle deck is where you can get your breath back, with various multimedia stations explaining how the tower fits in with the history of the harbour, the cradle of Britain's naval fleet. In 1545, Henry VIII watched aghast from the top of Southsea Castle as his flagship, the *Mary Rose*, sank in the harbour while engaging French forces. If only the Spinnaker Tower had been around then, he would have had a far better view. As it is, you can now look down at the new Mary Rose Museum, lying in wait at the nearby Historic Dockyard.

Need to know
Spinnaker Tower, Gunwharf Quays, Portsmouth, Hampshire ☎023/9285 7520, Ⓦ www.spinnakertower.co.uk. Daily: Sept–July 10am–6pm; Aug Sun–Thurs 10am–7pm, Fri & Sat 10am–6pm. £7.25.
Map 2, D6

A weird and wonderful trip around THE EAST END

Long associated with beloved fictional matriarchs Pat Butcher and Peggy Mitchell, today London's East End is well and truly on the visitors' map. But instead of flocking with the Ripper-tour herds to Spitalfields and Brick Lane, you might prefer to visit a few alternative haunts. These five take in a Victorian childhood, a miniature farm, candlelit drinks in a nineteenth-century Turkish bathhouse, retro clubbing and a highly unusual hostelry.

005 The Ragged School Museum

Go back to school Victorian-style with an interactive lesson in one of philanthropist Dr Barnardo's Ragged School classrooms. Thousands of poverty-stricken East End children were schooled and fed here between 1877 and 1908, and exhibits, a dressing-up case, writing slates and a rather severe Victorian schoolmistress help to put it all in context.

46–50 Copperfield Rd E3 Ⓦ *www.raggedschoolmuseum.org.uk. Museum only Wed & Thurs 10am–5pm, museum & interactive class 1st Sun of month 2–5pm. Free. Map 1, F4*

006 Hackney City Farm

Set back from the decidedly non-rural Hackney Road, with its uninspiring residential sprawl and handbag wholesalers of dubious quality, is a charming little enclave giving off a strong whiff of the countryside. It's free to wander around this tiny farm and visit the goats, rabbits, chickens, chinchillas and possibly the biggest pigs you'll ever see. It also has a decent café where you can feast on bacon sandwiches safely out of sight of the pig pen.

1a Goldsmiths Row E2 Ⓦ *www.hackneycityfarm.co.uk. Tues–Sun & bank hols 10am–4.30pm. Free. Map 1, F1*

007 The Bathhouse

Wander back through the Spitalfields crowds to the more corporate surrounds of Liverpool Street for a rather more elegant stopoff: a sumptuous subterranean bar-restaurant and cabaret space in a renovated Victorian bathhouse. Gleaming tiles, classy cocktails, flickering candle flames, a grand piano and birdcage decorations all add up to a romantic, quirky place to drink and dine.

7–8 Bishopsgate Churchyard EC2 Ⓦ *www.thebathhouseavenue.com. Bar & restaurant Tues–Sat. Map 1, E2*

008 Bethnal Green Working Men's Club

For the ultimate oddball night out, there's no finer choice than one of the throwback soirées at this working men's club. Fifties prom nights, sleazy Sixties discos replete with go-go dancing demoiselles and madcap retro circus-themed bashes are among the delights in store. Dressing up is a serious affair – think "your Mum way back when" rather than "fancy dress".

42–44 Pollard Row E2 Ⓦ *www.workersplaytime.net. Events most evenings, entry price varies. Map 1, F2*

009 40 Winks

And so to bed, and where better to hole up than the supremely eccentric *40 Winks*, incongruously sited in a Stepney townhouse. With just two offbeat, indulgently appointed guest rooms, it's a small affair with bags of style; each space in the house has been interpreted inch by inch by the resident interior designer, and there's a magical little garden out back.

109 Mile End Rd E1 Ⓦ *www.40winks.org. Single £90, double £130. Map 1, F2*

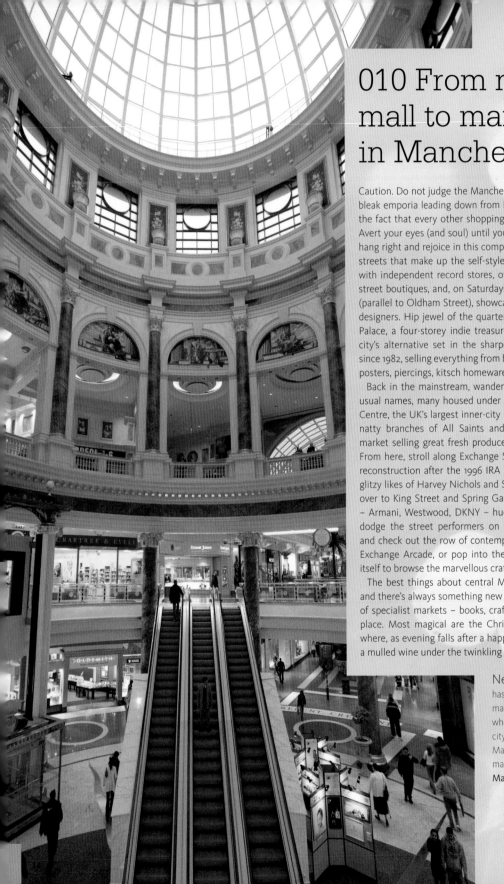

010 From mega-mall to market stall in Manchester

Caution. Do not judge the Manchester shopping experience by the bleak emporia leading down from Piccadilly train station, nor from the fact that every other shopping bag seems to be from Primark. Avert your eyes (and soul) until you reach Oldham Street and then hang right and rejoice in this compact, quirky retail scene. The few streets that make up the self-styled Northern Quarter are packed with independent record stores, off-kilter Oxfam shops, retro and street boutiques, and, on Saturdays, the Tib Street Fashion Market (parallel to Oldham Street), showcase for the region's funkiest new designers. Hip jewel of the quarter's crown is the mighty Affleck's Palace, a four-storey indie treasure-trove that's been keeping the city's alternative set in the sharpest vintage and street clothing since 1982, selling everything from bowler hats to bovver boots, plus posters, piercings, kitsch homewares and more.

Back in the mainstream, wander along Market Street for all the usual names, many housed under the sizeable roof of the Arndale Centre, the UK's largest inner-city mall, with 240 outlets, including natty branches of All Saints and Urban Outfitters, and a food market selling great fresh produce and a range of world cuisines. From here, stroll along Exchange Square, created during the city's reconstruction after the 1996 IRA bombing, and now home to the glitzy likes of Harvey Nichols and Selfridges. For proper posh, head over to King Street and Spring Gardens, where the biggest names – Armani, Westwood, DKNY – huddle in a snooty clique. Nearby, dodge the street performers on pedestrianized St Ann's Square and check out the row of contemporary jewellers inside the Royal Exchange Arcade, or pop into the buzzy Royal Exchange Theatre itself to browse the marvellous craft shop.

The best things about central Manchester are that it's walkable and there's always something new to see, with a changing calendar of specialist markets – books, crafts, jewellery, food – all over the place. Most magical are the Christmas markets (from mid-Nov), where, as evening falls after a happy day's shopping, you can enjoy a mulled wine under the twinkling lights of this magnificent city.

Need to know Manchester has three main train stations, the main one being Piccadilly, from where it's a short walk into the city centre. For information on Manchester's markets visit Ⓦ www.manchestermarkets.com.
Map 3, C10

011 Birmingham beats Venice?
Cycling the Black Country's canals

Venice may be famous for its canals, but Birmingham has more – though no one should stretch the comparisons too far. There are no fewer than eight canals and 32 miles of waterway within Birmingham's boundaries and together they weave a complicated pattern through the city and connect it with the neighbouring towns of the Black Country.

Birmingham's canals have a long and intriguing history. Until the arrival of the railways in the nineteenth century, almost all heavy goods were transported by water. The railways made the canals uneconomic, but they struggled on until the 1970s when tourism gave them a new lease of life; today herds of brightly painted narrowboats nose and nudge their way across them and hundreds of cyclists pedal along the old canal towpaths.

Of all the area's cycle routes, the Birmingham and Black Country Cycleway is the most enjoyable. A fifteen-and-a-half-mile route that follows the Birmingham Canal Main Line, it starts at Gas Street Basin at the heart of Birmingham – an attractive junction of waterways surrounded by an immaculately restored medley of red-brick buildings – and ends in Wolverhampton. The cycleway stays close to the Birmingham–Wolverhampton rail line, so if the rain comes down you can hop on the train at any one of half-a-dozen stations.

The Birmingham Canal Main Line was designed by Thomas Telford in the 1820s to replace longer, more convoluted waterways. The new canal was a great success, though the imposing industrial landscape was not to everyone's liking – Queen Victoria is said to have drawn the curtains of her railway carriage when she passed this way in the 1840s.

The cycleway uses the old (but upgraded) canal towpath as it threads its way through cuttings and embankments, tunnels and locks, warehouses and old factories. For the most part, the going is easy, but the tunnels need some care, especially the longest, the dark and dank Coseley Tunnel. Up above are dozens of bridges, the most impressive of which is Thomas Telford's mighty Galton Bridge of 1829, once the world's longest single-span, cast-iron bridge over what was at the time the world's largest man-made excavation.

Need to know The Birmingham and Black Country Cycleway begins at the Gas Street Basin, a 10min walk from New Street train station, and ends in the centre of Wolverhampton, a short walk from the train station. You need to obtain a free cycle permit from British Waterways from ⓦ www.waterscape.com/things-to-do/cycling/permit. Map 3, C11

012 On the piste in the steel city

You don't have to be posh to go on the piste in Sheffield. Its dry ski slope, high above the city, is like Sheffield itself – untidy yet vital. You drive up a steep potholed road and park next to what looks like a working men's club. If it's not a busy time, it can seem forlorn. Out of season it's positively depressing. But get up there when the students or ski clubs are doing their stuff, or even better at weekends when there are kids' parties, wedding celebrations, local families, even groups of youths necking Dutch courage at the bar, and the place positively thrums.

Not everybody is there for the skiing – there's an eight-lane bowling alley, indoor and outdoor play areas for kids and quad biking. But it's the skiing, snowboarding and tobogganing that hit the spot. The artificial slopes – they're stained and down-at-heel like most you'll come across – are thronged with people sweeping down the gigantic main incline, throwing themselves around on the snowboarding run (padded, thank God but watch those youngsters go), hurtling down the toboggan run, or taking their lurching first slithers on the nursery slope. Hear the shouts of the kids, the oil-slick hum of the lift machinery.

And then there's the view. The city lies below, like a Lego blanket thrown over the Pennine foothills, with its slowly turning city-centre Ferris wheel, its tower blocks and steelworks, its church tower, with the Peak District's patchwork fields beyond. Not Alps, not snow, not beautiful, but...interesting.

This is Sheffield, not Chamonix, honest industry not village lodges and alpine scenery, pints not *demi-pression*, happy hour not après-ski. Forget the serenity of the mountains – this is loud, noisy, working-class fun for all the family. But just in case you miss the point, climb to the top of the main slope, look down its majestic sinuous sweep against the city far below, and, if you've got the skill and the bottle (and the skis), swoop down its wide undulating, frightening, exhilarating plunge.

Need to know Sheffield Ski Village, 4 Vale Rd, Sheffield ⓣ 0114/276 0044, ⓦ www.sheffieldskivillage.co.uk. Hours vary for different attractions. £14.80/hr, up to £31.40/day. Map 3, D10

013 All change: London's docklands

Take a trip out east from central London on the Docklands Light Railway (DLR) – high over the interesting borderland between the City of London and the east - to a city of enormous forms, vast symmetries and rapid change. Every few months a whole new crop of buildings appears with minimum fuss, usefully filling an awkward space. First stop is Canary Wharf, the most mature of all the Docklands developments, a place given over to the generation of wealth like nowhere else – it's a lot of fun to wander around and enjoy the feeling of being in a place where the superficial effect is everything.

Next, continue your journey on the DLR to Pontoon Dock on the Woolwich Arsenal branch, where a very pleasant and imaginative park has been built alongside the river – right next to the Thames Barrier, London's defence against its mighty river and a fascinating structure in its own right. Alight again and return to Canning Town, changing to the Beckton branch for Custom House or Royal Victoria stations and the highlight of the whole area: the Royal Docks. The scale of these docks is awe-inspiring. Nowhere else in the city is there a feeling of such tremendous space: vistas that stretch to the vanishing point like an illustration in a manual of technical drawing.

If you have more time, keep walking further east to the Royal Albert Dock, where you can watch the planes landing on a narrow strip with water on either side at London City Airport. Further east again, at Cyprus DLR, you can stand at the eastern end of the docks and look west towards Canary Wharf and the rest of London – there's a real edge-of-the-world feeling in this particular spot.

Come back west via Canada Water on the Jubilee Line (changing at Canary Wharf) and take a stroll along the river's south bank, again with superb Thames views. Near the *Mayflower* pub in Rotherhithe (117 Rotherhithe St), there's a charming statue of a pilgrim staring in wonder at a newspaper that shows him what will happen in America in the centuries to come. He could express as much amazement about the future of the place he's leaving: a stretch of London's historic riverside that continues to change with astonishing speed.

Need to know DLR trains run every 5–10min; standard London underground fares apply. See Ⓦ www.tfl.gov.uk.
Map 1, F4

014 From Arthur's Seat to Sheep Heid Inn

New York has Central Park; London wouldn't be London without the Serpentine and Speakers' Corner; but no city save Edinburgh sits cheek-by-jowl with an urban wilderness quite like Arthur's Seat. An ice-age relic ringed by an asphalt moat, this cluster of green slopes and sheer rock has served as the city's lungs since the days when belching chimneys earned the place its smoky sobriquet, Auld Reekie.

With the smog clouds long dispersed, views from the basalt eyries of Salisbury Crags, on the massif's eastern flank, are intoxicating, arcing across the New Town's genteel cobbles and across the Forth estuary to Fife. Shorten the angle of your gaze, if you dare, and the architectural incongruity of the Scottish Parliament just across the road hoves into view; shorten it further and you risk inducing vertigo. Not for nothing are there crimson-trimmed triangles warning of falling rocks, while, further up the crag's dizzying crescent, helmeted climbers limber up for something scarier.

The 820ft crest of Arthur's Seat itself is easier on the inner ear, though the 360-degree panoramas are just as breathtaking. The climate is gentler and crowds thinner – often non-existent – down in the lee of the peak, at the bottom of glorious, glacier-scoured slopes lined by young trees and ravishingly scented gorse; sit on the right stone at the right angle, and not a trace of Edinburgh's skyline is visible: the ultimate urban escape.

From here it's an easy meander over the lower flanks of the volcano's tail and down a stone stairway to Duddingston village, a venerable enclave guarded by a twelfth-century church and home to Scotland's oldest pub, the *Sheep Heid Inn*. It certainly feels antiquated, its atmosphere thickened by fraying tomes, a roaring fire and the knowledge of those who've drunk here before, regulars like James VI and Mary Queen of Scots, not to mention Bonnie Prince Charlie. None of them, alas, can have enjoyed a post-hike pint quite as satisfying as a *Sheep Heid* Guinness.

Need to know Holyrood Park, Edinburgh ☎ 0131/652 8150, Ⓦ www.historic-scotland.gov.uk. Parking available. Road closed Sun 8.30am–6pm. Maps and leaflets available from Holyrood Lodge Information Centre, next to Scottish Parliament (daily 9.30am–3pm). The *Sheep Heid Inn*, 43–45 The Causeway, Duddingston ☎ 0131/661 7974, Ⓦ www. sheepheid.co.uk.
Map 4, D14

015 Punting on the Cam

The experienced professional punter – propelling boatloads of tourists along Cambridge's River Cam – speaks of the simple sensory pleasure in the interaction of the firm riverbed, the massive punting pole (wielded with a masterful delicacy) and the punt itself, pushing against the springy upthrust of the gentle waters. In fact, it is like driving a people carrier with a joystick from a seat where the luggage would usually go.

Your punt will naturally be attracted to other punts, blocking the river under the sarcastic gaze of the city's youth, who stop to watch your ineptitude from one of the many pretty bridges. Your response should be to affect an ironic detachment; something achieved more easily when you console yourself with the idea that perhaps punting was never meant to be done well. The point is to drift with languorous unconcern, admiring the beautiful college gardens and architecture, while disguising incompetence as abstraction and reverie.

This slow river is lined with some of the grandest architecture in the country. You recline almost at the water's level as the great buildings rear around you in a succession of noble set pieces. Perhaps the two most notable sights are the chapel at King's College, a structure of forbidding single-minded authority, and Christopher Wren's library for Trinity College, which has the same rigorous perfection that some may find refreshing (others overwhelming).

When you're done punting, the colleges are wonderful places to explore, if they'll let you in; the rules of access vary from college to college and season to season, although you can always behave as if you have a perfect right to walk wherever you like and see what happens.

Need to know Punts can be rented from stations at Mill Lane and Magdalene Bridge, and at other points in the city centre; it costs around £18/hr (for a punt for six), chauffeured punts are around £12/hr per person, £50 minimum. Map 3, E12

016 Perfect pleasures: a hedonistic weekend in Brighton

Just as the Sixties generation didn't really invent sex, Brighton didn't really invent the dirty weekend. But this fun-loving city never tires of claiming it did. It all started with George, the lascivious Prince Regent: at the turn of the nineteenth century, he and his outré entourage couldn't get enough of the place. It was quite a switch for a former fishing village whose early popularity was based on health-giving attractions such as sea-bathing and natural cures made of bugs in brine.

Brighton has always had its ups and downs, but ever since it gained city status in 2000, it's been riding high. With a nip here and a tuck there, it has transformed itself into a haven of seaside cool – sophisticated but with masses of the kooky, rebellious spirit that's always been its trademark – and its busy shops, pubs, clubs and boutique B&Bs lure thousands of visitors every weekend.

Dive into The Lanes, the maze of quirky shopping streets immediately northwest of the pier, and let the indulgence begin. Muscle your way past the doe-eyed couples sighing over engagement rings in the jewellery shop windows and you can browse bespoke shoes, vintage vinyl and the sauciest of silk kimonos in one-of-a-kind boutiques. Chocoholics beware: Duke Street, on the west side of The Lanes, offers a feast of temptations including gorgeous, locally made truffles from Montezuma's and ludicrously extravagant creations from Choccywoccydoodah.

Come the evening, you'll want to whirl you way around a few cocktail bars or ancient, low-beamed pubs – in the centre, try *Merkaba* for a futuristic feel, or *The Basketmakers Arms* for something old-school, with excellent ale – before making your mark on clubland, at an indie gig, a comedy show, a throbbing techno club or a wild night of burlesque cabaret and daring dressing-up. The latest hot ticket is the *Brighton Ballroom* in Kemptown, but things change fast in this fashion-mad city, so keep your eyes and ears open.

You're never going to make it to breakfast the next morning, so opt for brunch in the North Laine instead. *Bill's* sets the benchmark for huge plates of super-fresh deli-style food in a warehouse-style space, but *Farm*, with its beautifully selective menu of locally sourced produce, is a fine contender, too.

The perfect pad? There are plenty to choose from, but for sensory overload you can't beat *Hotel Pelirocco*, whose high-kitsch rooms include a Play Suite with a huge ceiling mirror and a pole for you to try out your raunchiest dance routines.

Need to know *Merkaba*, 17 Jubilee St ☎01273/900300, Ⓦwww.merkababrighton.com; *The Basketmakers Arms*, 39 Cheltenham Place ☎01273/689006, Ⓦwww.thebasketmakersarms.co.uk; *Brighton Ballroom* ☎01273/605789, Ⓦwww.brightonballroom.com; *Bill's*, 100 North Rd ☎01273/692894, Ⓦwww.billsproducestore.co.uk; *Farm*, 99 North Rd ☎01273/623143, Ⓦwww.farmsussex.co.uk. *Hotel Pelirocco*, 10 Regency Square ☎01273/327055, Ⓦwww.hotelpelirocco.co.uk; doubles start at £115. Map 2, E6

017 Jingle them bells: Lincoln's Christmas market

Need to know Lincoln Christmas Market, first weekend in Dec: Thurs 4–9.30pm; Fri & Sat 10am–9.30pm; Sun 10am–7pm. Tourist information ☎ 01522/545458, Ⓦ www.visitlincolnshire.com. There's no parking near the Christmas Market; park-and-ride is at Lincolnshire Showground just off the A15 north of Lincoln.
Map 3, D10

For four days in early December a quarter of a million visitors descend on the handsome cathedral city of Lincoln to enjoy its famous Christmas Market. From modest beginnings as a German-style traditional market with just eleven stalls, this festive market has expanded to three hundred stalls, selling just about everything seasonal you can think of – and then some. There are stalls selling photographs, paintings and ceramics, jewellery and hand-blown glass, candles and handmade wooden toys, with many of the most distinctive items coming from Germany and Scandinavia. Nor is there any lack of things to eat and drink: chestnuts roast on charcoal fires, mulled wine steams in giant vats and whopping German sausages turn golden brown. In the background, carol singers, dressed in Victorian costume, entertain the crowd, as does the brass band. And then there's the Ferris wheel, the largest of several fairground rides. Father Christmas gets in the act too, venturing out from the North Pole to sit himself by the fire in the Judge's Lodgings along with his merry band of elves, but without his reindeer, who – as everyone knows – have to rest up in early December.

The setting for the market is hard to beat, its fairy-lit stalls clambering up the steep cobbled lanes that connect the newer part of Lincoln with the older part up above. Here, at the top of the hill, the severe, stone walls of Lincoln Castle are on one side, the cathedral, one of England's most beautiful churches, is on the other. Pop inside the church to peek at the town's mascot, the Lincoln Imp, a finely carved little chap attached to a column in the Angel Choir. No one took much notice of him until the 1880s when a local jeweller, James Ward Usher, devised a legend and then, with real entrepreneurial flair, sold the trinkets to match. Usher's tale had a couple of imps hopping around the cathedral, until one of them is turned to stone for trying to talk to the angels carved into the roof of the Angel Choir. His chum made a hasty exit on the back of a witch, but the wind is still supposed to haunt the cathedral awaiting their return.

018 Let the deva take you to Chester

People flock to Chester from throughout the northwest for serious retail therapy, for the glitz of Browns department store and the *Grosvenor Hotel*, the *grande dame* of luxury in these parts. But beyond these genteel modern attractions you can also discover some seriously impressive history dating back to Chester's foundation as the Roman fortress of Deva Victrix. From the amphitheatre to its Tudor-fronted pubs and the ancient River Dee, Chester has mastered the art of nurturing its glorious past.

The Roman city walls are in remarkably good condition – two miles of walkways, peppered with turrets, towers and gateways that take no more than an hour to wander. From the western stretch, there's an exceptional view of the Roodee – the oldest horse-racing venue in the country. But whatever you do, don't be fooled by locals who tell you that it's legal to shoot a Welshman with a bow and arrow from the walls on a Sunday – this arcane bylaw was finally repealed in the 1970s.

A later addition to Chester's cityscape is the Rows, a unique second storey of arcades on all four of the main shopping streets, which were first constructed sometime after a thirteenth-century fire devastated the city. A few of the galleries you see today are Tudor, though many are highly convincing Victorian reproductions. Either way, while chain stores predominate on ground level, a walk up the steep steps to the Rows brings you a fine array of one-off, family-run stores selling everything from antique jewellery to gourmet coffee beans. Be sure to check out Lowe & Sons, the silversmiths, and the Scented Garden spa, both on the Rows above Bridge Street – both bespoke gems, one ancient, one contemporary.

The city's Roman amphitheatre is reputed to be the largest in the country, and is the closest Chester gets to a theatre. Only half of it has been excavated, though there's more than enough uncovered to get a sense of what it must have been like during one of the cockfights, military drills or gladiatorial combats that took place here in the first century. There's nothing nearly so bloodthirsty here now, though occasional outdoor summer concerts make sure that, far from being neglected, Chester keeps the incredible legacy of its past very much alive. Just be sure to put away that bow and arrow before you arrive.

Need to know The stores and cafés on Chester's Rows keep normal shopping hours. The city walls and Roman amphitheatre are free and open 24 hours a day.
Map 3, B10

019 Burrow deep into Liverpool's underground kingdom

Liverpool may be known as a city of quite exceptional stature when it comes to enterprise, its heyday of construction producing such grand edifices as the Albert Dock and the Liver Building, but for one of the city's lesser-known attractions – and the most peculiar enterprise of all – you need to look far below.

The Williamson Tunnels, located deep under the ground in the Edge Hill suburbs, are not only a work of quite remarkable folly they're also an incredible mystery. To this day nobody knows what tobacco merchant Joseph Williamson had in mind when he ordered this labyrinth of underground tunnels to be built in the early 1800s.

Some say that Williamson wanted to build an underground shrine to his wife, others that he feared the end of the world was nigh and wished to survive the apocalypse deep underground. Yet another theory is that it was a surreal gesture to soldiers returning from the Napoleonic Wars, a work creation scheme on a huge scale. It's all conjecture, however, and visitors are left simply marvelling at how such a vast project was created on one man's whim.

Though the building work was described in local papers at the time, mainly as a nuisance that interfered with the sewage and drainage systems, the tunnels slowly dropped off the radar and were regarded as an urban myth for many years.

It's only recently that parts of this bizarre network of corridors, some barely wide enough to walk through, others leading out into huge banqueting halls, have been opened to visitors. The tunnels are dry, creepy and full of random artefacts such as huge collections of crockery dating from the 1830s. Look out too for graffiti dating from the 1960s, the work of illicit adventurers who would have been lowered down by rope.

Perhaps the most extraordinary thing about this bizarre experiment is that there are believed to be many more tunnels, which haven't yet been unearthed, and that two hundred years on, we're no closer to understanding Williamson's strange underground kingdom, and his motives behind it.

Need to know Williamson Tunnels, 15–17 Chatham Place, Edge Hill, Liverpool ☎ 0151/475 9833, Ⓦ www.williamsontunntels. com. Thurs–Sun 10am–5pm. £4.
Map 3, B10

020 On the Front Bench: take a tour of the Houses of Parliament

Need to know Houses of Parliament, London SW1. Tours last 75 minutes and run throughout August (Mon, Tues & Fri 9.15am–4.30pm, Wed & Thurs 1.15–4.30pm), and on most Saturdays throughout the year. Tickets can be bought at Ⓦ www.ticketmaster.com or see Ⓦ www.parliament.uk.
Map 1, D4

It's so small. That's what most people say when they enter the chamber of the House of Commons. It's as if the heart of the British parliamentary system and the cradle of modern democracy should be epic in scale. In fact, it isn't even big enough to hold all the UK's 650 Members of Parliament.

The chamber is grand, however, and on tour days it resonates with hushed importance. The ribbed, green-leather benches – which you're strictly told must never be sat upon – step up from the green-carpeted floor. The two sides of the house are divided by thick red lines that, it's said, are two swords' length apart. Above, ornamented wooden galleries rise steeply towards a faux-medieval roof. The chamber of the House of Lords, just down the hall, is more sumptuous still, with its red, buttoned-leather benches and utterly resplendent gold throne, which is used by the Queen on the one day in the year when she's allowed in: for the State opening.

You can visit these twin chambers, at the Victorian heart of the Palace of Westminster, on Parliament's summer tours. For Joe or Jo Public, who knows that he or she will never be elected as an MP (or, indeed elevated to the Lords), there's a satisfying sense of getting at something that's usually off-limits. That feeling gets even more intense when you're shown the Queen's gorgeously neo-Gothic robing room, or the Division Lobbies, either side of the Commons chamber, where MPs line up before getting their vote counted. The walls are lined with bound copies of the parliamentary archives, with an old phone directory lurking haphazardly in a corner, some bills and posters announcing committee activities on notice boards, and a sign in old-fashioned script announcing "All demonstrations by strangers in the gallery are out of order".

You never get to climb Big Ben, unfortunately, but the tour has one surprise at the end: the huge, medieval Westminster Hall. Its astonishing, lofty timber roof has presided over everything from coronation banquets to the trials of Guy Fawkes and Charles I and, while the Hall isn't now used for anything of real governmental importance, it is breathtakingly, humblingly vast.

021 Behind Oxford's walls

Oxford has some truly grand vistas: the college-lined curve of The High; the generous piazza of Broad Street, overlooked by the Bodleian Library and the classic student pub, the *King's Arms*; the tree-lined avenues leading across the grassy flats of Christchurch Meadow to the river.

Oxford's finest moments, however, need seeking out. The dome of its centrepiece library, the honey-coloured Radcliffe Camera, rises out of a plaza that is virtually walled in by forbiddingly machicolated ranks of colleges and libraries. Approaching from the west, and college-crowded Turl Street, you squeeze down Brasenose Lane between the ranks of student bicycles. From the north, it's best to approach via the gargoyle-watched gates of the Sheldonian Theatre, then duck through the passageways and hushed courtyard of the Bodleian Library. From The High (as Oxonians call the High Street), the most atmospheric route is via the winding, palpably medieval Queen's Lane, passing between high, blank walls, then under the so-called Bridge of Sighs.

Magdalen College is best known for its magnificent chapel (where the professional-standard choir sings evensong, daily), but its treasures are the deer park and water meadows – and to get to them you have to bypass the chapel, traverse the hushed Cloister and cross a small stream. The confusingly ancient New College (which has another superb choir), hides its arcaded medieval cloisters at the end of a passage leading off Front Quad – and to get there, you have to pass through the disconcertingly fortress-like New College Lane Gate.

Even the best pubs are hidden away, in Oxford. *The Turf*, with its courtyard gardens and absurdly low-ceilinged bars, is buried in a warren of backstreets behind New College's ancient tower. *The Bear*, a cosily ancient pocket pub, lurks at the end of Alfred Street, among the cobbled lanes that surround Oriel College. And the *White Horse*, though bang in the middle of Broad Street, is so tiny that you could be forgiven for missing it altogether.

Need to know New College (daily; Easter to early Oct 11am–5pm; winter 2–4pm; £2); Magdalen (daily; July–Sept noon–7pm, Oct–June 1pm to dusk; £4.50); Choral evensong is sung on weekdays at 6.15pm (New) and 6pm (Magdalen).
Map 2, D5

Retreat from the bustle:
FIVE CITY INDULGENCES

022 Tea at The Langham

Afternoon tea at a posh old London hotel can be like slipping back a good three generations. With English food, this is not necessarily wise, but at *The Langham*'s Palm Court, nostalgia plays with the contemporary. So tiny bite-sized sandwiches of coronation chicken jostle on a plate with duck egg and mustard cress, and scones vie with zingy mini-morsels of, say, orange carrot cake with violet frosting. The teas are adventurous, too: oolongs and Cornish blends. Ensconced under the high ceiling as the piano noodles discreetly, you could lose happy hours.

The Langham, 1c Portland Place, London W1 Ⓦ www.palm-court.co.uk. From 2pm. Map 1, C2

023 A close shave at Trumper's

The attraction of a barber-shop shave is not cut-throat-razor scraping, it's the experience. At the elegant Trumper's of Mayfair, you take your seat at a private, wood-panelled booth. Your face is massaged with sandalwood-scented "skin food" then wrapped in sumptuously hot towels, perfumed with spicy bay rum. The shave is courteous, attentive and deft – and you'll learn from it. The "shaving school" sessions are popular with the young gentlemen, they say.

Geo. F. Trumper, 9 Curzon St, London W1 Ⓦ www.trumpers.com. Map 1, C3

024 Harrogate's Turkish baths

Spas are everywhere now. What you won't find on your high street, however, is the grandeur of Harrogate's Turkish baths. The combination of bright, Moorish-style decor and restored Victorian detailing is beguiling, and the palatial scale of the place – there are three grades of hot room as well as a steam room – is breathtaking.

Parliament St, Harrogate, North Yorkshire Ⓦ www.harrogate.gov.uk/ turkishbaths. Map 3, C9

025 Watsu at Thermae Bath Spa

At Bath, you feel tradition almost bubbling up through the cobbles. The Thermae Spa at the city's honeyed heart may be in a splendid Georgian building, but it's also slick and sleek, with glass-cylinder steam rooms and a daring rooftop pool. The most exciting experience, however, is surely the signature "Watsu" treatment. You're taken alone into a private, octagonal pool in a classical courtyard where, in the warm, dripping silence, a therapist cradles you in her arms, pulling you gently this way and that, letting the warm water itself unpick and untwist every muscle in your body. If you can handle the intimacy, this is the sort of intense treatment you'll dream about for years to come.

6–8 Hot Bath St, Bath Ⓦ www.thermaebathspa.com. Map 2, C5

026 The perfect Martini at Dukes

You may never get to drive an Aston Martin, or enjoy a dalliance with a beautiful Russian spy, but one sure-fire way to indulge in a little James Bond fantasy is to savour one of the exquisite Martinis at *Dukes Bar*, a regular haunt of Ian Fleming and said to be his inspiration for 007's favourite tipple. The Vesper (Crown Jewel gin, Potocki vodka, Angostura bitters) was Fleming's Martini of choice, but this elegant hotel bar, located in a discreet corner of St James's, offers a wide selection, including the fiery Tiger Tanaka: for genuine action heroes only.

Dukes Hotel, St James's Place, London SW1 Ⓦ www.campbellgrayhotels. com. Map 1, C3

027 Dancing to dubstep in London

Every Thursday night, dubstep devotees make the pilgrimage to East London club *Plastic People* for a night of dark, distorted bass – channelled through a soundsystem big enough to make your ribcage rattle. FWD>>, running since 2001, has played a pivotal role in dubstep's ascendancy from the urban music underground to the remix genre of choice for hip-hop stars such as Snoop Dogg and Eve. But in the small, barely lit basement of *Plastic People*, the glitz of mainstream hip-hop is nowhere in sight; the room is steeped in reverberating sub-bass as silhouetted figures dance through the darkness, surrounding the MCs in full-flow on stage.

A Croydon born-and-bred fusion of UK garage, jungle and dub, over the past decade dubstep has emerged from its South London roots to become a familiar sound at club nights from Berlin to New York. Yet there's still no night quite like the capital's FWD>> for showcasing both new and established talent. Big names such as Skream and Kode9 appeared here early on and continue to feature on impressive line-ups alongside dubstep icons like Benga and Plastician. Inside the music takes hold: the crowd are passionate, whether they're listening to genre-defining anthems like Benga and Coki's *Night* or new white labels being played for the first time. In the silence before the bass drops the tension is electric.

Alongside FWD>>, the DMZ night hosted every other month by seminal collective Digital Mystikz at *Mass*, a converted church in Brixton, is one of the most atmospheric places to surrender to some body-shaking beats. It regularly provides a platform for new DJs and MCs, though DMZ's long queues are legendary.

Its popularity bolstered by pirate radio, a Mercury Prize nomination for artist Burial's superbly sparse, haunting album *Untrue* in 2007, mainstream chart success and a dynamic club scene, dubstep's star continues to rise – and there's no better place to encounter its raw, moody energy than at the London club nights which shaped the genre.

Need to know FWD>> runs every Thursday night 9.30pm–2am at *Plastic People*, 147–149 Curtain Rd, London EC2 (£7; ⓦwww.ilovefwd.com). For DMZ see ⓦwww.dmzuk.com.
Map 1, E2

028 A different sort of museum: the Imperial War Museum North

Plenty of museums teach you things, but not many museums make you feel something. At the Imperial War Museum in Manchester there are no dusty weapon displays, no dioramas of glorious battles with toy soldiers, no bullet-ridden flags and no regimental histories.

What makes this museum really different is the Big Picture. There's no need to look for the theatre – the whole museum becomes one. Every hour, the museum galleries are transformed by a series of audiovisual shows, hypnotic presentations that explore the impact of war on people and society. As the lights dim in the main exhibition hall, everyone shuffles to a halt while images begin to splash over the tanks and guns, the walls, floors and even the ceiling, and voices boom out of the darkness. The images and stories, told by real people, are often very moving. This is not a history of great battles, victorious generals and grand armies. You'll hear soldiers, civilians and observers talk about war as it is, as they experienced it. Their testimonies are personal, harrowing and disturbing. Some visitors are merely impressed, some are shocked and some even weep, but everyone speaks a little more softly afterwards.

Of the three presentations (they rotate through the day), *Weapons of War* is the most detailed, showing not just how weapons have been manufactured over the last hundred years or so, but how they were used – how their victims experienced and feared them, the part you never hear about on the news. The *War at Home* focuses on the homefront in World War II, the story of how the British public kept going despite the threat of bombs, rations and terrible loss. Finally, and perhaps the most poignant of all, is *Children and War*, which explores the experience of children in Britain and Germany during World War II, contrasting that with experiences of war up to the present day. You don't need a degree in history to appreciate any of this – just an open mind.

Need to know Imperial War Museum North, The Quays, Trafford Wharf Rd, Trafford Park, Manchester ℡ 0161/836 4000, Ⓦ north.iwm.org.uk. Daily: March–Oct 10am–6pm; Nov–Feb 10am–5pm. Free.
Map 3, C10

IMPERIAL WAR MUSEUM NORTH

029 Unearth Auld Reekie's dark side

"Who indeed that has once seen Edinburgh," wrote Charlotte Brontë, "but must see it again in dreams waking or sleeping?" And, perhaps, in nightmares too, for Edinburgh – although forever associated with the rationality of the sciences, philosophy and medicine – is also steeped in the supernatural.

This duality is expressed most famously in *The Strange Case of Dr Jekyll and Mr Hyde* by Robert Louis Stevenson. One of his inspirations was Deacon Brodie, who lived in Edinburgh during the seventeenth century, spending his days as a respectable businessman and his nights as a thief and murderer.

The tale of Deacon Brodie is told on the many night-time walking tours of Edinburgh that explore the city's dark side. These ghost tours take place in the atmospheric Old Town, which is filled with dramatic Reformation-era architecture, cobbled streets, forbidding buildings, churches and graveyards. The charismatic and theatrical guides tell the tales of Auld Reekie's murderers, plague victims, witches and ghouls, as well as the city's nineteenth-century bodysnatchers, who would steal the corpses of the recently departed and sell them to local medical schools.

These tours have their fair share of scares, but if you are after a truly terrifying experience head to the Edinburgh Vaults. Situated beneath an arch of the South Bridge, this labyrinth of eighteenth-century tunnels originally housed taverns, tradesmen and – reportedly – the victims of notorious Edinburgh serial killers Burke and Hare. As conditions declined, the businesses were replaced by the city's poorest citizens, before the atrocious surroundings forced even them to depart.

These dark, dank and often claustrophobic vaults are now the site of overnight "vigils" where intrepid visitors are led by guides equipped with "ghost-hunting equipment" in search of paranormal activity. Frequently they find what they are looking for: small children have been sighted; people have reported being grabbed; strange smells, lights and sounds have appeared; and torches and cameras have suddenly failed.

Before you head into the vaults, however, one piece of advice: be sure to take a good look at your guide – an apparition named "The Watcher" has been spotted on several occasions and has been mistaken for a guide by some unfortunate visitors.

Need to know Mercat Tours is one of several companies that run daily ghost tours (℡ 0131/225 5445, Ⓦ www.mercattours. com; 1–2hr; £8–12/person). Edinburgh Vaults vigils are run every few months by Ghost Events (℡ 01236/615300, Ⓦ www. ghostevents.co.uk; £55 for a midnight–6am visit).
Map 4, D14

030 Finding Enlightenment at the British Museum

With its three full miles of objects produced by the world's greatest civilizations, the British Museum is nothing if not daunting. And from the ancient unknowability of a 13,000-year-old carved mammoth tusk to the dazzling modern lines of Lord Foster's Great Court, it can on occasion be, well, just a little too much.

Thank goodness, then, for the Enlightenment Room, where, as the library of George III, the British Museum began its days. With its warm parquet flooring and elegant Neoclassical lines, this reassuringly old-fashioned – and gratifyingly quiet – space has an immediately soothing effect. Themed displays offer a whistlestop tour through not only the museum's collection, but also the impulses that led to the collection; the lofty ideals of the great age of Enlightenment, with its compulsion to acquire, classify and understand the world. There are no towering Egyptian gods or perfectly hewn Assyrian reliefs here, no colossal Greek statues peering down at you through the centuries. Instead you can browse themed cabinets of curiosities and treasures, following either a reasoned enquiry, aided (very Enlightenment-style) by succinct captions or your own magpie instincts. Between high glass cases lined with wonderful old tomes – from Burnes' *Travels into Bokhara* to Boswell's *Account of Corsica* – you can see a hummingbird's nest found during one of Captain Cook's voyages, fossils once believed to be the devil's toenails, and compounds of ground mummies' fingers, used by Sir Hans Sloane, the physician-collector who founded the museum, to treat bruises. You'll also find a distressed-looking "merman" (in fact a withered monkey's head sewn onto a fish tail), Mesopotamian clay bricks inscribed for the Babylonian king Nebuchadnezzar II and an exquisite Roman mosaic of writhing sea life. You can peruse a shopping list, written on limestone, from Thebes (1100 BC) and read ancient Egyptian poetry complete with the scribe's editorial corrections. You can even touch a copy of the Rosetta Stone, which is a surprising thrill.

Taken back to seeing as those early collectors did, with fresh and curious eyes, you are restored, ready to battle through the crowds in the other, better-known rooms of the museum. Better still, you might even find yourself ready to discover the world, and the endless scope of human achievement, anew.

Need to know The Enlightenment Room is on the ground floor, just off the Great Court. The British Museum, Great Russell St, London WC1 🌐 www.britishmuseum.org. Daily 10am–5.30pm. Free.
Map 1, D2

031 From old-school glitz to techno blitz in Glasgow's club scene

Widely recognized as one of the UK's most vibrant and rascally centres for clubbing, Glasgow offers an eclectic mix of venues and vibes for the discerning clubber. Glasvegas might be a long-established, wryly affectionate nickname for this dirty old town but on a somewhat nondescript stretch of the Clyde, the gloriously retro Vegas truly swings. Since establishing itself in 2000, the increasingly sporadic club night alternates between several venues in Glasgow and Edinburgh but truly comes into its own as a riverside Sin City when hosted at the *Ferry*, two levels of gambling and dancing encased inside the boat's glass atrium. With an eclectic array of tunes spun by the sharply attired DJ trio of Frankie Sumatra, Dino Martini and Bugsy Siegel, the playlist incorporates everything from Fifties and Sixties pop, soul, funk, dancefloor jazz and Latin to occasional country and western standards, with special emphasis on classic film and TV themes, swing and Rat Pack favourites.

If you prefer your nights out not quite so glamorously kitsch, maybe Numbers is for you. Run by a collective of DJs, designers and promoters, it attracts an informed techno crowd and invariably boasts a roster of eye-catching guests. One of Glasgow's most versatile spaces is *The Arches*, a series of vaulted halls beneath the city's Central Station that hosts five big regular nights, including Pressure, a full-on house and techno blitz, and Death Disco, which drapes itself in the Day-Glo stylistic interpretation of disco while fixing its sound firmly in contemporary electro. Resident Hushpuppy also moonlights on the decks at R-P-Z, where live performers join the scampish blend of "digital disco, hi-nrg punk rhythms and junk rock attitude" catering to a predominantly studenty crowd.

Then for the city's indie kids there's Spitfire, once held at the Royal Air Force Association club in Glasgow's West End, now housed in the *Merchant City*, and a haven for those who enjoy a broad smorgasbord of punk, pop, Motown and various electronica.

And if all this choice renders you hopelessly indecisive, once a month Point 4 at the *Soundhaus* hosts any four of Glasgow's most popular club nights in three of its spaces over the course of a single night.

Need to know Vegas, *The Ferry*, 25 Anderston Quay, varied dates and venues 🌐 www.vegasscotland.co.uk; Numbers, first Fri of month, *Sub Club*, 22 Jamaica St ☎ 0141/248 4600; Pressure, last Fri of month, *The Arches*, 253 Argyle St ☎ 0141/565 1000; Death Disco, third Sat of month, *The Arches*; R-P-Z, last Sat of month, *Stereo*, 20–28 Renfield Lane ☎ 0141/222 2254; Spitfire, second Fri of month, *Blackfriars Basement*, 36 Bell St ☎ 0141/552 5924; Point 4, third Fri of the month, *Soundhaus*, 47 Hydepark St ☎ 0141/221 4659.
Map 4, C14

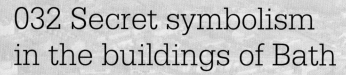

032 Secret symbolism in the buildings of Bath

Blanketed in soft, honey-coloured stone, Bath is one of the most beautiful cities in England. But it was never always thus. Its transformation from a seasonal resort of just two thousand people in 1700 was thanks largely to the work of two architects: John Wood the Elder, a Freemason whose set-piece designs are studded with symbology and built using the geometric rules of pagan Britons; and his son, John Wood the Younger.

The Circus, considered by many to be Wood the Elder's finest work, forms a tight perimeter of magnificent townhouses at the top of Bath. Taking the shape of a circle, an ancient sacred symbol – Wood wrote that "the works of the Divine Architect tend to a circular form"– it has a much smaller inner ring, where trees now grow; a circle with a central dot is historically associated with sun worship. More intriguing, however, is that the diameter of the Circus is exactly the same (316ft) as the diameter of the stone circles both at Stonehenge and at nearby Stanton Drew.

Draw three lines connecting the three points of entry into the Circus and you get a triangle within a circle – for Freemasons, the representation of the Trinity in Eternity. Masonic symbology, however, is far more evident in the buildings' details themselves. The spectacular carved frieze that runs around the entire length of the Circus is decorated with over five hundred emblems: look out for compasses (a feature of the Freemason's shield), the moon and sun (classic Masonic images when given faces, as they are here) and "circular" snakes – known as Ouroboros, the snake devouring its own tail represents eternity and is found on numerous Masonic seals.

If the Circus is the sun, then you need only walk a few hundred metres to find the moon, Wood the Younger's Royal Crescent, a grand arc just to the west, and the earth, Queen Square, south along Gay Street, designed by his father. Queen Square's sides measure 316ft (again, just like Stonehenge), and at its centre stands an obelisk, another Freemason favourite. But the most striking symbology of all is invisible at ground level – when viewed from the air the Circus, Queens Square and Gay Street form the shape of a key, a Masonic symbol indicating knowledge that should be kept secret. The question is: what was their secret?

Need to know Queen Square, the Circus and the Royal Crescent are in Bath's Upper Town; you can get a bird's-eye view of their layout from the replica model at the Building of Bath Collection, on the Paragon (℡ 01225/333895, Ⓦ www. bath-preservation-trust.org. uk; Easter–Nov Mon, Sat & Sun 10.30am–5pm; £4).
Map 2, C5

TO THE MANOR BORN

houses, castles and gardens

There's a British obsession with the concept of home that's hard to explain to visitors, and harder still to explain to ourselves. We cherish our privacy, pull up the drawbridges, pour our personalities into our houses and lovingly tend our gardens – and then for pleasure like nothing better than to poke around someone else's house and garden, great or small, with gasps of delight or tuts of disapproval depending on our view and mood. The castle, the stately home, the country house, the botanic garden, all form an integral part of the tourist experience and in no other country in the world is there such a rich, well-cared-for domestic fabric that has endured for centuries. Partly, it's to do with that very British embrace of tradition and continuity. After all, castles from central Scotland to southern England and the Welsh borders were also once simply homes, cared for by generations of (admittedly wealthy) families. The same instinct explains the survival – indeed, the thriving – of glorious country houses like Chatsworth. However, there's also an ongoing fascination in seeing how the other half lives that drives much of the house-and-garden industry, whether it's marvelling at the theatrical opulence of a royal palace or – at the other extreme – imagining life in a Victorian back-to-back. In between castle and cottage are idiosyncratic townhouses, ruined abbeys, curious follies and quirky country manors that all have something to say about British domestic life, past and present, though it's perhaps out in the garden that the national character finds its most eloquent expression. There's sobriety in the manicured grounds and formal gardens of stately homes, pride in extensive national botanic collections, jollity in highly personal private gardens and sheer British invention in stand-alone attractions like Cornwall's pioneering Eden Project. Not all these living and leisure spaces are National Trust properties (though a great many are under the care of that charitable body), but there is a wider sense that the British house and home – handsomely preserved and protected – is always held in the national trust.

033 Through the keyhole at Dennis Severs' House

When sitting idly at home, do you ever try to picture who has lived there before you? Dennis Severs did. In fact, his imagination gripped him so powerfully that, when he bought a run-down eighteenth-century house on a narrow, cobbled street in London's East End, he re-created a living image of its Georgian and Victorian pasts, furnished and ornamented in meticulous period detail, and filled it with a cast of fictional characters. He then opened it to guests, inviting them to partake in a unique theatrical experience.

Stepping across the threshold of 18 Folgate St is like passing through a picture-frame into a painting. As your eye readjusts to the candlelit gloom, your nostrils to the burning tallow, and you move through the shadows across the hall's creaking floorboards, it becomes obvious that this is no museum. A dark-clad, slightly sinister gentleman introduces "the game" that's about to unfold: the house's owners, the Jervises, a family of Huguenot master silk-weavers, have departed suddenly, moments before your arrival. You're about to be immersed in their world.

As you explore, the spaces – both temporal and mental – between you and your surroundings seem to dissipate. In the kitchen, a teacake browns in front of the crackling fire; lulled by the warmth, the house cat curls contentedly on a chair. In the parlour the rich aroma of bubbling gravy fills the air, and a half-eaten pomegranate and almost-drained glass of claret sit abandoned on the table; did you interrupt Mr Jervis's meal? In another room, a Hogarthian tableau – the aftermath of a drinking party – is re-created: the punch bowl is empty, chairs are overturned, tobacco strewn across the table. You're rather sorry you missed it.

Wandering in mesmerized silence, you'll feel as though you're taking part in a story – of which Dennis himself, though long dead, is the narrator. Playful, cryptic notes, artfully left on sideboards and mantelpieces, encourage you to take part in this "adventure of the imagination". And as imagination takes over, you become as much a part of this otherworldly house as the Jervises themselves.

Need to know Dennis Severs' House, 18 Folgate St, London E1 ☎ 020/7247 4013, ⊛ dennissevershouse.co.uk. Sun noon–4pm, £8; Mon following the 1st and 3rd Sun of the month noon–2pm, £5. Book ahead for the Monday evening "Silent Night" (6–9pm, £12; plus additional dates over Christmas, £15). A drink in the *Water Poet* opposite makes for a suitably Gothic add-on to a visit. Map 1, E2

034 A glimpse of Eden

Whichever way you consider it, the Eden Project is extraordinary. For one, it's an amazing sight – its golf-ball-like conservatories seemingly submerged in the earth, a flash of postmodernism in the Cornish countryside. Second, its construction was unthinkable – built in a 197ft-deep disused clay pit, it required 1.8 million tonnes of debris to be shifted and 83,000 tonnes of soil to be created out of mineral waste from the mines. And its aims, to showcase the richness of the world's natural environments and educate visitors in the properties of plants and how to live more sustainably, has been a runaway success.

The stars of the show are the two indoor "biomes" – the geodesic domes in which the climates of the Mediterranean and rainforest are re-created. The former is scattered with olive, citrus, fig and peach trees, lending the air a rich flavour of the South; Californian and Cape species get a look in too. In the rainforest biome, automated misters keep the daytime humidity at 60 percent; a tumbling cascade powered by recycled water adds to the effect. It's interesting to see acai and rubber trees up close, but equally fascinating to learn about the many uses tropical species can be put to. Did you know, for example, that pineapples are used to make cloth and cashews to make brake pads? All the more sobering, then, to discover that an area of rainforest equal in size to the dome is destroyed every ten seconds.

As well as the biomes, the Eden Project also has an education and arts hub called The Core – with films, school workshops and exhibitions on the importance of plants – and a stage that hosts theatre, comedy and live music. The Eden Sessions, a series of one-day music festivals, pulls in big names from Martha Wainwright to Mika. Eden really does have something for everyone – and its mission, to make us more respectful of our environment, is an increasingly critical one for everyone to grasp.

Need to know The Eden Project, Bodelva, St Austell, Cornwall ℡ 01726/811911, Ⓦ www.edenproject.com. Daily: March–Oct 10am–6pm; Nov–Feb 10am–4.30pm. £17.50, £4 discount if you arrive by foot or bike.
Map 2, A7

035 Aberglasney Gardens: paradise found

Aberglasney's horticultural curators describe it as "a garden lost in time". It's a romantic image for a site that is part stately mansion, part archeological dig. But the truth is not quite as tragic as the phrase suggests: while much has been lost, much has been found, too.

Once a grand Carmarthenshire estate, Aberglasney fell on hard times during the twentieth century and by the mid-1990s the house was totally derelict: its windows empty sockets, its masonry crumbling and its gardens choked with weeds.

Just when it seemed doomed to collapse, a Restoration Trust stepped in, led by a team of experts who were determined to patch up the damage and perhaps reveal some of the glories of the past. The gardens were the main focus of their interest: they were known to date back well over 500 years, making them a perfect candidate for research. Their hunch has already paid off: little by little they have made some astonishing discoveries.

One of the earliest revelations was a real breakthrough. Carefully, the team excavated the stone-walled cloisters immediately west of the mansion, digging down through the centuries to discover a formal garden dating back to late Tudor or early Stuart times. Even more astonishingly, coins dating back to 1288 were found among the debris.

Now that a re-creation of the early seventeenth-century layout is in place, you can wander the raised stone path that tops the cloister walls to admire its geometric lawns and think yourself back to the grandeur of the era. In spring and autumn, the grass is "enamelled" with flowering bulbs, a splash of colour that, at the time, would have seemed extremely exotic – and a sure-fire way to impress the most distinguished of visitors.

On the south side of the house is another superb development: the ruined masonry of an ancient courtyard has been shrouded in glass, creating a subtropical hothouse. Named the Ninfarium after the glorious Italian gardens of Ninfa, there's a Zen-like calm to its shady, orderly pathways. Healthy palms reach high into the atrium, sheltering cycads, magnolias and orchids, their petals as delicate as a cloud of butterflies.

Need to know Aberglasney Gardens, Llangathen, Carmarthenshire ℡ 01558/668998, Ⓦ www.aberglasney.org. Daily: April–Sept 10am–6pm; Oct–March 10.30am–4pm. £7.
Map 2, B5

036 Peacocks and a parterre at Drummond Castle Gardens

The long beech-enclosed drive that leads to Drummond Castle has a sense of drama, but gives no inkling of the exotic vision ahead. The castle itself is a bluff medieval keep surrounded by turreted domestic buildings, all heavily restored in the nineteenth century. You pass through a courtyard to access a wide stone terrace, and the garden is suddenly revealed: a symmetrical and stately Italianate vision in the shape of Scotland's flag, a St Andrew's Cross. The lines of the cross are punctuated by urns and Classical statues, and at their centre is a seventeenth-century obelisk sundial. It's an artful garden in every sense: steep steps lead down to the sundial, and beyond the topiary and the neat flower beds a wide avenue cuts though dense woodland, continuing the line of the parterre's central path but making a visual connection between the formal garden and wider, wilder estate.

Although the garden conjures visions of an old French chateau or an Italian palazzo, in its current form it's a relatively modern creation: the ornamental garden and the terracing were designed by Lewis Kennedy in the early nineteenth century. But the origins of the garden are much older – the first Lord Drummond began building the castle in the late fifteenth century, and in 1508 there is evidence that the estate supplied cherries to James IV when he was on a hunting trip. The sundial created by Charles I's master mason was put in place in 1630; in the following century the family was more preoccupied with assisting the Jacobite uprising than pruning the roses, but in calmer times in 1842 Queen Victoria planted two copper beeches here, and enjoyed walks in the garden with Albert. It remains in feel very much a courtly garden. The paths seem tailor-made for stately strolling, giving you the space and time to admire the marble statuary, snooty peacocks and neatly clipped foliage. And when you've explored the parterre, don't miss the abundant blooms in the glasshouses, and the impressive kitchen garden.

Need to know Drummond Castle Gardens, near Muthill in Crieff, Perth & Kinross ☎ 01764/681433, Ⓦ www. drummondcastlegardens.co.uk. Easter weekend & May–Oct daily 1–6pm. £5. Map 4, C13

037 Regency splendour: Brighton's Royal Pavilion

Brightonians love the Royal Pavilion – it appeals to their enduring affection for all things quirky, nonconformist and fun. But over the centuries, it's had many a detractor. One of the earliest and loudest was the nineteenth-century political activist William Cobbett, to whom it looked far too much like the Kremlin or, at best, a random assortment of turnips and flower bulbs arranged on a box.

For its devotees, the ostentatious, multi-domed Pavilion is a unique expression of Regency romance and of one man's right to indulge his own fantasies. The man concerned was George, the fifty-something Prince Regent; keen to spend more time on the south coast, he commissioned John Nash to concoct the ultimate playboy pad. It was the 1810s, an era of untrammelled individualism, with figures as diverse as Napoleon and Byron each riding their own personality cults; George, meanwhile, was simply enjoying a life of ludicrous excess, with pleasure his unashamed priority.

Everything about the Pavilion is so overblown, it's hard not to laugh out loud. The dining room is a masterpiece of opulence, with gilded dragons adorning the architraves and leering down from a massive chandelier, said to weigh over a ton; the reception rooms are stuffed with painted chinoiserie. The Great Kitchen is a revelation, kitted out with state-of-the-art Regency technology such as steam-powered heating and a pump to provide a constant water supply. Thus equipped, staff were expected to produce menus of up to seventy dishes for the Prince's lavish banquets.

As a museum, it's fascinating, but as a venue, it's all too easy for the decor to steal the show. Undeterred, in recent years, couples have been vying for a wedding or civil partnership slot in the Red Drawing Room. Every May, the organizers of the annual Brighton Festival have enabled concert-goers to appreciate the full glories of the richly decorated, impeccably restored Music Room by staging a handful of events there; with artists as diverse as string quartets, lieder singers and the electronica genius Talvin Singh, they've been refreshingly free of stiffness or stuffiness. The Prince Regent would surely have approved.

Need to know The Royal Pavilion, Pavilion Buildings, Brighton ☎ 03000/290290, Ⓦ www.royalpavilion.org.uk. Daily: Oct–March 10am–5.15pm; April–Sept 9.30am–5.45pm. £9.50.

Map 2, E6

038 Imaginary spaces: Sir John Soane's Museum

Sir John Soane was a dreamer when it came to architecture, likening it to poetry and claiming it should "keep the imagination awake". Lofty ideals indeed for this ambitious son of a brickie who through graft, luck and marrying a rich woman, became one of Britain's most original architects. He may have spent nearly fifty years designing the Bank of England, but it's his home, where he lived from 1813 to 1837, that offers the most exciting journey into the imagination of this quirky genius.

Soane gathered inspirations like a magpie. Like his contemporaries, he had a soft spot for the ancient Romans, but found beauty everywhere, judging objects only by their emotional impact. As you burrow through the crannies of his creaking old house, a riot of busts and scrolls, statuettes and urns, tiles and plaques confront you. Some are originals, others casts – "authenticity" is irrelevant in this Looking Glass world where imagination rules the roost.

First, the light. Soane filtered London's pearly grey through yellow skylights, bathing Italian marbles in the kind of golden Mediterranean sunshine they'd have grown up with. Boxy rooms are lit by convex mirrors bulging from unexpected surfaces – on the backs of shutters, embedded in the ceiling – like giant water droplets reflecting imaginary rooms. Imaginary rooms do exist here, too: the tiny Picture Room, for example, lined ceiling to floor with Soane's favourite paintings, including Hogarth's *Rake's Progress* sequence. With a dramatic flourish the guide swings open the walls – delighted gasps – to reveal another panelled wall, more pictures, more engravings. Unbelievably, that panel is also pulled back – gasps again – to reveal...what? A gallery? Mezzanine? It can't be seen from below – so is it an extension of the Picture Room? Can it be called a room if it has no ceiling, walls or floor? Dizzying stuff, literally, with Turner paintings and a classical nymph presiding over a model of the Bank of England, all seeming to float in front of you.

Head down into the cellar, which Soane cluttered with crumbling statuary, centred on a giant Egyptian sarcophagus and called a crypt. Or to the "monk's parlour", a folly built for the architect's alter ego, the solitary "Padre Giovanni". Here the imagination drifts into loopy humour, with gloomy Gothic trappings including a giant, ostentatious tomb for a tiny dog called Fanny.

Need to know Sir John Soane's Museum, 13 Lincoln's Inn Fields, London WC2 ☎ 020/7405 2107, Ⓦ www.soane.org. Tues–Sat 10am–5pm, free; Sat tours 11am, £5. Map 1, D2

039 Frightfully genteel: Warwick Castle

On the surface, Warwick Castle looks like an ideal place to spend a genteel, quintessentially English day out. The wonderfully restored medieval castle, built in 1068 by William the Conquerer on the site of an older earthen rampart near the River Avon, houses an opulent hall lined with suits of armour, state rooms packed with period furniture, lavish royal chambers and a tower that could have been plucked straight out of a fairy tale. Surrounding the castle, meanwhile, are 690 acres of immaculate gardens, landscaped in the eighteenth century by Lancelot "Capability" Brown.

However, the castle is also home to what one British newspaper has dubbed the scariest tourist attraction in the country. The castle dungeon, where senior Royalists were detained during the English Civil War, now has a Black Death theme, complete with strikingly realistic decaying bodies, torture chamber and medieval medical equipment, not to mention crowds of leeches, creepy chanting monks and gallons of (fake) blood. It is all brought to life by a devilish cast of actors, who take obvious delight in creating a gloomy and ghoulish atmosphere.

For some, the dungeon can prove too scary: during its first month, fifteen people fainted, four threw up and many others fled, prompting staff to tone down some of the most gruesome elements. It still packs quite a punch, however, and children under 15 must be accompanied by an adult (something that many adults may also find comforting). For those with steadier nerves, by contrast, extra scary night-time visits can be arranged.

If you're after a less traumatizing experience, however, the grounds are perfect for an idle wander. There is a beautiful Victorian rose garden, a conservatory of exotic plants and flocks of stately peacocks strolling by. As well as the world's largest trebuchet (a 59ft-high catapult weighing 22 tonnes), which is fired twice daily, regular archery, falconry and sword-fighting demonstrations are staged. The highlights, however, are the eye-catching jousting displays. Performed at speed by agile latter-day knights on thrusting steeds, they provide just as many thrills as the castle dungeon, but considerably less gore.

Need to know Warwick Castle, Warwick ☎ 0871 265 2000, Ⓦ www.warwick-castle.co.uk. Daily: Oct–March 10am–5pm; April–Sept 10am–6pm. On the door, a one-day adult ticket, covering entry to the castle, the grounds and the dungeon, costs £25.45, but it's cheaper to book online. Map 3, C12

TOP 5 >>

FOLLIES

Follies pop up everywhere in the grand parks and gardens of Britain's stately homes. Built for decoration, not use – thus the name – they exude wild ambition and delightful eccentricity.

040 Stourhead

The gardens at Stourhead are an artificial paradise, but a gorgeous one. A collection of exquisite eighteenth-century follies, along with a host of exotic trees, shrubs and flowers, stand around a lake created in a fold of the Wiltshire hills. A Temple of Flora, a mini-Pantheon and various grottoes and Gothic ruins gaze at each other across the lake, adding grandeur – and a touch of whimsy – to this loveliest of landscapes.

Ⓦ *www.nationaltrust.org.uk/stourhead. Map 2, C6*

041 Rushton Triangular Lodge

Rushton Triangular Lodge, in Northamptonshire, was built by the rebelliously Catholic Sir Thomas Tresham in the 1590s, when it was dangerous not to be a confirmed Anglican. The Holy Trinity is honoured in every stone: the three walls are 33ft long, and the three floors are inscribed with three Latin quotations of 33 letters each. Some say the symbolism honours Tresham too: his wife called him "Tres", the Latin for three. Maybe so, but the Lodge exudes spiritual depth today, not vanity.

Ⓦ *www.english-heritage.org.uk/rushton. Map 3, D11*

042 Fuller's Follies, Brightling

"Mad Jack" Fuller sponsored the young scientist Michael Faraday, gave Beachy Head its first lighthouse, rescued the ruinous Bodiam Castle and, while an MP, in 1810, had a drunken spat with the Commons' Speaker. His maddest legacy, however, is the collection of follies on his estate at Brightling in East Sussex, among them a giant obelisk, a hollow tower built to remind him of Bodiam and the conical Sugar Loaf, supposedly created to win a bet that he could see a nearby church spire from his window. His grave, in Brightling churchyard, is an impressive 25ft pyramid. *Map 2, F6*

043 Wainhouse Tower, Halifax

When the 253ft-high stone shaft of the Wainhouse Tower was begun, in the early 1870s, it was destined to be an unusually fine factory chimney. When John Wainhouse sold his factory, however, the new owner refused to complete it. Undeterred, Wainhouse took on the project himself; he said it was to be an astronomical observatory, but some think he wanted to annoy a rival local industrialist, who didn't like chimneys.

Ⓦ *www.calderdale.gov.uk. Map 3, C10*

044 The National Monument, Calton Hill

The most conspicuous of all follies, Edinburgh's National Monument was never meant to be one. Built in the early 1820s as a grand replica of Athens' Parthenon, it was supposed to commemorate the Scottish dead of the Napoleonic Wars. Unfortunately, not enough money was raised, so only twelve columns were ever erected. They now gaze down over the city: offering a grand view, and a stark commentary on pride and ambition. *Map 4, D14*

045 Somewhere to breathe: Mottisfont's old roses

Before you even get to the roses at Mottisfont Abbey – which is, after all, the point of the visit – you encounter some sensuous temptations. First you cross the River Test, arguably the finest chalk stream in England, which runs clear and shallow through gentle meadows fringed by grassy downland. This is the place for walks (the Test Way passes by here), or quiet sitting – or trout fishing, if you can afford it.

You then walk through Mottisfont's lovely grounds, a grassy haven bordered by chalk streams and studded with old oaks, sweet chestnuts and the improbably massive great plane. Then there's the Abbey itself, a mellow pile with Tudor wings and Georgian frontages and a stately drawing room whose eccentric trompe l'oeil decor – all painted swags and smoking stoves sketched in grisaille – was created by the English prewar artist, Rex Whistler.

But beyond the river and the house and the grounds lies Mottisfont's heart: its twin walled rose gardens. They are fabulous, harbouring one of the finest collections of old roses in the world. Among the six-hundred-odd varieties you'll find names that hint at exotic beauty, such as Reine de Violette, Tuscany Superb and Ispahan, and names that suggest a more blushing Englishness, such as Eglantine and the Common Moss Rose. Climbers, noisettes and ramblers trace glorious patterns on the high brick walls, cross pergolas or spill up into apple and pear trees. The shrub roses, meanwhile, crowd noisily between the box hedges and lawns and lavender pathways, jostling among the hosts of bulbs and perennials. There is something to see, then, right through spring and summer. But come on a warm, still, humid afternoon in June (that's when the perfume lingers most intensely in the air), find somewhere to sit, and simply breathe.

Need to know Mottisfont, five miles north of Romsey, Hampshire ☏ 01794/340757. Ⓦ www. nationaltrust.org.uk. Broadly, the house and gardens are open March–Oct daily except Fri 11am–5pm. For part of June, when the roses are at their best, the gardens are also open until 8pm, and on Fri. The gardens (but not the house) are also open Nov, Dec & Feb Sat & Sun 11am–4pm. £7.60.
Map 2, D6

046 An Englishman's home: Bodiam Castle

Ask any five-year-old to draw you a castle and you'll probably end up with a version of Bodiam Castle in East Sussex. With its fairy-tale battlements, arrow slits, portcullis and moat, it is the very image of a forbidding medieval fortress and undoubtedly one of England's most evocative, especially in the early morning mist with the caws of crows rasping in the air. Yet while it certainly looks the part, Bodiam may be, whisper it, something of a fraud.

Historians, you see, can be a tad sniffy about Bodiam, claiming it's little more than a beefed-up manor house rather than a "proper" castle. For starters the moat, seemingly a tricky barrier for the assumed French invaders, could have been drained in a few hours by a man with a shovel. Then there are the thin walls, the vulnerable large windows and the lack of a proper drawbridge. Yet gripes like these rather miss the point.

Its owner, local bigwig Sir Edward Dallingridge, had little intention of holing up inside and pouring boiling oil through the murder holes when the castle was completed in 1385. For him Bodiam was about impressing the neighbours and displaying the new-found wealth he had obtained by plundering French villages. Instead of a defensive keep he opted for thirty en-suite bedrooms set around a pleasant courtyard. And though little remains inside today, you can still make out the vast kitchen and pantry and climb the steep spiral stairs to Sir Edward's bedchamber (complete with attached chapel).

What really sets Bodiam apart, though, is its unspoilt exterior and the sweeping views from its battlements. It's a location manager's dream (it played a key role in *Monty Python and the Holy Grail*) and just a few hours here will set your imagination into overdrive – you half expect toothless peasants to be tilling the fields or to see a dragon swoop overhead. For the kids, there are plenty of ye olde activities to take part in, from dressing up in medieval garb to archery and falconry displays.

Need to know Bodiam Castle, near Robertsbridge, East Sussex ☎ 01580/830196, ⓦ www.nationaltrust.org.uk/bodiamcastle. Daily mid-Feb to end Oct, with reduced opening times in winter. £5.80.
Map 2, F6

047 English Baroque: Blenheim Palace and gardens

The estate of one of Britain's pre-eminent families, and one of the most magnificent houses in the country, Blenheim is grand and impressive more than lovable, a monument to great men rather than a family home. Its history is bookended by two great military tales, and two men bearing the illustrious name Churchill. The first was John Churchill, first Duke of Marlborough, whose reward for his military success on behalf of Queen Anne in the 1702 Battle of Blenheim was the land and resources to build this palace. The result is a colossal Baroque pile designed by John Vanbrugh, and filled with art, artefacts and ornamentation.

Throughout the house the story of his military brilliance is told – in portraits, in tapestries of him in battle, painted on the ceiling of the saloon, crafted in a huge silver ornament depicting him on horseback at the moment of victory, in the overblown memorial in the chapel – and atop a Victory Column in the grounds. The palace's highlight, though, is less bellicose: the light and elegant Hawksmoor-designed long library, housing 10,000 books and a large organ that you may occasionally hear played.

Later dukes were less illustrious, with a habit of squandering the family wealth (the ninth Duke married an American heiress, Consuelo Vanderbilt, to rectify the situation). It took nearly two hundred years for the family to produce another man quite so celebrated, but it was worth the wait. On November 30, 1874, Winston Leonard Spencer Churchill was born in a downstairs room here. It's preserved as it was at the time, as part of a fascinating exhibition that includes some of his paintings and letters.

While the buildings impress and inform, the gardens and parklands are sheer pleasure – beautiful formal arrangements, including water terraces, a rose garden and "secret" garden, and over 2000 acres of lakeside parkland landscaped by Capability Brown. It's well worth going on a sunny day and spending a couple of hours outside, not least for the views back to the house. Follow one of the three suggested walks or take the little train to the pleasure gardens, which includes a maze and butterfly house.

Need to know Blenheim Palace, Woodstock, Oxfordshire ☎ 0800 849650, ⓦ www.blenheimpalace.co.uk. Palace and gardens: mid-Feb to Oct daily 10.30am–5.30pm; Nov to mid-Dec Wed–Sun 10.30am–5.30pm; park: 9am–4.45pm. Palace, park and gardens £18.50; park and gardens £10.30.
Map 2, D5

048 Bears and beers at Traquair House

Tall, turreted Traquair House turns its face away from visitors – the entrance gates, topped with statues of bears supporting shields, were locked in 1745 following a visit by Bonnie Prince Charlie. The then owner, the fifth Earl, swore they would remain that way until a Stuart king sat on the throne.

The tale is possibly apocryphal, but it does reveal something of Traquair's history of rebellion; it sheltered Catholic priests from persecution – the priest's hole and secret staircase can still be explored – and the family fervently supported Mary Queen of Scots as well as the doomed Jacobite campaign. The fourth Earl's sister-in-law launched a famously bold and successful rescue of her husband, William Nisdale; he was imprisoned in the Tower during the Jacobite Rebellion and she visited the day before his execution, disguised him as a woman and whisked him to safety.

The genesis of the ancient house is more peaceable: it was built as a hunting lodge for Alexander I in the early twelfth century – the court made forays from here into Ettrick Forest to hunt boar, bears and wild cats – and it was also used as a centre of administration and justice. During the thirteenth-century Wars of Independence Traquair was remodelled along military lines, with a defensive pele tower. It wasn't till the sixteenth century that the lairdship of Traquair was established, and the house took on its current domestic role.

And it is the personal effects and family portraits that make a visit to Traquair so special: you can see the cradle used by Mary Queen of Scots to rock her son James when she visited in 1566, and there are rich tapestries, illuminated books, Jacobite glass and a rare working harpsichord from 1651.

In more recent times, the eighteenth-century brewery was revived: make sure you sample a Bear Ale or a Traquair Jacobite Ale in the *1745 Cottage Restaurant*, set in an old walled garden, before leaving this idiosyncratic and beautiful home.

049 Snowshill Manor: curiosities in the Cotswolds

Elegantly painted on the postbox outside Snowshill Manor are the words *Nequid pereat* – "Let nothing perish" – a mantra for compulsive hoarders everywhere, and an appropriate motto for this treasury of trinkets, curios, *objets trouvés* and gorgeous gewgaws from around the world.

After an inheritance freed him from the tedium of earning a living, the illustrator and architect Charles Paget Wade (1883–1956) dedicated his time to the acquisition of beautiful works of craftsmanship that he restored and exhibited in this pale-gold Cotswold manor house outside Broadway.

The house is emphatically not a museum, but an idiosyncratic private collection, for Wade's own enjoyment and that of any connoisseur of fine things who happened to be passing, including such eminent visitors as J.B. Priestley, Virginia Woolf and John Betjeman. Wade himself lived in an adjacent cottage.

The fruits of his labours – some 22,000 items in all – are displayed from floor to ceiling of the twenty rooms here, stuffed into every niche, nook and cranny, a veritable cornucopia of the weird and the wonderful: Bedouin cloaks, Balinese masks, Cantonese lacquer cabinets, eighteenth-century model ships, a Chinese opium press, astronomical aids, figures used in Japanese *No* theatre, exotic musical instruments, gaudy toys, Samurai armour, Victorian dolls, and in the attic, rooms devoted to ancient bicycles (think boneshakers and penny-farthings) and spinning wheels. The lighting is subdued and mysterious, and labelling is scarce, which increases the element of serendipity, though National Trust volunteers – positively oozing enthusiasm – are stationed in every room to answer questions. "They are rooms to linger in," wrote Wade, "rooms one must return to; rooms where there is always something to discover; rooms which inspire a thousand fancies."

Such an abundance of riches leaves the head swimming, and Snowshill's terraced gardens are the perfect antidote. Largely the work of the Arts and Crafts designer M.H. Baillie Scott, the grounds are a delight, with gushing flowers and apple and pear orchards, all organically grown, and with views over the Vale of Evesham to one side. Next stop: the antiques shops and flea markets of the Cotswolds.

050 Lost in history at Hampton Court

Ghosts stalk the corridors of Hampton Court Palace: Catherine Howard, dragged back to her rooms after being accused of adultery, not long before her execution at the Tower of London, is apparently seen screaming in the appropriately named Haunted Gallery; while Henry VIII's favourite wife, Jane Seymour, has been spotted walking through Clock Court, carrying a lighted taper. Whether or not you believe in ghosts – or are fortunate enough to see one – there's no denying that the palace is so rich in history that there seems to be more to it than just the many visitors that wander through its rooms.

It was Thomas Wolsey, during the reign of Henry VIII, who transformed what was a large private house – built as a grange for the Knights Hostpitallers in the thirteenth century – into the impressive complex that we see today. The palace was a striking, modern centrepiece for the king's rule, used to impress and entertain foreign dignitaries and, of course, house his various wives in lavish rooms.

Even today, it's impossible not to be enchanted by the architecture and design of the buildings and grounds – in the medieval Great Hall, with carved wooden beams above and sumptuous tapestries on the walls, it's easy to imagine the King's Men, Shakespeare's theatre company, performing for King James I, the room reverberating with music and chatter. Yet it is perhaps the chapel that steals the show, with its ornate, vivid blue ceiling; time your visit with a choral service on a Sunday and you'll find yourself transported back in time by the atmospheric music.

Rivalling the ghosts as the palace's most famous attraction is the trapezoidal maze, planted at the end of the seventeenth century as a place for courtiers to lose themselves when needing to escape palace politics. Though its size may seem a little underwhelming on first glance, even the most thoughtful of explorations here can leave you stumbling around blindly. Perhaps, you'll wonder, the palace's ghosts are nothing more than hapless tourists who've never found their way out.

Need to know Hampton Court Palace, Hampton Court, Surrey ℡ 0844 482 7777, Ⓦ www. hrp.org.uk/hamptoncourtpalace. Daily: 27 March–30 Oct 10am–6pm; 31 Oct–26 March 10am–4.30pm. Palace, maze & gardens £14. Trains run to Hampton Court station from London Waterloo every 30min; more regular trains run to nearby Kingston, from where it's a short bus journey to the palace (#111, #216, #411, #451, #R68, #513).
Map 1, E4

051 Back to basics at the back-to-backs

The sheer scale of the industrial boom that gripped nineteenth-century Birmingham is astonishing, but the raw statistics speak for themselves: in 1811, there were just 85,000 Brummies, a century later there were ten times more. Inevitably, the city's infrastructure could barely cope and as wages were low – sometimes desperately so – the demand for cheap housing was intense. It was this demand that spawned the back-to-backs, quickly erected brick dwellings that were one room deep and two, sometimes three floors high, built in groups ("courts") around a courtyard where the communal toilets were located. Such crowded conditions bred a strong sense of community – and a pithy, ironic sense of humour – but even by the standards of the time it was all pretty grim. As early as the 1870s Birmingham council banned the construction of any more, though it took several decades to clear those that had already been built.

The last Birmingham courts were bulldozed in the 1970s; this set, which was lived in until 1966, has been painstakingly restored by the National Trust to give a fascinating insight into Britain's immediate past. The guided tour wends its way through four separate homes, each of which represents a different period from the early nineteenth century onwards, with all sorts of anecdotal tidbits about the people who lived here and lots of period bygones to touch and feel. Learn about the Mitchells, locksmiths and bell-hangers, several generations of whom lived here for almost one hundred years, and about Sophia Hudson, a widow and pearl-button driller and her five children, and about Herbert Oldfield, a glass-eye maker who dwelled in the back-to-backs with his wife and eight kids.

To truly get to grips with back-to-back basics, though, you should consider staying here, just a brief walk away from the city centre: the complex offers two small "cottages" – really terraced houses – kitted out in Victorian period style. True authenticity, however, is sacrificed for comfort, with the addition of en-suite and self-catering facilities; you'll be thankful of it, even if poor old Herbert Oldfield is turning in his grave.

Need to know Birmingham Back-to-Backs, 55–63 Hurst St & 50–54 Inge St, Birmingham ☎ 0121/666 7671, Ⓦ www.nationaltrust.org.uk/main/w-birmingham-backtobacks 1hr tours Feb–Dec Tues–Sun 10am–5pm. £5.45, National Trust members free. Two-person "cottages" can be rented for two nights minimum (☎ 0844 800 2070, Ⓦ www.nationaltrustcottages.co.uk; £165 in Jan, £246 in July).

Map 3, C11

052 Stowe: Enlightenment landscape

Few places in Britain can match Stowe when it comes to illuminating the Enlightenment ideals of nature tamed, ordered and generally improved upon. The house and grounds were created by the upwardly mobile Temple family, said to be richer than the king of England, and the names of those who worked here read like a Who's Who of eighteenth-century design. Charles Bridgeman and architect John Vanburgh (creator of Blenheim Palace and Castle Howard) laid out the original grounds, succeeded by William Kent and Lancelot "Capability" Brown, the two greatest British landscape gardeners of their age, while Vanburgh, Robert Adam and Thomas Pitt all lent a hand in the house's design. The fame of the gardens rapidly spread across Europe – 1748 even saw the publication of a guidebook, *Les Charmes de Stow*, to cater to the large number of French visitors. Jonathan Swift, John Gay, William Congreve and Jean-Jacques Rousseau all came to pay their respects, while Alexander Pope was a regular guest, opining that: "If anything under Paradise could set me beyond all earthly cogitations, Stowe might do it".

Stowe remains as captivating as ever: an idyllic swathe of beautifully landscaped countryside dotted with a quirky collection of statues, monuments and assorted architectural curiosities. Triumphal arches mark the entrance to the estate, from where long driveways converge on the superb house (now home to the prestigous Stowe School). Beyond here stretch the rolling gardens themselves, arranged around the Octagon Lake, with artfully contrived vistas revealing strategically placed archways, rotundas, temples and assorted follies interspersed with allegorical statues, monuments and solemn busts of assorted notables – Socrates, Shakespeare, Queen Elizabeth I – designed to affirm the Temple family's upstanding Whig political credentials. Over forty structures survive, ranging from the beautiful Palladian Bridge through to a string of rather grand Neoclassical temples – an unlikely vision of classical Greece in the depths of Buckinghamshire. It's worth stretching your legs to reach some of the more whimsical creations scattered around the grounds, including the tiny Chinese House, the hilltop Gothic Temple, and, further afield, Stowe Castle – which isn't a castle at all, but a line of cottages, artfully disguised with battlements and towers.

Need to know Stowe, Buckingham, Buckinghamshire. The gardens are owned by the National Trust ☎ 01494/755568, Ⓦ www.nationaltrust.org.uk/ stowegardens. March–Oct Wed–Sun 10.30am–5.30pm, Nov to mid-Dec, Jan & Feb Sat & Sun 10.30am–4pm. £6.50. The house is owned by Stowe School (☎ 01280/818166, Ⓦ www.stowe. co.uk/house; £4.40).
Map 3, D12

053 Step back into a golden age at Plas Mawr

The reign of Queen Elizabeth I (1558–1603) is often regarded as a golden era – a short-lived period of peace and prosperity when the English Renaissance flourished, Sir Francis Drake circumnavigated the globe and Shakespeare composed his plays. Plas Mawr is the finest surviving home from this period. On a cobbled street in the heart of Conwy – a beautiful walled town on the north Wales coast – Plas Mawr (Welsh for "big house") was built between 1575 and 1586 for wealthy merchant and local MP Robert Wynn.

Thanks to £2-million-worth of repairs and restoration work, the townhouse is in remarkable condition, with tall sandy-coloured lime-rendered walls, turrets and a stately courtyard. As you walk through the kitchen, pantry, dairy, bedchambers, reception rooms and grand dining halls, it is easy to imagine yourself back in Elizabethan times. There are colourful (and sometimes gaudy) friezes, many decorated with the over-the-top Wynn family crest (which features regal lions and topless maidens); elaborate plasterwork ceilings; and innumerable original heirlooms, including an aged Welsh Bible, kitchen utensils and a mighty four-poster bed. Plas Mawr is also a fun place for kids: there are countless nooks and crannies to explore, a romantic tower to climb and light-hearted interactive displays on aspects of Tudor and Stuart life, including their bodily functions, superstitions and diet.

Perhaps the most evocative part of the house is the watchtower. With panoramic views of Conwy Castle, the town walls and out to sea, it was here that Lady Wynn would await her husband's return from his many trips overseas. One stormy night in 1598, Lady Wynn – with a child in her arms – stumbled down the watchtower's stairs and fell to her death. A doctor was summoned, but after panicking and trying to flee, was locked in a room by a maid. He later disappeared without trace.

When Wynn returned home to find his wife and child dead, he was so distraught that he ended his own life. Since then there have been several alleged ghostly sightings of him, Lady Wynn and even the mysterious missing doctor.

Need to know Plas Mawr, Conwy ☎ 01492/580167, Ⓦ www. conwy.com/plasmawr.html. Tues– Sun: 27 March–30 Sept 9am–5pm; Oct 9.30am–4pm. £4.95.
Map 3, B10

054 Glendurgan:
a tropical hideaway

Cornwall is not short of fabulous gardens. Lamorran, Trewithen, Trevarno, The Lost Gardens of Heligan – all would be standout attractions in any other county, but Cornwall has so many of these horticultural highlights that it's tough to know where to point one's green finger. Should you prefer a country estate to accompany your rhododendrons, Lanhydrock is a good choice. You're a bamboo nut? Head to Carwinion, which has over 140 varieties of the panda snack. If, on the other hand, you like your gardens subtropical, riverside and with plenty to keep the kids entertained, then look no further than Glendurgan.

The valley above the Helford River in which it lies was bought in 1820 by Alfred Fox, a Quaker businessman who owned a shipping company in nearby Falmouth, which provided the perfect vehicle for importing exotic plants. Over the next two decades he worked tirelessly on his vision of a slice of the tropics in Cornwall, including the cherry laurel maze that looks from above like a coiled serpent and is a hit with children. Look out too for some of the less obvious quirks of Fox's design, such as Holy Corner, filled with species associated with the Bible such as yews, olives and a Judas tree. And be sure to follow the sloping paths down to the beach beside the tiny fishing village of Durgan; it makes for a perfect picnic stop and a chance to get your toes wet.

Late spring is perhaps the best time to visit, when Glendurgan's many camellias and magnolias emerge in a splash of cherry pink, violet and cream, and the air is scented with cedar and pine. While you're in the area, try to make time to see what the rest of the Foxes were up to: Alfred's brother Robert created Penjerrick Garden (about 2.5 miles north) and other brother Charles was responsible for Trebah (about a third of a mile to the west). The family connection lives on today: descendants of Alfred still live in the house at the top of the valley, and on Sunday and Monday Glendurgan is usually closed to the public so the family can enjoy it privately.

Need to know Glendurgan is at Mawnan Smith, near Falmouth, Cornwall ℡ 01326/252020, Ⓦ www. nationaltrust.org.uk/main/w-glendurgangarden. Tues–Sat 10.30am–5.30pm, also Mon in Aug and bank holidays. £6, free for National Trust members.
Map 2, A7

WELSH CASTLES

With over a hundred extant castles (and evidence of 300 ex-castles), Wales has valid claim to being the world's castle capital. None may be as mighty as Windsor or as flamboyant as Bavaria's Schloss Neuschwanstein, but there's a fine, gritty quality to them all.

055 Conwy Castle

For sheer grey-stone solidity, nothing beats Conwy Castle with its eight massive round towers arranged squarely on the banks of the Conwy Estuary. Completed in 1287, this "Iron Ring" edifice was finished in less than five years, complete with associated "bastide" town. The two worked in symbiosis: the castle was kept supplied by the merchants who were protected by the mile-long ring of town walls. The wall walk still gives the best views of both castle and town.

Ⓦ *www.cadw.wales.gov.uk. Open daily; £4.60. Map 3, B10*

056 Carreg Cennen Castle

Carreg Cennen is the most romantically sited of all native Welsh castles, perched on its craggy, limestone hill, often with mist swirling around the lower slopes. There's something wild and preternaturally Welsh about this isolated locale on the edge of the heather-purpled Black Mountains. On the south side a steep cliff plummets down to the bucolic valley of the River Cennen below; you can descend via a vertiginous stairway tunnel cut into the cliff face.

Ⓦ *www.cadw.wales.gov.uk. Open daily; £3.60. Map 2, B5*

057 Castell Dinas Brân

The ruinous state of Dinas Brân – Crow's Fortress Castle – high above the town of Llangollen, almost puts it out of contention as a castle. It is really just a short stretch of crumbling thirteenth-century masonry and a few vaulted arches, but there are few better places in Wales to watch the sun set over the bucolic Dee Valley and ponder the English–Welsh power struggles that gave rise to this borderlands relic.

Open daily; free. Map 3, B11

058 Penrhyn Castle

More like a Welsh chateau than a real castle, Penrhyn stands as a testament to nineteenth-century class divisions. While the workers hacked away at the nearby slate quarries, their masters created a vulgar but compelling neo-Norman fancy complete with five-storey keep. Everything is on a massive scale, from the 3ft-thick oak doors and halls of fine art – Canaletto, Gainsborough, Rembrandt – to a slate bed, designed for Queen Victoria's visit.

Ⓦ *www.nationaltrust.org.uk. Mid-Feb to Oct daily except Tues; £10. Map 3, B10*

059 Caernarfon Castle

Caernarfon Castle is both the most recognized Welsh castle and its least typical. It eschews the ancient square form and stronger rounded fortifications in favour of distinctive polygonal towers, the supreme development of "Iron Ring" architect James of St George. The largely intact walls are riddled with passageways that eventually deliver you to the ramparts, with fabulous views of the ancient town of Caernarfon to Snowdonia beyond.

Ⓦ *www.caernarfon.com. Open daily; £5. Map 3, A11*

060 Keeping it in the family at Chatsworth

There aren't many stately homes where "stately" plays second fiddle to "home", but at Chatsworth – ancestral pile of the Dukes of Devonshire, handed down through sixteen generations – family still comes first. Sure, it's an estate on a vast scale, employing hundreds of people and attracting a million paying visitors a year, but there's still a tangible sense of the Cavendish family at home in the grandiose rooms, halls and chambers. You can feel it in the ornate, carved, seventeenth-century chapel, used for family christenings, or in the charming paintings of the sixth Duke's favourite dogs. Pictures of assorted nobles and royals in their finery might appear to be of mere, stuffy, long-gone toffs, but these portraits across the centuries are of intimate family friends – something that's more immediately apparent in the clever, contemporary, colour-changing digital portrait of the current Duke's daughter-in-law.

Everything, of course, is on a grand scale, and what the Dukes of Devonshire have always thought of as home is less a house and more a stunning Baroque palace, with magnificent gardens by Capability Brown complete with maze and tumbling cascade. A nine-mile-long wall encloses the thousand-acre grounds that are studded with big-ticket sculptures, an imperial fountain shoots a spear of water into the sky, while the eighteenth-century stables (now housing restaurants and shops) were once the fanciest horse lodgings in the country.

But despite the theatrical opulence of the house there's nothing too precious about an estate where staff are only too keen to share their knowledge, whether it's the gardeners, herdsmen or housekeepers. There are daily milking demonstrations on the farm, animals to pet, home-made preserves to buy, storytelling and dressing-up in the house, and den-building for kids in the woods. It's a refreshingly open approach that derives directly from the family's enthusiasm – "if you see us about the place, please say hello", invite the current Duke and Duchess. Baroque it may be, boring never.

Need to know Chatsworth House, near Bakewell, Derbyshire ☎01246/565300, Ⓦwww.chatsworth.org. House & garden mid March till Christmas daily 11am–5.30pm, garden until 6pm, last admission 1hr before closing. All-inclusive Discovery Ticket from £15.50, family ticket from £46. Admission is cheaper if you book online, and there's separate house-and-garden and garden-only admission too.

Map 3, C10

061 English eccentrics at Stokesay Castle

Ringed by the remains of a moat and looking like a half-timbered country cottage on steroids, Stokesay is one of the most unusual and intriguing castles in England.

In fact, this is not really a castle at all, but a fortified manor house, built by socially aspiring wool-merchant Lawrence of Ludlow in 1281 and completed in ten years by the same team of carpenters. Before this time it was a "stoke", or dairy farm, owned by the Lacy family; eventually the words stoke and lacy were fused into Stokesay.

Sitting in lush Shropshire countryside, all dense hedgerows and patchwork arable land, Stokesay is comprised of a harmonious cluster of buildings: the original honey-coloured and crenellated fortifications, topped with a weathered slate roof; an Elizabethan half-timbered gatehouse decorated with carvings of Adam and Eve; and a little country church with canopied pews. Edward I granted the licence to fortify, but it's likely the steep castle walls were designed with aesthetics in mind, rather than to keep marauding Welshmen at bay; the castle was built during a lull in the border battles.

And it is the domestic rather than military nature of Stokesay that gives it its particular charm, and enables it to sit so very prettily in this verdant landscape. The great hall, which dates from Lawrence's time, is spanned by a massive timber-framed roof, and still has its original interior staircase. Instead of a fireplace, there's an octagonal hearth in the centre of the room. Elsewhere, the north tower has its original tiled floor, and the gatehouse features seventeenth-century wall paintings; until the time of Charles I, Lawrence's descendants were responsible for the attractive development of the castle.

After this point, Stokesay was used as base for the king during the Civil War, and was then handed to the parliamentarians without any significant fighting taking place. Having survived its long history conflict-free, this overwhelmingly attractive and eccentric collection of buildings was thus preserved for future visitors.

Need to know Stokesay is 7 miles northwest of Ludlow, Shropshire ☏ 01588/672544, Ⓦ www.english-heritage.org.uk. April–Sept daily 10am–5pm; Oct Wed–Sun 10am–4pm; Nov–Feb Thurs–Sun 10am–4pm; March Wed–Sun 10am–5pm. £5.50, free for English Heritage members.
Map 3, C11

062 We Shall Remember Them: The National Memorial Arboretum

There is something fittingly low-profile about the National Memorial Arboretum. Tucked away off a busy A-road, it announces itself with just a simple sign; no fuss, no show. If you didn't know it was there you could drive quite happily past it, unaware of the 50,000 trees and 160 memorials that dot the neatly manicured grounds. It's a perfect metaphor for the many who have lost someone in the conflicts that have blighted the last century, who bear their grief quietly whilst appearing to live normal lives.

For them, and for all those who have been touched by war, the NMA is a place of pilgrimage; tranquil, respectful and committed to honouring the memory of those who have died in war. The grounds are separated into different areas; tree-lined walks, rose gardens, and dozens of memorials to individual regiments and battalions. It is a place to stroll, to sit and contemplate, to learn a little history and, most importantly, to pay respect.

At the heart of the Arboretum lies the imposing Armed Forces Memorial, a vast open stone circle with a central obelisk dedicated to those who have died in service since the end of World War II. The memorial is designed so that a shaft of sunlight will fall across the sculpted wreath in the centre of the circle at exactly 11am on the eleventh of November. What makes it particularly moving are the 16,000 names carved into the circular walls; a personal remembrance of every serviceman and -woman. It's a sobering sight, and helps to make the sheer scale of the losses an individualized reality.

Many who visit the NMA will do so in memory of someone, but it's an equally worthwhile experience for those who haven't suffered any personal loss. Many of the trees are still young (planting began in 1997) but in the years to come it will be lushly beautiful, and a fitting monument to those who lost their lives.

Need to know The National Memorial Arboretum, Croxall Rd, Alrewas, Staffordshire ☏ 01283/792333, Ⓦ www.thenma.org.uk. Daily 9am–5pm. Free; guided walks 11.30am & 2.30pm, £2. **Map 3, C11**

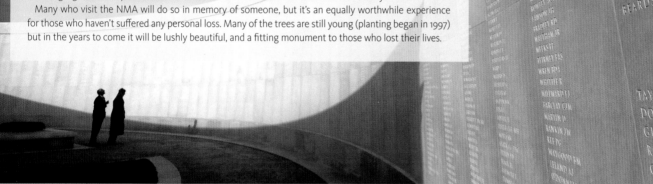

063 Cheshire's gardens of distinction

A strong contender for Britain's prettiest and most demure county, Cheshire is an opulent treasure-trove of verdant greenery, hiding away some of the nation's most glorious gardens.

Arley Hall near Nantwich is a staggeringly ornate Jacobean pile with some of the finest gardens in England. Amid the acres of immaculate lawn, parkland and avenues of lime trees lies one of the country's first herbaceous borders – dating back to the 1830s – and a prewar kitchen garden which still grows crab apples and vegetables for Viscount Ashbrook and his family who live in the hall today. If things look somewhat familiar that may be because, as well as episodes of *The Forsyte Saga*, there have been two *Coronation Street* weddings filmed here.

For a view of some of the more exotic plants nature has to offer, head for Ness Gardens on the Wirral – created by Victorian philanthropist Arthur Kilpin Bulley, who travelled the world in search of rare plant species to bring home to his botanic gardens. The fruits of his travels are still on show today, with rare species from China and South America including the dazzling purple flowers of the Himalayan magnolia and the modish sharp blues and greens of the Chinese *Gentiana sino-ornata*.

For sheer unfettered romance, perhaps the greatest park in all England lies in the grounds of Cholmondeley Castle. Here lies nature at its most ravishing, with a temple water garden complete with koi carp, nature trails, lily ponds and rose gardens plus lebanon, oak and chestnut trees galore, all in the grounds of a nineteenth-century castle. The grounds were used as a Czech army camp during World War II; every year on the first Sunday in July Czechs from all over Great Britain come to give thanks at this, the *crème de la crème* of Cheshire's historic and stunningly well-maintained gardens.

Need to know Arley Hall and Gardens, Northwich, Cheshire (☏ 01565/777353, Ⓦ www.arleyhallandgardens.com; April–Oct Tues–Sun & bank holidays 11am–5pm; Nov Sat & Sun 11am–5pm; £6); Cholmondeley Castle, Malpas, Cheshire (☏ 01829/720 383, Ⓦ www.cholmondeleycastle.com; April–Sept Wed, Thurs, Sun & bank holidays 11am–5pm; £5); Ness Gardens, Neston, Merseyside (☏ 0151/353 0123, Ⓦ www.nessgardens.org.uk; daily: Feb–Oct 10am–5pm, Nov–Jan 10am–4.30pm; £6.50). **Map 3, B10, C10 & C11**

064 Fountains Abbey: a medieval powerhouse

Of all England's monastic ruins, Fountains Abbey best exemplifies the thriving world of the great medieval religious houses. From humble beginnings in 1132 – thirteen monks, scratching a living in a sheltered Yorkshire valley – the Cistercian abbey became one of Europe's richest foundations, at the centre of a vast entrepreneurial business that farmed sheep, sold wool to Italian merchants, grew vegetables, bred horses, mined metals and milled corn. Hardly any wonder that Henry VIII fixed an avaricious eye on England's monastic estates and, with their Dissolution in the 1530s, Fountains Abbey and others went into savage decline – the monks dispersed, industries broken up, and the very abbey stones plundered for other buildings.

So it's remarkable that so much has survived at Fountains Abbey – more than enough, in fact, to put yourself in the sandals of a medieval monk as they lived, worked and prayed in the deep Yorkshire countryside. The dramatic open-to-the-sky ruins of the abbey church and soaring tower give the first hint of the scale of the operation, which was as much working village as place of worship, with an enormous dormitory with vaulted cellars underneath, plus kitchens, refectory, infirmary, meeting room and even prison. At the nearby abbey mill bread was made for the brothers and for the surrounding villages and farmsteads – it stayed in continuous operation for eight centuries (and was still working in the 1920s).

Walk past the picnicking families, down the lawns and across the riverside fields, and the abbey shimmers in the distance like a landscape artist's dream – absolutely no accident, as it happens, since the adjoining Georgian water gardens and deer park of Studley Royal were developed in the eighteenth century to form a single, glorious, harmonious whole. The monks were long gone by then of course, but there's a serenity in these geometric ponds, canals, temple follies and curving paths that is entirely in keeping with the silent habits of the Cistercian "White Monks". Meanwhile, the National Trust – which owns the estate, now a World Heritage Site – does much to bring the abbey ruins to life, hosting medieval re-enactments and candlelit Christmas carol concerts.

Need to know Fountains Abbey and Studley Royal, Ripon, North Yorkshire ☎ 01765/608888, Ⓦ www.fountainsabbey.org.uk. Feb, March & Oct daily 10am–4pm; April–Sept daily 10am–5pm; Nov–Jan Mon–Thurs, Sat & Sun 10am–4pm. From £7.70.
Map 3, C9

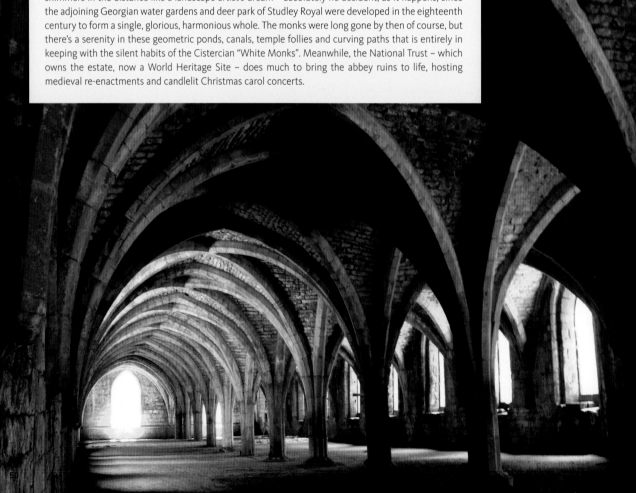

065 Alnwick Poison Garden

It makes sense to lock up dangerous criminals and wild animals, perhaps – but plants? Well, yes, when we're talking about these plants. Within the 40-acre Alnwick Garden, the botanical annexe to Alnwick Castle, lies a sullen little plot of deadly flowers and bushes deemed so dangerous that they too are kept behind bars. Visitors to this cultivated collection of botanical death should be wary. Don't sniff too hard, perhaps... Though one suspects their deadly pollen and spores could permeate even the ominous wrought-iron gates, fronted with skull and bone signs, that declare: "These plants can kill".

Unlike the rest of Alnwick Garden, the poison garden can only be visited on a guided tour. The heavy iron gates are locked behind you. This is serious stuff. Flame-shaped beds are planted with tobacco, mandrake, hemlock – and innocent-looking rhubarb, the stalks of which make lovely crumble, but whose lush green leaves can kill. Maximum security is applied to coca (for cocaine), cannabis plants and poppies, the heads of which contain all that's required to make opium, heroin and morphine. Plants are only as dangerous as the ends to which they're put, of course. And some of these nasties have been used to heal, also. Or to transform. In the nineteenth century, Victorian nannies kept children unseen and unheard by dropping laudanum, the tincture of opium that was then widely available, into their milk.

Weaving through the garden, guides debunk myths, tell old wives' tales and impart ancient wisdom. Learn here about Old Man's Beard, rubbed by professional beggars into sores to make them weep piteously. Or the hallucinogenic properties of Deadly Nightshade. Chewing a humble laburnum leaf, you are told, will lead you to froth at the mouth and wildly convulse.

When the tour is done, you are left to drift through a long, dappled ivy tunnel and out into Alnwick Garden proper, where the pretty cascade of water pools, high stone wall and lush, sweetly scented rose garden will obliterate all thoughts of death and deadly addiction.

Need to know Alnwick Garden, Denwick Lane, Alnwick, Northumberland ☎ 01665/511350, Ⓦ www.alnwickgarden.com. Daily: Nov–March 10am–4pm; April–Oct 10am–6pm. £10.50, £20.80 with castle. Trains stop at Alnmouth, four miles away.
Map 4, E15

066 The passionate gardens of RHS Wisley

As you walk through the brick entrance arch at Wisley, you're hit by scented air wafting through from the flourishing acres beyond. And there really are acres and acres here – 240 of them, to be exact, all lovingly, scrupulously, passionately tended. Ahead lies the serene canal and walled garden; beyond, secretive paths lead through the Wild Garden's woodlands to the staggering new glasshouse, which rises out of an entire lake. The preternaturally heated interior heaves with tropical ferns and palms and creepers, all fighting their way towards the glass. There's even an indoor waterfall.

But why go straight on? A left turn takes you up a breathtaking avenue of lawn, between 20ft-deep mixed borders from which English cottage garden flowers dance and nod in coloured ranks. Beyond, there's the elegant rose garden, and beyond again what seems like an entire ecosystem of rhododendrons and magnolias on Battleston Hill. And beyond that, the Jubilee Arboretum rises back up towards the Fruit Field, which is really an entire hillside combed with 450 types of apple, plum and pear, many of them rare and rich varieties. It's not exactly encouraged, but on an early autumn day you could even quietly taste a windfall pear or two – or buy them in the shop later.

Turning right from the entrance takes you towards the pleasant parkland of the Seven Acres and the Pinetum – which is surely one of Wisley's highlights. The spires of firs, pines and redwoods rocket improbably towards the Surrey skies, while yews and cedars spread their skirts vastly, transforming the springy lawns underneath into mossy, needle-scented shade.

Wisley isn't all about loveliness, though, or even drama. Instead, it's alive with passion and energy. The Royal Horticultural Society is dedicated to research and education, so you'll see guided tours pausing to consider a fine clematis, enthusiasts gleaning tips from the model allotment, or maybe volunteers weeding through a host of experimental pumpkins. In the thrumming Trials Field, you might even stumble upon an entire committee earnestly deliberating which of a host of narcissus varieties should be given the Society's coveted Award of Garden Merit. At Wisley, garden enthusiasm is deliciously infectious.

Need to know RHS Garden Wisley, Surrey ☎ 0845 260 9000, Ⓦ www.rhs.org.uk/wisley. March–Oct Mon–Fri 10am–5pm, Sat & Sun 9am–5pm; Nov–Feb closes 3.30pm. £9.50.
Map 2, E6

067 By Royal Appointment: touring Highgrove Gardens

It's amazing what a few words of encouragement can do. When the Prince of Wales bought Highgrove House, his family home near Tetbury in Gloucestershire, the estate didn't even have a lawn. Some thirty years later, what was once an empty landscape is now one of the most innovative gardens in Britain. Clearly, Charles has spent a lot of time talking to these plants.

Tours start at Highgrove House itself, surrounded by scented plants such as wisteria, honeysuckle, jasmine, holboellia and thyme, and meander for two miles through a series of interlinked gardens, from the immaculate Sundial Garden, fronting the house, to the Arboretum. Most eye-catching in its marriage of form and function is the Prince's Islamic-style Carpet Garden, a medal winner at the Chelsea Flower Show, whose colour and appearance – which includes fountains decked in elaborate zelij tiling – were based on the patterns of Persian carpets within the house. Look out for the slim, dark conifers, so important to the atmosphere of an Islamic garden, and the fig, pomegranate and olive trees, mentioned in the Koran as being present in Paradise.

Arguably the most interesting sections, though, are the Wildflower Meadow and the Walled Kitchen Garden. The former was co-designed with one of the UK's leading biodiversity experts, and – as an organically sustained initiative that also helps preserve the country's native flora and fauna – is a living example of the philosophy that underlines much of Highgrove and the Prince's nearby Duchy Home Farm. The meadow features more than thirty varieties of British wildflowers – ox-eye daisies, yellow rattle and ragged robin among them – and is home to some of the National Collection of Beech Trees, part of a conservation programme that safeguards the diversity of the country's plant heritage.

Vegetables in the Walled Kitchen Garden are grown in the cottage-garden tradition, a key factor in Highgrove's self-sufficiency. Evidently, Charles is rather partial to Charlotte potatoes and Hapil strawberries, a big, soft, juicy berry, but among the various fruit and vegetables busily growing here are a number of rare and endangered varieties, including some cooking apples that are now virtually extinct. Sometimes, it seems, it's good to talk.

Need to know Highgrove House, Doughton, Tetbury, Gloucestershire. Tours (1hr 30min) of Highgrove Gardens are conducted in groups of 25, and must be pre-booked, enquiries ☎ 01666/503203, bookings ☎ 020/7766 7310, Ⓦ www.highgrovegardens.com. £15. Proceeds go to The Prince's Charities Foundation.
Map 2, C5

068 Victorian excess at Mount Stuart

Make sure you go to the loo before you visit Mount Stuart. The loo in question is in Rothesay on the Isle of Bute, a magnificent Victorian gents' built by Twyfords in 1899 and featuring ceramic tiles, mosaic floors, copper pipes and grand enamel urinals that have been described as "jewels in the sanitarian's crown".

Four miles south of here, the sumptuous theme is continued at Mount Stuart, a Victorian ancestral pile built by the third Marquess of Bute, with several tonnes of Italian marble that required a new railway line to ferry it down the coast. The Marquess, who had a strong interest in architecture, commissioned pseudo-medieval Cardiff Castle before getting to work on the family seat. Mount Stuart was built from red stone in high Gothic style, with pointed window arches, tall chimneys and the chapel spire that renders the palatial exterior asymettrical. Throughout, the architect fused the Classical (marble columns and echoes of ancient Rome and Byzantium) and the Romantic; the exterior is festooned with a Juliet balcony and pointy turrets.

As you enter the house, the vaulted, cathedral-like Marble Hall is lit with stained glass depicting the signs of the zodiac and rises three storeys high. Upstairs, the Horoscope Room also demonstrates the Marquess's interest in astrology; the ceiling depicts the position of the stars on the day he was born in 1847. (In fact the current ceiling is a faithful 1980s replica, with the insertion of Pluto, which hadn't been discovered when the decorative scheme was created.) Clearly a stranger to modesty and restraint, the Marquess also commissioned Scotland's first private heated pool; this was also the first house in Scotland to have electricity and it even features its own Italian chapel, in gleaming white Carrara marble.

From some, the opulence of Mount Stuart tips over into decadence. But the 300-acre estate provides a wonderful counter to the drapes and the marble, with stretches of wilderness, a spacious Victorian kitchen garden and a tumbling rock garden.

Need to know Mount Stuart, Isle of Bute ☎ 01700/503877, Ⓦ www.mountstuart.com. May–Sept Mon–Fri & Sun 11am–5pm, Sat 10am–1.30pm. £8. The Rothesay loos are open daily (Easter–Sept 8am–7.45pm; Oct–Easter 9am–4.45pm; 20p).
Map 4, C14

069 Dawyck: meetings with well-travelled trees

Edinburgh's famous Botanic Garden may get the royal seal and most of the press, yet a mere 45-minute drive south, on the B712 near Stobo, stands what is arguably the world's most exquisite arboretum. Sequestered in one of the most scenic corners of the Scottish Borders, Dawyck is a veritable masterpiece of horticultural passion and creativity, matured over three centuries into a stunning sixty acres of botanic forest.

The secret of this place lies in its range of species from climatically similar corners of the globe. As in Scotland as a whole, one of the best times to visit is in spring, when you're welcomed by the Himalayan feast that is the Azalea Walk in full bloom. Over the brow of the hill, 300-year-old giant redwoods tower next to a rustling brook. Incredibly, these are actually infant trees, just a tenth of the way through their lives, and mere striplings compared to their 300ft-tall Californian forebears. Nevertheless, as the world's largest species, their size and nigh-on cosmic timescale cannot fail to impress anyone able to crane their neck back far enough.

Just beyond the upward curve of the burn another giant hoves into view: the rhubarb-like gunnera plant feels truly exotic, even tropical, a South American specimen with foliage as big as a golf umbrella. Yet tropical this garden is not, and when the September sun shines the heat of a stalling summer, Dawyck puts on one of the finest displays in nature: Eurasian sorbis and American acers mount a flaring foliage of reds, oranges and yellows subdued only by the rusty native beech, refracting the steaming dew and supplying photo opportunities galore.

Atmospheric features like the old chapel, the stone humpback bridge or Dawyck House, relics of the garden's heritage as part of the Dawyck estate, give purpose to those panoramic shots, or you could zoom in to the striking snakeskin bark of the Manchurian striped maple, possibly an evolutionary disguise to protect saplings. Even if you forget your camera, Dawyck will imprint itself on your grey matter anyway, a humbling lesson in the glorious potential of landscape.

Need to know Dawyck Botanic Garden, Stobo, near Peebles, Borders ☎01721/760254. Ⓦwww.rbge.org.uk/the-gardens/dawyck. Daily: Feb & Nov 10am–4pm; March & Oct 10am–5pm; April–Sept 10am–6pm. £5, families £10. Free parking; good wheelchair access; no dogs except guide dogs. Map 4, D15

070 Re-imagining the Scottish past at Stirling Castle

Few castles can claim so much bloody history, and yet so much exquisite artistry. It's true that Mel Gibson came here to raise a glass (or several) to celebrate the premiere of his epic movie, *Braveheart* in 1995, but Stirling Castle has seen far more influential masters.

Perched on a jagged outcrop of granite, and framed by heather-smothered hills, it looks like the classical impregnable fortress, its bleak, stolid walls witness to a long history of murder and mayhem. Thanks to *Braveheart*, almost everyone in the world knows about William Wallace and the Battle of Stirling Bridge where he trounced the English in that memorable (and bloody) battle scene. Disappointingly for Wallace fans, little remains of the castle he took in 1297; after another hero, Robert Bruce, decisively beat the English again at Bannockburn in 1314, the castle was effectively destroyed and then rebuilt. The oldest surviving part of the castle today is the stern North Gate, built in 1381 during the reign of Robert II.

Yet the castle's later history is wonderfully preserved, offering an alternative to that blood-and-guts image. Mary, Queen of Scots was crowned in the Chapel Royal in 1543, and the Great Hall where she held lavish feasts is still there. It remains a majestic space, with enormous walls, high oriel windows, and a fine oak hammer-beam roof, encrusted with vivid stone carvings. Mary would have slept inside the section of the castle known as the Palace, built in 1540; after restoration, the walls will gleam with elaborate hand-woven tapestries, and the queen's bedchamber will feature a magnificent four-poster bed. The castle is also painstakingly reproducing the set of 33 gorgeous hand-carved oak medallions that once adorned the ceilings of the Palace. The replicas will eventually return to the ceiling of the King's Presence Hall, while a special gallery is being created for the originals.

Then there are the famous Hunt of the Unicorn tapestries, medieval gems being recreated for the castle by weavers at West Dean College. It remains to be seen if Gibson, or the ghost of William Wallace, will make an appearance at the unveiling in 2014.

Need to know Stirling Castle, Castle Wynd, Stirling ☎ 01786/450000, Ⓦ www. stirlingcastle.gov.uk. Daily: April–Sept 9.30am–6pm; Oct–March 9.30am–5pm. £9, guided tours included.

Map 4, C14

071 Wandering the paths of Sissinghurst

White flowers against green foliage have such a simple elegance. Strip the colour scheme of an ornamental garden down to these barest of essentials, and your measure of horticultural splendour changes. It's like being shown a photograph of a familiar person in black and white, and feeling you're seeing them anew. Without the distracting dazzle of colour, you instead concentrate on textures, contrasts and the subtle interplay of light and shade.

The famous White Garden at Sissinghurst Castle pours texture upon texture, shape within shape, and is equally fascinating both at a distance and close up. There are several angles from which to admire it – framed by a shady arch, for example, or backed by the weathered walls of the Priest's House – and there's fresh beauty in every white iris, lupin and sunny-centred daisy.

It's one of a series of room-like areas of planting with which the poet Vita Sackville-West and her husband Harold Nicolson, a diplomat-turned-politician, adorned the grounds of Sissinghurst. When they arrived in 1930, the site was derelict, but Vita, who had an ancestral connection with the castle, saw in it an opportunity to shake off some of the sadness she felt at being shut out of the inheritance of her childhood home, Knole, simply because she was a woman.

The couple had different approaches to gardening: Harold enjoyed the discipline of orderly spaces separated by brick walls, yew trees and box hedges, while Vita was a romantic who enjoyed creating mysteries and surprises. In 1938, they opened the garden for an entrance fee of a shilling. When Vita died at the age of 70, Harold handed it to the National Trust, causing waves of tension within the family; however today, thanks to the efforts both of the Trust and of Vita and Harold's single-minded grandson, Adam, who has lived there all his life, it's the most visited garden in Britain, with a productive mixed farm.

The romantic-looking Elizabethan Tower that dominates the estate was originally a lookout; for the Nicolsons, it was the perfect vantage from which to survey their leafy domain. Climb up to its highest windows and you can see how beautifully the gardens, orchards and vegetable plots nestle within the Wealden countryside, complementing it just as they intended.

Need to know The garden at Sissinghurst Castle, Biddenden Road, near Cranbrook, Kent ☏ 01580/710701, Ⓦ www. nationaltrust.org.uk. Mid-March to Oct Fri–Tues 11am–6pm. £10.50. Map 2, F6

072 Power-mad at Cragside

Wealthy Victorian industrialists showed off in a way that is entirely recognizable even today – they built huge, inappropriate mansions in the bucolic English countryside, and William Armstrong's faux-Tudor Cragside, near Rothbury in Nothumberland, is typical of the type. But Armstrong himself (later the first Baron Armstrong) was far from the stereotypical, more-money-than-sense fat cat, and his house – though brash for its time – was also bold and innovative. For the fabulously rich arms manufacturer was also a pioneering hydraulic and hydroelectric engineer who pursued his dream of renewable energy more than a century before the wider world woke up to its potential.

Armstrong had society architect Richard Norman Shaw design him a lavish country seat at which he entertained the Prince and Princess of Wales and other A-list guests. The royal couple doubtless marvelled at Cragside's Turkish baths, and enjoyed meals from the state-of-the-art kitchen with its electric spit, beneficiaries of Armstrong's extraordinary project that turned Cragside into the first house in the world powered by hydroelectricity. Run now by the National Trust, the house itself offers a fascinating glimpse of a high-Victorian opulence that echoes down through the ages – Armstrong's impressive billiard parlour is the equal of any modern-day mansion games zone, while today's WAGs would feel right at home in the over-the-top marble drawing room.

But it was all made possible by what Armstrong did outside the house. The "water wizard", as the National Trust dubs him, landscaped an entire craggy valley, built artificial lakes, installed hydraulic machinery and a Pump House, and powered the whole shebang from his Power House, down in the estate gardens. It's this technology at the heart of Cragside that makes it more than just another country house, and, in the end, it's the wonderful forested grounds rather than the house that makes for a hugely enjoyable day out. There are trees by the thousand, looping trails and a labyrinth, and one of Europe's largest man-made rock gardens, while Armstrong's Orchard House represents one final blow of his technological trumpet – fruit still grows here, despite the challenging Northumberland weather.

Need to know Cragside, Rothbury, Northumberland ☏ 01669/620333, Ⓦ www. nationaltrust.org.uk. House Easter–Oct Tues–Sun 1–5pm (bank holidays, half-term and summer school holidays from 11am); gardens and estate Easter–Oct Tues–Sun 10.30am–5pm, Nov & Dec Wed–Sun 11am–4pm. £12.60/ family ticket £31.50, gardens and estate only £8.10/19.60. Map 4, E15

EAT, DRINK
AND BE MERRY

food and drink

Once upon a time – in the culinary Dark Ages of prawn cocktail and Black Forest gateau – who would have believed that cooking in Britain would be the new rock and roll, that one day you wouldn't be able to move for Michelin stars in Shropshire and Cumbria? A current generation of British chefs is rocking the world, from Heston Blumenthal and his ethereal "molecular gastronomy" to the nose-to-tail philosophy of meat-and-offal enthusiast Fergus Henderson. True, not quite everyone in Britain slow-roasts their own vine-grown tomatoes before heading out to pick hedgerow herbs for dinner. But there's no denying the dramatic shift in attitude over the last twenty years that has led to better, more nourishing British food in both homes and restaurants – whether it's higher welfare, sustainably sourced, locally grown or artisan-made. But there's a deeper, hidden truth too, which is that – despite the glib jibes from foreigners and past culinary horrors – Britain has always had fantastic food and drink. It's easy to forget that once upon a time all markets were farmers' markets. It wasn't fashion that led Cornish tin miners to knock up a tasty meat-and-vegetable pasty for their underground lunch, and it wasn't Jamie or Nigella who suggested that the Wensleydale monks might like to try their hand at making amazing cheese. There's been a sensational fish market in London for as long as there's been a London – the Romans were bringing in salted anchovies two thousand years before the *River Café* started banging on about them – and whisky has been distilled in Scotland for centuries. So in our regional celebration of British food we give you the unsurpassed Melton Mowbray pork pie, oysters from Whitstable and Herefordshire cider. We want you to eat chips made from potatoes in God's own Lancashire potato belt, tuck into Somerset eels and flavour your meals with Isle of Wight garlic. Across the nation there are fantastic food festivals, cookery masterclasses and gastropubs galore, and whether you're into eating fry-ups or Fat Rascals, tracking down Slow Food or wild food, you can guarantee Britain is the place to find it.

073 Guzzling garlic on the Isle of Wight

Need to know The Isle of Wight Garlic Festival (@www.garlic-festival.co.uk) takes place every August at Fighting Cocks Crossroads, Bathingbourne Lane, Sandown. Tickets cost £7.50 for adults, £4 for children. The showground is open from 10am to 6pm. Wightlink (@www.wightlink.co.uk) runs ferries and catamarans from Portsmouth to Fishbourne.

Map 2, D6

In 1948, Angelo Pellegrini, the great Italian food writer, claimed that garlic "blesses and ennobles everything it touches – with the possible exception of ice cream and pie". And he was right: the pungent plant tastes far better with bolognaise than banoffee. But more than sixty years later, at Britain's smelliest food event, garlic-flavoured puddings are snapped up by the bowlful.

The Isle of Wight Garlic Festival, which makes a corner of the island hum with the sour, buttery pong of garlic for two days every August, began as a local school fundraiser in the 1980s. Nowadays it's a much bigger deal, attracting around 20,000 visitors a year and giving locals a chance to showcase the island's best produce – including great husk-covered bulbs of garlic that taste so good, even the French have started importing them.

There are stalls selling tongue-tingling garlic beer, sickly-sweet garlic fudge and yes – Pellegrini would be turning in his grave – even sugary garlic ice cream. But you can also get your chops around dishes that make use of the stinky allium in much more conventional ways. From striped blue and white tipis, apron-clad vendors serve up barbecued ears of sweetcorn, smothered in butter and infused with delicate garlic. Nearby there are chefs sautéing seafood over bright-blue gas flames, causing wonderfully heady clouds of garlic smoke to billow slowly over the crowds of foodies. And everywhere you look, there are bundles of purply-white cloves waiting to be thrown into pots and pans of deliciously piquant sauces.

With the best will in the world, however, there's only so much garlic you can eat in one day. So when you feel it seeping through your pores and out into the warm summer air, take a walk through the rest of the festival site. Here you'll find plenty of garlic-free food to enjoy, like locally produced fruit juices and award-winning meat and dairy. Away from the food stalls altogether, there are live bands, magic shows and circus acts to keep you entertained, plus huge marquees full of local arts and crafts.

After all that exertion, you may feel your garlic breath is beginning to fade away. But honestly, even if you only sampled a few of the garlicky treats on offer, you're going to smell bad for at least twenty-four hours.

074 Tea with a Rascal

A dozen pairs of shining, ruby-red eyes peer out from among the neat rows of creamy chocolate éclairs, glistening fruit tarts and crumbly Yorkshire shortbread. On closer inspection, the eyes turn out to be sticky, glacé cherries atop a large raisin bun and are accompanied by a toothy, blanched almond grin. This cheeky face belongs to the celebrated Fat Rascal, the best-known and arguably most delicious cake served up at Harrogate's – and Yorkshire's – most famous tearooms, *Bettys*. A cross between a rock bun and a scone, the Rascal is made with a tempting concoction of dried fruit, nutmeg, cinnamon, orange and lemon zest. Washed down with a steaming cup of tea, it's the ultimate teatime treat.

Bettys Tearooms was established in 1919 by Swiss confectioner Frederick Belmont, who, after arriving in London from his motherland, lost his document with the address of his destination. After remembering that the place sounded like "bratwurst", and with the help of many a station controller, Frederick managed to find the correct train to Bradford. He decided to stay in Yorkshire, and went about realizing his dream of setting up his own confectionery business. The fashionable spa town of Harrogate became the location for his flagship store, and nowadays Yorkshire is blessed with six tearoom outlets.

Need to know *Bettys'* flagship branch is at 1 Parliament St, Harrogate, North Yorkshire (open daily 9am–9pm), and there are outlets in Ilkley, Harlow Carr, Northallerton and two branches in York. Details of cookery classes at *Bettys* can be found at @www.bettys.co.uk.

Map 3, C9

It's rare to see *Bettys* without a long queue of tourists and locals, who flock to indulge in its unusual, hybrid menu of Swiss–Yorkshire cuisine – expect anything from raclette rösti and Gruyère-cheese omelettes to Yorkshire sausages or Wensleydale and watercress quiche. Inside, the café oozes Art Deco elegance with its pretty, etched- and stained-glass windows, smooth marble tables and modish wood panelling. To a backdrop of gently chinking glasses, the soft hum of conversation and hot tea flowing from china teapots, uniformed waiters and waitresses in crisp, high-collared white shirts and spotless aprons flit efficiently from table to table. Those with a particularly sweet tooth should drop by for a genteel afternoon tea on Sunday afternoons; as the smart pianist in white gloves tickles the ivories in the background, you can tuck into soft, currant-filled scones with lashings of cream and sweet strawberry jam. And if you can't bear to tear yourself away from the tearoom's tasty treats, why not take part in their regular cooking classes, where you can learn how to rustle up your very own Fat Rascal.

075 Underneath the arches at Britain's best food market

A half-wheel of gooey Somerset Ogleshield cheese bubbles on the griddle, its rich, tangy aromas clogging the air; smeared over a plate of crumbly Charlotte potatoes it makes for a sublime raclette. Across the way at Baxter's, a dozen or so amply sized bangers – venison, ostrich, wild boar – brown gently, spitting and smoking their way to perfection. Or how about half a dozen of Richard Haward's native oysters – they sit so temptingly on a bed of bladderwrack – freshly harvested from the shallow creeks of Essex's Mersea Island, where they've been gathered since Roman times? It's lunchtime, you're starving – but never has decision-making proved so difficult. And you haven't even reached the serious part of the market yet.

Nowhere demonstrates Britain's new-found passion, zest and confidence in food and drink better than Borough Market. A market has existed on this site, nestling beneath the footings of London Bridge, since the twelfth century, and the distinctive green wrought-ironwork of its current buildings is unmistakeably Victorian, but it wasn't until the market's renaissance as a retail outlet in the late 1990s that Borough established its reputation as a foodie haven. Today, alongside its wholesale role – the bustling fruit and veg market continues to operate during the early hours every weekday morning – it stands as the finest source of exceptional produce in Britain.

It's also a superb repository of food knowledge and expertise. Passionate stallholders will enthusiastically discuss provenance or cooking techniques, all the while – like all good market traders – gently coaxing your purse strings open. Some of the stalls of the labyrinthine Middle Market are works of art in themselves, from the huge fishing-net-garlanded stone counter at Furness Fish & Game, to the irresistibly French Le Marché du Quartier, where a full-size 2CV provides the backdrop to an array of low-cal delicacies – Périgord truffles, goose fat and *confit de canard*. But don't ignore the smaller, simpler stalls of the newly covered Jubilee Market: you won't find more powerful, meatier Polish sausage than at Topolski, displayed with typical Slavic lack of fuss, or a finer, creamier blue-veined cheese than Nottinghamshire's Stichelton, on sale at Rennet and Press.

And most importantly, don't be afraid to try and haggle: it is a market after all.

Need to know Borough Market, 8 Southwark St, London SE1 Ⓦ www.boroughmarket.org. uk. Wholesale market Mon–Fri roughly 2–8am. Retail market Thurs 11am–5pm, Fri noon–6pm & Sat 8am–5pm, though note that not all stalls operate every day.
Map 1, E3

BRITISH FOOD FESTIVALS

From Land's End to John O'Groats, and East Anglia to the Welsh coast, there's not a part of the country that doesn't champion its local food and drink. The burgeoning number of food festivals is a sure sign that Britain now takes its tucker seriously, and while our pick of the national crop ranges from classic to quirky, there are endless other local affairs that celebrate everything from the humble spud to the classiest seafood.

076 British Asparagus Festival, Worcestershire

It only has the shortest of seasons, but England's noblest veg, the mighty asparagus, yields to none in taste and texture. In the prime growing area of the Worcestershire's Vale of Evesham, experience eight weeks of "asparagus-related fun", from auctions of the finest spears to cooking demos, tastings, farmers' markets and tours of the region on the "Asparabus" – not to mention the ever-present Gus, a man dressed as (come on, keep up) a giant asparagus.

Ⓦ *www.britishasparagusfestival.org; April–June. Map 3, C12*

077 Flavour of Shetland

The best regional food festivals link their celebration of local produce to the surrounding countryside, crafts and culture, and nowhere is this done more effectively than in Lerwick, capital and main port of the Shetland Islands and the "bridge" between Britain and Scandinavia. All the traditional eat-and-drink ingredients are present, from food stalls to demo sessions, but in between you can catch a rollicking fiddle band, talk to Shetland knitters, listen to the Old Norse Saga stories and witness the march of the Viking warriors.

Ⓦ *www.flavourofshetland.com; June. Map 5, F18*

078 Pontefract Liquorice Festival, Yorkshire

Quite how a small West Yorkshire market town ended up inextricably linked to the root-sap of a Middle Eastern herbal plant is hard to say (returning Crusaders may have had something to do with it), but Pontefract is proud to be England's Liquorice Capital, and has the sweets to prove it. Sample the famed splendours of the Pontefract Cake, plus more herbal-flavoured food and drink than you can shake a liquorice stick at at this one-day summer event.

Ⓦ *www.experiencewakefield.co.uk; July. Map 3, D10*

079 Great British Cheese Festival, Cardiff

No doubt the French would have something to say about it, but a) Britain produces nearly twice as many types of cheese as France, and b) who cares what the French say? Britain's biggest and best cheese festival is held in the majestic surroundings of Cardiff Castle, where hundreds of producers offer tastings, cookery demos and masterclasses, while bands play, artisan ale, wine and cider are drunk, and the drama of the World Cheese-Tossing Championship unfolds.

Ⓦ *www.greatbritishcheesefestival.co.uk; Sept. Map 2, C5*

080 Aldeburgh Food & Drink Festival, Suffolk

The Suffolk coast's annual foodie fixture is a two-week celebration of all things local in and around charming, arty Aldeburgh. The main two-day event is held at the old Victorian malthouses at nearby Snape (concert venue for the town's biggest bash, the Benjamin Britten-focused Aldeburgh Festival) and, despite being relatively new, has rapidly acquired a reputation as one of the best food fests in the country – a field-to-fork showcase in stunning East Anglian countryside for local producers, restauranteurs, chefs, farmers and food writers.

Ⓦ *www.aldeburghfoodanddrink.co.uk; Sept/Oct. Map 3, F12*

081 Eating offal at St John

It's fair to say that twenty years ago, the only place you'd expect to see a squirrel was in the park, and that bone marrow was something fit only for the dog – neither would have been thought fair game for the dinner table. Tried-and-tested cuts of meat – sirloin and rump, cutlet and chop – were on the whole served in the same familiar, undemanding ways that had been popular for decades. Nose-to-tail eating would have been thought something from the Middle Ages.

Fergus Henderson changed all that when he opened *St John* on the site of a former smokehouse in then unfashionable Farringdon, just north of the City of London. The design for the new restaurant was simple: rickety wooden tables and plain white walls, in keeping with the building's former role. And the cooking was even simpler. No garnishes, sauces or reductions here – instead, the emphasis was on impeccably sourced British ingredients served without fanfare. Great British dishes – smoked eel, saddle of hare, pork belly – all made a triumphant return to the menu.

What really set tongues wagging, though, was Fergus's conviction that virtually all parts of an animal could – and should – be consumed, a return to the thrifty rural traditions of Britain's past. A starter of chitterlings or rolled pig spleen, for example. could be followed by blood cakes and fried eggs or ox heart and carrots – with squirrel (it's like tender wild rabbit) making a seasonal appearance. The new generation of Young British Artists flocking to the area at the time, including Tracey Emin, loved it; the rest of London was quick to follow suit.

Fifteen years on, and *St John* has gone from strength to strength, with a sister branch, *Bread and Wine*, in Spitalfields and a hotel in the West End. The formula remains resolute however, with some dishes – such as the unctuous roast bone marrow and parsley salad – gracing the menu just as they did on opening day in 1994. It's robust eating, and certainly not for the faint of heart, but *St John* has proved instrumental in spurring the current nationwide use of high-quality local ingredients, everywhere from five-star hotel restaurants to country gastropubs. And that's offally good news for us all.

Need to know *St John Bar & Restaurant*, 26 St John St, London EC1; *St John Bread & Wine*, 94–96 Commercial St, London E1. All reservations on ☎ 020/7251 0848, ⓦ www.st.johnrestaurant.com.. **Map 1, E2, F2**

082 Three cheers for beer

For five days of the year each summer, the somewhat soulless exhibition centre in Earls Court is transformed into a giant pub. Or at least that's what it feels like. Gone are the trade stalls and suited delegates, replaced by an army of (mostly bearded) volunteers manning hundreds of kegs, dispensing beers few people have ever heard of to thousands of squiffy punters – a lot of whom are wearing traffic-cone hats or sombreros for no apparent reason. People line up to play skittles or shuffleboard, or to grab a bag of pork scratchings, an ostrich burger or a T-shirt saying "Who drank my lunch?". Welcome to the Great British Beer Festival, a celebration of home-grown ale and its resurgence in popularity.

Beer is back on the menu in Britain – there are more breweries in operation since 1939 and cask-ale sales are rising year on year – and if you were to judge purely by the GBBF, you'd think we'd never stopped loving it. More than twelve thousand people pour through the doors every day to sample over five hundred different ales, from a Pitstop Penelope to a Radgie Gadgie. If you somehow get tired of those and are still able to stand upright, there are a hundred or so ciders and perries to imbibe, plus a large range of international beers (including some truly excellent ones from the US).

But what makes the GBBF a class apart from other beer festivals is that there's more to it than just showing up, drinking and playing spot-the-best-beer-belly. Those yet to be convinced of the hoppy stuff can take part in tutored tastings or a "Girls' Guide to Beer" tour; connoisseurs will appreciate the book signings and collectors-item beer mats for sale. Folk and country musicians occupy the stage and when the band's not playing, a pleasing rumble of chatter fills the hall. Basically, it's like being in a pub with more choice than you could ever imagine and quirky people who you wouldn't meet anywhere else. Convinced? Great. Mine's a Red MacGregor.

Need to know The festival takes place over five days in early August at Earls Court Exhibition Centre, Warwick Rd, London SW5. For details of the event, including opening hours on each day, visit CAMRA's website (ⓦ www.camra. org.uk). Tickets £10 (£8 for CAMRA members); £2 discount if booked in advance. **Map 1, A4**

POTs OF SEAFOOD
LARGE . SMALL
COCKLES £2·00 . £1·00
WHELKS £2·00 . £1·00
PRAWNs (PEELED) £2·50 . £1·50
CRAY FISH £2·50 . £1·50
JELLY EEL £2·50
MUSSLES £2·00 . £1·00
CRAB STICKs 15P EACH OR 10 £1·00
ROII MOPS 80P Sour 60P SWEET
ANCHOVIES £2·50 . £1·50
CHILLY, GARLIC, PLAIN.
SEAFOOD MIX £2·50 . £1·50
IN OIL OR PLAIN.
PINXS 25P EACH OR 5 for £1·00
LOBSTER TAIL £1·20P EACH

083 Oyster adulation on the Kent coast

Dedicating a week-long festival to the humble oyster might seem a tough act to pull off. But Whitstable, now synonymous with the world's clammiest delicacy, more than manages, luring in tens of thousands of visitors each July. Of course it's not *all* about the bivalves – there's music, poetry, art and plenty of booze sloshing around – but it's rude to leave town without sampling the star of the show, cold, quivering and freshly "shucked" from its shell.

"But, oysters in *July*?" you say. And it's true, the *crème de la crème*, the native Whitstable Oyster (once a favourite of Roman emperors) is at its succulent best in autumn and winter. Instead you'll most likely be slurping down locally grown European oysters, and perfectly acceptable they are too. The festival's quirky timing, apart from promising half-decent weather, is a legacy of St James's Day (July 25), traditionally marked with a thanksgiving service on the beach in honour of the patron saint of, you guessed it, oysters.

The sea duly pacified, the gluttony can begin as dozens of oyster stalls open for business and the punters arrive en masse (don't even think about driving in, use the free park and ride service). As well as the oyster tasting (£4.50 for six), there's a giant farmers' market and beer festival, impromptu performance art (everything from sea shanties to comedy) and a crab-catching competition for the kids. Perhaps the highlight, though, is the oyster-eating contest where iron-stomached participants sacrifice their dignity by downing four oysters and half a pint of stout in the fastest time possible.

Though the festival shouldn't be missed, you'll find Whitstable is an eminently likeable resort year-round. It preserves a rare weather-beaten charm and mercifully lacks the rows of amusement arcades and "deep-fried everything" restaurants that can blight the Kentish seaside. While seafood is its *raison d'être* (and you half expect a Rick Stein or Jamie Oliver to lay claim to the place as their own personal fiefdom), the huge skies, lingering light and cute beach huts will keep you coming back, whatever your feelings on raw molluscs.

Need to know Whitstable Oyster Festival is held annually, starting on or near July 25. For exact dates see Ⓦ www. whitstableoysterfestival.com, which also provides links to shops, restaurants and accommodation open year-round.

Map 2, F5

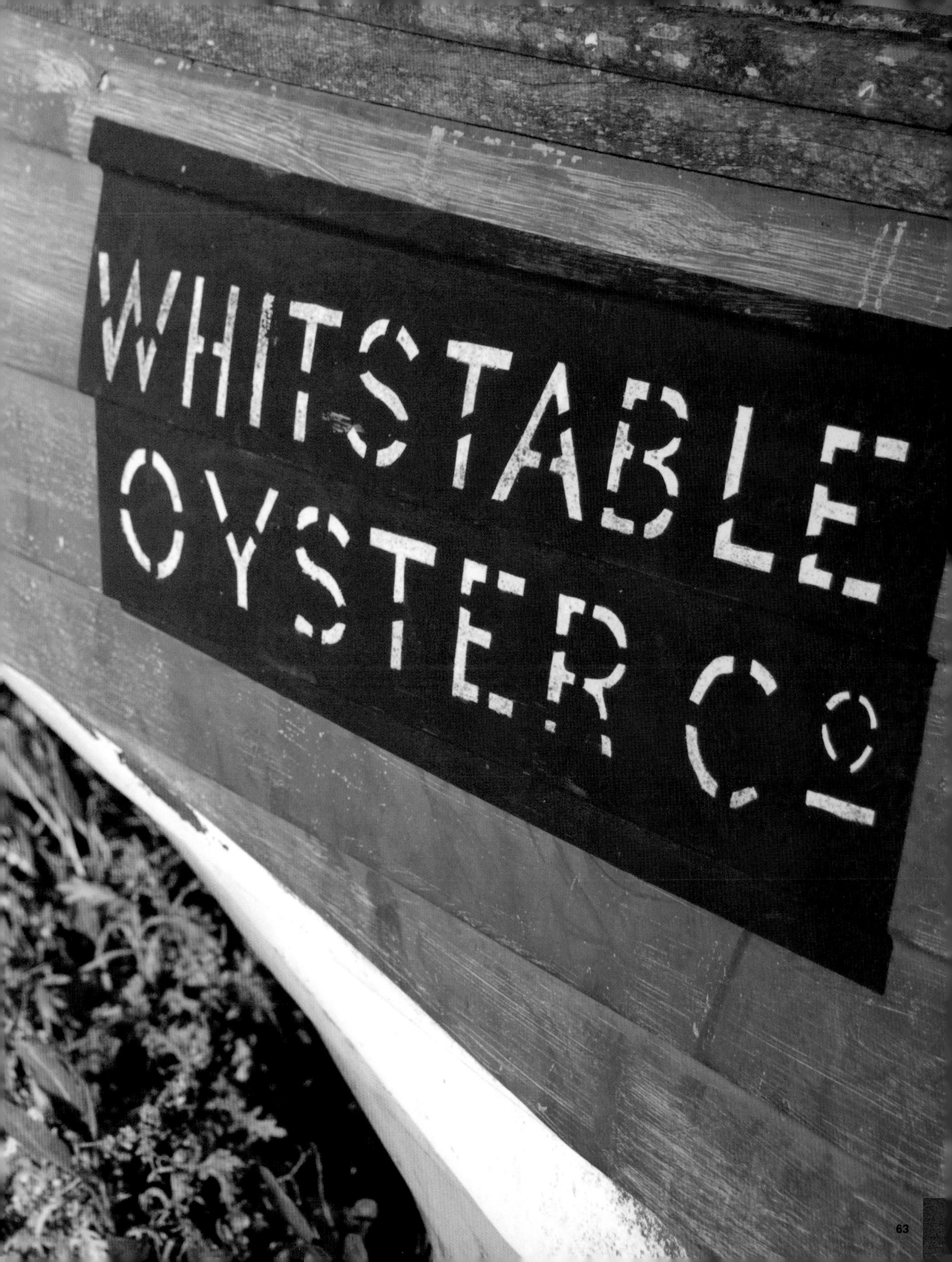
WHITSTABLE
OYSTER Co

084 Smoke gets in your adenoids: sipping Islay's world-class whisky

With their famous brand names framed on a rocky foreshore, the distilleries of Islay are among the Hebrides' most conspicuous landmarks, the whitewashed cardinal points of any self-respecting whisky tour. And just as their kiln chimneys seem wrought from some displaced seam of Orientalism, so their smoky single malts have proclaimed a new Lordship of the Isles with an export dominion extending right across the globe. Laphroaig... Lagavulin... as whisky names go, they're undeniably evocative and as redolent of luxury as they are of wind-lashed Highland romance.

Prize for Islay's most bracingly distinctive spirit belongs, most would agree, to Laphroaig, a dram of which is probably best enjoyed *in situ* at their distillery near Port Ellen on the island's south coast. If you're arriving by ferry from the Kintyre peninsula, you can't miss the bold black lettering, though that's nothing compared to the boldness of the whisky's bouquet, a remedial dose of peat and kelp that smokes the senses and tars the tongue. It mightn't be love at first taste, but it's one you won't forget, a mystery residing in moss, heather, storm-driven seaweed and an eminently soft water drawn from a loch the company have fought court battles over to keep. Also near Port Ellen is the even older and equally iconic Lagavulin, a venerable 16-year-old malt with a similarly peat-smoky if not quite so medicinal finish. Lagavulin is also the sponsor of Islay's acclaimed September jazz festival, itself a connoisseur's dream of single malt and music, with intimate gigs in local inns and even distilleries.

Further east is Ardbeg, a dramatically sited huddle of pipes and stills dating to the early nineteenth century, definitively saved from oblivion in the late twentieth and famously described by whisky authority Jim Murray as "the greatest distillery to be found on earth". Perhaps, and there can be few pleasures as heady as a dram of deeply peaty, citrus-hinted Ardbeg in their kiln-sequestered café. Oldest of all Islay distilleries, however, is Bowmore, a beach-fringed northern stalwart whose lighter strain of peat-reek is perfect for newbies. Just don't forget to add water.

Need to know Up-to-date tour times and prices are available on the individual distillery websites: Ⓦ www.laphroaig.com; Ⓦ www.discovering-distilleries.com/Lagavulin; Ⓦ www.ardbeg.com; Ⓦ www.bowmore.co.uk. Note that many distilleries close in July and August. For the jazz festival line-up see Ⓦ www.islayjazzfestival.co.uk.

Map 4, B14

085 Ludlow: take it easy in Britain's Slow Food capital

The Slow Food movement – champion of local production, traditional cuisine and, above all, good food – may have its origins in Italy but since the 1990s has become firmly established in Britain, with nine member towns across the country. The first to join, in 2003, was the charming Shropshire market town of Ludlow, which has strong claims to be at the vanguard of this particular epicurean revolution. With its string of much-lauded restaurants, celebrated food festival, and stupendous array of delis, butchers and speciality food and drink stores, it's something close to Eden for anyone with a serious interest in their grub.

Try to come in mid-September if you can, when the imposing ruins of the town's Norman-built castle play host to one of Britain's biggest and best food festivals, with over a hundred small local producers offering their wares in huge marquees. A highlight is the sausage trail, which takes you to every butcher in town to sample a banger. Locals swear by D.W. Wall & Son, champion of rare breed meat and game, which with its tiled interior and wooden chopping boards feels like something from another age. The beef is the thing here, from Red Poll to Longhorn, and their beef sausages are simply the finest you'll find in the UK.

Don't fret if you miss out on the festival, as Ludlow is a gastronomic delight at any time. There's a farmers' market twice a month, and the market square is packed with stalls four days a week. Then there are the inspirational shops – three superb bakers (try Price & Sons), two cheese shops (The Mousetrap is a fine bet) and a chocolatier (The Chocolate Gourmet) – not to mention the brace of Michelin-starred restaurants, *Mr Underhill's* and *La Bécasse*, in town, and several others in the surrounding Marches.

The final stage of the foodie pilgrimage is out to the town's northern outskirts, where the Ludlow Food Centre, housed in a vast converted barn, sells a magnificent array of superb local produce, much of it from the Earl of Plymouth's surrounding estate – ask any keen gastronome in town what to buy here and expect a long conversation. The local Bromfield Priory cheese, famed Shropshire "fidget" pies, home-made Seville marmalade and Victoria Sponge made by Anna in the bakery department – all are enough to make you pause before ever entering a supermarket again.

Need to know The Ludlow Food Festival (Ⓦ www.foodfestival.co.uk) is held over three days in mid-September, and the farmers' market on the second and fourth Thurs of each month. D.W. Wall & Son, 14 High St, Ludlow ☎ 01584/872060, Ⓦ www.wallsbutchers.co.uk; Ludlow Food Centre, Bromfield, Ludlow ☎ 01584/856000, Ⓦ www.ludlowfoodcentre.co.uk. See Ⓦ www.ludlow.org.uk for details of other shops and restaurants.

Map 3, C12

086 Glasgow's Italian soft spot

On paper, it doesn't look like the best business plan: hawking ice cream in the most infamously cold and damp of climates. Yet for hundreds of Italian immigrants at the turn of the twentieth century, the prospect of pushing a handcart up and down the mean streets of Britain's industrial cities was a more attractive option than the grinding rural poverty back home. Many gravitated to Glasgow, engine room of the empire with a working populace ripe for conversion to what was then an exotic foreign luxury. As such, this frozen marvel was to cause no end of controversy, blamed for everything from Sunday trading to juvenile delinquency. Yet with more than 300 shops operating by 1905 alone, ice-cream cones – and the families who sold them – were to become an integral and much loved fixture of Scottish life.

Today, though the traditional Italian café has become something of an endangered species, there can't be many Glaswegians who don't know their Knickerbocker Glory from their 99, and, basking in the humble bustle of a place like *University Café*, in the city's West End, it's difficult to imagine what all the fuss was about. Open since 1918, the place could win a prize for its vintage-kitsch window display alone. Inside, shelves groan with glass jars, the wood panelling goes back generations and the mirrored walls reflect one of the most loyal clienteles in the city, some slurping away at the prize-winning, home-made vanilla, chocolate or strawberry, others tucking into pretension-free pasta.

Just as treasured, and perhaps even more atmospheric, is *Café D'Jaconelli* in Maryhill, opened in 1924. With its seriously old-school frontage, boiled sweeties and glass door etching of sundae-with-smoking ashtray, it's become something of a city icon, famously frequented by the likes of Billy Connolly and the subject of cameos in films such as *Carla's Song* and *Trainspotting*. *Jaconelli*'s claims its ice cream as the best in the city – and they may just be right. Enjoy it in a red leather booth against the luminous glow of a fish tank, and you'll experience the very essence of a guilty pleasure that's defied the Glasgow drizzle for nigh on a century.

Need to know *University Café*, 87 Byres Rd, Glasgow ☎0141/339 5217. *Café D'Jaconelli*, 570 Maryhill Rd, Glasgow ☎0141/946 1124. Even the most decadent sundae won't set you back more than a fiver in either place.
Map 4, C14

087 Padstein and beyond: seafood and sparkling wine on the Cornish coast

There remain few places more idyllic than the quay at Padstow to tuck into a mountainous portion of fish and chips. With the ocean so close, it's little surprise that seafood is the speciality: your fish might have been caught just hours before by the boats in view, or landed that very morning in nearby Falmouth or Newlyn. And pick up your fish supper from *Stein's Fish and Chips*, part of the ever-expanding portfolio of the area's best-known piscatorial magnate, and it's not just cod or haddock on the menu. On a typical day at Stein's quayside chippie there's also a choice of sea bream, hake, lemon sole and even monkfish.

Padstow and its environs are full of fabulous food – from pasty shops to delis, ice-cream parlours to gastropubs – but this chic little fishing village is best known for its high-class restaurants. The seeds for Padstow's much-lauded dining scene were planted when Stein opened his flagship *Seafood Restaurant* opened back in 1975. Arguably still Padstow's headliner, here you are treated to a seafood extravaganza – ranging from classic fruits de mer or lobster Thermidor to melt-in-the-mouth scallop, sea bass and salmon sashimi, and gorgeously messy Singapore chilli crab – in classy, modern but unpretentious surroundings. It still gets booked out well ahead – proof the experience is worth splashing out for. But there's more to Steinland than the *Seafood Restaurant*, and you can also sample the celeb chef's eminent cuisine – at more affordable prices – at the less fish-dominated *Stein's Café* and *St Petroc's Bistro*.

While it's easy to bang on about Stein, the town's foodie credentials have long been boosted by competition to Rick's monopoly, and a number of serious rivals are drawing the gastronomes elsewhere. Helmed by Paul Ainsworth, one of Gordon Ramsay's protégés, the esteemed *Number 6 Restaurant* is one such place, a stylish and sophisticated outfit showcasing local produce in innovative dishes. Meanwhile, across the harbour in Rock, Nathan Outlaw pulls in foodies in the know to his outstanding signature restaurant at the *St Enodoc Hotel*.

The seafood may be out of this world, but hemmed by Atlantic coastline *and* the lush Camel Valley, there are acres of farmland to support high-quality locally reared and grown meat, veg and dairy – the Padstow Farm Shop has a superb selection. And, as if the culinary credentials aren't enough to pull you in, nearby Camel Valley Vineyard produces award-winning vintages that have proved a phenomenal success on the international wine scene.

Need to know Rick Stein's restaurants ⊛www.rickstein.com; *Number 6 Restaurant* ⊛www.number6inpadstow.co.uk; *Nathan Outlaw* ⊛www.nathan-outlaw.co.uk; Padstow Farm Shop ⊛www.padstowfarmshop.co.uk; Camel Valley Vineyard ⊛www.camelvalley.com. Check out ⊛www.padstowlive.com for general info on Padstow.
Map 2, A7

088 Leeds Corn Exchange: welcome to the gastrodome

On first acquaintance, the magnificence of Leeds Corn Exchange can be a tad intimidating. Great elliptical roof, balconies, banisters, flights of steps and a riot of wrought iron – the sheer Victorian scale and exuberance of the place is breathtaking. But be not faint of heart, for this is a polished gastronomic gem.

Dinky boutiques now colonize its upper levels, but descend to the piazza floor and you'll see beautifully lit food shops tucked under the arches off to the right. The Patisserie glories in its cupcakes and muffins – mouth-melting perfection; the Fromagerie is temperature and humidity controlled to protect its artisan cheeses; why the Chocolaterie includes a holding room is a mystery – who'd want to escape? And the bakery just smells like heaven. Beyond the shops, there's a café and a champagne bar, both achingly cool.

As you enter the restaurant itself, spacious beneath its soaring dome, you'll find that, despite the grand surroundings, the attitude of the young staff is pitch-perfect: friendly, enthusiastic, well informed yet unobsequious. Staff selection and training must be spot on.

Then you'll notice how good the food is. Not pretentious (though courtesy of *Masterchef* and others, we all know our monkfish ceviche from our sous-vide mackerel), but beautifully cooked, locally sourced and delicious.

When you look at what Anthony Flinn and his family (dad, sister, partner) have done in a few short years for eating out in Leeds, you wonder why nobody thought of it before. Top-quality food, with ingredients sourced from the lush surrounding Yorkshire countryside, aimed at every level of eating out – from lunchtime coffee and a cake in the Victoria Quarter patisserie to the fine dining of the Boar Lane restaurant. It's *Piazza by Anthony* though, aimed somewhere in between, that's really got tongues wagging. Brought to you by two innovative, ambitious young men – thirty-something Cuthbert Broderick, who designed the building in 1860, and twenty-something Anthony, who rejuvenated the city's dining scene a century and a half later – it takes pride of place among Leeds' culinary experiences.

Fine dining is the new rock'n'roll, they say, chefs the new guitar heroes. Let's drink (and eat) to that.

Need to know *Piazza by Anthony*, The Corn Exchange, Call Lane, Leeds ☎ 0113/247 0995, ⓦ www.anthonysrestaurant.co.uk. The restaurant is open daily Mon–Thurs 10am–10pm, Fri & Sat 10am–10.30pm, Sun 10am–9pm. Hours for the café and champagne bar differ.
Map 3, C10

089 A feast of fish at Billingsgate Market

Forget fish and chips. Set your alarm – deep breath – for around 4am, pull on a pair of wellies (or at least turn up your trousers) and make for Billingsgate Market in the heart of London's Docklands for an unbeatable hands-on shopping experience and the chance to stock up for many a fish dinner to come.

A tolling bell declares Billingsgate open for business at 5am, but in fact the market never really sleeps – the porters and merchants start work well before dawn and deliveries of up to 150 or so varieties of fish and shellfish arrive throughout the night from all over the UK and beyond. With only a few hours of trading each day, activity is frenetic, competition between merchants fierce and the banter brusque and bawdy. You won't feel drowsy for long – if the bright lights and clamour of voices don't wake you up, you can guarantee the writhing racks of eels, inky trays of cuttlefish, perhaps even the unmistakeable spike of a swordfish poking from a passing porter's trolley will set your head in a spin.

Although the market has only been in its present home beneath Canary Wharf since 1982, when it moved from the City of London, its origins stretch back to Roman times. Fishing and delivery methods and the sheer range of stock may have changed beyond recognition but you can still rely on the merchants, many of whom come from generations of Billingsgate traders, to fill you in on how and where the fish was caught, as well as how best to cook it. They're not pulling your leg when they tell you about sightings of other marine life in these parts, either – there really is a resident, very well-fed seal who bobs around in the dock waters behind the market.

Unless you own a sizeable freezer, visiting with a group of friends is a good bet as you'll need to buy in bulk – a whole salmon, say, or a tray of pearlescent octopus – and you may well get carried away. Post-shopping you can refuel with a fry-up at one of the market cafés, be on your way home before most of the city is waking up and, after a well-deserved siesta, reconvene for a delicious fish feast.

Need to know Billingsgate Market, Trafalgar Way, London E14 ⓦ www.billingsgate-market.org.uk Open Tues–Sat 5–8.30am. Fish cookery courses are available at the on-site Billingsgate Seafood Training School (☎020/7517 3548, ⓔinfo@seafoodtraining.org).
Map 1, F4

090 Sup a pint in England's oldest pub

During the Middle Ages, the water quality in Nottingham – as elsewhere across the kingdom – was notoriously poor. Locals often resorted to brewing ale because the fermentation process created a palatable, nutritious product safe to drink – albeit one with alcoholic benefits. And so, when Nottingham Castle was built for William the Conquerer in 1068, a brewhouse was one of its first additions. The sandstone caves at the base of the castle proved an ideal location as they provided the steady, cool temperature required for brewing.

Thankfully, Nottingham's water quality has improved over the past thousand years, so locals and visitors have to think of another excuse for stopping off for a pint at *Ye Olde Trip to Jerusalem*, which occupies the brewhouse site and claims (alongside twenty or so rivals) to be the oldest pub in England. Dating back to 1189, *Ye Olde Trip*'s curious name would seem to support its case: it derives from the era of the Crusades, when Richard the Lionheart's knights would stop off at the inn for sustenance before the long journey to the Holy Land ("trip" in those days meaning a resting place, rather than a journey).

Although the black-and-white-timbered exterior dates from the seventeenth century, the interior is wonderfully evocative of the pub's more ancient heritage: there's a distinctly cave-like feel, with stone walls, aged wooden beams, narrow passageways and cramped alcoves. Downstairs in the cellar, where the beer barrels are now stored, are the remains of an old castle jail cell, as well as a former cockfighting pit (call the pub beforehand if you want to take a look down here). Sadly, the pub ceased its brewing role years ago, but there is a fine range of beers, ales and stouts on offer. The perfect thing to sup – of course – is Olde Trip, a rich and faintly fruity ale brewed for the pub by Greene King.

If you've developed a taste for Nottingham's subterranean medieval history, head up to the castle from where you can tour the labyrinth of man-made caves and tunnels that lie beneath it. There are a wealth of intriguing sites to explore, including the Duke of Newcastle's wine cellar, King David of Scotland's dungeon and Mortimer's Hole, through which King Edward III's supporters snuck into the castle and captured the treacherous Roger Mortimer, who had organized the murder of the young king's father, Edward II, in 1327.

Need to know *Ye Olde Trip to Jerusalem*, Brewhouse Yard, Nottingham ☎0115/947 3171, ⓦwww.triptojerusalem.com. Open Mon–Thurs & Sun 10am–11pm, Fri & Sat 10am–midnight. For details of tours of Nottingham Castle Caves, see ⓦwww.nottinghamcity.gov.uk.
Map 3, D11

091 Wallace's favourite cheese

Wallace: Won't you come in? We're about to have some cheese.
Wendoline: Oh no, not cheese. Sorry. Brings me out in a rash. Can't stand the stuff.
Wallace: (gulp) Not even Wensleydale?

Fans of Nick Park's amusing clay-based tales will know that toothy Wallace is an ardent cheese-lover, and his particular favourite is the deliciously crumbly, tangy Wensleydale. When he chose to highlight the cheese, Park was unaware that the Wensleydale Creamery, based in Hawes, deep in the Yorkshire Dales, was suffering such low sales that production of the cheese was close to suspension. PR played its part though, and with the creation of a special Wallace and Gromit-branded cheese, the Creamery's sales soared.

Film works aside, Wensleydale cheese has been a long-standing member of Yorkshire's culinary heritage. Cheese-making was introduced into the area in the twelfth century by French Cistercian monks, and their recipes and techniques were handed down through the generations. In 1897, a farmer based in Hawes went one step further: he decided to use cow's milk sourced solely from Wensleydale to make cheese on a large scale. Popularity of the cheese grew steadily, but then came the 1930s Depression, which killed off many Dales dairies and farms. Battling against this backdrop was Yorkshire businessman Kit Calvert, who cobbled together enough capital and local support to save the dairy in Hawes. Today, after a brief closure in 1992, the Creamery is a thriving business, as well as a popular visitor centre.

Located a couple of minutes' walk from the centre of the village, the Creamery includes a small museum outlining the history of the cheese, with charming reconstructions of milking parlours – complete with milking stools, pails and bottles – and a typical Yorkshire kitchen equipped with bygone cooking implements and a cosy hearth. Next, visitors access the viewing gallery, where glass windows overlook massive vats filled with swirling milk; you can also watch factory workers pressing and cutting the cheese by hand. Final stop is the cheese shop, where samples are on offer – including varieties such as Wensleydale with sweet apricot, pungent garlic or spicy ginger. With creamy Jervaulx Blue their latest achievement, the Wensleydale Creamery has – thanks to Kit Calvert's dogged determination and Nick Park's little clay friends – firmly established itself on the English cheese board.

Need to know Wensleydale
Creamery, Gayle Lane, Hawes,
Wensleydale, North Yorkshire
Ⓦwww.wensleydale.co.uk. Open
daily: museum 10am–4pm; cheese
shop 9am–5.30pm. Museum £2.50.
Cheeses from £2.50.
Map 3, C9

092 The proof is in the pudding

Thick, heavy, covered in sickly sauce and drowned with lashings of custard – few things are as downright delightful as the great British pudding. And in a time of health-food fads and waistline watching, few things need celebrating more. Which is precisely what happens every Friday in the *Three Ways House Hotel* in north Gloucestershire, where the Pudding Club pays homage to bygone tarts and old-school sponges.

Founded in 1985, Pudding Club has become something of a culinary cult, and now each "meeting" is attended by some seventy dessert devotees. Like a glutinous version of *Fight Club*, the club has its rules: you may eat only one pudding at a time; you must finish your pudding before moving on to the next one; you cannot go up to the pudding table out of turn. There are others (and you most certainly *can* talk about Pudding Club), but more important is the unwritten rule to go easy on the meal served beforehand. Most veterans skip this stage altogether, and you'll see why when the main event arrives: seven sticky, fluffy, baked or steamed traditional British puds, paraded through the dining room with the pomp and ceremony of a royal arrival.

The selection varies week to week, but it's always an interesting spread, rich in history as much as taste. Pudding Club favourite Sticky Toffee and Date is usually in there, oozing with hot toffee sauce, though as it was created in the 1970s (at the *Sharrow Bay Hotel* in the Lake District, where it was originally called Icky Sticky Toffee Sponge), it's a comparative youngster. Spotted Dick, whose name derives from its raisin content and a corruption of the word "pudding" (puddink, puddick, dick) has more of a heritage, its recipe first appearing in print in 1851.

Look out, too, for Cumberland Rum Nicky, a sticky tart whose exotic ingredients – dates, ginger and rum – are a nod to the area's trade with the West Indies in the early 1900s, and, of course, Bread and Butter Pudding, which stems from the early seventeenth century, when stale bread was steamed, fruit, meat and any other leftovers added, and the whole thing baked in an oven.

Tradition never tasted this good.

Need to know Pudding Club (Ⓦ www.puddingclub.com) costs £34 per person and is held at 7.30pm every Friday at the *Three Ways House Hotel*, Mickleton, Gloucestershire (Ⓦ www.threewayshousehotel.com).
Map 3, C12

093 Drink with the dockers in Liverpool

Away from the rejuvenated city centre, Liverpool's docks can be eerily quiet these days. Though iconic Albert Dock – home to Tate Liverpool, the Mersey Maritime Museum and a host of other attractions – was magnificently restored in the 1980s, much of this vast former fulcrum of industry remains a sad picture of postindustrial decline, with acres of warehouses, locks and offices lying empty and forlorn. Liverpool's waterfront is now UNESCO World Heritage listed, but many of its buildings stand elegiacally derelict, not least the incredible tobacco warehouse on neglected Stanley Dock – the largest brick warehouse in the world. It's simply too big for any developers to take on.

   Many of the hundreds of pubs in this once teeming area have also met a predictable fate. Some have been boarded up for decades, victims of the decline of the docking industry. There are, however, a few beautiful old-timers that somehow still manage to flourish. Step into *The Atlantic* on Regent Road and you'll feel like you're entering a Liverpool that has never heard of Steven Gerrard, Paul O'Grady or even the Fab Four. Firmly stuck in the early 1950s, this one-room pub still has sawdust on its floors and a skiffle band in the corner on Sunday lunchtime. Retired dockers sup pints of spectacularly cheap ale, joined by families and in-the-know traditionalists who simply refuse to see such an important slice of Liverpool social life die out.

   Back towards the city centre and stop off at *The Baltic Fleet*, shaped like a ship, and the only pub on Merseyside with its own brewery. Minutes can slip into hours when settled into the bijou drinking area, complete with a real wood stove; you can even partake in a pinch of snuff tobacco, available at the bar. This is also the best place to sample Liverpool's most famous dish – Scouse. Still popular today, this stew served with bread and beetroot was in former times a welcome taste of home for returning sailors after months at sea, or for fatigued dockers after a nightshift unloading cargo from distant shores.

   One day, dozen more pubs along here may reopen their doors, but for now, the majority of visitors to Liverpool are too wrapped up in the bar scene in Concert Square to venture into this forgotten spot. Come for a pint and drink a toast to the dockers who made Liverpool one of the most important trading centres on earth.

Need to know *The Atlantic*, 162 Regent Rd, Liverpool ☎0151/922 9815; *The Baltic Fleet*, 33 Wapping, Liverpool ☎0151/709 3116. Both are open daily from noon to 11pm.
Map 3, B10

094 Eel of fortune: gourmand gold in the Somerset Levels

Each spring, they arrive in their thousands, wriggling their way up through the rhynes and ditches that crisscross the Somerset Levels. It's taken a year to get here, the warm currents of the Gulf Stream carrying them some three thousand miles across the Atlantic from their breeding grounds in the Sargasso Sea near Bermuda. No one really knows why the European eel makes such a mammoth journey, only to return when fully mature, to spawn and die. Or what triggers their transformations on the way that take them from larvae to "glass" eel to elver. In fact, not much is known at all about this mysterious creature, other than they don't half taste good.

   Elvers (baby eels) have been a central Somerset delicacy for hundreds of years: covered in flour and deep-fried, cooked with bacon and served in an omelette or, best of all, smoked. At Brown & Forrest, a family-run smokery in the heart of the Levels, they've been hand-smoking eels for over thirty years, using a system that goes back a hundred. The eels, pulled from the nearby River Parrett, are hot-smoked over beech and apple wood. It's a short process but a fine art: the eels are roasted over an open fire, which is then blanketed with sawdust to create more fumes, resulting in a succulent fish with a tantalizing hint of salt and smoke. Beech brings out their delicate flavour – oak, used for smoking salmon and trout, would overpower the eel's natural taste – while apple gives them a mellow sweetness.

   The coppery-skinned creatures are then whipped out of the smokery, aromatic clouds billowing about them, and served fresh on rye bread at the on-site restaurant, or vacuum-packed for the deli next door. Add a squeeze of lemon and a pinch of pepper (or, for the smoked-eel aficionado, a dash of horseradish), but not too much – you still want to taste the briny tang of the Sargasso Sea.

Need to know
Brown & Forrest is at Bowden Farm Smokery, Hambridge, Somerset ☎01458/250875, ✆www.smokedeel.co.uk; the shop and restaurant are open Mon–Sat 10am–4pm. A 200g packet of hot-smoked eel over beech and apple costs £2.
Map 2, C6

LOCALLY GROWN WATERCRESS 80p BUNCH

095 The fat of the land:
from water buffalo to watercress in Winchester

In a small English cathedral town there is a corner of a car park that is, well, forever France. Or it is every second or third Sunday, anyway. This is when the Hampshire Farmers' Market comes to Winchester, drawing with it a host of discerning foodies. But the Frenchness of this event has nothing to do with the customers. The uniform here – think green wellies, jumbo cords and a battered fleece – is definitively Middle England. No, the Frenchness of this market is all about the proudly, rampantly regional produce.

The market rules say that all stallholders have to farm (or bake, or brew, or pickle) their produce in Hampshire, or within ten miles of the county borders. Hampshire has some of the finest farmland in Britain, and the stalls here are the exquisite proof. For meat alone, you could stock up on water buffalo steaks, a leg of muntjac venison, some wood pigeon breasts, Longhorn beef sausages (though they often sell out) and a roll of organic topside beef. The cheesemaker will offer you some Lyburn Gold as you walk buy, but ask for the Old Winchester; it's the connoisseur's choice. Sea fish comes up with the fishermen from Portsmouth, and it's not your usual supermarket choice of cod, salmon or tuna: think turbot, clams and cuttlefish. The river fish is pulled out of Hampshire's unique chalk streams (some salmon, but mostly trout – either fresh, smoked or turned into delicious pâté) as is the wealth of local watercress.

There are stalls from the Isle of Wight devoted to tomatoes, and garlic. There are home-made cakes and pickles and jams and soaps and an array of artisanal breads that would put France to shame. Even the Hampshire wines, such as Fonthill Glebe, are making a reputation, and of course there are ciders and bitters and a particularly good stall selling rare-variety apple juice. This being well-to-do Winchester, even the snacks are a cut above. The Broughton water buffalo burgers are utterly delicious. If you baulk at buffalo, try the watercress scones, or the free-range hog roast in a bun.

Need to know The market tours Hampshire, usually returning to Winchester on the second and last Sunday of every month (see Ⓦ www.hampshirefarmersmarkets. co.uk for dates). The venue is a central car park, five minutes' walk from the cathedral, ten from the train station.

Map 2, D6

096 Deep-fried heaven in Glasgow

Need to know Kings Café, 71 Elmbank St, Glasgow ☎ 0141/332 3247; Pizza Crolla, 156 Buchanan St, Glasgow ☎ 0141/333 0016; Glasgow Royal Infirmary, 84 Castle St ☎ 0141/211 4000.

Map 4, C14

Despite Scotland's burgeoning food culture, prompting unprecedented interest in local produce, global cuisine and environmental health, the Glaswegian diet remains something of a national joke, the city's reputation as Europe's heart attack capital a source of frequently ill-disguised civic pride. Certainly, it's gallows humour that led one of the city's more upmarket West End restaurants to be christened The Ubiquitous Chip. Mind you, nobody deep-fries it better.

There's strong evidence to suggest that Glasgow's signature dish, the deep-fried Mars bar, started off predominantly as an urban myth, but the concept intrigued so many it became a widespread reality. Either way, there's no escaping the fact that the combination of soft, gooey chocolatey caramel and slightly savoury crisp exterior is horribly compelling – though you wouldn't want a second (and, let's face it, you'll struggle to finish a first). Kings Café, just off Sauchiehall Street's main drinking drag, is a proud purveyor – though in truth, takeaways throughout the city will usually deep-fry any confectionery you like for a modestly negotiated fee.

Battered Creme eggs are also prized, but their popularity – and that of the deep-fried Mars bar – was preceded by that of the deep-fried pizza, a dubious by-product of Glasgow's sizeable Italian population – at least the healthy Mediterranean diet is making inroads somehow. For a "pizza supper" a whole or half portion is typically dunked in oil without batter (accompanied of course by Irn-Bru), but Pizza Crolla are renowned for their less health-conscious variation, the battered Pizza Crunch. If this isn't quite enough to soak up the booze, you can always cut the pizza in half and fill it with chips – hey presto, a pizza and chip sandwich.

Tastiest of all, however, and undisputed king of all Glaswegian battered dishes, is the deep-fried haggis. Though it may look and sound as appetizing as its affectionate nickname, the "scabby dick", for many Glaswegians chowing down a deep-fried version of this winning blend of sheep's heart, liver and lungs, oatmeal and spices equates to a patriotic duty. Would Robert Burns, Scotland's best-loved bard and author of the immortal "Address to a Haggis" have approved? You bet he would.

097 Breakfasting like a king at an East End institution

It's 11am on Saturday morning at the *E Pellicci* café on Bethnal Green Road, and everyone is bloody hungry. There's a queue out the door, and ravenous customers poke their heads in periodically, desperate for an available seat. From the outside, it's hard to see what the fuss is about. But behind the unassuming exterior of this little building lies a wonderful Art Deco-style interior (a postwar addition responsible for the current Grade II listing), with stained-glass panels bearing the name of the family who have run the place since 1900. Even more enticing are the huge plates of home-cooked food that await you inside.

Once you've bagged a seat, wave for the menu of Italian and British staples. Above your head, the staff banter oscillates between Cockney and Italian, and customers clamour to order over the bilingual bellows. For an idea of those who've dined here before you, look up at the signed framed photos of EastEnders actors dotting the walls, and the snapshots of other famous faces peeking out from behind the steaming tea urn. *Pellicci*'s breakfast menu features all the permutations of a classic full English, plus loads of extras for a build-your-own feast. Unlike mediocre greasy spoons with their limp, oily no. 3 breakfasts, what you get here is of superior quality, and service comes extra-friendly with a healthy dose of mickey-taking. If the fry-up doesn't appeal, there's plenty more to choose from: steak pies, fish and chip specials, scampi and more, as well as mouthwatering Italian favourites – standard pasta dishes, cannelloni and mountainous servings of lasagne. Best of all are the famous hand-cut chips (finish 'em, or you'll be outed as a lightweight).

Clearly, the drawback of eating at such a popular establishment is that you have to wait your turn. Punters stare murderously at plates that arrive before their own. Another full English bangs down a tantalizing few inches away. And just when you're beginning to wonder why on earth you came to sit in a small, hot room full of chatter and other people's food, yours arrives, and it's the heartiest portion yet. You may need to lie down for an hour afterwards, and you probably won't be on speaking terms with your arteries, but yes, it is the finest breakfast in London.

Need to know *E Pellicci*, 332 Bethnal Green Rd, London E2 ☎ 020/7739 4873; Mon–Sat 7am–4pm; closed Aug.
Map 1, F2

098 Miner's delight: the Cornish pasty

Cornwall's gastronomic reputation thrives on the bounty of the sea, but the county's most famous food export was, for centuries, taken deep into the bowels of the earth. The pasty (or *oggy* in the Cornish dialect) was the staple lunch of tin miners, who could hold the crimped crust in their grubby hands and throw that part away after eating the filling, which used to consist of meat and veg on one side and jam on the other. The discarded crusts were also said to be the favourite snack of the knockers – capricious spirits who had to be appeased to keep the men safe from danger. Miners' wives would etch their husband's name into his pasty; even today, some bakeries will mark a customer's initials on a pre-ordered batch.

At its best, the pasty is the ultimate comfort food. Hot from the oven and golden brown, with steam escaping from the cracks, it's wonderfully satisfying on a winter's day. Three million of these gut-busting snacks are made every week in Cornwall, though as any local will tell you, many of them ain't proper. To be considered genuine, it must be crimped to one side rather than on top, must have no filling other than chuck steak, sliced potato, onion and swede, and these ingredients must be raw prior to baking. Purists roll their eyes at carrots and such abominations as lamb and mint. Imagine the controversy, then, when in 2009 a Devonshire company won "Best Cornish Pasty" at the British Pie Awards. Fortunately order was restored when the Proper Cornish Food Company wrested the title back over the Tamar the following year.

Perhaps the best place to make a pilgrimage is Ann's Pasties, a small shop in The Lizard that made its name when it was featured on Rick Stein's TV series *Food Heroes*. Here, at the mainland's southern tip, Ann Muller sells sublime pasties loaded with beef sourced from nearby cows and potatoes and swede grown by Roland Hill, a farmer in the village. If you're planning on walking the South West Coast Path, this makes for a perfect picnic stop.

Need to know Ann's Pasties, Sunny Corner, 3 Beacon Terrace, The Lizard, Cornwall ☎01326/290889, Ⓦwww.annspasties.co.uk. The shop opens at 9am Mon–Sat (closed Mon Nov–Easter) and shuts when they sell the last pasty.
Map 2, A7

099 A toast to England: wine-tasting in Kent

With the industry dominated by Old World heavyweights France and Italy, and New World upstarts like Chile and California, it's hardly surprising that English wine has always struggled to gain a foothold in the global wine market. But put that glass of champagne down: not any more. Though wine has been made in England since the Normans – some say since the Romans – it wasn't until the 1960s that vines began to be grown on a commercial scale. Since then the industry has expanded exponentially and now produces wines to rival even the most established competitors. English sparkling wine has been the most successful so far: with a soil and topography not dissimilar from the chalky *terroir* of the Champagne basin, the vineyards of the South Downs have produced some award-winning fizz in recent years. But numerous whites, rosés and even reds are following in their wake.

There are now over four hundred vineyards in England, mainly concentrated in the sunny southern counties. Many are open to the public for tours and tastings. One of the best of the bunch is Kent's oldest commercial vineyard at Biddenden, a family-run concern producing wines from ten varieties of grape of Germanic origin, including Ortega, Dornfelder and Schonburger. Currently producing around 80,000 bottles a year, Biddenden has won numerous prizes, including English Wine of the Year in 2008, awarded to its medium-bodied white wine, Ortega.

Visitors are free to wander round the vineyard at their leisure, or join the free tour that takes place on various weekends throughout the year. A friendly guide leads you past neat rows of straight, beautifully pruned vines, explaining the history of the business and the ins and outs of viticulture. The best time to visit the vineyard is during the harvest (Sept–Nov), when you can watch harvesters busily picking juicy bunches of grapes. The tour then moves to the barns, where the grapes are pulped, ready for bottling.

After all the walking and talking it's time to get down to the business of tasting. Free samples of the wine you've just seen growing in the fields are on offer, from the deliciously light Gribble Bridge rosé made from Dornfelder to the sparkling white, a refreshing blend of Reichensteiner, Pinot Noir and Scheurebe – and of course there's the opportunity to purchase a few bottles. Roll over Bordeaux, it's time to celebrate the English grape – cheers!

Need to know Biddenden Vineyards, Gribble Bridge Lane, Biddenden, Kent ☎ 01580/291726, 🌐 www.biddendenvineyards.com. The winery is open Mon–Sat 10am–5pm, Sun 11am–5pm (closed Sun in Jan & Feb). Check the website for details of tours.
Map 2, F6

100 Pint-sized: beer in a Nutshell

Which is the smallest pub in Britain? Well, you'd think that would be an easy enough argument to settle, but not so – and publicans have been arguing the toss forever. What can't be disputed is just how small *The Nutshell*, in the heart of the pretty Suffolk town of Bury St Edmunds, actually is. Just fifteen feet by seven, it's big enough for twelve customers or maybe fifteen – but only if they can raise a pint without raising their elbows (though for a charity gig no less than 102 drinkers managed to squeeze inside on one splendid occasion in the 1980s). As you might expect, successive landlords have warmed to the theme of the pub's rather diminutive size and the antique interior, with its wood panelling, benches and gnarled bar, has at one time or another held the world's smallest dartboard and the world's smallest snooker table.

So why is the pub so minuscule? Because it was an afterthought: in the 1850s, a local pawnbroker by the name of John Stebbings decided to diversify, buying the premises next door to his shop to sell fruit, veg and ales – and so *The Nutshell* was born. Since then, it's accumulated all sorts of tall tales and is supposedly haunted by no fewer than four ghosts, including a pair of illicit lovers, a monk and a pregnant nun in the cellar, and a boy who appears in the bath in which he was murdered up above on the third floor. As if that were not enough, the desiccated body of a dried cat hangs from the ceiling – the result of an old builders' custom to wall in cats behind the fireplace to ward off the evil eye; the poor old feline was found during renovations.

As for the brews on sale, *The Nutshell* is owned by Bury's very own Greene King brewery, which provides some sterling beers. Stop in for a pint of the full-bodied Abbot Ale, superb Old Speckled Hen, a ruddy ale with a tangy zip, or the lighter IPA – India Pale Ale, named after the days when it was exported by the barrel load to British expatriates sweltering in the heat of India. Just don't bring all your mates.

Need to know The Nutshell, The Traverse, Bury St Edmunds, Suffolk ☎ 01284/764867, 🌐 www.thenutshellpub.co.uk. The pub is open daily 11am–11pm.
Map 3, E12

BRITAIN'S PROTECTED FOODS

They may not be as internationally renowned as Parma ham, Greek feta or champagne, but Britain boasts an increasing range of tasty regional produce whose "unique heritage, character and reputation" is protected by the EU. Here are five of the best.

101 Herefordshire cider

Cider's come a long way since the days of The Wurzels, and these days Brits consume more cider per head than any other nation on earth. Herefordshire – one of three counties where production is protected – grows 20 percent of the UK's cider apples, some of which of course go into mass-produced fizz, but you can still experience the real thing at award-winning Westons, a family firm set up in 1880 using apples from their own orchards. Tour its visitor centre in the village of Much Marcle to admire one of the largest bottle collections in the world and sample a drop of potent Old Rosie – at 8.2 percent, she'll blow your socks off.

Ⓦ www.westons-cider.co.uk. Tours run three times daily and cost £6 for adults. Map 3, C12

102 Arbroath Smokie

Surely the finest smoked haddock anywhere can be found in the North Sea town of Arbroath, where the Arbroath Smokie defies Scotland's dubious culinary reputation. The best way to eat the delicately textured and aromatic, copper-brown fish, which is salted, dried and then smoke-cured over smouldering hardwood chips, is straight from the barrel at one of the family-run smokehouses overlooking the town's harbour. With thick smoke billowing daily out of its smokehouse, tiny, whitewashed M&M Spink is one of the most congenial and atmospheric spots to try it.

Ⓦ www.arbroathsmokies.co.uk. Map 4, D13

103 Stilton cheese

Stilton proves that the French don't have a monopoly on pungent and wickedly delicious cheese. *The Bell Inn* in the Cambridgeshire village of Stilton lays claim to being the birthplace of the "English Parmesan" (as Defoe described it); the village was once a trading post on the London–York coaching road, and the pub can certainly be credited with popularizing the cheese with passing travellers. Though Stilton is no longer made in the village – only producers in Nottinghamshire, Leicestershire and Derbyshire are allowed to use the name – the inn still serves a fine selection of cheeses, and the village still celebrates its formative role with an annual Stilton-rolling competition along the High Street in May.

Ⓦ www.thebellstilton.co.uk. For a list of producers see Ⓦ www.stiltoncheese. com. Map 3, D11

104 Yorkshire forced rhubarb

In the seventeenth century, rhubarb was seen as a wonder drug, capable of curing everything from excessive freckles to cancer, and sold for three times the price of opium. The tangy and versatile plant thrives in an area known as The Rhubarb Triangle, between Wakefield, Morley and Rothwell in West Yorkshire. You can sample the produce at Wakefield's Festival of Food, Drink and Rhubarb in February, or find out about how the plant is "forced" in darkened sheds – producing tender, early-flowering stems – and harvested by candlelight during a tour of one of the largest producers, E. Oldroyd & Sons.

Ⓦ www.yorkshirerhubarb.co.uk. Tours run Jan–March (£7.50). See Ⓦ www. wakefield.gov.uk for more on Wakefield's food festival. Map 3, C10

105 Melton Mowbray pork pie

Rather like Marmite, most people either love or hate this quintessentially English snack of chopped uncured pork sealed in jelly and wrapped in a thick crust. These days only nine producers based around the Leicestershire town of Melton Mowbray are allowed to make the classic pie, one of the oldest being Dickinson & Morris, who have been baking them since 1851. Gawp at the mouthwatering array of pies – from tiny to enormous – at their Old Pork Pie Shoppe, drop in for a demonstration, or even have a crack at hand-crafting a pie of your own at one of their "Pork Pie Evening Experiences". The pies are baked overnight, ready to be picked up the following day.

Ⓦ www.porkpie.co.uk. Map 3, D11

106 Wild and free: foraging in Wales

Hunter-gatherers that we once were, there is little more satisfying than coming home with a basket of food you've found and picked yourself – particularly if it's free. Wales may be full of sheep, but it's also prime foraging territory, with vast crenellated stretches of coastline, clean rivers, ancient oak woodlands, craggy mountains and rugged moorland all teeming with edible wild plants. Once a pursuit for hippies, foraging is nowadays more an activity for the gastronome – Wales's wild foods are rich and intensely flavoured and almost all of the edibles mentioned below cost a small fortune to buy. Snowdonia and the Cambrian coastline are an excellent place to start off – an area steeped in history and myth, this was once the stomping ground of legendary Welsh ruler Owain Glyndŵr. The scenery is stunning – all soaring mountains, glacial cwms and hidden waterfalls – and the place names hereabouts are as much a mouthful as the food. All you need to begin is a good identification book and a keen eye.

Between April and June, you will often catch the hot odour of wild garlic (or ramsons), a relative of chives, in the woods, and common sorrel and hairy bitter-cress also thrive – all make a tasty addition to salads. Autumn, "season of mists and mellow fruitfulness", heralds the arrival of edible fungi; Britain has over a hundred edible species, and poking through the crisp forest floor you can find delicious yellow chanterelles, elegant parasol mushrooms, remarkable giant puffballs and crispy Jew's ears, used in Asian cooking. Handsome, bulbous ceps (also known as porcini) are a gem of a find – they're best fried in oodles of butter and served on toast. Beginners should try an organized foray as a small proportion of Britain's mushrooms are lethal.

For dessert head up to the mountaintop heaths and moors to look for Tolkienesque-sounding bilberries – they taste zingier than their cousin, the American blueberry, and stain your mouth a dark plum colour. And when you're done picking, don't forget to lie back in the heather and soak up the views – you may even catch the sight of a red kite or buzzard soaring overhead.

Need to know The Centre for Alternative Technology (Ⓦwww.cat.org.uk), near Machynlleth, Powys, runs fungi and wild food identification courses. Never eat anything you are unsure of, dig up the root of a plant or strip it of its leaves, flowers or seeds. Richard Mabey's *Food for Free* is an excellent resource.
Map 3, B11

107 Bessie pours a mean pint at the Dyffryn Arms

Need to know *Dyffryn Arms*, Gwaun Valley Rd, Pontfaen, Pembrokeshire ☎ 08721/077077. The pub is open most afternoons and evenings – unless it isn't.

Map 3, A12

If you're travelling in Pembrokeshire's delightful Cwm Gwaun – the Gwaun Valley – in very rural west Wales, one experience not to miss is to nip in for a pint at the *Dyffryn Arms*, a slate-roofed free house in the tiny village of Pontfaen, tucked into a fold of the Preseli Hills. There's not much to this classic local: just one diminutive front-parlour room with a chequerboard-tiled floor, three tables, a couple of old church pews, yellowing prints on the walls, a dartboard and a cosy coal fire. A gastropub this ain't – a few packets of peanuts, crisps and a jar of picked eggs are more the *menu du jour*. No, what gives the *Dyffryn Arms* its legendary status is its owner, affable octogenarian Bessie Davies, whose family have been running the pub – known locally simply as *Bessie's* – since 1840. Bessie herself has been in charge for pushing forty of those years, and still holds fort at the sliding hatch at the back of the room, one elbow on the worn sill, the other raised pouring beer from a jug into the plainest of glasses, and a plastic-checked pinny her protection against spillage. Once you've sunk your pint ask for a refill and Bessie will reach behind to the only barrel behind the bar, fill the jug from the spigot and decant the Bass into your glass. She's always got time for a bit of chinwag with the local farmers – for this diminutive room is pretty much the valley's social hub – and the occasional curious tourist.

It isn't just the pub that's time-warped. The entire valley clings to a relic of bygone times, namely the pre-1752 Julian calendar, which decrees that the residents of Cwm Gwaun celebrate New Year, or "Hen Galan", on January 13. Riots occurred across Britain when the change took place, and a few places resisted the twelve-day switch. It's only Hen Galan that's been retained in Cwm Gwaun, so you won't need to reset your watches when you visit. But if you're here on that day, the place to be is *Bessie's*.

108 Molecular gastronomy at The Fat Duck

The best restaurant in Britain? Well, for once, the critics seem to agree. For three years, it's beaten off competition from Gordon, Marcus, Raymond to hold top spot from the *Good Food Guide*; and, even more remarkably, for six – and counting – it's never dropped out of the San Pellegrino Awards' world top three. Yet really *The Fat Duck*, the famed two-storey former pub in the rural hamlet of Bray, is as much about theatre as dining, with two performances daily at lunch and dinnertime. Each show takes the form of a tasting menu of twelve or more courses, and takes around four hours to unfold. It's a long time for a meal but then there's a lot to take in.

Tastes, textures and sensations of dishes are assembled to wrongfoot expectations (a "jelly of orange and beetroot" is a serving of two separate jellies, in which the orange tastes of beetroot and the red of orange) or startle with unexpected flavour combinations (the notorious snail porridge and smoked bacon and egg ice cream) or just plain confound (edible sand?). Typically, several courses will involve elaborate table-side preparations, like the palette-cleansing mousse of lime and green tea poached in front of diners in a fog of liquid nitrogen, or the gold pocketwatch plucked out of a wooden case by a server and dunked in your bowl where you observe it dissolve in hot water poured from a teapot to complete a mock turtle soup. And there are the props, including iPod nanos, seashells and picture frames.

The mad hatter in the kitchen is, of course, Heston Blumenthal, a man with a unique talent for conjuring up the feasts of dreams (jam-filled Queen of Hearts playing cards, for example) and putting them on a plate. In doing so he reduces diners to a state of childlike wonder. But as whimsical as it all sounds, make no mistake, this is seriously brilliant food. The tastes are exquisite, and the level of sheer technical ability and artistry that goes into the preparation of each and every dish is astounding. Really, those awards people don't dish out their accolades for nothing.

After dining you could walk a few doors down the lane to the local pub to come back down to earth – but, perhaps not, because Blumenthal owns that place as well.

Need to know *The Fat Duck*, High St, Bray, Berkshire (☎01628/580333, ⓦwww. thefatduck.co.uk) is a ten-minute taxi ride from Maidenhead train station. The tasting menu costs £160 per head.

Map 2, E5

109 A taste of Brum: The Balti Triangle

Just a couple of kilometres southeast of Birmingham city centre lies a microcosm of north Indian and Pakistani life. Clothes shops stock saris, salwar kameezes and pashminas; halal butchers' stand beside grocers' with Asian fruit, vegetables and spices; jewellers sell elaborate gold creations by the weight, while other stores offer a bewildering array of multicoloured beads and bangles. Locals switch between Urdu and Punjabi and English – though whichever language is spoken a distinct Brummie twang remains. Above all, the air is thick with intoxicating aromas.

This area, centred on three roads – Ladypool Road, Stoney Lane and Stratford Road – is home to something just as iconic to Birmingham as the Bullring and the Rotunda: the balti. Invented by the area's Pakistani and Kashmiri community in the mid-1970s, balti is best thought of as a style of cooking, rather than a single dish. (There is some disagreement about the origins of the name: balti means "bucket" or "cooking utensil" in Hindi and Punjabi, though there is also a region of north Indian and Pakistan called Baltistan.)

Baltis are cooked and served in the same balti bowl, a small thin-pressed steel wok that allows for a swift cooking time (baltis take around eight minutes to cook, far quicker than a curry). Vegetable oil and fresh herbs and spices are used, rather than ghee and curry pastes, giving the dish a lighter, fresher taste. And naan, instead of rice, is the accompaniment of choice.

The Balti Triangle, as it's been dubbed, has around a dozen authentic balti restaurants (as well as many traditional Indian restaurants): among the best are *Punjab Palace*, *Al Frash* and *Shabab*, all on Ladypool Road, and *Shahi Nan Kebab House* on Stratford Road. There's a wide range of baltis on offer (most costing around £6), though two dishes really stand out: chicken and mushroom, and lamb and aubergine. Ask for "desi style" if you want your food authentically hot. Few restaurants are licensed, but the vast majority allow diners to bring their own alcohol (corkage is rarely charged).

For dessert, head to one of the many local sweet shops (Royal Sweet Centre on Ladypool Road is particularly good), which offer toothsome *burfi* (similar to fudge), *gulab jamun* (deep-fried dough balls soaked in syrup) and *kulfi* (Indian ice cream).

Need to know The Balti Triangle is spread over the Sparkhill, Balsall Heath and Moseley neighbourhoods and is easily accessible from the city centre. Visit ⓦwww.balti-birmingham.co.uk and ⓦwww.visitbirmingham.com for maps, transport details, restaurant reviews and tours.

Map 3, C11

110 Tibbie, queen of lochs

There aren't many centuries-old coaching inns left intact in Scotland, and none with so sublime a setting as *Tibbie Shiels'*. Perched on the edge of St Mary's Loch in the heart of the Scottish Borders, with the Loch of the Lowes fanning out behind it, this is a place to dream into your ale. Its handful of loch-side benches may have been beaten by the Borders weather, but the views alone, unbroken across the water's inky expanse and the sheet-glass summits reflected on its surface, render the term beer garden perhaps just a little inadequate.

The *Inn* itself, or at least the oldest portion of it, is the epitome of Borders vernacular, white-painted stone with low windows and – hanging baskets notwithstanding – a certain austerity, appropriately enough, perhaps, given this area's historical reputation as a Covenanting stronghold. Founder Isabella (Tibbie) Shiel herself was, by all accounts, as devout as they come, and, if the forbidding portrait in the inn's entrance hall ("headroom 5ft 10in") is anything to go by, more than a match for her clientele. Nineteenth-century regulars famously included Sir Walter Scott and his friend and Gothic novelist James Hogg, shepherd in the parallel valley of Ettrick, and a writer whose influence has been cited, in recent years, by such prominent Scottish literary figures such as Irvine Welsh.

The patrons mightn't be quite as influential these days, but they're still quick with a great line, and the pub's as friendly as any in the region – probably just as well given the intimacy of the bar itself, a tiny counter lined with single malts and a blackboard chalking up the kitchen's home-made specials. Lamb, pheasant and venison are all locally sourced, and they also do the usual pub-grub standbys including a ravishingly creamy mushroom lasagne. While the dining room comes with loch views and the beneficent gaze of Scott and Hogg, you're more than welcome to eat in the open air, though a word to the wise: the midges, under the right conditions, are wont to be as ardent as the Convenanters.

Need to know
Tibbie Shiels Inn, St Mary's Loch, Selkirkshire, Scottish Borders ☎01750/42231, ⓦwwwtibbieshiels.com. Open April–Oct daily 9am–midnight, Nov–April Thurs–Sun 9am–midnight; food served noon–8.30pm. En-suite accommodation at £38 per person for a double room. Camping and tepee hire also available, plus rental of fishing boats. Map 4, D15

111 Tracking down the perfect chippy in Lancashire

It's a battle almost as old as the Wars of the Roses. Where should you go for the best fish and chips in Britain? Yorkshire and Lancashire both lay claim to the title, but for both sheer quantity of choice and the local pride taken in serving the finest haddock and chips (cod is most definitely a southern thing), it's the northwest that has the edge. Lancashire has more chippies than anywhere else in the UK, and there's a strong claim that the county is home to the first ever fish and chip shop, opened on the site of Oldham's Tommyfield Market in 1863.

That original chippie is today long gone, and these days it's Blackpool's sea air that provides the ideal atmosphere for devouring a wrapped paper bag full of deep-fried goodness. Standout among the resort's chippies is *Seniors*, where the fish is bought fresh each morning from nearby Fleetwood's fish market, and delicacies including hake and turbot are often on offer alongside the standard choices.

If Blackpool feels a little too bellicose an environment for sampling the perfect fish and chips, then head a few miles south to the tiny village of Lytham, where *Whelan's* has been frequented by the likes of Rick Stein, who loved this bijou gem so much he wrote about it in his *Seafood Lovers Guide*. Here, the haddock is fried in beef dripping and the chips have a deeply satisfying crunch. Local patrons insist that visitors also sample the home-made cheese and onion pie, made with local Butler's cheese – though whether you'll have any stomach capacity left after a jumbo haddock and chips is another matter.

Perhaps the most revered of all the northwest's chippies, though, can be found up the coast in the sleepy county town of Lancaster. Here lies *Hodgson's*, celebrated by its adoring fans with an "I love Hodgson's" Facebook page and proud recipient of a garland of awards including the National Federation of Fryers' "Fish and Chip Shop of the Year". There's more than just the usual hearty, robust haddock and chips on offer here. Swift service makes the inevitable long queues bearable and there's a strict quality control – only fish from sustainable stocks and locally grown potatoes from nearby Garstang are used. Like all the best chip shops in this area, you'll struggle to find gravy, spring rolls or microwaved pies. What you will find is an authentic slice of northern hospitality and gargantuan portions. Just keep any references to Yorkshire strictly critical.

Need to know *Seniors*,
106 Normoss Rd, Blackpool ☎01253/393529, ⓦwww.thinkseniors.com; closed Sun; *Whelans*, 26 Clifton St, Lytham ☎01253/735188, ⓦwww.whelansfishandchips.co.uk; *Hodgson's*, 96 Prospect St, Lancaster ☎01524/67763, ⓦhodgsonschippy.com; closed Sun.
Map 3, B9, B10

112 Become a vegetarian masterchef in Bath

Discreetly tucked away on a side street near Bath's grand Gothic abbey, *Demuths* restaurant serves vegetarian food so delicious it can convert steadfast carnivores. Locally sourced vegetables star in expertly prepared dishes – try stuffed courgette flowers, or tomato *upma* with baked pineapple – influenced by owner Rachel Demuth's extensive international travels.

For a more hands-on experience, however, you can draw on the chefs' alchemical skills at *Demuths'* Vegetarian Cookery School, centrally located in one of the city's elegant Georgian buildings. Each of the deservedly popular day and evening courses here attracts up to sixteen enthusiastic cooks (of mixed ability), and the intimate classes ensure that everyone experiments with inspiring new recipes. Courses cover an impressive range of global cuisines, from the spicy flavours of a south Indian *thali* and the Moorish-influenced tastes of Andalucian tapas, to intense, hot Mexican classics – enhanced by chillies from neighbouring Dorset.

You'll need to book well in advance for "No time to cook – Fast and Delicious", salvation for anyone who struggles to think outside the pasta and pesto box after a long day at work. Students leave this hands-on day having created ten seasonal dishes – you may find yourself able to bake soda bread or prepare a wonderful halloumi and quinoa salad in little more time than it takes to microwave a ready meal. Relaxed morning coffee sets the tone for the day and experienced, charismatic chefs guide groups through each dish – before long you'll be assuredly creating calzones bursting with vegetables or preparing mango and rosewater rice pudding of exquisite delicacy. Instruction is by a mixture of demonstration and cooking in small groups, with plenty of opportunities to ask questions and sample your creations along the way. You'll also find your confidence in the kitchen boosted by numerous invaluable tips, including useful training in knife skills and advice on where to source the best ingredients.

Such evocative sights and smells are sure to encourage a hearty appetite and a late lunch showcasing the day's dishes, complemented by organic wine, is the perfect way to celebrate your culinary efforts.

Need to know *Demuths Restaurant*, 2 North Parade Passage, Bath ☎01225/446059. Vegetarian Cookery School, 6 Terrace Walk, Bath ☎01225/427938, ⍟www. vegetariancookeryschool.com. Day courses 10am–4.30pm; £125. Evening courses 6–9pm; £45. Map 2, C5

113 A cold wind to Valhalla: sup Britain's most northerly pint

The dark days are over. It's official: British brewing is enjoying a renaissance. And nowhere is there greater cause for celebration than north of the border, where a succession of craft- and microbrewers have exploded onto the market in recent years. From the classic oak-fermented ales of Traquair House in the Borders to the aggressively iconoclastic Fraserburgh-based BrewDog ("beer for punks"), Scotland is producing some of the nation's most exciting brews. And to find one of the most innovative of artisanal brewers you have to travel very far north indeed – in fact almost until you drop off the edge of the country.

In Shetland's most northerly island of Unst, with its dramatic cliffs and fine sandy beaches, Britain certainly goes out with a bang. Amid the rolling landscape of heath and moor, and crumbling old crofters' cottages, stands the former RAF radar base of Saxa Vord – now the warm and welcoming *Saxa Vord Resort*. It's home to Valhalla, Britain's most northerly brewery.

Valhalla belongs to the affable Sonny Priest, who started the brewery a decade and a half ago when cutbacks at the RAF base reduced his hours. It's a small, homespun operation, with production largely by hand, as you'll soon discover if you take a tour – until recently the equipment only allowed two beers to be bottled at a time, with caps put on by hand – but its focus on the artisanal creates ales of exceptional quality. The range of six beers include the dark and earthy Auld Rock, which derives its name from Shetlanders' own term for the island; the unique Island Bere, an oddity made with an ancient grain called bere brought to these islands by the Vikings; and the light Old Scatness, which combines bere, wheat and oats with heather and honey. It gets its name from an archeological dig that revealed evidence of beer-making in Shetland over two millennia ago.

Once you've fortified yourself with a couple of samples – you'll need them up here when the nights draw in and the wind increases in strength – make your way up to the bleak headland of Hermaness, home to puffins, gannets and "bonxies" (great skuas). From here you can look onto the jagged rocks known as Muckle Flagga, site of one of the most dramatically set lighthouses you could imagine, and across to Out Stack. North of here there's nothing until you reach the North Pole.

Need to know Valhalla Brewery (⍟www.valhallabrewery. co.uk) moves into *Saxa Vord Resort*, Unst, Shetland (⍟www. saxavord.com) in early 2011; call ☎01957/711658 to arrange a visit. For more information on Unst, including how to get there, see ⍟www.unst.org. Map 5, F17

THE GOOD OLD DAYS

myth, heritage and nostalgia

04

The British are often accused of wallowing in the past – lamenting the passing of more innocent times, incessantly raking over the glory days of Empire, insatiably consuming period costume dramas and royal biographies, and invoking the spirit of the Blitz at the slightest inconvenience. There's some truth in the charge, but let's be fair – with more than five thousand years of settled history, and a proud record of stability, democracy and invention, there's an awful lot of the British past to wallow in and be nostalgic about. Was everything better way back when? Well, that's a different question, but there's no shortage of places in the British Isles to find out if the Sixties really did swing or if Tudor life would have suited you down to the ground. Heritage has its own thriving industry these days and there's scarcely a stately home or historic attraction that doesn't have a living history programme of activities designed to show you the past in exhaustive, authentic detail. What's more, Britain is really good at this stuff – open-air museums, restored villages, battle re-enactments, protected ancient monuments, nostalgia collections, archeological digs, vintage industry and transport, folklore tours and more. Every week, thousands of otherwise perfectly normal people willingly give up their spare time to tinker with steam engines, don a Roman tunic or join a morris-dancing group, while period and traditional festivals go from strength to strength. Sometimes, admittedly, it's all just an excuse for a bit of fun – tongues are firmly in whiskered cheeks at London's Chap Olympiad – and occasionally the good old days turn out to have been not so great after all. But in the end, it's often the land itself that speaks to the ages and certain places right across Britain retain an innate capacity to take you back in time, without the need for fancy costumes and festivals: you'll see what we mean as your childhood comes flooding back on the golden sands at Bridlington or as you huddle from the elements among the windswept Neolithic buildings of Skara Brae.

114 Bekonscot Model Village: 1930s England in miniature

The largest model village in the world, Bekonscot offers an idealized version of prewar England in miniature. Morris dancers parade in the town square, a troop of Brownies tie a maypole, farmworkers gather up stooks of hay, two horses turn an old-fashioned cider press and a brass band plays at the end of the pier. Look carefully, though, and you'll find little splashes of period comedy, like the small boy in Bekonscot Hospital with his head wedged in a saucepan, while on a nearby village green a careless workman drops a paint pot on the head of a passing vicar and an even more careless garage attendant stands brandishing a petrol hose with a cigarette in his mouth.

Bekonscot "village" actually consists of six Lilliputian towns – Greenhaily, Bekonscot, Maryloo, Hanton, Wychwood and Evenlode. It's a wonderful pint-sized vision of rural England, with half-timbered houses, quaint village greens, flinty churches, rugged castles and diminutive high streets dotted with little shops bearing ludicrous names (Sam and Ella's Butchers, Chris P. Lettis Greengrocers, Leekey Plumbers Merchants, and so on). Dozens of miniature trains shuttle around the complex, connecting the various towns – some have been in service for over fifty years, and each covers an astonishing two thousand miles every year (locals like to joke that it's the only railway network in the country where the trains still run on time).

Bekonscot was created in the 1920s by accountant Roland Callingham in what was then his back garden – assisted by his gardener, chauffeur and housekeeper (the name is a conflation of Beaconsfield, the town in which the village is situated, and Ascot, Callingham's former home). The swimming pool became the village "lake", the rockeries were turned into hills, while Bassett-Lowke were commissioned to add a large-scale model railway. Callingham's model village rapidly began to attract visitors, as well as inspiring a string of similar creations elsewhere in England and providing, it's said, the inspiration for Enid Blyton's Toytown. Blyton herself in fact was another former Beaconsfield resident: a miniature replica of her old house, Green Hedges, can also be seen in the village with a diminutive Noddy outside – a quaint example of life imitating art imitating life.

Need to know Bekonscot Model Village, Warwick Rd, Beaconsfield, Buckinghamshire Ⓦ www.bekonscot.co.uk. Open mid-Feb to Oct daily 10am–5pm. Adults £8.50, children £5, under 2s free. Map 2, E5

115 Gin and jousting: clash of the dandies at the Chap Olympiad

One day in July, something downright silly happens in a leafy, cultured corner of Bloomsbury. As you pick your way through the calm residential streets around Bedford Square, you'll see clusters of finely dressed ladies and gents gathering for a rather special sports day. Now, those who didn't excel in the athletic arts back when they were in short trousers may wilt at the idea, but the Chap Olympiad offers a refreshing concept: a day of cheerful non-athleticism in full period get-up.

Put on by *The Chap* magazine and nostalgia party organizers Bourne & Hollingsworth, the Olympiad encourages vintage-style dressing up, taking sartorial inspiration from Victoriana up to the 1940s. This is no half-hearted fancy-dress day out: chaps and chapettes are painstakingly attired down to the last pearl and tiepin (apart from the occasional doubter in jeans and T-shirt, looking outrageously out of place) and look worthy of an invitation to a knees-up chez Gatsby.

On to the games themselves. Umbrella Jousting provides an early highlight: your chariot is an old bike; your sword a trusty black brolly; your only protection a newspaper shield (the *FT* naturally), and your wits. Then there's the Three-Trousered Limbo: two athletes climb into an enormous pair of three-legged tweeds, race off with a silly walk, then attempt to limbo their way under a gradually lowered pole. Now the Cucumber Sandwich Discus begins, and it's all eyes on how far the mighty snack lands from the plate. It's a tense time.

With our Olympic heroes behaving with the formal civility of yesteryear, it's safe to say that this is far from your average British festival. You can be sure that no one here is trying to overturn a portaloo or writhing about in mud – one's brogues would be ruined. Throughout, contestants show a sanguine lackadaisical sportsmanship. To break a sweat would just be poor show; posing, smoking, drinking gin and cheating your way to the prize (with a theatrical flourish of course) are the marks of a true sporting champ.

Naturally, there isn't room for everyone to compete on the day – get there at the very start if you want to. Besides, if you retire to the sidelines you'll have more time to groom your moustache, eat thoroughly British sandwiches and get legless. If only sports day had always been thus.

Need to know The Chap Olympiad takes place annually at Bedford Square in Bloomsbury, London WC1; entry costs £15. See ⓦ www.thechapolympiad.com for further details.
Map 1, C2

116 Soaking up the Saxon past at Sutton Hoo

It's just a mound covered in scruffy yellow grass – nothing much, you think. But then your guide clambers up the slope, looking for something. When he gets to the top he pauses for a second, nods, then suddenly lies down, legs fully extended with his back flat on the ground. He lies there in silence; you wonder if he's having a breakdown or a heart attack. But then he slowly lifts his left shoulder off the grass, and holds the position. "This is how we found the body," he whispers, "just like this, right below this spot".

When unearthed more than seventy years ago, the burial mounds at Sutton Hoo yielded some of the richest Anglo-Saxon treasure ever found. Treasure-hunters had been digging here for centuries without much luck. By the time Edith May Pretty bought the nearby property in 1926, tales of gold were just rumours, whispered stories told by the old men of the village. Yet Edith was intrigued, and finally, in 1938, she invited local archeologist Basil Brown to excavate the site. On his second dig the following year, Brown uncovered the remains of a vast burial chamber, later identified as a seventh-century Saxon ship – perhaps the last resting-place of King Redwald of East Anglia.

The site today, on a bluff above the River Deben, remains a wild, unkempt heath, open to the wind. Visit on a cool November morning, when the mist lingers on the river and a light frost smothers the burial mounds like ice on miniature mountains, and it's easy to imagine a fleet of longships drifting towards the marshy banks of the Deben, the men in furs groaning as they dragged the wooden bow up the slope, and the solemn ceremony that laid a king to rest.

Though Sutton Hoo's main treasures have long since moved to the British Museum, the site's absorbing visitor centre houses finds from subsequent digs, as well as reproductions of the main pieces and a life-sized re-creation of the burial chamber and contents. But don't miss out on the main attraction; and remember it really isn't "just a mound".

Need to know Sutton Hoo (☎ 01394/389700, ⓦ www.nationaltrust.org.uk) is off the B1083 Woodbridge to Bawdsey Road in Suffolk – follow the signs from the A12. Open April–Oct daily 10.30am–5pm; Nov–March times vary (see website). Adults £5.50.
Map 3, F12

BRITISH ICONS

What makes a true British icon? As you'll see from our favourites below, there's no rulebook. But one thing is clear: it's what makes us stand out from the crowd that we hold most dear. In the 1800s it was the bowler hat. In the Sixties, it was the miniskirt. Nowadays, while the rest of Europe obsesses over coffee, it's the fact that tea remains resolutely the national drink. To the outside world we must seem like a funny bunch, but most of us wouldn't have it any other way.

117 Bond . . . James Bond

Played by two Englishmen, a Scotsman and a Welshman, Bond perhaps is the ultimate British icon. From Keswick with Love may not have quite the same ring to it, but deep in the Lake District, near the breeze-rippled surface of Derwent Water, there's a car collection with a licence to thrill. The Bond Museum's best exhibits include the gun-topped Aston Martin Vanquish V12 from *Die Another Day*, and the ultra-sleek Lotus Esprit S1, which transforms into a submarine in *The Spy Who Loved Me*. Pay them a visit – they've been expecting you.

The Bond Museum, Southey Hull Trading Estate, Keswick, Cumbria ☎ 01768/775007, ⓦ www.thebondmuseum.com. Map 4, D16

118 Royal Ascot

Part racing event, part fashion show: Royal Ascot is unlike any other meeting in the horse-racing calendar. And although there's more than £3m in prize money at stake over the five-day event, most of the attention seems to be focused on the dress sense of the champagne-quaffing attendees – especially on Ladies' Day, when a sea of flamboyant hats and fascinators makes it tricky to see the track.

For tickets and travel information, visit ⓦ www.ascot.co.uk. Royal Ascot is held annually in June. Map 2, E5

119 Sherlock Holmes

Baker Street may have changed beyond recognition since Victorian times, but one address – 221b – has been left in the early 1900s as a tribute to Conan Doyle's fictional detective. Behind the piano-black front door, you'll find the great sleuth's leather-bound books and brass-studded armchairs, and, of course, a terrific collection of pipes. You can even don a deerstalker and pretend to be the great man himself.

The Sherlock Holmes Museum, 221b Baker St, London NW1 ☎ 020/7224 3688, ⓦ www.sherlock-holmes.co.uk. Admission is £6 for adults. Map 1, B2

120 The bowler hat

Long before it became the preserve of the suited city banker, the bowler hat was worn by men from all backgrounds – rich and poor. Not only did it look good, it protected their heads from low-hanging branches on those countryside horse rides. James Lock & Co, the St James's Street boutique that designed the first bowler in 1850, is still open today. Shop there, you'll feel every inch a true English gent.

James Lock & Co, 6 St James's St, London SW1 ☎ 020/7930 8874, ⓦ www. lockhatters.co.uk. Map 1, C3

121 The miniskirt

Even in the swinging Sixties, the miniskirt raised eyebrows. Older people detested it, saying it was sleazy, but the younger generation – male and female – couldn't get enough of it. One thing most agree on is that the miniskirt was invented (or at least popularized) by British designer Mary Quant, and her collection at the V&A in London is a study in liberated mod styling.

V&A, Cromwell Rd, London SW7 ☎ 020/7942 2000, ⓦ www.vam.ac.uk. Admission free. Map 1, B4

122 The Spitfire

The single-seater Spitfire didn't just help to win the Battle of Britain; it was the most graceful fighter plane of its day. And when you hear the throb of its propeller beating through the air, you'll see why it's still so popular. Head along to one of the air shows hosted by the Imperial War Museum in Duxford to see one of these magnificent beasts in action.

Imperial War Museum, Duxford, Cambridgeshire. Admission costs £16.50 for adults. Air shows take place several times a year; for more details, visit ⓦduxford.iwm.org.uk. Map 3, E12

123 A cuppa

Ahh, tea. For a commodity that's produced thousands of miles from home, it couldn't be more British. As a nation, we took it to our hearts and then added milk and two sugars. But down in the laidback southwest, taking tea on its own was never quite leisurely enough. So clotted cream, scones and ruby-red jam were added to the ritual, and the cream tea was born. Try it at Otterton Mill in Devon, where the flour for the scones is milled on site, and the setting – in a glorious rolling valley – beats any city hotel.

Otterton Mill, near Budleigh Salterton, Devon ☎01395/567041, ⓦwww. ottertonmill.com. Map 2, C6

124 Auntie Beeb

When Television Centre opened back in 1960, people couldn't believe its size. Now, more than fifty years later, people can't believe it's still standing. Sure, its brick-and-glass facade has seen better days, but the building is now protected by law. Not because of how it looks, but because of the cultural gems it houses – from *EastEnders* props to the *Blue Peter* studio. As you walk its ageing corridors, it's worth keeping your eyes peeled: you might just spot a Dalek.

BBC Television Centre, Wood Lane, London W12. Tours cost £9.95 per adult. For more information see ⓦwww.bbc.co.uk/tours. Map 1, E4

125 Peter Rabbit

Beatrix Potter's fictional bunny might not seem an obvious choice as a British icon, but try telling that to the Japanese, who love him so much that they've re-created the author's slate-grey Lakeland cottage, brick for brick, just outside Tokyo. When a warm summer's breeze parts the ferns that lead to the real Hill Top, and you catch your first glimpse of the working farm where these enchanting tales were set, you'll find little has changed here since Potter's time. Wandering through the cluttered house and its herb-scented gardens, you'll get the feeling she could walk right back in at any moment.

Hill Top, Near Sawrey, Cumbria. See ⓦwww.nationaltrust.org.uk for more information. Map 3, B9

126 The Mini

Union Jack, chequerboard, or just plain white: whatever's painted on the roof, the car underneath is unmisteakably a Mini. At the Heritage Motor Centre's annual Mini Festival, it's hard to stand out from the crowd. But that doesn't stop enthusiasts from trying; there are Minis with spoilers, stretch limo Minis, and even Minis with hot tubs where their boots should be.

The Mini Festival takes place each July at the Heritage Motor Centre, Gaydon, Warwickshire. For visitor information, see ⓦwww.minifestival. co.uk. Map 3, D12

127 The fertile plains of Cerne Abbas

The soft chalk downland of southern Britain has, for millennia, proved a tempting canvas for creative interventions into the country's rolling hills – Uffington in Oxfordshire boasts an ancient white horse with a recently proven 3000-year history; a nineteenth-century horseback geoglyph just outside Weymouth, Dorset, is said to represent King George III; and a hillside lion etched in 1933 beckons visitors to Whipsnade Zoo.

But most celebrated of all the chalk carvings has to be the Cerne Abbas giant, just north of Dorchester in Dorset. He's been used in adverts peddling jeans, condoms and bicycles, and in 2007 shared the hill with a giant doughnut-wielding Homer Simpson (there was a movie to promote), but he's attracted interest for a lot longer than that. And no prizes for guessing why: for this fellow, the "Rude Man" as he's also known, is possessed of a rather alluring and unashamedly large phallus.

Legends explaining his significance run back to ancient times: he was a Roman tribute to Hercules; a Celtic British icon; a Saxon deity; and a slain Danish giant. But as there's no written evidence of his existence till the late seventeenth century, most of these stories can be relegated to folklore. More convincing interpretations place him during the English Civil War, when he was carved as an insulting caricature of Oliver Cromwell – the local landowner of the time was a sworn enemy – while others suggest he was a parody of Abbot Thomas Corton, expelled for malpractice from the nearby Benedictine Monastery.

Whatever his genesis, however, it is his status as a fertility symbol that has always resonated most strongly with visitors to the site. Childless couples used to dance around a maypole erected on nearby Trendle Hill, and it is said that if you make love on the carving – particularly on the tip of his phallus – your chances of conception will be greatly enhanced. This is, of course, if you decide to ignore the notice from the National Trust who now own and maintain the site: the public are politely requested to remain outside the perimeter fence. Just how many locals have ignored this plea is a matter of debate, however, as it was revealed by the National Statistics Office in 2010 that North Dorset has the highest average birth rate in the country, nearly double that of central London. A mere coincidence, perhaps, or proof that even the most outlandish of legends are founded on a grain of truth?

Need to know The best place to see the giant in his full glory is from the viewing area just off the A352 south of the village of Cerne Abbas.
Map 2, C6

128 Dig a little deeper: amateur archeology on Hadrian's Wall

Indiana Jones never had it this hard. Not once, in any of the films, do you see him stooped over a designated plot of turf, back aching and fingernails crudded with dirt, as a fine drizzle sweeps in from the North Sea. But then, this is rural Northumberland, not some studio set in LA, and the huge garrison fort that you're helping excavate is very real indeed – a two-thousand-year-old medley of military quarters, bathhouses and civilian homes that constitutes the largest collection of Roman buildings on Hadrian's Wall.

Built in 122 AD, the Wall ran 76 miles from the Tyne to the Solway Firth, its entire length dotted with milecastles, turrets and, as at Vindolanda, forts. The garrison here was home to around five hundred soldiers, whose daily lives are being pieced together by a similar number of volunteers each summer – unlike other historic sites, who work only with trained researchers, Vindolanda opens what's left of its doors to everyone, giving ordinary members of the public the chance to play intrepid archeologist.

It's tough work – you can get stuck into the topsoil with a spade, but the next four feet need delicate sifting with a hand trowel and brush – and you'll probably shift a fair few barrow-loads of disappointingly empty earth before finding anything. But when you do, gingerly extracting a clogged piece of wood that was once a lady's hair comb or a rotting strip of leather that turns out to be an archer's thumb guard, the sense of discovery is electrifying. The backache vanishes. The rain seems to disappear.

Finds like this will pepper your week (most volunteers come for longer), as you work closely with a professional archeologist, perfecting your dig skills and enhancing your understanding of Roman Frontier Britain. Many such discoveries end up in the on-site museum, which houses the largest collection of leather, textiles and basketry found anywhere in the Roman Empire. The famed writing tablets, the earliest archive of writing in the country, however, made it into the British Museum itself. Now, not even Dr Jones managed that.

Need to know Vindolanda (Ⓦ www.vindolanda.com) is 35 miles west of Newcastle. Excavations run from April to September (booking from Nov 1) and cost £55 per person (minimum age 16 years) for one or two weeks. **Map 4, E15**

129 Hunkering down in a nuclear bunker

As tourist attractions go, Fife's Secret Bunker – with its unmistakeable hazard and barbed-wire logo – must be one of Scotland's most unconventional. It's certainly one of the most unnerving, not to mention claustrophobic. For those of a certain vintage, who shivered through the ever-looming catastrophe of the Cold War years, this place brings home the reality of a nuclear strike with all the visceral force of a punch to the guts, a sensation all the more powerful if you happened to live in the bunker's back yard without even really knowing for certain it was there. Yet even if you're too young to remember the Cuban Missile Crisis or the beautiful, disturbing animated film *When the Wind Blows*, this is a grimly fascinating window on a time when vaporization was but a push-button away.

The bunker's entrance lies deep within the bowels of a wooded rise, which – incongruously – overlooks some of Britain's most scenic coast and bucolic countryside. It's cunningly disguised within a kind of neo-vernacular farm building, which leads to a reinforced concrete walkway that goes down... and down... and horribly down further, till it feels like you're on a particularly clammy bad trip to the proverbial centre of the earth. Once you've finally reached the shelter itself, no less than a hundred feet underground, it's more like *Das Boot* meets *Tomorrow's World*, with corridors, dorms and antechambers – two whole football pitches' worth – glaring in submarinal sterility. Rows of spartan bunk beds sit primed for uneasy dreams, while a plant room straight out of a 50s B-movie processes the bunker's air and generates its electricity.

Most unsettling of all is the main control room, still equipped with its primitive computers and control panels, military maps and clunky old red telephones hotwired for that fatal call. And if you weren't one of the great and good spared in the interests of subterranean government, you'd more than likely have ended up – in lieu of any physical trace – as a number in one of the ominous-looking filing cabinets ready to record death tolls from every region of Scotland.

Need to know The bunker is located at Troywood, some three miles north of Anstruther, on the B940 near Crail, Fife ☎ 01333/310301, Ⓦ www. secretbunker.co.uk. If you're coming from St Andrews, look out for the not-so-secret sign at the junction with the B9131. Open daily March–Oct 10am–5pm; £9.50. **Map 4, D14**

130 Good, old-fashioned seaside fun at Bridlington

Despite reports of its demise, the traditional English seaside holiday is alive and well in Bridlington, dear old Brid, the southernmost resort on the Yorkshire coast. It's long been a family favourite – where your parents came if they thought that Scarborough was too brash or Filey too genteel, and where generations of children built their first sand castle on golden sands that seemed to stretch for ever. The seafront promenades have been smartened up over the years, and asking for a cappuccino no longer risks a blank look, but in many ways Bridlington is a throwback to more traditional times – and it would take a hard heart not to dive gleefully into its nostalgic charms.

The harbour is still at the heart of things, splitting the bays to north and south. The curving proms and regimented backstreets behind are lined with guesthouses with wistful, wildly inappropriate names (*San Marino*, *Balmoral*, *The Edelweiss*) for a break in a bracing Yorkshire coastal town. Meanwhile, down at the Bridlington Spa – an Edwardian hall and theatre wrapped in a contemporary carapace – the summer sun never sets on its classic diet of pop acts, tribute bands, vintage rockers and virtuoso ventriloquists.

Get someone to hand over some pocket money and you're really in business, in a *Life on Mars*, is-that-all kind of way. Thirty pence gets you into the Harbour Heritage Museum for the history of Bridlington harbour – here for a thousand years – and another pound buys a fifteen-minute trip aboard the seagoing pirate ship ("wreaths and ashes scattered at sea"). It's under a quid for a Mr Whippy, and just two pounds for a bag of willy-shaped rock, and although inflation has seen off the Penny Falls in the arcades, a fistful of two-pence pieces might just get you that precariously balanced plastic keyring. Then it's on to the waltzers, dodgems, vintage carousel and log flume in the seafront fun park, before finally tearing off your shoes and plodding across the beach to build the world's largest sand castle. Come on, admit it, what's not to like?

Need to know See ⓦwww.realyorkshire.co.uk for more information about Bridlington and the East Yorkshire coast. For acts at the Spa, call the box office on ☎01262/678528 or check ⓦwww.spabridtickets.com.
Map 3, D9

131 Into the gloom of the Jersey War Tunnels

Head north from St Aubin's Bay up Jersey's main valley road to St Lawrence, and you can step back nearly seventy years to the saddest and most poignant period in the island's history. Jersey was occupied by German troops for most of World War II, from 1940 until Liberation in 1945. These five long years were a time of isolation and struggle during which over three hundred islanders were sentenced to prison or sent to concentration camps. Many suffered severe malnutrition.

The Germans carried out a number of defensive construction and engineering projects in the Channel Islands but the excavation of Hohlgangsanlage 8 (Ho8), a series of hillside tunnels in central Jersey, was by far the most elaborate and dangerous. Totalling over a kilometre in length, the complex was originally designed to be a weapons store sturdy enough to last a thousand years – the constant, cool temperature provided optimum conditions – but as the war drew on and casualties increased, the Germans converted it into an impregnable hospital.

Creating the tunnels was a gruelling task. The unfortunates lighting the gunpowder and wielding the hand-tools were a motley crew of over five thousand Russian, Polish, French and Spanish slaves and civilian prisoners, many of whom were maltreated by their captors – exhaustion and disease were horribly common. Others were injured in accidents, and some simply disappeared.

Today Ho8 is a museum of wartime Jersey, sometimes simply called the Jersey War Tunnels. The displays are stuffed with memorabilia relating to the harsh realities of German occupation: little details, such as the make-do-and-mend shoes and the handmade clothes and cosmetics, speak volumes about the resourcefulness of the islanders at a time of deprivation. There are also film clips to watch, and a reconstruction of the hospital's operating theatre and wards. Some unfinished sections of the complex have been revealed, to give you a sense of the conditions the slave labourers had to suffer.

It's an engrossing experience with a strong anti-war message, but it's chilling too – some even say the tunnels are haunted – so when you emerge, you'll be glad to see daylight once more.

Need to know Jersey War Tunnels, Les Charrières Malorey, St Lawrence, Jersey, Channel Islands ☎01534/860808, ⓦwww.jerseywartunnels.com. Open March–Nov daily 10am–6pm. £10.50.
Map 2, C8

132 "Be seeing you" at Portmeirion

There should be more places like Portmeirion, a "Home for Fallen Buildings" on the crook of Cardigan Bay. Sometimes grand old edifices can't be preserved in their entirety, so why not pilfer some of the best bits and arrange them into something new? It's a concept that worked a treat for Welsh architect Clough Williams-Ellis who was less interested in individual buildings than in their effect en masse. Over half a century (from 1925 until just before his death in 1978) he constructed his own private "village", ingeniously incorporating unloved mullioned windows, discarded entranceways, a Jacobean ceiling, even in some cases whole structures. The result: an extraordinary – and unique – pastiche of an idealized Italianate village, incongruously set on the west Welsh coast. In the wrong hands, of course, it could all have gone terribly awry. It's not everyone who would think to place a Siamese figurine on top of an Ionic column, centre it in a Mediterranean piazza and flank the whole with a 1760 colonnade rescued from a bomb-damaged bathhouse in Bristol. And yet it works. Wonderfully.

The setting helps. Williams-Ellis scoured Britain for a suitable site for his project but settled on this forested cove, just four miles from his family home. When the tide is out, broad sands stretch right across the Dwyryd Estuary, where Patrick McGoohan was forever being chased by a giant beachball in the 1967 cult TV series, *The Prisoner*. The show's exteriors were all shot at Portmeirion, and the memory is marked by an annual convention (in April) – and a little merchandising.

Though certainly a delightfully theatrical place, Portmeirion can feel plain bizarre on a grim rainy day, so come when the sun is shining and let the Italianate atmosphere seep into you. Warm days attract large crowds, however, so the key is to stay overnight on the estate, either at *Castell Deudraeth*, a Victorian crenellated manor fashioned into a boutique hotel, at the waterside *Hotel Portmeirion*, or in any of the numerous self-contained cottages Williams-Ellis constructed around the village. Guests get free rein around Portmeirion after the day visitors have gone, the most peaceful time of all to explore.

Need to know Portmeirion is three miles east of Porthmadog, Gwynedd. For more information and accommodation bookings, call ☎01766/770000 or see ⓦwww.portmeirion-village.com. Open daily 9.30am–5.30pm; adults £8; Nov–Feb free entry with voucher downloaded from the website.
Map 3, A11

133 Into the time tunnel at the Museum of Brands

If you give a 16-year-old boy a packet of Munchies, that's probably the last you'll hear of it. But for the young Robert Opie, now a consumer historian, that was the first of a dumbfounding collection of artefacts, now exhibited in West London's fascinating Museum of Brands, Packaging and Advertising.

The main part of the collection comprises an enthralling chronological social history, represented by a vast assemblage of domestic products, toiletries, clothing, food, toys and more. Items range from the Victorian era to the present, laid out in a low-lit "time tunnel". The earlier decades take you through a fascinating haul of human trappings, from the first Lyle's Golden Syrup tin to World War II-era cosmetics – posters reveal the advertising campaigns of the day, with brands such as Pond's appealing to wartime women's sense of aesthetic in a time of national disquiet.

It's absorbing stuff, but when you start to recognize items from your own lifetime it gets particularly compelling. Browsing retro Daz, Britvic, Bisto and Kellogg's packaging, you'll be amazed at how these everyday objects resonate with the child in you. The toys are the stuff of collectors' dreams: heaps of *Star Wars* paraphernalia, *Planet of the Apes* and *Jim'll Fix It* board games, and the mighty Buckaroo. In the 80s section, up pop those god-awful dancing sunflowers, while the 90s ushers in bottles of former teen-favourite scent Charlie Red. You might find that the impact fades in the 2000s display, but in a few years it will no doubt prompt someone else's stroll down memory lane.

The second stage of the museum is a study in brand development. And believe it or not, it's engrossing to watch Robinson's Barley Water morph from a tin of lemon-flavoured crystals to the familiar plastic bottle, and Saxa table salt grow from a cardboard packet to today's ubiquitous stout red cylinder.

The winding route means you can lose yourself in the detailed displays, emerging hours later, awed and blinking, into the lobby. From the Mary Quant stockings to the Toilet Duck, Opie's collection is a historical account, a nostalgia trip and a clever study of advertising all in one.

Need to know Museum of Brands, Packaging and Advertising, 2 Colville Mews, Lonsdale Rd, London W11 ☎020/7908 0880, ⓦwww.museumofbrands.com. Open Tues–Sat 10am–6pm, Sun 11am–5pm; £5.80.
Map 1, A3

134 Pride of Bristol: the SS Great Britain

Isambard Kingdom Brunel – the very name is as stirring as Bobby Moore lifting the World Cup or the union flags waving at the Last Night of the Proms. The great Victorian civil engineer gave Britain some of its greatest and grandest tunnels, bridges, stations and ships, leaving such a significant mark on Bristol, in particular, that it's commonly assumed he was a local lad. He wasn't, he was born in Portsmouth, but he certainly seems to have been inspired by this booming, outward-looking southwestern city.

He commenced his most conspicuous projects, Temple Meads railway station and the splendid Clifton Suspension Bridge, while he was still in his twenties; both are monuments to the supreme confidence of the 1830s. A decade later, with interest in travel to American and Australia growing apace, he turned his attention to shipping. Because his great masterpiece, the SS *Great Britain*, was built in Bristol's Floating Harbour, the city residents have always felt it belongs exclusively to them. After many years' absence, they reclaimed it in 1970, lovingly restored it, and turned it into a museum which has since been showered with awards.

Designed to have the grace of a galleon, it was nonetheless breathtakingly modern. Highly ambitious, Brunel built his steamship for both size and speed; on its maiden voyage in 1843, it was easily the world's largest vessel, revolutionizing intercontinental travel as resoundingly as Concorde did in the 1970s.

Engineering buffs will be fascinated by the massive iron hull and propeller, brilliantly displayed in the *Great Britain*'s original dry dock, now carefully sealed and climate-controlled. If you're interested in social history, you'll want to linger over the introductory displays, where you'll find ephemera relating to the people that voyaged in the ship during its many years of service. Among the vintage photos, tickets and sketchbook pages are letters describing life on board, from the quality of the porridge to the terror of a mid-Atlantic storm.

Promenade on the open deck and you can imagine yourself breathing in the salty air of the high seas, just as the passengers did – strictly segregated by class. There's more powerful evidence of the class divide downstairs, where first-class passengers enjoyed comfortable cabins and sumptuous banquets, while those in steerage were crammed into a lively but shanty-like arrangement of bunks. An excellent audioguide brings the whole visit to life with sound effects such as the grinding of machinery and the clucking or mooing of livestock, while diary snippets give voice to characters as diverse as stokers, merchants and Royal Marines.

Need to know The SS *Great Britain* sits in Bristol's Great Western Dockyard ☏ 0117/926 0680, ⓦ www.ssgreatbritain. org. Open daily: April–Oct 10am–5.30pm; Nov–March 10am–4.30pm; £11.95, including free return visits for twelve months. Map 2, C5

135 Seek out the most remote chapel in Wales

Some say Soar-y-Mynydd chapel is the most remote in Wales. Maybe it is, maybe it isn't. It really doesn't matter except that you'll certainly need some patience to navigate here along the winding moorland roads of Mynydd Eppynt, west of the town of Tregaron. A red kite circles overhead and a few sheep huddle for shelter under craggy rowan trees, but there's no habitation to be seen. In fact you could easily miss it, almost hidden in a small copse at the foot of some bald hills.

From the outside the chapel appears little more sophisticated than a barn – just a long, stone, whitewashed building with a simple pitched slate roof. Two chimneys rise from one end where the two storeys point to the chapel's domestic role, while just the "Capel Soar Y Mynydd" sign on the gable end and a pair of semicircular-headed windows give any indication of its religious purpose.

Out here, it's hard to imagine there were ever enough people around to maintain a congregation. But the 1820s, when the chapel was built, were more God-fearing times. It should be derelict by now, but the widely scattered community of Calvinist Methodists has just managed to keep the place viable, even using it as a schoolhouse until the 1940s.

Doors either side of the altar lead into a plain, white interior with a small maze of box pews, all nicely worn by nearly two centuries of devotion. Typically Calvinistic simplicity is the theme here – only *Duw Cariad Yw* ("God is Love") written in scroll behind the pulpit signals the divine presence. On a busy Sunday they might once have squeezed in a hundred of the faithful, but by the end of the last war the congregation had shrunk to fifty and by the 1960s less than ten attended regularly. Visit during the week and the chances are that you'll be here all alone, but on summer Sundays pilgrims still come from far and wide to hear itinerant ministers from all over Wales preach the gospel in the fervent style of old.

Need to know Soar-y-Mynydd Chapel, Llanddewi Brefi, Ceredigion. The chapel is generally left open during the daytime. Sunday services are held in summer. Map 3, B12

136 Mead and murder at the Battle of Tewkesbury

A medieval drummer beats out a sombre military pattern, marching the men – knights in full body armour, gunners, flag-bearers and men-at-arms – towards their positions. Some two thousand troops – representing the Houses of York and Lancaster – advance to their battle lines, facing each other across an open field. The roar of a cannon shot tears the sky, then a whoosh of arrows as the archers fire their longbows. Lord Somerset's Yorkist forces advance towards the enemy lines, but they're countered as the Lancastrians launch a full-on charge, lunging deep into the Yorkist lines. As the bodies enmesh in combat, amid battle cries and the clash of steel, the first casualties drop from the melee.

For one weekend every summer, the genteel Gloucestershire town of Tewkesbury turns the clock back to 1471, hosting in a field nearby a re-enactment of the bloody Battle of Tewkesbury, a decisive moment in the Wars of the Roses (for the record, the Yorkists soundly thrashed the Lancastrians). It's the centrepiece of the annual Tewkesbury Medieval Festival, the largest event of its kind in Europe.

Most participants – anyone can attend the festival, but you need an invitation to take part – are sticklers for authenticity. Many spend the weekend as their medieval counterparts would have, living in tents, cooking over fires and so on. Spectators, however, are free to live a less ascetic lifestyle, sampling hearty food like hog roasts and traditional beers and meads, watching jousting and archery contests, and wandering among the colourful array of jesters, acrobats, jugglers, falconers, magicians, fire-eaters and storytellers. History buffs can go on guided tours of the battlefield site, and there's much to keep kids entertained, from treasure hunts to the chance to make their own shields and wimples.

Meanwhile, Tewkesbury itself hosts numerous events, giving the town the feel of a film set for the weekend. Once the battle is decided late on Saturday afternoon, the victorious Yorkists advance to storm Tewkesbury Abbey, an event swiftly followed by the trials and (thankfully mock) beheadings of the captured Lancastrian soldiers.

For many, however, the most enjoyable parts of the weekend are the comical juxtapositions of medieval and modern life. A frequent entrant into the local "in bloom" competition, Tewkesbury treats visitors to the incongruous sight of coats of arms fluttering alongside hanging baskets and knights in full armour lumbering past colourful floral displays.

Need to know The Tewkesbury Medieval Festival (Ⓦwww.tewkesburymedievalfestival.org) is held annually on the second weekend in July. Entry is free.
Map 3, C12

137 Dyb dyb dyb: cast away on Brownsea Island

Need to know Brownsea Island is situated in Poole Harbour, Dorset, and run by the National Trust (Ⓦwww. nationaltrust.org.uk); entry costs £5.50 for adults. The island is only accessible by ferry (late March to Oct only; Ⓦwww. brownseaislandferries.com). See Ⓦwww.nationaltrustcottages. co.uk for details of the one cottage available to rent on the island (from £444 for two nights; sleeps 4).

Map 2, D6

There aren't many opportunities to play Robinson Crusoe in Britain, but on Brownsea Island you can be cast away totally self-sufficient for a night or two, almost alone – that is, unless the scouts have got there first. Once the last ferry-load of day-trippers has left, this beautiful island off the Dorset coast reverts to peace and seclusion, populated (apart from the odd guest at its Henry VIII-built castle) only by wildlife, including a thriving colony of the endangered red squirrel. You can stay at its National Trust cottage – but you'll have to bag it quick.

For much of the last century, the island was owned by one Mary Bonham Christie, the "demon of Brownsea". A fierce recluse who chased away visitors, she inspired Enid Blyton to set one of her Famous Five stories here – Blyton rechristened it Whispering Island. For all her unpopularity, Christie's obdurance proved to be Brownsea's salvation, as the island was allowed to revert to a natural wilderness, a state that the National Trust has helped maintain since it took over ownership half a century ago. Today, Brownsea retains an air of mystery: most visitors feel a real sense of adventure and discovery as they explore its confusing network of footpaths through dense woodland and out into sunny heath. There are lakes and lagoons here, and some fine beaches, though many lie tantalizingly out of reach, hidden below low cliffs or accessible only by hard-to-find steps.

No wonder Robert Baden-Powell was so taken with the place. In 1907, he saw it as a suitable testing ground for the 22 working-class lads he ferried over from the mainland to fend for themselves at a camp on the island's south coast. This adventure gave birth to the Scout Movement, and his original camping spot is still used by various scout and girl-guide groups. It's also something of a pilgrimage site, and wooden signposts display the messages of hundreds of scout troops that have since visited from all corners of the globe.

There's a fantastic beach in the south of the island, which scouts have dotted with improvised shelters made from propped-up tree branches. Boats lured here usually get caught out, grounded in the deceptively shallow waters some way offshore. Stay for the night and you can lie back, dip into your *Scouting for Boys* and smugly enjoy your island hideaway as the mainlanders are towed away by the coastguard.

138 Culloden Moor: the last battle

Need to know Culloden Moor, Inverness, Highland ☎0844 493 2159, Ⓦwww.nts.org. uk/culloden. Open Feb, March, Nov & Dec daily 10am–4pm; April–Oct daily 9am–6pm. Adults £10, concession £7.50, family £24; battlefield PDA included in price

Map 5, C19

Even amid Scotland's grisly back pages, the Battle of Culloden stands as one of the cruellest. Faced with the glowering expanse of Drumossie Moor today, it's hard to believe that Nairn, the sun-blessed Brighton of the North, lies only a few kilometres to the northeast. For though a state-of-the-art visitor centre boasts computer-simulated combat, Culloden remains a place forever ruminating on a darker age, when brother fought against brother in the last tooth-and-nail battle on British soil.

With loyalties so divided, sometimes within the same family, it also remains, unsurprisingly, one of the most controversial, recalling a pivotal clash between competing dynasties: the House of Stuart, represented by Bonnie Prince Charlie and a Jacobite army comprised largely of Highland clansmen; and the governing House of Hanover, represented by a Duke of Cumberland-led British army that included both Lowland and Highland Scots. Suffice to say that on April 16, 1746, the conflict's political, constitutional and religious complexities boiled down to a brutally swift conclusion; in less than an hour, the Jacobite army was annihilated, many of its soldiers mown down by government grapeshot.

As Charlie legged it to the Hebrides, the remnants of the Jacobite army met with as little mercy as ordinary Highlanders. Indiscriminate killing and economic devastation followed as government forces attempted to purge the region of both its Jacobite sympathies and its cultural identity. Tartan bit the dust, as did, ultimately, the whole clan system. And whether the Highland Clearances were an inevitable consequence of the battle or not, what strikes you more than anything about Culloden two and a half centuries on is its haunting sense of absence, a microcosm of countless straths and glens ceded to the wild, or to sheep.

It's an absence as vast as the burial cairns are squat, magnified by the removal, in recent years, of much of the site's tree cover. And though the concrete walkways threading the heather and gorse lend somewhat surreal intimations of a city park, it's the wind-flayed desolation that lingers. GPS audioguides may offer the last word in historical tourism, yet the essence of this place surely lies in the depths of its silence.

139 Back to the Industrial Revolution at Ironbridge

On paper, it may not sound exactly fun: a UNESCO World Heritage Site dedicated to showcasing the extraordinary industrial heritage of a small slice of the Shropshire countryside. But if learning about the history of iron-smelting doesn't sound like a top day out, be reassured: the mix of interactive exhibitions, historic re-creation and general light approach means there is much to enjoy at Ironbridge.

Most people make a beeline for the iconic Iron Bridge itself, designed by Abraham Darby in the late 1780s, but it's a good idea to visit some of the museums first to get a sense of why and how the world's first cast-iron-built bridge – a material previously far too expensive to use on such a scale – came to be constructed here. There are ten museums scattered over an area of six square miles, each dedicated to a different aspect of industry – from iron-smelting to tile-making and ceramics. Between them they create the most extensive industrial heritage site in the whole of England.

The Coalbrookdale Museums are a good place to start: the Museum of Iron sets out the importance of the early iron industry, and is also home to the original Old Furnace, where Abraham Darby produced the first iron smelted from coke rather than charcoal. His discovery made iron integral to the Industrial Revolution, and close by are the Darby Houses, where the wealthy family lived. Also nearby is Enginuity, an interactive exhibition offering the chance to really get involved with industrial processes, from using a little ingenuity to pull a locomotive to generating power by hand.

The other big draw is Blists Hill Victorian Town, a 52-acre re-creation of a working town at the turn of the twentieth century. Authentic shopfronts have been transported to the site, and visitors can change their twenty-first-century sterling for pounds, shillings and pence in the bank, before visiting the pharmacy, sweetshop and haberdashers, all which mix antique items with gifts for sale. All of the shops are staffed by characters in period dress, who are on hand to give an insight into life during the Victorian era. Most visitors don't make it to all ten museums in one day, but the good-value "passport" ticket allows unlimited entry to them all for a whole year – you may just find your interest sparked, and plan a return trip before too long.

Need to know Ironbridge Gorge, Shropshire ☎01952/884391, ⓦwww.ironbridge.org.uk. Open daily 10am–5pm. A passport ticket costs £21.95 for adults, £14.25 for children. Tickets to individual sites are also available.
Map 3, C11

140 Dancing with druids at dawn: the Summer Solstice at Stonehenge

Stonehenge is mind-boggling. Both its great age and the feat of human endeavour evidently involved in its construction are awesome to consider. But this colossal structure is never more astonishing than on the summer and winter solstices, when it is perfectly aligned to the points of sunrise and sunset.

Archeologists are still unsure why Stonehenge was built. Theories abound and conflict. It could have been an astronomical calculator, or a place for ritual sacrifice, a royal palace or even a UFO landing site – but for modern-day Druids who follow the Celtic Pagan systems of faith, Stonehenge is not only a mysterious site to marvel at, but a living, functioning temple. They, along with thousands of others, visit annually to witness sunrise on the longest day of the year, a significant date in the Pagan calendar.

The Summer Solstice is a mass gathering. If the sun is out, around 30,000 people grab the rare opportunity to experience the view from inside the henge. Cars and camper vans line up in thousands in a nearby field and the festival feeling kicks in. Druids in their traditional white robes and headdresses stride down the muddy lane towards the site alongside mystified tourists, families with enchanted youngsters, musicians, performance artists and a handful of cider-fuelled Wiltshire teenagers there for the all-night party.

Inside the circle it is madness, crammed with bodies. Some are naked, clambering up onto the formations to dance and sing; some chant and meditate; others hug the cold sandstone. But most just stare in wonder at the ancient edifice around them. The celebration is typically peaceful, if eventful for the security guards, who are better practised at pacing the circuit on dark, lonely nights.

There are concerns about the effect this revelry has on the prehistoric construction. Druids fear for the corrosion of the stones, and that the spiritual meaning of the occasion is diluted. But as the sunlight spills over the edge of Salisbury Plain, and breaks behind the Heel Stone, there is only common joy and appreciation for the remarkable orientation of these incredible lumps of rock.

Need to know See Ⓦ www. english-heritage.org.uk for more information. Entry is free, with access from 7pm the evening before the solstice. A bus service operates from Salisbury; expect traffic queues. Future dates: June 21 (2011), 20 (2012) and 21 (2013).
Map 2, D6

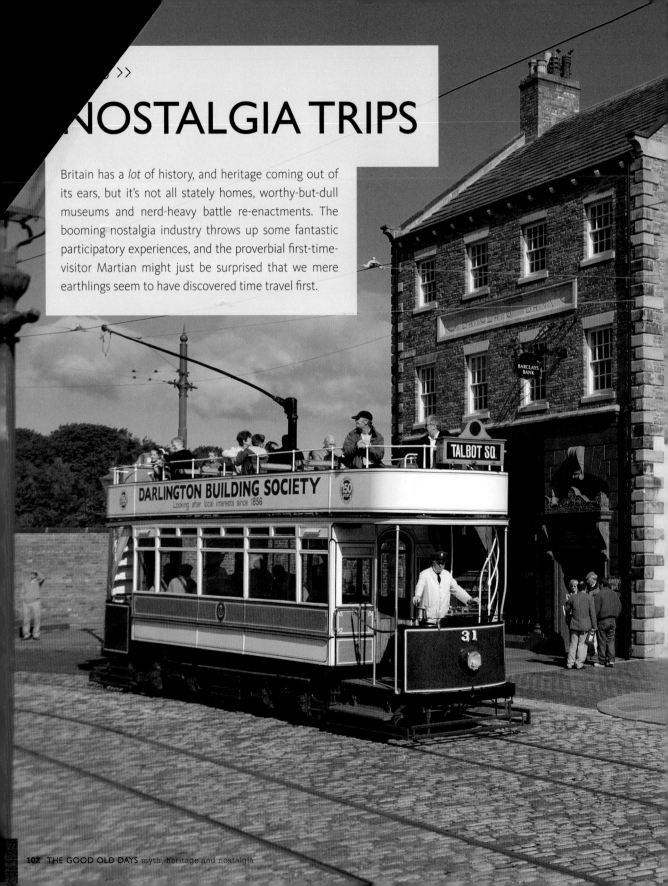

NOSTALGIA TRIPS

Britain has a *lot* of history, and heritage coming out of its ears, but it's not all stately homes, worthy-but-dull museums and nerd-heavy battle re-enactments. The booming nostalgia industry throws up some fantastic participatory experiences, and the proverbial first-time-visitor Martian might just be surprised that we mere earthlings seem to have discovered time travel first.

142 Wartime Weekend, Ramsbottom, Greater Manchester

The 1940s go with a real swing, from the afternoon tea dance to big band night, in Ramsbottom's fabulous annual dress-up-and-join-in wartime festival. Steam trains on the East Lancashire Railway heritage line take enthusiasts right back to the days of starched uniforms and flouncy dresses (vintage gear is de rigueur), complete with jive competitions, marching bands, church coffee mornings, wartime markets and sassy troop entertainers. This is one place where you *do* mention the war.

Ⓦ*www.east-lancs-rly.co.uk*, Ⓦ*www.ramsbottomonline.com. Spring Bank Holiday weekend. Map 3, C10*

143 Kentwell Hall, Long Melford, Suffolk

There's only one place to get the lowdown on sixteenth-century fashion, or hear about the latest, newfangled farming implement, and that's at Kentwell's meticulously observed re-creations of daily Tudor life. It's a full-immersion experience, with living, working, talking Tudor folk, rich and poor, going about their daily lives – right down to a steadfast incomprehension if asked about anything from a later age. Want to learn about spinning? There's no app for that so you'll have to listen carefully.

Ⓦ*www.kentwell.co.uk. Map 3, E12*

144 Eastbourne Victorian Festival, Sussex

Relive the glory days of the Empire in Eastbourne, when Britannia ruled the waves, bodices were big and whiskers even bigger. The town's annual Victorian festival is an excuse for dressing up and showing off, whether you're joining the icy sea-dip or attending music-hall gala night at the theatre – and Queen Victoria herself arrives by train to be met by singing schoolchildren and local dignitaries.

Ⓦ*www.eastbournevictorianfestival.org.uk; Sept. Map 2, E6*

145 Hartlepool's Maritime Experience

Sword-fighting sailors and roaming press gangs add a real whiff of authenticity to Hartlepool's eighteenth-century seaport, where the oldest British warship still afloat, the HMS *Trincomalee*, takes pride of place. Quayside guides in period get-up point out the highlights, from a dramatic sea battle in the Fighting Ships show to good old-fashioned games of hopscotch and skittles. Cause any trouble, and you'll be on eighteenth-century community service (that's rat-catching duty, landlubbers).

Ⓦ*www.hartlepoolsmaritimeexperience.com. Map 4, E16*

141 Beamish, County Durham

Britain's best open-air museum puts you right in the middle of daily life a century or two ago, with painstakingly reassembled buildings and re-created streets showcasing the years 1825 and 1913, from manor house to pit village. Any puzzling questions (What was *that* used for? What age can my kids start down the mine?) are fielded by costumed guides who share an absolute passion for their regional history, whether they're driving the steam locos or serving in the sweet shop.

Ⓦ*www.beamish.org.uk. Map 4, E16*

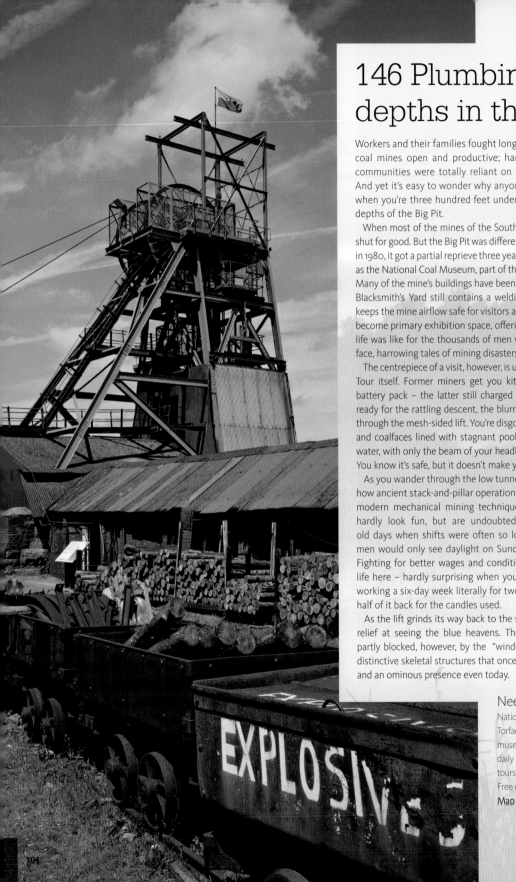

146 Plumbing the depths in the Big Pit

Workers and their families fought long and hard to keep the Welsh coal mines open and productive; hardly surprising when whole communities were totally reliant on the pits' economic viability. And yet it's easy to wonder why anyone would want a miner's job when you're three hundred feet underground in the cold, clammy depths of the Big Pit.

When most of the mines of the South Wales Coalfield closed, they shut for good. But the Big Pit was different: having stopped operations in 1980, it got a partial reprieve three years later and in 2001 started life as the National Coal Museum, part of the National Museum of Wales. Many of the mine's buildings have been left exactly as they were. The Blacksmith's Yard still contains a welding shop, the Fan House still keeps the mine airflow safe for visitors and the old Pithead Baths have become primary exhibition space, offering a unique insight into what life was like for the thousands of men who picked away at the coalface, harrowing tales of mining disasters and all.

The centrepiece of a visit, however, is undoubtedly the Underground Tour itself. Former miners get you kitted up in helmet, lamp and battery pack – the latter still charged in the former Lamp Room – ready for the rattling descent, the blurred rock face just inches away through the mesh-sided lift. You're disgorged into a labyrinth of shafts and coalfaces lined with stagnant pools and streams of dank, rusty water, with only the beam of your headlamp to fend off the darkness. You know it's safe, but it doesn't make you feel any less uneasy.

As you wander through the low tunnels your miner-guide explains how ancient stack-and-pillar operations gradually gave way to more modern mechanical mining techniques. Such advanced methods hardly look fun, but are undoubtedly an improvement on the old days when shifts were often so long that during winter most men would only see daylight on Sunday between visits to chapel. Fighting for better wages and conditions has always been part of life here – hardly surprising when you hear tales of small children working a six-day week literally for twopence – only to have to pay half of it back for the candles used.

As the lift grinds its way back to the surface, you'll likely feel some relief at seeing the blue heavens. The view of the rolling hills is partly blocked, however, by the "winder" – one of the last of these distinctive skeletal structures that once dotted the coalfield's skyline, and an ominous presence even today.

Need to know Big Pit National Coal Museum, Blaenafon, Torfaen ☎ 01495/790311, ⓦ www.museumwales.ac.uk/en/bigpit. Open daily 9.30am–5pm; 1hr underground tours start frequently 10am–3.30pm. Free entry.
Map 2, C5

147 Baldrick and bells: learning to morris dance on the Isle of Wight

If someone were to organize a Eurovision Dance Contest for the over-60s, who would win? The Spanish would be strong contenders: they'd just have to enter some agelessly glamorous flamenco dancers with wiry torsos and don't-mess-with-me flounces. The Ukrainians could easily wow the judges with some fearsome Cossack dancers, lunging and leaping with as much bravado as their creaking knees allow. The English, however, would probably field a gang of tubby blokes with a penchant for synchronized skipping. They'd have a laugh, but they wouldn't have a hope.

Daft though their hankie-waving, bell-jingling antics may seem, England's morris dancers – all 14,000 of them – enjoy their many traditions so thoroughly that they're not bothered by the occasional chortle or sneer. Morris men have been dancing their way through the rural calendar since the fifteenth century: commemorating St George in April, seeing in the dawn on May Day, blessing the hop harvest in August and adding colour to country fairs all through the year. Their routines may be eccentric, but they're always delivered with a generous dollop of good humour, since morris men are above all a jovial lot. It must be the regular exercise, convivial company and post-performance pints of real ale.

If you reckon you've got what it takes to be a morris man (or woman, since you ask), you could sign up for a class at Britain's first school of folk culture, the Carnival Learning Centre in Ryde. Why Ryde? Because the Isle of Wight is a hotbed of morris madness, with no less than six active troupes – or sides, a they're known in the biz. Don't worry, you don't have to be over 60 – all ages are welcome.

Morris is a new departure for CLC which until recently specialized in global traditions such as African drumming and samba dancing. Waving the flag for English folk dance is Brian Reeves from the Men of Wight, with a repertoire of favourites such as Balance the Straw and Broad Cupid. He'll soon have you strapping on your baldrick (that's your sash) and bells, stomping your feet and clomping your stick with glee.

Need to know The Carnival Learning Centre, Westridge, Brading Rd, Ryde, Isle of Wight (℡01983/817280, Ⓦwww. thecarnivallearningcentre.org) runs morris dancing classes on Thursday mornings between February and April (£4 per two-hour session).
Map 2, D6

148 Guinevere and the grail: uncovering myths in Glastonbury

Towering over the Somerset Levels, a lone pinnacle in an open expanse of marshland, the five-hundred-foot-high mound of Glastonbury Tor has invited myth and conjecture for centuries. The tower-topped hill is visible for miles around, and has (allegedly) served as everything from the Land of the Dead to a meeting point for UFOs.

Glastonbury's most fabled legend is its association with the mysterious Isle of Avalon – water levels around here are now much lower than they were in the past, meaning the Tor *was* probably once an island – and it was to Avalon that King Arthur was allegedly brought following his mortal wounding at the Battle of Camlan in the mid-sixth century. Arthur lay buried at Glastonbury Abbey until 1191, when, shortly following its gutting by a great fire, monks "discovered" his body, along with Queen Guinevere's, under a leaden cross bearing the inscription "Here lies the renown King Arthur in the Isle of Avalon". Experts argue over how old the writing is, and the cross itself was lost centuries ago, though it is beyond doubt that the resulting influx of pilgrims provided the finance necessary for the abbey's restoration. In 1278, the bones of Arthur and Guinevere were transferred to the abbey but disappeared after the Dissolution of the Monasteries in 1539 – a plaque near the High Altar marks the spot where their black marble tomb lay.

Many of Glastonbury's legends overlap, and so Arthurian tales are intertwined with another enduring local myth: the Holy Grail. Finding the Grail was the ultimate quest for King Arthur and the Knights of the Round Table, though it would seem that they didn't have too far to look. Legend has it that Joseph of Arimathea, attempting to establish Christianity in this heathen corner of the Roman Empire, buried the Grail at the foot of the Tor. The spring of blood that miraculously flowed forth is now marked by the Chalice Well, though the waters' red colouring has more to do with its rich iron content than any sacred symbolism.

It was just below the Tor, too, on Wearyall Hill, that a tired Joseph, with his disciples ("Weary, All"), was said to have stuck his thorn staff into the ground to rest; by morning, it had taken root. Descendants of this sacred Glastonbury Thorn still grow in the abbey grounds, blossoming around Christmas each year – the only other hawthorns that do this are, interestingly, in the Middle East....

Need to know Glastonbury Abbey (Ⓦwww.glastonburyabbey. com; daily 9.30am to dusk, Jan, Feb & Dec from 10am, June–Aug from 9am; £5.50) is on Magdalene Street in the town centre. Glastonbury Tor (open year-round; free; Ⓦwww. nationaltrust.org) and the Chalice Well and Gardens (daily 10am–5.30pm, Nov–March till 4pm; £3.50; Ⓦwww.chalicewell.org.uk) are less than a mile to the east.
Map 2, C6

149 Cloud-watching at Skara Brae

Need to know Skara Brae is situated in the parish of Sandwick on the western mainland of Orkney. Open daily: April–Sept 9.30am–5.30pm; Oct–March 9.30am–4.30pm. £6.70.

Map 5, D17

The Orkney Islands, exposed and almost totally treeless, are the kind of place where you can see the weather coming from a long way off: heavy cloud and rain are frequent visitors, sweeping in from the Atlantic Ocean. And so it was that one night in 1850, a violent storm hit the white-sand Bay of Skaill, tore into a grassy mound on the shoreline, and revealed one of the world's great archeological treasures: the Neolithic village of Skara Brae.

Paths lead you round the grass-topped complex, from where you can look down into the site's eight stone-built constructions. They are immediately recognizable as homes, furnished in period style with stone shelves, beds and square hearths. The adjacent visitor centre re-creates one of the homes for a walk-through experience, but in fact the real thing gives an equally vivid sense of the lives of the people who farmed and fished here five thousand years ago.

A remarkable amount has been discovered about the inhabitants from the midden – or waste – pile that sheltered the houses; though the windowless homes would have been dark and smoky, in other ways life was pretty comfortable here. The diet was varied, consisting of shellfish, beef, red deer, boar, mutton, barley, wheat and sea-bird eggs. Flint for tools was collected from the seashore, and animal bones provided the raw materials for other implements: needles, knives, pins and axes. The inhabitants slept in their cosy-looking stone beds on a mattress of straw or heather, with animal skins – and the fire – to ward off winter chills. A complex drainage system has been unearthed, and some early form of toilet may have been one of the mod cons on offer. The houses follow an identical layout and were connected by low passageways, suggesting a close and non-hierarchical settlement.

And Skara Brae must have been a successful community: it was inhabited for six hundred years before being abandoned, to disappear under the soil for more than four thousand years. But as the weather conspired to reveal Skara Brae, so it threatens to wash away and eclipse this vulnerable coastal site. Take a ferry to Orkney, and see it while you can.

150 Don't panic! Whistles and whimsy at Bressingham

Need to know

Bressingham Steam & Gardens (☎01379/686900, ⓦwww.bressingham.co.uk) is 2.5 miles west of Diss along the A1066. Open Easter–Oct daily 10.30am–5pm (June–Aug till 5.30pm), plus mid-Feb to Easter daily for Dads Army Museum & Winter Garden only. Non-steam days (Mon & Tues) £9.50; steam days (Weds–Sun; daily mid-July to early Sept) £12.

Map 3, F11

When the Norfolk market town of Diss joined the Cittaslow movement a few years ago to become Britain's third Slow Town, it didn't have to brake very hard. What more perfect place, with its winsome old town and idyllic village green, could there be for a museum dedicated to that most British of anachronisms – the steam railway?

And Bressingham Steam and Gardens, full of gentle surprises, is a steam museum *par excellence*. It's clear that this is going to be a fun day as soon as you arrive, when from behind a white picket fence a cheerful whistle pierces the air, accompanied by a tangy waft of warm, oily steam. With an impressive plume of vapour, the comically small *Alan Bloom* trundles into its hanging-basket-festooned station; it's one of several pristine miniature locomotives taking visitors along Bressingham's four narrow-gauge railway lines, each exploring in stately fashion a different section of the magnificent grounds.

There are full-size trains here too: in the Royal Coaches and Locomotives shed, you can peer into Edward VII's claret Royal Saloon carriage, awash with Javan teak and silk-brocaded upholstery – just the ticket for the sprint down to Epsom for the Derby. And the paean to steam extends beyond the locos: every so often there's an energetic calliope burst of *The Sailor's Hornpipe* or *Life on the Ocean Waves* as the lovingly restored steam-driven Victorian gallopers (carousels) spring into life.

It's all unashamedly nostalgic, but then Bressingham takes a turn for the whimsical. Wander through the Exhibition Hall and you arrive at a gaslit wartime-era shopping street. Peer up at the shopfront names: Frazer Funerals' Director; Jones the Butcher; the Walmington-on-Sea Post Office. Of course – you've arrived at the official home of the Dad's Army Appreciation Society. Perhaps that's why there was a bright yellow double-decker by the entrance, with the words "Trotters Ethnic Tours" emblazoned on the side – *Only Fools and Horses* clearly gets a look-in too.

The sitcom displays may seem a bit raggedy, but not so Bressingham's *pièce de résistance*: its spectacular gardens. The immaculately tended herbaceous borders are a riot of colour at any time of year, with some delightfully eccentric touches, not least the cute stone bridges and Anglo-Saxon huts of The Dell.

Bressingham, surprises at every turn, is the sort of place that makes you chuckle contentedly for much of the day. And three cheers to that.

151 Trace the horrors of the Pendle Witch Trials

It's Sunday evening around the campfire, and the drumming is intensifying. Entranced by the rhythm, half-naked girls are dancing wildly around the fire, leaping through the flames. Pentacle flags flap in the wind, and a shaman summons the spirits. It's summer solstice at the Pendle Witch Camp, and it's clear that four hundred years after the most notorious witch trial in Britain, bleak, windswept Pendle Hill has lost none of its powers to enchant.

The year was 1612, nine years after King James of Scotland ascended the English throne. Both fascinated and terrified by witchcraft, the paranoid king brought in harsh statutes for anyone found guilty of covenanting with the spirits or uttering spells. And so when ten women and two men, mainly from two rival peasant families from villages on the slopes of Pendle Hill, were forced into lurid confessions of witchcraft – drinking blood, burning effigies and using black magic to cause paralysis and even death – they didn't have a hope. After five months of imprisonment in the jail at Lancaster Castle, all but one was found guilty and hanged in front of huge crowds on Lancaster's Gallows Hill.

With its sinister history, it's fitting that this isolated part of Lancashire should remain some of the most wild and unspoiled areas of the country, the brooding landscape of the ancient Forest of Bowland, of which flat-topped Pendle Hill forms an outlier, starkly at odds with the industrial cityscapes further south. Once roamed by wolves and wild boar, this terrain of verdant pastures, steep valleys and dramatic expanses of open moorland, dotted with stone-built farms and villages, is magnificent walking country. You can also explore the area – visiting sites connected to the witches – by car on the 45-mile Pendle Witches Trail, which leads from the Pendle Heritage Centre, where you can read up on the trial, through the bucolic Ribble Valley – inspiration to both Conan Doyle and Tolkien – and over the heather-clad slopes of the Trough of Bowland. The Trail concludes with the dramatic descent to Lancaster, where a tour of the castle brings the horrors of the trials to life. Still a working prison, in parts it retains an exceptional atmosphere of gloom: tours take in the thirteenth-century Adrian's Tower, hung with manacles and leg-irons; the old cells, where you'll experience what it's like to be locked in yourself; and the drop room, final step on the road to the gallows where so many met the hangman's noose.

Need to know For more information, see ⓦwww.visitlancashire.com and ⓦwww.forestofbowland.com. Lancaster Castle is open daily 10am–5pm; £5. The Pendle Witch Camp (ⓦwww.penwitchcamp.co.uk), an annual gathering of modern pagans, takes place over summer solstice weekend and costs £30; a year-long programme of activities is planned for 2012 to celebrate the four-hundredth anniversary of the trial.
Map 3, C9

152 Do the dashing white sergeant in Ullapool

Homely, boisterous – and, above all, huge fun – the ceilidh has its origins in small Highland communities, in the days when folk music, dance and song were the only available forms of entertainment. A ceilidh can take many forms, but the essential elements remain common to all: catchy fiddle music, a caller to describe the dances to bewildered visitors, and a willingness on the part of the participants not to mind making a fool of themselves, whether they're making up an eightsome reel or belting out a party piece.

One of the best venues for a local ceilidh is The Ceilidh Place in the Highland town of Ullapool on the eastern shore of Loch Broom. This renowned arts centre – which also offers cosy accommodation and a café-bar – was created in 1970 by actor Robert Urquhart in the house he was born in. It originated as a simple café with a sign outside inviting passing musicians to play for their supper, but, as its popularity grew, eventually expanded to take the vibrant form it has today, with a packed programme of events that includes dance, storytelling, Celtic song, rafter-raising traditional music and the odd dash of jazz or classical music. The original café now has Fairtrade status, and they are pleased to serve "fish from the pier, tatties from the lochside and herbs from the garden".

And all in the unlikely setting of a little fishing town, built on a neat grid at the height of the herring boom in the 1780s; its rows of handsome little cottages look out to sea, dwarfed by the CalMac ferry that ploughs across the waters to Lewis. The surrounding country is fabled Wester Ross, with its soaring mountains, high passes, island vistas and rugged hiking up peaks such as Suilven, Cul Mor and Stac Pollaidh. The rugged hiking here is unmissable – but make sure you keep enough energy in reserve, once you've kicked off your walking boots, to put on your dancing shoes for some homespun entertainment, Scottish style.

Need to know The Ceilidh Place, 14 West Argyle St, Ullapool, Highland ☎01854/612103, ⓦwww.theceilidhplace.com. It has thirteen simple en-suite bedrooms, which are telly-free but feature a radio and mini library. The neighbouring bunkhouse (sleeps 32) offers more basic, cheaper accommodation. Ceilidhs are held regularly in summer.
Map 5, C19

THRILLS AND SPILLS

outdoor adventures

Think outdoor adventures and heart-pumping thrills, and chances are it's holidays in New Zealand, Australia and North America that spring to mind. Now look closer to home and think whitewater rafting, river-tubing, skiing, caving and alpine climbing – let no one tell you that Britain isn't made for adventure. There has to be something about the great British outdoors that first inspired the likes of Livingstone, Shackleton, Mallory, Bonington and Pen Hadow – to name just a few of the Brits who have gone higher, further and longer than anyone else. But whatever it is that's special, it's certainly not the superlatives that others can claim. On a world scale, British rivers are mere trickles, our canyons are cracks and the mountains are puny – Ben Nevis, Britain's highest mountain, checks in at 4409ft (which sounds respectable until you realize that there are 150 other countries in the world that can do better than that). Instead, what Britain has – in spades – is astonishing geographical variety packed into its modest proportions. The Lake District, for example, is only thirty miles across but it features sixteen major lakes, dozens of challenging peaks and endless opportunities for adrenaline junkies. In Wales, there's world-class mountain biking, kayaking and rafting – and this in a land area that's only 160 miles by 50. There are exceptions, and big-sky adventurers can push themselves surprisingly hard in Britain, particularly by immersion in the raw landscapes of the Scottish Highlands, one of the last great European wildernesses; across the country though, there are dramatic long-distance hiking routes that border on the epic. Meanwhile, the booming popularity of wild swimming, bushcraft courses and back-country camping suggests a modern reconnection with nature and the outdoors, as the largely urban British rediscover the simple joys of their own backyard. Combine a passion for local exploration with typical British ingenuity, and you get all sorts of unexpected thrills in some unexpected places, whether it's husky rides in Norfolk, zorbing in Dorset or paddle-boarding in the Fenlands. It's all here in Britain, so buckle up, strap in, hang on and enjoy.

153 Towers of granite: tackling Cornwall's Commando Ridge

It was at the turn of the twentieth century that the daddy of rock climbing, A.W. Andrews, put the far-western Cornish peninsula of Penwith down in history as the epicentre of sea-cliff climbing. It's a dramatic landscape, where scrub-topped granite cliffs and gaping zawns (or sea inlets) plummet into the azure sea, and one which presents climbers with some thrilling challenges. The longest ascent in this rock-monkey's playground is Bosigran Ridge, where climbers take on 198 metres of serrated rock that yawns from the hissing cauldron of the Atlantic up onto wild heathland.

Famously dubbed Commando Ridge for its role as a training ground for marines during World War II, the route is adrenaline inducing without being a reckless undertaking. Waves lick your heels on the vertical slab jutting skyward from Porthmoina Cove, after which the gradient eases and the dragon's back of rock arcs landward.

When it's basking under clear skies Commando Ridge is one the most picturesque coastal routes imaginable, with views curling west to Pendeen Watch Lighthouse, Cape Cornwall and Land's End. But when a sea mist rolls in the territory becomes eerie and perilous – on his first visit here in 1902, Andrews likened catching sight of the vanishing and reappearing rock to glimpsing pale ghosts as the dense curtain rose and fell.

While routes this awesome are often only accessible to experts, what makes the ridge a classic is that it accommodates all levels of climbers and offers lots of exit and entry points where less competent – or weary – climbers can dip in and out. Excellent hand- and footholds etched into the granite invite even novice climbers to have a go (in the hands of an expert), and there are several shorter climbs on the western side of the ridge.

Being such a popular spot Bosigran is home to the only climbers' club hut in Cornwall, offering basic accommodation for groups. And it isn't only climbers that flock here – the cliffs around Bosigran are also popular with sea birds including peregrines and the rare chough.

Need to know

Bosigran is between Zennor and Morvah – there is a National Trust car park by Carn Galver mine on the B3306. Hotrock Climbs (☎07729 091380, ⓦhotrockclimbs.com) can organize rock-climbing courses and trips to the ridge. The *Count House* Climbers' Club Hut can be booked by BMC clubs and climbing groups on ⓦwww.climbers-club.co.uk. Map 2, A7

154 Legendary labyrinths below Castleton's hills

Need to know For caving information contact the Peak District Information Centre, Buxton Rd, Castleton, Derbyshire (☎01629/816572, ⓦwww.peakdistrict.gov.uk; April–Oct 9.30am–5.30pm, Nov–March 10am–5pm). All the caves are within a forty-minute walk of Castleton, which is a pleasant two-mile walk or bus ride from Hope train station.

Map 3, C10

Odin Mine, Giant's Hole, Suicide Cave, Windy Knoll: the names on the map around cavern-riddled Castleton conjure images of a subterranean system to rival Middle Earth's Mines of Moria.

The caves here reach storybook proportions: as vast as speleological Britain gets. The 140-metre shaft of recently discovered Titan, indeed, is big enough to swallow St Paul's Cathedral several times. Yet Castleton's underground adventure playground of chambers, crawls, waterfalls and squeezes has long been synonymous with the otherworldly.

Even three hundred years ago, when tourists first started arriving for cave tours, locals were already hyping the caves' awe-inspiring atmosphere. The river that flowed though Peak Cavern, the area's caving hotspot, got renamed the Styx; later the entire cavern was evocatively rebranded "the Devil's Arse". More recently, even the BBC jumped on the bandwagon, immortalizing the current showcave's rear end as the descent to Underland in *The Chronicles of Narnia*.

It's the colourful history as well as the mind-blowing geology that puts Castleton's caverns a cut above the UK's other caving complexes. Two centuries of mining bolstered the subterranean network: now caving odysseys can feature boating along a nineteenth-century lead-miners' tunnel (Speedwell Cavern), or stalactite-spying amid the world's only naturally occurring Blue John (Treak Cliff Cavern).

If your appetite for the cavernous is whetted by the four showcaves here, you've got another thirteen miles of more serious subterranean to explore. Passages cut down through the labyrinthine limestone nearly 250m, and divers can venture deeper still. The eerie graffiti of the poor souls who mined here adorns cave walls, along with glimmers of the galena and rare Blue John they risked their lives to find. There's even an ancient miner's boat wedged in Speedwell Cavern. Hypogean highlights include the 65-metre Leviathan pitch in Titan and potholing paradise Giant's Hole, with whitewater rapids and grottoes aplenty en route. And for the toughest tunnelling around? Odin Mine's dangerous reputation was such that even ore-desperate miners regularly refused work there, recruiting (so the story goes) convicts to do the dirty work. Be warned.

155 Husky heaven: riding with dogs in Thetford Forest

Need to know Contact ⓦwww.huskyracing.org.uk for more information about husky rides.

Map 3, E11

It's a crisp, cold morning, not yet light, and we pull up on the edge of the forest. Two women appear from the shadows and we know we're in the right place. Not only because it's 6am and there's no one else around, but because we can hear a restless rustling and yelping in the back of their van. As we follow them into the forest the din gets louder...

Britain is full of fringe outdoor activities pursued tirelessly by committed enthusiasts, but this one really is unusual – even for Norfolk. It's husky riding, East Anglian-style: teams of Siberian huskies are raced through the expansive heath and woodland of Thetford Forest, pulling excited participants not on sledges (it doesn't get cold regularly enough for that), but purpose-built "rigs". It's ideal terrain for taking the dogs out, and a great way for them to keep exercised on winter mornings. Be aware though that the huskies like it best when it's really, really cold.

Husky barking is a mixture of yelping and howling that isn't easy on the ear, and it rises to a crescendo once the dogs are harnessed up. It can only be quelled by one thing: running. We jump onto the back of the disabled quad bike used for training and all of a sudden the noise cuts out because we're off. The huskies are ecstatic as we accelerate down the track, eight dogs scampering along in front and Sally the driver directing operations behind, with shouts of "Haw!" and "Gee!" – Inuit for left and right.

It's a great feeling, surging through the forest at speed, powered only by the dogs. We take the corners tightly and sometimes at a terrifying pace, but the animals are in complete harmony and control with each other, and indeed with Sally, who sprinkles her commands with words of praise and encouragement. We cover about four miles in fifteen minutes or so, and are soon back where we started, where the dogs froth, pant and noisily lap water from tin bowls, before having the foam gently wiped from their snouts with a towel and a short walk to warm down. They've had fun, and are content to be loaded back in the van, with the prospect of breakfast and a snooze when they get home. It's pure husky heaven, and they're as happy as can be until the next morning's run.

WILD SWIMMING

Rule Britannia! We Brits advocated the health benefits of sea-water bathing a century or so before our continental cousins, and in recent years we've spurned the municipal pool to rediscover the childhood thrill of wild swimming. Tropical this island is not, of course. But from magical Scottish streams to lazy East Anglian rivers and tiny tarns in Wales, this wild bunch prove aquatic adventures await anyone hardy to embrace the climate. And isn't that what being British is all about?

156 Faerie Pools, Glen Brittle, Isle of Skye

Fairy-tale enchantment is the last thing you might expect in this Gothic landscape. Yet at the heart of the brooding moorland and mist-wreathed mountains of majestic Glen Brittle lie waters that are pure magic: a series of glorious gin-clear plunge pools worn smooth over millennia by the cascading Allt Coir' a' Mhadaidh River, which on sunny days glow with a tropical turquoise hue. You might end up the same colour, too – water temperatures hover stubbornly around 8°C – but don't let that deter you from pushing upstream, where an underwater arch awaits. Dive in, swim through and you'll emerge grinning from ear to ear. *Map 5, B20*

157 Burton Bradstock, Dorset

Durdle Door just along the coast is spectacular but who wants to wild-swim with holiday parks? At Burton Bradstock, star of the Jurassic Coast, there are no caravans, no car parks, just a pebble beach and crumbling cliffs that stretch into the distance enticing you to swim just that little bit further. Don't stray too far, though – once you're dried off and warm, you shouldn't miss the upmarket *Hive Beach Café* on a bluff above the beach, which prepares some of the freshest seafood and fish in the country. *Map 2, C6*

158 River Waveney, Suffolk

With its languidly flowing water and lush landscapes, the River Waveney encapsulates all that's idyllic about wild swimming in rural Suffolk. Slip in where the river curves around Outney Common, near Bungay, and you'll soon be stroking slowly past flower-fringed banks while swallows swoop over the surface and startled cows stop and stare. If there's a more perfect place for a dip on a sultry midsummer's day then they're keeping it quiet. *Map 3, F11*

159 Llyn Idwal, Snowdonia

Tarn-swimming in North Wales puts the wild into wild swimming. It's a truly challenging activity, where to reach your high-altitude blue-green glacial lake you'll need to hike through an ice-shattered mountainscape. And nor is it just the cold water that's breathtaking. At Llyn Idwal, in the Nant Ffrancon Valley (park by Llyn Ogwen lake and walk up for a mile), you wade from a pebble beach into deep clear water, dwarfed by high crags, rock slabs and scree. Better still, the lake is (theoretically at least) open to sunshine. Who knows, you might even see some. *Map 3, B11*

160 Crummock Water, Lake District

He was in a boat, which was cheating, but Wordsworth was dead right – there are few better views than that from the centre of Crummock Water. Cormorants glide over the placid surface and the bulks of Mellbreak and Grasmoor rise above. Alongside its good looks and lack of motorboats, Crummock Water takes top billing in the Lake District's wild-swimming wonderland because of its small scale, easy-access shoreline and shallow water that's a mite warmer than surrounding lakes. You might not want to dispense with the wet suit just yet, though. *Map 4, D16*

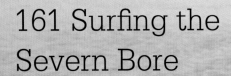

161 Surfing the Severn Bore

Autumn mist swirls across the placid waters of the River Severn, and a kingfisher flits along the riverbank in a spark of colour. Gradually, from downriver, a noise like the murmuring of a distant crowd develops into a roar, then suddenly a mighty wall of brown water appears across the entire width of the river, topped here and there by a creamy curl where the wave is racing to get ahead of itself.

This is the Severn Bore, one of the longest and biggest tidal bores in the world. It's a startling spectacle when you're watching from the riverbank. If you're actually in the river, it can be terrifying.

The river, though, is where you'll be if you choose to surf the Bore. Since the Sixties, surfers from all over the world have made their way to the Severn to catch this remarkable wave. It occurs on the biggest tides of the year when Atlantic waters from the Bristol Channel surge up the Severn Estuary at as much as 12mph and become funnelled between the ever-narrowing riverbanks to create one of Britain's most bizarre natural phenomena.

If the equinoxes coincide with big Atlantic swells, the wave may be as much as six feet high, tearing off overhanging tree branches, sweeping away sections of riverbank and providing a ride that can last for several miles. It's a challenge even for a competent surfer. Non-surfers will want to stay bankside, from where the Bore is simply a strange and magnificent sight.

Need to know The largest bores occur at the September and March equinoxes. Go to Ⓦ www.riverseveraore.co.uk for more details.

Map 2, C5

162 Two wheels, four abbeys: cycling the heart of the Scottish Borders

Hauling a bike across Borders country may not be for the faintest of heart – cyclists are often glimpsed in luminous grimace set against driving rain, pitted roads and punishing gradients – but you don't need to be Tour de France material to tackle the Four Abbeys Route. The region's flagship circuit, this 55-mile round trip, mainly along minor roads, is the most cultured of cycle jaunts and a gently potted history lesson in its own right. Straddling the rivers Tweed and Teviot, it carves through the heart of the Borders, past the castles, towers and ruined abbeys that tell the stories of this fiercely contested land.

And, with the distinctive, heather-bunched triumvirate of the Eildon Hills as a backcloth, abbeys don't come much more elegantly ruinous than Melrose. In common with its contemporaries, much of the abbey's salmon-coloured stone dates to successive reconstructions, its beleaguered monks having borne the pyromaniacal brunt of cross-border incursions. Setting out from the abbey car park, the only incursion you're likely to face these days is heavy traffic on the busy A68, though the route quickly shears off on a more bucolic course to nearby Dryburgh Abbey. On atmosphere and location alone – a cloistered bow in the River Tweed, just north of St Boswells – Dryburgh has a claim as the most compelling historic monument in the Borders, its intimacy heightened by some unexpectedly well-preserved nooks and crannies. Of more starkly practical purpose is Smailholm Tower, mounted in an unlikely rash of crags just off the B6397 as you flank the Tweed on its northeasterly canter to Kelso. While Smailholm was often visited by a young Walter Scott, nearby Floors Castle was the one-time celluloid abode of Lord Greystoke, making up in pepperpot-turreted whimsy what Kelso's once mighty abbey – abbey no.3 – lost in war.

From here, the route rolls south on a twenty-mile loop, initially tracing the fertile banks of the Teviot before climbing to bisect the old Roman road from York and finally descending into Jedburgh, where the ostentatious Augustinian abbey still holds it church nigh-on intact. This might be the place to beg succour for a final climb back over the Eildons, or at least invoke divine protection against those pesky potholes.

Need to know To make the most of the sights, Four Abbeys is best completed over two days, though experienced cyclists could easily do it in one. A full description and route map are available at ⓦ www.visitscottishborders.com, and you'll also need OS Landranger Maps #73 and #74.
Map 4, D15

163 Hoist the sails in Cornwall

Big yachts, little yachts, sleek yachts and working boats – the south coast of Cornwall comes alive with billowing sails when the wind doth blow. As home to the world's third deepest natural harbour, an expansive bay, the wending estuaries of the Carrick Roads, the River Fal and the Helford Passage, Falmouth and its surrounds are a haven for yachties of all calibres. Once you're gliding along the ramps of the open seas, the jewel-studded coastline in sight and the spatter of salt water on your face, you too will fall prey to the addiction to sailing these waters that's gripped seamen for centuries.

Perhaps nowhere is more apposite to begin a water-bound expedition than Mylor, home to the new Olympic training facility and a convenient base from which Mylor Boat Hire rents out dinghies, day boats and pocket cruisers. With some basic sailing experience under your belt, the River Fal is ideal for a day-trip: spot herons and peregrines on wooded banks, drop anchor in chic St Mawes, visit the National Trust's Trelissick Gardens and, if the tide is on your side, sail to the city of Truro. And when the briny air summons up a hearty appetite, why not stop for cream tea at the *Smugglers* in Philleigh or moor up for a waterside pint and posh pub-grub at the *Pandora Inn*?

For novice sailors a Clovelly Picarooner is the perfect vessel for creek crawling, while those with more experience who want a zippier ride can opt for a Devon Yawl. Sailing aficionados can navigate beyond the Fal on a multi-day trip into Falmouth Bay and the Helford Passage. Between manning the helm, hauling the sheets and plotting your course, you can sleep under the stars in secret coves, seek out the *Ferry Boat Inn* and explore Frenchman's Creek – immortalized by Daphne du Maurier's novel.

Experiencing Cornwall under sail is the perfect marriage between a blast on the water and full-on coastal exploration. Even if you arrive here with no sailing experience you can quickly learn the ropes for fair-weather conditions – or plump for a family motorboat. Better still, though, acquire your sea-dog qualifications right here in Mylor.

Need to know Mylor Boat Hire, Mylor Yacht Harbour, near Falmouth, Cornwall ☎01326/377745, ⓦ www.mylorboathire.co.uk. Sailing (and motor-) boats can be rented from £25 per hour to £500 per week. Mylor Sailing School (☎01326/377633, ⓦ www.mylorsailingschool.co.uk) runs a full range of RYA courses.
Map 2, A7

164 Gliding at Sutton Bank

One of the most spectacular viewpoints in Yorkshire, Sutton Bank is also easily reached – which means that you'll likely share its huge and panoramic vistas with scores of others. That is, unless you decide to get a little higher than the hoi polloi. Thanks to the Yorkshire Gliding Club, located atop the bank, this is easily done. What better place to take off and soar up into the Yorkshire skies?

You may wonder quite what you've let yourself in for as your glider is "aero-towed" up into the clear blue behind a small single-engine plane. But relax: this is the time to make the most of the view as it unfolds below you – before long, you'll be in charge, and there'll be more pressing matters on your mind. And some view it is – on a clear day the whole of the Vale of York flattens itself out beneath your wings, green fields interspersed with glinting rivers, darker smudges of villages and towns and off in the distance the ancient city of York. Look to the west and you'll see the outline of the Pennines and the Yorkshire Dales; over your shoulder are the purple-heather-covered North York Moors; and away in the east the deep blue of the North Sea.

It's a lot to take in, but now it's time to concentrate. Once the cable connecting the glider to the plane is cast adrift, your instructor sets about demonstrating the basics of flying. You'll be invited first to share dual control, but no sooner have you learnt to appreciate the subtle movements for yourself, then the words, "OK, you're in control now" ring in your ear, your instructor lets go of the joystick, and the glider is yours to fly all alone.

It's an exhilarating, slightly terrifying feeling to be in control, but as the elements whistle past the fuselage try not to flip straight into panic mode – after all, you're two thousand feet up in the sky and it's your responsibility to make sure you stay there. Yes, you really are flying . . .

Handle the joystick smoothly but firmly, keeping regular check on the instruments, and you'll find that it's not actually so difficult. This of course is the easy bit – your instructor will take over again for the trickier task of getting back down to terra firma. But even this brief twenty-minute flit through the Yorkshire skies is enough to see why humankind spent millennia trying to get airborne.

Need to know Yorkshire Gliding Club, Sutton Bank, Thirsk, North Yorkshire (℡01845/597237, Ⓦwww.ygc.co.uk) offers twenty-minute trial lessons for £89 per person. For more information on gliding see the British Gliding Association's website (Ⓦwww.gliding.co.uk).

Map 3, D9

165 Back to white: rediscovering Scotland's ski resorts

Until recently, the unique exhilarations of skiing – the sensation of falling through space, propelled by nothing but gravity and abandon – looked destined to become solely a foreign pleasure. That was until the winter of 2009/10. Every snow cloud, it seems, has a silver lining, at least in the Highlands: while the rest of us slipped and skidded to work, cursing through some of the worst winter weather in decades, the Scottish ski resorts struck gold, with superlative cover right into summer, under blue skies bordering on the alpine. With a dismal exchange rate making foreign resorts even pricier, moreover, Scotland's resurgence couldn't have come at a better time. New runs were built, and beginners took up skiing like never before. It was a joy to see those slushy, rock-laced runs reborn.

Whether you're an absolute beginner or an old hand, on snowboard or skis, you'll do well to make your first stop Glenshee, the clan chief of Scotland's resorts with an impressive 36 runs and 40km of piste, and a location readily accessible from Edinburgh. Though nearby Cairngorm boasts a funicular railway, and beginners' favourite The Lecht the best snowmaking facilities, this place, on the edge of the Grampians, has been hosting skiers since the 1930s, and, if you're lucky enough to experience blue skies instead of a klaxon-sounding whiteout, can almost feel like a continental day-trip. Comparatively speaking, and considering the range of runs, the price of a day pass (£25) is great value for money.

That said, there's nothing quite like Glencoe, a small but perfectly formed resort that, despite having faced serious financial difficulties during the lean years, reported the most extensive covering of new snow in the world at the height of the 2010 season, and one – at least on a sunny day – that offers an entirely different perspective on a glen otherwise infamous for its history and harsh climate. With the steepest run in the country (the ominously named Fly Paper), Glencoe is likewise a favourite with adrenaline junkies, as are – snow conditions permitting – the world-class off-piste expanses of the Back Corries in the nearby Nevis Range. Whatever you do, get it while the skiing's good – let's hope we can stave off those Mediterranean winters, at least on the slopes, for a little while yet.

Need to know More information can be found at Ⓦwww.ski-glenshee.co.uk; Ⓦwww.lecht.co.uk; Ⓦwww.cairngormmountain.co.uk; Ⓦwww.glencoemountain.co.uk; and Ⓦwww.nevisrange.co.uk. Skis, snowboards, boots and clothing can be hired at all resorts for around £35–40.
Map 4, C13, D13; Map 5, D20

HIKES IN THE GREAT OUTDOORS

Our green and boggy isle may be small, but one thing's for certain: it's home to some of the most magnificent landscapes in Europe, if not the world. Sure, our much lamented climate means you'll likely get a soaking or three (four if you're in Scotland), but with everything from coastal strolls to fearsome scrambles, British boots were, surely, made for some serious walking.

166 Hadrian's Wall Path

From the suburbs of Newcastle to the Solway Firth, Britain's most iconic Roman monument doubles as perhaps its most compelling long-distance path, marching some 84 miles across northern England's most bracing and barren terrain. Sure, you'll need some imaginative licence in places but enough stones remain unturned – and forts excavated – to project the rather ascetic lot of a second-century legionnaire, blistered feet no doubt included.

Ⓦ www.nationaltrail.co.uk/hadrianswall. Map 4, D15–E15

167 West Highland Way

As Scotland's inaugural long-distance path, the 95-mile West Highland Way did much to raise the profile of the hiking opportunities on Glasgow's doorstep. It's a rites-of-passage trek that segues beautifully from city suburbs to the forests of Loch Lomond, the desolation of Rannoch Moor and the drama of Devil's Staircase, eventually winding up near the foot of Ben Nevis: all in all, a perfect introduction to the Scottish Highlands. In high summer, though, it's also a potentially not-so-perfect introduction to the dastardly Highland midge. Forget that repellent at your peril...

Ⓦ www.west-highland-way.co.uk. Map 4, B13–C14

168 Lizard Peninsula, Cornwall

You likely won't see any lizards on this Cornish peninsula (the name rather has its roots in the native tongue), but you will breeze through some of Britain's most spectacular coastline, complete with exotic subtropical plants, rugged caves and exquisite coves, and an endlessly churning sea. And though it makes up a mere fraction of the marathon six-hundred-mile South West Coast Path you could happily spend days exploring its serpentine nooks and filmic crannies.

Ⓦ www.southwestcoastpath.com. Map 2, A7

169 Wester Ross, Scottish Highlands

Since Monty Halls turned his back on the twenty-first century in favour of the simple life as a crofter in *The Great Escape*, the coast of Wester Ross has become as popular with would-be escapees as its mighty Munros have long been with hill-walkers and climbers. While both Applecross and the Loch Torridon settlements of Shieldaig and Diabaig all make great bases for some gloriously scenic and relatively easy-going sea walks, the ancient, fortress-like peaks of Torridon itself, not least the twin-pronged bulk of Liathach, the famous horns of Beinn Alligin and the gleaming, quartzite-crowned massif of Beinn Eighe, offer some of the most dramatic ascents on the British mainland.

Ⓦ www.visitwester-ross.com. Map 5, B19

170 Helvellyn, Lake District

It's not the highest peak in the Lake District but it can still stake a claim as the most romantic, with a capital "r" or otherwise. Beloved of Wordsworth, Wainwright and generations of walkers, England's most popular mountain is a study in contrast, its summit flat enough to land a plane and its deceptively named western arête, Striding Edge, sharp enough – terrifyingly so – to evoke the Sublime in even the most hardened scrambler.

Ⓦ www.helvellyn.com, Ⓦ www.lakedistrict.gov.uk. Map 4, D16

171 Wessex Ridgeway

A different kind of ridge entirely from the arêtes of Lakeland, if no less steeped in history, this archaic highway has been chalking up foot traffic for centuries, threading as it does into an old Devon to Norfolk trade route. Its 137-mile course passes through some of the loveliest landscapes in southern England – think intimate woods, hidden valleys and open downlands with views that go on forever – taking in Avebury's stone circles, the fringes of Salisbury Plain and ancient droving trails in Hardy's Dorset, en route to the chalk giant of Cerne Abbas and the coast.

Ⓦ www.ldwa.org.uk. Map 2, D6–C6

172 Tryfan, Snowdonia

It may slop and squelch under some of the heaviest rainfalls in Britain, but, for those who prefer their hiking hands, Snowdonia is hard to beat. Its serrated, slate-lined peaks cater for a range of abilities, yet it's also home to the only mountain on the British mainland that demands scrambling as part of the main ascent: regal Tryfan. The famous north ridge route in fact pans out far less intimidatingly than its razor-like fin suggests from the ground, but once you reach the summit – and leap the five-foot gap between the iconic Adam and Eve rocks – you'll feel like a true mountaineer.

Ⓦ *www.snowdonia-npa.gov.uk. Map 3, B11*

173 Southern Upland Way, Borders

The Scottish Borders are perhaps still more identified with horseriding than hoofing it, but this coast-to-coast, Irish to North Sea odyssey – 212 miles in total – may one day change that. And while the dome-like hills of the Southern Uplands mightn't match the Highlands for drama, they more than match them for sheer remoteness – chances are you'll have your trail to yourself, even in summer. If you don't fancy hiking the full hog, the thirty-odd-mile Moffat to Traquair stretch makes for an evocative sampler, encompassing the ancient remnants of the Ettrick Forest, St Mary's Loch and the splendours of Traquair House.

Ⓦ *www.southernuplandway.gov.uk. Map 4, B16–D14*

174 South Downs Way

Cradling a hundred-mile swathe from the historic city of Winchester to the spectacular white cliffs of Beachy Head, this clement landscape of ancient woodland, open heath and chalky downs may lend itself more to rambling, cycling and horseriding than hardcore hiking, but its recently awarded national park status reflects a rural charm wholly distinct from Britain's remoter corners. Tackle it from west to east to take advantage of the prevailing wind, and the psychological appeal of finishing at those vertiginous cliffs.

Ⓦ *www.nationaltrail.co.uk/southdowns,* Ⓦ *www.southdowns.gov.uk. Map 2, D6–E6*

175 Stanage Edge, Peak District

A kind of Peak District Table Mountain in miniature, the four miles of gritstone cliff that make up Stanage Edge have been scaled since the nineteenth century, while the surrounding dry-stone dykes, historic buildings and emaciated moors have been sewn into England's cultural and literary landscape for much longer. Various walks take in the famous escarpment, most conveniently setting out from the village of Hathersage. Whichever route you take, though, you'll be rewarded by spectacular views, not to mention the haunting debris of long-abandoned millstones and the hair-raising sight of people inching up the Edge's profusion of iconic climbs – you may even be tempted to don a hard hat yourself.

Ⓦ *www.visitpeakdistrict.com. Map 3, C10*

176 Single-track thrills in the King's Forest

Coed-y-Brenin is Britain's original mountain-biking forest, and still hogs poll position as one of the country's best. Here, amid nine thousand acres of spectacular Snowdonia scenery, you'll find exhilarating mountain-biking routes ranging from roller-coaster single-track, technical rocky sections to a wide, flowing family trail. There are mellow loops, white-knuckle drop-offs, and steep uphills and thrilling downhills that will have all levels of mountain bikers grinning from ear to ear.

Gold, bronze and copper mining were once the centre of activity hereabouts, but these days it's nature that has the upper hand. Wildlife abounds with wood warblers, skylarks and buzzards soaring in treetops, below which bikers glide alongside rivers and swoop down rocky stacks. The trails all emerge from the superbly equipped new visitor centre, home to a cosy café, on-site bike hire, showers, a bike wash and an accessories shop.

Coed-y-Brenin's seven routes range from an easy green to difficult reds and severe blacks, six of them demanding a competent level of fitness and ability. The popular Yr Afon is ideal for families and novices, contouring the hillsides along forest track that takes in the majestic Gain and Mawddach waterfalls. In contrast, the super-technical 30km Dragon's Back is billed for more accomplished riders with steep ascents and ripping descents. If you're a true master of your wheels there's only joy to be had on the burns and rock steps of Temtiwr, the streambeds of the MBR Trail, the single-track racecourse of Tarw, the epic climbs of the Beast of Brenin and the fast-riding Cyflym Coch. Be warned if you're nowt but an average rider that even the red runs will have you quaking in your cycling shorts.

But whatever your skill level there's fun to be had. Suck in the scenery from the top of the trails, the forest picnic area or the all-ability walking routes. And since Go Ape opened here you can even take in Coed-y-Brenin from a high ropes course in the treetops.

Need to know Coed-y-Brenin is near Dolgellau, Gwynedd (℡01341/440747, ⓦwww.mbwales.com/coed_y_brenin and ⓦwww.forestry.gov.uk/wales; MP3 audio trails are available for download on the latter). The visitor centre is open daily 9.30am–4.30pm. For public transport see ⓦwww.traveline-cymru.info.
Map 3, B11

177 Four legs good on Exmoor

Picture this: a mist rising above an undulating expanse of fern and purple heather, the early-morning chatter of birdsong and the gurgle of a hidden rill, a hazy prospect of sea to the north, and the contented snort of ponies picking their way along the grassy track. That's Exmoor on horseback, the most romantic way of experiencing the lush wilderness that straddles the Somerset–Devon border. There's much to be said for exploring the moor on foot, on trail bike, in a canoe or by 4x4 on a wildlife safari, but no other means captures the spirit of Exmoor so harmoniously.

Horses and Exmoor are a natural match: it's long been a favourite terrain for hunting – a source of pleasure to some, embarrassment to others – and the habitat of the stocky Exmoor ponies that roam wild. More than three hundred miles of bridleways intertwine across the moor, allowing you to take in such beauty spots as Tarr Steps, Porlock Vale and Selworthy Beacon, and views stretching across to the Quantock Hills and over the Bristol Channel to South Wales. On the way you'll catch sight of wild red deer (the largest concentration in England) and the occasional fox and hare, while buzzards, hawks and skylarks swoop high above and heath fritillary butterflies weave among the woods. The varied landscape takes in high heather moorland and ancient oak woodlands, sliced through by peaty streams and steep combes, and dotted with sequestered villages and farms. The colours can be spectacular, with the ground carpeted in primroses and bluebells in spring, purple flowering heather in mid- to late summer and bright russet swathes of deer sedge in autumn.

Roads on Exmoor are scarce but access to its wildest depths is comparatively easy on four legs. Horses and ponies are readily hired from riding schools and stables that offer everything from simple treks and escorted rides for novices to more ambitious half-day hacks for experienced riders. At some point in your rambles, let rip and feel the rapture of a mad gallop over the heather. Sometimes exhausting but always exhilarating, there's no better way of experiencing the moor.

Need to know Stables include West Lynch Farm, Allerford, near Porlock, Minehead, Somerset (℡01643/862816, Ⓦexmoor-riding.co.uk) and Spirit of Exmoor, High Bullen Farm, Ilkerton, Barbrook, Lynton, Devon (℡01598/753318, Ⓦwww.spiritofexmoor.com). Rides cost around £30 for an hour, £60 for a half day. See also Ⓦwww.exmoor-nationalpark.gov.uk and Ⓦwww.activeexmoor.com.
Map 2, B6

178 Canoeing on the River Wye

The peaceful River Wye, which for part of its length forms the Anglo–Welsh border, runs through some of the greenest and most luxuriant countryside in Britain. On a lazy summer's day, paddling through its tree-fringed waters in a canoe or kayak, stopping by a country pub for lunch, is one of the most relaxing experiences imaginable.

It's also a novel way to access some of the attractions, both bucolic and cultural, in the area. From the antiquarian bookshops of Hay-on-Wye to Chepstow Castle to Tintern Abbey, there are some great reasons to hop out of your canoe along the way. You can rent a canoe for part of a day, or organize a multi-day trip, sleeping in guesthouses or campsites en route. The 31-mile stretch between Hereford and the market town of Ross-on-Wye has no rapids to negotiate, making it good for learners and kids.

The Canoe Hire Company in Ross can organize a three-day trip between the two towns, with suggestions for pub stopoffs and campsite stays. Make sure you take some time to explore Hereford before you hit the water; its patchwork cathedral contains the legendary medieval map, the Mappa Mundi. Day two takes you past an Iron Age hillfort, and ends at handsome little Hoarwithy, where you can stay at the idyllically rural riverside *Tresseck Campsite* and indulge in a spot of fishing. There's also a village inn and an incongruous but imposing Italianate church.

On day three you negotiate salmon pools and ruined railway bridges to reach the market town of Ross-on-Wye. This was held to be the birthplace of the English tourist industry – in the eighteenth century, lovers of the Picturesque were taken on trips from here down the Wye to admire its steep sylvan slopes, abbeys and castles.

If canoes aren't your thing you can explore the area easily on foot: the 136-mile Wye Valley Walk connects Hereford with Ross-on-Wye – the route is signed with a leaping salmon logo and incorporates ravine woodland as well as gentle pastures.

Need to know Canoe Hire Company, Ross-on-Wye, Herefordshire ℡01600/890470, Ⓦwww.thecanoehirecompany.co.uk; prices start at £30 for a day, and £90 for a three-day trip. *Tresseck Campsite,* Hoarwithy, Herefordshire ℡01432/840235, Ⓦwww.tresseckcampsite.co.uk. See Ⓦwww.wyevalleywalk.org for information on walking.
Map 3, C12

179 Having a laugh: zorbing in Dorchester

If laughter is the best medicine then someone should petition the government – were it prescribed on the NHS, zorbing could make Britain the healthiest nation in Europe. Developed in New Zealand in the mid-Nineties then franchised worldwide in the last decade, this curious pastime involves little effort, no skill and it ticks off trails in seconds – mountain biking this is not. Yet if there is a more giggle-inducing way of passing the time, they're keeping it quiet.

Zorbing, or sphering as it is sometimes known, is generally pigeonholed as an extreme sport – but don't let that put you off. The Concise OED defines it as "a sport in which a participant is secured inside an inner capsule in a transparent ball which is then rolled along the ground". In an inflatable nutshell, it is the gloriously silly pursuit of travel inside an oversized beach ball, and the longest run in England is at Dorchester-based Zorbing South UK.

A clever piece of design sees two intrepid zorbonauts dive through an access window in the side of the transparent orb into the smaller inner ball, which is connected to the outer sphere by nylon cords. Here, seemingly suspended in space, they are strapped opposite each other into harnesses – go with a friend for double the fun – then eased to the lip of a grass piste. There are no brakes, no going back.

There should also be no surprise to discover that cartwheeling at speeds in excess of 20mph over more than 200 yards causes utter disorientation. Within a bounce or two, you lose all sense of direction. Yet nausea is rarely a problem for first-time zorbonauts, say Zorbing South operators. Extreme hilarity is.

For those of a more delicate disposition, Zorbing South also provides gentler hydro zorbing. In this slower, harness-free variation you free-ride, either on foot or sprawled on the floor, and can zorb solo with just a couple of buckets of water for company – warm on chilly days, fortunately. Wear your dirty clothes – it's like being inside a quick rinse at the launderette.

Kids' stuff, hardcore adrenaline-junkies will doubtless snipe. It's their loss. This is one activity that really is all about having a laugh. Amen to that.

Need to know Zorbing South UK (☎01929/426595, ⓦwww.zorbsouth.co.uk) operates from late March to October. Rides cost £45 for a two-person harness ride or £30 for a solo hydro ride (£45 for a dual hydro ride).

Map 2, C6

180 Messing about in boats on the Norfolk Broads

Need to know The Norfolk Broads Yachting Company, Southgates Boatyard, Lower Street, Horning (☎01692/631330, 🅦www.norfolk-broads.com) rents out proper old-fashioned Broads sailing boats; the Canoe Man (☎01603/499177, 🅦www.thecanoeman.com) offers canoe rental and guided canoe and wildlife trails; and Barnes Brinkcraft, Riverside Rd, Wroxham (☎01603/782625, 🅦www.barnesbrinkcraft.co.uk) have motorboats for hire.

Map 3, F11

Stand on the green in the riverside village of Horning and look out onto the water: the marshes on the far side are a forest of masts; in the background you can hear the lazy chug of a motor as a boat searches for an evening mooring; while to your right a mass of sails glides downstream back to the sailing club. If you had stood here fifty years ago the view would have been much the same. Welcome to the timeless landscape of the Norfolk Broads.

Horning lies right at the heart of the Broads, the largest wetland area in the country, stretching from Norwich all the way east to the coast. It's a haunting, eerie wilderness of lake and river, reedbed and marsh, a flat landscape of huge skies and distant horizons cut only by windmills and the gaff-rigged sails of far-off yachts. Run by the Broads Authority, and with the status of a national park, it's a haven for bird- and wildlife, and you can see grebes, herons and if you're lucky a kingfisher or two; you might also catch a glimpse of the rare swallowtail butterfly, which is unique to the area, and it's not unusual to spy an otter poking its whiskered snout out of the water.

But most of all it's the perfect place to mess about in a boat. You don't need any experience – at least if you opt for an engine rather than sail, which is what most people do. Not surprisingly, it's very busy in peak season. But the Broads have a Tardis-like ability to absorb visitors, and even in the height of summer it's possible to escape the crowds. Better yet, get out in a canoe and explore the smaller waterways that aren't navigable by larger craft. You really will feel like you're in the middle of nowhere.

181 Pedalling around the New Forest

The gorgeous pocket of green between Southampton in Hampshire and Christchurch in Dorset is much more than just a forest. Protected as the New Forest National Park since 2005, it also encompasses open, grassy heathlands with waist-high patches of bracken and gorse. Here and there are boggy wetlands, their ponds crammed with frogspawn in spring; to the south, the coastline is visited by rare black-headed gulls and flocks of waders. Its woodland areas are scattered, and enchanting – sun-dappled spaces where insects dance overhead and leaves and twigs crunch underfoot.

While much of the park has a wilderness feel, you'd never call the Forest untamed – this is a busy, working landscape, dotted with towns, villages and campsites and well trodden by locals and visitors alike. In many ways, this accessibility adds greatly to its appeal. As it's crisscrossed by roads, it's easy to navigate by car; but by far the most rewarding way to enjoy the beautiful, gently undulating landscape and its appealing sounds and smells is to jump on a bike. It's easy to leave the roads behind: a network of way-marked off-road cycle routes totalling over a hundred miles in length weave their way through the most scenic spots.

Brockenhurst, in the heart of the forest, makes an ideal base. It has a friendly and helpful local bike shop, Cyclex, which sells everything you could possibly need, and also offers a complete hire service including helmet, tool kit, route maps and emergency backup. It's owned and run by keen riders who are actively involved in New Forest cycling and conservation issues. On request, they will deliver to any home, hotel or campsite.

If you're not in the mood for a plain old mountain bike, you could try hiring a variant such as a Yellowbike electric bike – perfect for anyone aged 14 years or over wanting to boost their pedal power a notch or three – or an adult-sized trike or Dawes tandem. There are even some handy extras, such as attachments which allow you to tow babies and children. Best of all for dog-lovers is the DogKab – a rainproof pull-along pod that'll guarantee a fun excursion for any dog who can't quite keep up with your top speed.

Need to know Cyclex (New Forest Cycle Hire), Downside Car Park, Brockenhurst Station, Hampshire (☎01590/624204, ⓦwww.newforestcyclehire.co.uk) is open 362 days a year. Bike hire starts at £13 per day for adults, £6 for kids. Other hire shops include AA Bike Hire (☎023/8028 3349, ⓦwww.aabikehirenewforest. co.uk) in Lyndhurst and Forest Leisure (☎01425/403584, ⓦwww. forestleisurecycling.co.uk) in Burley Map 2, D6

182 Scrabbling up big Ben's cold shoulder

Nowhere epitomizes the Scottish Highlands better than Ben Nevis. Massive and broad-shouldered, with a north face that plummets 650m from its 1344-metre summit, "the Ben" is an imposing sight, particularly in winter when snow drapes its ledges and buttresses, and ice falls transform its gullies and ridges into an ice-climbing playground.

There are numerous ways to ascend the mountain, longest of which is the classic 600-metre Tower Ridge route. It's not too technically demanding, but it's not easy either, and you should have had some experience of winter hill scrambling (at the very least) before taking it on – wise heads employ the services of a guide.

As you set out en route to the crag you'll have plenty of time to ponder the lie of the land and the wisdom of what you're about to attempt. Ice climbing requires a mix of technique and brute strength – and you'll soon be tested on whether you have sufficient of each.

Once the guide gives the go ahead, it's time to get stuck in. As you swing, the pick of your ice axes should sink securely into the ice with a satisfying thunk; your feet meanwhile will perform a little ballet to ensure the two tiny metal fangs at the front of your crampons engage firmly with the giant icicle you're balancing on. Executed correctly this provides a remarkably secure hold when you consider that your entire body weight is being supported by just a couple of centimetres of sharp steel frozen into the glassy ice – along with a rope for safety, of course. The less skilled tend to smash raggedly at the ice, which depletes energy reserves very quickly – not recommended on Tower Ridge since you'll need all your strength for the series of challenging steps that climb inexorably to the summit plateau, each one opening up ever more expansive views across the Western Highlands.

There's very little let up in the exposure or the excitement, and throbbing forearms and wobbly thigh and calf muscles are unavoidable. Errors of judgement on the ridge have seen parties benighted, or worse. But when you eventually emerge onto the summit and out of the icy blue shadows of the north face you'll have the sense of having engaged with the mountain's winter personality in a way no mere walker ever could. And clad in your rugged gear, having conquered the summit, you'll feel a bit of a mountaineering hero too.

Need to know Ice Factor, Leven Rd, Kinlochleven, Lochaber, Highland (☎01855/831100, ⓦwww. ice-factor.co.uk), close to Fort William, has the largest indoor climbing wall in the world and offers both indoor and outdoor climbing courses, including trips to Ben Nevis, from £150 per day (including guide fees and all equipment). The ice-climbing season runs from January to April depending on conditions. Map 4, C13

183 Scuba in Scapa

Need to know Seasoned cold-water divers will get the most out of Scapa on a diving charter with an experienced skipper: try Halton Charters (☎01856/851532 ⊛www.mvhalton.co.uk), based in Stromness, Orkney. For tuition or dive guides contact Scapa Scuba (☎01856/851218, ⊛www.scapascuba.co.uk). Divers and non-divers will enjoy the exhibitions at the Scapa Flow Visitor Centre at Lyness on the island of Hoy (⊛www.scapaflow.co.uk/sfvc.htm).
Map 5, D17

Surrounded by the windswept Orkney Islands, one of the world's great natural harbours conceals a dramatic episode of naval history that's ripe for underwater exploration. Scapa Flow, Britain's finest dive site, inspires awe in the most blasé of Aussie Scuba instructors and commands respect from seasoned deep-sea rig divers. In fact plunging deep into these chilly Scottish waters to explore the shipwrecks of Scapa is an unforgettable experience for anyone with the courage to attempt it.

This is the last resting place of the German High Seas Fleet interned by the British at the end of World War I. Rather than see the flotilla broken up, Rear-Admiral von Reuter ordered its scuttling – all 74 ships – on June 21, 1919, thus denying the Allies valuable spoils of war. Salt water, tidal currents and salvage efforts have all conspired in the intervening years to erode the fleet, but a dozen or so vessels still cling to the seabed, accessible to all with sufficient diving qualifications, equipment – and nerve.

Sunk in peacetime, and by their own commanders, these wrecks are not war graves, but even knowing that they conceal no ghosts, the ships have a powerful effect on the imagination. The intimidating scale alone of a dreadnought in dark waters sets the pulse racing. Finning over the seemingly endless hull of a rusting battle-cruiser, orange-grey and carpeted with anemones, your torchlight picks out the deadly detail of a gun in the green gloom. Swimming through the *Brummer*, from the bridge to the bowels of her boiler room, you'll find yourself in awe of the brave men who sailed in her, and their brothers who went down with many of her sister ships in battle.

Over almost a century these ruins have become mature reefs. Encouraged by the northern summer sunshine, "dead men's fingers" and blooming plumose anemones swathe the wrecks in bouquets of cream and orange. Conger eels, crabs and octopus have made these sunken beasts their home, while silvery shoals, colourful wrasse and seals patrol with a proprietary air; all keep a close eye on visiting divers.

184 Fishing for your supper

Succulent, creamy-white chunks of cod flake softly at the touch of your knife. A quick squeeze of lemon is all it needs to enhance the flavour, delicate and impossibly fresh. Your supper has been plucked from the Atlantic just two hours ago, by your own fair hands – or to be more exact, rod.

A world away from often wasteful commercial fishing, sport fishing is something of a fine art and, heavily regulated, has minimal impact on fish stocks. For big game – halibut, cod, ling, pollock and the like – the Cornish coastline is the place to try your hand. Based in Penzance, Bite Adventures run daily fishing trips on their 32ft vessel, steaming up to 20 miles from the shore onto the Cornish waters. With weather conditions inclement at the best of times, wrap up warmly – wear a hat, a pair of thick-soled boots and lots of waterproofs. A tough stomach is a useful asset, as riding waves whipped by gale-force winds can be pretty hairy. All the tackle is provided on board, from rods and lines to the bait (most often mackerel or squid). All you need to bring is a couple of durable bags, ready to hold your catch.

Bite Adventures focus on wreck fishing, which can throw up some exciting – and very challenging – sport. Once hooked, the fish will dart in and out of the wreck, requiring fast line work and a strong and steady hand. For still more of a challenge, opt for the conger eel fishing trip, which involves anchoring the boat above the wreck and dangling the bait deep below; conger eels can grow up to 200lb (although it's more normal to come across a sub-100lb specimen) and are tough opponents.

Need to know Bite Adventures, 2 Menwidden Cottages, Ludgven, Penzance, Cornwall ☎01736/741254, ⊛www.biteadventures.com. Wreck fishing trips can be organized year-round, but the best catch is from March to July. They cost £45 per person, or £400 for a private charter.
Map 2, A7

The big daddy of them all is the shark. Cornwall is home to many toothy critters, from the Porbeagle, with its pointy snout, to the sharp-toothed Mako. Fishing for shark stretches even the most experienced fishermen – it takes patience and a heck of a lot of strength. Lines and rods are heavier, at 50lb, and the hook is designed to dissolve in the fish if it's lost in a fight. When a shark is caught, it'll have its picture taken and then be released back into the water as soon as possible.

Unsurprisingly, big-game fishing is more suitable for experienced fishermen, but if you're a beginner, or a child – or both – there are shorter trips of two to four hours. That's more than enough time to fish for your supper.

185 Become a bushman on the Gower peninsula

Whether it's the urge to escape a high-stress, low-risk urbanized society, the growing acceptance of alternative lifestyles – or simply down to all the survival TV shows – more of us are going bush than ever. But you can admire Ray Mears's fire skills over a TV dinner on the sofa all you like – there's no substitute for hands-on guidance from an expert.

Experts like Andrew Price, enthusiastic founder of Dryad Bushcraft on Wales's Gower peninsula. Having learned traditional skills from indigenous peoples worldwide and worked as an outdoor pursuits teacher, Andrew cast a new eye over his home turf. An authentic bushcraft experience relies on a low population density and scenic diversity, and the Gower – a world in miniature with upland heath, forests, cliffs and coast all easily accessible – excels in both. After all, it's hard to feel like Bear Grylls when the *Dog & Duck* twinkles at the bottom of a Surrey woodland.

As well as scenic beauty, the appeal of Dryad is that it is more bushcamp than boot camp. Leave forest survival fantasies to Rambo – on the weekend Practical Woodsman course, you get to learn the craft of bushcraft. It's not that Andrew, a resident expert for *Bushcraft and Survival Skills* magazine, doesn't teach survival skills; it's just that he also emphasizes the value of tuning into nature. And there's a lot of that on the 400 acres in which Dryad operates.

Parked up, you head into the woods to learn the bushman essentials – knife, saw and axe technique. With these mastered the fun begins. There's more incentive to build a perfect wickiup shelter from branches and leaf-litter when it's your roof for the night, and gorgeous countryside takes on a deeper significance when you need its nettles for fibres and its food for supper. And can there be a finer reward for fire-lighting with a bowdrill than a hot cuppa? Sure, a brew takes an hour or so but that's half the point – to slow down and reconnect with the environment.

One-day courses cater to families or nervous novices, while experienced survivalist types can vanish into the Welsh wilds for seven days or live out *Robinson Crusoe* fantasies on a remote stretch of Gower coast.

Need to know Dryad
Bushcraft (☎01792/547213, ⓦwww.dryadbushcraft.co.uk) holds courses year-round on the Gower peninsula. The weekend Practical Woodsman course costs £190, which includes all food and hot drinks.
Map 2, B5

186 Riding a whitewater roller coaster: rafting in Bala

River Tryweryn looks so peaceful as you approach. Outside a visitor centre a youngster sucks on an ice cream with mum, Birdsong emanates from deep within the mossy oak forest that blankets the river. A sense of Arcadian bliss in a timeless Welsh landscape reigns. That is, at least until a scream rends the air – just another satisfied customer of the National White Water Centre.

The UK's first commercial whitewater-rafting operation when it opened a quarter of a century ago, the National White Water Centre, located near Bala in North Wales, is now, by a quirk of hydrography, also the largest. While most British rafting rivers dry to a trickle in summer, the Tryweryn is fed by a dam release. On around two hundred days each year, courtesy of the Environment Agency, some 9–16 cubic metres of water per second pour into the river from the large Llyn Celyn reservoir, controversially constructed in the 1960s to provide water for Liverpool, transforming its upper and middle sections into an aquatic funfair, complete with dodgems, bucking bronco and waltzer.

All it takes to ride some of the country's finest whitewater roller coasters is moderate fitness, an ability to swim and a willingness to get wet. Very wet if you're at the front. Technical sections like the laconically titled Graveyard, a thrillingly wild two-kilometre stretch of rapids, see the shallowing river slingshot your raft through a swift channel. Rocks flash by on either side as your guide urges you on – "Hard forward! Hard, hard! Lean in! Hold on!" – but at least it is dry. On rapids such as the Ski Jump, you speed off a lip and land waist-deep in an impromptu bathtub as the raft fills with foaming water. And that's only halfway down – the largest drop is still to come.

On a two-hour session you'll have time for four trips. Sounds repetitive? Then opt for the Orca Adventure. After an hour's guided rafting, you'll take to an inflatable canoe to tackle the rapids alone, chaperoned by a guide in a kayak. Good luck and don't forget to scream.

Need to know The National White Water Centre, Frongoch, Bala, Gwynedd ☎01678/521083, ⊛www.ukrafting.co.uk. Check the website or phone the water information line (☎01678/520826) a few days in advance for dam opening times. A two-hour session costs £60; the Orca Adventure costs £82 for a half day; wet-suit hire costs £5.

Map 3, B11

187 Paddleboarding in The Fens

Deep in the Cambridgeshire fenland there's a pub called the *Five Miles From Anywhere (And No Hurry) Inn*. Head a little deeper into the countryside to Wicken Fen, one of the last fenland wildernesses left in Britain, and you'll know what they mean.

Bought for a snip in 1899, Wicken Fen is the oldest nature reserve in the National Trust's portfolio. In terms of British landscapes it is unique. Only 0.1 percent of the undrained wetland – once an area of quaking bogs and marshland – that made up the East Anglian fens until the early 1800s remains. The rest has gone to carrots and spuds.

With over 99 percent of the traditional habitat lost to intensive agriculture – draining of the Fens created one of the most fertile agricultural areas in Europe – Wicken Fen represents a Noah's Ark for native species. Over 8000 varieties have been recorded at the nature reserve by Cambridge University scientists, making this the most biodiverse location in Britain. No wonder Charles Darwin sourced samples from local reed-cutters while he was a Cambridge student.

Until recently, you could only experience the fen from a hide or via a network of boardwalks. Trouble is, some of the most interesting wildlife lies beside waterways that crosshatch the area. Motorboats would disturb the fragile ecosystem, and that's where the Fen Paddle comes in. Stand-up paddle surfing – an ancient form of Hawaiian surfing that has caught the imaginations of J-Lo and Cornish surfers alike – provides a minimum-impact way to experience these otherwise inaccessible parts of the reserve. Who needs waves when such natural beauty abounds?

After a quick lesson in board basics, you are off on surfari with a conservation warden, sculling gently through water lilies across Wicken Lode, the fen's principal watercourse, with a single paddle. Fish dart just below your feet and brilliant, jewel-like damselflies and dragonflies hitch a lift. Within the reedbeds fringing the banks flit a spotter's book of water birds. Marsh harriers circle in the huge sky above. Peace reigns supreme, broken only by the swish of your board through the water and the whisper of reeds. It's hard to believe your core muscles are getting a workout.

Hard too to believe that Cambridge is only ten miles away – you feel so far from anywhere. And in no hurry to get back.

Need to know Wicken Fen
(☎01353/720274, ⊛www.wicken.
org.uk; daily 10am–5pm; £5.75)
is near Wicken village, midway
between Ely and Cambridge; there
is no public transport to the village.
Fen Paddle (☎01353/664750,
⊛www.fenpaddle.co.uk) operates
hour-long trips daily (£15) and
three-hour trips (£50) weekly in
Wicken Fen during the school
summer holidays and June half-
term.
Map 3, E12

188 Taking a dunking in a doughnut: tubing Pitlochry

Floating downstream in a giant, inflatable doughnut amidst the stunning Perthshire woodland scenery around Pitlochry might sound relaxing, but the deceptively strong currents of the River Garry mean that Scotland's only adventure tubing experience is not for the lily-livered. Sure, once your wet-suited and booted there'll be some reflective moments as you drift through the deep, dark pools of chilly tranquillity. Elsewhere, however, your pulse will quicken as you navigate logs and rocks through escalating rapids in one of Scotland's most exhilarating water slaloms.

Even in webbed gloves, you'll find a half-day's tubing requires a surprising degree of exertion – you'll certainly feel your shoulder muscles pleasantly aching afterwards – not least because these surfing vessels are ill-designed for hanging ten: you'll be pitching into the drink and having to hoist yourself back into your ring more times than you'll be able to count.

Some parts of the river are too hazardous to negotiate by inflatable, while others afford a chance to try jumping from the surrounding cliffs. Guides will occasionally steer you landwards and towards a series of craggy precipices, such as Soldier's Leap. One of several elevated spots, ranging from a mere plop to over 3m high, from which tubers are encouraged to precede their tube into the water, the gorge takes its name from the 1689 Battle of Killiecrankie: legend has it that fleeing Redcoat Donald MacBean evaded capture by the victorious Jacobites by hurling himself across the five-and-a-half-metre-wide gorge. It's a thrilling plummet, best approached as if a Jacobite blade was at your backside.

Such plunges are optional, so you needn't jump if you don't fancy it. But where's the fun in that? Better still to go the whole hog and book yourself into an even more intense experience: whitewater tubing through the foaming spume of the River Tummel. Now that certainly won't leave you with much time to relax.

Need to know Nae
Limits, Ballinluig, near Pitlochry,
Perthshire ☎0845 178177 or
01796/482600, ⊛www.naelimits.
co.uk. April–Sept only. Both
adventure tubing (with optional
cliff jumping session) and
whitewater adventure tubing
normally cost £50 per half day.
Map 4, C13

189 Climb every mountain: the Via Ferrata at Honister

Famously, the Lake District features England's highest peak (Scafell Pike) and its deepest lake (Wast Water) – and to that you can add the country's most ridiculously thrilling high-mountain adventure, the Via Ferrata. The owners of Borrowdale's Honister Slate Mine have taken a traditional alpine "Iron Way" fixed-cable system and married it to the precarious route that Lakeland miners once took as they scrambled up the rock face of Fleetwith Pike. Result? You get a hard hat, a clip-on belt and harness, and a safety briefing, and within twenty minutes find yourself hanging on for dear life two thousand feet up a Cumbrian mountain.

And it all starts off so innocently, trudging up the path from the visitor centre with the guide. There's a bit of hands-and-feet scrambling as you first clip your belt onto the cable, and some walking and some un-clipping, and some more clipping and some fine views, and then . . . ah, yes, that would be the steel rungs and ladder across the exposed rock face would it? Everyone inches across, grimacing, hands white against the iron bars, not – under any circumstances – looking down, despite the cheery exhortations of the preposterously nimble guide to do exactly that. All right, maybe you sneak a peak, down a thousand feet of sheer rock wall to the snaking road in the valley below, knowing (reassuring tug on the harness) that you can't actually fall off, though not quite believing it.

The route continues up and around the rocks and crevices, and it beggars belief that Victorian miners did this without a safety harness, leaping from one foothold to the next. Still, at least they weren't confronted by the please-tell-us-you're-joking zip-wire ride across the gorge that prefaces the final climb to the summit. Frankly, it's eyes closed for most at this point, but the adrenaline rush afterwards is indescribable and another fifteen minutes or so sees you standing on top of Fleetwith Pike, grinning like a loon. Never has 2126 feet seemed so impossibly high – or so dramatically alluring that you can't wait to do it all over again.

Need to know Via Ferrata at Honister Slate Mine, Honister Pass, Borrowdale, Cumbria ☎017687/77714, Ⓦ www.honister. com. Advance bookings essential; departures 1 or 2 times a day. Adults £25, or £35 including zip-wire ride.
Map 4, D16

FORTY WINKS

great places to stay

Looking back on Britain in the 1970s in his *Notes from a Small Island*, travel writer Bill Bryson recalled with a shudder the ghastly guesthouse landlady, the petty rules and regulations ("like joining the Army") and the downright discomfort that once went hand in hand with an overnight stay in the UK. Anyone in Britain of a certain age recognizes the description of the inhospitality industry with glee – and probably has their own *Fawlty Towers* holiday memory of deranged hoteliers, faulty plumbing and terrible service. Goodness, how things have changed. We may not like the clumsy word but the "staycation" – the holiday at home – is doing wonders for accommodation across Britain. B&Bs in particular have been forced to raise their game, as punters increasingly demand the service and facilities they are used to getting abroad. Out go the cheerless decor, the chintz, the bone-hard beds, the UHT milk pots and the greasy fry-ups. In come boutique styling, fancy linen, whirlpool baths, herbal teas and organic breakfasts. In contemporary hotels, spas and cool bars are de rigueur, and if you ask for a menu you're as likely to get one for pillows as for the restaurant these days. Designers, restorers and conservationists have invested their considerable talents in converting neglected or historic properties across Britain, while even camping has had a makeover – it's no longer just a tent in a field but "glamping" in rug-strewn, stove-warmed yurts and teepees. Britain now has some of the world's finest accommodation, from lavish and luxurious to ineffably hip, and if prices have inevitably risen over the years (a common complaint), then so – unarguably – have standards and expectations. And if you're looking for somewhere just that bit different then Britain really does have the market sewn up, from historic inns, cosy castles and country-house hotels to a where-else-in-the-world roster of converted lighthouses, windmills, follies, towers, schools and train stations. Check out our star picks, and whether it's a rock'n'roll hotel or a Scottish wilderness lodge, there's no better place to grab forty winks.

190 The Scarlet: eco-luxury in Cornwall

Scarlet by name, green by nature, this sleekly designed eco-hotel, back-lit by the Atlantic, is indulgent, relaxed and deservedly proud of its sustainable skin: proof that caring about the environment doesn't mean scrimping on style. The hotel flaunts an array of quirky luxuries to seduce guests into a state of utter well-being. Here you can ease into the rhythms of Mother Nature in a wood-fired hot tub perched on the edge of the beach; dare a dip in the outdoor pool purified by reed-bed vegetation; kick back with a cocktail on the rooftop terrace; undergo soothing treatments in the Ayurvedic spa, or swim in a solar-heated pool that seems to stretch almost to the ocean.

The Scarlet's design emphasizes the natural environment throughout. The roof garden is planted with native sea thrift, and each uber-stylish room looks out onto a panorama of crashing waves, staggering cliffs and pearly sands. Hotel conventions are challenged too: there is no reception desk behind which staff stand on ceremony (instead they magically appear on your arrival), children are an absolute no-no and every interlinking space throws up an opportunity to take the weight off your feet and sink into the surroundings.

To ensure peace and harmony infiltrates not only your senses but also your state of mind, plenty of relaxation aids have been introduced. In the Ayurvedic spa you can curl up in a hanging canvas pod, get messy with a mud treatment or treat yourself to a rebalancing spa journey. If you prefer to work out in the arms of nature, go wild swimming with a private coach, try surfing or walk the hotel dog along the South West Coast Path. But though the likes of Bedruthan Steps, Watergate Bay and *Fifteen Cornwall* await within walking distance, you may find it a wrench to stray too far from this seaside sanctuary. Besides, your on-site Michelin chef, Ben Tunnicliffe, conjures up excellent seasonal dishes that rival Jamie Oliver's offerings.

Since opening its doors in 2009, *The Scarlet* has exceeded its vision to provide "delicious food, Cornish art and quirky stuff to make people smile". This place is sublime and squeaky-green to its core.

Need to know *The Scarlet*, Tredragon Rd, Mawgan Porth, near Newquay, Cornwall ☎ 01637/861800, Ⓦ www. scarlethotel.co.uk. Rooms cost £180–395 per night (ten percent first-night discount if you arrive by foot, bike or public transport). Dinner £32.50/£39.50 (2/3 courses); spa experiences from £60 per hour.
Map 2, A7

191 Penthouse camping in Wales

The problem with camping in Britain is not just the weather, it's that so many campsites take style tips from suburbia. And then there's the endless packing and unpacking to factor in. So raise your enamel mug to *fforestcamp* in Wales's Teifi Valley. It takes the best bits of hotel accommodation – comfy beds, interior design, real breakfasts, faultless staff – and adapts them to the outdoors. The result is camping for softies: a 200-acre hotel with canvas rooms and woodland corridors. Oh, and room service.

Purists needn't choke on their Kendal mint cake quite yet. It may draw from the world of brick-and-mortar hotels, but *fforest* is founded upon a love of getting under canvas, as the range of high-quality tents ready-pitched in wildflower meadows testifies. Love to go back to basics? Then there are traditional Nomad tunnel-tents. "Threepis" – like a miniature tipi "but three times better", the owners say – up the ante in comfort. But even they are not a patch on the geodesic domes. These futuristic structures qualify as tents because of their canvas skins. Actually, though, they're camping's penthouse suites: nearly 4m high by 6m across, flooded with natural light and featuring real decor like polished wood floors, rustic-chic beds with featherdown duvets, the odd retro furnishing and a recycled wood-stove. All have an attached alfresco kitchen, as do the crog lofts, four effortlessly hip, retro-modern mezzanine apartments carved from a former barn. No one said you had to camp, after all.

Nor do you have to cook. A communal lodge provides fresh meals a few times a week, plus excellent breakfasts – that's for those who haven't pre-ordered "tent service", a breakfast hamper and a cafetiere delivered to your tent flap. Other site facilities include a Scandinavian barrel sauna and an artfully shabby bar stuffed with mismatched furnishings and rustic charm.

You could call *fforest* inspiring. You can certainly call it cool. Just don't call it glamping. Because for all its style, *fforest* remains dedicated to the great Welsh outdoors. That's why numbers are limited to a hundred guests despite its two hundred acres. It's also why daily programmes of activities, from canoeing to bushcraft, are scheduled to entertain the kids, making this a family playground as much as an adult retreat. Who would've thought a campsite could encompass so much?

Need to know *Fforestcamp*, Cwnplysgog, Cilgerran, Cardigan ☎ 01239/623633, Ⓦ www.coldatnight.co.uk. Open for camping April–Oct; crog lofts are open year-round. Bookings can be made for three-night weekend stays, four-night midweek stays, or for a minimum of a week during school holidays. Prices for a midweek stay start from £185 for a Nomad tent; from £245 in a Threepi; from £345 in a Dome; and from £395 in a crog loft. Activities are not included.

Map 3, A12

192 Townhouse chic at Hotel du Vin

Glasgow may not be a byword for luxury and indulgence, but it is known for its wonderful architecture. The small and exclusive hotel chain *Hotel du Vin* have capitalized on this, turning an Edwardian pale-sandstone terraced hotel into one of the country's most chic accommodation destinations. And the famous wit and friendliness of the local population is evident: Glasgow's *Hotel du Vin* is warmer and more welcoming than many a landmark posh hotel, from the friendly tartan-clad doorman to the approachable restaurant staff.

The style is cool minimalism with a good dash of excess, evident in the velvet drapes, plasma-screen tellies, Egyptian linen and the sheer size of the suites. Throughout, original architectural features have been retained, including hand-carved wood-panelling, cornices and dramatic stained-glass panels. There are 49 rooms and suites to choose from. You may want to ask for one with an antique four-poster bed, while for maximum extravagance the enormous Mews Suite even has its own gym and sauna. Classic Room Catena Zapata, meanwhile, has a roll-top bath which sits in front of the bay window. Meals too are well out of the ordinary. The modestly titled *Bistro* serves modern European food cooked with local ingredients: velouté of langoustine to start, perhaps, followed by roast beef in red wine sauce, roast Dornoch lamb or Shetland skate wing. There's a 600-bin wine cellar plus a choice of 300 whiskies that may limit your powers to explore the city.

But one of the chief pleasures of a stay here is to walk the backstreets of the cosmopolitan West End, hilly thoroughfares with red- and honey-coloured tenements rising to either side. From the nearby Botanic Gardens you can walk along the banks of the Kelvin, which cuts an unexpectedly verdant swathe through the city. To the south, Byres Road is home to some outstanding independent boutiques, delis and cafés, while parallel Ashton Lane makes for a classic Glasgow night out: you can crisscross from bar to bar, and then head up the cobbled lane for a movie at the arthouse cinema.

Need to know *Hotel du Vin*, 1 Devonshire Gardens, Great Western Rd, Glasgow ☎0141/339 2001, Ⓦwww.hotelduvin.com. The tariff starts at £150 for a standard room, soaring to £960 for the Mews Suite.
Map 4, C14

193 Underleigh House: the Peak of perfection

It's the small things that make a B&B truly great. A slab of home-made cake and freshly made tea on arrival, a generous tea-tray with a jug of cold milk in the room, slouchy sofas to sink into and an agreeable cat pottering around, happy to curl up on a complete stranger. *Underleigh House* in the Peak District scores on every one: homely without being chichi; pleasingly indulgent without straying into boutique hotel territory.

Much of this is down to the warm welcome and careful management of Philip and Vivienne, who seem to run *Underleigh* with real love. Vivienne is on hand when guests arrive, and is a great source of local information, from the best pubs for dinner to the best walking routes to explore the stunning surrounding countryside. The fact that many guests return year after year is testament to their hospitality; they're happy to run tired walkers down to the pub for supper, arrange taxis back or even make up the numbers for the local pub quiz if required.

The B&B's location is particularly lovely; tucked away up a small lane, with views that stretch out across the surrounding hills, unhindered by the modern world. The pretty village of Hope is within walking distance and the famous caves at Castleton are just five minutes' drive away. On summer evenings, *Underleigh*'s pretty garden is the perfect spot for a chilled glass – fridges in each room are helpfully provided so guests can bring their own beer and wine.

But it's the mornings that really make the place special. Breakfasts are spectacular, taken at one long table that groans under jugs of fresh juice, bowls of slow-cooked porridge and plates of locally sourced sausage and bacon, melt-in-the-mouth mushrooms and tomatoes from the garden. To one side, another table offers bowl after bowl of breakfast treats: apricots and raisins steeped in alcohol, home-made muesli, fresh fruits, local yoghurt, toasted nuts and seeds. It's a full-on feast, best taken slowly with a large pot of coffee, piles of hot toast and an internal promise to walk it all off later in the day.

Need to know *Underleigh House*, Lose Hill Lane, Hope, Hope Valley, Derbyshire ☎ 01433/621372, Ⓦwww.underleighhouse.co.uk. Doubles from £87 per room per night.
Map 3, C10

TOP 10 >>
UNUSUAL PLACES TO STAY

From ornate Victorian water towers to wave-battered houses in the sea, our little island is bursting with unusual places to stay. Try one from our list below, and you'll refuse to stay in a *Travelodge* ever again.

194 Livingstone Safari Lodge, Kent

Stick your neck out of *Livingstone Safari Lodge* at Port Lympne Wild Animal Park and you might see a giraffe sniffing around in the early morning light. Here, in the hundred or so acres of Kent countryside that rolls away from your private veranda, there are herds of grazing wildebeest, zebra and antelope. Keep your eyes on the glistening watering-holes and you might even spot a hippo poking its nostrils above the surface. The accommodation is fairly basic, who cares when you're waking up to one of the best views this side of Africa?

Ⓦ *www.totallywild.net. Open March–Oct. From £115 per person per night Map 2, F6*

195 La Rosa, Whitby, North Yorkshire

Way before the "glamping" revolution, a campsite near Whitby started putting people up in vintage caravans, ranging from an Elvis-themed period piece to an authentic chrome Roma full of etched glass. The kitsch factor proved so popular they've now opened a hotel in town and stuffed it full of high-camp Victoriana – think Naughty Nineties meets eBay – with themed rooms dedicated to everyone from Bram Stoker to Angela Carter.

Ⓦ *www.larosa.co.uk. Camping costs £30 per person per night (£28 if you arrive by public transport); rooms at La Rosa Hotel cost from £80 per double Map 4, F16*

196 Appleton Water Tower, Norfolk

The Victorians were a clever bunch. Instead of wasting their energy on a heating system to stop water towers from freezing, they just re-routed flues from below, channelling hot smoke up through the centre of the tanks. But as the ornate iron railings and twisting staircases of *Appleton Water Tower* attest, they still had a taste for fanciful design. When you gaze out over the Sandringham Estate from your warm octagonal bedroom, you might just thank them for it.

Ⓦ *www.landmarktrust.org.uk. Expect to pay around £600 for a midweek stay in summer. Map 3, E11*

197 Old Railway Station, West Sussex

There used to be a time when train travel was fun, even glamorous – and a far cry from today's dreaded commuter run. At the *Old Railway Station* at Petworth, near Chichester, the golden age of rail lingers on, from the gorgeous vaulted guest hall, once a busy ticket office, to the chocolate-brown Edwardian Pullman carriages, which house colonial-style guest rooms. All that's missing, in fact, is the railway line, which closed in 1966. So drop your bags, stop for a cream tea, and thank God you've got nowhere to go.

Ⓦ *www.old-station.co.uk. Rooms start at £99, but cheaper late deals may be available. Map 2, E6*

198 The House in the Sea, Cornwall

A short walk from the bawdy nightclubs of Newquay, there's a private island for hire. Perched atop a large granite rock and cut off from the mainland by swirling, aqua-blue surf, the red-roofed *House in the Sea* is reachable only by a 70ft-high suspension bridge. It was once home to Sir Oliver Joseph Lodge, the bright chap who invented the spark plug. Now it's a luxurious B&B with its own wonderfully isolated stargazing terrace.

Ⓦ *www.uniquehomestays.com. From £170 per night. Sleeps two. Map 2, A7*

199 Cley Windmill, Holt, Norfolk

The flat, marshy landscape of north Norfolk does wonders for *Cley Windmill*. Those white latticed sails just wouldn't stand out as well among rolling green hills. But the flat terrain has caused problems too; in the 1950s, a great flood put the mill under eight feet of water. Now, the eighteenth-century tower has been graciously restored, and guests are invited to curl up with a book under the beamed ceiling of its circular sitting room.

Ⓦ *www.cleywindmill.co.uk. Rooms start at £80 per night. Map 3, F11*

200 Badrallach Bothy, Wester Ross

When you're trekking in the cold and rugged Scottish Highlands, finding somewhere warm to spend the night can be a matter of life and death. Step forward the splendid Mountain Bothies Association, who have converted dozens of ruined old buildings into bothies – simple, free shelters left open to all. Though it continues the tradition, *Badrallach*'s bothy, in remotest Wester Ross, is a little more homely than most, with smouldering, peat-fired stoves warming the cold stone walls, but you'll still need to cook for yourself – and bring your own sleeping bag.

Ⓦ *www.badrallach.com. Bothy from £7 per person per night. See* Ⓦ *www. mountainbothies.org.uk for more on bothies. Map 5, B19*

201 Star Castle Hotel, Isles of Scilly

From down on the ground, it's not immediately obvious where *Star Castle* got its name from. But arrive on St Mary's by whirring helicopter and you'll see its jagged outer walls etching an eight-pointed Cornish star into the hilltop. The garrison was built in 1593 to protect the islands from the Spanish Armada and subtle reminders of its tumultuous history can still be spotted to this day.

Ⓦ *www.star-castle.co.uk. Doubles start at £162 per night, including dinner. Map 2, A8*

202 Hotel Pelirocco, Brighton

Hotels don't usually mix well with rock'n'roll – just think of all those TVs that have crashed out of bedroom windows. But at *Hotel Pelirocco*, near Brighton's pebble-fringed seafront, the rock star ethos has been embraced, drizzled with sauciness, and then packaged into nineteen uniquely sexy bedrooms. There's the flagship sleazy Play Room, with an eight-foot-wide circular bed (complete with mirrored canopy) and an in-room pole-dancing area. Then there's the Pin-up Parlour, where tasselled lampshades and drapes pay homage to Fifties bombshell Diana Dors. Or maybe the Nookii Room's more your style, drenched in black satin, with its own peep-show sign.

Ⓦ *www.hotelpelirocco.co.uk. Rooms start from £50 per night. Map 2, E6*

203 Clavell Tower, Dorset

If nature was given its way, *Clavell Tower*, near Wareham, would probably be somewhere at the bottom of the English Channel by now. But in 2006, the Landmark Trust embarked on a project to restore the 180-year-old folly and rebuild it 82 feet back from the crumbling cliffs of the Purbeck coast. It worked, and nearly £900,000 later, it's available to rent – a dinky little house with unparalleled views.

Ⓦ *www.landmarktrust.org.uk. Sleeps two. Expect to pay upwards of £450 for a three-night weekend stay. Map 2, D7*

204 Marble muses at Carbisdale Castle

A weekend country retreat in a Highland castle graced with a sculpture gallery and acres of woodland to explore is the stuff that dreams are made of – if only you had the cash.... But at *Carbisdale* you won't have to reach for your credit card: a night's stay at this impressive baronial castle will cost you less than twenty quid.

Now the proud flagship of the Scottish Youth Hostel Association, *Carbisdale Castle* was built between 1906 and 1917 by the Duchess of Sutherland. She built the soaring Scots baronial pile with money from her divorce settlement, granted on the condition that she should settle outside Sutherland lands. The duchess agreed to the terms, but placed the castle on a steep hillside so that it should be as visible as possible to the disgruntled Sutherlands. The castle tower is faced on only three sides by a clock – the Sutherland side left blank as the duchess, quite literally, wouldn't give them the time of day. *Carbisdale* was bought in 1933 by the wealthy Salvesen family; they sheltered the king of Norway here during the Nazi occupation of his country, and then generously gifted the castle to the SYHA in 1945.

Aside from fellow hostellers, you may encounter occupants of a spectral variety: a phantom bagpiper; a lady in white; a distressed wraith still angry from the routing of the Royalist forces of the Marquis of Montrose, which occurred just down the hill in 1650.... Spooks aside, there's plenty to keep you occupied at *Carbisdale*, whether you're admiring the shapely forms of the white marble maidens in the sculpture gallery, perusing the impressive art collection (now mostly replaced by reproductions, so don't look too closely) or hiking and biking in the surrounding hills.

Just hanging out in the library is a pleasure, with a ceiling so encrusted with stucco if looks as if it's dripping white icing. Bring a book to the primrose yellow and pink lounge, wreathed with moulding; take to the shining wooden floor of the ballroom; or gaze wistfully out of the picture windows to the Kyle of Sutherland and the distant hills.... Half close your eyes to block out the institutional hostel furniture and the tartan carpets, and you can really imagine how the other half lives.

Need to know *Carbisdale Castle YH* is near Culrain in Sutherland, Highland ☎ 01549/421232, Ⓦ www.syha.org.uk. Dorm beds cost from £19.50 per person; standard twin rooms from £50 per couple.
Map 5, C19

205 The Lord Poulett Arms: Somerset's perfect pub?

Pretty little Hinton St George, a peaceful cluster of soft hamstone houses in deepest Somerset, is the type of village you wander into expecting to find the perfect country inn but rarely do. The thatched roofs, the harmonious brickwork, all crying out to be topped off by a local that marries a boisterous bar with a fine-dining restaurant, and modern bedrooms with traditional hospitality. But Hinton St George is different. For Hinton St George has the *Lord Poulett Arms*.

And the *Lord Poulett Arms* has the kind of rooms you'd want to live in – classy but comfortable, with antique beds, seagrass floors, and gilded mirrors set against exposed hamstone or Osborne & Little wallpaper. Some have a roll-top bath in the middle, all have the sort of thoughtful touches that only come with small-scale lodgings: Roberts radios rather than satellite TV, home-made biscuits in place of tartan-packeted shortbread.

You can make these your base for exploring south Somerset, but there are closer attractions to visit. The award-winning restaurant – one half bare flagstones, the other rich wooden floorboards – serves game from Exmoor and fish from Dorset. Lunch runs along the lines of gourmet sarnies with triple-cooked chips or home-made herb gnocchi. Dinner features dishes such as gilt-head bream with celeriac purée or pan-roasted venison. In the cosy bar area, decked in dried hops and decorated with flickering candles, you can get Somerset ale from the barrel, cider from a jug and, in season, home-made sloe gin or mulled wine. In summer, regulars play boules on the lavender-fringed piste out back; in winter, open fires crackle with contentment.

The only debate about the *Lord Poulett Arms* is whether it's a great pub with lovely bedrooms, or lovely bedrooms with a great pub. The fact that you can't quite tell is part of its appeal, though – the balance of rooms and restaurant, of service and atmosphere, is spot on. Either way, it's a winner. Maybe that's because it's a local pub for local people, whose reputation just happens to be good enough to attract custom from far and wide. Or maybe it's because pretty little Hinton St George is the type of village you wander into expecting to find the perfect country inn....

Need to know *Lord Poulett Arms*, High St, Hinton St George, Somerset ☎ 01460/73149, Ⓦ www.lordpoulettarms.com. Doubles cost £89–95 (private or en-suite bathroom) per night, including breakfast.
Map 2, C6

206 Playing lighthouse keeper at the Belle Tout

Perched in glorious isolation on top of a vertiginous sea cliff, the *Belle Tout Lighthouse* is a B&B with a difference. Just 70ft lies between you and the crumbling cliff edge – and a dizzying drop of 300ft to the crashing waves below. The views from this doughty little tower are, as you'd expect, something special, giving a 360-degree panorama over Sussex's most beautiful stretch of coastline: east to soaring Beachy Head, the country's highest sea cliff, west to the Seven Sisters, south across the English Channel, and north over the rolling South Downs. For once, the promise of a room with a view doesn't disappoint.

The lighthouse – named after the Belle Tout ("beautiful head") headland on which it stands – was erected in 1832 and remained operational until 1902, when a more effective replacement was built at the foot of nearby Beachy Head. After a lifetime of being variously shot at, abandoned, filmed and restored, it hit the headlines in 1999 when its then owners, faced with the prospect of their home tumbling into the sea after a series of rock falls brought the cliff edge just 10ft from their patio garden, had the 850-tonne building lifted up onto runners and slid back onto safer ground – an astonishing feat of engineering by any stretch of the imagination.

Inside, there are six smartly contemporary bedrooms, most with large picture windows making the most of the glorious views, a comfy lounge with capacious leather sofas and toasty open fire, and a lovely breakfast room where you can munch on your Sussex sausages while gazing out to sea. But it's the lamp room at the top of the lighthouse that's the real highlight of any stay. It's been converted into a cosy and stylish lookout, with white leather banquettes and sky-blue woodwork, and music (there's a CD player) and candles to enhance atmosphere – but it's the fabulous 360-degree views that steal the show. By day the surrounding countryside is busy with hikers striding along the undulating South Downs Way, but as evening comes the people drift away and the *Belle Tout*'s only neighbours are the occasional rabbit. Whether hunkered up here on a stormy day, listening to the wind growling around the tower, or gazing out onto a perfect summer's day sunset, you'll never want to leave.

Need to know *Belle Tout Lighthouse*, Beachy Head, Eastbourne, East Sussex 01323/423185, Ⓦ www.belletout. co.uk. Doubles cost £145–190; 2-night minimum stay. **Map 2, E6**

The approach to luxurious *Alladale Wilderness Reserve* is low-key – no signs, no fancy gates and no fanfare – just a long lane that narrows to a dirt path, then runs uphill to a handsome Victorian lodge. Contrary to what you may have heard, there are no bears or wolves in them thar hills – at least not yet.

Alladale is the passion of Paul Lister, an MDF millionaire who used his riches to buy 23,500 acres of land and restore it to something resembling its pristine state: richly wooded and alive with animal and birdlife. The surroundings here – high-sided valleys cloaked with heather and dotted with Caledonian pine – are undeniably impressive, but after a little time with one of the reserve's expert rangers you'll realize that the landscape is unnaturally, almost uncannily, empty. The deforestation of areas like this was compounded by the Clearances, when crofters were mercilessly pushed out of the surrounding glens in favour of sheep, who guzzled the ground vegetation. And deer, with their natural predators – wolves – long disposed of by man, have grown in impossible numbers.

Lister has begun to reverse some of this damage, with a project that aims to restore the area – predators and all. He has encountered numerous obstacles, not least a media-fuelled hysteria that paints Alladale as a lupine disaster waiting to happen – a Scottish Jurassic Park. In the background, the serious work of large-scale tree planting has begun, and Oxford University has studied the introduction of wild boar here.

All this is the background to a deluxe accommodation experience – Lister wants to prove that his reserve can be a money-spinner, and can engage visitors with more than the traditional hunting, shooting and fishing. All these are in fact on offer, alongside nature walks, spa treatments, bike rides and pony trekking. Groups can hole up in the gorgeous lodge, which is decked out in rich colours and sumptuous textiles and comes complete with roaring fires, spacious dining room, billiard room, gym and a friendly chef catering to your every need. Otherwise, head to one of the two more remote stone "bothies" which give more of a wilderness feel. But spartan they are not: think flat-screen TVs, wind-powered wi-fi, splendid evening meals waiting in the fridge and tasteful tweed-covered furnishings. The juxtaposition of luxury and wilderness may be jarring to some, but a stay at *Alladale* is an intriguing and inspiring experience.

Need to know *Alladale Wilderness Lodge and Reserve* (**T** 01863/755388, **W** www.alladale. com) is an hour's drive north of Inverness, near Ardgay. Group stays in the lodge average £206.25 per person per night in high season; the bothies cost £162.50 per person per night.
Map 5, C19

208 Back to school in Northumberland

Need to know *The Old School*, Newton-on-the-Moor, Alnwick, Northumberland ☎ 01665/575767, Ⓦ www.northumberlandbedandbreakfast.co.uk. Rooms cost £105 per night. Map 4, E15

Lying deep in the heart of the Northumbrian countryside, Newton-on-the-Moor is a peaceful little village with a pleasing array of pretty, flower-bedecked cottages. It has a small village hall, a popular pub (*The Cook and Barker*) and a great B&B called *The Old School*. In fact, it's not just great – it's the best B&B in England.

Winner of the coveted Enjoy England Award for Excellence (2010), *The Old School* sits on the edge of the village, enjoying far-reaching views over to the rolling Cheviot Hills. As the names suggests, it occupies an old schoolhouse building, which dates back to the eighteenth century. From the outside, it's possible to make out its disciplinary roots, as sensitive renovation over the years by owners Malcolm and Kath Downes has left period features in place – one playground now doubles up as parking space, the other is the front garden, while the old headmaster's house, erstwhile residence for the big boss, his wife and children, is now a bedroom.

But the interior is far from institutional. Four bedrooms – one on the ground floor, three upstairs – are luxurious and comfortable. The cosy ground-floor room, billed as a "study", is decked out in cool beige and cream tones, and has an enormous bed, iPod dock, flat-screen TV, and sleek en-suite bathroom. Upstairs, the rooms are larger and a little more country chic, each with soft quilts, exposed walls, and chocolate-brown wooden beams. A little balcony upstairs overlooks the rose-filled garden and sun terrace, often occupied by resident cat, Tess.

The snug breakfast room, with separate dining tables, is the perfect setting for a delicious breakfast lovingly cooked to order by Malcolm. All produce is organic and locally sourced, including honey (from Chainbridge Honey Farm in Berwick), back bacon (from Longframlington) and salty kippers (from the fishing village of Craster). Plump for the Omelette Arnold Bennett, a hearty concoction of free-range eggs from Detchant Farm, and Craster's smoked haddock.

Location-wise, *The Old School* couldn't be better – just a few minutes' drive to the east is the coast and its gloriously sandy beaches, while westwards is a medley of picturesque villages, stately homes and craggy castles, as well as the hills, valleys, rivers and forests of the Northumberland National Park. So, what are you waiting for? It's time to go back to school....

209 Country life at the Devonshire Arms

Need to know *Devonshire Arms Country House Hotel & Spa*, Bolton Abbey, Skipton, North Yorkshire ☎ 01756/710441, Ⓦ www.thedevonshirearms.co.uk. Double rooms start from £238, weekends from £258, though the website has special offers. Meals in the *Brasserie* (daily, lunch and dinner) cost £20–35 per head; *Burlington Restaurant* (Tues–Sun dinner & Sun lunch) menus at £65, £72 and £85. Map 3, C9

You know you're moving in different circles when you come upon the hotel sign that says "Helicopters are left entirely at their owners' risk". However, that's pretty much the only brash note at the *Devonshire Arms*, the wonderfully understated country-house hotel sited on the Duke of Devonshire's 30,000-acre Bolton Abbey Estate in the Yorkshire Dales. Originally a coaching inn, it's been extended over the centuries but remains agreeably small in scale (forty guest rooms and suites) yet big on atmosphere and personal service.

The hotel's setting is as quintessentially English as it gets – a babbling river with old stone bridge, village cricket pitch, manicured lawns and rolling green fields. A rack of fishing rods at the door and a crackling fire in the lobby put you firmly in the country mood, and the dog-friendly credentials are impeccable – you've got to love a place that provides a dog-washing bucket and sponge and dog-food ordering service. If you prefer to pamper yourself rather than the family mutt, wander across to the spa where stylish pool, sauna, gym and therapy suites sit under the rafters of a converted barn.

Rural-chic rooms, no two the same, make the most of the views, with accommodation split between the original building and the newer wing – in the old part you get wooden four-poster beds made by carpenters from the Devonshire's family pile at Chatsworth (the same stately home is also the source of many of the paintings on the walls in the hotel). Blankets instead of duvets, fresh milk, a bedtime hot choccie, a hot-water bottle – you only have to ask and up trots a cheery member of staff in double-quick time.

The two hotel restaurants source locally and organically where they can, and make use of the *Devonshire*'s own kitchen gardens. The bright and breezy *Brasserie and Bar* gets the informal vote, and has an outdoor summer terrace. The *Burlington Restaurant*, meanwhile, flaunts a Michelin star under chef Steve Smith, whose gorgeously presented dishes sit well on the polished, candlelit tables under more Devonshire family art.

210 Under the Thatch: cosying up in rural Wales

Driving up the beautiful Glyn Ceiriog Valley from its thirteenth-century stronghold, Chirk Castle, you catch occasional glimpses of the glossy Ceiriog River, tumbling along over smooth-polished stones. But you'll rarely see another car. Take a sharp right onto an uphill track flanked by steep pasture and eventually you reach Plas Pennant – a North Wales manor house in miniature, with white-gold stone walls, a cascade of lawns and glorious valley views.

To one side, in a cobbled courtyard, is the old *popty*, or bakehouse, now a simple stone cottage with honeysuckle around the door. Just a few years ago this modest little building was barely a shell, but its owners saw its potential and set about restoring it using traditional methods and authentic materials: flagstones for the floor, limewash in soft, earthy colours for the timbers and walls. They tucked a cosy bedroom into the old crog-loft mezzanine and created a simple, gingham-trimmed kitchen next to the living space below. The result is a delightful holiday hideaway.

Like the sound of that? There's more. Next, they transformed Plas Pennant's disued chapel into another gorgeous cottage, furnishing it with vintage oddments and style-magazine flair. Both cottages are now available through specialist letting agency Under The Thatch.

The people behind Under The Thatch are passionate about rescuing humble historic buildings from dereliction, conserving them, restoring them and making them beautiful once more. By staying in one of the farms, cottages and crofts they represent, not only are you boosting the rural economy, you're also helping preserve a part of Britain's architectural heritage that's all too often overlooked.

The project which started it all was *Ffynnon-Oer Isaf*, a magically rustic Aeron Valley cottage with a shaggy thatched roof; more recent additions to the portfolio include character properties such as *Popty* and *Capel Pennant*, a watermill and several colourful, bow-topped Romany gypsy caravans.

Also on the books are some wonderful old Welsh farmhouses, such as *Dolau Canol* in the Teifi Valley and *Treberfedd* near Aberaeron. *Trehilyn Isaf* near Strumble Head is much in demand; it's owned by Griff Rhys-Jones, who recorded the process of restoring it for a BBC documentary. Browse any of the cottages' visitors books, and you'll find them stuffed with glowing comments from guests who come back time and time again.

Need to know Under the Thatch (Ⓦ www.underthethatch. co.uk) offers a choice of over 70 self-catering cottages, houses and character properties sleeping two to ten, from £120 for two people for two nights. Most are located in rural Wales.

Map 3, B11

211 Langar Hall:
a pilgrimage of taste

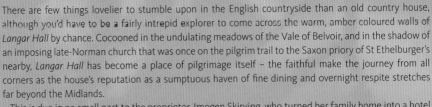

Need to know *Langar Hall*, Langar, Nottinghamshire ☎ 01949/860559, Ⓦ www.langarhall.com. Prices for one night in a double room, with breakfast, start at £195 midweek.

Map 3, D11

There are few things lovelier to stumble upon in the English countryside than an old country house, although you'd have to be a fairly intrepid explorer to come across the warm, amber coloured walls of *Langar Hall* by chance. Cocooned in the undulating meadows of the Vale of Belvoir, and in the shadow of an imposing late-Norman church that was once on the pilgrim trail to the Saxon priory of St Ethelburger's nearby, *Langar Hall* has become a place of pilgrimage itself – the faithful make the journey from all corners as the house's reputation as a sumptuous haven of fine dining and overnight respite stretches far beyond the Midlands.

This is due in no small part to the proprietor, Imogen Skirving, who turned her family home into a hotel 25 years ago with taste and great attention to detail. She has the kind of personal approach to hosting, mirrored by her staff, that leaves guests feeling well cared for but not mollycoddled, and is undoubtedly *Langar Hall*'s heart and soul.

Many noted guests have stayed here, from David Bowie to Barbara Cartland, who famously took the same room, subsequently named after her, every time she made the trip between the Scottish Highlands and her home in Hertfordshire (it is resolutely not pink, but extremely comfortable). The remaining eleven en-suite bedrooms are also individually named and decorated – from the opulent romance of Bohemia, a favourite of honeymooners, to the refined, understated furnishings of Cricketers – all boasting views of rolling countryside or the pretty church garden. You will wake up refreshed and ready for a hearty breakfast, although dinner is the real highlight of a stay here. The evening begins with an aperitif in the sitting room, recently upholstered by local designer and family friend Paul Smith, as Imogen, and Michael her expansive maître d', chat to guests while they peruse the menu and admire views over the deer park. The dining room next door is an intimate setting to enjoy some fine cuisine – deliciously plump roast wood pigeon stuffed with foie gras on a bed of puy lentils is one of the signature dishes – that should, on its own, be enough to warrant a return visit.

212 Pen-y-Dyffryn: go wild in the country

The phrase "country house hotel" can be one to strike fear into the heart of modern travellers, threatening chintzy bedrooms, warm G&Ts and a terrifying overuse of tweed. *Pen-y-Dyffryn* avoids such clichés, and mixes a peaceful old-fashioned feel with enough twenty-first-century comforts to keep it feeling pleasantly contemporary. Rooms are cosy and comfortable, with small flat-screen TVs, chic bathrooms with a nice line in toiletries and pleasingly squishy-but-firm beds.

Tucked away in a dip between the steeply rolling hills of the Anglo–Welsh border, the hotel is just three miles from the town of Oswestry, yet feels delightfully rural. A stay here is more about walking boots than slingbacks, with many a walk from the hotel's front door ranging from a gentle stroll to a full day's hike.

In the evenings, the hearty outdoorsy feel is exchanged for simple elegance, as pre-dinner drinks are served in the cosy bar before a top-notch supper. Food is integral to a stay at *Pen*: free afternoon tea is offered on arrival, and the dinner menu changes frequently according to what can be sourced locally. Slivers of local beef carpaccio, pan-fried scallops and buttery lemon sole are typical, all served up with considerable panache. The indulgent desserts – crispy brûlée, oozing fondants, creamy pannacotta – are a particular high spot, and an added motivation for a next-day ramble across the hills.

In spite of its isolated location, the hotel makes a great base for exploring. As border country, these lands have been fought over for centuries and there are ruined castles and dramatic National Trust properties to explore. Further afield, the atmospheric Lake Vrynwy and dramatic peaks of the Snowdonia National Park are ideal for a day-trip.

Pen is a hotel that morphs and changes throughout the week. Quieter and more staid on weekdays, when the guests tend to be older and the dining room may have emptied by 9pm, it's buzzy at weekends, when urban escapees keep the bar open till late, and breakfasts are something of a bleary affair. Whenever you visit, though, *Pen-y-Dyffryn* remains a blissful rural escape.

Need to know *Pen-y-Dyffryn Country Hotel*, Rhydycroesau, Oswestry, Shropshire ☎01691/653700, Ⓦ www.peny.co.uk. Doubles from £172 per night, high tea, dinner, bed and breakfast included.
Map 3, B11

213 Sleeping with the bishops at Durham Castle

Short, squat and somewhat unprepossessing, Durham Castle takes a bit of a back seat beside its large – and rather more beautiful – neighbour, the cathedral. But together they make up a UNESCO World Heritage site, and are without doubt the highlight of a visit to the city. Despite today's neat and tidy appearance, the bastion has certainly been through the mill over the years, and – to add insult to injury – it's now home to over one hundred exuberant university students belonging to Durham's University College.

Built on the site of an eleventh-century fortress commissioned by William The Conqueror, Durham Castle has spent most of its existence inhabited by a succession of Prince Bishops. The so-called "Kings of County Durham", these Bishops enjoyed power akin to the king of England, and had their own justice system, mint and army. Using their well-stocked coffer, they primped and preened their home, adding a chapel, halls, kitchens and a crenellated keep. In the fourteenth century, however, they ran out of steam: the office's finances dried up and the building fell into disrepair. Seized by Oliver Cromwell during the Civil War and Commonwealth, handed to the major of London, and passed back to the Bishops again, the castle was a complete ruin by 1836, when Bishop Van Mildert bequeathed it to the university.

It makes a pretty impressive student digs today, with a rabbit warren of bedrooms in the keep, an eleventh-century wood-panelled Great Hall that now functions as a dining room and the all-important college bar in the cellars. Fortunately, castle living isn't confined to the students: during university holidays the college rents out a selection of the rooms for B&B. Choose from the no-frills single and double rooms in the keep, or splash out on one of the two State Rooms (available year-round). Best of the two is the Bishop's Suite, a sumptuous complex hung with seventeenth-century tapestries, furnished with a beautiful four-poster bed and boasting wonderful views over the River Wear. There's also the second State Room – the Chaplain's Suite, with a private bathroom – as well as twin bedrooms in the medieval gatehouse and some more overlooking the castle gardens. In such majestic settings it's easy to forget that your room with a castle view will soon belong to next term's disorderly student.

Need to know University College, Durham Castle, Palace Green, Durham Ⓦ www.dur.ac.uk/university.college. Rates for B&B range from £28.50 to £95 per night.
Map 4, E16

214 High Society at The Savoy

Grande dame of the capital's hotels, *The Savoy* was opened in 1889 by theatre impresario Richard D'Oyly Carte with the proceeds from his hugely successful Gilbert and Sullivan operas. The capital's first luxury hotel, it featured such unheard-of indulgences as hot and cold running water, electric lighting, "ascending rooms" (lifts) and even rudimentary room service by means of "speaking tubes" connected to the restaurant. Carte hired celebrity chef Auguste Escoffier and hotshot hotelier César Ritz, who came up with the novel concept of playing music while guests dined, "to cover the silence which hangs like a pall over an English dining table". The pair transformed *The Savoy* into a bastion of impeccable service, heady glamour and English eccentricity, and from the turn of the century to its Art Deco makeover in the 1920s and beyond, the hotel attracted an endless stream of the great and the good. Claude Monet painted the Thames from his bedroom window; Oscar Wilde conducted his affair with Lord Alfred Douglas in rooms 346–362; Laurence Olivier and Vivien Leigh first clapped eyes on each other in the lobby; Winston Churchill regularly treated his cabinet to lunch here during World War II; Marlene Dietrich made love in the ballroom; Fred Astaire danced on the roof; and The Beatles dropped in to visit Bob Dylan (and ordered porridge and pea sandwiches).

When the hotel closed its hallowed doors for refurbishment in December 2007, its contents, from chandeliers and grand pianos to butlers' plates and asparagus tongs, went up for auction. Emptied of its treasures and entrusted to a fancy French design firm, *The Savoy* seemed destined for an unseemly glitz-over. But three years and £220 million later, the hotel revealed its surprising new look: just like before, only better. Much-loved features such as the *American Bar* remain, while the bedrooms retain their Edwardian and Art Deco aesthetics, but the design is complemented by some harmonious new additions. A beautiful glass dome now floods the Thames foyer with sunlight; the shadowy *Beaufort Bar*, embellished with £38,000-worth of gold leaf, seems designed for illicit liaisons; and the *River Room* restaurant, decked out like a 1920s ocean liner, serves modern French cuisine. *Pièce de résistance* is the eight-room, £10,000-a-night Royal Suite, swathed in pale-yellow silk and twinkling with Murano glass chandeliers, which takes up an entire floor overlooking the river, offering bird's-eye views of the hoi polloi on the South Bank below.

Need to know *The Savoy*, The Strand, London WC2 ☎ 020/7420 2405, Ⓦ www.the-savoy.com. Doubles start from £350.

Map 1, D3

215 Woodlands Country House: quirky splendour in north Cornwall

Need to know *Woodlands Country House*, Treator, near Padstow, Cornwall ☎ 01841/532426, Ⓦ www. woodlands-padstow.co.uk. Doubles cost from £98 for a standard room out of season up to £150 for the Beach Room over the summer. **Map 2, A7**

The moment you're welcomed by an utterly charming gentleman sporting a luxuriant walrus moustache, you know *Woodlands Country House* isn't going to be your average guesthouse. Built in 1884, this grand yet homely Victorian house is not only beautifully maintained and stuffed with interesting family heirlooms, but its hosts, Hugo and Pippa Woolley, offer hospitality with bells on – you'll feel part of the fold for the duration of your stay. Dogs or kids? No problem. Muddy walking boots? Come on in. Need a lift to a restaurant? I'll just get the car keys.

Exuding the ambience more of a civilized house party than a strait-laced B&B, this isn't the sort of place where you're relegated to your bedroom. Downstairs the communal Blue Room is decked out with plump sofas, an honesty bar and a mountain of reading material, while outside there's a croquet lawn by the fountains and plenty of space for four-legged friends to run about. The eight opulent bedrooms range from the classic four-poster Bay Room to the more contemporary, colossal Beach Room with ocean views, an indulgent bathroom and cosy sitting area with a luxurious day-bed. As well as wi-fi, tea and coffee (fresh milk, hoorah), rooms are thoughtfully kitted out with trays for walking boots and super-comfy beds dressed in Italian Frette linen.

Since it's situated minutes' drive from gastronomers' Padstow, it matters not a jot that *Woodlands* doesn't serve evening meals: with Stein's eateries, Paul Ainsworth's *Number 6* and Nathan Outlaw's fine-dining gaff at Rock, there's more than enough choice in the vicinity. Yet harking from a chef's background and having penned his own book on breakfasts, Hugo makes his own foodie contribution with legendary, locally sourced breakfast feasts – often accompanied by his baritone melodies booming from the kitchen. There's crunchy home-made granola, Cornish Hog's Pudding, daily specials from pancakes to kedgeree and always a fresh batch of home-baked treats. Lucky, then, that nearby awaits the South West Coast Path and seven pearly bays on which to hike or surf your way to a hearty appetite.

Voted South West England's B&B of the Year 2009–10, *Woodland*'s combination of affordable glamour and affable hosts will no doubt keep this country house on lists of special places to stay for many years to come.

216 Sleep under medieval beams, Lavenham

Need to know *Lavenham Priory*, Water St, Lavenham, Sudbury, Suffolk ☎ 01787/247404, Ⓦ www.lavenhampriory.co.uk. Rooms start at £105 per night (based on two sharing), although lower rates are available for single occupancy. **Map 3, E12**

At the beginning of the twentieth century, Lavenham's medieval buildings were being dismantled – beam by beam – and rebuilt elsewhere. Some were even being shipped abroad. But when developers began picking apart the half-timbered Wool Hall, which had once been at the centre of the village's lucrative cloth trade, local reverend Henry Taylor knew he had to act. He enlisted the help of a wealthy patron, Princess Louise (a daughter of Queen Victoria), who paid off the developers and had the Wool Hall rebuilt in its original position. Without even realizing it, the pair had kick-started Britain's preservation movement.

So when you're ducking in and out of Lavenham's wonky, firelit pubs, spare a thought for Taylor and his princess. Without them, this place might be more humdrum than historic. There are now more than three hundred listed buildings in the village – that's one for every half a dozen people– and plenty of them have gorgeous guest rooms for you to sleep in.

The most atmospheric by far are at *Lavenham Priory*, a Grade I-listed house set in a three-acre garden of walnut trees, mint and lavender. The building was founded in the thirteenth century (almost certainly on profits from the wool trade) but it took three centuries of extensions to reach its present size. When you step into the Great Hall, you'll see guests snuggled up next to the 480-year-old inglenook fireplace, sipping warm whisky from the owners' splendid honesty bar. Climb up the creaking Jacobean staircase and you'll find spacious bedchambers equipped with French armoires, four-poster beds and – to remind you what century you're in – flat-screen TVs. Lofty white ceilings are dissected by wide beams, warped by centuries of subsidence, while great red rugs cover the original floorboards. Each bedroom has its quirks, and a quick investigation may reveal medieval wall paintings, Elizabethan strapwork designs and even see-through floor panels that look down into a swirling freshwater culvert. When you're happy there's nothing you've missed, clamber into your ornate four-poster, lay your head down for the night, and thank goodness for Reverend Taylor.

SUITE DREAMS:
Blow-the-budget hotels

217 Babington House, Somerset

Babington House, near Frome, pioneered the modern brand of country-house chic back in 1998, when its seductive mix of heritage, pampering and cool design, set against a backdrop of rolling Somerset hills, convinced hordes of burnt-out media types to ditch their Barcelona mini-breaks in favour of a fashionable weekend in the sticks. It remains as popular ever, thanks to its relaxed, home-from-home vibe. Children are positively encouraged – it even has an on-site crèche – and there's plenty to entertain big kids too, from a classic film in the cosy cinema to a massage for two in the Cowshed spa.

Ⓦ *www.babingtonhouse.co.uk. Doubles from £220. Map 2, C6*

218 The Balmoral, Edinburgh

Grande dame of Edinburgh hotels, the landmark *Balmoral* was once a grand railway hotel (its famous clock is still set three minutes fast), and it's still the city's best address for a splurge: kilted doormen welcome you into the balustraded entrance hall, and the best rooms come with sweeping views of the castle. J.K. Rowling was so enamoured with the place that she holed up here to write the last of the *Harry Potter* books; room 552 – complete with owl door-knocker – has been renamed in her honour.

Ⓦ *www.thebalmoralhotel.com. Doubles from £170. Map 4, D14*

219 Lucknam Park, Wiltshire

Standing at the end of a mile-long avenue of lime and beech trees, and boasting the requisite dovecote, croquet lawn and herb garden, this stately Georgian pile, just six miles from Bath, is the perfect place to indulge your Jane Austen fantasies. And if you tire of the Michelin-starred restaurant and award-winning spa, you can take one of the stables' suitably glossy horses on a hack round the estate's 500 acres of unspoilt parkland. Here's hoping you meet Mr Darcy en route.

Ⓦ *www.lucknampark.co.uk. Doubles from £295. Map 2, C5*

220 Barnsley House, Gloucestershire

Built by the village squire in 1697 – his initials are carved in the creamy Cotswold stone above the front door – *Barnsley House*, near Cirencester, is the English country-house retreat par excellence. It's famous for its glorious gardens – the work of garden designer Rosemary Verey – which now hold an unashamedly twenty-first-century spa. The rooms, meanwhile, are all boutique elegance, exquisitely furnished and with real log fires, while the bathrooms come with plasma-screen TVs, so you can channel-hop from the comfort of your bubble bath.

Ⓦ *www.barnsleyhouse.com. Doubles from £275. Map 2, D5*

221 Hipping Hall, Cumbria

With bucolic scenes on all sides – the Yorkshire Dales and Lake District are within easy reach – this seventeenth-century manor, near Kirkby Lonsdale, is the perfect spot for walkers who want somewhere plush to rest their weary limbs at the end of the day. The all-white bedrooms are soothing and restful, with decadent limestone bathrooms, and there's a fantastic restaurant too. An imposing fifteenth-century hall hung with tapestries, it makes a memorable setting for dinner: refined but gutsy cuisine to satisfy the heartiest of hikers' appetites.

Ⓦ *www.hippinghall.com. Doubles from £200. Map 3, C9*

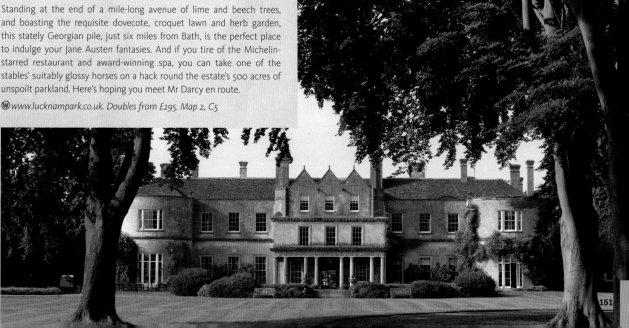

222 Augill: king of the castles

Need to know *Augill Castle*, South Stainmore, Kirkby Stephen, Cumbria ☎ 01768/341937, Ⓦ www.stayinacastle.com. Double or twin rooms including breakfast start from £160; dinner from £20 per person, children's suppers £7.50.

Map 4, E16

"Is it a real castle?" is pretty much the first question everyone asks, as turrets and crenellated facade hove into view amid the rolling fields of the Eden Valley. Emphatically yes is the answer, though quite what else *Augill Castle* is is a matter of some debate. It simply won't do to describe it as a mere bed and breakfast, or even country guesthouse, but neither is it a hotel in any regular sense. In fact, it's the home of Simon and Wendy Bennett, who rescued the decaying Victorian's gentleman's retreat in 1997 and set about its restoration, planning to take in a few paying guests along the way. Now there are fourteen rooms and suites offering a classy but wonderfully informal take on castle living, with the tone set by a boisterous welcome from Holly the dog, the house chickens scratching in the grounds and a pile of wellies at the door.

Rooms are boutiquey without being precious – think crisp linen; thick drapes; vibrant wallpaper; sturdy, reassuring furniture that you can lounge about on; and interesting curios from stacked packing cases to carriage clocks. Wood panelling, stained glass, four-poster beds and roll-top baths proliferate, and while you won't find a trouser press you will meet with glee the sherry decanter on the table and the tea tray with Assam, Earl Grey and proper ground coffee. Three of the rooms have a working fireplace and if you've always fancied a turret of your own, one turns up as a wardrobe and another as a dressing room.

The make-yourself-at-home feel continues throughout, from the family photos on the grand piano to the well-stocked honesty bar in the library. An open fire's always on the go, while breakfast and dinner are taken house-party style around a positively baronial dining table, overseen by your jovial hosts-cum-chefs. Young children are given an earlier high tea and then whisked away for games, DVDs and popcorn. It might all sound relentlessly familial and communal but there's more than enough space to do your own thing, either in the castle's own fifteen acres (complete with tennis court, tree house, trampoline and giant Jenga) or further afield in the nearby Yorkshire Dales and Lake District.

223 Rubbing shoulders with literary greats at Hazlitt's

Need to know *Hazlitt's*, 6 Frith St, Soho Square, London W1 ☎ 020/7434 1771, Ⓦ www. hazlittshotel.com. Rooms start at £175 per night (without breakfast), rising to £850 per night for the Duke of Monmouth Suite.

Map 1, C3

Hazlitt's, a portrait-filled townhouse tucked away on Frith Street in London's Soho, is a difficult hotel to write about. Not because there aren't stories hiding behind the drapes of its heavy red and gold curtains – on the contrary. But because everywhere you look, literary greats stare back at you.

Entering the lobby, for example, you're greeted by a dark, candlelit self-portrait of the hotel's Georgian namesake, William Hazlitt, who lived and died in one of the hotel's buildings when it was still a boarding house. And upstairs in one of the guest rooms, hanging high above a carved wooden desk, there's a painting of *Gulliver's Travels'* author Jonathan Swift, who often used to visit this part of Frith Street.

Take time to chat with the waistcoat-clad staff at *Hazlitt's* and you'll realize the literary connections run still deeper. Poet Mary Barker also used to live within these walls, as did William Duncombe, famed for his Latin translations of plays. You'll also discover that when Hazlitt's old house opened as a hotel in 1986, the writers kept on coming. Now, page after page of them, from Bill Bryson to JK Rowling, have made this place their temporary home in London. In fact, so many writers come here, there's even a cabinet in the ground-floor sitting room for them to leave signed copies of their books in.

If you can afford it, check into the Duke of Monmouth Suite, with its private roof terrace, working fireplaces and gleaming marble bath, filled up via the beak of a life-sized metal eagle. Or seek inspiration in the ultra-feminine Teresa Cornelys Suite, named after a famous eighteenth-century courtesan, where gilded, hand-carved cherubs cling to the enormous bedposts. In fact, there are 23 different rooms for guests to choose from, each named after people who lived in, or had some connection to, these grand old buildings.

There's no restaurant at *Hazlitt's* though, nor are there any of the usual trappings of a luxury hotel in London. Breakfast (fruit granola with hot coffee and crumbly-warm pastries) is carried into your room at a time that suits you, and the bar is a self-service affair. There's not even a doorman to hold the front door open for you when you leave. But with characters like Hazlitt and Swift for company, you'll probably be happy to stay inside.

224 The simple life at Caerfai Farm

It wasn't so long ago that Wyn Evans was mocked by his peers as an "eccentric nutter". No one's laughing anymore. The dairy farmer has gone from crank to crusader as the zeitgeist has caught up with the organic farming he pioneered over twenty years ago. For all the forward thinking of his farming, however, it's simplicity and understatement that make his campsite one of the most appealing in Wales. Without fuss or fanfare, *Caerfai Farm*, a mile from pocket-sized city of St David's, gets just about everything right.

It's the cliff-top location that draws people back time and again. Spread before every pitch is the mesmerizing seascape of St Bride's Bay; a shifting palette of greys, greens and, yes, even turquoise when Welsh weather gods smile. Beneath you is Caerfai Bay, one of the nicest notches of sand in Pembrokeshire, and virtually empty by day; for *Caerfai* campers, a path descends direct to the beach from the site.

With stupendous views, a beach in the backyard and space to spare, *Caerfai* is a firm favourite with young families. They also appreciate the sort of details that make or break a camping trip with tots: amenities include ample showers and family rooms, and a store that sells the farm's delicious cheeses alongside fresh croissants, local cakes and organic veggies. Yum.

The farm's environmental credentials only add to the feel-good factor. Catch Evans as he pedals around the site on his bike and he'll explain how cow slurry powers the milk sterilization unit or discuss the kilowatt hours of the ground-source heat pumps that combine with solar panels to heat water. Yet part of the farm's charm is that you'd never know – this is eco for ethics not avarice.

On the downside *Caerfai* is no place to camp when a gale slingshots across the bay – a perfect excuse to rent one of its four cottages, their stone walls and cracked beams exuding the character of this centuries-old farmstead.

Evans often wonders why people return year after year. Why don't they go somewhere else, he asks. And leave behind a site that ticks all boxes? Makes you wonder if there isn't something eccentric about him after all.

Need to know *Caerfai Farm*, St David's, Pembrokeshire ☏01437/720548, Ⓦwww.cawscaerfai.co.uk. Open Whitsun–Sept. Camping £7 per person per night; £4.50 without a motor vehicle; minimum seven-day stay during school holidays. Cottages from £245 per week.
Map 2, A5

225 The Temple: A folly of epic proportions

If you like a challenge, try arriving at *The Temple* at night. Tucked away down a long tree-lined carriageway that once led to stately Badger Hall, it was designed as an elegant folly in the country mansion's grounds. The house has long since disappeared, gutted by fire and finally demolished in the 1950s, but *The Temple* has been rebuilt and restored to the pristine state in which it began life in the 1780s.

Originally, the main purpose of this Greek Revival architectural ornament was to provide somewhere for afternoon gatherings, for guests to sit and take tea on the terrace that looks out across picturesque Badger Dingle. In those days, the dingle was carefully landscaped with pools, ravines and footpaths, designed by William Emes, a pupil of Capability Brown. The vista is wilder now, the dingle a tangle of greenery flanked by fir, chestnut and spruce trees, but there is something romantic in its unkemptness, and sitting on the colonnaded terrace, drink in hand, is still as pleasurable as its original architect intended.

The accommodation itself is quirky: the elegant upstairs sitting room opens out onto a balcony, furnished with high-backed armchairs and painted furniture inspired by the original designs. At the back of the room a spiral staircase leads down to a compact bedroom, slick shower room and neat kitchen that manages to squeeze in all the modern essentials: microwave, dishwasher and electric cooker.

As a romantic getaway it's ideal. In the summer months the terrace is idyllic, perfect for evening barbecues and lazy afternoons, and in autumn and winter there is a cosiness to being tucked away somewhere so utterly isolated. There is, however, plenty to explore in the surrounding area. Ironbridge Gorge and the historic town of Bridgnorth are both just a short drive away, and Wenlock Edge and the twin hills of Titterstone Clee and Brown Clee offer fantastic walks. But you might find you want to stick to gentle strolls through Badger Dingle – it is after all your own private hideaway.

Need to know *The Temple*, Badger, Shropshire is six miles from Bridgnorth. It sleeps two and is bookable through the Vivat Trust (☏0845/090 0194, Ⓦwww.vivat.org.uk). A week's rental costs from £635, though in low season three-day breaks are available from £365. No children under 16.
Map 3, C11

THE BIRDS AND THE BEES

wildlife and nature

Britain may be a crowded, urbanized nation, but we were once all farmers and the siren pull of the land still stirs something elemental in us. We go to great lengths to look after our remaining natural habitats, whether it's a cherished patch of back garden or one of the fifteen national parks that conserve our mountains and moorland, forests and wetlands. And beyond our parks and gardens there's a long British affinity with nature that expresses itself in many ways – an obsession with the weather, the visceral battle over fox-hunting, the poetry of William Wordsworth or Ted Hughes; and of course we're famous for treating our dogs better than our children. In the absence of lions and tigers and bears, the British celebrate the unsung corners of nature and in doing so find genuine delight – where else in the world do armies of twitchers assemble for the prospect of spotting a little brown bird? Or do the first daffodils of the year spark letters to the national press? Out in the country, there's much to experience that requires little effort and expense – think of the joy of bluebell woods in May, for example, or of fragrant lavender fields in July. Nature reserves, and protected woodland and wetland areas, are found even within the biggest towns and cities, while successful conservation projects drive tourism in some of the most beautiful parts of the British Isles – from wild osprey viewing in the Lake District to the world's first bumblebee sanctuary in Perth and Kinross. And if only the big beasts will do, you can start with the great bustard (the world's heaviest flying bird, half the size of a man), now being reintroduced to Wiltshire, before making your way to see Northumberland's ancient wild cattle, tracked on foot through the fields at a safe distance. This is as close to big game as indigenous British wildlife gets, though for heart-in-the-mouth thrills nothing beats a trip to Britain's whale-watching capital, the Isle of Mull, or to Cardigan Bay to see dolphins leaping through your boat's bow wave.

226 Getting cute: the seals of Blakeney Point

Huge, innocent black eyes, feathery whiskers and a blubbery, white body rolling around on the sand: is there anything cuter than a baby seal?

Healthy populations of seals live in colonies all along Britain's coastline, but one of the most rewarding spots to view them is Blakeney Point in Norfolk, which has been protected by the National Trust since 1912. Boat trips run out to the three-and-a-half-mile spit of sand that shelters Blakeney Harbour, where a colony of around five hundred can usually be found basking on the beach.

Boats drift right up to the colony, engines cut, where the honking, snorting and wriggling goes on throughout the year. There are grey and common seals here – most simply ignore the cameras, their huge, fat bodies seemingly glued to the beach, but others entertain their guests with shows of speed and agility. Comically torpid on land, seals are explosive in the water, splashing and diving right past the boat, close enough to touch (don't, though – seal bites are far from cute).

Come between June and August and you'll spy loveable common seal pups (the greys breed in November and December), occasionally peering at the boat with mournful, wide eyes; some look as if they are about to burst into tears. You might cry yourself if you forget your coat – the flat marsh and dunes that surround the point are hammered by North Sea breezes, even in summer. Weather allowing, trips also include a stop at the end of the spit where an information centre is housed in an old lifeboat station; terns, plovers and oystercatchers are regular visitors outside.

If this was Australia a high-tech catamaran would be conducting tours of the "Seal Experience". But this is Norfolk. Experienced skippers like Jim Temple run trips in small open-top boats and the *Anchor Pub* at Morston doubles as the ticket office. Boats go out every day, but times are not fixed and vary according to the tides; ask at the pub for details.

Need to know Temples Seal Trips (T 01263/740791, W www.sealtrips.co.uk) is based at Morston Quay, on the A149 just outside Blakeney, Norfolk. Trips run daily April to October and last 1hr, but call ahead to confirm times. They cost £8 per adult. Map 3, E11

227 Twitching in the suburbs

The London suburbs are probably the last place you'd expect to find one of Europe's most important ecological areas. The hazy lassitude of a summer's day in leafy, sedate Barnes is briefly disturbed every few minutes as planes from Heathrow roar overhead, but the jets aren't the only ones using this flightpath. Over two hundred species of birds now call this unlikely spot – the London Wetland Centre – home, including lapwing, sparrowhawk, redshank, teal and even the elusive bittern; it's a roll call that's enough to make any serious twitcher prick up their binoculars. But far from being the preserve of serious bird aficionados alone, a day out in this hundred-acre oasis of conservation, created from the old Thames Water reservoir a decade ago, offers millions of Londoners the chance to experience wildlife unparalled in a major capital; to swap the grey city pigeon for the dazzling blue flash of a kingfisher, buzzing bluebottles for the electric-green dragonfly, and urban rat-runs for water vole colonies. What better way to spend a lazy country day out without leaving the city?

The emphasis at the centre is firmly on conservation rather than jaw-dropping avian displays – more *Springwatch* than *Planet Earth* – and while pondlife, reedbeds and wader scrapes may not seem particularly sexy as the natural world goes the free hourly guided tours by passionate volunteers bring the quirks of the various species and their habitats to fascinating full colour. Asian rice paddies and other wetlands of the world have been lovingly re-created to attract non-native species, and from the three-storey observation tower, your patience may be rewarded with a rare sighting of a passing feathered visitor from sunnier climes.

Afterwards, wander the paths that crisscross the wetlands, sidestepping an adorable line of ducklings as they scuttle across, and pausing to watch shovelers ducking and diving in the streams. As you settle down in a sunny spot to enjoy a pondside pinic the importance of closing all those gates suddenly becomes clear – the last thing you want is that arctic goose you were admiring earlier to take a sudden fancy to the sandwiches.

Need to know London Wetland Centre, Queen Elizabeth Walk, London SW13 ☎ 020/8409 4400, Ⓦ www.wwt.org.uk/london. Open daily: summer 9.30am–6pm; winter 9.30am–5pm. Adults £10, children £5.50.
Map 1, E4

228 Peering into the Devil's Beef Tub

"A deep, black, blackguard-looking abyss of a hole it is, and goes straight down from the roadside, as perpendicular as it can do". For Walter Scott, as for countless other Borders chroniclers, the Devil's Beef Tub, a sheer scree 500-foot hollow looming out of an emerald landscape due north of Moffat, was fertile literary territory, devilish in name and often nature, and rich in lore.

A cartographical oddity even among the *cleuchs* and *dods* of Tweedsmuir, the Devil's Beef Tub takes its rather gruesome title from its reputation as a hideout for stolen cattle, in the days when the Borders was akin to a Scottish Wild West. It was also at various times a refuge to such diverse mythical and historical figures as Merlin ("with hair growing so grime, fearful to see", as one account put it), Robert the Bruce and William Wallace. But make no mistake: this is one of southern Scotland's most dramatic sights, both from its approach by road, and – if you have the nerve – close up from the higher reaches of the Tub's eastern flanks.

Driving up the A701 from Moffat, the "abyss" falls away from the right-hand lane, a hazard more obvious when looking back at the road from up above the Tub itself, as lorry after articulated lorry precariously skirts the hollow's western crown. Back in the Beeftub's turbulent past, at least one wretched soul tipped himself in, a Jacobite who, according to legend, escaped from his captors by rolling down the chasm "like a hedgehog" in his plaid. Peering down from the precipitous track below Great Hill, gashed at regular intervals by chutes of loose rock, it's obvious he can't have taken such a leap lightly.

As the track tails down to the hollow's southern extremities, so the vertigo lessens and the bracken thickens. With the admirable endeavours of the Borders Forest Trust set to return much of the area to its natural woodland habitat, though, this Devil, in the not too distant future, may well wear another face entirely.

Need to know The Devil's Beef Tub is just off the A701, approximately five miles north of Moffat in Dumfries and Galloway. Access is via the gate on the right-hand side of the road, just beyond the viewpoint on Ericstane Hill; look out for the Annandale Way sign. For more information, see Ⓦ www.bordersforesttrust.org.
Map 4, D15

229 Shags, skuas and twites: birdwatching in Shetland

Shetland's isolation amid some of the richest fishing grounds in Europe make it a very special place for sea birds. In fact, over a million – more than ten percent of Britain and Ireland's total as a whole – make the archipelago their home during the summer breeding months. The sheer diversity of what's on offer, combined with some jaw-dropping scenery, make birdwatching here an exhilarating experience for both dedicated twitcher and the intrigued amateur alike.

One of the first places you catch sight of if you arrive by air, the RSPB reserve at Sumburgh Head is a dramatic introduction to Shetland's Mainland, rising sharply out of the land only to plunge a sheer 300ft into the ocean. It's a steep yet accessible ascent to the Robert Stevenson-built lighthouse that tops the spur, a focus for circling twites and a perfect place to survey this rich birding ground. Between May and August, guillemots pack into the rocky lower ledges of the cliff face alongside the raggedy nests of shags, while further up, kittiwakes and razorbills can be spied in the cracks and crevices. Squadrons of gannets fly overhead to feeding grounds elsewhere, great and Arctic skuas fill the skies, while fulmars congregate at the cliff's highest points. Amidst a cacophonous chorus of noise, the undoubted stars of the show are the wonderfully comic puffins ("tammy nories"), which can hold more than sixty small fish in their beaks at any one time and will let you within arm's length.

And it's not just the RSPB reserve that makes Sumburgh Head such a memorable wildlife experience. Grey seals bask at the foot of the cliffs, an occasional target for killer whales, while in summer the seas are sometimes home to minke whales and harbour porpoises. Sightings are largely down to luck but you're advised to take a specially tailored tour to increase your chances. And on clear days you can see to the mighty cliffs of isolated Fair Isle, whose own vast bird population is frequently augmented by lost migrants, blown onto the island from their travels to more exotic climes.

Need to know Shetland Nature (℡ 01597/733372, Ⓦ www.shetlandnature.net) include Sumburgh Head as part of their Mainland Biodiversity Tour (£75 per person; max 6 in a group). Telescopes and binoculars are provided, warm clothing and rugged footwear essential. See Ⓦ www.rspb.org.uk/reserves and Ⓦ www.visitscotland.com for more information.
Map 5, F18

Few places in Britain juxtapose so violently the destructive impulses of man and the timeless fecundity of nature as Orford Ness. This wild and remote shingle spit, stretching for some ten miles along the bleak Suffolk coastline, is an ecologically unique nature reserve of brackish lagoons, mud flats, grassland, salt marsh and, above all, shifting swales and ridges of shingle. Home to wildfowl and waders, the spit preserves flora of such scarcity that it's the most important of its type in Europe. But while Orford Ness, protected by the National Trust, today fulfils a crucial conservation role, for much of the past century this lonely, wind-battered stretch of shore, off-limits to all but a handful of boffins, concealed some of Britain's darkest and most sinister military secrets.

It's nearly twenty years since "the island", as it's known hereabouts, was purchased from the Ministry of Defence, but the place still sends shivers down the spines of locals old enough to remember when intruders were kept at bay with security fences and police watchtowers. Though rumour was rife, nothing was known of the purpose of the enigmatic shapes, a series of spectral pavilions that still pierce the flat horizon.

The history of Orford Ness traces the paranoia of the twentieth century. For seventy years it was a hub of intensive military experimentation, testing bomb ballistics, radar and more. As Cold War fears gripped, laboratories were constructed to test the components of nuclear weapons, and by 1968 it was the nerve-centre of Cobra Mist, an Anglo–American radar system that could penetrate deep into Soviet territory.

So it's with some trepidation that you clamber from the ferry onto the island jetty, and hike across the tussocky marsh grass towards the huddle of abandoned buildings that flank the ness's old airfield. It's a scene of apocalyptic dereliction: rusting, leaky hangars caked in mildew and guano; rotting prefabs, reclaimed by Triffid-like bracken. It becomes even more desolate as you venture across a narrow creek onto the shingle itself, and trudge towards the ghostly "pagodas", constructed over the nuclear-testing pits. Jagged metal spikes jut from disembodied concrete walls; a lonely watchtower punctures the gun-metal sky.

Yet amid this dystopia, nature doesn't just cling on – it thrives. Undisturbed by man, rare sea pea flourishes along the drift line of the beach; graceful avocets and oystercatchers flock to the rippling lagoons; a merlin skims across the verdant marshes. As wilderness reclaims this hostile, grimly compelling place, there can be few more elegiac statements on the transience of man.

Need to know Orford Ness (☎ 01728/648024, Ⓦ www.nationaltrust.org.uk; £7.20) is accessible only by National Trust ferry from Orford Quay (April–June & Oct Sat only; July–Sept Tues–Sat; outward boats run 10am–2pm; last boat back 5pm). It's best visited from early August when all three of the colour-coded trails that crisscross the island are open; stick to the paths as unexploded ordnance still litters the site.
Map 3, F12

231 In the shadow of ancient oaks in Epping Forest

Need to know Epping Forest stretches for twelve miles from east London to southwest Essex, and can be accessed via the central line stations of Loughton, Theydon Bois or Epping. For more information contact the visitors' centre in High Beech (☎ 020/8508 0028).

Map 2, E5

Queen Victoria would probably have disapproved of paintballing. In 1882 when that redoubtable lady declared Epping Forest would henceforth be protected for "the use and enjoyment of my people for all time", she almost certainly had rather more sedate entertainments in mind. Today, the London area's largest open space remains a uniquely safeguarded area, as ecologically vital as it is historically significant, and with six thousand acres the activities of a day out are limited only by your imagination and the vagaries of the weather.

One of the last remaining vestiges of the ancient woodland that once blanketed England, Epping appears in local annals from at least the twelfth century. By Tudor times it had become the playground of royalty, and, later, of highwaymen (the outlaw Dick Turpin infamously used it as a hideout during the Essex Gang's reign of terror in the 1730s). For kings and killers and everyone in between, it truly has been "The People's Forest". Rambling along sandy, dappled paths on foot, galloping on horseback through meadows of waist-high grass, or splashing cross-country through muddy puddles on a dirt bike, it seems impossible that you are not, in fact, deep in the countryside, but only thirty-five minutes away from the city.

Though exploring by bike or on horseback gives you a sense of the sheer scale of the forest, the greatest pleasure is in meandering through Epping's 50,000 veteran trees, twisted by pollarding into living sculptures, which rise in spring from a sea of pristine bluebells. A popular route begins at Queen Elizabeth's Hunting Lodge, now somewhat marooned by the side of a busy road in Chingford. A peek inside reveals lovingly re-created royal hunting feasts and other displays that bring the bonhomie of a Tudor hunting party to life. From here it's a delightful stroll across lush meadows where longhorn cattle graze and rare butterflies flutter by, down to Connaught Water, one of many wetland areas in the forest, thronged with reeds, water lilies and royal ferns. Ambling on through mature hornbeam, beech, and ash, look out for the wild service tree, a true indicator of an ancient forest. Gazing skywards at gnarled oaks (home to more species of birds, mammals and insects than any other tree in Britain) marvel that when Henry VIII was bounding on horseback in pursuit of a stag through these same shadowy glades, some of these behemoths were but tiny acorns.

232 In the land of the Big Grey Man

Need to know Affleck Gray's long-out-of-print *The Big Grey Man of Ben MacDhui, Myth or Monster?* remains the definitive book on the subject, and a fascinating repository of related Highland hauntings. Ⓦ www.biggreyman.co.uk is a dedicated website, with an excellent short film shot on wintry location.

Map 5, D20

More elusive than Bigfoot, more abominable than the Yeti, the Big Grey Man of Ben MacDhui – Am Fear Liath Mòr in Gaelic – has been stalking the Cairngorms for at least a century. He's more often heard than seen – an irregular crunch-crunch of snow or scree, in queasy-making stilted parallel to the walker's own steps – and just as often experienced as heard – as an overpowering feeling of uneasiness or even sheer terror. He's big (up to 30ft tall according to one early witness), possibly more brown than grey, and pretty hairy – in short, not the kind of guy you'd want to meet down a dark sub-arctic plateau of an evening, be he hominid, haunting, hallucination or otherwise.

The account that really set the legend in motion came from one Norman Collie in the mid-1920s, a highly respected climber and professor at the University of London. He described how as the eerie footsteps sounded behind him, he "was seized with terror and took to my heels, staggering blindly among the boulders for four or five miles". A string of walkers, climbers and writers followed suit with their own uncanny encounters, sealing MacDhui's reputation as the Edinburgh Castle of Scottish mountains.

The Big Grey Man may be antisocial, but there's no denying the desolate allure of the Big Grey Man's beat, extending down from MacDhui's summit to the Lairig Ghru pass, the inky fathoms of Loch A'an and the cosmic bulk of the Shelter Stone. This last is a 1700-tonne rock that sheared off the crags at the end of the last ice age, creating a natural redoubt against the savagery of the Cairngorm climate; a night spent beneath it is an unforgettable experience in itself.

For whether you're drawn by the myth or just the landscape, the place wields a magnetic pull like few others in the Highlands, drawing hikers, climbers and wilderness seekers back year after year. But be warned: if, among the moss-rimed peat hags and ramparts of black granite, you hear that telltale crunch-crunch it may just be your last visit...

233 Wild ponies in the New Forest

Where else but Britain would a royal hunting ground that's almost a thousand years old still be called the New Forest? It was William I (the Conqueror) who claimed and named this large patch of southern wilderness, grabbing the rights to its deer and wild pigs with scant regard for local tradition. Commoners who had lived off the land for generations were summarily forbidden from trapping or shooting animals, or putting up fences to protect their crops. It was harsh, but they were offered one consolation: the right to let their livestock wander throughout the forest, grazing freely. This tradition endures today.

There are still plenty of wild fallow, roe and red deer in the New Forest, but they're rather elusive. The forest's famous ponies, however, are quite the opposite. Challenge your companions to a first-to-spot-the-pony competition as you enter by car, and you'll be doling out the honours within half a mile. Just peer between the trees and you'll soon see one munching away in a grassy clearing; drive through any of the villages and there's likely to be a mare ambling along the high street with a foal following closely behind. Shopkeepers have to be vigilant – it's a brave (or foolhardy) greengrocer or florist who displays their wares within reach.

The ponies' remarkable nonchalance is down to the fact that they have a pretty easy life. They're free to roam the forest like wild animals, but they're cared for by the present-day New Forest Commoners, who either own or rent forest land with common rights attached. Practising Commoners can also allow their sheep, cattle and donkeys to nibble the forest pasture, and let their pigs loose to forage for acorns.

Most New Forest Ponies are handsome, fuzzy-faced creatures, either chestnut or bay, which have been carefully bred to preserve the purity of the line. The only blight in their cheerful existence is the ever-increasing traffic on the forest roads, many of which are unlit: accidents occur with distressing regularity. However, a new policy of kitting ponies out in reflective collars is helping protect them – and the effect, though a little spooky, is arguably rather stylish.

Need to know For New Forest tourist information, visit Ⓦ www.thenewforest.co.uk or the information centres at Lyndhurst, Lymington and Ringwood.
Map 2, D6

234 On the rocks at Malham Cove

The soaring, curving grey-white amphitheatre walls of Malham Cove soon hove into view as you approach across the green Yorkshire fields. A 260-foot-high waterfall without the water, formed fifty thousand years ago when the outflow from a melting glacier poured over the lip of a high limestone cliff, it's a truly grand sight, on a different scale from the surrounding dales. Artists hunched over easels (brollies at the ready in case of a downpour) amid the munching sheep are a familiar sight on the approach path.

It's an easy walk from Malham village – you can push a stroller all the way to the foot of the cove – but there's work to be done if you want to unlock Malham Cove's real secrets, which lie on top of the cliff, up the breath-sapping steps to the side. From here, the views down the dale are magnificent, while underfoot is an extraordinary limestone pavement fractured into broad slabs (known as clints) and deep fissures (grykes). This giant's crazy paving captures water, moisture and shade, and has developed into a habitat for rare ferns and plants with names (hart's tongue fern, enchanter's nightshade) right out of the *Harry Potter* handbook. In early summer peregrine falcons swoop around the cove, hunting and feeding, while a squelchy tramp across the moorland beyond leads to England's highest lake, Malham Tarn, where a wetland reserve and viewing hides await.

To complete the circuit you can descend back to Malham via Gordale Scar, a deep ravine that requires strong nerves and a head for heights – the last part is nothing less than a hands-and-feet scramble down a waterfall. If you find yourself praying to the moorland spirits, you can thank them for your safe descent in nearby Janet's Foss, a mossy, wooded dell rich with the scent of wild garlic, where dippers and wagtails flit over the pool of a charming waterfall. And if shrieking kids are plunging into the water, ruining the peace and quiet? Tell them the pool has always been used as a sheep-dip. That usually does the trick.

Need to know
Malham National Park Centre (T 01729/833200, W www.yorkshiredales.org.uk) has maps and route guides for local walks, including the Malham Cove, Malham Tarn and Gordale Scar circuit. A staffed RSPB peregrine viewpoint at the base of Malham Cove operates between April and August. There's lots more information about Malham on W www.malhamdale.com.
Map 3, C9

235 Geography teacher heaven in the Peak District

Wedged between Sheffield, Manchester and Derby, it's no surprise that the Peak District is Britain's most visited national park. The park divides into two areas: the brooding Dark Peak in the north and the gentler White Peak in the south, each named on account of their different geologies. That may sound dull – but when you get out and explore, you'll find it's quite the opposite.

For these two geologies produce very different yet equally enticing landscapes, both of which can be easily explored in a weekend. Higher and wilder, the Dark Peak is formed of tracts of wind-whipped moorland interspersed with "edges", outcrops of the underlying millstone grit that create dramatic escarpments such as Stanage Edge. Although modest in height they still offer panoramic views across seemingly endless miles of heather and grass. There's little human habitation here – this barren landscape is the lonely home only to sheep, grouse, rabbits and hares.

Windswept and inhospitable though these edges may be, they're popular not just with hikers (the Pennine Way courses through) but with climbers too – the coarse-grained grit gives excellent friction and has led to the development here of some of the world's hardest technical rock climbs.

The White Peak's carboniferous limestone presents a more bucolic landscape of deep, verdant valleys – Monsal Dale is typical – and rolling hills divided into fields hatched by dry-stone walls – look carefully at a field wall and there's every chance you'll find fossil shells and plants embedded in the stones.

This fossil-rich rock also makes for great climbing on the various crags that dot the area – the attractive village of Castleton, set beside a babbling brook, makes an ideal base for exploring some of the White Peak's finest landscapes. Here you'll find the small but impressive chasm of Winnats Pass, and just to the north, the ever-shifting landslip beneath the vertiginous face of Mam Tor, which marks the boundary between the White and Dark peaks.

At the bottom of Winnats Pass is Blue John Cavern, a showcave where blue john, a rare form of blue fluorspar, was mined in the past. In fact, the limestone hills all around Castleton are pocked with water-worn cave systems for the intrepid to explore.

Need to know See Ⓦ www.visitpeakdistrict.com for more information.
Map 3, C10

236 A bird's-eye view of the Bassenthwaite ospreys

Just north of Keswick, from a clearing in the trees of forested Dodd Wood there are sparkling views down to the waters of Bassenthwaite Lake. The native red squirrel still has a foothold here, and magical spring days see blue-washed skies framing the Lakeland fells beyond. Against all odds, it's by this Cumbrian lake that a pair of wild ospreys have returned to nest and breed – flying from their African wintering grounds, en route to Scandinavia, the Bassenthwaite ospreys have holed up here instead every year since 2001, encouraged by a nest platform built for them by the Lake District Osprey Project.

The ospreys are a particularly unexpected sight in a compact region of small lakes and truncated horizons like the Lake District. These are big birds of prey, with a wingspan of up to 1.7m, famous for the way they hunt, plunging into shallow water feet-and-talons first to grab live fish to take back to the nest. Trout, pike, perch, even eels – all suffer the sharp hammer-blow from above that tells them they're just about to become dinner for an osprey mate and her chicks. After a six-week incubation it's another seven or eight weeks before the fledglings leave the nest, with the whole magnificent cycle – from arrival in early April to migration south again in September – available in close-up for anyone prepared to make the short hike through Dodd Wood to the two open-air osprey viewing platforms.

High-powered telescopes get you as close as you'd want to be to talons like that, and on most days during the season you'll see the ospreys going about their business, flying, feeding, fishing and washing, with staff on hand to answer your questions. For an even more personal view, though, make your way from Dodd Wood the few miles west to the Forestry Commission's Whinlatter Forest Park, whose visitor centre has a live video feed streamed direct from the nest. It's *Big Brother* for Bassenthwaite's birds, who successfully raise a brood a year in blissful ignorance of the Whinlatter nest-cam.

Need to know Lake District Osprey Project (Ⓦ www.ospreywatch.co.uk), Dodd Wood, Cumbria, is three miles north of Keswick, off the A591. Viewpoints are open daily 10am–5pm while the ospreys are present (usually April–Sept; check website); free access, though parking fee charged. Whinlatter Forest Park, Whinlatter Pass, Cumbria (daily 10am–5pm; Ⓣ 017687/78469, Ⓦ www.forestry.gov.uk).
Map 4, D16

GREAT BRITISH WILDLIFE EXPERIENCES

237 Selkirk's salmon leap

Ettrick Weir, near Selkirk in Scotland, is one of the best places in the world to witness one of nature's greatest phenomena: the spectacular salmon leap. Each autumn thousands of salmon make the arduous journey from as far away as Greenland back to the gravel beds where they were born at the upper end of the Ettrick River, a tributary of the Tweed. So determined are they to reach their destination that they will leap over any obstacle in their way – an awesome muscular display. You can enjoy a salmon's-eye view of it at the Philiphaugh Salmon Viewing Centre, which has an underwater camera to catch the takeoffs.

Ⓦ *www.salmonviewingcentre.com. May, June & Sept–Nov are the best months for viewing. Map 4, D15*

238 Badgered in Devon

Watching badgers feed is a mesmerizing sight, especially when they are with their cubs. From the ingeniously concealed hide at Devon Badger Watch, near Tiverton, you can watch the antics of these reclusive animals as they play and feed around their sett. Best of all, the badgers usually appear well before dusk, so if you're quiet you should be rewarded with a good view.

Ⓦ *www.devonbadgerwatch.co.uk. Open April–Oct Mon–Sat; £10. Map 2, B6*

239 On the trail of Squirrel Nutkin in Yorkshire

Though it clings on in Scotland, the much-loved red squirrel remains in catastrophic decline across much of England and Wales: the larger grey now outnumbers the native species by twenty to one. To arrest its demise, numerous reserves have been set up across the country; the densely forested Widdale Squirrel Reserve in Yorkshire is one of the best, with a special viewing area set up for you to admire the fluffy-tailed beauties as they feed. The nine-mile Snaizeholme Trail crosses delightful Dales countryside to the viewpoint from the Wensleydale town of Hawes.

Ⓦ *www.yorkshiredales.org.uk/snaizeholme-red-squirrel-trail.htm. Map 3, C9*

240 Flying high on Mull

The magnificent golden eagle breeds across the expansive hunting grounds of the Scottish Highlands and Islands, but is easiest to spot in western areas, such as the Isle of Mull, where the open moorland they favour stretches down to sea level. The island is also home to the rare white-tailed eagle (or sea eagle), Britain's largest bird of prey, recently reintroduced following its extinction in the early twentieth century. Ranger-led walks are arranged by the island's RSPB visitor centre between April and October to spot the beautiful birds, and chances are you will also catch sight of otters and deer.

Craignure Visitor Information Centre Ⓣ *01680/812556,* Ⓦ *www.rspb.org.uk/datewithnature/sites/mull. Map 4, B13*

241 Starling work on the Somerset Levels

An eerie sight greets visitors to the Somerset Levels in late autumn and winter. At dusk between November and January a swirling mass, like a colossal black cloud, fills the sky, collecting and dispersing in bizarre, ever-changing patterns. This astonishing event is laid on by thousands of starlings – residents joined by millions of migrants from northern and eastern Europe, visiting for the UK's milder winters – who gather, for safety in numbers, to roost for the night. Westhay Moor, Ham Wall and Shapwick Heath are all good places to witness the displays.

Ⓦ *www.somersetwildlife.org/westhay_moor.html,* Ⓦ *www.rspb.org.uk/hamwall and* Ⓦ *www.naturalengland.org.uk/ourwork/conservation/designatedareas/nnr/1006131.aspx. Map 2, C6*

242 Boar-n again in the Forest of Dean

Venture too far into the woods of the Forest of Dean and you might be in for a hairy surprise. Bar a short-lived reintroduction in the seventeenth century, wild boar were extinct in Britain from the 1200s until the 1980s, when farming of these master foragers began. Since then, there have been numerous escapes – and a handful of deliberate releases – and now significant breeding populations of wild boar have established themselves, notably on the Kent/East Sussex border and in the Forest of Dean. Destructive and occasionally aggressive, they're not popular with everyone, though – the first cull took place in 2010 – so go find them while you can.

See  www.britishwildboar.org.uk for more information. Map 2, C5

243 Prehistoric cattle at Chillingham

Fierce and primeval – indeed they look like the sort of animal painted by prehistoric man – wild Chillingham cattle once roamed free through the forests of Britain. Today, these handsome beasts survive only within the extensive parkland of Chillingham Castle in Northumberland, where they've remained astonishingly genetically isolated for centuries. Visit the Chillingham herd, which today numbers around ninety, and it'll be the closest thing to big-game spotting you get in England.

Chillingham Wild Cattle Park (W www.chillinghamwildcattle.com) is open Easter–Oct; tours run regularly daily except Sat; £5. Map 4, E15

244 Puffin spotting on Skomer

Lying just off the Pembrokeshire coast, spectacular Skomer Island, the second largest in Wales, is home to a huge breeding sea-bird population, including one of the UK's most important colonies of puffins. Up to six thousand of these endearing, comical birds roost here in colonies in early summer, nesting in cliff-top burrows often poached from rabbits. Come in May, when the island is carpeted in a sea of bluebells and red campion flourishes in sheltered areas.

The island is accessible from April to Oct. See W www.visitpembrokeshire. com for details of boat trips. Map 2, A5

245 Glorious bustards on Salisbury Plain

In 2009, Salisbury Plain saw the UK's first birth of a great bustard chick for over 170 years in a breeding programme designed to reintroduce the world's heaviest flying bird to our shores. Up to 3ft tall with a wingspan of 8ft, these are impressive giants, and it's quite a thrill to observe the small population of twenty or so birds, introduced from Russia in 2004, on a trip to the project's secretly located hideout in the Plain's chalky grassland.

W www.greatbustard.org. Call T 07817/971327 to prearrange ninety-minute guided tours of the project; £10. Map 2, D6

246 Avocets at Minsmere

With its long legs, distinctive pied colouring and elegant upward-curving beak, the avocet is perhaps behind only the mute swan as the most graceful of our native bird species; indeed its comely looks have made it world-famous as the emblem of the RSPB. There's no better place to watch these beautiful waders than on the Scrape, a man-made lagoon at Minsmere RSPB reserve in Suffolk, where about a hundred pairs nest annually each spring. While you're here, listen out for the distinctive boom of the bittern, Britain's rarest bird – Minsmere's reedbeds shelter around 30 percent of the UK's breeding population.

W www.rspb.org/minsmere; £5. Map 3, F12

247 On the otter trail in Devon

It takes a little skill, a lot of patience and a heap of luck to spot an otter, but the payback is sublime – a glimpse at something so rare and precious that it will leave you feeling elated. In fact, despite the difficulties, the chances of glimpsing an otter are now better than they have been for some time. After decades of decline, the British otter is alive and well and now constitutes one of the healthiest populations in Europe. Its near extinction on these isles was accountable to the usual suspects – hunting, habitat loss and pollution – but careful land management and conservancy measures have helped bring about a comeback. Devon, a stronghold of otters in Britain, makes a great place to attempt a sighting.

Playful, inquisitive, and intelligent, otters are never still; in fact, their fascination with the world around them seems almost childlike – one reason why they make for such compelling viewing. When you're on the prowl, the first factor to weigh up is that the only species found in the UK, the European otter, is mainly nocturnal, so dawn or dusk are the best times for a viewing. You also need to choose your terrain well: Devon's otters are found along rivers, streams, lakes and marshes throughout the county, but focus on the Sid, Otter and Axe rivers in East Devon, and your chances of a spotting go up significantly. Dartmoor is another place to try, as are the Taw and Torridge valleys in north Devon – "the country of the two rivers", as described in Henry Williamson's *Tarka the Otter* (1927), one of the finest pieces of nature writing in the English language, and set around here. Whilst out and about, look for soft soil near a waterway, or the distinctive paw print in mud – a round pad, about an inch long, perhaps with some evidence of webbing around the five toes. And keep your eyes open for spraint – otter poo – often on a smooth rock or a small mound. This may contain shreds of bone or fish scales and, unusually, actually has quite a pleasant aroma (it's often been compared to jasmine).

Even if you come away without a glimpse of Tarka's descendants, chances are you won't feel too downhearted, as its habitats happen to be some of the most glorious patches of countryside you'll ever have the privilege of splashing about in.

Need to know
The Tarka Trail (Ⓦ www.devon.gov.uk/tarkatrail), a 180-mile route for walkers and cyclists in north Devon, offers good opportunities for otter-watching. Butterfly Farm and Otter Sanctuary, Buckfastleigh (Ⓣ 01364/642916, Ⓦ www.ottersandbutterflies.co.uk) is a good place to view otters if you can't see them in the wild.

Map 2, B6–B7

248 Purple haze at Norfolk Lavender

Visit in high summer, when the fields hum with bees and the fragrant aroma of a million blooming flower buds permeates the air. Beyond the farmhouses an ocean of lilacs, purples and blues, row after row of neatly pruned bushes, stretches to the horizon. You can stroll into the middle of the fields along dried mud paths and just stand there, breathing it in. These are simple pleasures: there are no mountains, waterfalls or gorgeous vistas in this corner of Norfolk, but it's hard to resist the subtle magic of the lavender fields.

Used in balms, perfumes, headache cures and sleeping aids for centuries, lavender is common in English gardens, but rarely farmed like this: founded in 1932, Norfolk Lavender has nearly 100 acres under cultivation. Yet it's hard to get a sense of the smells and colours from the road, and driving into the busy car park you might think it's just another garden centre with a shop and café. Don't be put off – this is very different.

For starters, not all lavender is the same: the complex is home to the grandly titled national collection of lavender, a bewildering assortment of over two hundred lavender cultivars (sourced from three different species), many with their own distinctive smell. And during the harvest – July or early August depending on the weather – you can visit the nearby distillery, where heaps of dried lavender flowers yield precious oil used in a variety of speciality perfumes and toiletries. Insomniacs take note: the rich scent of lavender is particularly intense here. The site also maintains a large aromatic herb garden, and for those eager for an olfactory change of pace, a rare breed collection featuring jumpy wallabies, dopey alpacas and horned sheep (lots of fun for the little ones). But really, this is all about the lavender and those endless fields of purple haze. You can even eat it too: real aficionados will, naturally enough, end up with a cup of tea at the café, accompanied by lavender cake, lavender scones and delicious lavender jam.

Need to know Norfolk Lavender, Caley Mill, Heacham, King's Lynn, Norfolk ☎ 01485/570384, Ⓦ www.norfolk-lavender.co.uk. The grounds are usually open all year round, Mon–Fri 9am–6pm, Sat 9am–5pm, Sun 10am–4pm, but call ahead to confirm. The main site is free; the Rare Breeds Animal Centre and Meadow Gardens cost £3.50. Map 3, E11

249 Lundy: wild isolation on Puffin Island

There aren't many wilder places in Britain than Lundy. Arriving on this windswept island, a 400ft hulk of granite, you'll feel like you've been cast away: it's hard to believe you're just eleven miles from the Devon coast. Swarming with wildlife and fringed by the kelp forests of a marine nature reserve, it's an island where nature provides the entertainment.

The experience begins as you slip away from the mainland aboard MS *Oldenburg*. If you're lucky dolphins will ride the bow waves, and you might even spot a basking shark. You disembark in a place with only a score of permanent residents, and little regard for modern trappings. Walking is the only means of transport – a fact emphasized by the gruelling incline to the verdant plateau that caps the island.

Lundy is Norse for "Puffin Island", and these bright-beaked birds can be spotted during April and May. But at any time of year the wildlife quota far outnumbers human traffic. The shrill of sea-bird colonies – shags, guillemots, razorbills and Manx shearwaters to name but a few – echoes along the rugged west coast, while Soay sheep, Sika deer, mountain goats and Lundy ponies roam the wild terrain, grazing where the endemic Lundy Cabbage grows.

During summer an exhausting list of guided activities bring you face to face with the island's wildlife: explore rock pools on rocky shore rambles, spot seals on boat trips or don a mask and snorkel for a close-up view of some of the richest marine life outside the tropics. With its crystal-clear waters, 216 shipwrecks and coral reefs, this is also one of the UK's finest diving sites.

Aside from the wildlife, it's the wild terrain that people come here for. Walkers can discover caves and gawp at rock-stacks, crags and buttresses. Climbers test their nerves on the high seaward-plummeting walls of granite; challenging routes include the ominous-sounding Devil's Slide. Or, for a less extreme test climb the 147 steps of the decommissioned Old Lighthouse, for a dizzying panorama – at sunset orange skies silhouette the surrounding coastlines of Wales, Cornwall, Devon and Somerset.

This is real-deal island life, and once the ferry departs with its flock of day visitors the magic of Lundy's wild isolation intensifies. There are all sorts of places to stay from a converted pigsty to a castle – but why not be a true Robinson Crusoe and camp out under the stars?

Need to know The MS *Oldenburg* departs for Lundy (frequencies vary) from Bideford and Ilfracombe in Devon between March and October, costing £32.50 for a day-return. From November to mid-March a helicopter service runs from Hartland Point. See Ⓦ www.lundyisland.co.uk for more information, including accommodation. Map 2, A6

250 Seeing blue in the green wood, Hampshire

When blue is as intense and violet-tinged as this, something odd happens to the eyes: it's as if the colour is restlessly strobing at the very edge of the visual spectrum. The dappled light filtering through the beech leaves above makes the light still more diffuse and strange.

This is an extraordinary sight, by any standards. Here, in Hampshire's Micheldever Wood, tens of thousands of tiny blue flowers are spreading away into the depths of the forest. People talk about a "sea" of bluebells, or a "carpet" but neither word is anything like adequate. You wouldn't dare wade among these blossoms, still less walk on them. The effect is more like the way mist hugs the ground on a certain sort of morning – except that this mist is charged with extraordinary colour.

Like mist, bluebells in bloom are elusive, transient, almost spooky. There's something delightfully humble about them, too: perhaps it's the way their heads hang gently down to one side. This strange mixture of gentleness and grandeur perhaps explains why a bluebell wood is one of the most cherished of all English scenes: these are the ladies and gentlemen of flowers. They fit the English ideal of a soft, temperate landscape, filled with grace and ancient secrets.

It helps that bluebells really are a national treasure: somewhere between a third and a half of the world bluebell population is found in England. Of course, the English worry that their bluebells are under threat from foreign invaders. The enemy this time is the assertively upright Spanish bluebell, whose florets bristle on all sides instead of bowing meekly sideways, in the proper English way – and which likes to mate with the native form to make a more vigorous hybrid. Picking an English bluebell is forbidden by law, but you're encouraged to root out as many Spaniards as you can find.

Need to know In late April or early May you can see bluebells all over Britain, but they thrive best in woodland shade. At Micheldever Wood in Hampshire (seven miles north of Winchester, off the A33) you can just walk freely into acres of shimmering blue.
Map 2, D6

251 Site of the bumblebee: exploring Vane Farm

Need to know Vane Farm, Loch Leven, Kinross, Perth & Kinross (☎ 01577/862355, ⓦ www.rspb.org.uk/vanefarm), is accessed via the M90, Junction 5; follow signs for Vane Farm. Open daily 10am–5pm; adults £3, children 50p.
Map 4, D14

Four and a half centuries after Mary, Queen of Scots reluctantly abdicated her throne on Loch Leven's Castle Island, a new and quite different type of queen has taken up residence. It's all down to the joint efforts of the RSPB, originally in partnership with the Bumblebee Conservation Trust, who have created the world's very first bumblebee reserve, a newly sewn, twenty-acre wildflower meadow providing nourishment and – with numbers declining elsewhere at an alarming rate – much-needed habitat for these ecologically vital insects.

The meadow forms part of Vane Farm, a long-established nature reserve on the Fife–Kinross border, and, while it may still be in its infancy, it's already carpeted with an abundant supply of both annual and perennial wildflowers. As a result, rare blaeberry bumblebees (or mountain bees) have already been spotted buzzing down from the nearby birch-covered hills to feed before the berries ripen. While the bees patrol inside the meadow, you can spy swallows skimming a little way above, picking off insects to take back to their nests, many of which are attached to Vane Farm's visitor centre.

Higher up, peregrines, buzzards and kestrels circle in search of mice, frogs or carrion though the big news is the recent sighting of sea eagles. With their beclouding eight-foot wingspan, this recently reintroduced species would make a thrilling sight for a lucky visitor, though their arrival is a rather less welcome development for the reserve's longer-residing waterfowl. In fact, the loch is a twitcher's delight of birdlife, and a crucial pit stop for numerous species, including both pink-footed and greylag geese. Three hides provide front-row access to all the action on the loch, marshes and lagoons. And if you forget your flask, head to the RSPB's first-floor café, where there's also a large viewing window overlooking the entire loch with free telescopes and live camera footage.

It's also possible to get a closer perspective on the wildlife courtesy of weekend pond-dipping, with nets provided by the enthusiastic staff and volunteers. And with numerous other activities such as treasure hunts and bumblebee spotting forays, Vane Farm is a guaranteed buzz for all the family.

252 Brave the waves to the Calf of Man

Need to know Day-excursion boats depart from Port Erin (usually twice daily May–Sept). Tickets cost £20 return, and you should check in advance as landing numbers are limited (☎ 01624/832339; call between 5pm and 8pm). There's more information on the Manx National Heritage website (ⓦ www.gov.im/mnh).
Map 3, A9

The narrow channel between the Isle of Man and the tiny Calf of Man islet, off the isle's southwestern tip, may only be a few hundred yards wide, but it might just be the trickiest boat crossing you ever make. The tide races through the Calf Sound, as it's known, and with the wind up and the currents swirling it's a challenge for even the most experienced boatsmen. Safely in the harbour, you can breathe again – and start to appreciate perhaps the country's most remote bird sanctuary, breeding ground of the red-legged chough and Manx shearwater, not to mention its gulls, puffins, kittiwakes, shags and storm petrels.

Early farming families attempted to scratch a living here, while the Calf also hid the occasional fugitive in former times. These days, though, the only human residents are the wardens, who spend a great part of each year recording the migration patterns of the birds. They'll tell you what there is to see, and point out any current restricted areas, but other than that you're on your own to follow the paths that fan out across the rabbit-cropped heath and grassland. There's hardly a tree to be seen on this exposed patch of land – not much more than a mile across – but the spring wildflowers and late-summer purple heather add a splash of colour to the cliff-ringed terrain. Grey seals bask on the rocks below (they might even have come out to greet you as your boat inched in to harbour), while native Manx sheep pick a precarious living from the land.

There are hints of hard lives past in the various abandoned buildings, and in the empty lighthouses, while one of the former farmhouses is now the Bird Observatory. It's a bleak place in many ways, but also strangely compelling, and the hours slip away until it's time to leave. Even then there may be a twist, as there's a final, fingers-crossed, will-it-won't-it moment as the boat approaches – in bad weather, it's not unheard of for the boat pick-up to be impossible, at which point the Calf of Man's "no shops, no toilets, no camping" warnings really do become interesting.

253 Dolphin spotting in Cardigan Bay

Tumbling down the steep road to New Quay in Cardigan Bay on a bright summer's day, the sea beneath you glittering like a mirror, makes you feel glad to be alive. But this is as nothing compared to how you'll feel when you get out onto the bay. For this picturesque harbour, once the home of writer Dylan Thomas, is the access point for one of the most exciting wildlife displays in Britain.

Dophins appear up and down Britain's coastline throughout the year. But there are only two known resident bottlenose populations – one north of the border in Moray Firth, the other here in Cardigan Bay. Take a trip out aboard the Cardigan Bay Marine Wildlife Centre's survey boat, the 33ft *Sulaire*, and if fortunes smiles you may just find yourself spectacularly rewarded.

Rolling through the waves beneath the grand cliffs of the Cambrian coast, the boat engine chugging gently on, it feels at first as though you're searching for a needle in a very large (and very wet) haystack. But then, as if from nowhere, a torpedo of shimmering grey-black bursts out of the glassy ocean swell as a large male dolphin comes to play in your bow wave, the swoosh from his blowhole an electrifying blast of life. Then two, three, ten, now dozens more dolphins join him, the bigger males playfully bow-riding, leaping clear of the sea and snaking beneath the boat's keel.

It's a muscular display of sheer exuberance, and the energy of these enchanting show-offs is instantly transferred to the spectators on the deck. Giggles and whoops of sheer joy fill the boat, and smiles are irrepressible – the powerful sense that the dolphins are trying to form a connection with you is an unforgettable, sublime experience.

A display like this may go on for a few minutes or an hour or more, and as hippy-dippy as it sounds, it'll will put you in a good mood for the rest of the day. Who needs Prozac when there are dolphins in Cardigan Bay?

Need to know Boat trips on the *Sulaire* start at £18 for adults, £10 children for two hours (T 01545/560032, W www.new-quay.com/surveyboat). For more on the Cardigan Bay Marine Wildlife Centre, see W www.cbmwc.org. The best period for dolphin spotting is May–Oct. Map 3, A12

ECO EXPERIENCES

Whether seeking a dose of The Good Life or wanting to do your bit to keep Britain a green and pleasant land, connecting with the environment can help revive the spirit of even the weariest urban dweller. Spend some quality time in the countryside and nurture self-sufficiency skills for a brave new eco-world.

254 Wwoofing in Norfolk

Not a stuttering dog impersonation but World Wide Opportunities on Organic Farms. Discover the realities of rural life on Fincham's Farm, an isolated smallholding near the village of Garboldisham Ling in south Norfolk, from early starts to milk the goats to the intricacies of sheep-shearing. No agricultural expertise is necessary to sign up for a short break, but you're bound to glean some tips on mulching and pesticide-free ways of growing before you leave. It's a family affair where everyone chips in to earn their board and meals – and giving your food a hand on its journey from garden to plate makes it extra flavoursome.

Ⓦ *www.wwoof.org.uk. Individual UK membership costs £20 per year. Meals and accommodation on Fincham's Farm free in exchange for about five hours' work a day. Map 3, E11*

255 Centre for Alternative Technology, Wales

Nestled in the foothills of Snowdonia just three miles north of Machynlleth, this interactive shrine to sustainable living shows you exactly what an eco-home looks like. Sunshine and breezes are harnessed to keep the lights on and the rooms cosy, while water is recycled in clever ways to meet your washing needs. After a comfort break in the compost toilet, take a stroll in the permaculture garden to learn planet-friendly ways of feeding yourself. It's an inspiring vision to ponder over a glass of chilled organic wine in the eco-café.

Ⓦ *www.cat.org.uk. Adult entry £8.50 summer, £6.50 winter. Map 3, B11*

256 Dry-stone walling in Northumberland

A sunny hillside overlooking a patchwork of fields near the village of Rothbury is a scenic spot for a lesson in the ancient craft of dry-stone walling. Experienced traditional builder John Wilson demonstrates how no mortar is needed to assemble a solid, durable wall the Incas would be proud of. Selecting the right shaped stone to lock together in a neat jigsaw is slow but satisfying work – and the finished wall not only stops sheep wandering off but is a piece of living history.

Ⓦ *www.drystonewallingcumbria.co.uk. Day courses £60 per person; weekend courses £140. Map 4, E15*

257 Spot wild daffodils in Yorkshire

Spotting the first daffodils of the year is just one way of adding to the Woodland Trust's online record of how climate change is affecting Britain's wildlife and nature. Take a springtime walk in the Farndale valley by the River Dove in North Yorkshire to see a mass of yellow blooms carpeting the banks.

Ⓦ *naturescalendar.org.uk. Map 3, D9*

258 Beachsweeping in Cornwall

From putting up a fence around a cider apple orchard to hacking through gorse in the Peak District to give the wildflowers space to bloom, BTCV's charity-run conservation holidays are a chance to blow away the city cobwebs and get your hands dirty. The week-long Cornish Beachsweep in Falmouth is one of the most rewarding: after a day combing the magnificent beaches, batten down for the evening in Tregedna Farm's stylish converted barn for a communal meal with like-minded volunteers.

Ⓦ *shop.btcv.org.uk. The Cornish Beachsweep costs £290, including board and accommodation. Map 2, A7*

259 Chasing waterfalls at Pistyll Rhaeadr

The sense of detachment increases the further you go along the lane. Houses stutter then fall behind. The broad valley narrows and becomes secretive. Soft hills steepen into bluffs. Then at the valley head, with Llanrhaeadr village four miles back, you glimpse Pistyll Rhaeadr above the trees. Welcome to the highest waterfall in Wales, a majestic cascade that tumbles down over 230ft of Silurian cliff-face, and one of the most enchanting locations in this most magical country.

It's not only today's visitors who think so. In legend, the waterfall represented the gateway between the living in the pastoral valley downstream and the dead in the Berwyn Mountains – the Rhos y Beddau or "moor of graves" whose thrillingly empty hills peel away behind. The original Celtic King Arthur is said to have (war) lorded it over these bleak uplands, perhaps erecting some of the stone circles that can be reached on little-tramped trails. Another tale relates that the valley beneath the waterfall was a sacred space for the druids. Who can blame them with scenery straight from a mythic blockbuster?

The focus for day-trippers who arrive in their hundreds in summer is a café beneath the waterfall, originally built as a religious retreat in the eighteenth century. Yet to appreciate the ancient soul of Pistyll Rhaeadr you have to escape the happy crowds, forgo the cream teas and take to the trail. Climb up behind the café to peer over the lip of the cascade or ascend Berwyn Ridge to Arthur's Saddle. Only in solitude can you sense the stillness of a landscape that is steeped in myth.

Better still, stay overnight. The café offers bed, breakfast and balconies with a view of the waterfall, or you can bunk down in a lovely circus caravan, lined with conker-hued varnished wood. Best of all is to get under canvas in the wonderful *Retreat Campsite* beneath the waterfall. Pitched beside the Rhaeadr River at dusk, the real world seems to recede and the valley spins a cocoon of silence around itself, slowly vanishing into darkness save for the glow of your campfire.

Need to know Pistyll Rhaeadr is signposted from Llanrhaeadr, Powys. The café and members-only *Retreat Campsite* (both ☎ 01691/780392, Ⓦ www.pistyllrhaeadr.co.uk) are open all year; annual membership for the campsite (£25) is available on site or in advance.
Map 3, B11

260 A highland fling with the minke whales of Mull

A Roman-nosed grey seal looks on quizzically, nostrils flared, as the *Sula Beag* slips quietly out of Tobermory's colourful harbour. A motivational Mars bar hangs from its mast – a prize for the first person to spot a whale. This is no lazy pleasure cruise though; all on board are soon issued with a pair of binoculars and briefed on how to recognize telltale signs of cetacean activity by the enthusiastic guides, veterans of Britain's longest established whale-watching company.

Soon all eyes are fixed on the sea surrounding northern Mull, scouring the waves for the mirror-like glint of a minke whale; the search is interrupted only briefly to look for the pair of rare white-tailed sea eagles that nest on a passing headland. Glengorm Castle peers down from the island's isolated cliffs, the stepped mountains behind an autumnal riot of fawny browns and mossy greens. The craggy isles of Eigg, Skye and Rum slowly appear on the horizon as the boat plies out into whale country beyond Ardnamurchan, mainland Britain's most westerly point. The clear waters here are astonishingly rich with plankton, and attract not only many minkes but also sea birds, harbour porpoises, dolphins, basking sharks – at up to 30ft long, true leviathans of the seas – and very occasionally killer whales.

"Whale, whale", comes the cry and all heads turn to catch a glimpse of the slender dorsal fin nearby as it disappears on a deep dive. Eyes scan the water intensely as the engine goes silent. In time a pale band becomes visible in the blue, then a flipper, and soon the minke surfaces gracefully with a puff of fishy breath. It rolls its body through the water in a graceful arc, dips down, but then returns again – and again – to continue its gentle investigation of the boat. As if playing to its captive audience the whale rolls over elegantly, exposing a long, slender white belly before finally bidding the boat adieu and vanishing almost as suddenly as it came. Passing back into harbour, the seals are still draped across the basalt columns of Seal Island, but as the year draws to a close the minkes disappear altogether; the location of their winter home remains a mystery.

Need to know Sea Life Surveys are based in Tobermory harbour on the Isle of Mull (☎ 01688/302916, Ⓦ www.sealifesurveys.co.uk). Whale-watching trips run from Easter to mid-October; a four-hour trip costs £39 per adult.
Map 4, B13

261 In search of the northern lights

Aurora borealis: it's an exotic sounding name – and an experience, you'd imagine, limited to travellers on exotic expeditions to the Arctic north. Yet with perseverance and not a little luck, it is actually just about possible to catch a glimpse of this extraordinary phenomenon on home soil.

Dubbed the Dance of the Spirits by Native Americans, the northern lights are a spectacular cosmic show caused by an atomic powwow, a rarefied encounter between solar wind (streams of particles charged by the sun) and the earth's atmosphere. As the particles are borne down the lines of the earth's magnetic field, the resultant emissions paint the night sky with shimmering tapestries of colour; different hues light up as different elements hit the plasma shield – blue for nitrogen, yellow-green or even red for oxygen.

The most ravishing displays tend to occur north of the Arctic Circle, yet around the spring and autumn equinoxes, geomagnetic storms can drive the aurora into sight of more temperate climes – Britain, and most often northern Scotland, included. Subzero temperatures and clear skies are a prerequisite for the best shows – it goes without saying that light pollution is a no-no – and to maximize your chances you'll need to get as far from human habitation as possible, and the further north the better. You still mightn't get the spectacle of a vaulting stellar genie or *Close Encounters of the Third Kind*-esque epiphany witnessed near the poles, but even the faintest glimpse of electric-green, violet-pink or laser-orange is veritable manna from heaven, a just reward for sitting up shivering all night.

Good places to catch the northern lights include the wilds of Cape Wrath, Knoydart or even the Cairngorms; Orkney, Shetland and the Hebrides are all possibilities too. Or you might want to brave the subarctic heights of Ben Hope in Sutherland, Scotland's most northerly Munro and surely as exhilarating a vantage point as any. The curtain may rise at any time from sundown to the wee hours of the morning, though the period immediately before and after midnight – when the sky is at its darkest – is the most likely. And, if you've kept vigil thus far in vain, take heart; the coming of a solar maximum – when the solar wind is at its strongest – raises the odds dramatically of seeing the northern lights in our own backyard in the near future.

Need to know The next solar maximum is currently forecast for spring 2013. To monitor geomagnetic activity in real time, check out Lancaster University's AuroraWatch at www.dcs.lancs.ac.uk/iono/aurorawatch; as well as a striking gallery, they offer free alerts of imminent aurora by email and text.
Map 5, C18

ARE WE NEARLY THERE YET?

adventures for kids

There's never been a better time to be a child in Britain – and we're not talking about health, education and prosperity, but about kids' stuff, plain and simple. Long gone are the times when a family day out meant a visit to the dull local museum or, heaven forbid, the dreaded walk in the country. No more hushed corridors of portraits, or gloomy halls full of dusty display cases – these days, any family attraction worth its salt is high tech, hands-on and interactive, whether it's exploring the visceral thrills of the dinosaur age or the explosive elements in a former steelworks. The "look, don't touch" approach in museums, galleries and historic houses has been largely abandoned (even the National Trust is now encouraging active participation at their properties), and across Britain children are positively urged to join in – from making their own art-works and meeting their favourite authors to digging up the past and feeding the animals. Big kids (ie, grown-ups) aren't neglected either, since many of Britain's best attractions and activities are geared towards engaging the whole family, whether it's walking among the treetops at Kew Gardens, marvelling at the ocean depths in The Deep or negotiating the underground maze and water-traps at the Forbidden Corner. Meanwhile, the great British outdoors just begs kids to get wet, dirty and thoroughly excited – off-road biking, sea-kayaking, fossil-hunting, rock-pooling are all Grade A activities, guaranteed to bring a smile to otherwise dyed-in-the-wool, Wii-obsessed, online-world refuseniks. Some things need no introduction, like the thrilling rides at Alton Towers, Britain's largest theme park, or the magnificent creations at Legoland. Others, from playing Poohsticks to a visit to the panto, reverberate through the ages – gentle activities that link the generations. Gather the family, ignore the eternal, impatient cry from the back seat – "Are we nearly there yet?" – and discover the best that Britain can do for its children.

262 York's Viking time machine

York needs no introduction – the stone walls, medieval halls, Minster, tea shops and tour guides – but there's a hidden secret under the streets that archeologists have spent decades exploring. A thousand years ago York was a thriving Viking city known as Jorvik, its vitality, wealth and scope clear from the myriad buildings and artefacts found in the 1970s during work on the new Coppergate shopping centre.

After an initial five-year dig, and a couple of subsequent multi-million-pound developments (the latest in 2010), visitors to Jorvik Viking Centre get an innovative, close-up look at Viking society on the very site where the excavations took place. If you were ever going to get kids interested in the past, this is the place, with its interactive museum exhibits, role-playing Vikings and touch-screen learning, but the best bit comes right at the beginning as you descend beneath the modern-day streets and are clunk-clicked into a ghost-train-style "time capsule", which then lurches off through the streets of Viking York.

It's a clever and classy conceit that grabs you from the start, as your ride takes you right inside the excavated houses, shops and backyards, with animatronic figures hailing you in Old Norse, smoke blasting from a blacksmith's furnace, and Viking builders enjoying a tea break (no change there then). Children hunker down to play a board game, dogs fight in the street, and a rat peeks his head out from among the bloody hunks on the butcher's table. The building timbers are those discovered *in situ*, and every object – from cooking pot to amber jewellery – is a Jorvik original. Neatly redressing the one thing missing from every period-piece movie – the smell – you get decidedly authentic wafts from both farmyard and market, while every child's favourite attraction is the furiously straining Viking gent astride the outdoor latrine. This is (ahem) bottom-up history at its best.

Need to know Jorvik Viking Centre, Coppergate, York ☎ 01904/615505, Ⓦ www.jorvik-viking-centre.co.uk. Open daily 10am–5pm (4pm in winter). Adults £8.95, family ticket from £26; advance tickets (by phone or online) are advised to beat the queues.

Map 3, D9

263 Tunnel your way to the Ilfracombe's tidal pool

Kit up first with picnic rugs, wet suits, buckets, spades, snorkels and crabbing nets. Accessed via a series of long subterranean tunnels, carved through the lofty rocky cliffs, Ilfracombe's spectacular Tunnels Beaches are one of the jewels of the Devon coast. Emerge around low tide into the sunlight onto the sheltered sand and pebble beach, and you'll be able to take a dip in the magnificent tidal sea-water swimming pool, a haven for little ones. Add in an abundance of rock pools rich with sealife, the opportunity for kayaking out to a secret cove, and all the facilities you need, from a stylish family café to an indoor soft play area, and you have a superb family day out.

It was early in the nineteenth century – when the art of bathing was fully in vogue – that the tunnels were created, hand-carved by a team of Welsh miners. The beaches opened to the public in 1824, drawing gentry from far and wide to indulge in the health-giving pastime of sea-water bathing. In those days, bathing was strictly segregated: women were transported to the water's edge in horse-drawn bathing machines in order to preserve their modesty, while the men, who bathed naked, were conducted by boat to a separate pool. And just to ensure decorum was observed at all times, a bugler sat between the ladies' and gentlemen's pools, ready to blow his horn in case an errant fellow attempted to spy on the bathing belles.

Of three original tidal pools at the Tunnels Beaches only the ladies' pool has survived the ravages of storms to this day, its inviting glassy shallows twinkling with Blue Flag purity. And once the little ones have had their fill of splashing about, there's plenty more to keep them entertained. Numerous rock pools teem with weird and wonderful species: limpets and top shells, periwinkles and anemones among many. Look further afield and bigger creatures abound: seals and porpoises are often spotted from the rocky spits jutting seaward, while sea bass, pollock and conger eels are sometimes seen darting beneath snorkellers. There really can't be many better ways to spend a day in the West Country.

Need to know Tunnels Beaches, Ilfracombe, Devon Ⓦ www.tunnelsbeaches.co.uk. Open Easter hols to Sept daily 10am–6pm (summer hols until 7pm); Oct (except half-term) Tues–Thurs, Sat & Sun 10am–5pm. Adults £1.95, children £1.50, under-3s free. The tidal pool is visible three hours before and after low tide – check website for tide times.

Map 2, B6

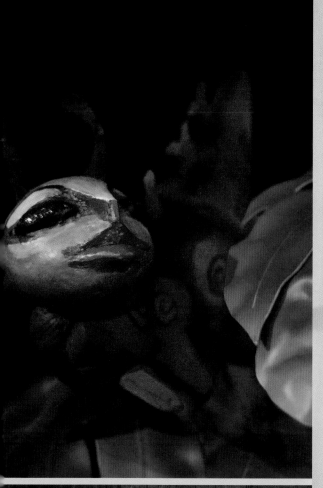

264 Spellbound at the Little Angel Puppet Theatre

It is dark, save for several bouncing streaks of DayGlo colour. Three caterpillars are singing in three-part harmonies, and somewhere in the mix is a gang of angry strawberries. You are not insane, but an audience member at Islington's wonderful Little Angel Puppet Theatre. And next time, you and your brood will be shoving the other kids out of the way so you can get to the front.

The setting is a dark, slightly draughty room, a former temperance hall with a high ceiling and wooden pews. Expert lighting illuminates the tiny set and its characters, to a playful, enduringly catchy score. The black-clad puppeteers are in full view, but soon melt away until all you see are the expertly manipulated stars of the show. There's much humour in the telling, with more than one joke thrown in for the benefit of watching parents, many a foreign accent and character stereotype, and myriad visual gags. The puppeteers, who sing, act and perform intricate manoeuvres, connect beautifully with the rapt kids (all nicely hypnotized and quiet), and although most performances are aimed at very young children, the accompanying adults cannot fail to be equally enchanted.

Little Angel has been running puppet shows here since 1961, when it was set up by innovative puppeteers John and Lyndie Wright. The hall seats a hundred, but feels much more intimate, and the workshop at the back is where many of the puppets are born. The above-mentioned caterpillars are characters from Barb Jungr's *The Fabulous Flutterbys*, but the programme features many other productions throughout the year, some of them recurring favourites, such as *Fantastic Mr Fox* and *Cindermouse*. The same show normally runs for several months, so there's plenty of time to book the family in; it's also truly affordable, with ticket prices ranging from a fiver to £12 or so.

The magical glow of the lights, the resonating voices, the accessible melodies and the artistry of the movements – it all makes the prosaic slapstick of the old Punch and Judy shows seem rather flat. And so, as the dancing DayGlo blobs flit about, and the surrounding children's eyes grow vast with wonder, even the most sensible soul in the room will just give in, sit back and listen to what the singing caterpillars have to say.

Need to know Little Angel Puppet Theatre, 14 Dagmar Passage, London N1 ☎ 020/7226 1787, Ⓦ www.littleangeltheatre.com. Map 1, E1

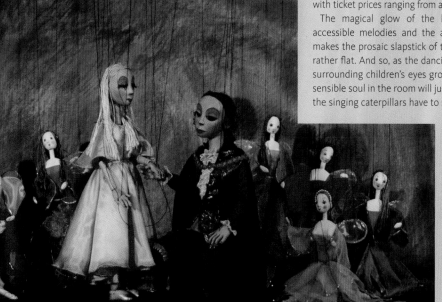

265 Getting in touch with your inner bear

Now approaching his 85th birthday, A.A. Milne's "bear of very little brain" has become a global phenomenon, with the original stories translated into fifty languages and Pooh, Tigger, Eeyore, Piglet and co featuring on duvet covers from Beijing to Barcelona. While the Disney films might have given him a jarring US accent, Pooh is, of course, a quintessentially English bear and the geography of his world is based firmly around Milne's home in deepest Sussex.

Here among the open heathland and pine trees of Ashdown Forest you'll find many of the locations – the Hundred Acre Wood, the Enchanted Place and the Heffalump Trap – captured so beautifully in the books by illustrator E.H. Shephard. Most are within a short drive of the village of Hartfield which functioned as Milne's country escape from the 1920s until his death in 1956. The bear associations have not been lost on local entrepreneurs – at the end of the high street you'll find the "Pooh Corner" shop and tearoom, home to the world's largest selection of "Pooh-phernalia" and often packed with rapt Japanese teenagers ("Pooh-san", even outsells Hello Kitty in the land of the rising sun).

From Hartfield, pilgrimage can be made to the various Pooh-related sites. Best of all is Poohsticks bridge, a perfect representation of the bridge where Pooh invented a new game by absent-mindedly dropping pine cones off the side. Today, you will struggle to find a pine cone or even a stick within a hundred yards of the bridge so it's worth bringing along your own. The rules are simple – face upstream, release your sticks from an equal height (throwing is strictly forbidden), then rush over to the other side to see whose comes out first. On a fine day, with the sound of birdsong and the lazy flow of water in your ears you can't help imagining Pooh and Christopher Robin in the same spot. In the words of the latter: "I think we *all* ought to play Poohsticks".

Need to know Ashdown Forest Area of Outstanding Natural Beauty covers 6400 acres of the High Weald in East Sussex (Ⓦ www.ashdownforest.org). The House at Pooh Corner in Hartfield (Ⓦ www.houseatpoohcorner.com) offers tours and information on "Pooh Country".
Map 2, E6

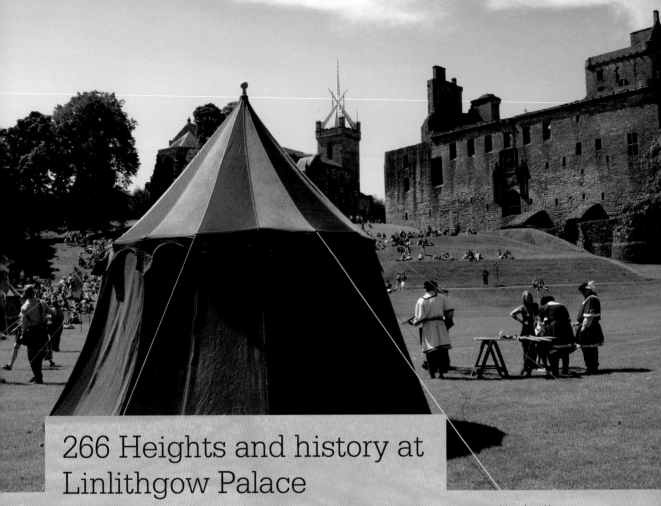

266 Heights and history at Linlithgow Palace

Fifteenth-century Linlithgow Palace may be in ruins, its windows open to the sky, but it has enough hidden spiralling staircases, stony dungeons and vertiginous walkways to keep adventurous kids happy for a good couple of hours, and the huge roofless Great Hall is a marvellous place to run amok.

There's plenty of child-friendly entertainment in the summer, from staged medieval games and jousting to falconry, displays of weaponry skills and tours by costumed guides. But at any time of year there's plenty to engage kids actively in the castle's history. You can encourage them to look for the remnants of the drawbridge and the other means and devices that kept intruders at bay and prisoners confined. In the courtyard, children will love the flamboyant carvings of mermaids, shepherds and animals on the three-tiered octagonal fountain; it now runs with water every Sunday in July and August, but was made to flow with wine when King James V married Mary of Guise in 1538. Looking up, what appear to be window slits above were in fact privvies, a fact that's bound to go down well.

On the domestic front, peering at the huge fireplace in the kitchens helps you imagine how the castle's lavish banquets were produced, with meat being turned on spits by little boys who were called "turnbrochies". From the kitchen, chutes propelled rubbish into the surrounding dry – and doubtless very smelly – moat.

Continuing to the Great Hall, infant jaws will drop at a fireplace so big it required whole tree trunks to fuel it. And don't forget to point out the minstrel's gallery, where party entertainment was provided and you can still see the hooks from were tapestries were hung. Beyond are the bedrooms, and the lofty heights of Queen Mary's Bower, with sweeping loch views and a satisfyingly dizzying perspective on the castle itself.

Need to Know Linlithgow Palace, Kirkgate, Linlithgow, West Lothian ☎ 01506/842896, Ⓦ www. historic-scotland.gov.uk. Open daily: April–Sept 9.30am–5.30pm; Oct–March 9.30am–4.30pm. Adults £5.20, children £3.10.

Map 4, D14

267 Children's stories on seven storeys

If you don't have a child, kidnap one. And then take that child (and yourself) straight to Seven Stories, Britain's only museum dedicated to celebrating the art of children's literature. Tucked beneath the Byker Bridge in Newcastle's Ouseburn Valley, the inviting, bright white building is called Seven Stories (a) because it's got seven storeys and (b) because there are, reputedly, only seven types of story you can tell.

The entrance level, Level Three, houses an enormous bookshop rammed with all sorts of wonderful children's books – from charming Paddington Bear stories by Michael Bond to Jacqueline Wilson's most recent *Tracy Beaker* tales. But before delving in, head upstairs to Level 4, The Sebastian Walker Gallery, where changing exhibitions bring children's picture books to life using hands-on, interactive games, quizzes and models. Past exhibitions have included "Green Drops and Moonsquirters", a celebration of Lauren Child, creator of the beloved *Charlie and Lola* and an imaginative retelling of Hans Christian Andersen's *The Princess and the Pea*. Children could sit at Charlie and Lola's kitchen table, dress up in Charlie and Lola outfits, play with dolls' houses and perform *Princess and the Pea*-themed puppet shows to their friends and family. Tattered manuscripts and original illustrations are also dotted about up here – look out for those by Quentin Blake, most famous for his illustrations of Roald Dahl's stories, as well as the little pencil-etchings of ballerinas by Ruth Gervis, sister of *Ballet Shoes* author, Noel Streatfeild. Fans of Philip Pullman will love the manuscripts of the *His Dark Materials* trilogy while the younger generation can pore over Geraldine McCaughrean's lively early versions of *The Kite Rider*.

Pop upstairs to Level 5, the Robert Westall Gallery, named after the Tyneside-born writer with a penchant for tales of cats, war, the supernatural and love, an intriguing combination that's explored further through old photographs, manuscripts and original artwork of all of his most familiar stories – don't miss the mock 1940s radio that has recordings of the author himself reading from his books. While the adults examine these scripts, kids can chill out in the Book Den with a good book or two. And if that isn't enough, check the timetable for talks by authors on Level 7: recent speakers include Francesca Simon, author of the *Horrid Henry* series. Don't forget to stop by the bookshop on the way out. Oh, and give that kidnapped child back.

Need to know Seven Stories, 30 Lime St, Newcastle upon Tyne (T 0845 271 0777, W www.sevenstories.org.uk) is accessible by bus #22 from Central Station (stop "Tanner's Arms"). Open Mon–Sat 10am–5pm, Sun 10am–4pm. Adults £6, children £5, under-3s free. Map 4, E15

CHILD-FRIENDLY MUSEUMS

Britain's museums and galleries have upped their game, now entertaining and enthralling young visitors as well as educating them. Where "don't touch" used to be a common command, these days children are positively encouraged to interact, often involving some mind-blowing hands-on displays. Here are some of our favourites.

268 Roald Dahl Museum and Story Centre, Great Missenden

This is no straight-laced museum but a place for a phizz-whizzingly good time. Children can dress up as Dahl's characters, make up funny words, smell walls that look like chocolate and create illustrated tales. As well as meeting the great storyteller through pictures and manuscripts, you can even sit in his chair and jot down your own swizzfiggling story ideas.

Ⓦ *www.roalddahlmuseum.org. Open Tues–Fri 10am–5pm; Sat & Sun 11am–5pm. Adults £6, children £4. Map 2, E5*

269 Natural History Museum & Darwin Centre, London

Did your kids see *Night at the Museum*? Well this is where prehistoric creatures, science and nature truly come to life before your eyes. Come face to face with the animatronic T Rex, stand beneath the world's largest mammal and feel the ground move in an earthquake. Witness giant tarantulas among the specimens in the Darwin Centre's Cocoon, and discover just how humans are changing the environment. Inspirational for all ages.

Ⓦ *www.nhm.ac.uk. Open daily 10am–5.50pm. Free. Map 1, B4*

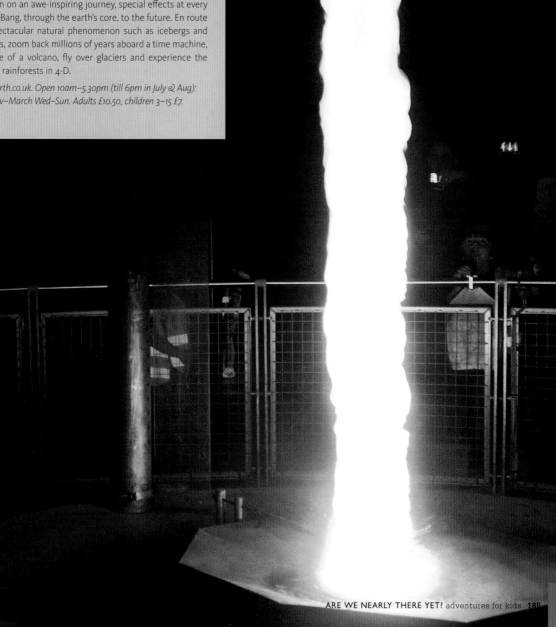

270 Manchester Art Gallery

With their highbrow culture and silent exhibition halls, art galleries were once fun-free zones for kids. But Manchester Art Gallery is just one place where things have changed. Dressing up in imitation of the artworks, chariot racing and a gallery filled with tactile objects all bring art into creative young hands. Here you get backpacks stuffed with activities for 7- to 12-year-olds and tool belts with binoculars and magnifying glasses for younger children. All this, plus a calendar packed with workshops and events, in a buggy-friendly venue with a decent family café.

Ⓦ *www.manchestergalleries.org. Open Tues–Sun 10am–5pm. Free. Map 3, C10*

271 Our Dynamic Earth, Edinburgh

ODE takes children on an awe-inspiring journey, special effects at every turn, from the Big Bang, through the earth's core, to the future. En route they'll witness spectacular natural phenomenon such as icebergs and the Aurora Borealis, zoom back millions of years aboard a time machine, stand on the edge of a volcano, fly over glaciers and experience the Arctic, oceans and rainforests in 4-D.

Ⓦ *www.dynamicearth.co.uk. Open 10am–5.30pm (till 6pm in July & Aug): April–Oct daily; Nov–March Wed–Sun. Adults £10.50, children 3–15 £7. Map 4, D14*

272 Magna Science Adventure Centre, Rotherham

Learn all about the elements on a high-octane, interactive adventure through fire, water, earth and air. Make waves, squirt cannons and get rained on. Dry off by a towering fire tornado and experience a ground-shaking pyrotechnic display. Drive a JCB and explode a rock face. Spin on a gyroscopic chairs and play on trampolines, spinning bowls and tilted roundabouts – all in the interest of science, of course.

Ⓦ *www.visitmagna.co.uk. Open daily 10am–5pm (closed Mon Nov–March). Adults £9.85, children £7.95. Map 3, D10*

273 Up to the forest canopy at Kew's Treetop Walkway

They may not look too high from below, but once you've climbed the 118 steps to the Xstrata Treetop Walkway and are standing, heart pounding, 60ft above the ground, you suddenly realize just how tall the trees really are. From here, the views stretch across Kew Gardens – a vast swathe of lush greenery, with the Victorian Temperate House reduced to the size of a doll's house – and beyond, towards Richmond Park and central London.

For kids, there's a real freedom in being up so high, the walkway feeling almost precarious beneath their feet as they pound enthusiastically along. Up in the tree canopy, you're able to notice things that you couldn't from the ground: the emerging blossom in spring, the budding of the spiky sweet chestnuts, and more varieties of green than you could have imagined existed. The walkway enables you to really appreciate the landscaping of the Botanic Gardens, and to study arboreal nature at close quarters – the insects and squirrels that make their home among them, not to mention the chattering green ring-necked parakeets that have populated this leafy part of southwest London.

When you've had your fill of being up in the sky, the trouble is knowing what to do next – the three-hundred-acre gardens are such a treasure-trove of delights that it would be impossible to squeeze everything into one visit. If being up in the trees has left the kids desperate for more clambering about, head underground to experience Kew's labyrinthine, human-sized badger sett; or to Climbers and Creepers, where they can pretend to be insects inside carnivorous (well, wooden) plants.

Though spring – with the purple flush of bluebells and dusky blossoms colouring the grounds – is undeniably a wonderful time to visit Kew, the gardens are a joy at any time of year, and the tropical climes of the Palm House will keep you warm on even the chilliest of days. The little ones, of course, with their heads in the trees, won't even begin to notice the weather.

Need to know Kew Gardens, Surrey ☎ 020/8332 5655, Ⓦ www. kew.org. Open Feb & March daily 9.30am–5.30pm; April–Aug Mon–Fri 9.30am–6.30pm, Sat & Sun 9.30am–7.30pm; Sept & Oct daily 9.30am–6.30pm; Nov–Jan daily 9.30am–4.15pm; last entry to Xstrata Treetop Walkway 1hr before closing. Adults £13.50, children under 17 free.
Map 1, E4

274 A day out with Thomas at Kirklees

A whistle toots, clouds of smoke and steam billow skywards, and parents with their kids stream down from the car park. Children throng the playground, throw themselves around on bouncy castles, have their faces painted. There's usually something going on at Kirklees Light Railway, but today it has a special buzz: for Thomas the Tank Engine and his friends have come to town.

On the platform, the little blue-engine hisses, parents jockey (politely – this is England) to snap him with their self-conscious children, the Fat Controller (can you still say that?) looks at his pocket watch and taps his foot. Doors clatter shut, the whistle screeches, the couplings take up the slack, and with a crescendo of clanks and chuffs brave little Thomas hauls the carriages through an untidy sprawl of factory buildings and derelict land. The strains of "Thomas and Friends" bounce cheerfully down from ceiling-mounted speakers.

Suddenly, you're cruising through glorious Yorkshire countryside as the little train sails out onto an embankment, smoke streaming back from its stack. From bridges and far away in fields people wave. It's like *The Railway Children*. Oak, ash, sycamore, fireweed, ferns and foxgloves line the track, as the train swoops down then up towards the tallest freestanding building in the UK, majestic Elmley Moor Transmitting Station.

The train thunders into a deep cutting – faceted rock hewn by men long dead. Flying buttresses of sunlight slant down through the trees and smoke. The cutting becomes a tunnel – too big, surely, for Thomas and his friends, a serious piece of civil engineering. Finally, 25 minutes after setting off, the train pulls into Shelley station. More bouncy castles, coffee and soft drinks, burgers and doughnuts. Engines huff and puff, turntables turn, points are thrown, water is taken on, and the return journey begins.

Great for children, for families, for train spotters. But that little slice through the Yorkshire landscape, the steel rails and permanent way planned, financed and executed a long time ago, the embankment and cutting and tunnel, is more than kids' stuff. This is what Britain was built on.

Not bad for a day out with the kids.

Need to know Kirklees Light Railway, Clayton West, near Huddersfield, West Yorkshire ☎ 01484/865727, Ⓦ www. kirkleeslightrailway.com. Thomas and friends visit for one weekend per month (May–Aug & Nov; departures every 30min 10am–4pm). Adults £9.50, children aged 2–15 £7.50, under-2s free.
Map 3, C10

275 Stacks of fun at Legoland

Did you know the word Lego comes from the Danish *leg gohdt*, meaning to "play well"? Well, there are no limits to the possibilities for play in this plastic fantastic land constructed from over 25 million bricks. Around every corner across the park's ten kingdoms await grin-inducing creations: Lego wildlife, Lego knights, Lego pirates, Lego dinosaurs. In Miniland you'll even find Lego reproductions of famous landmarks such as the Moulin Rouge and London's skyline, the latter including a 16-foot-high Canary Wharf made from 200,000 bricks.

It may be the Lego that makes it unique (at least within Britain), but really Legoland is all about good old-fashioned theme park fun. Aimed primarily at 3- to 12-year-olds, the park boasts a dizzying array of roller coasters, water rides, trains and merry-go-rounds spun into its 150-acre labyrinth. But, unlike most theme parks, it's not just geared up for adrenaline junkies: there's plenty to amuse younger tots too. Children who break the 3'6" barrier pretty much have free reign and will no doubt be rushing for the Pirate Falls log flume, The Dragon roller coaster and the Jolly Rocker pirate ship. But even precious cargo under 3' can get high at Balloon School, spot Lego wildlife on the Orient Expedition and skipper a battery-powered boat around the lake.

Kids keen to get behind the wheel can earn their Lego licence at Driving School or power a fire engine at Fire Academy, while computer addicts can get a fix in the Xbox 360° Gaming Zone. True Lego fans will be lured by the Imagination Centre where they can pull themselves up the Space Tower for a bird's-eye view, build and test Lego models in the workshops and experience 4-D special effects in the movie theatre.

With so many attractions to cram in, be prepared for a big (and expensive) day out. Splashing out an extra £15-plus per person for a Q-Bot means you can max out on the experience by queuing remotely and saving oodles of time. And, from 2012, you'll be able to extend the experience with a sleepover at the *Legoland Hotel* currently under construction.

Need to know

Legoland, Windsor, Berkshire
☏ 01753/626182, Ⓦ www.legoland.co.uk. Open daily mid-March to early Nov; closed some Tues & Wed in April, May, Sept & Oct; opening hours vary – see website. Adults £38, children £29. Q-Bot virtual queuing device £15–40 per head.
Map 2, E5

276 Strange ways in the woods at The Forbidden Corner

As greetings go, the entrance tower gives you a pretty good impression of what is to come. Huge blinking eyes and a gaping mouth invite you on a walk down a giant tongue-tunnel, complete with reverberating, digestive burp – cue screams and laughter as the kids charge further on into the self-styled "Strangest Place in the World". It certainly defies straightforward description – call it a woodland maze within a secret walled garden, wrapped up as an eye-popping folly, and you're only halfway to understanding what makes The Forbidden Corner such a hoot.

It's a labour of love by owner and folly enthusiast Colin Armstrong and his architect friend Malcolm Tempest, who have turned part of the Tupgill Park Estate, just outside Middleham in North Yorkshire, into a highly eccentric family attraction. Trick fountains, oak-carved giants, misleading gateways, frog fountains and talking statues are just the start of it, since the maze effectively continues underground as well, with an underworld labyrinth entered through a full-sized Classical temple facade. This is an extraordinary place of revolving floors, blank doors, secret passages and subterranean forests, where nothing is quite as it seems – dare to walk through the underground waterfall, for example, and the waters miraculously part, while if out of curiosity you try the door marked "staff only", out shoots a hand accompanied by a gruff invitation to clear off.

By the time you emerge, back into the gardens for another round of japes and follies, you'll be drenched (no opportunity's missed to squirt you with water) and any children in the vicinity will be approaching a count of ten on the Shriek-o-meter. The Forbidden Corner does have paths and signs, and a maze guide written in rhyming couplets, but to be frank, any prospect of following a formal route disappears once the first large talking mouse tells you a joke. And if, at the end of the day, you've learned anything, it is never, ever to go back down the dungeon corridor and see what's making that terrible banging noise on the door.

Need to know The Forbidden Corner, Tupgill Park Estate, Coverham, Middleham, North Yorkshire ☎ 01969/640638, ⓦ www.theforbiddencorner. co.uk. Open Easter–Oct Mon–Sat noon–6pm, Sun 10am–6pm; Nov–Christmas Sun only 10am–6pm. Adults £10, children aged 4–15 £8, under-4s free, family ticket £34. Advance booking for timed entry is essential, by phone or online.
Map 3, C9

WILDLIFE FOR KIDS

Despite the prolific wildlife native to our isle, we've always had a penchant for the globe's more exotic animals. A day out amid these wild things is a hands-down winner with kids.

277 Africa Alive!, Suffolk

It turns out the UK's Sunrise Coast isn't as far from Africa as you thought. You need a good imagination to picture the African savannah in Lowestoft, but you can spot rhinos, giraffes and ostriches roaming here. Walk with lemurs and ride the Safari Roadtrain, while for a special treat over-14s can feed the lions, or even be a keeper for the day.

Ⓦ *www.africa-alive.co.uk. Daily from 10am. "Meet the lions" costs £100 for 1hr; "Keeper for the day" costs £95 per half-day. Map 3, F11*

278 The Deep, Hull

Seeing a shark swim past your ear you might think your time had come. Yet as you stroll through the deepest underwater viewing tunnel in Europe, and ride in the glass elevator, a close encounter with sharks and rays is just part of the experience. The Deep's oceanic odyssey will take you into a deep-sea research station and to the ice-cold Polar Gallery, but don't miss the feeding in the lagoon or the daily dive presentation.

Ⓦ *www.thedeep.co.uk. Daily 10am–6pm. Adults £9.50, children £7.50. Map 3, D10*

279 Durrell Wildlife Conservation Trust, Jersey

Set up to save endangered species from extinction, the Trust uses its Jersey Wildlife Park to provide a window into its global conservation work, showcasing some of the planet's most exotic – and at-risk – species in habitats ranging from Madagascan dry forest to the Discovery Desert. As well as visiting the animals, kids can get involved in numerous other ways, from half-term workshops to three-day courses for older children considering wildlife conservation as a career.

Ⓦ *www.durrell.org/wildlife-park. Daily: summer 9.30am–6pm; winter 9.30am–5pm. Adults £12.90, children aged 4–16 £9.40. Map 2, C8*

280 Longleat Safari Park, Wiltshire

Longleat invariably crops up amongst the UK's top tourist haunts; after all, its combination of exquisite country house, Capability Brown gardens and full-blown safari park is pretty irresistible. Vast in acreage, the grounds have plenty of space for giraffes and zebras, rhinos and hippos, and the drive-through safari, a world first when it opened in the 1960s, is still one of the country's wildest and most exciting. Alight in Wallaby Walkthough but you'll want the windows firmly shut in Tiger Territory and Lion Country.

Ⓦ *www.longleat.co.uk. Safari Park open Feb–Oct. Adults £12, children £8; passport ticket to all attractions £24/£17. Map 2, C6*

281 Monkey World, Dorset

Few animals have the capacity to mesmerize children like primates, and at this superb rescue centre you can meet the largest group of chimpanzees outside of Africa. Alongside the resident chimps, orang-utans, gibbons and monkeys, there's plenty of rope ladders and climbing frames to keep kids amused. Be prepared to fall in love so much you might adopt your own primate.

Ⓦ *www.monkeyworld.org. July & Aug 10am–6pm; Sept–June 10am–5pm. Adults £10.75, children £7.50. Map 2, C6*

282 Buried treasure: fossil hunting in Lyme Regis

Need to know Discovering
Fossils (book online at Ⓦwww.
discoveringfossils.co.uk) runs expert-
led fossil hunts in Lyme Regis,
Dorset (£10 for adults, £6 for under-
10s). See Ⓦwww.dinosaurland.
co.uk, Ⓦwww.lymeregismuseum.
co.uk and Ⓦwww.lymeregis.org for
further information.

Map 2, C6

To any child who loves dinosaurs (are there any who don't?) the Jurassic Coast must sound like a dream destination. At its most celebrated spot, Lyme Regis in Dorset, 12-year-old fossil hunter Mary Anning found the near-perfect skeleton of a massive ichthyosaurus, revealed by a rock fall. Could such a miracle happen again?

Mary discovered her specimen, a 200-million-year-old cross between a fish and a lizard, in 1811, almost half a century before Charles Darwin first published his *Origin of Species*. This was a time when there was little scientific evidence to challenge the literal truth of the biblical account of creation. One young girl's lucky find turned the world upside down.

Elsewhere in Britain, the erosion of cliffs is a worry or even a tragedy, but on the rugged Devon and Dorset coast it's a process which keeps offering up fresh gifts. Visit Lyme Regis today and you may not, perhaps, find so much as a sniff of an ichthyosaurus, but traces of their contemporaries are there in abundance, embedded within layer upon layer of blue lias rock. Every day, the tide uncovers fresh material, laden with history.

Fossil-hunting is such a mainstay of the Lyme Regis tourist industry that the town goes all out to advertise and encourage it: even the lampposts are adorned with elegant, ammonite-shaped ironwork. It's now generally frowned upon (and somewhat dangerous) to hack away at the cliffs, but you just need to sift through the fallen shards that litter the beach, chiselling large pieces open, to find the petrified bodies of primitive shellfish and reptiles. To get an expert's eye view of this treasure-trove, kids can sign up for an organized fossil hunt with a professional palaeontologist.

To find out more about Mary Anning and her many achievements, it's worth dropping in at the church where she was baptized: it's now a fascinating little museum called Dinosaurland. Despite the Disney-sounding name, there's a serious educational side to its lively reconstructions of prehistoric habitats. If, after that, you're still hungry for more, then scoot over to the Lyme Regis Museum, where an ammonite-inspired spiral staircase and displays of many famous local finds take pride of place.

283 Frolicking on Coram's Fields

Need to know Coram's
Fields, 93 Guilford St, London
WC1 (Ⓣ020/7837 6138, Ⓦwww.
coramsfields.org; 9am–7pm in
summer; 9am–dusk in winter; free,
best for ages 2–8). The Foundling
Museum, 40 Brunswick Square,
London, WC1 (Ⓣ020/7841 3600,
Ⓦwww.foundlingmuseum.org.uk;
Tues–Sat 10am–5pm, Sun 11am–
5pm; adults £7.50, under 16s free).

Map 1, D2

Hidden away amid the relentless urbanity of north Holborn, Coram's Fields is a haven for little ones, so poorly served in this area of Georgian terraces and office blocks. Beyond the whitewashed gateway, two lawns shaded by ancient chestnut trees open out and the urge to gambol is irresistible – toddlers roam unfettered and young families loll on the grass. On the very hottest days a paddling pool fills with squeals and splashes. The stricture of "no unaccompanied adults" gives the Fields a carefree air – kids rule here, and very young ones at that.

With plenty of sand to pile and dump, and water to pump and divert, single-minded industriousness sets in for the under-8s, and much of the sandpit becomes a glorious mud bath. Numerous climbing frames cater for every level of physical development, with slides, rope bridges and ladders galore. If you've got a spread of ages in tow, you couldn't ask for a better place to allow them all to blow off steam.

But there's something else at play here... the colonnaded building that runs the perimeter and the Georgian gateway at the entrance hint at a history of heartbreak. Coram's Fields lies on the site of the Foundling Hospital, a children's home opened by Captain Thomas Coram (1668–1751), where distressed mothers could leave their unwanted babies. In eighteenth-century London a place at the Hospital would save an infant from perishing on the street, and before a lottery admissions system was introduced fights would break out among the women desperate to secure a place for their baby. Children could also be left anonymously in a wickerwork basket, set into an alcove in the gateway. Those lucky enough to secure a place would eventually learn essential skills for work. Girls were taught sewing and domestic work, while boys twisted ropes for fishing nets. The Foundling Museum, just north of the Fields, movingly portrays the history of the hospital, and also includes a collection devoted to the composer George Frideric Handel, who held concerts in the Hospital's chapel to help raise funds.

The struggle for funds continues at Coram's Fields, evident in a few run-down buildings and an inadequate city farm, but the importance of this place for the children of London is unquestionable – patients from the adjacent Great Ormond Street Children's Hospital are its most enthusiastic users.

284 Eureka!

As you approach Eureka!, the only purpose-built children's discovery centre in the UK, the echoes of *The Wizard of Oz* are unmistakeable. You follow the yellow brick road and leave behind Kansas-monochrome Halifax for the vivid colours of Oz. There's even a multi-hued windmill on top of the building, like a psychedelic water pump on a Midwest prairie ranch. Indeed, Eureka! owes a debt of gratitude to the States in general, where similar museums have sprouted everywhere since the 1960s. But in Britain they somehow didn't take. Except here in Halifax.

Once inside, it's all primary colours. The kids are primary, too – Eureka! is designed specifically for children up to the age of 11. In fact, adults aren't allowed in on their own.

As you enter, to the right Archimedes waits to be dunked in his bath. Our Global Garden provides an early highlight, ranging across six world environments, from the jungle to the arctic; at either end, toddlers' sections encourage under-5s to roam and explore. In Living & Working Together, a role-play area teaches older kids how to get to grips with grown-up life – in the bank (Halifax of course) they can take cash out of an ATM, sit on a chair made of a million pounds (not, alas, real notes) and dodge the alarms in the bank vaults. A hundred other hands-on activities crowd the M&S shop, a post office, a garage. Everything – phone box, lift, front door – is used to elucidate and explain and educate.

The two big blasts of the museum, though, are SoundSpace and Me and My Body. The first caters for both the science geek and the music buff (how do ears work? What's the connection between music and emotion?). The second investigates every aspect of the human body – how tall, wide, heavy are you? What happens when you eat? The high point, though, is the cycling skeleton. Sit on the bike next to the mirror and start pedalling. Slowly your reflection begins to fade, the mirror becomes a window, and there's your bony doppelganger, pedalling away like mad beside you with a devilish grin on his face.

Need to know Eureka! The National Children's Museum, Discovery Road, Halifax, West Yorkshire ☎ 01422/330069, ⓦ www.eureka.org.uk. Open term time Tues–Fri 10am–4pm, Sat & Sun 10am–5pm; school hols daily 10am–5pm. Adults and children aged 3–11 £8.95, children aged 1–2 £2.95, under-1s free.
Map 3, C10

285 Wet and wild on the Pembrokeshire coast

There are family days out that involve being a spectator or sitting down for a ride. And then there are family days out with Preseli Venture. The enthusiastic team at this outdoor adventure specialist have cooked up an adrenaline-packed day for families (or half-day if you're not sure you'll all hack the pace) that's all about getting active, getting wet and getting fully immersed in the natural environment. Pick two out of three activities – coasteering, sea kayaking and surfing – then don wet suits and take the plunge to explore the beautiful Pembrokeshire coast.

The day usually starts with coasteering, which involves grappling, climbing and jumping and swimming your way along some of the most rugged and isolated parts of the coastline. Expert hands introduce the kids to all the sorts of activities you'd normally warn them to avoid – swimming through rock gullies, leaping from granite stacks and washing up with the swell in idyllic coves.

Hearts racing, hair wet, have a pit stop at Preseli's *Eco Lodge* for lunch or take a jaunt to the village pub and refuel for an afternoon of sea kayaking or surfing. Kayakers of all levels can paddle out in Fishguard harbour or Abercastle Bay, then journey along the coastline exploring hidden coves and sea caves and spotting seals and sea birds along the cliffs. Alternatively join the surfing craze and ride the tumbling waves at Newgale or along one of an abundance of Blue Flag beaches.

What makes the whole day sheer joy is that the instructors take on the responsibility of the tuition, kit and safety, leaving families with the freedom to focus on having fun together. All trips set out from Preseli Venture's impressive *Eco Lodge* (look no further if you're looking for cosy family-friendly accommodation), and if there are any family members who don't fancy the adrenaline hit – or haven't yet reached the minimum age of ten – there's plenty to do nearby: stroll to the beach at Aber Mawr, drive out to Strumble Head lighthouse, cycle country lanes or visit dinky St David's, Britain's smallest city.

Need to know Preseli Venture, Parcynole Fach, Mathry, Haverfordwest, Pembrokeshire ☎01348/837709, Ⓦ www. preseliventure.co.uk. The Endorphin Blaster Adventure Day costs £49/£98 half/full day per adult, £35/£70 per child. Children must be 10 years or over, at least 3'9" tall, reasonably fit and able to swim.
Map 3, A12

286 Pigs on parade: wallowing around Jimmy's Farm

Need to know Jimmy's
Farm, Pannington Hall Lane,
Wherstead, Ipswich, Suffolk
☏ 0844/493 8088, Ⓦ www.
jimmysfarm.com. Open April–Oct
daily 9.30am–5.30pm; Nov–March
Mon–Fri & Sun 9.30am–4pm,
Sat 9.30am–5pm. Nature Trail:
adults £4.50, children (under-
16s) £3.50, family ticket £15; rest
of farm free. Weekend tickets
for Harvest at Jimmy's (Ⓦ www.
harvestatjimmys.com) cost £100
per adult, £30 per child (6–17
years); single-day tickets also
available.
Map 3, F12

Who would've thought it possible – a derelict farm revived, hundreds of pigs raised, a range of food products, numerous TV shows, a book, a butterfly house and a restaurant, all within seven years. The amount of work that has gone into Jimmy Doherty's farm since he bought it in 2003 is staggering, and still he builds and expands and adds. Once you've arrived, checked out the farm shop and herb garden and had a snack in the *Field Kitchen*, head through into the heart of the farm via the "Nature Trail", where the fun really begins. Well-thought-through fun. With pigs.

Ooohhh the pigs! Over 400 wallow and stamp in knee-deep mud – their pens stretch into the distance and each of the rare-breed beauties has a good-sized plot to themselves. From the lookout point, kids can watch Essex pigs, Gloucestershire Old Spots and Saddlebacks, and if it's the right time of year, plenty of piglets run and jump and fight and squeal. The pigs alone (and the pork pie) would be reason enough to come to Jimmy's, but there's more.

In the steamy butterfly house, caterpillars munch through the foliage and butterflies emerge from cocoons, testing their soft unfolding wings, flitting and floating through the foliage, and resting on sleeves and tops of heads. Guinea pigs live in grand Lilliputian style in their village of brightly painted houses, and the pygmy goats and Jacob sheep are reliably curious about anyone who wanders close to their pens. Ferrets peep out of hollowed-out logs, and on the chicken safari, rare-breed poultry frantically try to avoid the advances of curious toddlers. A woodland walk wends its ways through the trees, leading to the perfect spot to build a den – or to shelter in one constructed by a previous adventurer.

And still there's more: for a weekend each September, Jimmy's is taken over by sound systems and food stalls. At Harvest at Jimmy's, kids can get up to the usual farm antics plus take cooking lessons, catch a puppet play and dance dance dance. Celebrity chefs present their tastes, and Michelin-starred gourmands give special workshops. And the live music and DJs continue throughout the day and deep into the night.

Jimmy's beats the pants off of any city farm. Bring your wellies and don't leave without bacon.

287 If you go down to the woods today...

Just outside the pretty Broadland village of Horning, there are weird creatures lurking in the forests and swamps. Some of them bask in the reeds, waiting for unsuspecting small children to come by; others have built small houses in the trees, where they hide until it's quiet, only emerging to pick up litter, which they hate. And there's a marsh boggle called Swampy, who loves to eat and to sleep, and tries to be brave but is sometimes scared by the mysterious goings-on in the deeper parts of the woods.

Welcome to Bewilderwood, a homespun fantasy world that is one of Britain's most unusual attractions for children. Based on a series of books by local author Tom Blofeld, it's the reedy, watery environment of the Broads brought to life for kids – both a land of make-believe based on the characters in the books and an overgrown adventure playground full of rope bridges and ladders, zip wires and rickety tree houses. You get around by way of marshland walkways and forest paths, and a boat takes you around a tiny broad where Mildred the lisping vegetarian crocklebog blows water at you.

It has its drawbacks: in summer it's hugely popular and there are queues to get in and for more or less everything inside the park. But its mixture of spooky fantasy and adventure has something for kids of all ages, from toddlers to daredevil teenagers, and there's a wittiness to the whole thing that is refreshing and fun. It also has admirable environmental credentials: everything is made of wood, rope or other sustainable resources, for example, and the boats run on electricity. And the whole place evokes a bygone age of kids staying out late and coming home exhausted (although oddly the book and park's creator claims to have been inspired by the computer game Myst). Whatever his inspiration, it's such a good, old-fashioned day out that the only way to follow it is with lashings of cake and ginger beer.

Need to know
Bewilderwood, Horning
Rd, Hoveton, Norfolk
☏ 01603/783900, Ⓦ www.
bewilderwood.co.uk. Opening
times are complicated – check
the website. Adults and children
over 3' 6" pay £11.50, children
3'–3' 6" £7, and children under 3'
go free.
Map 3, F11

288 Mud and mayhem at Shambala Festival

Pitch your tent, pull on some wellies, don a pair of fluorescent tights, a set of wings and some facial hair, and you're all set for four days of unabashed wackiness at Britain's most family-friendly festival. Set in a secret location and with a line-up of undisclosed musical acts, Shambala remains – despite its growing reputation – small in scale (capacity 7000), free of corporate sponsorship, strongly ecologically sound and retains an inclusive ethos that embraces both families and serious partiers. Whether tracking down bands, joining dance lessons, or whipping up something arty or crafty, you'll soon realize that this festival is all about discovery, taking part and letting loose in a rather childlike manner.

The organizers of Shambala excel at pleasing everyone, with adult stuff that pleases kids – radical circus performances, thumping dance music, site-specific art – and kids' stuff that pleases adults – hula hooping, crazy golf, even advanced tree climbing (with nets and pullies to help you reach new heights). Still, most families with kids under 8 find themselves hanging out in the children's area, where they can get busy with messy play at Artful Splodgers, baking and straw flower-making at Biddie's Bingo Hall, and enjoy the clownish antics of the performers in the Big Top. Trampolining, parachute shaking and making a serious racket with the oversized chimes and xylophones keeps kids occupied for hours, and it's a wrench to get them back to the campsite (or to that act you were hoping to catch).

For the young party-heads, it all culminates in the mad Saturday carnival procession (thoughtfully scheduled at 5.30pm – before cranky time), when they get down with every other costumed Shambala-ite. As the sun goes down, little eyes grow wide at the manic mash-up of sound systems, lights and loonily attired revellers, and just when you're thinking perhaps it's time to tone things down, the bubblologist appears, drawing squeals of delight from your children by practically encasing them in bubbles. When little-uns do need a breather, there are chill-out yurts with a family spin, evening campfires with a cup of cocoa and Rub-a-dub Tub, blissful baths for under-2s – with keyboard accompaniment, of course.

Leaving Shambala, you'll wonder how to keep the kids, happily exhausted and seriously muddy, occupied until next year's festival – perfecting their newly learned samba moves and raku firing techniques should keep them busy. Oh, and planning a loopier costume for next year.

Need to know Ⓦ www. shambalafestival.org. Location: undisclosed as yet (though the grounds of a Northamptonshire stately home are a pretty good bet). The festival takes place over the August bank holiday weekend. Adult tickets cost around £100, kids aged 15–17 £60, 5–14s £25 and 0–4s free; car pass or live-in vehicle pass extra. Map 3, D11

289 Driving your own JCB at Diggerland

Isn't driving a JCB every boy's dream? Well it's not just boys of all ages clamouring to get behind the wheel of construction machinery at Diggerland Devon: the girls and even grannies and grandpas are flocking for a piece of the action. The series of muddy fields that make up Diggerland may not be a beauty hotspot. But to any kid for whom messing about in tractors, dumping some dirt and excavating terrain is just about a perfect day out, it is a simple and brilliant invention.

There are JCBs, tractors, dumper trucks, giant diggers, dirt diggers and more to get behind the wheel of. But even then the fun is far from over. Get high in the flying bucket of the Spindizzy, hop on the Dig-a-Round and take in a bird's-eye view from the vertiginous Sky Shuttle. Young drivers can legally joyride as they navigate a 4WD police car around a bumpy course, while pre-teens can drive battery-powered Land Rovers. If you prefer an expert behind the wheel experience the ups and downs – over hills and through water – of a Land Rover Safari, or refine your own skills on a challenge to excavate buried treasure or play skittles in a digger.

While most of the rides are made for tractor-crazed children over 3, a little effort has been made to amuse tiny tots and any tag-alongs not worked into a frenzy by the T-word. As well as the Diggerland train, bumper cars and go-karts, there's an indoor play area with a bouncy castle, and outside there are zip lines, slides and play equipment. Yet sticking fast to its digger niche has served the park well – it retains a small and friendly ambience, with few queues even in the summer holidays.

There are currently four Diggerlands in the UK – the others are in Durham, Kent and Yorkshire – but Devon has come up trumps with a basic campsite adjoining the park, so you can be first at the door once the sun's up or last out without having to endure the long journey home. Unless your family is tractor-bonkers you can dig your way to a heady smile in just half a day, leaving plenty of time to spin off around a few more of Devon's attractions including Killerton House and Knightshayes Court, both run by the National Trust, Tiverton Castle or Crealy Great Adventure Park.

Need to know Diggerland Devon, Verbeer Manor, Cullompton, Devon ☎ 0871/227 7007, Ⓦ www.diggerland.com. Open Sat, Sun & school hols: Feb & Oct 10am–4pm; March–Sept 10am–5pm. Admission £15, under-3s free. See Ⓦ www.visitdevon.co.uk for more on Devon's visitor attractions.
Map 2, C6

290 Falling into Oblivion at Alton Towers

Try to imagine yourself as an astronaut. Not the peaceful part when you're suspended miles above the earth in a gleaming white capsule, surrounded by an ocean of calm. And not the really fun-looking bit we've all seen on grainy footage of the Apollo missions, when space explorers bounced clumsily along the surface of the moon, collecting rock samples and pushing flagpoles into the powder-fine surface.

No, imagine yourself during the launch: facing upwards, strapped into a fire-breathing space shuttle, with 3Gs of force squeezing down on every fibre of your body. You'd probably be terrified. Reverse this situation so you're facing downwards, and then pile on another 1.5Gs of force, and you're some way to describing how it feels to ride Oblivion, the world's first vertical roller coaster.

Admittedly, the ride can't compete with a space shuttle's 17,500mph top speed. But you don't need any training to enjoy it. All you have to do is join the queue and begin preparing yourself for a 150ft drop into a steaming black hole. Now and then, the clunks and whirs of the ride grab your attention, only to be drowned out by the screams of passengers who've already rocketed down the rails. All the while, you'll hear people telling each other how to deal with the scariest part of the ride, the bit when you're held on the brink of all that G-force for what seems aeons. "Don't look down" is the phrase most used.

But eyes open or eyes closed, that drop feels incredible. For the first second or two of carefree euphoria, you'll surge straight down towards the earth. Then you'll tunnel below the surface on a terrifyingly gloomy section of track, before emerging into the daylight for a 190-degree banked turn that makes your skin rumble with delight. Right then, even without a space shuttle, you'll feel like a hero.

Need to know Alton Towers, Staffordshire (Ⓦ www.altontowers.com) is open daily from mid-March to early Nov (times vary; check website); adults £30.40, children under 12 £23.20. Oblivion, located in the park's X-Sector, has a minimum height restriction of 4'6".
Map 3, C11

291 Cycling the Camel Trail, Cornwall

Following eighteen miles of blissfully level, mostly traffic-free disused railway track from pretty-as-a-picture Padstow to the foot of Bodmin Moor, Cornwall's Camel Trail is about as perfect a cycle route for families as it's possible to imagine. Families flock here because it's easy-going for little legs, and for even littler passengers in bike seats, trailers or on tag-alongs, all of which are available from cycle hire outlets.

It's not just the accessibility that's inviting; this is a stunning trail along which the landscape changes character continuously as you roll from the sandbanks and rocky shores (Betjeman called the route along the spectacular Camel Estuary "the most beautiful train journey I know"), through wooded valley thickets to granite-studded moorland. Peer out to creeks and sandbanks to see egrets, herons and oystercatchers; wow at water skiers on the Camel Estuary; stop for a Cornish ice cream; and take a detour to Camel Valley Vineyard for an award-winning tipple (a perk for parents).

The ride is staggered into three main sections – Padstow to Wadebridge (5 miles), Wadebridge to Bodmin (5.8 miles) and Bodmin to Wenfordbridge (7.5 miles). The beauty is that you can bite off a chunk to suit your time frame and ability, and there are plenty of picnic spots, watering-holes and food stops on the way. At the mouth of the Camel Estuary, Padstow marks one end of the trail and is, of course, a compulsory stopping-off point for foodies. The hub of the trail though is the market town of Wadebridge, once a pivotal settlement for its crossing point over the River Camel, now useful for its plentiful bike hire outlets, cafés and amenities. Beyond Wadebridge the trail wends through enchanting woodland to Bodmin, site of a historic jail, ultimately fetching up at the isolated hamlet of Wenfordbridge, at the western edge of wild Bodmin Moor.

Need to know A map and leaflet of the route can be downloaded from ⓦ www.visitcornwall.com. Bike hire outlets include Padstow Cycle Hire (ⓦ www.padstowcylehire.com); Trail Bike Hire, Padstow (ⓦ www.trailbikehire.co.uk); Camel Trail Cycle Hire, Wadebridge (ⓦ cameltrailcyclehire.co.uk); Bridge Bike Hire, Wadebridge (ⓦ www.bridgebikehire.co.uk); and Bodmin Bikes (ⓦ www.bodminbikes.co.uk). Some outlets offer one-way hire with pick-up/drop-off service.

Map 2, A7

292 Pools of bright water on Marloes Sands

Whether you're hiking the Pembrokeshire Coast Path or simply dipping into southwest Wales for the day, you'll have seen plenty of fine national park scenery by the time you arrive at Marloes Sands, not far from the country's westernmost point. Even so, this glorious sweep of silver-beige sand will take your breath away.

So generous in extent that you'll scarcely believe your luck, Marloes Sands is a beach for kids to cartwheel, hopscotch and run until their hearts pound as loudly as the waves. Utterly unspoilt, it's also perfect for swimming on warm, sunny days. One glimpse of the water from the clifftop – clear, turquoise and very enticing – and they won't be able to get down to the shore fast enough. It's just as beautiful in dull weather, when the sand, sea and sky are daubed in the muted colours of a Farrow & Ball paint chart, and oystercatchers fuss, undisturbed, along the water's edge.

The slanted cliffs that frame the sand are particularly striking, their angles and creases streaked with russet, purple and gold. Over 400 million years old, they're studded with remnants of long-dead sea creatures – trilobites, brachiopods and scraps of fossilized coral. Pick your way along the rocks strewn at their foot, and you'll find some of these creatures' present-day descendants, very much alive.

Peering into a rock pool feels rather like gazing at an underwater miniature garden, bright with fronds of seaweed. The deeper pools, replenished by each tide, are always busy with creatures that need to stay submerged to survive; look carefully enough and you may see tiny shrimps and gobies, perfectly camouflaged to match the sand. Hiding among the smaller stones and strands of weed may be shore crabs, sea spiders and insect-like sea slaters; mussels, limpets and barnacles hold fast to the rocks and anenomes cling on, too, their tentacles drawn in so they look like dollops of damson jam.

Equipped with a net, a bucket, a magnifying glass and an identification chart, kids can count up the species, scoring points as they go. If they're competitive, they'll want to check the periwinkle shells, just in case there's a hermit crab tucked inside – definitely worth a bonus score.

Need to know Close to the northern end of the beach is a National Trust car park (£4 per car; free to members). Pembrokeshire Coastal Bus #315, the Puffin Shuttle, runs to Marloes Sands from Haverfordwest and Milford Haven, the nearest train stations, three times a day.
Map 2, A5

293 Tallulah, Tudors and tractors at Tatton Park

With one Mr G. Osborne as its MP and a resident population of the bejewelled and perma-tanned, Tatton, in leafy Cheshire, is among the UK's wealthiest constituencies. At its heart sits Tatton Park, a vast estate that's one of the greatest days out in the northwest.

The herds of deer roaming the 1000-acre park will make children's heads swivel on the drive through the gates, while the mansion and formal gardens are glorious, but the big attractions for kids are the well-designed Adventure Playground, with over thirty rides, and the Home Farm, an authentic 1930s working farm with Rare Breeds Accreditation. Here children can stroke, feed, groom and cuddle an assortment of goats, hens, ducks, pigs, horses and donkeys and visit a period cottage and a working pottery. Stars of the show are Tallulah the massive Tamworth pig (such a celebrity she has her own Twitter page), Blossom the Clydesdale and Rosie the Red Poll, each with adorable offspring. There's a strong educational element, with hands-on demonstrations, workshops and well-written, informative signs, and plenty of summer-holiday activities. Any child with even a vague interest in animals will love it, and if they've fallen for a particular creature they can revisit/stalk it online, thanks to the farm's webcams, or even adopt one of the Big Three. The barns are all sheltered and there's a covered playbarn equipped with a fleet of ride-on tractors (toys, obviously), so there's plenty to do even when it's chucking it down.

The other area of interest to older kids, particularly those with a bent for history, is the (allegedly haunted) Tudor Old Hall, its rooms tricked out as they would have been from Tudor times up until the late 1950s. The guided tours are fascinating enough, but even better are the wonderful historical re-enactment events – 1940s weekends, medieval fayres, American Civil War weekends, Viking days and so on – when you (and the kids) can turn up in costume, try your hands at all sorts of bygone activities and even watch a thrillingly realistic simulated battle – they'll learn more in an afternoon here than in a whole term at school.

Need to know Tatton Park, Knutsford, Cheshire (℡ 01625/374431, 🌐 www.tattonpark.org.uk). Entry is £5 per car; attractions £4.50, £2.50 (5–15), family ticket £11.50; NT members receive half-price farm entry. Most attractions are closed Monday; see website for full hours and ticket details.
Map 3, C10

294 Make a date for panto in Glasgow

With spectacular colourful costumes, beautiful princesses, valiant heroes, raucous sing-alongs, slapstick and communal shouting, pantomime is undoubtedly fabulous no-holds-barred entertainment for kids, with even the smallest and shyest shedding their inhibitions to boo the baddies, applaud the goodies, laugh heartily as custard pies shoot back and forth across the stage, and belt out songs with the Pantomime Dame. The fast-talking Dame – invariably a man despite the name – rules over this particular brand of chaos, with the most outrageous outfits and by far the best and funniest lines.

There are no better fast-talkers than Glaswegians, which makes the city a great venue for panto fun at Christmas. For the traditional panto experience, head to the King's Theatre, where classics such as *Snow White*, *Cinderella* and *Jack and the Beanstalk* will introduce the nippers to both frolicsome entertainment and fairy-tale archetypes. Meanwhile, the much-loved Citizens Theatre, the second oldest working theatre in the UK and a venue with a strong reputation for innovation and diversity, has refined its panto tradition into what they prefer to term a Christmas Show. The Citz is not a place for washed-up soap stars to cling to their flagging careers: their recent *Cinderella* was an artful retelling of the Grimm tale, which stuck close to the dark original tale of Cinders' loss and loneliness, and eschewed entertainment of the "Oh yes he is, Oh no he isn't!" variety.

But with its celebs, mild sexual innuendo, not to mention the often tight-fitting clothes of its leads, even panto in its traditional form has plenty to appeal to adults. The writer Angela Carter described its language as "everyday discourse dipped in the infinite richness of a dirty mind", and there's always a joyously subversive and gender-bending edge, from the "principal boy", a young woman who generally wears long boots and woos the maiden, to the transvestite glory of the Dame. Now, everyone, after three: "Watch out, he's behind you...!".

Need to know The King's Theatre, 297 Bath St, Glasgow ℡ 0844 871 7648, 🌐 www.ambassadortickets.com; tickets cost around £25. The Citizens Theatre, 119 Gorbals St, Glasgow ℡ 0141/429 0022, 🌐 citz.co.uk; family tickets (for 2 adults and 2 children) start at £32, adult tickets cost £11–18 and child tickets £6–10.
Map 4, C14

THE SEA,
THE SEA

beaches and coastline

First some figures. The length of the coastline of Great Britain (ie, around the main island of England, Scotland and Wales) is usually reckoned to be a shade above 11,000 miles. Add the offshore islands (and there are at least a thousand of those) and the total coastline jumps to closer to 20,000 miles. And then consider that nowhere in slender, elongated Britain is more than 75 miles from the coast. So it's perhaps not surprising that if we're looking for a natural symbol that defines this island nation, it's the sea that sits foremost in British hearts and minds – that sustained our ancestors, that nurtured our greatest explorer, Captain James Cook, and that helped defy the Armada, Napoleon and Hitler. A single coastal image – the iconic white cliffs of Dover – has long stood for the immutability of the nation, while the most stirring wartime story is actually that of a British retreat, back from Dunkirk across the sea to the safety of home. With the protective coast and its waters thus buried deep in the British consciousness, there isn't a bay, beach, cliff or creek that doesn't have a loyal following, whether it's a hidden cove or surf spot that only a local would know or the golden strands of resort beaches that still attract millions of visitors a year. You can swim or sail or kayak in the sea for a different view of Britain, and you can walk the coastal paths, north, south, east and west, for an ever-changing vista of the encircling ocean. You can island-hop in the Scillies and Hebrides or explore mighty shoreline castles; you can sit by a candy-striped beach hut or sing sea-shanties in a fishermen's pub; you can go kitesurfing or coasteering, sand-castle building or rock-pool exploring. But in the end, what you can't do is ignore the ever-present lap of the waves and call of the gulls in Shakespeare's "fortress built by nature for herself...this precious stone set in the silver sea".

295 Samphire and sea birds on the North Norfolk coast

"Terribly flat, Norfolk", Noel Coward wrote, and it's true that the North Norfolk Coastal Path, which runs from Hunstanton in the west to Cromer in the east, won't provide high vistas or a huge physical challenge. What it does is take you round a little-known and unique stretch of the British coastline. Forget buckets and spades, and think instead of wooden boats stranded at high tide on clumps of moss and grass-green samphire, crab-fishing from battered wooden piers, and some outstanding bird-watching.

The shoreline path allows you to explore this unusual semi-watery landscape, and to access some of the quirkiest settlements in the country. At Wells next-the-Sea, the dinky narrow-gauge Wells Harbour Railway chugs back and forwards between the lively, rackety town and the shore every fifteen minutes in high season.

Next stop is the village of Stiffkey, a gorgeous little place with red-brick and flint houses, narrow streets, antique shops and the *Red Lion*, which serves Norfolk ales and seafood. The medieval church is worth a look, and adjoins the fairy-tale buildings of sixteenth-century Stiffkey Hall. The village is famous for cockles, known as "Stewkey Blues" for their grey-blue shells, and for Harold Davidson, who was rector here in the 1930s. He had a penchant for nipping off to Soho to minister to fallen women; his motives were deemed to be less than altruistic, however, and he was eventually defrocked.

Perhaps the high point of the route is the resort town of Blakeney, with its bobbing dinghies, canoes, and riotously competitive crab-catching contests. Take time off from the walk for a boat trip to view the common and grey seals – a colony of five hundred loll on the sandbanks at the end of Blakeney Point, which is also a breeding place for migrant birds including terns, oystercatchers and plovers. Just to the east, near Cley-next-the-Sea, you'll find excellent tearooms at Wiveton Hall, housed in a brightly painted wooden building with outdoor seating and PYO raspberries and strawberries in season.

The end point of the walk, Cromer is a Victorian resort town with all the requisite attractions: a sandy beach, a pier, fish and chip shops and a carnival held in August.

Need to know See 🆆 www. nationaltrail.co.uk/peddarsway for further details.
Map 3, E11–F11

296 Scrambling the Cuillin Ridge

The Black Cuillin on the Isle of Skye offer some of the most exciting and challenging mountain terrain in Britain. Much of it requires rock-climbing skills and all the associated paraphernalia. But there's plenty too for those who prefer to keep their feet firmly on the ground, with the Fionn Choire Horseshoe above Sligachan offering truly magnificent mountain scenery (weather permitting, of course – this is Scotland's west coast after all).

Despite being just nine miles long, the famous Cuillin Ridge offers a reasonably challenging hike. You'll be taking on rough terrain, with more than 3250ft of ascent, and in bad weather you absolutely must know how to navigate – among other possible hazards, the gabbro you're tramping across is magnetic and can deflect compass needles away from true north.

But if the day is set fair you're in for a treat. Take your time over the strenuous hike up onto the ridge – the rewards are well worth it, with the ascent gradually revealing ever more magnificent views across the Western Isles and the blue hills of the evocatively named islands of Rhum, Eigg and Muck to the south, with row upon row of high peaks back on the mainland.

Once you reach the ridge the route will present you with exciting, but not overly intimidating, walking. Stop for a while to gaze upon the infamous Bhasteir Tooth, an imposing rocky pinnacle where those hardy souls who are taking on the entire length of the Cuillin Ridge "proper" can be seen climbing and abseiling.

Non-climbers can bypass the Tooth easily enough, and as you thread your way onwards you're surrounded by rugged mountain landscapes that plunge away to shadowed corries and the sparkling blue Atlantic beyond. Such wild and spectacular scenery is comparable to any in the world.

The eventual descent is rather tough on what will by now be tired legs, but on a hot summer day there's a lovely payoff – the final swoop down the Allt Dearg Mor offers rushing waterfalls and streams into which you can plunge and cool off.

Need to know *Sligachan Hotel*, Sligachan, Skye ☎ 01478/650204, 🆆 www. sligachan.co.uk. Bunkhouse £16 per night, campsite £5 per night, lodge sleeping 14 £1450 per week. The best period for walking is summer, but weather is unpredictable year-round. Take spare clothes, food and drink. Guiding available at 🆆 www. climbskye.co.uk.
Map 5, B20

297 Unlocking the secrets of the Margate Shell Grotto

Margate is a many-headed beast. Rough-and-ready seaside resort of chippies, slot machines and tattoo parlours? 'Fraid so. Quirky, bohemian retreat with a delightful Georgian old town that's luring artistic types in their droves from the capital? Well, thanks to the spectacular new Turner Contemporary, gentrification is well on its way. Pre-Christian centre for the cult worship of a Phoenician fertility goddess? Or medieval focus for the Knights Templar's Masonic rituals? Erm…

Anyone unaware of Margate's associations with mystic cults and secret sects clearly hasn't explored the town's extraordinary Shell Grotto, concealed in its chalky underbelly beneath an unassuming suburban Victorian street. This mysterious subterranean chamber, its walls teeming with bizarre mosaics formed of millions upon millions of shells, has baffled all-comers since its accidental discovery by workmen in 1835. Over 170 years on, it has lost none of its power to amaze.

It takes just a few short seconds, but as you descend from street level down through a moss-covered arch into the grotto's dank, gloomy ante-passage, the transition from the mundane to the strange feels deliciously unsettling. The sinuous tunnel turns another bend and you catch your tantalizing first glimpse of opalescent shell-studded cave wall. You find yourself in an ethereal pagan temple, its walls shimmering with a swirling profusion of symbols and mysterious shapes. Is that an owl? A ram's head? A skeleton? Crossing a tiny domed space – lit by a pale shaft of light – and following an uneven serpentine passage, you strive to make sense of it all: who built this? Why? And when? The tunnel stops dead in an enclosed chamber, or altar room. Was this, you wonder, the scene of sacrificial offerings?

The beauty, of course, is that nobody knows. It's a mystery when the grotto was built – the shells, covered in layers of Victorian soot, are impossible to carbon-date – and a mystery why. For some it's a pagan shrine used for sun worship; for others a Mithraic temple. Most likely, it's an eighteenth-century folly, dating from the era when the taste for the trappings of the mystical East verged on obsession. One thing's for certain: the grotto's secrets will bamboozle and bewilder for a good while yet.

Need to know
Shell Grotto, Grotto Hill, Margate, Kent ☎ 01843/220008. Ⓦ www.shellgrotto.co.uk. Easter–Oct daily 10am–5pm; Nov–Easter Sat & Sun 11am–4pm. £3.
Map 2, F5

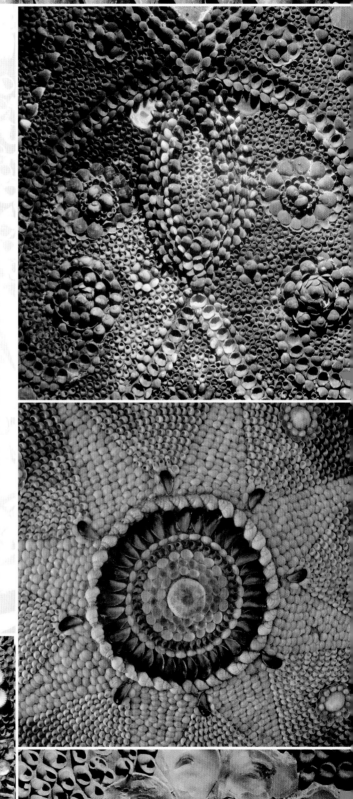

Ffordd Aaron
Tyddewi St. David's 12

298 Hiking the Pembrokeshire coast

There comes a moment when every walker on the Pembrokeshire Coastal Path breaks stride and stops to gaze in wonder. It could be an epic white beach that does it, perhaps a trail over a cliff carpeted with wildflowers, a whirlwind of sea birds or dolphins dipping in a bay. For first-timers, the route is a revelation. Call it the Eureka moment.

In Welsh, *Pen-fro*, which was anglicized to create Pembrokeshire, means "land's end". While the coast at Wales's southern tip bears a passing resemblance to Cornwall, it is nowhere near as famous – indeed, the Pembrokeshire Coastal Path may be the best long-distance walk in Britain that no one knows. For now.

The trail follows the shoreline of Britain's only coastal national park. Most walkers set aside a fortnight to complete the 186-mile route from Poppit Sands at St Dogmaels near Cardigan to Amroth by the seaside resort of Tenby, passing west to east from solitary cliffs to family-holiday favourites. Tracks are good throughout, campsites are abundant, and you'll never be more than two days' walk from fresh supplies.

For Bear Grylls-style bush-bashing head to the Highlands. For the rest of us, however, the sheer variety of scenery makes the Pembrokeshire Coastal Path a superb tramp, especially in the bloom of late spring. Most of the way you cling to the clifftops, teetering along fabulous coastlines around Fishguard, St David's Head and Marloes, and occasionally dipping down to one of the 58 beaches en route, where low-tide crossings at Dale and Sandy Haven keep things interesting. Seals and sea birds are abundant – a side-trip to bird sanctuary Skomer Island is a must for any nature enthusiast – but this is also a walk through human history: you'll see Neolithic cromlechs, early Celtic chapels like St Govan's near Bosherton, and the fabulous cathedral of Britain's smallest city, St David's.

So what's the catch involved in these fourteen glorious days? Perhaps just one: in 2010, readers of the BBC's *Coast* magazine named the path the best coastal route in the UK. Get there soon: it seems eureka moments are on the up.

Need to know The path is managed by the Pembrokeshire Coast National Park Authority (Ⓦ www.pcnpa.org.uk); see also Ⓦ www.visitpembrokeshire.com. Amroth is reached by bus from Tenby, which is on the train line from Cardiff. Travel to Cardigan is easiest by bus from Carmarthen, also on the Cardiff Railway. Walkers' buses link routes in summer (Ⓦ www. pembrokeshire.gov.uk/coastbus). Map 3, A12

299 Tintagel: landscape of legends

The ancient past is infused into the landscape around Tintagel. In this wild section of the north Cornish coast, the weft and weave of modernity seems to loosen, and you sense instead an older truth of Celtic legend. Breakers surge around ancient headlands into tiny half-moon bays. Sea birds cartwheel over shattered black-slate cliffs. Forgotten secrets seem to lie in sea caves.

The very name Tintagel is steeped in myth. Just about anywhere west of Wiltshire claims a connection with the legend of King Arthur, but since Geoffrey of Monmouth's twelfth-century *Historia Regum Britanniae* (*History of the Kings of Britain*) most Brits believe that it was in the island stronghold of Tintagel that the legendary sixth-century king was conceived. Excavations had already unearthed evidence of a powerful contemporary Celtic court here when, in 1998, archeologists discovered a tablet bearing the name "Artognou".

Clinging to a cliff above a sandy bay, the toothy remains of today's fort date from the thirteenth century. Catch it on a quiet day – or better still when an Atlantic gale lashes Barras Nose headland beyond the battlements – and it is impossibly evocative. In high season, however, it can feel like a theme park, and that's when you must seek the soul of this ancient landscape on foot.

The long-distance South West Coast Path tracks the shoreline above a fabulously fractured coastline. How far you follow it is up to you. Head south from the castle and you pass the Norman church of St Materiana's and Glebe Cliff – site of the dynastic Celtic cemetery, they say – then dip down after a mile or so to Trebarwith Strand, an Arthurian film set of cliffs, caves and golden sand. Better still is to find your stride and continue eleven miles to Crackington Haven. Beyond Barras Nose at Lye Rock, you gaze along one of the most glorious coastlines in Britain. A succession of headlands, harbours and lonely beaches awaits, reached on a path that clings to the cliffs and ducks through a natural arch at Ladies Window near Boscastle. The company's not bad either: seals, puffins, razorbills, guillemots, peregrine falcons. All in all, a walk of legends.

Need to know OS Explorer Map 111 covers the South West Coast Path (Ⓦwww.southwestcoastpath.com). Tintagel Castle (Ⓣ 01840/770328, Ⓦwww.english-heritage.org.uk) is open daily year-round. Bus #594 links Tintagel to Boscastle, seven miles away. Bus #595 links Crackington Haven to Boscastle.
Map 2, A6

300 Ramble on: the Fife Coastal Path

The coast of Fife, on a good day, is one of Britain's most postcard-perfect peripheries. And as an official way-marked route, spanning 65 miles from the Forth to Tay bridges, it's often thronged by day-packed ramblers.

On a cloudless late-autumn afternoon, however, you might just have it to yourself: suspended between sun-fired wheat stubble and a cobalt North Sea, it's a dreamscape of Scotland at its most benign. This is the polar opposite of the country's wilder stereotypes; the rolling geometry of a heavily farmed plain bound by successive swathes of Blue Flag beach, cliffs and golf courses is akin to a more rugged East Anglia, an impression compounded by the unlikely vision of an eighteenth-century windmill near the village of St Monans, a relic of a time when coal-fired pans evaporated sea water to produce salt.

In fact, the evidence of Fife's industrial past is apparent all along the trail, from the skeleton shipyards of Burntisland to the modernist ghost of Leven's recently demolished power station – a heritage in stark, fascinating contrast to the gabled film set that is the East Neuk, and never starker than the shingled arc stretching from Leven's shorefront to the East Neuk's western outpost, Lower Largo. If Largo's tiny harbour and narrow skeins of beachfront cottage weren't romantic enough, a solitary signpost points to the impossibly distant Juan Fernández Islands, once home to the town's most famous son, Alexander Selkirk (inspiration for Robinson Crusoe).

Even more of a contrast is Elie and Earlsferry a few miles further north, a wonderfully genteel enclave of mansions and old money, where you might catch a game of cricket on the sand below one of the most charming beer gardens in Scotland, the *Ship Inn*. The traditional, unfailingly picturesque fishing villages of Pittenweem, Anstruther and Crail, meanwhile, have famously become a magnet for artists and musicians, inspired, perhaps, by the same boundless horizons as the ramblers, and braced by the same edge of Europe air that makes this coast so endlessly alluring.

Need to know Ⓦwww.fifecoastalpath.co.uk. The coast is well served by buses, most conveniently the Stagecoach #X60 service between Edinburgh and St Andrews, and also regular trains between Edinburgh and Kirkcaldy.
Map 4, D13–D14

301 Beside the seaside in Southwold

Ranks of jolly beach huts, golden sands split by wooden groynes, a slender pier reaching into the sea... the little town of Southwold on the Suffolk coast has all the traditional British seaside enticements, plus a dash of vintage chic that's all its own. The only blot on the landscape – literally – is the hulking Sizewell nuclear power station on the coast to the south. It provides a surreal backdrop to the beach activity, however, and does little to detract from the town's quirky, retro charm.

Tilly's on the High Street is a temple to the English high tea, with staff in fetching 1920s maid's outfits serving lovely "layered teas" – tall tiers of scones, cucumber sandwiches and cakes. And while most small towns have allowed their ageing cinemas to expire, Southwold has the bijou *Electric Picture Palace*, done up in plush Edwardian style, all red velvet, vintage seats and a tiny Wurlitzer organ.

As well as kite-flying, fish and chip eating and very bracing North Sea swimming, Southwold is a great place for drinking: Adnams ales have their brewery in the town centre, and you can sample their renowned regular and seasonal ales at the cosy *Swan* or the *Crown* hotel pubs on the High Street.

Strolling the prom and the pier, whose uniquely inventive Under the Pier Show is not to be missed, provide good antidotes to high teas and beer, but there are scenic walks in all directions – not least around the town's backstreets and green spaces. There's a rich mixture of Victorian terraces and Georgian villas, with a gleaming white lighthouse looming over the rooftops – a fire in 1659 destroyed many of the buildings, and several plots were left open to evolve into attractive open greens.

Longer walks crisscross the unspoilt surroundings, including a three-hour route south across the River Blythe (via a little ferry) into the ancient village of Walberswick, where you can have a restorative pint at the 600-year-old *Bell Inn*. In August the village hosts the British Open Crabbing Championship, with a medal, a silver salver and 50 quid for the person who catches the heaviest crab. Good British fun at its best.

Need to know Southwold has no train station; the nearest stations are Lowestoft (45min) or Halesworth (30min), from where you can continue the journey by bus.
Map 3, F11

302 Exploring Guernsey's hidden coves

Guernsey lives up to its reputation as a sleepy place of soft-eyed cows, warm scones, ripe tomatoes and rambling country lanes. But it does have a wild side, too. Not wild as in hectic, brash or flash – wild as in waveswept, unspoilt and thrillingly remote.

South of St Peter Port, the coast of St Martin is edged by steep cliffs of ancient, granite-like gneiss, crinkled by time. Farmland and woodland flows down to the clifftops, to be met by a wilderness laced with more than 28 miles of glorious paths. The views are of lush coastal greenery and cornflower-blue sea; head out to the points – Icart or Jerbourg – to enjoy the full drama. Protected from development since the 1920s, this entire coast is a rambler's paradise to match the very best corners of Sussex, Dorset, Devon or Pembrokeshire.

Walk along the cliffs in early spring when daisies, foxgloves, thrift and delicate wild orchids speckle the scene, and you'll hear birds warbling for all they're worth; here and there you'll come across hides from which to get a better view. Return in summer and the air will be thick with sunshine and pollen, with bees buzzing drunkenly around the flowering gorse.

Pick your way down one of the steep, rocky descents, and you'll find yourself on a perfect little scrap of beach, its pale sand washed clean by the sparkling tide. There's a string of these beauties, from those shown on the map – Petit Bôt Bay, La Bette Bay, Saints Bay, Moulin Huet, Petit Port – to the tiny, secret strands that only the locals and aficionados know. To reach the most secluded, clothing-optional spots, you may have to scramble across from a neighbouring cove.

Moulin Huet is particularly delightful, its bay dotted with shade-dappled rocks, each of which have names. It's a scene that's scarcely changed since 1883, when Pierre-Auguste Renoir spent a month lodging in St Peter Port. Heading down to the coast, he propped up his easel on the sand to capture the beautiful, restless sea in oils, with bathers strolling in the shallows.

Need to know Guernsey's southeast coast is around two miles from the capital, St Peter Port, and easy to reach on foot or by bicycle, car or bus. See Ⓦ www.visitguernsey.com for more information.
Map 2, C8

303 Sauce-free seaside at Filey

There's something about the traditional British seaside (think Blackpool, Margate or Skegness) that encourages a back-to-basics hedonism of rowdy amusements, raucous entertainment and near-the-knuckle double-entendres. It's a winning format that's been exported to the Brits-abroad costas, and you either love it or hate it, but it turns out that not all seaside resorts are cut from the same gaudy cloth.

Filey – perched elegantly on the North Yorkshire coast between bigger, brasher Scarborough and down-to-earth Bridlington. Like many northern resorts, it first flourished in Victorian times and later boomed in the 1950s and 1960s as a cheap holiday destination for English workers – Butlin's, the archetypal postwar holiday camp, had a huge resort here, complete with its own railway station. When Butlin's went in the 1980s Filey might have been expected to struggle for trade, but the rather genteel small town kept its eye on its attributes (ooh er, as they'd say in Scarborough).

There's a long, wide sandy beach – that's par for the course in this neck of the woods – but the promenade of houses and villas behind doesn't feature a single amusement arcade. Donkeys plod up and down the sands, a pristine paddling pool sits below the town's beautifully maintained Victorian crescent and gardens, while families explore the rocks and pools of nearby Filey Brigg coastal nature reserve. It's improbably wholesome and unexpectedly refreshing – the raciest the seafront gets is by the harbour where you can buy fish and chips and watch the kids trundle round on the carousel. The harbourside notice board, meanwhile, advertises the week's hot tickets – to an afternoon tea dance or a date with country and gospel singer Paul Wheater ("Yorkshire's Jim Reeves").

Things come to a head during the annual Filey Festival, which reinforces the yesteryear feel of a town at ease with its image. There's a festival queen, bandstand concerts, a craft market, Punch and Judy shows, strawberry teas and a family fun day on the last Sunday. And the Filey sound of summer? It's the traditional festival curtain-closer that is the Last Night of the Proms at the Methodist Church.

Need to know Filey Tourist Information Centre, John St, Filey, North Yorkshire ☎ 01723/383636, Ⓦ www.discoveryorkshirecoast. co.uk. May–July daily 9.30am–5pm; Oct–April Mon–Fri 9.30am–5pm, Sat & Sun 10am–4pm. Details of the Filey Festival in late June/early July on Ⓦ www.fileytownfestival.co.uk. Map 3, D9

304 Songs by the sea: Port Isaac's Fisherman's Friends

Stop by at Port Isaac on a summer's Friday evening, and an ethereal sound will rise to meet you: the vigorous roar of a male voice choir. As you follow the lane down to the minuscule shingle-beached harbour of this North Cornwall village, the sound swells, fills the air, and there, right on the harbour, is the source of the fulsome blend of bass, baritones and tenors: a circle of burly, middle-aged blokes giving their all to shanties, seafaring folk tales and blubbery ballads. Yes, it's the Fisherman's Friends, enthusiastically performing their weekly ritual of songs by the sea.

Port Isaac, otherwise a sleepy, picturesque village of some thousand souls, was already on the map following its appearance in the British TV series *Poldark* and *Doc Martin*, both of which were set here. Fans trickled in, the pubs recorded an upturn in business, and locals – or some of them – scratched their heads and smiled. But in 2010 something strange happened: the local a cappella choir (one of many in Cornwall) signed a million-pound deal with Universal Music and released a hit album.

The ten-man band was Fisherman's Friends, formed from local fishermen, RNLI members, boatyard workers and Coastguard or Cliff Rescue staff, and all living within half a nautical mile of each other. They had already released two self-financed a cappella albums, but since the deal the band has gone viral, playing every festival on the circuit (including Glasto).

Port Isaac has much more to offer, of course: the dark cliffs between which the village is squeezed provide some sublime coastal walking – northeast, to Tintagel and Boscastle, southwest to the fashionable sands of the Camel estuary – while a cluster of more-than-decent pubs, restaurants, B&Bs and hotels keep you comfy. A spell in these parts provides the perfect tonic for jaded city-dwellers – but you'll have to join in a rousing chorus of "Pass Around the Grog", "Haul Away, Joe", "The Lifeboat Girl" or "Home from the Sea" to truly feel Port Isaac's peculiar brand of full-throated exuberance.

Need to know The Fisherman's Friends (Ⓦ www. fishermansfriendsportisaac.co.uk) perform every Friday evening between June and September at around 8pm. Map 2, A7

SURF SPOTS

There are times when Britain's wet and windy climate comes in very handy – such as, for instance, when you're a surfer. All that wind and wet blowing in off the surrounding seas produces surprisingly consistent and varied surf year-round, and thanks to the combination of Gulf Stream warmth and high-tech wet suits conditions are rarely too chilly to handle. Here's something for everyone from frantic young groms to seasoned barrel-riders.

305 Woolacombe, Devon

A two-mile-long beach that draws in consistent Atlantic swells; numbers in the water decrease if you walk south for a few hundred yards. On strong south and southwesterly winds, head to nearby Putsborough, which is very sheltered. Cheerful Woolacombe village is extremely surfer-friendly, with plenty of gear shops and a good surfers' pub, the *Red Barn*.

Ⓦ *www.eyeball-surfcheck.co.uk for surf conditions. Map 2, B6*

306 Llangennith, Gower

Beautiful Rhossili beach runs north into Llangennith, one of the biggest beaches in Wales and the focal point for Gower surfing. The beach picks up plenty of swell to suit all levels of ability, although it can be hard work paddling out in larger swells. Most visiting surfers hone in on the lively *Hillend Camping and Caravan Park* in the dunes at Llangennith, where board rental and lessons are available, while nearby in Llangennith village is the legendary PJ's surf shop and the equally venerable *King's Head* pub.

Ⓦ *www.pjsurfshop.co.uk. Map 2, B5*

307 Saltburn-by-the-Sea, North Yorkshire

One of the original centres of the northeastern surfing scene, there's an enthusiastic and friendly vibe at Saltburn, with everyone from complete beginners to salty experts making the most of the local waves. It's always busy when there's a swell running, but there are lots of uncrowded waves in the area too if you're prepared to explore. This stretch of the North Sea coast is surprisingly consistent – though pretty chilly at times.

Ⓦ *www.saltburnsurfcam.com. Map 4, F16*

308 Thurso, Highland

Thurso's reef break is a world-class right-hander that has hosted international pro contests and provides a fast, barrelling ride to triple overhead and bigger. Less experienced surfers can hit the town's beach, and if you want to explore there are world-class reef and beach breaks all along Scotland's northern coast. Take a good wet suit though...

Ⓦ *www.magicseaweed.com for surf conditions. Map 5, D18*

309 Watergate Bay, Cornwall

Watergate has quality beach breaks for all levels of ability – and when the tide drops, it reveals a two-mile expanse of beach. This gives you a chance to get away from the crowds in front of the beach car park, which is where you'll find the wildly popular (some say overhyped...) Xtreme Academy watersports resort, along with Jamie Oliver's *Fifteen Cornwall* restaurant.

Ⓦ *www.watergatebay.co.uk. Map 2, A7*

310 Tidal triumphs: Durdle Door and Lulworth Cove

Need to know ⓦ www.
lulworth.com. Both sites are
near West Lulworth, Dorset and
signposted on the A352 from
Dorchester to Wareham. Parking
(7am–7pm) costs £5 for 4 hours
plus. If you wish to avoid the
steep trail to Durdle Door, take
the shorter, flatter route from the
Durdle Door Holiday Park.
Map 2, C7

It's easy enough to see how Durdle Door earned its name – but less straightforward to get to see it in the first place. From Lulworth Cove car park, the white chalk trail to the site stretches up a mile or so over the hills. Admittedly it looks a fair distance on first glance, but it's only when you're a third of the way along, huffing, puffing and drawing sympathetic glances from walkers on their way down, that you really begin to wonder if you're nearly there yet. Push on: the reward is worth it.

At the summit, the iconic door emerges below, carved out of the limestone by the unrelenting strength of the sea. A precarious set of steps, crumbling like cinder toffee from the cliff side, lead to the shore. The beach is typically brimming with families, picnicking, paddling and watching the surf crash through the arch. Some people attempt to "swim the door", but on all but the calmest days it's a fool's game – the waves, that will one day reduce the door to a stack of stones, fling swimmers around like so much flotsam and jetsam.

Back up on the clifftop track, the peaks of the ragged chalk hills stretch out like a giant dinosaur's spine – rather apt for such a famous area of the Jurassic Coast. It's easier heading down the path, and the views are glorious. The turquoise water of Lulworth Cove – another dramatic landform sculpted by the erosive power of the English Channel – shimmers at the foot of the trail. It should be your next stop.

It took hundreds of thousands of years for the sea to eat away at the sandstone cliffs to create Lulworth Cove. The scallop-shell-shaped bay attracts half a million visitors annually and the locals have embraced tourism wholeheartedly, but without a dash of kiss-me-quick vulgarity. Lulworth is a place for classic pleasures, not least creamy Dorset ice cream scooped into chunky waffle cones – just made to be devoured on the pebble beach while recovering from that considerable walk.

311 Isolation on the east coast: Shingle Street

Nothing symbolizes the precarious nature of the Suffolk coastline like Shingle Street, a haunting row of cottages on a thin, shifting spit of land where the River Ore meets the swirling black water of the North Sea. This coast has been receding for centuries, picked apart, stone by stone, by fierce currents and storms – whole towns have fallen into the sea. It's hard to imagine a lonelier, more inhospitable place to build a village, not least when driving to it along the narrow lane from Hollesley, across the sluice and over the marsh.

In the nineteenth century this was a thriving fishing community, where skiffs and nets smothered the beach and wooden smokehouses dotted the shoreline. Today you can wander along the massive bank of shingle accompanied by nothing more than the crash of murky waves and squawking gulls. Behind you flat marshland bleeds into scrubby heath, beneath the vast skies that Suffolk is famous for – ahead lies the bleak North Sea, dotted with giant containers steaming south to Felixstowe. In summer the drabness is broken by clusters of wildflowers, but come in midwinter for the full effect, a powerful sense of complete end-of-the-earth isolation.

Little remains of the village, but a few people still live here; a row of neat, whitewashed coastguard cottages, the red-brick single-storey German Ocean Mansion, a couple of clapboard houses further along the spit and a lonely Martello Tower surveying the scene. The local pub was destroyed by a stray bomb in World War II, and indeed the war has provided the hamlet with much of its recent fame, involving conspiracy theories of phoney German invasions. Yet the sea remains its bitterest foe. The village could disappear within twenty years if new defences are not erected.

Until then, it's easy to imagine George Crabbe's *Peter Grimes* prowling the beach two hundred years ago:
*Here dull and hopeless he'd lie down and trace
Or sadly listen to the tuneless cry
Of fishing gull or clanging golden-eye;
And the loud bittern, from the bulrush home,
Gave from the salt-ditch side the bellowing boom.*

Need to know The hamlet
of Shingle Street lies at the end
of a lane (also Shingle Street) a
few miles south of Hollesley and
the B1083 between Woodbridge
and Bawdsey; you'll find two car
parks, but little else, on arrival.
Map 3, F12

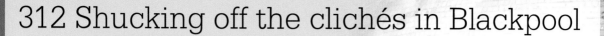

312 Shucking off the clichés in Blackpool

For better or for worse, the clichés are all intact. Kiss-me-quick hats, "fresh air" sold in a jar, dubious-looking burger stands and high-velocity roller-coaster rides. But, even if you prefer your entertainment *not* to be of the eyebrow-raising ironic variety, Blackpool Pleasure Beach provides big thrills.

First, the old-fashioned fun. The Big One is the ride to end all rides in Britain's most famous seaside resort. Nobody who has ever dared ride the world's fastest roller coaster (it gets up to 85mph) will forget it – for good reasons or for bad. If your need for speed isn't quite so acute then head for the good-looking antique rides, the pick of the bunch being the original wooden Big Dipper, which has been swooping and dipping since 1923, or the Grand National, where you race against another car next to you on parallel tracks.

Grotty B&Bs still abound, of course, along with a newer flurry of boutique options – blazing the trail is *Number One South Beach*, where rooms come with Egyptian cotton sheets and hot tubs and where the in-house restaurant serves up the likes of locally sourced haddock with poached egg (a superior old-school fry-up is also available, naturally – this is still Blackpool, after all).

Perhaps the biggest surprise for unsuspecting fun-seekers is the impressive collection of modern art scattered around town, including the largest disco ball in the world (entitled "They don't shoot horses do they?") on South Beach promenade, and a huge steel tower in the middle of revamped St John's Square with a swimmer diving off the top. This – Lucy Glendinning's "The Wave" – encapsulates best what Blackpool is aspiring to become – a resort town where the trad attractions of sea and sand aren't discarded, but that can pull in those of us who hanker for a side order with culture to go with our candyfloss.

Need to know Blackpool Pleasure Beach (Ⓦ www.blackpoolpleasurebeach.com; March–Oct 11am till late; free). Rides are priced individually; unlimited ride passes cost £15–28 and can be bought online. *Number One South Beach*, 4 Harrowside West, Blackpool (Ⓣ 01253/343900; Ⓦ numberonesouthbeach.com) offers B&B from £135. Map 3, B10

BEACHES

Oh we do like to be beside the seaside, us Brits; we do like to be beside the sea. Fortunately, there's a lot of coastline wrapped around this isle – over ten thousand miles of it, in fact. Factor in Britain's astonishing variety of landscapes and you have a country whose beaches range from epic strands to tiny notches chipped from cliffs, wilderness islands to prim Edwardian resorts.

313 Porthcurno, Cornwall

Small but exquisitely formed, Porthcurno's wedge of white sand, surrounded by ragged cliffs and framing a sapphire bay, creates an improbably idyllic scene. Nor is Porthcurno just a pretty face; the cliff-top Minack Theatre hosts open-air performances, while a museum celebrates the birth of transatlantic telegraphy here in 1870. Staggering beauty, culture and history all in one spot. *Map 2, A7*

314 Par Beach, St Martin's, Isles of Scilly

St Martin's seems to lie at the end of the world. Rawer and wilder than neighbour Tresco, this is an island for connoisseurs, a fertile fuzz of green fringed by sugar-white beaches that swell as the tide drops. Don't forget your mask and snorkel: seals bob among kelp forests in the clearest bluest water in the archipelago. *Map 2, A8*

315 Barafundle, Pembrokeshire

Royal Ascot? No, thanks. Glyndebourne? Too noisy. In 2006, readers of *Country Life* magazine, the glossy bible for posh pastoral folk, named this sensational beach scalloped into the Pembrokeshire cliffs as their favourite British picnic spot. Space has a lot to do with it; the walk here from Stackpole Quay keeps crowds to a minimum and gives Barafundle the frisson of a shared secret. Shallow seas and shelter from prevailing winds also score points. But the clincher? Superlative sands that are just perfect for sand castles. *Map 2, A5*

316 Bamburgh, Northumberland

There's no better model for sand-castle-making than the storybook silhouette of Bamburgh Castle. It rises behind the pale sand of this pristine beach, which stretches into the distance beneath a pale pure sky and extends a mile out to sea at low water. Add in the romantic outline of Holy Island at its northern end and it is a magnificent vista fit for Viking longships, one not nearly as well known as it should be. (That's half the reason to go.) *Map 4, E15*

317 West Wittering, West Sussex

Keith Richards may have a beach hut here, but West Wittering excels in peace'n'quiet rather than rock'n'roll. Swish through the dunes to emerge onto 55 acres of unspoilt sand that somehow swallows 10,000 visitors on sun-drenched summer bank holidays. Wind- and kitesurfers love it. So do kids, splashing in sandy pools or crabbing at low tide. Everyone else loves it, too – just dawdling or gazing out at the Channel with a cuppa. Keith's probably doing the same. *Map 2, E6*

318 Bantham, Devon

With its pristine sands, old thatched cottages and lack of commercialism, the south Devon village of Bantham is a small timewarp, preserved from much development over the past sixty years by its staunchly protective owners, the Evans Estate. The waves are popular with surfers but the beach, with its shallow waters and wide expanse of sand, is also good for the bucket-and-spade brigade, and there are rock pools and dunes to explore. *Map 2, B7*

319 Scarista, Harris, Western Isles

Beaches are about escapism, and Scarista on the Isle of Harris has it in buckets and spades. As if the adventure of getting to the Outer Hebrides wasn't enough, the wide-open vistas of rolling hills and empty seascapes from this raw, elemental beach give you a walk on the wild side at the outer edge of civilization. Sparkling white sands and vivid blue water add to the appeal. *Map 5, A19*

320 Holkham, Norfolk

Let's hear it for Holkham: white-gold sands (a rarity among Norfolk's more usual shingle), shells and starfish, a fringe of aromatic pine woodland and a nature reserve teeming with saltings and water birds. Gwyneth Paltrow strode its shoreline alone in the closing scene of *Shakespeare in Love*, and for good reason: there's an introspective intensity to this minimalist landscape, a romantic Turner-esque vista of empty sea and sky stung by the North Sea breeze. *Map 3, E11*

321 Crosby, Merseyside

A public petition in 2007 ensures that Crosby remains the permanent gallery for artist Antony Gormley's *Another Place* installation; a hundred life-size iron men who stare to the open sea either side of the tide line. Some are now half-buried in sand. Others are dressed in a coat of weeds. Gormley says his work tackles themes of migration and illustrates that every landscape has a social dimension. We say it creates the most haunting beach in Britain. *Map 3, B10*

322 Studland Bay, Dorset

Studland Bay is not as famous as the Jurassic Coast (which starts at the tip of this lovely bay as Old Harry's Rocks) – reason enough to visit. Another is the astonishing natural beauty preserved under the aegis of the National Trust. Tramping along trails through dunes and woods behind the bay you may spy deer, while in the heath you could uniquely spot all six British reptiles. There's a catch, of course: walking the trail means dragging yourself away from Middle Beach, with its charmingly ramshackle beach-hut café and sheltered water perfect for swimming. *Map 2, D6*

323 Peaks, paddles and golden beaches: Scotland by sea kayak

The glens and hills that define the Highlands, tramped by millions and immortalized on countless tins of shortcake, are undeniably grand. But Scotland's far northwest is different. The region of Assynt, just shy of Britain's northern edge, is mostly flat and mostly empty. From its moorlands, crofting fields and slender lochs rise strange, isolated sandstone peaks that offer hikers splendid scrambles along tortuous, crumbling ridges and great views of the Western Isles and much of northern Scotland.

The weather isn't always clear of course, and water is never far away. Get on a kayak, and a whole range of possibilities are at your disposal. You really appreciate the great stretch of the Scottish coast when you're bobbing off its rocky shores, paddling past sea birds and seals to abandoned huts and gold-sand beaches that look almost Caribbean – until you dash into their clear waters to come up gasping and twitching with an ice-cream headache and a thudding heart.

The kayaking itself isn't particularly technical: you may find yourself meandering at first, but before long your paddle will be dropping with a satisfying splash as you pull yourself forward into the vast sea. It gets tiring, but there are ample opportunities to pause – indeed, that's half the fun, letting the waves roll your craft up and down as you look up to the sky and back to the shore and contemplate everything and nothing.

Having a good instructor helps – ours brewed tea on a fire of grass and driftwood, told stories about local eccentrics and led us on a ramble up a hill to point out wildflowers. The adventurous can head inland along Loch Veyatie and Fionn Loch to the base of domed Suilven (2398ft) – a practical as well as intrepid route in, since no roads approach the mountain. But you don't have to be an iron man to enjoy this stunning corner of the world. Go in summer, when the days seem not to darken as much as thin into an eerie haze around midnight and the water temperature is almost bearable, and it's hard not to wax lyrical.

Need to know Norwest Sea Kayaking (Ⓦ www. norwestseakayaking.com) in the village of Lochinver, Sutherland, is just one of several operators. There's accommodation in Lochinver, Achiltibuie and Ullapool. You'll need your own vehicle to explore.
Map 5, B18

324 Life on the edge: the White Cliffs of Dover

There is a cliff whose high and bending head
Looks fearfully in the confinèd deep.
Bring me but to the very brim of it
        Shakespeare, *King Lear*, Act 4, Scene 1

From Shakespeare to Vera Lynn, the towering White Cliffs of Dover have always fired the British imagination. They're arguably our most iconic natural symbol: from the Armada through Napoleon to Hitler, their reassuring solidity invoked whenever our island nation has felt threatened. The full scale of the cliffs – all sixteen miles of them – is best appreciated several miles out at sea, but to experience their dramatic views and sheer drops there's no substitute for striding out along the clifftops themselves. Head west, towards Shakespeare Cliff – named in honour of its starring role in *Lear* – and you can descend to the tranquil nature reserve of Samphire Hoe; constructed from the spoils of the Channel Tunnel, it's one of the newest parts of the kingdom.

Walking along the North Downs Way takes you though the fascinating Western Heights, a vast network of fortifications constructed to withstand the Napoleonic threat; part is given over to the ominously titled Dover Immigration Removal Centre, suggesting a purpose that's no more friendly today. From here, the panorama across the shimmering-green Dover Straits – and even to France on a clear day – is spectacular.

The calf-busting route up to Shakespeare Cliff is not for the faint-hearted. Viewed from alongside, the cliffs slope backwards as if about to spring an attack, like a giant rearing white horse. The clifftop path frequently edges within a perilous few feet of the vertiginous drop. To peer over the precipice down to the rocky beach, hundreds of feet below, you'll want to fall forward into the long grass and inch on all fours towards the edge like a sniper.

The descent to Samphire Hoe drops through a long, dark passage excavated in the 1880s for an unsuccessful forebear of the Chunnel. The hoe itself is a delight: an ethereal landscape of gently undulating chalk meadow, framed by the awesome backdrop of Shakespeare Cliff, with a sense of wilderness that belies its recent man-made origins. It's a magical place from which to survey these magnificent towers of chalk.

Need to know Shakespeare Cliff and Samphire Hoe (Ⓦwww.samphirehoe.co.uk; daily 7am–dusk; free) lie three miles west of Dover, along the North Downs Way, National Cycle Route 2 or A20.

Map 2, F6

325 Close encounters with Llandudno's Great Orme

Riding the train along the North Wales coast, try to imagine how the two-mile-long, 679ft-high hunk of limestone headland that is the Great Orme might have appeared to Viking raiders a thousand years ago. With its smaller acolyte, the Little Orme, you can just about picture them as a giant Nessie-style monster. An impossible-to-prove theory derives Orme from the Old Norse word for sea serpent – and is the root for the word "worm".

Whatever its etymology, the Great Orme (*Y Gogarth* in Welsh) is inextricably linked with Llandudno, hunkered below its southern flank. As the Victorian middle classes flocked to this self-styled queen of the Welsh resorts for a little sea bathing and promenading, entrepreneurs devised ways to separate them from their holiday spending money, many of them involving the Orme. The views from the summit plateau across the Conwy Estuary to Snowdonia are just fabulous, and the Victorians have ensured that getting there is half the fun.

The essential tour is along Marine Drive, a four-mile circumnavigation via a wonderfully scenic one-way toll road, much of it cut into the limestone cliffs. Rock climbers scale the crumpled faces above, while on the right, the bank drops precipitously down to fisherfolk casting from the wave-pounded rocks below. Partway round, a side road winds up past St Tudno's Church – the parish's twelfth-century original – to the summit.

Another lovely alternative is to take the Great Orme Tramway, a San Francisco-style cable car hauled up Llandudno's steep streets and then out onto the open plateau. It's a pleasure to sit back and enjoy the ride in the blue-and-gold open cars, rattling their way up here as they have done since 1902; you might catch a glimpse of the herds of Kashmir goats that Queen Victoria gifted to the town. Stop at the Halfway Station for a short walk to the Great Orme Copper Mines, an important source of Bronze Age metal and later reworked by the Romans. Grab a hard hat and take the self-guided tour into the tunnels, making sure to stop by the burial site of three cats, sacrificed and interred here by superstitious miners.

Need to know Marine Drive's toll costs £2.50; parking included. Great Orme Tramway Victoria Station, Church Walks, Llandudno, Conwy (Ⓣ01492/879306, Ⓦwww.greatormetramway.co.uk; adults £5.60 return). Great Orme Mines (Ⓣ01492/870447, Ⓦwww.greatormemines.info; adults £6).

Map 3, B10

326 Little Maui: kitesurfing Camber Sands

No one in their right mind could describe the Channel as tropical, and there's not a grass skirt or a palm tree in sight. Camber Sands earned its "Little Maui" nickname not from any physical similarity to that exotic Hawaiian paradise, but because this backwater of Sussex – just ninety minutes from London – is the premier kitesurfing destination in the southeast.

A local wind anomaly helps. Whether it is caused by a gravel substrata that rapidly radiates heat to generate a sea breeze, or by the winds that channel onshore through Romney Marsh, this undeveloped crescent of powdery sand and shingle often experiences solid Force 3 to 4 conditions. It's no coincidence that one of the largest wind farms in Britain is sited here.

Along with those reliable winds, the quirks of Camber Sands' geography make it a natural playground for kitesurfing. For a start, the prevailing onshore conditions provide four miles of south-facing beach to rip past. Then there are the regular slow-rolling waves to leap when a swell barrels in. Best of all, Camber's size and relative isolation swallows all but the heaviest crowds. Fly your kite here and south coast hotspots such as Brighton, Wittering, Poole or Weymouth seem crowded (not to mention expensive, given the large free car park, Jury's Gap, a couple of miles beyond Camber village) in comparison.

Tides add a new dimension to a beach that can be surfed three hours either side of low water. Surfing is dangerous at high water, when groynes are submerged. At low water, though, sand bars create shallow, flat lagoons – perfect for speed-freaks to get an adrenaline fix. Just as appealing for novices, too, who will appreciate the gently shelving bottom that never leaves them literally out of their depth – always a good thing when being body-dragged through the sea by a powerful kite for the first time. Kitesurfing at its best, then. Just don't expect grass skirts.

Need to know Camber Sands is beyond Camber village, two miles west of Rye, East Sussex. From Easter to late October, Rye Watersports (☎ 01797/225238, Ⓦ www.ryewatersports.co.uk) schools everyone from novices to experienced surfers. Two- or three-day beginners' courses start at £179; you will never have more than two students per instructor. Map 2, F6.

327 Bardsey: island of 20,000 saints

You might get more than you bargain for if you're out for a breath of fresh air on the island of 20,000 saints – better known as Bardsey Island. Not so long ago a group of seventeen trippers found themselves stranded here for two weeks when the weather turned nasty.

But in mellower conditions there's nothing better for shaking off the cobwebs than an excursion to this small isle (*Ynys Enlli* in Welsh), around two miles off the Llŷn Peninsula in North Wales. The rocky splinter acquired its popular name from the number of pilgrims supposedly buried here in the Dark Ages, when it ranked alongside Lindisfarne and Iona as a destination for the devout, though nowadays the pilgrims are more likely to be birders and wildlife enthusiasts.

The main draw is the resident bird colonies, including razorbills, choughs, oystercatchers and Manx shearwaters, but people also come in spring and autumn to observe such migratory visitors as willow warblers, chiffchaffs and goldcrests. Others come just for a ramble or a spot of fishing or rock climbing (the Bardsey Ripple is a classic climb). Along the shore, you might spot a family of Atlantic grey seals, the pups basking on the rocks, or be satisfied with crabbing in the rock pools and squelching in the seaweed. If you're feeling energetic, take a hike through gorse, purple heather and bracken up the slopes of Mynydd Enlli, which at 547ft dominates the scene. Views encompass the ruins of St Mary's Abbey in the north of the island, a tiny traditional Welsh chapel from 1875 and the square lighthouse at the southern tip.

To get immersed in Bardsey life, consider a week's stay in a farmhouse – all lighting is by gas or candle and you'll have to venture outside to visit the loo. As night falls the only sounds are the squawk of birds and the pounding of waves on the shore. You'll have lots of space to yourself – the population is sparse to say the least, dwindling to fewer than ten in the off-season.

Need to know For boat access from Pwllheli or Porth Meudwy (weather dependent), contact Enlli Charters (℡ 0845 811 3655, Ⓦ www. enllicharter.co.uk) or Bardsey Boat Trips (℡ 07971 769895, Ⓦ www. bardseyboattrips.com). Adult fares cost £35 from Porth Meudwy. For farmhouse or cottage rentals, contact Bardsey Island Trust (℡ 0845 811 2233, Ⓦ www.bardsey. org). Hostel places for birdwatchers are available at Bardsey Bird and Field Observatory (Ⓦ www.bbfo. org.uk).
Map 3, A11

328 Taking the plunge on the North Devon coast

When you're inching your toes ever closer to the edge of a precipitous sea cliff, cold salt water dribbling out of your life jacket and into the razor-thin cuts you picked up on the ascent, taking time to admire the scenery is never your first priority.

But when you've leapt away from the cliff, plunged down into the churning Atlantic and struggled back up, gasping for a breath of briny ocean air, you can appreciate how beautiful it is on the North Devon coast. In this wild and ever-changing part of Great Britain, the sky, land and sea come together with spectacular results.

Craggy cliffs and remote caves are lashed by great undulating swathes of ocean, as they have been for millennia, and gently swirling winds hurl sand into every crevice of the rock face. Behind the cliffs, emerald hills roll off into the distance, creating a gem of a backdrop for coasteering – a nerve-rattling adventure pursuit that's as terrifying as it is thrilling.

The sport – if you can call it that – began as a distraction for bored surfers waiting for the next big swell, but has since become a major attraction in its own right. The aim is to swim, climb and jump your way along the barnacle-crusted coastline, which is fun, of course, even if the tamest sections are more suited to geology students than adrenaline junkies.

After an hour or so of warm-up jumps, you'll inevitably find yourself staring down at the sea from 25ft up. This presents you with a dilemma: do you turn around and scuttle back down the rocks like a frightened crab (to the possible amusement of other participants) or go against your every instinct and freefall into the ocean? Obviously, you jump.

As you get that stomach-in-your-mouth sensation of falling, falling, falling, through the air, like a sea bird dive-bombing its prey, everything's out of your control. Gravity sucks you into the water, causing a splash that floods the nostrils, and you're left to swim up through the tornado of blue-green bubbles you just created. When you surface, grinning, you'll already be scanning the shoreline for a higher cliff to conquer.

Need to know Barnstaple-based company Point Breaks (Ⓦ www.pointbreaks.com) runs coasteering trips on the North Devon coast from £30 per person.
Map 2, B6

329 Paying homage to the Old Man of Hoy

There are no long-distance views; you'll come across it quite suddenly. A soaring column stabbing out of the frothy ocean, precariously balanced on a ledge just offshore, a bit like a chopping knife, blade down. Catch your breath and soak in the view, the occasional puffin and the inevitable gaggle of super-human climbers, clinging to the rock like tiny red spiders. Even when it's snowing, the hostels are closed, and the only person you've seen all day is the old postman that seems to speak Swedish, you'll see climbers on the Old Man of Hoy. The stack was first conquered in 1966 by Chris Bonington, since when it's become a rite of passage for aspiring thrill-seekers.

Few visitors make the pilgrimage to the Old Man, the 449ft-high sea stack of red sandstone that pokes out of the North Atlantic; it's not somewhere you can simply pull up in the car and take a photo. Hoy is a lonely, rugged place with a handful of inhabitants and a couple of hostels off the "mainland" of Orkney, accessible only by ferry. Once here, you'll have to get hiking. From the pier at Moaness you must troll up the pass that hugs Ward Hill, then down the South Burn to weathered Rackwick Bay. It's a wild and often bleak walk along the narrow "main" road, so don't feel bad about accepting a lift from one of the locals – ancient tattooed sailors in 1970s Ford Escorts, local fiddlers on their way to the pub, and old ladies with cakes...on their way to the pub.

Rackwick, an old crofting and fishing village squeezed between towering sandstone cliffs, is a great place to stay. Buffeted by Atlantic gales most of the year, it transforms into a pleasant cove and beach in summer. From here it's another three-mile round-trip slog on a rocky path to the Old Man itself, hidden further along the coastline. Take in the astonishing vision while you can – erosion continues, and some experts believe that the great Old Man may soon collapse into the sea.

Need to know Two ferries (W www.orkneyferries.co.uk) serve Hoy from Orkney: one from Stromness to Moaness pier (£3.60), and a car ferry from Houton to Lyness (£3.60, car £11.50). Orkney Hostels (W hostelsorkney.co.uk) run two SYHA-affiliated hostels in North Hoy from mid-March to mid-September: the *Hoy Centre* (£14) and the tiny *Rackwick Outdoor Centre* (£11.15).
Map 5, D17

330 Island hopping in paradise

The term "island hopping" brings somewhere like the Greek Islands to mind. Basking on deck, welcoming the briny spit of the wake, disembarking on pearly shores – is this really something people get up to on the British coast? On the Isles of Scilly it is.

This unique archipelago 28 miles off the south coast of Cornwall boasts one of the mildest, sunniest climates in the country. And in a place where two-thirds of the jaw-dropping landscape is water, the best way to explore is by boat. Don't be fooled into leaving your waterproofs at home, however – this being Britain, unpredictable weather will decide whether you experience the islands in their sunniest glory or at the brunt of a wild Atlantic storm.

Each morning the quayside on St Mary's – the main island – is a frenzy of activity as visitors queue for inter-island boat trips and tours to uninhabited isles. Meanwhile ferries also depart from Bryher, St Martin's, Tresco and St Agnes, each heading for another slice of paradise where passengers can witness an abundance of wildlife, discover ancient sites and pad barefoot along white-sand beaches.

On board, there's a palpable sense of sea-bound adventure. Binoculars are at the ready to spot seals, puffins, rare sea birds, porpoises, sunfish and basking sharks. On inclement days hoods are pulled tight around weather-beaten faces and passengers huddled inside strain for a glimpse of the scenery through steamed-up windows. With its five inhabited islands and hundreds of uninhabited islands and islets, the view is one of intoxicating beauty.

On the western extremities, Bishop's Rock lighthouse marks the edge of granite islets that peter out into 3000 miles of uninterrupted Atlantic. In contrast, hunkering in the shelter of the larger islands' shallow peaks are golden bays tickled by crystal waters. Each of the inhabited islands retains an individual character: there's the thriving hub of St Mary's, the vast beaches of St Martin's, the lush gardens of Tresco, wild little Bryher and the western outpost of St Agnes. So with regular passenger ferries running daily, you can island-hop to your heart's content.

Need to know Check
Ⓦ www.simplyscilly.co.uk for general information and travel to the islands. St Mary's Boatmen's Association (Ⓣ 01720/423999, Ⓦ www.scillyboating.co.uk), runs a fleet of boats from the main island, and each outer island has its own ferry travelling to different islands each day; return trip from £7.20.
Map 2, A8

331 Cruel Cruden Bay

Look at a map of Scotland, towards the top, and you'll see a wedge of granite jutting east into the North Sea. This is Buchan, a hard, flat region that, for all that it's just next door to the Highlands, feels a world away. There are no lochs and glens here, no blur of heather and soft rain. Instead, farmland stretches under vast skies towards a savage coast where cliffs alternate with sweeps of wind-lashed sand.

You feel the harsh beauty of this region most intensely at Cruden Bay. Bram Stoker certainly did: he stayed here while dreaming up *Dracula*.

The bay itself is a mile-and-a-half swoosh of stupendously white sand culminating at each end in jagged rocks – locals say it made Stoker think of a fanged mouth – backed by wild dunes bristling with leg-slashing marram grass. This is not a place for basking, then – the northeast does get an unfair share of Scotland's sunshine, but still, it only gets really hot for a few weeks of the year. This is a place, instead, for stirring walks.

One particularly Gothic hike leads north of the bay, skirting the golf course (one of the finest links courses in the world) and crossing a picturesquely rickety white footbridge, the Ladies Bridge, to the tiny village of Cruden Bay. Everything is built in the local pink granite, right down to the minuscule harbour at the end of the road. The main Buchan coast path climbs on for half a mile to Slains Castle, perched on the cliffs. In Stoker's day, this was a melodramatically situated Victorian mansion: an obvious inspiration for Dracula's castle. Since then, 100 years of northeastern weather have reduced it to a truly dramatic ruin. Following a roughish path two miles north, you come to a still more alarming landmark: the cliff cirque of the Bullers o' Buchan. The mewing of gulls and kittiwakes rises from this granite cauldron, along with the rhythmic pound of the sea as it smashes its way in through an arch. In such a place, you could be forgiven for thinking the sea itself is breathing.

Need to know Cruden Bay lies 23 miles north of Aberdeen (regular bus service). For local history and information, try the Cruden Bay Community Association (Ⓦ www.crudenbay.org.uk), or the enthusiast's website Ⓦ www.bullersofbuchan.me.uk.
Map 5, E19

332 Northumberland's castle coast

Thanks to centuries of border battles with its neighbours to the north, there are more castles in Northumberland than in any other region of the country. And what castles they are.

Watching over the River Coquet as it drains into the North Sea, a couple of miles up the coast from Amble, Warkworth Castle was once home to the powerful Percy family, the earls of Northumberland. The fourteenth-century pile is remarkably intact and has one of the finest keeps of its kind, a three-storey behemoth that lords it over the surrounding walls.

So is there a more impressive ruin in the country than Warkworth? Well. . . . Less than ten miles up the coast, the craggy ruins of Dunstanburgh Castle dominate the land in all directions. If anything, the keep here – converted from a twin-towered gatehouse to strengthen it against the Scots – is even more defiant, perched on a headland and cutting a desolate figure against the sea.

So is there a more romantic fortress in the country than Dunstanburgh? Funny you should say that. Bamburgh Castle, another seven miles or so up the coast, is the fortress of a thousand fairy tales, a brooding series of battlements that span nine acres of rocky plateau between town and beach. One of the largest inhabited castles in England, Bamburgh was home to the kings of Northumbria, and was completely restored in 1900 after its destruction during the Wars of the Roses. You can tour the interior, but it's equally lovely seen from the vast expanse of windswept Bamburgh Beach.

So is there a more atmospheric castle in the country than Bamburgh? You know, there might just be. Crowning the tip of Holy Island, twelve miles south of Berwick-upon-Tweed and only accessible at low tide, Lindisfarne Castle was built in the mid-sixteenth century to protect the island's harbour from (you guessed it) the Scots. Converted into a house in 1903 by Edwin Lutyens, its dinky rooms mix grand fireplaces and grandiose arches with the personal touches of a private home. So is there a more historic stretch of coast in the country than the 33 beautiful miles that run from Amble to Berwick-upon-Tweed? Ah. You've got us there.

Need to know Warkworth and Dunstanburgh castles are owned by English Heritage (Ⓦ www.english-heritage.org.uk), Bamburgh Castle is home to the Armstrong family (Ⓦ www.bamburghcastle.com), and Lindisfarne Castle belongs to the National Trust (Ⓦ www.nationaltrust.org.uk); check Ⓦ www.lindisfarne.org.uk for tide times.
Map 4, E15

333 A pint on the beach at Porth Dinllaen

The blue waters of Caernarfon Bay are lapping just a few steps away across the beach as you sit on the pub wall wiggling your toes in the golden sand and supping on a pint of real ale outside one of Wales' best-set pubs. Welcome to *Tŷ Coch Inn* – the red house – at Porth Dinllaen, a wonderfully quaint village of a dozen or so houses and a lifeboat station wedged between the beach and steep green hills. One of the many beauties of this place is that only residents can drive here. Everyone else comes on foot, either along the beach from nearby Morfa Nefyn, or half a mile across the Nefyn and District golf course. Braving the golf balls is a slightly surreal way to reach Porth Dinllaen, which despite being bought in its entirety by the National Trust in 1994, hasn't been turned it into some "Don't Walk on the Grass" museum piece.

Porth Dinllaen was once a thriving (if small) fishing port with its own shipbuilding yard and plenty of smuggling. At the beginning of the nineteenth century, proximity to Ireland made it a contender for the principal rail terminal and ferry port for Ireland. It hardly bears thinking about: this gorgeous little spot could have turned out like Holyhead – the eventual "winner" of the contest.

In summer the bay is usually packed with small boats plying the calm waters, shielded from the prevailing westerlies by the protective headland of Carreg Ddu. A delightful path wanders up to the point, giving fabulous views down to the village with the high peaks of Snowdonia framing the distant horizon. Stroll back down to the pub for a ploughman's lunch or a steak-and-kidney pie. On a blustery day it is cosy inside; at all other times, best settle down on the waterside benches. Some find it so hard to leave they hole up in one of the adjacent holiday homes for a wonderfully away-from-it-all few days

Need to know The village is owned by the National Trust (Ⓦ www.nationaltrust. org.uk), which has details of accommodation. *Tŷ Coch Inn*, Porth Dinllaen, Morfa Nefyn, Gwynedd (Ⓣ 01758/720498, Ⓦ www.tycoch. co.uk), is open daily in summer. Map 3, A11

10

ALL THE WORLD'S A STAGE

music, film, theatre and literature

When actor and writer Colin Welland won an Oscar for his *Chariots of Fire* screenplay, he memorably brandished the statuette, shouting "The British are coming!" It was a great soundbite, announcing a contemporary rush of British talent, but actually he was around a thousand years out of date. From the earliest church mystery plays, and devotional songs and chants, Britain has been giving its genius to the world – a colossal cultural and artistic outpouring that has spread across the globe. If you think that's too grand a statement, consider a world without the plays of the boy from Stratford, or without the songs of four lads from Liverpool. Consider the poetry of William Wordsworth or the novels of Thomas Hardy, rooted in a sense of place but speaking to a wider human condition – and imagine the countless millions who know something about the Lake District or Dorset despite never having been there. There's a British cultural bedrock – in literature, music, theatre, film and dance – that not only enriches our own lives but attracts visitors from far and wide, keen to seek the source of inspiration of their favourite writers and artists, whether it's Dylan Thomas's "heron priested shore" or Shakespeare's reconstructed Globe Theatre. There's also a vibrant contemporary cultural scene that still makes Britain a global player – we might not build ships or mine coal any more but we still have a big old clanking conveyor belt churning out first-class actors, directors, writers, dancers, singers and artists. The big cities, of course, have the most dynamic arts scenes – from ballet to bookslams, stand-up comedy to sit-down recitals – but genius will out, wherever it takes hold. A Welsh male voice choir, open-air opera in a Cornish Greek theatre, the director's cut in a regional art-house cinema, or the no-holds-barred fiddle-thrash of a Shetland folk gig – that's entertainment, and the British are still coming.

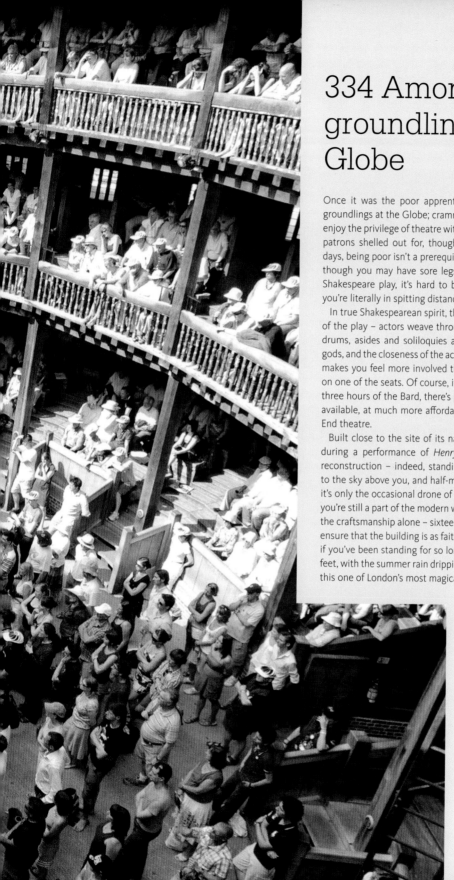

334 Among the groundlings at the Globe

Once it was the poor apprentices of London who made up the groundlings at the Globe; crammed into the Yard, they were able to enjoy the privilege of theatre without the price tag that the wealthier patrons shelled out for, though with none of the comfort. These days, being poor isn't a prerequisite of joining the groundlings – and though you may have sore legs from standing nonstop through a Shakespeare play, it's hard to beat this stage-side position, where you're literally in spitting distance of the action.

In true Shakespearean spirit, the audience is often an intrinsic part of the play – actors weave through the crowd bearing banners and drums, asides and soliloquies are directed at you rather than the gods, and the closeness of the action on the thrust stage immediately makes you feel more involved than you would if you were perched on one of the seats. Of course, if you don't think your legs are up to three hours of the Bard, there's plenty of more comfortable options available, at much more affordable prices than you'd pay in a West End theatre.

Built close to the site of its namesake, which burnt down in 1613 during a performance of *Henry VIII*, the Globe is an impressive reconstruction – indeed, standing in the yard, with the roof open to the sky above you, and half-moon tiers of seats surrounding you, it's only the occasional drone of an aeroplane that reminds you that you're still a part of the modern world. The theatre is worth a visit for the craftsmanship alone – sixteenth-century processes were used to ensure that the building is as faithful as possible to the original. Even if you've been standing for so long that you can no longer feel your feet, with the summer rain dripping down on you, it's hard not to find this one of London's most magical experiences.

Need to know

Shakespeare's Globe, 21 New Globe Walk, Bankside, London SE1 ℡ 020/7401 9919, Ⓦ www.shakespeares-globe.org. The Globe is open throughout the year for tours, but the theatre season runs from roughly April to October (with occasional performances some years at Christmas). Tickets: £5–35.
Map 1, E3

335 On Wessex Heights: a tour of Hardy country

Novelist, poet...architect. Thomas Hardy's early profession is his least known, and on first glance of Max Gate near Dorchester, the home he designed for himself in 1885, your first thought isn't of a talent wasted but slight relief that he turned to writing. It's a gloomy place, solid red brick – but this curiosity is an intriguing stop on the trail of Dorset's most famous son.

Dorset's towns and villages, landscape and language permeates all of Hardy's writing – so Dorchester itself is Hardy's Casterbridge, the coastal town of Bere Regis becomes Kingsbere and Cerne Abbas is Abbot's Cernel, the last two both featuring in *Tess of the D'Urbervilles*. A full tour of Hardy country would take in all these and more – certainly starting in Dorchester. But, more than visiting any individual town, it's when you explore deep into rural Dorset that Hardy's words most resonate: "There are some heights in Wessex, shaped as if by a kindly hand/For thinking, dreaming, dying on, and at crises when I stand,/Say, on Ingpen Beacon eastward, or on Wylls-Neck westwardly,/I seem where I was before my birth, and after death may be" (*Wessex Heights*, 1896).

At the centre of his Wessex Heights – which stretch roughly from the Wiltshire/Berkshire border in the east to the Quantocks to the west – is "homely Bulbarrow", a magnificent hill in north Dorset with an Iron Age fort, Rawlsbury Camp, and views across the county, including Blackmore Vale, Hardy's "vale of little dairies" and the home of Tess. It's fine walking country – the twelve-mile hike from here to Cerne Abbas is strenuous but doable in a day (stop at the thatched pub *The Brace of Pheasants* in Plush for lunch). Shorter is the walk up Bulbarrow and back from Ansty village (with a drink at *The Fox Inn* your reward); tramping along paths and across farmland around here is surely the closest you'll come to following in his characters' footsteps.

And the final stop is where his story started: the absurdly picturesque cob and thatch cottage in Higher Bockhampton, back towards Dorchester, where he was born in 1840, where he wrote his early novels, and which had been the Hardy family home for several generations. Nestled in among the trees, with an attractive garden, it's the archetype of rural Dorset cottage, and little altered since the family left – a perfect snapshot of his world.

Need to know Max Gate, Alington Ave, Dorchester (☎01297/489481; April–Sept Mon, Wed & Sun 2–5pm; £3); Hardy's Cottage, Higher Bockhampton (☎01305/262366; May–Oct Mon, & Thurs–Sun 11am–5pm; £4). Both are managed by the National Trust (Ⓦ www.nationaltrust. org.uk). *The Brace of Pheasants*, Plush (☎01300/348357, Ⓦwww. braceofpheasants.co.uk); *Fox Inn*, Ansty (☎01258/880328, Ⓦwww. anstyfoxinn.co.uk).

Map 2, C6

336 Learning how to live at the School of Life

The aim of the School of Life is so simple and so brilliant – to create a space where people can step back and consider life's most important questions: work, play, family, politics, love – you can't help but wonder if it has ever been attempted before. And the answer is that of course it has. As far back as 387 BC, Plato, pondering the same questions, set up his Academy, the very first institution of higher education. Not as a place to teach business administration or design technology, but to provoke thoughts, ideas and conversations among Athenians that might go some way to answering: "what is the right way to live?".

Fast forward several hundred years and similar conversations are being had among twenty-first-century Londoners in the back rooms of a small shop in Bloomsbury. The School of Life, set up in 2008, offers classes on subjects as diverse as "how to be a good friend" and "how to face death". The location in the heart of Bloomsbury is itself significant, with its mixed history of literary elitism and urban squalor. This is a place for the everyman: no entry qualifications required, just a decent bag-load of human experience.

Classes last two and a half hours, with a brief interlude for wine and cake, and are a mixture of lecture, pair work and group discussion. In effect, there are three teachers in the class: the teacher, the content of the class, and the ideas and experiences shared with your fellow classmates. There is no dogma here, instead the teacher offers up a smorgasbord of quotes, thoughts and ideas drawn from art, literature, film, music, history, psychology and philosophy, chosen to encourage the class to think deeply and differently – while you might not find the answer to the meaning of life, you are sure to uncover new ways of thinking about it.

If a class merely serves to whet your appetite, you can further your studies at one of the School's secular sermons, on subjects ranging from envy and adultery to kindness and humility. And for the very advanced student: an entire weekend away. Plato would be pleased.

Need to know School of Life, 70 Marchmont St, London WC1 ℡ 020/7833 1010, ⓦ www.theschooloflife.com. Classes Mon–Fri 6.30–9.30pm, £30. General opening hours for the School and bookshop Mon–Fri noon– 6pm. Map 1, D2

337 Beside the lake, beneath the trees: Wordsworth's daffodils

If William Wordsworth really did feel "lonely as a cloud" while strolling beside Ullswater in Cumbria on April 15, 1802, it was an abstract mood, as he wasn't alone that day: his companion was his devoted sister, Dorothy. Her journal records their delight at seeing a belt of daffodils "about the breadth of a country road". Two years later, her brother would use her notes as inspiration for *Daffodils*, a poem now stitched firmly into the fabric of English culture.

Make a pilgrimage to the same spot and you can't help but feel a cosy glow of recognition, mixed with a dash of dreamy romance. Every spring, thanks to the careful custodianship of the National Trust, a fresh "host of golden daffodils" – dainty little wild ones – appears in the dappled shade of Glencoyne Wood on Ullswater's peaceful shore. You can visit on foot, or cruise the lake aboard a Victorian steamer.

Dorothy's journal is on display at the Wordsworth Museum in Grasmere, where notebooks, publications, items of clothing and household objects help round out a picture not only of the Wordsworths but also of their close friend Samuel Taylor Coleridge and the other Romantics. There are more traces of their lives in Dove Cottage next door, home to William and Dorothy from 1799 to May 1808, a golden period for William's creativity. When William married his childhood friend Mary Hutchinson in 1802, the household grew to bursting point: three of their five children were born here. The small, simple rooms have been preserved as they might have been while the Wordsworths were in residence, and you can wander the steep garden where William retreated from the cramped conditions indoors to compose his poems.

Wordsworth considered Grasmere "the fairest place on earth", but eventually the growing family moved to a larger house, Rydal Mount, a few miles away, remaining there for 37 years. When their beloved daughter Dora died, he and Mary planted hundreds of daffodils at Rydal in her memory; these, too, still emerge every spring. There are more daffodils to admire in the churchyard of St Oswald's Church, Grasmere, near the Wordsworth family graves, where a community project has created a lovely garden of over 20,000 wild bulbs. Visit in late March or early April and you can see them "fluttering and dancing in the breeze" at their sprightly best.

Need to know Wordsworth Point in Glencoyne Wood is around seven miles south of Penrit (℡ 017684/82067, ⓦ www.nationaltrust.org.uk). Ullswater Steamers run cruises on the lake from Glenridding or Pooley Bridge to Howtown (℡ 017684/82229, ⓦ www.ullswater-steamers.co.uk; £9/£12.30). Dove Cottage and the Wordsworth Museum are in Grasmere (℡ 015394/35533, ⓦ www.wordsworth.org.uk; daily: March–Oct 9.30am–5.30pm; Nov–Feb 9.30am–4pm; £7.50). Rydal Mount is in Ambleside (℡ 015394/33002, ⓦ www.rydalmount.co.uk; March–Oct daily 9.30am–5pm; Nov–Feb Wed–Sun 11am–4pm; £6). Map 4, D16

338 Heritage in colour: York's Mystery Plays

It's not every Sunday night that you see your local butcher, draped in a strategically placed loincloth, his milk-bottle skin marbling in the chill of a northern English summer evening, being loudly jeered and hoisted onto a cross. You're ten plays and seven hours in, but moments like these still raise goosebumps. A hushed awe sweeps over the audience, sausage rolls pause halfway to mouths, hands stop tucking rugs around knees and kids who've given up trying to follow the language sit still and gape. Originally performed by York's powerful medieval guilds (the "mystery" refers to the secrets of each guild's own particular craft), today these colourful mini epics of religion and human nature continue to inspire, surprise and entertain as they have done for centuries.

Your medieval marathon begins at noon, when you settle down on the sun-dappled grass of Dean's Park, just out of the shadow of the towering Minster, and the first of the wooden wagons rolls into view. Accompanied by the beat of drums and the trills of tabor pipes, the *Creation of the World* (as enacted by the local Guild of Building) gets underway with much cheering, nodding, winking and audience interaction – a down-to-earth style that helps a modern viewer make sense of the Middle English text. Church congregations, theatre companies, local working guilds and other groups roll along one after another to present another of the 48 surviving plays, all based on Bible scenes. From the surprisingly bawdy pageantry of *Joseph's Troubles about Mary* to the modernist, almost Brechtian stylings of a local youth theatre group's *Massacre of the Innocents* – think *A Clockwork Orange* crossed with *Pilgrim's Progress,* all bowler hats, scary doll puppets and synchronized howling – it's clear that far from being relics these plays are living artefacts, continuing to weave themselves into the town's already embarrassingly rich cultural fabric. Every twenty minutes each episode concludes to raucous cheering that would make a medieval audience proud. The wagons then wend their way through twisting medieval lanes and cobbled squares to the next location, parting bemused seas of Italian teenagers and delighting tea-sipping tourists spooning clotted cream onto Fat Rascals in the wide windows of the legendary *Betty's* tearoom. As you follow this extraordinarily vibrant day-long pageant through the history-saturated city, as the sun climbs to its zenith and slowly sinks behind the spellbinding ruins of St Mary's Abbey, community theatre has never felt so theatrical, or so communal.

Need to know York Mystery Plays are held over two weekends every four years. The next cycle will be in July 2014. See Ⓦ www.yorkmysteryplays.co.uk for details.

Map 3, D9

FILM LOCATIONS

Britain crams an impressive array of landscapes, historical sites and urban environments into a relatively small area, making it a popular location for a wide range of films. Here's a selection of well-known film locations that also make for a great day out, whether you want a relaxing walk or a session in the surf.

339 Gladiator: Bourne Wood, Farnham, Surrey

The savage battle scene in "Germania" was shot in Bourne Wood, a somewhat unlikely location in the heart of the genteel Home Counties. However, visit on a damp and misty autumn day to enjoy one of the easy walking trails and it's not that hard to imagine yourself in the remote forests of central Europe some 2000 years ago. Director Ridley Scott obviously has a thing for Bourne Wood since he also used it as the location for "Castle Chalus" in *Robin Hood*, shot here nine years later.

Map 2, E6

340 Monty Python and The Holy Grail: Doune Castle, Stirling

Doune Castle was built in the late fourteenth century by Robert Stewart, earl of Albany and ruler of Scotland from 1388 to 1420, and makes for a great day out with its mix of stately rooms, interconnecting passageways and impressive fortifications. You may also recognize it as the castle upon which King Arthur and his men approach, coconut shells in hand, in *Monty Python and the Holy Grail*; it also stands in for Camelot, Swamp Castle and Castle Anthrax in the same film.

Ⓦ *www.historic-scotland.gov.uk. Map 4, C14*

341 The Railway Children: Haworth, West Yorkshire

This kids' favourite from 1970 made effective use of the Victorian towns and villages around Haworth, with all the train scenes shot on the Keighley & Worth Valley Steam Railway which runs through the area. Haworth's cobbled main street features heavily in the film, as does Brontë Parsonage where the eponymous authors lived. Take a trip on the train, a stroll through the village then a hike across the surrounding moors.

Ⓦ *www.kwvr.co.uk. Map 3, C10*

342 Hitchcock in London

Hitchcock may have set his most famous films in the US, but the Leytonstone-born master of suspense always remained a true Londoner. Classic early thrillers such as Jack the Ripper-influenced *The Lodger: A Story of the London Fog* (1927) and *Blackmail* (1929), which reaches its grisly denouement among the mummies of the British Museum, show him revelling in the macabre long before *Psycho*. Guided walks by Hitchcock expert Sandra Shevey explore the locations of three later films: courtroom melodrama *The Paradine Case* (1947), which features the Old Bailey's still bomb-damaged exterior; *The Man Who Knew Too Much* (1934; re-shot in colour in 1956), which moves from a Camden Town taxidermist's to its suspense-laden final scenes in the Royal Albert Hall; and gruesome serial murder thriller *Frenzy* (1972), set around Covent Garden. Filmed just before the fruit and veg market closed (where Hitchcock's dad had been a greengrocer), it's a typically dark love letter to a London on the verge of disappearing.

Ⓦ *sandrashevey.tripod.com/hitchcock.walks. Three-hour guided walks (Mon, Wed & Sat; £25). Map 1, D3*

343 Breaking the Waves: Lochailort, Highland

Not the cheeriest of films, Lars von Trier's 1996 production did at least locate itself amongst some of the most exhilarating landscapes in Scotland. The film's church scenes are shot just outside Mallaig at Lochailort, with further filming taking place in the town and at Neist Point, the most westerly location on the Isle of Skye. There's some fine easy walking around Lochailort and Mallaig, such as the stroll along the lovely white-sand beach of Camusdarach, while Skye's Cuillin Ridge offers some of the most spectacular and exciting hiking in Britain.

Map 5, B20

344 Robin Hood: Freshwater West, Pembrokeshire

Robin Hood features another spectacular battle scene from Ridley Scott, shot on the wide expanse of golden sands at Freshwater West in Pembrokeshire, one of Wales's best surfing beaches. This didn't go down too well with local surfers, who were banned from riding the waves for the period of filming. The waves caused some problems during the shoot with boats being swamped and both actors and extras being buffeted about in the swell – but if you're here with your surfboard this is, of course, exactly what you want.

Map 2, A5

345 The French Lieutenant's Woman: The Cobb, Lyme Regis, Dorset

The image of Meryl Streep draped in a large black cloak on the film's promotional poster was taken on The Cobb, a thirteenth-century breakwater built under the instruction of Edward I. This in itself makes for a fine albeit brief stroll, but you could also take a longer walk along the almost tropically dense Undercliff (which also appears in the film) to the west of The Cobb, or wander along the seashore to the east which is part of the famous Jurassic Coast.

Map 2, C6

346 The Libertine: Tretower Court, Crickhowell, Powys

Several major scenes from *The Libertine* were shot at Tretower Court, a finely renovated late medieval mansion and courtyard located a couple of miles from Crickhowell and tucked beneath the dramatic dark ridges of the Brecon Beacons' Black Mountains, which rise steeply to the north. During filming Johnny Depp was a regular at the lovely old *Bear Hotel* in Crickhowell, also well worth a visit.

Ⓦ *www.cadw.wales.gov.uk. Map 2, C5*

347 Harry Potter: Alnwick Castle, Northumberland

The magnificent bulk of Alnwick Castle – the second largest inhabited castle in Britain – was the setting for the Hogwarts School of Witchcraft and Wizardry, for broomstick flying lessons and for Quidditch matches. The imposing 700-year-old pile is everyone's idea of what a medieval castle should look like, hence its starring role in the first two Harry Potter films as well as *Elizabeth* and *Robin Hood Prince of Thieves* among others.

Ⓦ *www.alnwickcastle.com. Map 4, E15*

348 Withnail & I: Sleddale Hall, near Shap, Cumbria

The remote Crow Crag farmhouse where bibulous, out-of-work actors Withnail and narrator "I" find themselves "on holiday by mistake" is set on the side of the Shap Fells on the eastern edge of the Lake District. The farm, which makes for a pleasant half-day walk from the nearby village of Shap, has become a place of pilgrimage for fans of the film – and is a good place for escaping the busier fells and footpaths in the heart of the Lake District.

Map 4, D16

349 Those magnificent men with their music machines

Need to know Keith Harding's World of Mechanical Music, High St, Northleach, Gloucestershire. ☎ 01451/860181. ⓦ www.mechanicalmusic.co.uk. Daily 10am–5pm.
Map 2, D5

Once upon a time, before iPods or even CDs were thought of, the only recorded music available was that reproduced on automatic musical machines. The eminent horologist Keith Harding has gathered an intriguing and engrossing collection of self-playing musical instruments and other automata in the village of Northleach, a stone's throw from one of the grandest wool churches in the Cotswolds. Here, in a former schoolroom now adorned with William Morris wallpaper, you can join a tour by one of the impressively informed guides round a bewildering range of polyphons, antique musical boxes, player pianos, wax cylinder phonographs and horn gramophones, not to mention musical snuffboxes, cages with singing mechanical birds and a Steinway Reproducing Piano. The air resonates with tunes by the likes of Paderewsky, Rachmaninov and Gershwin, and you'll be entertained by jaunty bar-room jingles, folk melodies and contemporary airs and arias, from *Ave Maria* to *Come into the Garden, Maud* and *The Teddy Bears' Picnic* – sometimes by means of vigorous pumping and winding by the aforementioned staff. To hear Grieg play his own work (via a player piano) is truly spine-tingling.

Most of the instruments are nineteenth century, many of them are from Geneva or Paris, though the awkwardly named "Autoglockenpolyphon" – a sort of primitive jukebox – is from Leipzig. The technology astounds, making use of toothed cylinders, punched card discs and paper rolls, but the instruments are much more than mere machines – these meticulously crafted artefacts were prized additions to drawing rooms, the workings often encased within rosewood and walnut veneers with carved mouldings and intricate marquetry. Others are more frivolous: attention-grabbing fairground articles, brashly painted gypsy pipe organs, banjo-playing minstrels and miniature musical cottages.

Though many of the items on display are for sale, you might need to sell the car for some of them. A better option is to nose around the gift shop, packed with an irresistible collection of toys and devices, all exuding the same delight in nostalgia and gadgetry as the museum: pop-up books with sound effects, musical boxes, snoring and twitching fluffy pigs, and dozens of antique clocks. There's also a good selection of books on Cotswold architecture, crafts and customs, and, of course, on the art of mechanical music.

350 It's no croak: having a laugh at Manchester's Frog and Bucket

Need to know The Frog and Bucket, 96–102 Oldham St, Manchester ☎ 0161/236 9805, ⓦ www.frogandbucket.com. Daily from 7pm, check website for listings. Fri three comics £15, Sat £16, "Big value Thursdays" – five comics for £8.
Map 3, C10

The walls of Manchester's self-proclaimed "original home of comedy in the North" carry portraits of some very famous faces. Glance around The Frog and Bucket and you'll see Johnny Vegas and Peter Kay, just two of the huge stars that have launched their careers in the unassuming building on the corner of Oldham and Great Ancoats streets. Other past or present regulars include Dave Gorman, Richard Herring, Brendon Burns and Caroline Aherne, and the city's prodigal son Steve Coogan has been known to try out new comic characters here. People flock to The Frog because it has a long-standing commitment to comedy – especially alternative – and a friendly, welcoming vibe among audiences and comics alike. The cosy and welcoming venue started life in 1993 as a little pub on Newton Street where Peter Kay did one of his first ever stand-ups, but the comedy became so popular there the club moved to this larger place.

Inside you'll find a small stage, plenty of food and beer on offer and one big green frog. On a Monday night, which is free if you wander in and don't book a table, an array of upcoming comics have a five-minute slot each to "beat the frog" and prove they deserve a repeat booking. The standard is often remarkably high – and if it isn't the audience certainly let the performers know. If you prefer tried-and-trusted names, Thursdays are a good bet, when you get five nationally or internationally known comics on one bill. And at weekends you get some really top-class names, though it can get rather busy. Sometimes the audiences include comics themselves – regulars still turn misty-eyed at talk of Johnny Vegas's occasional off-the-cuff slots, delivered in varying degrees of (in)sobriety. But be warned – sit too close to the front and you just might find yourself a part of the show.

351 Small is beautiful: searching out the best music in London

London's concert venues are legendary. Try the *Hammersmith Palais*, where Joe Strummer had a famously dramatic time at a reggae night; *The Marquee*, where the Rolling Stones were baptized and Pete Townshend smashed up his guitar; Finsbury Park's *Rainbow/Astoria*, where Jimi Hendrix first lit his. You won't find any of them any more: the *Palais* is derelict, stuck in development limbo, *The Marquee* repeatedly moved and is now defunct and the *Rainbow* became a Brazilian Pentecostal church in 1985.

Then again, pop arguably should be temporary, should spark and then burn out. You can check out its current stars at the likes of the Brixton Academy, the Shepherd's Bush Empire and the vast O2. But if branding leaves you cold and expensive tickets with improbably large booking fees make you wince at your bank balance, London's smaller venues offer an appealing alternative, led by enthusiasm rather than beer sales. One of the most beautiful venues in the city is Islington's *Union Chapel*, a Grade-II listed Victorian Gothic chapel, which hosts a mixture of established acts, who often use the space for one-off gigs and special events, with showcases for new artists. Its regular Saturday lunchtime event, Daylight Music, features new bands that broadly fit within the folk moniker, which the echoing, atmospheric venue seems particularly well suited to.

The Windmill in Brixton is never going to win prizes for beauty, but like Daylight Music it seems, refreshingly, to pick bands it actually likes. Tucked away down a side street, this titchy, cheerfully battered pub hosts mixed line-ups, often broadly linked by genre, which means one evening might run from rockabilly to blues and another mix crunching rock and high-tempo punk. The result is that you feel you're at an evening with a vibe and a social function rather than an aircraft hangar filled with amps.

Herbal-tea-drinking chin-strokers wanting something a little more arty should find *Cafe OTO* – a Dalston café that serves Japanese food, avant-garde jazz, poetry, modern dance, dreamy electronica and the sort of droning post-rock that sounds like a droid in a washing machine – right up their street. Mellow during the day, its chairs, cushions and floor space soon fill up with obsessives come the evening, when it feels both keenly hip and straightforwardly welcoming: a place ripe for a happening.

Need to know *The Union Chapel*, Compton Ave, Islington N1 Ⓦ www.unionchapel.org.uk; *The Windmill*, 22 Blenheim Gardens, Brixton SW2 Ⓦ www.windmillbrixton.co.uk; *Cafe OTO*, 18–22 Ashwin St, Dalston E8 Ⓦ www.cafeoto.co.uk.
Map 1, D1, F3 & F4

352 Going to the ballet in Birmingham

Princess Aurora's delicately sequined bodice and fine tulle skirts are gorgeously illuminated as she pirouettes into the arms of her Prince. The dancers move gracefully through the sumptuous palace, rediscovered after one hundred years of being concealed in a thick forest conjured by the wicked fairy Carabosse. The delighted audience look on in awe, transported by Tchaikovsky's romantic score and Marius Petipa's sublime choreography.

But they are not seated in the expensive stalls of Covent Garden's Royal Opera House, for this lavish production of the great ballet classic *Sleeping Beauty* is being performed in one of British ballet's most important regional venues: the Birmingham Hippodrome. Located in the heart of the city, not far from the stylish shops of the Bull Ring and with the decent *Circle* restaurant on site, the recently redeveloped theatre is a cultural highlight of the city. Relatively affordable ticket prices ensure that the resident Birmingham Royal Ballet reaches increasingly broad audiences – and each of the comfortable seats has an excellent view of the stage. Artistic director David Bintley's internationally renowned BRB has made its home at the Hippodrome since it formed in 1990. Initially created as a sister company to Dame Ninette de Valois' London-based Royal Ballet, two decades later the BRB is now independent, but retains an excellent reputation on account of impressive stagings of both classical and avant-garde ballet.

Firm proof that regional ballet in the UK is in robust health, the BRB's outstanding repertory has expanded to include such productions as Prokofievs's magical fairy tale *Cinderella*, the enchanting story of *Coppélia*, the mechanical doll, and the charming Christmas classic, *The Nutcracker*. The company's world-class dancers have also successfully premiered exciting new works choreographed by David Bintley: from *Quantum Leaps* – dance ambitiously inspired by Einstein and the Cosmos, to *All That Jazz* – energetically performed with a live jazz orchestra. And it's not just lucky Brummies that get the chance to spend a spellbinding evening with the BRB, the company regularly tours the UK, so get booking to experience one of Britain's most dynamic ballet companies in performance.

Need to know The Birmingham Royal Ballet is based at the Birmingham Hippodrome and also tours throughout the UK. For further information, see Ⓦ www.brb.org.uk.
Map 3, C11

353 Dylan Thomas's "heron priested shore"

On a peaceful tree-lined lane in the shadow of the twelfth-century Laugharne Castle stands a simple, pitched-roof, green shed. Cup your eyes against the small window to reveal a few sketches pinned to the wall, a plain writing desk and a few pieces of balled-up paper scattered on the floor. It is as though Dylan Thomas has just popped out for a pint – "its live, white lather, its brass-bright depths" – at his favourite haunt, the snug at nearby *Brown's Hotel*.

Swansea's wild genius poet spent the last four years of his drink-shortened life in the small south Wales town of Laugharne producing some of his finest works from this shed. He'd wrestle over tight lines of poetry for five intense hours each afternoon before wandering along the lane to The Boathouse where he lived with his wife, Caitlin, and their three children. Today the boathouse is the focus of any Dylan Thomas pilgrimage. Until Dylan's death in 1953, aged just 39, the family lived in this gorgeously sited three-storey house with its views of the "heron priested shore" of the Taf Estuary. It hasn't changed much. There's a suitably Fifties feel to the furnishings, and the sonorous meter of Dylan Thomas's voice plays over an old radio set.

Thomas undoubtedly drew inspiration from this beautiful, peaceful spot, but his real muse was the town and people of Laugharne, which many credit as the model for the imaginary seaside town of Llareggub ("bugger all" backwards), in his classic *Under Milk Wood*. Walking the narrow streets of this "lazy little black-magical bedlam by the sea" almost sixty years on from the first performance of his "play for voices" it is hard to conjure up characters like Captain Cat, Mr Waldo and Myfanwy Price. Still, however much the town might be able to stake its inspirational claim, the greater part of the play was always the product of the master's fertile imagination.

The final station on the Dylan Thomas tour is the graveyard of St Martin's church. Here Dylan was joined by Caitlin in 1994, their twin graves marked by a plain white cross. It is perhaps fittingly underwhelming in a town that has always had a grudging love for its most famous son.

Need to know Dylan Thomas Boathouse, Dylan's Walk, Laugharne, Carmarthenshire Ⓣ 01994/427420, Ⓦ www.dylanthomasboathouse.com. Daily: Easter weekend & May–Oct 10am–5.30pm; Nov–April 10.30am–3.30pm, £3.75. *Brown's Hotel* is currently closed.
Map 2, B5

354 A dramatic cliffhanger

Building an open-air theatre in England was clearly an optimistic thing to do, but the woman who conceived the idea of the Minack – Rowena Cade – wasn't short on persistence either. From 1931 onwards she spent over half a century designing and assembling what is arguably England's most remarkable theatre – a Classical-style tiered auditorium constructed over a crag, from where spectators look down onto the stage and out to Porthcurno beach and the sea. It's not quite Land's End (that's about nine miles away) but it feels like it when you gaze over the ocean from your seat.

The first production here was, fittingly, *The Tempest*, Shakespeare's desert-island play. Since then The Bard's works have formed a regular part of the season, which lasts from May to September and includes a mix of amateur and professional dramatic companies. Part of the Minack's magic is that the second half of the performance usually takes place as dusk sets; so while the sun sinks into the horizon and washes the sea a deep tangerine, scenes are imagined as events at night, with candles and lighting used to full effect. And don't for one minute think that it will be cancelled if it's drizzling: the show must go on (barring a real tempest) and the sight of soaked actors declaiming to a drenched audience, with everyone pretending that it's all perfectly normal, is proof positive that British grit isn't dead yet.

The Minack is open year-round for visitors, and has some subtropical gardens and an exhibition on Rowena Cade as well as the auditorium itself, but it's one of those places where the play's the thing. Where else can you pre-order a pasty with your ticket, or listen to the murmur of the waves between acts? Good old Rowena. She might have been a bit eccentric but she had a vision of something truly special. And when the curtain comes down – metaphorically speaking – you'll share it too.

Need to know The Minack
Theatre, Porthcurno, Cornwall
℡ 01736/810181, Ⓦ www.minack.
com. April–Sept 9.30am–5.30pm;
Oct until 5pm; Nov–March
10am–3.30pm; £3.50. Performances
(May–Sept) are at 2pm or 8pm;
ticket prices £8–£9.50.. The Minack
is a 20min drive from Penzance;
parking is free. From Penzance
take buses #1, #1A or #504 to
Porthcurno valley.
Map 2, A7

One of the world's most dynamic dance houses, Sadler's Wells theatre has a well-earned reputation for showcasing some of the most exciting companies and innovative styles in contemporary dance. Though there has been an entertainment venue on the theatre's site in Islington, London, since Richard Sadler opened his "musick house" in 1683, the striking glass facade of the twenty-first-century Sadler's Wells is fittingly modern.

Perched inside the vertiginous 1560-seat main auditorium, audiences here are treated to performances that challenge and subvert traditional forms, from the strange, bold and sometimes violent choreography of the late Pina Bausch's company, to Akram Khan's compelling fusions of contemporary dance and traditional Kathak. Under current artistic director Alistair Spalding's watch, Sadler's Wells has ensured that its programme remains impressively avant-garde by commissioning several new pieces a year by leading choreographers, as well as establishing the annual "Global Dance Contest" to discover fresh talent. Quality control is set very high; associate artists and performers include celebrated contemporary ballet choreographer Christopher Wheeldon and Russell Maliphant, whose pioneering productions combine elements of ballet, yoga and capoeira. And the audiences reflect the variety of the performances; while classical ballet and opera can keep younger dance lovers at a distance with its high ticket prices and stuffy venues, during each interval Sadler's Wells' bars and galleries are packed with a diverse crowd.

For the uninitiated, contemporary dance can seem unappealing, often associated with jarring, difficult music and movements – but the breadth of programming at Sadler's Wells confounds this stereotype. At one end of the spectrum, esoteric pieces by smaller companies cater to purists, but other productions feature high-profile collaborations between mainstream dance companies, musicians and visual artists. Perhaps the best and cheapest (tickets £5–10) introduction to this star of London dance venues is *Sampled*, each January, where different companies perform short pieces in contemporary styles from hip-hop to ballet. Settled in your red-cushioned seat, watching the illuminated dancers spin, leap or somersault across the expansive stage, it's impossible not to feel inspired.

Need to know Sadler's Wells Theatre, Rosebery Ave, London EC1. For bookings and details of the programme: ☎ 0844 412 4300, Ⓦ www.sadlerswells.com. **Map 1, D2**

356 Fiddles and festivals in Shetland

Despite a surprisingly diverse live music scene, Shetland is best known for its world-class fiddle tradition. So venerated are its performers that the islands' mythical Trows are said to kidnap them for their nocturnal gatherings. In reality though, folk's pre-eminence owes a tremendous amount to the late Dr Tom Anderson, who formed the Shetland Fiddlers' Society in 1960, preserving an endangered art and teaching many skilled players, including the renowned Aly Bain.

Since 1981, local talent has been joined by performers from around the globe for the hugely popular Shetland Folk Festival. Hosted in large, well-maintained village halls across the islands, this springtime event spans four days with performances every day from early afternoon onwards. Attracting people of all ages and passionately supported by locals, not least because most people know many of the performers well, the early-evening concerts typically feature six or seven acts of various nationalities and styles. Initially sedate affairs that loosen up fast with the compere's dubious jokes, the lively jigs and reels are followed by supper and a dance until 1am. The emphasis tends to be on boisterous fun rather than steps being followed correctly – Shetland tunes are traditionally composed for dancing and locals pride themselves on playing faster than elsewhere in Scotland. But some of the best performances take place in the wee small hours, when well-oiled musicians and audiences trickle back from the outlying venues to the Festival Club in Shetland's capital, Lerwick, for ad hoc jams till 3 or 4am.

At festival time, pop into *The Lounge Bar* at lunchtime on Saturday to hear guest musicians join the relaxed sessions upstairs. If you're visiting at other times of the year, there's still always plenty on: try Wednesday and Thursday nights at *The Lounge* or Tuesdays in the nearby *Douglas Arms*. Other "folkie" festivals include the more inclusive Shetland Accordion and Fiddle Festival, which takes place in autumn, the Flavour of Shetland (mid-June), Fiddle Frenzy (early to mid-Aug), The Thomas Fraser Memorial Festival (mid-Nov) and The Peerie Willie Guitar Festival in mid-September. The controversial Mareel arts centre's opening on Lerwick quayside in 2011 should add another substantial string to Shetland's musical bow.

Need to know Shetland Folk Festival, late April to early May (Ⓣ 01595/694757, Ⓦ www.shetlandfolkfestival.com); Shetland Accordion and Fiddle Festival, early to mid-October (Ⓣ 01595/693162, Ⓦ www.shetlandaccordionandfiddle.com). Purchasing membership for both festivals is advised but not mandatory, though it is needed for entry to the Festival Club in Lerwick where many performances take place. Tickets are limited and sell out quite fast. *The Lounge Bar*, 4 Mounthooly St, Lerwick (Ⓣ 01595/692231); *The Douglas Arms*, 67 Commercial Rd, Lerwick (Ⓣ 01595/693787). See also Ⓦ www.visitscotland.com.
Map 5, F18

FILMHOUSES

If you want to join a good cross section of British society, get yourself to a filmhouse: rare is the place that finds boho indie hipsters, giggling teens, credits-scouring buffs and penny-pinching Orange Wednesday addicts settling down to share a genuinely communal experience. Along with a rash of cookiecutter multiplexes, film fans can also choose from a nice line in cool chains where plump armchairs, carrot cake and fancy wines are the norm, and quirky rep theatres that act as community hubs. There are even a few grubby fleapits for those of a nostalgic bent, though they're dying out fast.

357 Chapter Arts Centre, Cardiff

Films are just part of the deal at Cardiff's splendid arts centre, which opened in the late 1960s with a Pink Floyd concert. It's not quite as countercultural today, but the stylish creativity of its theatre, art exhibitions and live music extends to the screenings, with lots of indie and world cinema, panel discussions and even a monthly bad film club.

Market Rd, Cardiff ℡ 029/2031 1050, Ⓦ www.chapter.org. Map 2, C5

358 Duke of York's, Brighton

Brighton's Edwardian picture palace, now part of the hip national Picturehouse chain, celebrated its centenary in 2010. Snuggle down in the stylish, history-drenched auditorium – best of all, bag a sofa on the balcony – to soak up obscure and mainstream flicks, special screenings, themed premieres, all-nighters and funky parties.

Preston Circus, Brighton ℡ 0871 902 5728, Ⓦ www.picturehouses.co.uk. Map 2, E6

359 The Electric Cinema, Birmingham

The unprepossessing exterior, sandwiched between a couple of Chinese restaurants, belies the innate style of this classic old film theatre in Birmingham. Built in 1909 and remodelled in the 1930s, The Electric now offers art films, Art Deco style and absinthe from a vintage fountain – and an in-house orchestra that performs for special screenings.

47 Station St, Birmingham ℡ 0121/643 7879, Ⓦ www.theelectric.co.uk. Map 3, C11

360 Kinema in the Woods, Woodhall Spa

A charming, timewarped little place tucked among the pine trees, the Kinema is a genuinely populist filmhouse of the old school. Beginning its days as a concert pavilion to serve Lincolnshire's Woodhall Spa resort clients, today it shows mainstream films, with some popular classics, and hosts nostalgic, camper-than-camp sing-along organ concerts.

Coronation Rd, Woodhall Spa, Lincolnshire ℡ 01526/352166, Ⓦ www. thekinemainthewoods.co.uk. Map 3, D10

361 Tyneside Cinema, Newcastle

Opulent and with more than a touch of faded glamour, the Tyneside is as lively today as when it opened in 1937. The best current releases, world films and obscure indies are screened in a variety of rooms, from the cosy Roxy to the huge Electra, with a snug home-from-home ambience in the Digital Lounge. The sweet 1930s coffee shop serves tasty comfort food, while changing exhibitions, archive newsreel shows and film-related courses keep things energetic.

10 Pilgrim St, Newcastle upon Tyne ℡ 0845 217 9909, Ⓦ www. tynesidecinema.co.uk. Map 4, E15

362 Bloomsbury in Sussex

Daubs, swirls and blocks in earthy colours decorate lamp bases, table tops and chair-backs. Plump nudes recline under a mantelpiece scattered with sepia photos. Spilling over a chimney breast is a fluid mural including a still life, complete with painted-on frame. Who needs gilt frames, when your entire house is your canvas?

This is Charleston Farmhouse, the East Sussex home of post-Impressionist painters Vanessa Bell and Duncan Grant. Immaculately preserved, it's a museum to their unfettered creativity. It's also rich in memorabilia from the freethinking set of writers, artists and intellectuals to which they belonged: the Bloomsbury Group, friends who were far more than friends, their relationships passionately intertwined.

The couple moved to this calm corner of Sussex in 1916, amid the turbulence of World War I. Grant, a conscientious objector, had decided to run a fruit farm with his then-lover, Bunny Garnett. Even today, it's a blissfully peaceful spot, hidden from the busy Brighton-to-Eastbourne road. Visit in spring or summer and you'll find it adrift in a sea of green, floating serenely beside the soft, whale-backed bulk of the South Downs.

Friends, cousins and intimates from London gravitated to Charleston, John Maynard Keynes, Lytton Strachey, E.M. Forster among them. Vanessa's amicably estranged husband Clive and her younger sister, Virginia Woolf, practically lived there.

Virginia and her husband Leonard fell in love with Sussex so completely that within three years they acquired their own little pocket of green, The Monk's House, four miles to the west across the fields. It was in this pretty, weatherboarded cottage that Virginia wrote *Mrs Dalloway*, *To The Lighthouse* and *Orlando*, inspired by the object of her fascination, Vita Sackville-West. The downstairs rooms, which are open to the public, lovingly recreate the writer's presence.

The Bloomsbury Group's bond with the area lasted the rest of their lives and left a legacy that extended beyond their own homes. In the 1940s, Duncan Grant led Vanessa and her son Quentin in painting a set of Italian-influenced murals at St Michael and All Angels in the hamlet of Berwick. This modest, flint-walled church is a pleasant two-mile ramble from Charleston, conveniently close to a superb little country pub, *The Cricketers' Arms*, and the delightful Downland village of Alfriston.

Need to know Charleston Farmhouse, Firle, East Sussex (☎ 01323/811265, Ⓦ www.charleston.org.uk; April–Oct Wed–Sun & bank holiday Mon, times vary; £9); The Monk's House, Rodmell (☎ 01323/870001, Ⓦ www.nationaltrust.org.uk; April–Oct Wed & Sat 2–5.30pm; £4); *The Cricketers' Arms*, Berwick (☎ 01323/870469, Ⓦ www.cricketersberwick.co.uk). Map 2, E6

363 Move over Hay, welcome to Wigtown

Hay-on-Wye on the Wales/England border, long a name synonymous with bookshops, is usually thought of as being Britain's foremost town of books. It isn't, however, the only place in Britain where you'll find main streets bursting with bookshops and a calendar filled with literary events for every interest. Wigtown in Dumfries and Galloway is Scotland's answer to Hay and is every bit as quaint and bookish.

Officially designated Scotland's book town in 1998 after a Scotland-wide search for the perfect place to convert into a literary centre, the town boasts over twenty book-related businesses from The Book Shop, Scotland's largest for secondhand titles, with over a mile of shelving, to ReadingLasses – possibly the last bookshop specializing in women's studies left in the country – with a café serving delicious, mostly fair-trade and organic food. There are also smaller, specialist outfits like Byre Books, who focus on folklore and mythology, theatre, film and TV and Scottish interest.

A town of books wouldn't be complete without an annual literary festival and Wigtown's takes place over ten days in late September and early October. Speakers in previous years have included Roddy Doyle, Christopher Brookmyre, Iain Banks, David Aaronovitch, Irma Kurtz, Diana Athill, William Dalrymple and Louis de Bernières playing his mandolin and other bespoke instruments along to his poems and stories. There's music too, such as Burns' words sung chorally with harp accompaniment, and poetry, film screenings, creative writing workshops, late-night storytelling, cookery demonstrations by Scottish luminaries such as Nick Nairn and a fair amount of history, inspiration, celebration and tasting of the local whisky.

And all this takes place in a charming town just a stone's throw from a stretch of Scotland's stunning coast – Wigtown Bay is a rugged region of salt marsh and mud flat, a perfect stopoff for migratory birds. To the north of town is Galloway Forest park, with so little light pollution that it ranks as one of the darkest places on earth, an ideal place to view the night sky. Inspiration indeed for those of literary persuasion.

Need to know Wigtown Book Festival (W www. wigtownbookfestival.com) takes place in late September/early October. Events are ticketed and range in price from free to no more than £10. For more information, visit W www. wigtown-booktown.co.uk.
Map 4, C16

364 Adventure on the Dart: Agatha Christie's holiday home

Whether or not you're a fan of the Queen of Crime's oeuvre, there's something irresistible about the country-house settings, the sepia-tinted period and the aristocratic ambience of her numerous whodunnit yarns. All of these can be found in abundance at Greenway, a creamy Georgian mansion perched above the River Dart in South Devon, now run by the National Trust. This was her holiday home, which beautifully evokes the spirit of her sinister tales – it was in fact the setting of three of them: *Dead Man's Folly*, *Five Little Pigs* and *Ordeal by Innocence*.

Before the Mallowans (she was married to the archeologist Max Mallowan) took it on in 1938, the site had an illustrious history as home of the Gilbert dynasty, whose most famous scion, Sir Humphrey, was the soldier and navigator who claimed Newfoundland on behalf of Elizabeth I. The present building dates from around 1800 while its interior has the feel of a mid-twentieth-century rustic retreat, filled with baubles and knick-knacks from around the world. The most striking features include a frieze painted on the walls of the library by members of the US Coastguard billeted here during World War II, but it's the details that hold most interest – the Persian and Anatolian rugs, the Chinese screen made from kingfisher feathers, the Staffordshire stoneware and Meissen and Capo di Monte porcelain, and the various Buddhist and African sculptures.

On a more domestic note, you'll see piles of gardening hats, bound copies of the *Ladies' Magazine* from the turn of the eighteenth century, a wardrobe full of party clothes and a generously proportioned wooden WC. Traces of Agatha include dozens of the ornate wooden boxes that she collected, ranks of first editions of her books and tapes of the author discussing her method. And if you're lucky you'll come across one of the staff tinkling the ivories in the drawing room.

Outside is a gorgeous succession of walled gardens, old-fashioned greenhouses, fig and apple trees and hidden ponds, with the River Dart sparkling below. When you've had your fill, unwind with a leisurely round of croquet followed by tea and scones in the courtyard café.

But perhaps the most memorable feature of a visit to Greenway is arriving – a blissful river trip up from Dartmouth, followed by an ambling ascent through thick woods. Alternatively, there are glorious walking and cycling routes along the banks of the Dart.

Need to know
Greenway, Galmpton, Devon
T 01803/842382, W www. nationaltrust.org.uk. March to mid-July, Sept & Oct Wed–Sun 10.30am–5pm; mid-July to Aug Tues–Sun 10.30am–5pm. £8. Car-users must pre-book to use the car park; non-car-users get discounted entry. For details of the ferry from Dartmouth to Greenway see W www.greenwayferry.co.uk (May–Oct, roughly hourly; £6).
Map 2, B7

365 Raise the roof at a male voice choir performance

Mae Hen Wlad Fy Nhadau rings out from a grey chapel in the South Wales Valleys, bringing a tear to the eye of almost everyone in the hall. The National Anthem is in the repertoire of almost all Welsh male voice choirs either in Welsh or translated as *The Land Of My Fathers*.

The coal mines that spawned many of the choirs mostly shut up shop in the 1970s and 1980s, but even though many of the choristers may never have visited a pithead let alone worked a coalface, the choirs live on – indeed they thrive. There are over three hundred choirs in Wales, and the more exalted groups tour the concert halls of the world, vault CD recordings to the top of the charts (well, the classics charts anyway) and even act as curtain raisers for national rugby games.

Seeing a performance is a stupendously rousing experience – especially at somewhere like Cardiff's Millennium Stadium when seventy thousand fans join in. But what you gain in power you lose in the flavour and intimacy of a small-town recital in some nuggety Welsh village. Close harmony singing is very much part of Welsh tradition, and still binds local communities in a way rarely seen elsewhere. Appropriately, Welsh classics such as *Myfanwy* and *Men of Harlech* feature strongly, leavened with anything from John Lennon's *Imagine* to a medley of Tom Jones hits (perhaps half in Welsh, half in English). And it is all done in their best bib and tucker – creases sharp and shirts as white as they were when miners regularly headed to chapel of a Sunday.

The perfect complement to attending a performance is to head along to a midweek rehearsal, a much more casual affair where visitors are almost always welcome. Dress codes are relaxed and there's plenty of banter between tunes, but don't expect anything unprofessional once the singing starts. After all, no one wants to dishonour the land of his father.

Need to know The best-known choirs are Treorchy from the Valleys (Ⓦ www.treorchymalechoir. org) and the Swansea-based Morriston Orpheus (Ⓦ www. morristonorpheus.com) though Fron Choir from Froncysyllte, near Llangollen (Ⓦ www.fronchoir. com), have been very successful in recent years. Most charge for a performance, but rehearsals are free. For other listings see Ⓦ www. malevoicechoir.net.
Map 2, B5

366 In Wicker Man country

With *The Wicker Man* having long turned into Wickermania, there can't be many film fans who haven't grimaced at the prospect of Sergeant Howie's imminent roasting in one of the 1973 cult film's most iconic scenes. As the sun tumbles spectacularly off what looks like the horizon of the known world, *The Wicker Man* blazes its name into celluloid history; powerful stuff, but if you've ever wondered where exactly this scene was filmed, you might be surprised to learn that it wasn't some arcane Hebridean idyll but a clifftop on the Solway Firth. In fact, Dumfries and Galloway was the location for many of the film's most memorable scenes, and, if you're a fan, or even just vaguely curious, a browse around Galloway's dogleg coast can make for a fascinating day-trip. Historically a smuggler's paradise with easy access to a tax-free Isle of Man, the weathered ruts of Wigtown Bay are headed by the colour-flushed Georgian facades of Kirkcudbright, an unforgettable backdrop for the film's May Day shenanigans. This is where postmistress May Morrison (in what is now an art gallery) led Howie up one of many metaphorical blind alleys, and where the rest of Summerisle's wildly costumed citizenry led him on a wild goose chase around some real ones.

A few miles northwest, just off the A75, lies Gatehouse of Fleet, where Robert Burns famously penned *Scots Wha Hae*, and where the local estate office was used as the facade of the *Green Man* pub in the film. The pricelessly surreal interior scene – where assorted extras stomped along to a conspicuously less noble lyric – was actually shot in the bar of the *Ellangowan Hotel* in nearby Creetown, where you can still sup a nostalgically frothy ale today. From here the trail leads down the opposite side of the bay to Burrow Head, site of the aforementioned fiery climax, where, until recently, part of the original Wicker Man's legs were still standing. Nearby is St Ninian's cave, location of the film's sacrificial ruse, and the place where the fifth-century saint first began his mission to enlighten a heathen nation. He'd doubtless be appalled.

Need to know Various websites provide information on all *Wicker Man* locations, including many more Galloway scenes and those shot further afield; Ⓦ www.wicker-man.com and Ⓦ www.sw-scotland-screen.com are both fairly exhaustive. Music fans might also want to check out the Wicker Man Festival: Ⓦ www.thewickermanfestival.co.uk.
Map 4, C16

367 Shakespeare's Stratford

Shakespeare. Among schoolchildren, no other name evokes as many groans of boredom and disgruntlement. But back in Elizabethan Britain, when the Bard cast himself as the world's greatest playwright, having the opportunity to study plays – or study at all – was considered a great privilege. Of course, Shakespeare was one of the lucky ones (it's thought he studied Latin plays at a grammar school) but even so, most of his work was influenced by the world around him. Central to this was his beloved hometown, Stratford-upon-Avon, which still retains much of its sixteenth-century charm.

A walk down Henley Street, where Shakespeare grew up, reveals half-timbered buildings bedecked with lanterns, flags and striped canopies. From quaint tearooms you can hear the jingle-jangle of spoons on saucers, while the sweet smell of coffee – still an alien concept in Shakespeare's time – wafts its way unevenly through the crowds of tourists and street entertainers. Halfway up the street is the town's most famous building, Shakespeare's old house, complete with ornate leaded windows and splintered wooden flowerboxes that overflow with dazzling purple and red petunias.

Down by the River Avon, which ripples with the graceful paddles of swans, you can kick back with a book or explore the magnificent Bancroft Gardens. This part of town is also home to Stratford's crowning glory, the recently rebuilt Royal Shakespeare Theatre and adjacent Swan Theatre, and it'd be a tragedy not to attend at least one show. The Swan Theatre is in the round and the new main stage thrusts out into the auditorium, so in true Shakespearean style, every seat is within spitting distance of the performers, giving you the chance to enjoy plays like *Macbeth* in all their ghostly detail.

If that puts you in the mood for something spooky, you can amble up to Shrieve's House – supposedly Stratford's most haunted building – for a lantern-lit ghost tour. This is where the tortured soul of William Shrieve, an archer in King Henry VIII's army, is thought to roam restlessly. It's also where William Rogers, the inspiration for Shakespeare's comic character Falstaff, ran a popular tavern. Some visitors have reported feeling icy premonitions here, but it's known as one of Shakespeare's favourite places. And with such interesting characters around to influence him, you have to question whether he ever needed those Latin plays.

Need to know Stratford-upon-Avon is in Warwickshire. For tourist information and the latest on RSC shows, see Ⓦwww. visitstratforduponavon.co.uk and Ⓦwww.rsc.org.uk. Ghost tours at Shrieve's House run nightly (Ⓦwww. falstaffexperience.co.uk; £7.50). Map 3, C12

368 Singing St Cuthbert to sleep

The candlelight flickers gently in the gloom, shivering softly with the ebb and flow of the choristers' harmonious breath. The pure, clear chords of the Magnificat soar high into the cool cathedral air, dancing around the dark recesses of the lofty, vaulted ceiling. The service flows into the Nunc Dimittis, the serious and monotone Apostles Creed and an Anthem, and is drawn to a quiet close with a set of spoken prayers. This is Choral Evensong at Durham Cathedral, arguably the most magical and magnificent liturgy in Britain.

Evensong is usually a sung version of the traditional Anglican communion service (it can be spoken, too). The smart, white-robed choir consists of a twenty-strong, fresh-faced group of 8- to 13- year-old boys and girls belonging to the Durham Chorister School, whose premises are just behind the cathedral in Cathedral Close. The rest of the choral group is made up of twelve gentlemen – seven of whom are choral scholars of the university, and five lay clerks, who are unconnected to the university. The service is a musical feast for the ears; hymns tend to be a medley of glorious Renaissance melodies, alternated with a few Victorian tunes and some more contemporary works, which are often specially commissioned for the choir.

Durham Cathedral makes a suitably impressive venue for the sacred evening service: begun in 1093 in honour of the lowly monk-turned-saint Cuthbert, it's regarded as the finest Norman building in England. Cuthbert's shrine – originally an opulent green marble and gold monument, and today a simple grey slab of stone engraved with "Cuthbertus" – lies at the very top of the long nave, itself bordered by massive sand-coloured pillars. At 496 feet it's a huge building, but despite its size it's strangely cocoon-like, with a cosy and welcoming atmosphere – a quality that's accentuated during the intimate, candlelit Evensong service.

The congregation is made up of both locals and visitors, many of whom are pilgrims come to pay homage to the hallowed remains of St Cuthbert. During the university exam period, the number of worshippers doubles, added to by fraught students scared silly with exam stress; away from their textbooks, they seek solace, quiet and contemplation – with the sleeping St Cuthbert for company.

Need to know Evensong at Durham Cathedral is conducted at 5.15pm from Tuesday to Saturday and at 3.30pm on Sunday Ⓦ www.durhamcathedral.co.uk. Map 4, E16

369 Fab Four folklore in Liverpool

Take a walk down narrow Matthew Street, home of the original *Cavern* club in the centre of Liverpool, and it feels like the Fab Four never stopped playing. John, Paul, Ringo and George are still very much in evidence, though the souvenir shops and tacky statue of the lads are aimed squarely at tourists. For a more authentic experience of the Beatles' Liverpool head to the vibrant Hope Street area between the two cathedrals. Here, on tiny, residential Rice Street stands *Ye Cracke*, a wonderful, un-gentrified old boozer complete with various nooks and crannies where local students, office workers and garrulous pensioners hide away to sup pints of the local Cains beer. This is the pub where a very young John Lennon and original Beatles' member Stuart Sutcliffe would often drink at the end of the day, while attending Liverpool College of Art.

Around the same time, John and Paul first met at a local fête in 1957 in the pretty village of Woolton, where Lennon lived. The Mendips, his aunt Mimi's semi-detached house, is surprisingly genteel, situated on a quiet suburban street, and now restored to look exactly as it would have done when John lived here in the 1950s.

The blast furnace of creativity, however, was at McCartney's parents' council house at 20 Forthlin Rd in more humble Allerton, where the two young men composed dozens of their early hits in the front parlour, sitting "eyeball to eyeball" according to Lennon. This has also been restored to how it would have looked in austere postwar Britain, an immaculate re-creating of the plain 1950s interior. A twinge of sympathy must go to the caretaker, who lives in the house. McCartney himself has stopped by twice in recent years. On both occasions, he was out and Macca's old home was closed.

Ordinary in the extreme these locations may be, but the genius of the men who slept, worked, skived and drank here, renders them touching, if not especially fab-looking, testimonies to a group who, half a century on from their formation, are still the biggest on earth.

Need to know The Mendips and 20 Forthlin Rd are only accessible on a tour, run by the National Trust. They depart from the city centre and Speke Hall (Ⓣ 0844 800 4791, Ⓦ www.nationaltrust.org.uk/beatles; March–Nov, book in advance; £16.80, NT members £7.90). Map 3, B10

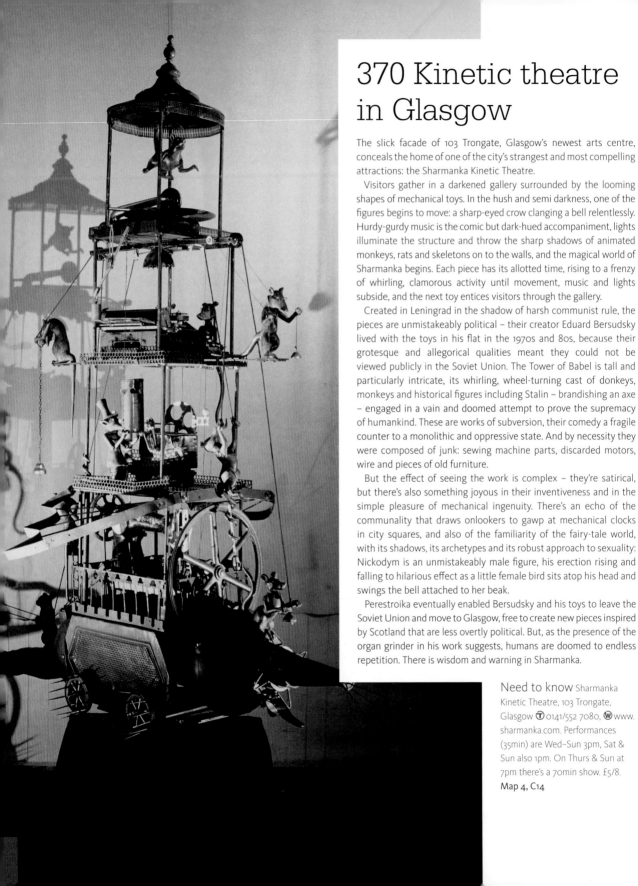

370 Kinetic theatre in Glasgow

The slick facade of 103 Trongate, Glasgow's newest arts centre, conceals the home of one of the city's strangest and most compelling attractions: the Sharmanka Kinetic Theatre.

Visitors gather in a darkened gallery surrounded by the looming shapes of mechanical toys. In the hush and semi darkness, one of the figures begins to move: a sharp-eyed crow clanging a bell relentlessly. Hurdy-gurdy music is the comic but dark-hued accompaniment, lights illuminate the structure and throw the sharp shadows of animated monkeys, rats and skeletons on to the walls, and the magical world of Sharmanka begins. Each piece has its allotted time, rising to a frenzy of whirling, clamorous activity until movement, music and lights subside, and the next toy entices visitors through the gallery.

Created in Leningrad in the shadow of harsh communist rule, the pieces are unmistakeably political – their creator Eduard Bersudsky lived with the toys in his flat in the 1970s and 80s, because their grotesque and allegorical qualities meant they could not be viewed publicly in the Soviet Union. The Tower of Babel is tall and particularly intricate, its whirling, wheel-turning cast of donkeys, monkeys and historical figures including Stalin – brandishing an axe – engaged in a vain and doomed attempt to prove the supremacy of humankind. These are works of subversion, their comedy a fragile counter to a monolithic and oppressive state. And by necessity they were composed of junk: sewing machine parts, discarded motors, wire and pieces of old furniture.

But the effect of seeing the work is complex – they're satirical, but there's also something joyous in their inventiveness and in the simple pleasure of mechanical ingenuity. There's an echo of the communality that draws onlookers to gawp at mechanical clocks in city squares, and also of the familiarity of the fairy-tale world, with its shadows, its archetypes and its robust approach to sexuality: Nickodym is an unmistakeably male figure, his erection rising and falling to hilarious effect as a little female bird sits atop his head and swings the bell attached to her beak.

Perestroika eventually enabled Bersudsky and his toys to leave the Soviet Union and move to Glasgow, free to create new pieces inspired by Scotland that are less overtly political. But, as the presence of the organ grinder in his work suggests, humans are doomed to endless repetition. There is wisdom and warning in Sharmanka.

Need to know Sharmanka Kinetic Theatre, 103 Trongate, Glasgow ☎ 0141/552 7080, Ⓦ www.sharmanka.com. Performances (35min) are Wed–Sun 3pm, Sat & Sun also 1pm. On Thurs & Sun at 7pm there's a 70min show. £5/8.
Map 4, C14

371 Word up: London's original literary nightclub

The phrase "spoken word" can strike fear into the heart of many a jaded observer of the London arts scene. Entering the imposing curved, red-brick structure of the Tabernacle community arts centre (and former evangelical church) in leafy Notting Hill for your first taste of Bookslam you may be excused the feeling of foreboding that it could all be a bit, well, pretentious. From the edge of the small stage, circular tables lit with flickering tea-lights fan out, around which the audience of hip young things cluster, tucking into posh plates from the buffet downstairs and murmuring excitedly over their white wines as the DJ sets up. The sense of anticipation is palpable. Lights are dimmed, the music blares out... hang on. They're playing Coolio? The resident Serbian DJ's love for bad Nineties hip-hop is your first inkling that far from being an exlusive, jazz clubby literary love-in, this book-club-meets-nightclub mash-up could actually be good old-fashioned fun.

Wandering onto the stage between acts to banter with the audience, wearing a hoodie and swigging from a can of Red Stripe, founder, host and compere Patrick Neate epitomizes the inclusive nature of the evening. A Whitbread-nominated author himself, his boundless enthusiasm for showcasing new writing and music has brought to Bookslam performers of a calibre that most literary festival organizers would give their eye teeth for. Established stars such as Will Self, Zadie Smith, Dave Eggers, Jonathan Safran Foer and Hanif Kureishi are never less than mesmeric, delivering vivid, thought-provoking readings that remind you how powerful storytelling can be. For all the big-name literary heavyweights, it's the diversity of the bill that as often as not provides the unexpected highlights: the furious pace of MOBO-award-winning rapper (and founder of the Hip Hop Shakespeare Company) Akala's delivery as he obliterates the boundary between music and poetry, the crystal-cut purity of up-and-coming singer-songwriter Valentina's dulcimer-accompanied voice or the agility of Doc Brown's rap-based stand-up comedy. Maybe it's literary genius by osmosis but somehow by the end you just feel smarter. Forget that usual morning-after feeling of having killed half your brain cells; this is one club night your head will actually thank you for.

Need to know Bookslam, The Tabernacle, Powis Square, London W11 Ⓦ www.bookslam.com. Usually the last Thursday of the month. Tickets are £8 in advance, £10 on the door.

Map 1, A3

A QUESTION OF SPORT

sport and games

"That's today's news. And now, sport". And with those few words, anyone British can safely switch off because we won't have won anything. Again. Some Pacific Island with a population of 43 will have held Wales to a draw in the football, and the latest tennis sensation will have gone out in the first round, making it 800 years without a Wimbledon win. Occasionally, due to a rift in the space-time continuum, one of our national teams or sporting heroes comes out on top, but it's an unsettling state of affairs. England, 2003 rugby world champions – how did that happen? What's most galling is that we invented or codified every single sport that matters – football, rugby, cricket, golf, tennis, rowing, boxing, you name it, a Brit once kicked a pig's bladder or thwacked a stone with a stick and thought, hang on a minute, that looks like it could be fun. And then within a few years the Germans were mastering the art of the penalty and the Australians were saying rude words to put us off our stroke, and it was all over. Of course, we hardly help ourselves as the home nations refuse to play nicely with each other – British national sports teams are as rare as hens' teeth – while other successful sporting countries, frankly, cheat by making up games that no one else plays, like baseball and American football. Mind you, we're not above that ourselves – darts, tossing the caber, outdoor wrestling in long johns, croquet on horseback, beat us at those if you can. However, what Britain does particularly well is not necessarily the sport itself but the sporting spectacle, from the rough-and-tumble horse race that is the Grand National to the intense, Glaswegian football fisticuffs when Celtic play Rangers. You can follow your chosen sport at its spine-tingling spiritual home – Lord's, St Andrews, Wimbledon, Aintree, the Millennium Stadium – and whether or not we clean up at the London Olympics in 2012 (the rather large and un-British 2008 medal haul was the best Olympics performance in a century), the show will be magnificent. Play on.

372 Blisters on the motorway: the Great North Run

Like any distance race, the views are a big part of the epic that is the Great North Run. The world's biggest half-marathon takes you over the great bridges of the Tyne, past homes and bandstands and an arcing, seemingly interminable stretch of motorway, to the coast at South Shields, where the horizon stretches into the North Sea and the wind takes the breath from your lungs and the kick from your legs. The views keep your head up, as do the splendid spectators, who line the route and hand out sweets and water and sympathy, but for many people, over much of the race, the main feeling is one of grim determination.

Unless you're superfit or you've trained to within an inch of your life, you're bound to have a painful spell at some point in the run, bound to wish yourself anywhere but here, bound to ask yourself that immortal question: "What the hell am I doing?" People run for different reasons: there's the challenge, of course, the chance to raise money, the comradeship, the big-day atmosphere. And the Great North Run, which began in 1981 and now attracts over 50,000 entrants, has the latter in spades: its mix of heroic, fancy-dress-clad fun runners and lycra-swathed athletes is a heady cocktail.

Its 13.1-mile stretch is neither quite as Zen nor quite as body-shattering as a full marathon, but unlike its London cousin you've a good chance of getting into this iconic race. Once here, standing in a queue of runners anxiously stretching and wondering whether they need to pee, you may look around you and again ask what the hell you're doing. It's at the end, as you totter from the finish line to your friends, your charity tent or a jam-packed pub, reeling from what feels like an out-of-body experience, with a big fat smile on your face and a goody bag in your hands, that you can pause, and give your answer: that's why I did it.

Need to know The Great North Run (W www.greatrun.org) takes place annually in September. It's worth applying for a place early in the year, especially if you're not running for charity. Aim to train for at least two months before undertaking a half-marathon.
Map 4, E15

373 Tossing the caber at the Braemar Gathering

No rain-lashed, midgie-ridden Scottish summer would be complete without the cornucopia of arcane sports that comprise a Highland Games. Held all over Scotland, not just in the Highlands, these are very much rural affairs, with rosetted ponies, curly-horned sheep and shaggy Highland cattle to the fore. But they're also devised as entertainment, with a comically competitive edge – kilted burly men toss the caber (that's a trimmed tree trunk to the uninitiated), drunken locals vie with each other in the tug-of-war, little girls high-step over crossed swords in country dances, and there might also be dressage, field races and even haggis hurling.

It's a traditional day out, and one which can have its longeurs as you nurse an alfresco beer or enjoy a spun sugar candyfloss while listening to the amplified drone of announcements regarding pipe bands and sack races to find out details of the next event. But even the most hardened kids will love the proximity of farm animals, from prize cattle to spruce ponies with their manes and tails plaited and done out in tartan ribbons. You might also see tiny kids in jodhpurs and jackets manoeuvring tiny ponies over high jumps.

Highland Games range from almost literally one-horse village affairs to the famous Braemar Gathering in Aberdeenshire, which has existed in one form or another for around 900 years. It was founded in the time of Malcolm III and, though suppressed along with many other aspects of Highland life following the Battle of Culloden, it resurfaced in the 1820s and was later attended by tartan-fetishist Queen Victoria. It still draws the Royals out in force; the monarch is traditionally the patron of the Braemar Royal Highland Society and the showground is handily located near to their summer retreat at Balmoral. As well as the usual shenanigans, the show in its current incarnation features the dramatic and deafening spectacle of massed pipe bands, and there's a military element too, with the armed forces competing in races and the tug-of-war, plus a punishing race up the nearby hill of Morrone. All this and all the sporrans you could toss a caber at.

Need to know The Braemar Gathering (Ⓦwww.braemargathering.org) is held on the first Saturday in September in the Princess Royal & Duke of Fife Memorial Park, Braemar, Aberdeenshire. Tickets cost £10–30. Map 5, D20

374 Racing in the Dales

Silhouetted against the cloud-blown sky and dwarfed by the mighty Hornby Castle in the distance, two horsemen on sturdy steeds linger on the brow of the hill, guarding a rowdy pack of baying hounds. Suddenly they turn and gallop, manes and tails flowing, towards the crowd, the hounds eagerly following the stirring blasts of the huntsman's horn. Spectators cheer with anticipation, knowing that the arrival of the hounds indicates the beginning of an exciting afternoon's point-to-pointing.

Originating over 250 years ago in Ireland, point-to-pointing is amateur steeplechase horse racing over 4ft-high brush hurdles. Horses are required to participate in at least four days' hunting with hounds before they are allowed to race, and if they show promise and potential, will earn the necessary qualifications to race under National Hunt rules (the glossy, top-dollar racing on television). Other point-to-pointers are often at the end of their National Hunt racing career, eking out the thrill of the chase in their old age. Point-to-points take place all over Britain, but one of the best is run by the local Bedale hunt at Hornby Castle in North Yorkshire. Overlooking the undulating racetrack that circles the verdant valley of Swaledale, the venerable fourteenth-century castle forms a magnificent backdrop to the area's most entertaining rural event.

Often cloaked in an ever-deepening layer of mud, the Bedale point-to-point isn't a place for Royal Ascot revellers in killer heels, top hats and tails – turn up in jeans and a robust pair of Wellington boots, with flat cap (not compulsory) and a dog and you'll fit right in. Don't forget to take a picnic – pork pies, quiche, the obligatory soggy sandwich – to eat before heading over to the parade ring to watch the leggy competitors limber up and then canter slowly down to the starting line. The best vantage points are up on the hills, from where you can see most of the race goings on – the commentator, hooked up to an ear-splitting tannoy system, enthusiastically fills in any gaps. After the race, head to the cluster of bars serving three or four local ales on tap, and for those with an appetite, there are vans doling out succulent bacon and sausage butties, chips and creamy Yorkshire-made ice cream. Meanwhile, competitors for Race 2 are marching around the parade ring, the bookies are yelling their odds and favourites, and the crowds are excitedly taking their positions on the hill. They're under starters' order and they're off!

Need to know Hornby Castle (privately owned) is six miles north of Bedale, North Yorkshire. Entry is £25 per car, plus £10 per single occupant. The Bedale point-to-point takes place once a year, normally on Easter Saturday. For more information see Ⓦwww.pointtopoint.co.uk. Map 3, C9

375 Having a right old shin dig at the Cotswolds Olimpicks

Dover's Hill, just outside the Gloucestershire market town of Chipping Campden, is archetypal rural England, a pretty hillock of National Trust-owned land that each spring echoes to the sound of birdsong – and to the crack of bone on bone as men in white coats try to kick each other in the shins.

Madcap as it may sound, whacking someone on the lower leg constitutes a serious sport in these parts, and shin-kicking is the marquee event at the annual Cotswolds Olimpicks – or Robert Dover's Cotswolds Olimpick Games, to give them their full title – held on this hill since the early seventeenth century. Named after the Norfolk earl who revived the games of Ancient Greece here in 1612, the Olimpicks are the ultimate compendium of sports you never knew existed.

Early competitions featured the long-gone games of singlestick, backswords and tumbling, and while today's events change every so often, you're guaranteed a selection of sporting spectacles – what makes it onto the schedule appears to be determined by either their names (the more bonkers, the better) or their rules (must be hazy at best), though a combination of both seems preferable.

As well as shin-kicking, recent events have included spurning the barre, akin to tossing the caber, and dwile flonking, which isn't really akin to anything, unless there are other games out there that revolve around trying to hit people with a beer-soaked cloth whilst dancing about. You can also catch gurning here – and not just any old gurning but gurning in a horse collar, no less – though perhaps too many years have passed for pig racing to make a comeback.

Need to know The Cotswold Olimpicks (Ⓦ www.olimpickgames. co.uk) kick off at 7.30pm on the Friday after the late May Bank Holiday; the next events will be on June 3, 2011 and June 8, 2012.
Map 3, C12

376 Playing the old course at St Andrews

Need to know Players need to enter a ballot to get a tee-off time – visit Ⓦ www.standrews.org.uk or call Ⓣ 01334/466666.
Map 4, D14

There are several courses where you have to play a round at least once to call yourself a true golf devotee (Pine Valley, Pebble Beach and Augusta National to name but a few), but the Old Course at St Andrews is still "the one". Just walking out onto the first tee sends shivers down the spine, as you think how many feet, legendary or otherwise, have squared up to send a ball hurtling into the blustery winds before you.

St Andrews is the home of golf – the game's equivalent to Wembley or Wimbledon, a venue that is part of the mythology of the sport. The contemporary view may be that golf courses should be manufactured, created and sculpted, but St Andrews had a very different designer of sorts, in the form of nature itself. Here, the landscape is the course. It may not have the charm or the aesthetics of its American counterparts but it has real character. There's barely a tree to be seen, so the atmosphere is quite different from many modern courses. Similarly, there's little water around aside from Swilcan Burn, which has to be traversed on the 18th fairway, and the adjacent bruise-black waters of the North Sea.

This perceived lack of obstacles doesn't mean there's little to test the most experienced of players though; the course is filled with hidden humps, bumps and dips, and there are man-made challenges, too – the infamous Road Hole Bunker on the 17th being the most notorious. Any obstacle that requires a ladder to escape from must be pretty hardcore.

They've been teeing off here for around three hundred years and you'd guess it hasn't changed much at all, which is one of the things that makes this such a unique sporting experience. Be sure to take a local caddie, though – that way, he can worry about whether you should be using a 9-iron or a pitching wedge, and you can concentrate on absorbing the significance of it all.

377 Visit the home of cricket: a day out at Lord's

Need to know Lord's Cricket Ground (Ⓣ 020/7432 1000, Ⓦ www.lords.org) is a ten-minute walk from St John's Wood tube station. Tours run at noon and 2pm year-round (also 10am April–Sept and 4pm Aug only), except on major match days, and cost £14 (£8 for children, students and seniors). Match ticket prices vary
Map 1, B2.

Former Australian Prime Minister John Howard once said that he considered Lord's "the cathedral of cricket". Nestled into your seat at a Test match among other worshippers of the game, waiting in reverential hush for the emergence of the teams at the start of a game, his pronouncement has a ring of truth. The players are no less affected by the almost sacred history of the place – all are desperate to score a century or take five wickets in an innings, thereby immortalizing themselves on the honours boards in the dressing rooms.

Why all this veneration? The answer lies in the history of the ground: it is one of the oldest in the world, built by Thomas Lord in 1814 at the request of the nobility, who had taken to cricket as a good excuse for gambling. They were getting annoyed by the crowds of plebs who came out to watch them in Islington and wanted a private pitch; Lord provided it. The Marylebone Cricket Club, which owns the ground, dates even further back to 1787 (making it one year older than the nation of Australia, as is gleefully pointed out when the Aussies play here). To this day, the MCC still decides on matters pertaining to the laws of the game.

Undoubtedly the best way to appreciate Lord's is to see a match here (preferably a Test, and most preferably an Ashes game, when the atmosphere is at fever pitch). But as a fallback, the tours are excellent. You'll get to see the Long Room, where the MCC members sit, and the Committee Room, from where the Queen watches when in attendance. The dressing rooms are included – so you can view the honours boards and stand on the balcony imagining the adulation of the crowd – as is a Real Tennis court, one of only 42 in the world. But the real highlight lies in the museum, where in a glass case lies the original Ashes urn, a gift presented to England captain the Hon. Ivo Bligh, possibly containing either a burnt ball or stump. He received it having beaten the Australians, following a defeat in 1882 that led one hack to write an obituary of English cricket, whose "body will be cremated and the ashes taken to Australia". That little six-inch-high jar is like the shrine within the cathedral; people come halfway across the world to see it. It's a daft game.

378 Arrows, Dutchmen and a whole lot of lager: darts at Lakeside

The doubters say that darts, whose practitioners never break out of a walk but often break sweat, isn't a sport. Yet even these killjoys might enjoy themselves at the BDO World Darts Championship, a competition that is as much about boozy good cheer as it is about the actual result. Hosted at a vast hotel-cum-pub complex in deepest Surrey, the competition packs over a thousand spectators onto a phalanx of long tables and gives them every opportunity to shout themselves stupid during all-day weekend sessions and weekday nights. Their voices join in a splendid cacophony with the thud of arrow into cork, the bellowed scores and blue jokes of a flamboyant umpire and the gulp of countless throats.

Don't look for too much sophistication here: the glasses are plastic, the food runs the full gamut from battered fish to burgers and the crowd perform for the cameras with gleeful enthusiasm, inching their way into TV footage and waving punning placards. But the vibe is supremely friendly. Being thrust onto a table with strangers makes it almost impossible not to socialize, especially when you might be sat alongside fanatical Dutch fans, fancy-dressed twentysomethings and elderly couples who've been coming since the year dot.

Look away from the busy bar and up from the sticky carpets, and there's some splendidly addictive sport going on. Darts' scoring system encourages a fine ebb and flow, legs and sets going from one side to the other as the competitors – Britain inevitably features heavily, but the Australians and the Dutch are vital presences – fire darts at the board, pausing with concentration to calculate the combinations they'll need to bring their score from 501 to zero. There are all manner of highlights – the vast cheer that comes with the perfect three-dart 180 or the rarer nine-dart finish, the edgy excitement that comes when a thrower misses double after double in pursuit of a finish. But what lingers in the memory is the merriment of it all, the friendly competitiveness of the players, who mean it when they hug at the end of games, and the sozzled happiness of a crowd that packs more mirth into a few hours than many football fans manage in a season.

Need to know The Lakeside BDO World Professional Darts Championships (Ⓦ www.lakesideworlddarts.co.uk) take place every January. Evening-only tickets cost £20, all-day tickets £40; it's best to apply by ballot several months in advance.

Map 2, E6

UNUSUAL OLYMPIC SPORTS

Every Olympics has its don't-miss headline races, but other, more unusual sports only emerge from obscurity when there's a new national hero to cheer on. Many are well worth watching – and absolute gems to play.

379 Archery

The perfect place for a taste of archery is undoubtedly Sherwood Forest, legendary home of Robin Hood, where the visitor centre runs occasional summer "have a go" sessions (£2 for 5 arrows) beside the giant 800-year-old Major Oak. Nearby, at Southwell, the Sherwood Archers club offers a six-hour beginners' course in target archery, the official Olympic version of the sport. But for the most Robin Hood-like experience, consider the Spirit of Sherwood field archery club: they hunt artificial, animal-shaped targets in the old forest itself.

Ⓦ www.nottinghamshire.gov.uk/home/leisure/countryparks/ sherwoodforestcp.htm; Ⓦ www.sherwoodarchers.co.uk; and Ⓦ www. freewebs.com/spiritofsherwood. Map 3, D10

380 Outdoor table tennis

Table tennis in Britain is derisively known as ping pong, but it's a serious sport, and making a comeback since the "Ping London" initiative set up outdoor tables all over the capital in 2010. Not all will return, but there are plenty of permanent tables in parks – there's one in Regent's Park, right by the tennis courts. Just bring a bat, and a ball or two.

See Ⓦ etta.tv/development-modules/find-an-outdoor-table to find a table near you. Map 1, B1

381 Real tennis, or jeu de paume

The saddest loss from the Olympic roster is surely real tennis, aka jeu de paume, aka court tennis, a superbly eccentric combination of squash and tennis which featured only in the Olympics of 1908. The sport is alive and well, however – as it has been for five hundred years. Famously, you can play it at Hampton Court Palace, but for a more modern experience make for the gleaming Millennium Court of the Middlesex Real Tennis Club in Hendon, north London.

Ⓦ www.murtc.co.uk. Monthly membership £25, plus court fee of £12/hr; beginners welcome. Map 1, E3

382 Fencing

Fencing venues, sadly, rarely occupy the Great Halls of castles. You won't find yourself skipping down the grand staircase so much as lunging along down the 2m-wide "piste" at a local leisure centre. Once you're actually girded up with your mask and foil (or epée, or sabre), questions of atmosphere are forgotten, however. This is a fast and agile sport which retains more than a whiff of the danger of yesteryear. The award-winning Truro Fencing Club is one of the few with its own dedicated salle.

Ⓦ www.trurofencing.com. See Ⓦ www.britishfencing.com/clubs to find a fencing club near you. Map 2, A7

383 Beach volleyball

Why *would* the Olympic Committee have voted to include beach volleyball in 1996? This is a sport in which bronzed and toned men and women in regulation-skimpy costumes dive around in golden sand, hugging and high-fiving. You can play it informally on any beach, but to try an Olympic-quality court, make for the Yellowave centre on Brighton beach. They run open sessions (for which you'll need to be at least quite sporty), or you can just book a court with friends.

Ⓦ *www.yellowave.co.uk. Open sessions on Sun (mixed) and Tues & Sat (women only); £3 for 2hr. Map 2, E6*

384 Pimms, polo and the art of posing

Need to know The Jack Wills Varsity Polo day (W www.jackwills.com) is held in early June at Guard's Polo Club, Windsor, Berkshire. Tickets £10 in advance, £20 on the day.

Map 2, E5

As Ralph Lauren spotted long ago, there's something inherently glamorous about polo. Whether it's the danger, the air of exotic exclusivity or simply the tight white trousers, it provides excitement and sex appeal in spades, and if you're lucky, the chance to see a minor royal fall on his arse. Most polo events, however, are rather crusty affairs – the kind of social gathering where you feel inadequate without having pulled up in a Range Rover with a Fortnum & Mason's hamper on the back seat.

Cleverly stepping into this gap is the Jack Wills Varsity Polo held at Guard's Polo Club in Windsor. Sponsored by the preppy, "Fabulously British" clothes brand, this event aims to attract the Facebook generation to the sport with, among other things, a bright red London bus dishing out Pimms, a live music tent and the chance to play BMX polo, all for the price of a Jack Wills sock. The "Varsity" part of the name comes from the participants – Oxford vs Cambridge, Harvard vs Yale and Eton vs Harrow all of which boast international-class players.

The game itself is surprisingly physical, a kind of equine hockey on steroids with the action thundering past in a blur of chestnut horse hair and swinging mallets. The pitch is so vast (it could accommodate nine football fields) that you're glad of the tannoy announcer explaining what's going on ("Tarquin Fairbrother has SCORED for Eton and it's the end of the chukkah!") and slightly regretting not bringing a pair of binoculars.

Like all great British sporting events, however, the actual sport is something of a sideshow. The real fun is had spotting Chelsy Davy or Prince Harry lookalikes or stepping onto the pitch for the traditional "treading of the divots" where spectators are asked to help replace chunks of dislodged turf. With the trophies handed out, the focus moves to the serious business of partying, capped off with a "silent disco" held in a giant marquee. Here you listen to DJs through a pair of headphones rather than thumping speakers. After all, there's no need to worry the horses.

385 The Old Firm: Scotland's most infamous derby

Need to know Though there's usually no public ticket sale, it's worth asking around the respective stadiums on match day. Alternatively, check out the club websites for hospitality deals: W www.celticfc.net and W www.rangers.co.uk.

Map 4, C14

Few would argue that these are dark days for Scottish football, with debt-wracked clubs, a struggling national side and attendances down across the board, but the Celtic vs Rangers fixture is still one of the world's most hotly anticipated derbies. It's almost always more high-noon showdown than beautiful game, but if you can get past the bilious rivalry it might just leave you on the edge of your seat: the dramatic 6-2/5-1 drubbings of the early noughties have already become legend, and while recent encounters have generally been closer and tighter, the tie's sheer unpredictability is what makes it so compulsive.

It's bitterly fought for a reason, of course; even the political baggage of Real Madrid vs Barcelona pales in comparison with the arcane antagonisms associated with this tie, rooted as they are in the mists of Irish/Scottish/British social, political and religious history. Given the extent to which Celtic and Rangers have dominated the Scottish game, moreover, such antagonisms have long cast a shadow. Yet with both the clubs and authorities taking a stand against sectarianism, the rivalry has thankfully been confined largely to the pitch in recent times, channelled into a match where the noise and the drama always seems several decibels louder than it did last time. Defeat for either side is, evidently, unthinkable, though this rarely translates into overly defensive drudgery, rather a headlong lunge for the finishing line.

So spare a thought for the non-native players, who, at least when they first arrive in Glasgow, can likely (and, perhaps, mercifully) have only the vaguest of notions as to what it's all about. All they know – or at least they will do after the first five minutes – is that it's played with an intensity they almost certainly won't have experienced at any other club, a manic tempo that often leaves them reeling. And for neutrals as well as die-hards, this is the thrill of it – a blue-green whirlwind lurching from end to end, streaked by shades of yellow and often red, and drowned in a cacophony of Glaswegian vowels. It isn't pretty, but then football rarely is.

386 Cowes Week: champagne and oysters at the sails

A quintessentially English seaside town on the Isle of Wight, Cowes is an attractive medley of historic pubs, narrow cobbled streets and boutiquey shops. Off season, it's decidedly quiet – the main sign of life is the queue at the local fish and chip shop – but come Cowes Week the place becomes party central.

Each year, some eight thousand sailors from all over the world descend on Cowes for the world's largest – and oldest – sailing regatta. Vast crowds of up to 100,000 cram into the narrow streets each morning to watch a spectacular array of sailing vessels gather in the Solent. There are up to forty high-octane races daily, competed by all sorts of sailors from amateurs to Olympians and Americas Cup veterans: with up to a thousand yachts taking part, you'll need to get used to the sporadic gunfire that marks the start of each class if you make the Royal Yacht Squadron, the official starting line, your vantage point. Alternatively, you can catch some of the action from the raised park known as The Green, but even from here, many of the racing boats quickly glide out of sight. So to get up close, catch one of the spectactor boats that leave from Trinity Landing. These pleasure craft weave around carefully so they don't cut up any competitors, but give you an insight into the sailors' incredible skill, especially when the wind's up and the yachts tip almost horizontally.

With so many to entertain, there's plenty more to Cowes Week than just sailing, and the regatta is a key part of the social calendar for yachties, celebs and the occasional splash of royalty alike: champagne and oysters are guzzled at balls, dinners and parties by the truckload. The waterfront Parade and Shepards Wharf Marina are packed with stalls and live entertainment by day, while after dark the action shifts to Cowes Yacht Haven (open to amateurs, professionals and ticketed spectators), where there are live bands and DJ sets until the small hours. The week closes with a truly awesome fireworks display, when the harbour is lit up by a giant explosion of sound and light – perhaps a fitting end to an event that was started to amuse King George IV between the racing at Goodwood and the Glorious Twelfth, the first day of the shooting season.

Need to know Cowes Week (Ⓦ www.cowesweek.co.uk) takes place in July/August, starting on the first Saturday after the last Tuesday in July. Spectator boats depart three times daily from Trinity Landing on Cowes Parade (£10, children £8). See Ⓦ www.islandbreaks.co.uk for info on transport to the Isle of Wight. Map 2, D6

387 Smell the glove: boxing at York Hall

Boxing's biggest bouts, with their pay-per-view screenings, pantomime press conferences and seats that stretch from celebs at the front to dots at the back, are all very well. But it's surprisingly hard, given boxing's current popularity as an activity among everyone from estate kids to office workers, to get close to the action. Most of Britain's smaller venues have died, the victims of redevelopment and a changing entertainment scene. York Hall, recently voted the sixth best place to watch boxing in the world, almost went the same way but, saved from closure by a cost-conscious local council in 2003, the iconic East London venue now hosts fifty fight nights a year.

Walk in – a stroll usually attempted after a few pints in the cheerfully spartan *Dundee Arms* across the road – and you arrive in a lovely old hall that dates from 1929, its polished boards staring up at an iron-banistered balcony and a great arch of gorgeous green-and-white ceiling. Half-gentrified Bethnal Green has seen successive waves of migrants and vast swathes of redevelopment since, and the venue's basement baths have morphed from traditional Eastern Europe steam rooms to a pricey spa. But the ring, shining beneath bright lights in the middle of all this unfussy elegance, remains York Hall's beating heart.

Around it, things are rowdy but friendly. Men with box-like shoulders cram the bar, drinking crap lager and throwing crisps down their throats. A hyper-tanned, scantily clad girl waves the cards between rounds. At the stage behind the ring, boxers warm up. And on that tall square itself, two men flex and sweat, feinting and swinging, some punches landing with an audible thump, heads drooping and eyes squinting as the rounds roll by. It's thrilling, visceral stuff: the beauty of York Hall is being in a place that's big enough to have a roaring atmosphere (its capacity is 1200) but small enough that you seem to be on top of the stage.

York Hall hosts it all, from kick boxing and occasional theatre to amateur white-collar events, friends and family yelling and pogoing in one corner of the venue. There are big fights too – David Haye, Joe Calzaghe and countless other names have walked these boards. But while there's hype aplenty here, this historic venue's rowdy embrace makes you feel a vital part of the action.

Need to know York Hall, 5–15 Old Ford Rd, London E2 (Ⓦ www. gll.org/centre/york-hall-leisure-centre.asp) is a few minutes' walk from Bethnal Green tube station in East London. Tickets (£10–£75) can often be bought on the door.
Map 1, F1

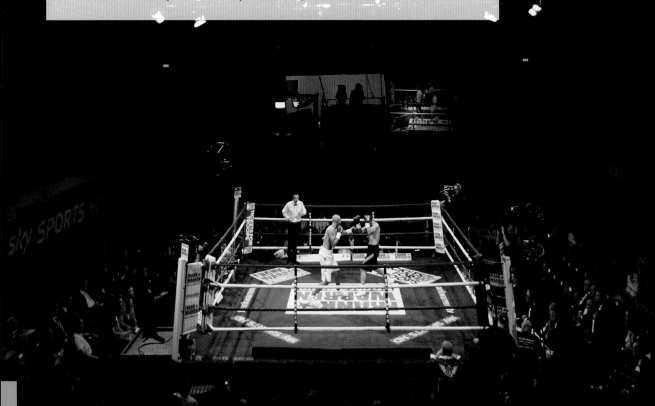

388 Beefcake brawls and soggy balls: medieval football in Derbyshire

Tis a glorious game, deny it who can/That tries the pluck of an Englishman.
Pluck is a bit of an understatement for the fearlessness required for an activity that has more in common with a medieval brawl than a modern sport. But this is a song sung in the Derbyshire town of Ashbourne – home to no-nonsense grit and the "glorious game" of Shrovetide football.

Played on Shrove Tuesday and Ash Wednesday, "Shrovie" is a relic of the rough-and-tumble sports of the Middle Ages – one theory states that the original "ball" was a severed head thrown to the crowd after an execution – and there have been moves to ban it since at least 1340, when Edward III complained that its noise disturbed his archery practice. You could see parallels with both football and rugby: there are two teams – the Up'ards and the Down'ards, formed of townsfolk from either side of Hemore Brook – and two goals. That, however, is where the similarity ends: discover that the game lasts for eight hours, that each team is a hundred or so strong, and that the goals are three miles apart on either side of the town centre, and you'll realize this is no mere kickabout. Nor do the rules leave much room for niceties: the ball can't be hidden or travel in a motorized vehicle, and murder and manslaughter are prohibited – but that's about it.

Instead, it goes like this: at 2pm sharp in central Shawcroft car park, following renditions of "Auld Lang Syne" and the national anthem, a ball (thankfully made of cork, rather than the pig's bladder – or human head – of yore) is thrown to the throng ("turned up" in local parlance) and the game is afoot. For the rest of the day it will be carried, thrown and kicked through town towards goal in a series of giant scrums, called "hugs", made up of burly players that even rugby beefcakes should treat with respect – however amiable the tussle, ribs can crack during the fight for possession. Get involved if you're hard enough, but most outsiders settle for spectating (not that you'll see much of the ball) from a respectable distance, and perhaps giving the hug an occasional shove to help it on its way. Wear stout boots, jeans and a rugby shirt, locals advise, and if you can find a smile when you end up in the river, wear that too.

And one final piece of advice: don't even think of parking in the town centre.

Need to know The next events will take place on February 21 & 22, 2012, and February 12 & 13, 2013. For more information, see Ⓦ www.ashbourne-town.com.
Map 3, C11

389 Watching Wales at the Millennium Stadium

Your Welsh friend invites you to Cardiff for the weekend to see the game. You quite like rugby and you've never been to the Millennium Stadium, so it sounds like a great idea. You arrive half an hour early, grab a beer and find your seat in the huge, canyon-like arena. But then something strange happens. Your friend starts to speak Welsh. He never speaks Welsh. In fact the stadium seems to be filled with a million Welsh supporters who have forgotten how to speak English. Then something even more astounding occurs: your friend starts to sing. In fact the whole stadium is singing, roaring with so much verve you think the roof might collapse. Tears are welling up in the eyes of the man next to you. "Gwlad! Gwlad! Pleidiol wyf i'm gwlad!" he bellows (roughly, "Nation, nation, I am faithful to my nation"). Overcome with emotion, you spontaneously erupt into stanzas of "Land of my Fathers".

Experiencing the world's largest and most patriotic choir has that effect. Watching Wales at the Millennium Stadium can be a mixture of ecstasy and pain for a Welsh supporter, but is more akin to an exotic cultural experience for everyone else. The singing, the sobbing, the angry curses and cries of unabashed joy create an unforgettable experience. You've never heard a national anthem sung like this before, 70,000 passionate voices united in Celtic pride. After the singing, the playing – a wall of red-shirts being urged on by near-hysterical fans. When Wales scores (and the team is pretty good these days), expect more songs, chants and roars.

Half-time offers some respite in the form of the stadium's 22 bars; thanks to high-tech "joy machines" that can serve twelve pints in eight seconds, the record stands at 77,184 pints of beer served during one nail-biting match. Suitably refreshed, the second half seems to pass much faster: the action seems more deadly, the players seem a couple of feet taller, and every attack seems like a pitched battle. Whatever the result, expect a long and detailed autopsy in the pub afterwards, where pints of locally brewed Brains cask ales are sure to flow freely.

Need to know Wales's home games in the Rugby Union Six Nations (Feb–March) take place at Cardiff's Millennium Stadium (Ⓣ 029/2082 2228, Ⓦ www.millenniumstadium.com); tickets are available through Ⓦ www.wru.co.uk or by calling Ⓣ 0844 277 7888.
Map 2, C5

390 Have a flutter at the world's greatest horse race

The Grand National is an event of superlatives: it's a dead cert as the world's most famous horse race; the prize money (nearly £1m for the winner of the main race) is the highest in Europe; and more is bet on it than any other event in the domestic racing calendar (upwards of £100 million in Britain alone).

But what makes the race, which dates back to 1839, unique is the atmosphere. The Grand National, perhaps more than any other British sporting event, attracts a real cross section of society – from royals in the VIP grandstands to locals in the budget enclosures – giving it an inclusive feel and a festive air. This helps to make the contest, the focal point of a three-day meeting held each April at Aintree Racecourse, uniquely popular with both racing enthusiasts and once-a-year punters alike. As does its unpredictability – the favourite rarely wins and 100/1 shots have triumphed on several occasions.

This unpredictability lends added emphasis to the traditional pre-race rituals: studying the racecard and weighing up the odds; visiting the paddock to check on the condition of the horses; and walking the course, past the famous Becher's Brook, the Canal Turn and the Chair fences. Of course for many, the event is simply an excuse for a great day out, a few drinks, a flutter and, above all, a dress-up. Many spectators don eye-catching – or eye-watering, depending on your point of view – outfits, and it is sometimes said, only half in jest, that the most eagerly anticipated contest at Aintree is the best-dressed racegoer competition.

However, as 4.15pm on the Saturday approaches, the 70,000 spectators focus their attention firmly on the Grand National itself and the forty horses that will race the four-and-a-half-mile course. While the ticktack men gesticulate wildly, last-minute bets are placed and silent prayers are offered, before a deafening cheer indicates the start of the race. The next ten minutes or so are filled with a crescendo of excitement before finally a winner emerges and – save for a fortunate few – thousands of torn-up betting slips are tossed in the air like confetti.

Need to know The Grand National takes place at Aintree Racecourse, Ormskirk Rd, Aintree, Liverpool (Ⓦ www.aintree.co.uk). Tickets (hotline ☎ 0844 579 3001) range from £18 to £95 per day, depending on the stand.
Map 3, B10

391 Reaching tennis nirvana in SW19

The first thing to remember about Wimbledon is that it's not a tennis tournament, it's a religious experience. For two weeks in high summer the faithful arrive with their tents and wet wipes, each harbouring a blind hope that they will enter the promised land and a British player will be crowned champion. The good news is that the promised land is within reach of anyone prepared to assemble at dawn at a golf club in SW19. As for the British champion, well, what's a faith without it being tested?

Aware of its devoted congregation, the All England Club has provided a set of commandments. Foremost among them is a 40-page guide to queuing for tickets (sample rules: "queue jumping will not be tolerated"; "takeaway pizzas shall be collected from designated areas"). Despite its nannyish tone, the result – the Wimbledon Queue – is a masterpiece of British fair play. There's no pushing, no touts and now, praise be, clean loos and fresh coffee thanks to its move from the pavements of Church Lane to the lawns of Wimbledon Park Golf Club.

The ideal time to arrive is early in the opening week before the hype reaches boiling point and that modern-day Passion play of a British player reaching the final round is acted out. Week one also provides a smorgasbord of talent from all corners of the globe and some of the tournament's greatest surprises, all on the cheaper ground courts. In 2010, for example, the longest match in history was ground out on lowly Court 18, a bloody-minded three-day epic finally won by 70 games to 68 in the final set.

As the more agnostic tennis fans begin to leave around 5pm your chances of reaching the inner sanctum increase. Returned Centre Court tickets are sold for just £5 – an amazing deal for seeing one of the greats of the game whether it's the swift-footed Spanish Achilles, the elegant Swiss Maestro or of course the Young Scottish Pretender, He who shall be crowned (one day).

Need to know Around 6000 Ground Admission tickets (£20) are available each day at Wimbledon, plus 500 show court tickets (from £34 up to £100 on finals day). If you can't face the queue try the public ballot for tickets (apply online at Ⓦ www.wimbledon.org).

Map 1, E4

392 Burning rubber at the Isle of Man TT

For fifty weeks of the year, the Isle of Man is a sleepy little place. Locals leave their doors unlocked, they stop to chat in the street, and they know the name of their next-door neighbour's cat. But for two weeks in summer, everything changes, as forty thousand visitors – with twelve thousand motorcycles – cross the Irish Sea and turn this quiet island into a rubber-burning, beer-swilling, eardrum-bursting maelstrom of a motorcycle festival.

The TT (Tourist Trophy) has been screeching round the Isle of Man for a hundred years, but only came about thanks to the island's political peculiarity. As a Crown Dependency, part of neither the UK nor the EU, the Isle of Man has its own parliament and can make its own laws. And so when, in the early days of the automobile, the UK forbade motor racing on its public roads and imposed a speed limit of 20mph, race organizers made their way over the water.

And they've never left, although the race they devised in 1907 would be impossible to initiate today. It's the kind of event that drives health and safety officers to drink: the 37-mile Mountain Course, which competitors lap several times, is no carefully cambered track – it's an ordinary road that winds its way through historic towns, screams along country roads, climbs up hills and takes in two hundred bends, many of which are not lined by grass or pavement but by bone-mashing, brain-spilling brick walls. And the fastest riders complete the course at an average speed of 120mph.

Sad to say, they don't all reach the finish line. Around two hundred riders have taken their final tumble on the roads of the TT, and islanders will delight in describing the details to you over a pint of local Bushey's beer. They'll also tell you that, while many of their fellow Manx folk love the adrenaline, the triumph and the tragedy of those two weeks in summer, others are less enthusiastic. The combination of road closures and roistering bikers drives these malcontents to blow the dust from their door keys, to lock up their homes and seek refuge elsewhere – taking their daughters with them.

Need to know TT race week is the first week of June; for more information, see Ⓦ www.iomtt.com.

Map 3, A9

393 Race the train on the Talyllyn Railway

Need to know ⓦ www. racethetrain.com. Race the Train takes place on the second or third Saturday in August in Tywyn, Gwynedd. Book early if you want to run (£25), or ride the train to watch the competitors (£12).

Map 3, B11

Legs aching, you're already running out of breath at the annual Race the Train event, and everything looks lost as belching clouds of smoke disappear into the distance ahead. Surely there's going to be no chance of catching up with the locomotive – at their best, the Talyllyn Railway's steam trains can rattle along at a spirited 15mph, and you'll never be able to keep that pace up for very long, especially not on a hilly course that is a continually changing mixture of gravel roads, narrow footpaths and rough pasture. But steam engines need to be topped up with water and there are passengers to pick up at stations along the way – Pentre, Rhydronen, Brynglas and Dolgoch Falls. So keep on going – there may be hope after all.

There's no question of letting the train take the strain today: it's more a question of whether you or the engine has the most puff. Each August almost a thousand runners pit themselves against the train on the often muddy fourteen-mile course from Tywyn Wharf station to the village of Abergynolwyn and back. The bucolic southern Gwynedd landscape along the way is gorgeous, but most aren't looking at the scenery. To be in serious contention you'll need to make the halfway turn well before the loco: the return journey is the tougher of the two halves. But since the runners' route largely follows the train line, you'll get plenty of encouragement along the way as friends and relatives on board cheer you along. In fact, just about everyone on the train will be yelling support anyway.

The train typically takes just under 1 hour 50 minutes, something only matched by the fastest hundred or so male runners (the men's record is 1hr 18min), and just a handful of women (the fastest taking 1hr 34min). Having started in 1984 with a mere 48 competitors, Race the Train has grown and grown to become a big family event. It is not all about superfit athletes, and there are several shorter races for those with more modest ambitions – 10km, 5.5km, 3.5km and even a Toddlers Trot. And now there's a post-race bash, and even a massage tent – so if the shouts of encouragement don't keep your pecker up, just focus on the soothing massage once it's all over.

394 Racing around Silverstone

Need to know Silverstone, Towcester, Northamptonshire (ⓦ www.silverstone.co.uk) runs two different single-seater race car experiences – one that lasts 50min, the other 2hr. Prices start at £99 per person and drivers must have held a full driving licence for at least a year by the time they take part. Height restrictions apply.

Map 3, D12

Soon after lowering yourself into the cabin of a single-seater racing machine, the panic sets in. What started as nervous excitement, buoyed by the throaty rasp of a Formula Ford engine, quickly reverts to fear. You know that soon, after clunking on your seatbelt, wiping your visor and adjusting your grip on the wheel one final time, you'll be told to floor the accelerator. And exactly 4.3 spine-jangling seconds later, you'll be tearing towards a hairpin bend at 60mph.

This is your introduction to racing, and your first chance to familiarize yourself with part of Great Britain's ultimate racecourse. This is where legends have been made (and broken), and as you screech your way around the track, red and white rumble strips blurring in the corners of your eyes, you'll soon realize why.

Silverstone's Stowe Circuit was built to test nerves. But it also tests your judgement. At every corner, you'll find yourself making frantic, split-second decisions about whether you should brake more, accelerate more or just tinker with your position on the track. Then of course there are the gears; if you change down too quickly or too slowly, you'll lose valuable seconds. But do nothing, and you'll skid hopelessly into the rough, sending an acrid cloud of dust and burnt rubber up into the grey Northamptonshire sky. The human brain wasn't meant to think this fast.

After a while though, you'll begin to get a feel for the course, and that's when you can really start testing yourself. With sweat staining the back of your overalls, and clammy palms struggling to grip the inside of your oil-stained gloves, you'll judder faster and faster into each bend, determined to beat your previous lap time. Now only one thing matters to you – speed – and you'll begin gunning for the car's 135mph limit.

But like the car, time flies. And at the end of your session, you'll have to ease off the accelerator before trundling to a stop and hoisting yourself back out of the hot car on excited, jelly-like arms. Looking back down into the cabin, you'll realize you're not scared anymore.

395 Hand to hand combat in the Lake District

A Lawrentian image of burly rural types locked in sweaty combat may not initially spring to mind when you think of the Lake District. But this manly, gritty pastime is an established Lakes tradition: Cumberland and Westmorland wrestling was hugely popular in the eighteenth and nineteenth centuries, though its origins probably date all the way back to the time of the Viking invasions.

Traditionally, participants wear rather unflattering garb: baggy shorts worn over white long johns with a shapeless vest. In the last few years though, athletic gear has been permitted, in a bid to entice the region's burly lassies to participate. At the start of the competition, the participants "tekk hod", linking their fingers together behind the opponent's back or neck – this hand hold needs to be maintained throughout the fight. Having tekken hod, the contestants spin around, locked in a close if rather awkward embrace, before one manages to hurl the other to the ground by means of one of the sport's esoterically named throws: a hype, a click or a cross-buttock. Otherwise, the rules are simple – the participants must always stay within the grassy ring, and the contest is decided on the basis of the best of three falls. The round ends, as it begins, with a polite handshake.

Wrestling is still a mainstay of country fairs such as the Cumberland Show held in Carlisle in July, September's Shepherds' Meet in Borrowdale, and the Egremont Crab Fair, which has been hosted at harvest time (the end of September) since 1267 – as well as wrestling, this idiosyncratic event gives space to pipe-smoking, the singing of hunting songs, and the great British art of gurning. Every two years, the sport is also part of the essential flavour of the Cockermouth Georgian Fair (May), which also features a costume parade, hurdy-gurdy music, morris dancing and sedan-chair racing. There's a vein of eccentricity in the Lakes, and the quaintly attired, gentlemanly participants in this ancient sport fit right in.

Need to know Look out for agricultural shows and country fairs across the region to see Cumberland and Westmorland wrestling: the Cumberland Show (Ⓦwww.cumberlandshow.co.uk), Shepherds' Meet (Ⓦwww.borrowdaleshow.org.uk), Egremont Crab Fair (Ⓦwww.egremontcrabfair.com), and the Cockermouth Georgian Fair (Ⓦwww.cockermouth.org.uk/georgianfair).
Map 4, D16

HIGH DAYS AND HOLIDAYS

festivals and events

Given that the standard British celebration is a nice cup of tea, and perhaps a digestive biscuit as well on a special occasion, many British festivals seem to belong to quite a different nation altogether. Burning pagan fires and bawdy maypole frolics hardly fit the buttoned-up stereotype, while otherwise sedate villages across the land succumb to an annual urge to chase a large cheese down a hill or set off fireworks into the small hours. In truth, the famous British reserve is largely a myth – it's far more likely to be a long, collective hangover following yet another almighty party, of which there are thousands each year in Britain. Pretty much every city, town and village has at least one big annual event, some with a history dating back centuries and others little more than an invented excuse for a booze-up. From the smallest village fête to Edinburgh, the world's largest cultural festival, there's a whale of a time to be had. Traditional song and dance are at the heart of many events, while another British tradition – the summer torrent of rain and mud – fails to dampen the enthusiasm of welly-wearing festival-goers. The number of music festivals has exploded in recent years, meaning you can find one to suit every musical taste. In a land shaped by immigration, cross-cultural celebrations have taken firm root – London's flamboyant Notting Hill Carnival is as much a fixture on the calendar as the Last Night of the Proms, while in Chinese New Year and Hogmanay the British get two new years for the price of one. British cliques and clans – goths, travellers, comedians, authors, sailors and opera singers – also come together to party in a succession of high-profile events, while Yorkshire, ever mindful of its position as "God's own county", puts on a national show of its own. There's no thread that links these festivals, save the enjoyment they provide – a day or two's escape from the everyday, and the perfect mini holiday.

396 Hitting the streets for the Notting Hill Carnival

It starts sometime in August, when the first of the after-party posters materialize along Ladbroke Grove and the plink-plonk rhythms of steelband rehearsals filter through the clamour of Portobello market. By the time the crowd barriers appear on street corners and the shop-owners begin covering their windows with party-scarred plywood, the feeling of anticipation is almost tangible: Carnival is coming. These familiar old streets are about to be transformed into a wash of colour, sound, movement and pure, unadulterated joy that makes this huge street festival the highlight of London's party calendar.

Carnival Sunday morning and in streets eerily emptied of cars, sound-system guys, still bleary-eyed from the excesses of last night's warm-up parties, wire up their towering stacks of speakers, while fragrant smoke wafts from the stalls of early-bird jerk chicken chefs. And then a bass line trembles through the morning air, and the trains begin to disgorge crowds of revellers, dressed to impress and brandishing their whistles and horns. Some head straight for the sound systems, spending the entire day moving from one to the other and stopping wherever the music takes them. Streets lined by mansion blocks become canyons of sound, and all you can see is a moving sea of people, jumping and blowing whistles as wave after wave of music ripples through the air.

But the backbone of Carnival is mas, the parade of costumed bands that winds its way through the centre of the event. Crowds line up along the route, and Ladbroke Grove becomes a seething throng of floats and flags, sequins and feathers, as the mas (masquerade) bands cruise along, their revellers dancing up a storm to the tunes bouncing from the music trucks. And for the next two days, the only thing that matters is the delicious, anarchic freedom of dancing on the London streets.

Need to know Notting Hill Carnival takes place on the Sunday and Monday of August bank holiday weekend See Ⓦ www. nottinghill-carnival.co.uk for a wealth of information on the carnival.

Map 1, A2

397 Remember, remember: Bonfire Night in Lewes

Need to know Lewes' Bonfire Society parades take place on the night of November 5. Firework displays take place at six sites around town, with tickets sold in local pubs in the preceding weeks; for details, see Ⓦ www.lewesbonfirecouncil.org.uk. The streets can be very crowded and therefore potentially dangerous. The town is closed to vehicles and drinking alcohol in the streets is not permitted.

Map 2, E6

Given that Bonfire Night is one of the few folk traditions that the English celebrate with gusto – and there's even a natty little rhyme about it – it's surprising that so many are hazy about its origins. Freedom fighter Guy Fawkes was the fall guy of the Gunpowder Plot, an English Catholic revolt led by Sir Robert Catesby. Enraged at the violent suppression of Catholics that had been commonplace for decades, the conspirators planned to blow up the State Opening of Parliament on November 5, 1605, assassinating King James I and insisting that his Catholic daughter Elizabeth be crowned Queen. They stockpiled explosives under the House of Lords, and left Fawkes to guard them.

Unluckily for Fawkes, he was caught red-handed in the early hours of the 5th. Later that day, Londoners were exhorted to light bonfires in thanksgiving for the King's lucky escape. Fawkes was condemned to be hanged, drawn and quartered, but escaped that agony by cheating the executioner, leaping from the scaffold to his death.

Ever since 1605, the celebration of Bonfire Night has continued unbroken, and these days, it's all about fireworks and fun, its sectarian origins largely forgotten. Not so in the Sussex market town of Lewes, though. This otherwise sleepy little place has been a hotbed of anti-Catholic feeling since the mid-1500s when it was Protestantism, not Catholicism, that was punishable by torture and death. Under Bloody Mary, seventeen Protestants were martyred here, burnt in barrels in the middle of town. The retaliating yells of "Burn the Pope!" that still ring out each Bonfire Night are enough to curdle the blood.

If you feel uneasy in crowds, freaked out by fire, scared of the dark or, worst of all, somewhat unsettled by sudden, ear-splitting explosions, don't even think about coming here – but if you love noise, smoke and fireworks, you'll be blown away. The town's seven Bonfire Societies raise funds all year, just to send it all up in smoke. Their Bonfire Boys parade through the streets carrying blazing torches and flaming crosses – seventeen of them, to honour the martyrs – to the steady beat of drums. Some drag barrels of smouldering tar, others parade huge satirical effigies of public figures, destined to be incinerated at the end of the night. Stirring speeches are read, bangers ricochet across the bonfire sites and, at the climax of proceedings, hundreds of rockets fill the sky.

398 Black tie, picnics and country house opera

Opera is supposed to be a highly emotional combination of theatre and music, yet all too often it's a byword for a corporate-funded, champagne-and-lobster lifestyle. If you're going to live the posh operatic experience, however, the country house opera festivals of the summer months are absolutely the way to go. You'll be among enthusiasts, not bankers, and driving out to a stately home and picnicking on the lawns between acts is infinitely more romantic than a rushed pre-theatre pizza and the tube home. And, of course, there's always the music, which, on a good night, can be the very finest.

The original and arguably most elite of the country opera venues is Glyndebourne, outside the town of Lewes in East Sussex. In fact, with its dedicated, 1200-seat auditorium, top stars and restaurants, Glyndebourne isn't all that different from a major opera house, even if many people still picnic during the interval.

Need to know For information on the opera festivals listed see: Ⓦ www.glyndebourne. com, Ⓦ www.garsingtonopera. org, Ⓦ www.grangeparkopera. co.uk, Ⓦ www.lfo.org.uk and Ⓦ www.ifordarts.co.uk. Booking is a matter of getting on the mailing list and acting fast when it opens. That said, returns can often be found, even for Glyndebourne.

Map 2, D5, D6 & E6

Garsington Opera has long been regarded as the more relaxed alternative, with its temporary stage open to the gardens at one side, allowing the sound of evening birdsong to compete deliciously with the singers. In 2011 Garsington is moving to a new, dedicated venue on the stunning estate at Wormsley, in Buckinghamshire, but it seems likely that the relatively laidback spirit will be maintained. A newish rival, Grange Park, has a heart-liftingly lovely setting in the grounds of a neo-Grecian stately home near Alresford, in Hampshire. The productions at the dedicated theatre can be ambitious: not everyone risks Prokofiev's surreal *Love for Three Oranges*.

As the big venues are drawn upmarket, there are rougher diamonds to consider. At Longborough, in the Gloucestershire Cotswolds, condensed performances of Wagner's Ring Cycle take place in a barn conversion – albeit a huge, classical one. And at the open-air Iford Festival in Wiltshire, which encourages young singers, there's room for fewer than a hundred people in the beautiful, cloistered setting, making this one of the most excitingly intimate settings for opera in the country.

399 Proms and circumstance

As much a part of the British summer as a rain-sodden Wimbledon, the Proms can also lay claim to being the biggest classical music festival on the planet: a 58-day epic watched by millions around the globe. Conceived in 1895 by the conductor Henry Wood with the aim of bringing classical music to the masses, the festival has stayed true to its egalitarian roots with a programme that mixes a familiar repertoire of Classic FM-friendly favourites with some long-forgotten works and bold new commissions. Aficionados come for the classical curveballs – a little Russian avant-garde constructivism or some baroque-techno fusion, say – but if you don't know your Arvo Pärt from your Elgar, there's plenty of lighter numbers on offer too. In recent years, Proms have been themed around John Williams' film scores and Rodgers and Hammerstein musicals, and the annual Doctor Who Prom – complete with daleks – is a sure-fire sell-out. Whichever concert you choose, the atmosphere of a packed Royal Albert Hall is almost worth the ticket price in itself, from the pin-drop silence as the conductor raises his baton to the last, dying note, when the spellbound hush of a five-thousand-strong audience is broken by a thunderclap of applause.

If you're planning to go to several concerts, it's more affordable to prom, which means queuing for a £5 standing ticket up in the gallery or in the arena, right by the stage. It's worth being aware of promming protocol: doors open 45 minutes before the performance starts, and there's no barging to the front if you arrive late, unless you want to unleash the fury of an army of more punctual prommers. And be ready to join in with the "prommers' stamp", the noisier equivalent of a standing ovation.

Eight weeks of concerts culminate in the raucous end-of-term party that is the Last Night, when a core of die-hard prommers – armed with Union Jacks and klaxons and sporting straw boaters – attempts to raise the roof with patriotic sing-alongs in the Rule, Britannia! vein. Last Night tickets are in high demand, so consider joining the misty-eyed, flag-waving hordes at the open-air Proms in the Park in London's Hyde Park and other cities nationwide for big-screen link-ups to the main event. All together now: "Land of Hope and Glory…".

Need to know The Proms, Royal Albert Hall, London SW7 Ⓦ www.bbc.co.uk/proms. Seated tickets cost £12–60; season tickets and weekend promming passes are available. At least 500 £5 promming tickets are sold on the door before each concert.
Map 1, B4

UNUSUAL COMPETITIONS

The British appetite for all things eccentric – particularly anything with a competitive element – ensures that on any given weekend you can find a bunch of people who lead otherwise sensible lives in a damp field somewhere snorkelling through bog water, racing pigs or chucking around black puddings. Here are the best ones to watch – from a safe and sensible distance of course.

400 Coal carrying

They breed them tough in Yorkshire. How else can you explain the idea of running for a mile with a sack of coal on your shoulders for fun? That's the challenge that's been laid down for the past 46 years in the World Coal Carrying Championships. Apparently the race started when two local coal merchants decided to settle a pub argument about who was fitter. It's exhausting, sweaty and very, very hard.

Gawthorpe, West Yorkshire Ⓦ www.gawthorpe.ndo.co.uk. Easter Mon. Map 3, C10

401 Pig racing

Wallowing around in the mud may be their favourite pastime, but pigs can actually pick up a fair head of steam too. The nippiest porkers and their owners gather at Bath Racecourse every April where they're put to the test to see who is the speediest piglet in the country. The pun-tastic "Ham National" involves eight pigs running around a track and jumping over some (very low) hurdles.

Bath Racecourse Ⓦ www.bath-racecourse.co.uk. April. Map 2, C5

402 Cheese-rolling

Cheese-rolling, an organized bout of cheese chasing down a grassy mound in Gloucestershire, is one of Britain's best-loved oddball events. It's certainly in the best spirit of British amateurism: anyone can enter and all they have to do is fling themselves down a precipitous hill after an eighteen-pound wheel of Double Gloucester. The first one to reach it wins – and no prizes for guessing what. The official event was cancelled in 2010, but enthusiasts ensured an unofficial one took place, and you can always take part on your iPhone – a cheese-rolling app has been developed.

Cooper's Hill, Gloucestershire. Ⓦ www.cheese-rolling.co.uk. Late May Bank Holiday. Map 2, C5

403 Pram racing

Having to drink seven pints of beer while covering two-thirds of a mile on foot doesn't sound like such an arduous challenge. And it isn't. Unless of course you're dressed up as a baby and pushing a fully grown man in a pram for the entire distance. The Oxted Pram Race, running since 1977, requires its competitors to race some sort of pram device – with their team-mate inside – through the market town of Oxted, stopping at seven pubs along the way where they have to down a pint in each. Prams tend to be of the home-made variety, constructed out of old armchairs, wooden boxes and giant fish tanks.

Oxted, Surrey Ⓦ www.oxtedpramrace.co.uk. July. Map 2, E6

404 Bog snorkelling

The reckless, fearless and the just plain filth-loving join in this competition each year, whereby participants must navigate their way through a 60ft-long peat bog without using any kind of conventional swimming strokes. Snorkels, masks and flippers are allowed but you're only allowed to raise your head above the gunk a maximum of four times. The perfect event for anyone who thinks that Glastonbury in the rain is just a bit too clean.

Llanwrtyd Wells, Powys Ⓦ www.green-events.co.uk. Aug. Map 3, B12

405 Bognor Birdman

Man has always wanted to fly, but unlike Icarus, who flew too close to the sun, the Birdmen of Bognor tend to spend most of their time flying far too close to and then very quickly downwards into the freezing sea water. Since 1971 contestants from across the world have come to the seaside resort town of Bognor to take part. The idea is to run off the end of the pier and attempt to fly as far as possible, usually in hang-gliders but often on bicycles, in Heath Robinson-esque wooden contraptions and in fancy dress. There's a cash prize for the winner, though nobody has ever yet gone as far as 100 metres – the closest contestant coming within centimetres of this in 2009.

Bognor Regis, West Sussex Ⓦ *www.birdman.org.uk. Sept. Map 2, E6*

406 Gravy wrestling

Just what are you to do with leftover gravy? You could always ask the *Rose 'n' Bowl* pub in Stacksteads, Lancashire, to take it off your hands. Every year they get hold of 440 gallons of gravy for the gravy wrestling championships. Wrestlers are required to take down their opponent in a paddling pool filled to the brim with the brown stuff. The mess is so bad that local firefighters are drafted in to hose down the Bisto barbarians afterwards.

Stacksteads, Lancashire Ⓦ *www.worldgravywrestling.com. Aug. Map 3, C10*

407 Gurning

The ultimate antidote to Miss World, the World Gurning Championships are an exercise in ugliness in which contestants must curl their lips and extend their jaws into a "gurn" that usually looks something like a constipated pit bull terrier lunging after a sausage. It takes place as part of a local fair that has been held in the town of Egremont in Cumbria since 1267. Anyone can enter, though be prepared for fellow competitors to make pretty serious sacrifices. One winner in the 1990s even had his front teeth removed to perfect his trophy-winning gurn. That's dedication. And frankly, that's just weird.

Egremont, Cumbria Ⓦ *www.egremontcrabfair.com. Sept. Map 4, D16*

408 Stone skimming

There's something beautifully pointless about chucking a stone into some water, but it's not a spectator sport in itself. Skimming on the other hand attracts hundreds of competitors to the tiny island of Easdale. The idea is to make a flat piece of slate stone go the furthest distance along the water while "skimming" the surface at least three times. The trick is to have the correct stance, to throw it at the correct angle and to find a stone of just the right smoothness. Children have their own contest as do people over 50, who can compete in the charmingly named "Old Tosser" section.

Easdale, near Oban, Argylle & Bute Ⓦ *www.stoneskimming.com. Sept. Map 4, B14*

409 Black pudding throwing

Cooked pig blood and fat wrapped in intestine has long been a favoured breakfast staple for Brits in the form of black pudding. They're quite handy weapons as well. The targets at the World Black Pudding Throwing Championships in Ramsbottom, near Manchester, are Yorkshire puddings, placed on top of a wall, which contestants aim to knock off by way of a well-thrown pud. Dating back to the 1850s, this is a contest that defies logic, but certainly leaves one wondering what other British foods could be used for sport. Spam tennis anyone?

Royal Oak pub, Bridge St, Ramsbottom, Greater Manchester Ⓦ *www.ramsbottomonline.com. Sept. Map 3, C10*

410 Take to the skies over Bristol

Those who have lived in Bristol for more than a summer or two are accustomed to seeing a giant turtle flying over their rooftops. Sometimes, you'll hear it before you see it – there's a roar, you look up, and suddenly, there it is, looming overhead – perhaps pursued by a monster chicken, a goggle-eyed bulldog or even a bagpiper in full highland regalia.

If you thought that hot-air balloons had to be balloon-shaped, then a visit to Bristol for the city's International Balloon Fiesta will reveal whole new horizons. For some time, cunning designers have been creating inflatables in all manner of shapes. Often, there's a commercial sponsor involved – hence the bulldog, a well-known insurance company's doleful mascot, and some surreal flying objects including a fire extinguisher and a wine box – but sometimes designers create novelty balloons just for fun. You name it, they'll hang a basket under it and see if it flies. As well as the turtle, family favourites such as Thomas the Tank Engine and Sonic the Hedgehog make regular appearances in the city skies.

Bristol, home to the world's largest balloon manufacturer, has been holding its annual Fiesta since 1979. Experienced pilots and teams from all over the world are invited to take part and as many as 150 teams show up. Even if you haven't booked a place on a flight, it's fascinating to join the throng, watching the park fill with colour as the balloons heave into shape.

A mass ascent is scheduled for 6am and 6pm each day. These are the calmest and best times to fly, but the vagaries of the British summer mean that sometimes the balloons can't take off at all. For visitors, this isn't necessarily a total disappointment, though – while they're grounded, you can see the balloons at close range and quiz the pilots about taking to the skies. There are plenty of other things going on, too, not least daredevil displays from stunt motorbike teams, helicopters and the Red Arrows.

Come the evening, things get funky. Roll up for the Nightglow and you can watch the balloons, illuminated by their burners, pulsate in time to top-volume chart music, while colourful rockets explode overhead.

Need to know The Bristol International Balloon Fiesta, Ashton Court, Long Ashton, Bristol (Ⓦ www.bristolfiesta.co.uk) takes place over a four-day weekend in early August (Thurs–Sun from 6am until late). There are Nightglow events on the Thursday and Sunday evenings. Entrance is free; champagne balloon flights cost from £180.
Map 2, C5

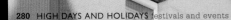

411 Hogmanay in Edinburgh

From the cascade of fireworks tipping over the castle rock to uninhibited displays of stranger-kissing as midnight chimes and the sight of the classical pillars of the Royal Scottish Academy being transformed into a giant urinal, Edinburgh consistently throws the world's most memorable New Year's Eve party. And it's a party on a grand scale, with around 80,000 people from around the world joining in.

The reasons for Scotland's particularly fervent embrace of New Year date back to the Protestant Reformation, when Christmas was regarded as a Papist imposition, and Hogmanay took over as the annual celebration. In fact, Edinburgh's celebrations kick off with a distinctly inauthentic, though enjoyable event that takes place four days before Hogmanay: Shetland's Up Helly Aa Vikings process up Calton Hill with thousands of participants, all carrying torches lighting the route from the Royal Mile to the classical temples on the hill.

On the night itself, a more traditional event to start the evening with is the candlelit concert in St Giles Cathedral, the hulking medieval church on the Royal Mile. From then on the tempo rises, with a massive street party on Princes Street and a boisterous ceilidh in the Princes Street Gardens, followed by a large-scale concert: past performers have included the Red Hot Chilli Peppers, Blondie and Madness, with support from artists such as the mournful but brilliant Scottish folk-rocker King Creosote. At midnight, the fireworks kick off, and from Calton Hill to Salisbury Crags, from the new town to the old town, from the pubs and from the castle esplanade, the whole city looks skywards and celebrates. Auld Lang Syne is belted out, and any last shreds of Presbyterian reserve are abandoned, as people bound around hugging and kissing each other.

The next day, one brave (or foolhardy) way to shift that hangover is to join in the quirky Loony Dook, a fancy-dress communal plunge into the uninviting ice-cold waters of the Forth at South Queensferry, accompanied by a pipe band and lots of merriment. It might be not everyone's idea of welcoming in the new year, but the setting under the rust-red Forth Rail Bridge is spectacular, and you certainly won't forget it in a hurry.

Need to know Edinburgh's Hogmanay is now a ticketed event, so book ahead both for entry and for accommodation. Ⓦ www.edinburghshogmanay. com.
Map 4, D14

412 Appleby Horse Fair

Anyone driving to the Appleby Horse Fair may find themselves following the disconcerting, seemingly ancient vision of young men riding horses bareback down the A66 dual carriageway. Every June, the Cumbrian town of Appleby-in-Westmorland and its 2500 residents play host to thousands of horses, around 10,000 Romanies and Travellers and over 30,000 other visitors, at one of the world's oldest horse fairs. The horses are everywhere – outside the town's shops and hotels, being washed en masse in the River Eden, being ridden in a display of outright speed along on the town's roads, and proudly on show, with the powerfully built black-and-white workhorses, bred over centuries and noted for their stamina, passivity and intelligence, standing nobly in fields and surrounded by admirers.

The horses and the fair are integral to the culture of the nomadic, tribal way of Romany life. Formally given a charter by King James II in 1685, some estimate the fair's age to be over a thousand years old, substantially predating the first arrival of Romanies to the British Isles. But the event has become sacred to the Romany community as the annual meeting point for gypsies, a celebration of their way of life, culture and language. However far-flung they are, many Romanies will make the journey to Appleby to meet up with families and friends who they may not see from one fair to the next. As one attendee said, the fair is *morra tan*, "our place".

Amid all this tradition, changes arise. Among the boot men, pot men and fortune-tellers are many non-gypsies who've come for the good trading opportunities and brought with them nought but tat. Alongside the fleets of the traditional, brightly painted "bow top" caravans are fields of the white modern versions. And the horses brought for show, or to be bought and sold, are no free roamers, with each horse needing a "horse passport" proving ownership, while all newborn foals and horses hitherto without passports must be micro-chipped. Nevertheless, seeing a vast nomadic tribe and their horses re-create this traditional world is a spectacular vision that harks back many centuries.

Need to know Appleby Horse Fair, Appleby-in-Westmorland, Cumbria Ⓦ www.applebyfair.org. First week of June from Thurs to the following Wed, with the main days on Fri, Sat & Sun. If June 1 is a Thurs, the fair starts on the following Thurs (June 8).
Map 4, D16

413 The greatest show in Yorkshire

Preparation begins months in advance: pigs' trotters are polished; sheep are shorn; hens fattened up; cows and horses groomed until they're silky smooth. And that's just the animal side of things – flower arrangements are practised again and again, cake recipes perfected and vegetables lovingly nurtured to become plump and juicy. Competitors and exhibits must be flawless by mid-July, in time for one of the most illustrious agricultural shows in Yorkshire, The Great Yorkshire Show.

Held just outside the well-to-do town of Harrogate and lasting three days, the Show is a celebration of all things country, from livestock and produce to traditions and arts and crafts. Don't expect to see the entire show in one day – it's spread out over a hefty 250 acres. Buy a programme and earmark a few must-see exhibits – depending on taste, you could admire gargantuan combine harvesters and tractors lined up in shiny rows, watch bakers calmly kneading their bread in the cookery tent, or gawp – from a safe distance – at sharp-taloned birds of prey in the falconry displays. Equine competitions – held in the neat, hedge-lined main ring – are particularly popular, while demonstrations of traditional country skills, such as sheepshearing, cow milking and blacksmithing, take place regularly throughout the day.

Livestock shows tend to attract the biggest crowds. Competition is fierce, with every animal – according to the rules of pedigree that date from the eighteenth century – displaying the qualities and traits that best define its breed. Classes are split up by way of breed, age and sex, and competitors are paraded around the main ring in front of keen-eyed judges in plain white coats: enormous bulls plod alongside their needfully muscular owners; eager sheepdogs corral quick-footed sheep into pens; rose-pink piglets run amok and induce soppy exclamations of "awww" from the crowd; and milk-white goats trot about, bleating loudly. They are all there to win, and while prize money isn't hefty, the honour of first place is unparalleled – those months of pampering and petting have paid off.

Come teatime, head to the home-produce stalls, where you can tuck into piles of soft, baked scones, gooey Victoria sponge cake and spicy gingerbread – all washed down with a cup of (what else?) Yorkshire tea.

Need to know Great Yorkshire Show, Harrogate, North Yorkshire Ⓦ www.greatyorkshireshow.co.uk. Showground open Tues & Wed 7.30am–7.30pm, Thurs 7.30am–6.30pm. Tickets £21 on the day, £18 advance purchase.
Map 3, C9

414 A global gathering in the Welsh hills

In the north Wales countryside a Filipino choir in pink and blue chiffon poses for a photo. Rajasthani musicians in turbans relax between shows, as a group of traditional Scottish dancers hurries by. Ukrainian folk singers enjoy the sunshine, while a gaggle of South African students head for lunch. A nervous Patagonian ensemble prepares to perform.

At first glance, it appears an unlikely scene. But every year, during the second week of July, around four thousand singers, dancers and musicians from more than fifty countries arrive in the verdant Dee Valley to compete in the six-day Llangollen International Musical Eisteddfod.

Eisteddfods are Welsh festivals of competitive music, literature and performance dating back to the twelfth century (eisteddfod means "to be sitting together", a reference to the audiences that once gathered to listen to competing bards). There are many Eisteddfods staged throughout Wales, but the Llangollen International Musical Eisteddfod is slightly different. It was first held in 1947 after British Council employee Harold Tudor came up with the idea of staging musical competitions to promote peace and understanding between nations in the aftermath of World War II. The event has been held annually ever since, and in 2004 it was nominated for the Nobel Peace Prize.

It is held just outside Llangollen town at the four-thousand-capacity Royal International Pavilion – which looks like a mini Millennium Dome – surrounded by smaller stages, craft stalls and food and drink vendors. In recent years "fringe" events have also sprung up in Llangollen itself.

During the days, accomplished performers compete in a range of categories, including choirs, folk dancing and instrumental works. Shortly afterwards, the judges reveal their "adjudications" – which range from technical jargon to acerbic asides – and announce the winners. In the evenings are the main concerts: Luciano Pavarotti, Ladysmith Black Mambazo, José Carreras, Kiri Te Kanawa and Joan Baez, as well as Welsh singers such as Katherine Jenkins and Bryn Terfel, have all graced the stage over the years.

But arguably the most enjoyable part of the Eisteddfod is simply wandering around outside the pavilion, watching the impromptu performances and taking in the melange of national costumes, languages and cultures.

Need to know Llangollen International Musical Eisteddfod, Dee Valley, Denbighshire. Day passes £9; reserved tickets in the pavilion are £12–15; tickets for the evening concerts £15–55. For more information visit Ⓦ www.international-eisteddfod.co.uk and Ⓦ www.llangollen.org.uk.
Map 3, B11

415 Lighting up Leicester: Diwali

One of the most dramatic stories in the Sanskrit epic the *Ramayana* is Lord Rama's liberation of his beloved wife Sita from the clutches of the demon king Ravana. When Lord Rama returned home to Ayodhya, local people celebrated the triumph of good over evil by lighting rows of clay lamps – an act repeated by hundreds of millions of people around the world each year during Diwali, the most important festival in the Hindu calendar.

The biggest celebration of Diwali – an abbreviation of "Deepavali", which means row of lamps – outside India takes place in Leicester, one of the UK's most diverse cities. Every autumn, tens of thousands of people – including followers of the Sikh and Jain religions, who also celebrate Diwali – crowd onto Belgrave Road in the heart of the city's Indian community to take part in the "festival of lights".

The celebrations start with the switch-on of the Diwali lights: after music, dancing and speeches (in English, Hindi and Gujarati) from local dignitaries, a noisy countdown starts, climaxing at 7.30pm with the switch-on of around 6500 multicoloured lights, an explosion of confetti and a cacophony of cheers. Eventually the crowd works its way down the road – dubbed the "Golden Mile" – to the nearby Cossington Street recreation ground where an extremely loud firework display ensues.

En route, tempting aromas waft out of the area's many Indian restaurants, and sampling the special Diwali dishes on offer is one of the great pleasures of the festivities. As sweets are traditionally given as presents during the festival, there's a huge variety of *gulab jamun* (small doughnuts soaked in syrup), *jalebi* (deep-fried, super-sweet twirls of batter) and more unusual dishes like *gajar ka halwa* (carrot halva) to choose from.

The end of the festival – Diwali Day – takes place around two weeks later, with similar levels of celebrations, fireworks and food. As the night draws to a close, the crowds slowly disperse, and for the final time that year people are guided home by thousands of flickering Diwali lights in houses across the city.

Need to know Diwali is based on the Hindu calendar so the date varies each year – it usually falls in October or November. For more information visit Ⓦ www.goleicestershire.com or call the Leicestershire tourist information line on ☎ 08448 885181.
Map 3, D11

416 Light your fire in Shetland's Viking ritual

Anybody who scorns films such as *The Wicker Man* as being fiction of the most fanciful variety needs to head to the capital of windswept Shetland in January. There may not be Christopher Lee marshalling a human sacrifice here, but most of the other ingredients of a pagan ritual are in place: fire, costumed revellers and a large intake of alcohol.

Up Helly Aa is a yearly tribute to Shetland's close geographical and historical connection to Scandinavia – Shetland was the property of Norway for over five hundred years – though the festival itself is a decidedly more recent invention. Developed in the 1870s from earlier winter festivities, which often involved rolling flaming tar barrels, locals came up with a novel plan to channel passions for fire and drinking into something positive, and the rituals and celebrations of Up Helly Aa were established.

Up Helly Aa has been thriving ever since. So on an invariably bitter cold night in January, Britain's most northerly town comes alive with locals bedecked in sheepskins, Viking helmets, shields, chain mail and axes. Incredibly, a 30ft-long replica Viking long boat, which takes local craftsmen over four months to build, is carried aloft through the narrow streets amid a cacophony of marching bands, whistles and a heck of a lot of shouting.

Out of the 5000-strong crowd more than 800 men, led by the Guizer Jarl, the leader of the main squad (there are 45 squads in total), carry flaming torches which are thrown onto the boat at the designated "torching point". As the boat slowly crumbles to a cinder the festival continues with theatre performances, singing and dancing. Be sure not to miss the enormous fireworks display nor the chance to engage in a late-night singsong inside one of the local boozers or the Town Hall, one of the main venues for entertainment.

Thankfully the next day is a public holiday in Shetland – essential for nursing sore heads, and getting to grips with memories of a night that combines pyrotechnics, history and copious whisky to utterly bizarre effect.

Need to know Up Helly Aa, Lerwick, Shetland Ⓦ uphellyaa.org. Takes place on the last Tuesday of January.
Map 5, F18

417 Books galore at Hay-on-Wye

Need to know Hay Festival of Literature and the Arts, Hay-on-Wye, Powys Ⓦwww.hayfestival.co.uk. Eleven days in late May or early June. Book accommodation months ahead.

Map 3, B12

Books, books, books! And a whole load more books. Hay-on-Wye is a lovely, little Welsh border town that is a pleasure to hang out in for a variety of perfectly good reasons. But it is really about books. Secondhand books. And antiquarian books. And book festivals. And bookshops filling the former cinema. And book cafés. In fact the whole town has been taken over by the book trade with over thirty bookshops packed into a town (really little more than a village) of around two thousand inhabitants.

It has become the world's largest secondhand and antiquarian book centre thanks largely to flamboyant local Richard Booth, who opened his first bookshop here in 1961. Others followed and by the late 1970s it was already Wales's "town of books". In 1977 (on April 1, of course) Booth whipped up a good bit of publicity by declaring himself ruler of the "independent kingdom of Hay-on-Wye"... a self-styled king, Richard Coeur de Livre.

A decade or so later, promoter Peter Florence launched the Hay Festival, an annual celebration of all things booky that Bill Clinton famously dubbed the "Woodstock of the mind". By the mid-1990s half of literary Britain (and stellar names from the worlds of art and politics) were decamping here annually for highbrow addresses, poetry readings and some good old-fashioned book promotion. A-list authors – the likes of Norman Mailer, Salman Rushdie and Martin Amis – became regular features, and Arundhati Roy and DBC Pierre effectively launched their careers here. Now, around fifty thousand festival-goers flock to a self-contained site on the outskirts of Hay-on-Wye, complete with massive marquees, stalls and cafés. When the weather is good (a rare occurrence) you'll find groups scattered on the grass de-constructing the last speaker's address.

Many talks are now broadcast or turned into podcasts, and the festival has even expanded to almost a dozen similar events in Mexico, Spain, the Maldives and India, but there's no substitute for experiencing the original.

418 Getting classical on the Suffolk coast: Aldeburgh Festival

Few composers have been so tied to a single place as Benjamin Britten, who loved the Suffolk coast his whole life: "I belong at home – there in Aldeburgh. I have tried to bring music to it in the shape of our local Festival; and all the music I write comes from it".

Today the Aldeburgh Festival remains very much Britten's baby, a celebration of classical music established by him in 1948, along with singer Peter Pears and writer Eric Crozier, and inspired by the same sky-domed landscapes. Indeed, little has changed in this part of Suffolk since Britten's day, a crumbling coast of shallow estuaries, grey seas and humble fishing towns. Snape Maltings, where the festival has been based since 1967, has also retained its Victorian character, despite evolving into a major tourist complex replete with shops, galleries, cafés and even boat tours up the Alde estuary.

Need to know The Aldeburgh Festival, Suffolk (Ⓦwww.aldeburgh.co.uk) takes place over two weeks in June, with concerts at Snape Maltings plus venues in Aldeburgh; programme and tickets are available several months in advance. Snape Maltings Concert Hall (Ⓦwww.snapemaltings.co.uk) is located at Snape, five miles inland from Aldeburgh (signposted off the A12), and approximately 30 minutes from Ipswich. It's best reached by car.

Map 3, F12

Britten's aim was to present new music and new interpretations of older or forgotten pieces, and today it's the festival's smaller concerts that reflect this heritage best. The young talent taking the Britten–Pears Programme composers course supply a range of new work, while the youthful Britten–Pears Orchestra offers fresh, dynamic takes on a range of classical pieces. Britten still features of course – many of his works were premiered at the festival (*A Midsummer Night's Dream* in 1960; *Death in Venice* in 1973), and his masterpiece, the opera *Peter Grimes*, remains a fan favourite; the chilling tale of an alienated and brutal dreamer never fails to mesmerize audiences, a powerful evocation of the struggle of the individual against the masses.

Today the festival is managed by Aldeburgh Music, which purchased Snape Maltings in 2006, ushering in what promises to be a new golden era, a "creative campus" for the world's most talented musicians. Yet, though he died in 1976, the festival is unlikely to shake the ghost of Britten anytime soon – his inspiration is everywhere. Just wander outside the hall on long summer evenings, along the wind-blown reeds of the River Alde, or stroll along the harsh, shingle shore of nearby Aldeburgh, and you'll get a sense of what drove him to write music.

419 Robin Hood Festival: family capers the medieval way

For the first week of August each year, in celebration of Nottinghamshire's legendary outlaw, Sherwood Forest is transported back to the thirteenth century. Although the now peaceful oak and birch woodland has been the backdrop to a thousand years of noble English history, it is for the legendary escapades of one local hero that families pour into the Robin Hood Festival in their thousands every year to experience life as it would have been for the loveable rogue and his band of arrow-wielding merry men.

Over a quarter of a century, the Robin Hood Festival has grown into a pop-up village of sorts, with stalls and attractions spread across about a square half-mile of woodland that can be circumnavigated comfortably in an hour or so. You have the choice of meandering along leafy tracks between spectacles, through the same woodland that Robin Hood himself allegedly roamed, or of following one of several entertaining guided adventures a little deeper into the forest. This might be a walk with a falconer and some of his proud, feathered friends, or a more exciting scrum to get to Robin Hood's secret woodland lair via a series of clues and some very colourful encounters en route. Just strolling, however, is the best way to take in the festivities – with mischievous japesters, dancing musicians, traditional craftsmen and fire-breathing jesters at every turn.

The itinerary changes a little every day but archery lessons are always on offer for a small fee, and most days host high-octane jousting (which frightens as many adults as it does children) and rather vicious skirmishing between Robin Hood and the evil Sheriff's men in the shade of the Major Oak, a gargantuan tree said to be over 800 years old, which attracts many visitors in its own right.

The festival is a paradise for little boys and girls who have always dreamed of being Robin Hood or Maid Marian. Green felt caps, bows and arrows and garlands of flowers are ubiquitous fancy-dress props, and every day there are opportunities for children to join in theatrical re-enactments of the Robin Hood story, to the hilarity of their parents.

Need to know Robin Hood Festival, Sherwood Forest Visitor Centre, Edwinstowe, Nottinghamshire (Ⓦwww.nottinghamshire.gov.uk/robinhoodfestival) takes place over the first week in August. Visitor Centre daily 10am–5pm, festival around 11am–4.30pm. Festival entry is free, small charge for some events and car parking £5. For food, there are a couple of nice pubs in the village of Edwinstone half a mile down the road.

Map 3, D10

420 Pride without prejudice in Brighton

Let's be clear about one thing, fun-lovers: the summertime Pride in Brighton and Hove festival is not the grandest of affairs. Yes, there's a sequin-sprinkled parade, but don't roll up expecting miles of elaborate floats and glitzy, Rio-style dance troupes. It's all much more down to earth than that – think gangs of friends and colleagues in thrown-together fancy dress, waving in time to cheesy pop or giggling their way through sketchy dance routines. And, yes, there's an all-afternoon dance party in the city's biggest park – but this isn't Ibiza. While there's a bit of strutting and posing, it's more about just hanging out with your mates, lobbing cheerful heckles at the cabaret acts and larking about on the funfair.

The one thing which Pride in Brighton and Hove has in spades is inclusiveness. Unlike Sydney, whose more militant lesbian, gay, bisexual and transgender groups have been known to spit fire at the thought of non-LGBT revellers muscling in on their Mardi Gras, Brighton is happy for anybody and everybody to join the party. Pride is a community event, in the best sense of the word; a whole array of local service providers make the effort to take part, from firemen to social workers, and alongside the same-sex couples and groups of friends in the cheerful crowds you'll see families, children and straight couples of all ages. Brightonians can't pretend they live in an absolute Utopia of open-mindedness and community spirit, but it's still one of the most easy-going cities in Britain – and that's worth celebrating.

You don't have to dress up, but if you'd like your photo to grace the galleries that pop up all over the web straight after the event, you most definitely should. Every year, the festival has a different theme – Carry On films, fairy tales and soap operas are favourites – but the best costumes are always the ones that go totally off-menu. So if you've ever fancied yourself as a stilt-walking goblin or (an ever-popular choice) as Dorothy, complete with ruby slippers, take the plunge. In 2010, one pair of attendees arrived dressed as a tea party. Both bearded and somewhat heftily built, they twirled around the grounds in crinoline dresses decked out with china plates, cupcakes and cucumber sandwiches. Very tasty.

Need to know The main events of the Pride in Brighton and Hove summer festival (W www.brightonpride.org) are on a Saturday in early July. The parade follows a route through the city centre; entrance to the afternoon festival party at Preston Park is free.
Map 2, E6

421 Vamping it up in Whitby

Irish writer Bram Stoker's seaside sojourns in atmospheric Whitby fired his imagination and, in his 1897 vampire novel *Dracula*, he found a character that would thereafter be associated with the town's stepped streets, brooding abbey ruins and clifftop graveyard. Surprisingly, perhaps, the town itself – a small fishing port with up-and-coming resort pretensions – wears the connection lightly. Apart from the harbourside "Dracula Experience" ("...as you enter a dreadful fear will come upon you") and a plaque on the house in which Stoker used to stay, there's little to suggest that Whitby is the centre of insatiable horrors from the grave. Little, that is, until you start to notice the number of shops flogging gothic clothes and jewellery and the preponderance of pasty-faced characters about town in Regency dress, flowing gowns and chains, and top hats and capes.

Matters come to a head twice a year (April and October) at the Whitby Gothic Weekend (or just "Whitby" to any self-respecting goth you might know), which has mushroomed from a meeting of friends to one of the most popular gothic gatherings on the world circuit. During the day in the Spa Pavilion – normally the preserve of tea dances and end-of-pier hypnotists – the Bizarre Bazaar flogs anything a goth might fancy, before the stalls are packed away in time for the nightly roster of bands.

Over four days and nights there are the club sessions, cabarets and gigs you might expect, but also plenty of events that defy the stereotype and make Whitby a hoot – from goth bingo to the annual grudge footy match between the local paper, the *Whitby Gazette*, and Real Gothic FC ("the world's premier all-goth football team").

During festival time, unofficial headquarters is the otherwise very traditional *Elsinore* pub on Flowergate, host of the very first gothic weekend in 1994. There's a decent pint of Tetley's here, and a welcome for voluptuous vamps and curious characters of all kinds – indeed, if you've not gone goth for the duration you'll very definitely be the odd one out as you sink a drink amongst the un-dead.

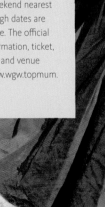

Need to know Whitby Gothic Weekends are usually held over the last weekend in April and the weekend nearest Halloween, though dates are subject to change. The official website, for information, ticket, accommodation and venue details, is Ⓦ www.wgw.topmum. co.uk.
Map 4, F16

422 Brass bands, pasties and the Red Arrows: Fowey and Polruan regattas

When you hear the word "regatta", it's easy to imagine fleets of salty Olympic hopefuls wearing too much Gore Tex, or floating gin palaces captained by florid men in blazers. On Cornwall's south coast, Fowey's homely regatta is like neither cliché. With its crab-catching and stranger-spotting competitions, its giant pasty ceremony and raucous carnival, it is heartfelt and refreshingly un-yachty.

The week-long calendar kicks off with a carnival that sets the tone for good-humoured silliness. Enthusiastic pub crews, families in themed costumes and semi-professional brass bands all parade noisily down the packed, narrow high street. A local girl, decked in the hydrangeas that flourish in Cornwall in August, is crowned Queen of the Carnival, and the day culminates in partying on the quays and a firework display that fills the estuary with light, noise and smoke.

It's this estuary, above all, that makes Fowey magic. The little town is scraped along the side of a miniature fjord that's a fantastic amphitheatre. When bands play or guns go off to announce races, the noises swirl and bounce around. When the big yachts sail in from Falmouth, or the gig boats race, oars swinging madly, or the torchlight boat procession passes on the last night, the boats all parade in full view along the waterfront. The small, local Troys and Fowey river boats even race in the harbour, dodging in and around the moored yachts.

Best of all, when the Red Arrows arrive on the Thursday evening (weather permitting), they use the estuary as their stage, appearing heart-stoppingly over the skyline before jetting up and down the harbour and disappearing with stunning speed, leaving trails of coloured smoke, cheers, applause and the noise of echoing boat horns.

If wholesome homeliness is the draw, consider also visiting the little-known regatta at Polruan, Fowey's villagey neighbour, which lies a two-minute ferry ride across the water. There's hymn- and shanty-singing, a sand-castle competition, a tombola in aid of the lifeboat, and a race of bouncing balls along the tiny street that cascades down the hill towards the harbour. It's like Britain in the 1950s – and none the worse for it.

Need to know Fowey Regatta (Ⓦ www.foweyroyalregatta.co.uk) is usually held on the third full week of August, culminating on the Saturday night. Polruan Regatta is held either the following week, or the one after that. Entertainments are mostly free, though charitable donations are de rigeur, and you'll pay to enter competitions. Map 2, B7

423 Horsing about at the Common Ridings

The Common Ridings of the Scottish Border towns of Hawick, Selkirk, Jedburgh and Lauder are one of Britain's best-kept secrets – an equestrian extravaganza that combines the danger of Pamplona's Fiesta de San Fermín and the drinking of Munich's Oktoberfest. Commemorating the days when the Scots needed early warnings of attacks from their expansionist neighbours, the focus of each event is a dawn horseback patrol of the commons and fields that mark each town's boundaries. Selkirk may boast the largest number of riders, and Lauder might be the oldest event, but Hawick is always the first – and the best attended – of them all.

At dawn on each day of the ridings, a colourful and incredibly noisy drum and fife band marches around the streets to shake people from their sleep and, more importantly, to allow plenty of time for the riders, and virtually the entire town population, to get down to the pub – they open at 6am – and stock up on the traditional breakfast of "Curds and Cream" (rum and milk). Suitably fortified, over two hundred riders – all exquisitely attired in cream jodhpurs, black riding boots, tweed jackets and white silk neckerchiefs – mount their horses and gallop at breakneck speed around the ancient lanes and narrow streets of town, before heading out into the fields to continue the racing in a slightly more organized manner.

By early evening, and with the racing done for the day, the spectators and riders stagger back into Hawick to reacquaint themselves with the town's pubs, an activity that most people approach with gusto. Stumbling out onto the street at well past midnight, you should have just enough time for an hour or two of shut-eye before the fife band strikes up once more and it's time to do it all over again.

Need to know The Common Ridings take place in the Scottish Borders and are usually held over a few days to a week in June. For more details, see Ⓦ www. hawickcommonriding.com or Ⓦ www.visitscottishborders.com. Map 4, D15

424 Fringe benefits

Need to know The
Edinburgh festivals are in late
summer every year, running
for most of August. Check
Ⓦ www.edfringe.com, Ⓦ www.
edinburghartfestival.com,
Ⓦ www.eif.co.uk and Ⓦ www.
edbookfest.co.uk. Book
accommodation as early as
possible.
Map 4, D14

Every year, the billboards go up, covering walls, fences and lampposts with the gurning mugs of quiz-show veterans and talking heads. Every year, flyers plastered with naked flesh and questionable quotes spew out of hands and into pockets and dustbins. Every year is bigger, brighter, bolder, with new taboos to break and more weird shows set everywhere from cabs and phone boxes to vast conference centres. Every year, punters stung by high prices and performers stung by bitter competition and bitterer reviews swear this year will be their last. Every year has an Edinburgh Festival, and you should go to at least one of them.

The Edinburgh Festival is, strictly speaking, about five festivals. There's the Book Festival, home to top authors and commentators and set in leafy Charlotte Square; the International Festival, which hosts lush, clever productions of the high arts; the Art Festival, which gathers together special exhibitions and regular galleries; and the Fringe, which is what most people mean when they talk airily of the Festival, bulging with all manner of comedy, theatre and music from pros and amateurs. The glory and terror of the Fringe – which, inevitably, has an unofficial fringe of its own – is that no one decides who becomes a part of it, performers just pay to be included in the programme. You can see students tackle *Hamlet* or *Bouncers* for a few quid, watch brilliantly clever or enormously stupid stand-up, check out splendid new work from daring playwrights or stand in a big top and watch a circus reinvent itself. The big venues – the Pleasance, the Assembly Rooms, C, the Underbelly and the Traverse – dominate, but performers sweep like spores through Edinburgh in August, colonizing the churches, broom cupboards and open spaces of this grand, gothic capital, sometimes earning their big break, sometimes performing, literally, to an empty house.

It's possible to have a fabulous time and see no shows at all, heading instead from temporary bar to venerable pub, nattering with the performers, punters and hangers-on that come here like moths to a month-long flame. But better to feel the heat of the action, wading through the drunks and the dross in the hope of spotting that rare and wonderful beast: genius making a name for itself.

425 Jig by the sea on the merry morning of May

Need to know Obby
Oss, Padstow, Cornwall. May 1
(unless this falls on a Sunday,
in which case the festival takes
place on Monday May 2). For
general information see Ⓦ www.
padstow.com. Padstow Museum
(Ⓣ 01841/532752, Ⓦ www.
padstowmuseum.co.uk).
Map 2, A7

Long before Rick Stein spurred Padstow into the gastronomic limelight, this Cornish seaside village had made its name for Obby Oss. One of the most distinctive May Day festivals in the country, Obby Oss (dialect for hobby horse) is a traditional community celebration that's been on Padstow's calendar for centuries.

In a unique ritual generally believed to be some sort of ancient Celtic fertility rite – May Day itself has its origins in the Celtic festival of Beltane – two Osses, monstrous, masked effigies with huge, hooped skirts, are paraded through the streets to the accompaniment of song, accordions and drums. It's best not to get too hung up on the meaning behind it all, and instead grab a pint and a pasty and get swept away in the festive ambience. Indeed it's impossible not to get swept away in the tangle of bunting-bedecked streets crammed with revellers.

The town barely sleeps from the first song at midnight on the last day in April until festivities peter out late into the following night. However, the real action kicks off when the Blue, or "peace" Oss is led out of its stable at 10am, followed by the Old Oss an hour later from the *Golden Lion Inn*. Teams of white-clothed Padstonians sporting red or blue sashes follow the Osses through town in a procession of rhythm and dance that comes to a climax at the towering, beautifully decorated, flower-covered maypole in the square. Day and night the festival's insistent beat is accompanied by the chant of folk songs as a merry celebration of these ancient rites.

If you visit Padstow on any day other than May Day, catch the spirit of Obby Oss through the archives and images in the Padstow Museum on Market Strand. While you're in the area you can also embrace the scenery that inspired the late poet laureate Sir John Betjeman, to trundle along the famous Camel Trail and dine in the foodie institutions that Rick Stein later made the town famous for.

426 Enter the dragon: Liverpool's Chinese New Year

With the oldest Chinese community in Europe, dating back to the mid-nineteenth century, and one of the largest in number as well, Liverpool makes an obvious destination to celebrate Chinese New Year without hopping on a plane to Shanghai, the city Liverpool has been twinned with for a decade.

The focal point for the celebrations is the city's magnificent Chinese arch on Nelson Street. Fifty feet tall, it was shipped piece by piece from Shanghai in 2000. With beautifully intricate decorations, including two hundred dragons, it has been positioned in accordance with feng shui principles to bring good luck to the community. During the new year festivities, the surrounding Nelson, Berry and Duke streets shake off their slightly rundown Georgian and Victorian primness to take on a distinctly oriental look, with lanterns festooned from the streetlights and flags from the People's Republic hung everywhere. The party starts early in the morning of the first day of the New Year, the date of which changes each year, with stunning lion, unicorn and dragon dances, fireworks galore in a daytime display on St George's Square, t'ai chi demonstrations and at least 18,000 carnival-goers who bring the centre of Liverpool to a standstill. The lion in particular is not to be missed – its red colouring is believed to bring good luck, hence the prevalence of red in all the decorations.

This is a great opportunity to get acquainted with some of the spectacular Chinese street food which is made to commemorate the beginning of a new year. Don't miss trying the chilli crab with egg noodles, the steamed mussels or a plate of crispy duck with apricot and plum sauce if you want your taste buds to tingle with the flavours of an authentic New Year feast Chinese-style.

Need to know Chinese New Year, Liverpool. The date changes every year. For information on the events organized see Ⓦ www. visitliverpool.com.
Map 3, B10

BRITAIN'S MUSIC FESTIVALS

From Marc Bolan and free milk to stadium rave and boutique festivals, this damp isle has long been a fine place for a party. It may have nothing quite as hot as Valencia's Benicàssim or as far-out as Nevada's Burning Man, but this wild bunch – from Butlins-brewed indie to Wiltshire-based world music, with stopoffs for classic metal and avante-garde electronica on the way – should satisfy anyone's hunger for music and thrills.

427 All Tomorrow's Parties

Over a decade after it began, ATP is full of contradictions. It brings drugs and rock'n'roll to the faux-suburbia of a Butlins holiday camp. It marries experimental music (ferocious hardcore, wonky electronica, sublime and silly prog-rock) with a hearty sense of nostalgia (indie-group reunions are a speciality). And it works: performers and audience alike are buffeted by waves of noise, offered horrific frankfurters and grim artificial cheese and wander from chalet to rock-out to beat-fest, safe in the knowledge a hot shower is a mere shout away.

Ⓦ www.atpfestival.com. Various dates, typically May & Dec. Map 2, B6

428 Bestival

Like many of the smaller festivals done good, this Isle of Wight wig-out's increased capacity has taken a little of its intimacy. But Bestival isn't taking itself too seriously yet. The line-up mixes indie, dance and hip-hop with classic pop in groovy mix-tape style, big-selling headliners and late-night DJs keeping things busy till long after nightfall. The joyous Saturday fancy-dress parade, meanwhile, sees Stormtroopers, strange animals, space hoppers and mashed up beat-seekers join forces in the festival's pleasantly wooded valley setting, offering one of the festival's season's definitive highlights.

Ⓦ www.bestival.net. Early Aug. Map 2, D6

429 Bloc

It may lack the field-filling, mega-selling likes of David Guetta and Tiësto (Creamfields handles that), but this 5000-strong, holiday-camp based rave-up's small size means it can push an entertaining bunch of old stars, erstwhile pioneers, noisy envelope-pushers and eclectic live acts – where else would you find crunching dubstep, old school techno, Salt 'N' Pepa and ten-pin bowling on the same bill?

Ⓦ www.blocweekend.com. March. Map 2, B6

430 Cambridge Folk Festival

Folk is enjoying a moment in fashion's spotlight thanks to the vigour and marketability of acts like Mumford & Sons, but it'll take more than that to change the Cambridge Folk Festival's mellow spots. With stripped-down narratives, foot-stamping, rootsy sing-alongs, more guest appearances than a chat show and the odd bit of blues, indie or reggae, this endearing, unpretentious festival looks as strong as ever, almost five decades after it began.

Ⓦ www.cambridgefolkfestival.co.uk. Late July/early Aug. Map 3, E12

431 Download

Donington Park, which has had had a metal connection since 1980's inaugural Monsters of Rock festival, has moved with the times and the current Download festival mixes ancient behemoths like Iron Maiden and AC/DC with newer acts and the odd indie or emo band, who usually risk having a plastic bottle or hundred flung their way.

Ⓦ www.downloadfestival.co.uk. June. Map 3, D11

434 Secret Garden Party

Though hotly tipped indie and dance bods are on stage throughout the weekend, you don't get many big-name acts here, but that's just fine: Secret Garden really is about more than just the music, man. A gorgeous lake, wacky art installations and all manner of half-organized weirdness distinguish this genial Cambridgeshire fancy-dress fandango.

Ⓦ uk.secretgardenparty.com. Mid-July. Map 3, E12

435 T in the Park

Heavily branded, sat near a stinking chicken farm and packed with drunk wee nippers, T in the Park may not be for everyone. But if you want up-for-it crowds, headline acts that often trump Glastonbury in their prestige and some often-glorious sunsets, breaking over the hills that fringe the main stage, you'll have a whale of a time in Perthshire.

Ⓦ www.tinthepark.com. Early July. Map 4, D14

436 WOMAD

Its current base may be a Cotswolds market town, but with spin-offs in Spain, New Zealand and Abu Dhabi and performers from every continent, WOMAD has never lacked ambition. Its thrillingly broad palette – you might hear Peruvian dance music, Chinese pop, urban African funk and English folk – is set alongside stalls, workshops and arts performances and lapped up by a mellow crowd.

Ⓦ www.womad.org. Late July. Map 2, D5

432 Glastonbury

"It's too big", moan the festival veterans. "It's too mainstream", grumble the music lovers. "It's too dodgy", weep the parents. Glastonbury may be all these things – and, with its big fence, chic VIP areas and visits from royals, it sometimes feels as countercultural as a cabinet minister – but it can still be a magical place. There are countless corners to explore: dance tents, pagan villages, kids' entertainers and, inevitably, some of the biggest bands the world has seen. You might even see some sunshine...

Ⓦ www.glastonburyfestivals.co.uk. Late June. Map 2, C6

433 Green Man

With a vibe somewhere between a farmers' market and a psychedelic freak-out, Green Man manages the neat trick of appealing to families and hedonists, its low-key vibe bolstered by a lovely setting on the edge of the Brecon Beacons. And the acts – hoary folk veterans, scuzzy rockers and mildly eccentric popsters – seem to enjoy it as much as the crowd.

Ⓦ www.greenman.net. Mid-Aug. Map 2, C5

GRAND DESIGNS

art and architecture

Britain – historic theme park or vibrant contemporary centre of art and architecture? In many ways it's the wrong question, since talent, skill, invention, ingenuity, call it what you will, is clearly evident in both medieval cathedral and modern art gallery – one might be more or less to your taste, but it's hard to deny the long unbroken line of genius that runs through British building, art and design. Much of it has been around so long that it forms part of the national fabric, and imagining York without its masterpiece Minster or London minus Wren's churches is to imagine two different cities entirely. Meanwhile, world-class museums in England, Scotland and Wales display unrivalled historic collections of art, applied art and sculpture, where you can see snapshots of the world's cultures and Britain's relationship with them. But there's also an embrace of the new that's at odds with the supposedly conservative, backward-looking British. Look how quickly *The Angel of the North* – the towering road-side Antony Gormley sculpture – went from eyesore to icon, and consider the transformative effect of striking new cultural buildings in towns and cities from Cardiff to Middlesbrough, Norwich to Nottingham. The big national and provincial attractions have never wanted for visitors, but when previously unsung places like Gateshead, Walsall and Folkestone start pulling in art-tourists and culture-seekers you know there's a booming cross-country interest in great art and grand designs. In fact, there's long been a very local engagement with many of Britain's best-known artists and sculptors – witness the enduring popularity of Salford's L.S. Lowry, Bradford's David Hockney or Castleford's Henry Moore, each of whom have a firm place in British hearts, museums, galleries and sculpture parks. Public art in all its guises could almost be said to be a British fascination – and one that shows no sign of abating, if the fuss about what goes on Trafalgar Square's Fourth Plinth, the phenomenal popularity of Tate Modern and Newcastle's Baltic or the search for the elusive Bristol street artist Banksy, is anything to go by.

437 Art on the Tyne: inspiration at Baltic

It's common enough, these days, for a company to adopt the name of its website. Punctuation fanatics may seethe, but brand-identity experts are all for it. If it's good for a company, why not for a city? Ever a fearless lot, the Geordies have taken the plunge. Welcome to NewcastleGateshead, an urban regeneration success story.

Not content with anything as modest as a minor face-lift, the twin cities of Newcastle upon Tyne and Gateshead have opted for total reinvention in some areas. This process accelerated in the 1990s and 2000s; shiny new waterfront flats, boutique hotels and buzzing, where-to-be-seen bars now line Newcastle's quayside, while across the River Tyne, confident cultural landmarks dominate the once-bleak Gateshead Quays. It's a powerful transformation: even the *Tuxedo Princess* – the downmarket cruiseship-nightclub that lurked on this stretch of the river for years – has been towed away.

Towering over the scene like a fortress is Baltic, Gateshead's striking contemporary art centre. Still emblazoned with the words Baltic Flour Mills, this uncompromisingly modernist building has just as much presence as London's Tate Modern – and even more volume – it claims to be the biggest gallery of its kind in the world. Best suited to large-scale installations, its four galleries host an exciting and ever-changing programme of shows including headline-grabbers such as works by Yoko Ono, "musical paintings" by Malcolm McLaren and a fresh dose of Damien Hirst's 1990s classic, *Pharmacy*.

Whatever the current crop of exhibitions, it's worth visiting for the views. Look down from the glass-fronted lifts, the viewing terraces or the rooftop restaurant and you can admire the elegant geometry of the Tyne Bridge. Modelled on the design for the Sydney Harbour Bridge in the 1920s, it's still a potent symbol of the city. Like its Australian counterpart, it now has a slinky performing arts centre for a neighbour: the miracle of computer-assisted architecture that is The Sage, nestling like a glossy-skinned pupa on the riverbank. Spanning the river in a graceful curve is the Gateshead Millennium Bridge, better known as the Blinking Eye – surely the wittiest modern bridge in Britain. The whole scene is so inspiring that avant-garde photographer Spencer Tunick has used it as a location; the resulting series of studies, created with the help of 1700 naked volunteers, is one of his best to date.

Need to know Baltic Centre for Contemporary Art, Gateshead Quays, South Shore Rd, Gateshead, is a 15min walk from Newcastle city centre (☎ 0191/478 1810, Ⓦ www.balticmill.com). Daily 10am–6pm, Tues opens 10.30am. Free. For local visitor information, see Ⓦ www.newcastlegateshead.com.
Map 4, E15

438 Essential art at the Sainsbury Centre

You approach the pared-down hangar-like Sainsbury Centre on the UEA campus across a lush lawn, and step into a modernist temple of art. The building, an early work by Norman Foster, has simplicity and functionality at its core; it was designed to showcase the superb collection of Robert and Lisa Sainsbury. High glass walls give space and light to the works, which are displayed not with an attempt to categorize or contextualize but to showcase each piece in its own right. This aesthetic approach sees an elongated Modigliani juxtaposed with an ancient marble figure from Cycladic Crete, with its long nose and neatly folded arms. There are moments of connection, and also of dislocation: your path through the gallery might take you from a silver Inca effigy of a llama to a carved wooden Polynesian icon or a masterful Roman portrait head. The eclectic layout is also particularly effective at highlighting the well-documented influence of ethnographic art on modern masters such as Henry Moore, represented by a rounded non-realist *Mother & Child*, and Picasso, whose early gouache nude shows a mask-like female figure.

One unexpected treasure of the collection is Degas' *Little Dancer*, a bronze of a pinched but touching ballerina, complete with fabric tutu. Another iconic bronze is one from Benin dating from the early 1500s, with its striking, exaggerated features and geometric headdress. On a smaller scale is a little green ceramic hippo from ancient Egypt, whose comically short legs and chubby body belie the fact that hippos were regarded as fearless beasts: the sculpture was placed in a grave to protect the deceased.

Elsewhere, temporary exhibitions explore contemporary photography, painting and ceramics, and there's usually space given to two other outstanding collections held by UEA. One is comprised of Constructivist painting, sculpture, graphics and furniture, including a Le Corbusier chair and Joseph Albers' *Homage to the Square*. And the Anderson Collection consists of rich Art Nouveau treasures, including a Tiffany vase and a shimmering Lalique buckle with butterflies flanking an opal beetle.

To round things off there's the excellent light-filled *Gallery Café* and a gallery shop selling genuinely covetable crafts and gifts.

Need to know The Sainsbury Centre is on the campus of the University of East Anglia, Norwich Ⓦ www.scva.org.uk Tues–Sun 10am–5pm; also "late shift" events when it's open after hours for live art, poetry, dance and film events. Free, but often a charge for special exhibitions.
Map 3, F11

439 Clean lines and crashing waves: the De la Warr Pavilion

Built in 1935 as a cultural house for the people – the vision of the ninth Earl De la Warr, the aristocratic, socialist Mayor of Bexhill – the De la Warr Pavilion is an architectural masterpiece by Erich Mendelsohn and Serge Chermayeff, and one of the first Modernist buildings in Britain. Curving, majestic but intimate and informal, it's worth the trip to the coast for the building alone. It stands in a marvellous setting right on Bexhill's beach, with an elegant spiral staircase protruding out towards the sea, huge glass windows, sleek terraces and a quirky, wavy bandstand.

The building's had a rocky history, and only spent a few years functioning as intended before World War II intervened. Wartime damage, unsympathetic alterations to the building and neglect followed. Finally, after being granted listed status in the 1980s, it was restored to close to its original appearance and reopened in 2005 as something akin to its intended purpose, and now thrives as a bustling, local arts centre.

There's nothing retro about this palace to recreation, and it hosts a packed and eclectic programme of events. The light, airy gallery shows contemporary art exhibitions, the auditorium attracts an impressive line-up of international artists and entertainers, and the pavilion offers courses and talks, summer Sunday gigs on the bandstand, and a host of imaginative events – what better use is there for a flat white Modernist exterior wall than to project films onto it on summer evenings (just bring a blanket)?

Seventy-five years after its inception, the pavilion is finally fulfilling the earl's ambition to create a home for a new industry: "the industry of giving that relaxation, that pleasure, that culture which hitherto the gloom and dreariness of British resorts have driven our fellow countrymen to seek in foreign lands." And on a sunny day, looking over Bexhill's broad beach from the crisp, stylish balconies of this Modernist masterpiece, it is hard to imagine why you'd ever wish to cross the sea for pleasure.

Need to know De la Warr Pavilion, on the seafront, Bexhill, East Sussex ☎ 01424/229111, Ⓦ www.dlwp.com. Daily 10am–6pm. Free.
Map 2, F6

440 Take a trip with Mackintosh to Glasgow School of Art

There aren't many opportunities to take a tour of a master building with the architect, especially when the architect in question has been dead for more than eighty years. But visiting the Glasgow School of Art, you have the uncanny feeling that its creator, Charles Rennie Mackintosh, is leading you around.

A pool of light illuminates the central staircase, pulling you into the building; the stained glass of the doors to either side depicts watchful eyes. And as you go up the staircase, you'll notice that the banister is unusually high, but by the top has become rather low, emphasizing the sensation that you are rising through space. An enclosed, glass corridor that runs along the back of the building has only one small square aperture to the outside – it's placed so that when you open it your eyes fall on an elegant, metal sculpture on the rooftop, depicting a tree, one of the symbols of Glasgow.

If you feel manipulated by these touches, it is manipulation of the most playful and romantic kind. And it is combined with an altogether more robust sensibility: this remains a working building, as the scuffed wooden floors, crowded corridors and bustle of student activity testify. An artist to his fingertips, Mackintosh was acutely aware of the needs of art students; this concern is perhaps most evident in the north light that floods the painting studios, where generations of students have worked.

And other elements are still very much used for the purposes they were designed for: the janitor's room which sits like a Japanese lantern in the stairwell; the director's office, in a suitably supervisory position over the front door; and the wooden desks dotted around at strategic points for students to sit at and sketch the city skyline.

The masterpiece of the building, though, is the library. Its tall, dark, wooden columns evoke the stillness and contemplative feel of a forest clearing, with irregularly hung lanterns illuminating the room like a sunburst. As the students who lead visitor tours will testify, the building, and the man, remain a vivid, living inspiration.

Need to know Glasgow School of Art, 167 Renfrew St, Glasgow ☎ 0141/353 4530, Ⓦ www. gsa.ac.uk. Student-led guided tours: April–Sept daily on the hour 10am–4pm; Oct–March Mon–Sat 11am, 2pm & 3pm, booking advised. £8.75.
Map 4, C14

441 Tate Modern: the largest art circus in town

From oversized upstart to national treasure in just ten years, Tate Modern has been adopted by the British public in a way that no one imagined possible for a gallery of modern art. Though its collection is an impressive survey of the big names of twentieth-century international art – including Monet, Matisse and Rothko – the real stars are the building itself, huge, grand and proudly displaying its industrial past as a power station, and Tate's ambitious and playful curating.

At the outset Tate Modern did away with stuffy, chronological displays, instead hanging its collection thematically in a thought-provoking and irreverent approach. Architecture and art as adventure come together most strikingly in the Turbine Hall, and its headline-grabbing commissions of the Unilever series. One vast installation after another has explored scale and size, transforming the space into a fairground for art, inviting thousands of visitors to hurtle down twisting slides (Carsten Höller's *Test Site*, 2006), explore vast gaping dark holes (Miroslaw Balka's *How It Is*, 2009) or be dwarfed by the otherworldly *Maman*, Louise Bourgeois's spider, which has reappeared in several guises since 2000. At least part of the story is the extraordinary and unexpected response of visitors, most notably in Olafur Eliasson's 2004 *The Weather Project*, the huge, glowing half-disc of light, with mirrors on the Turbine Hall's ceiling both creating a full "Sun" and reflecting back images of people far below – as they sat, picnicked, created designs and words with their laid-out bodies, and transformed the hazy, half-light hall into a mini festival site.

And Tate Modern continues to grow – literally. Three vast oil drums behind the main building are currently being excavated and will be turned into performance spaces and more galleries, while a Herzog & de Meuron-designed extension is planned above them. Such constant innovation, with regular re-hanging of the main displays, several blockbuster exhibitions a year and a plethora of events, not to mention the magnificent views across the river to St Paul's from several floors, ensures that, despite the crowds, Tate Modern always offers something worth returning for.

Need to know Tate Modern, London SE1 ℡ 020/7887 8888, Ⓦ www.tate.org.uk. Sun–Thurs 10am–6pm, Fri & Sat 10am–10pm. Main galleries free, special exhibitions around £10.
Map 1, E3

442 A village worth its salt

The belching mills and factories that fired the Industrial Revolution fouled Britain's expanding towns and cities, and forced workers into grim lodgings in fetid alleys under polluted skies. William Blake's "dark Satanic Mills" and the writings of Marx and Engels highlighted the social iniquities, but it took a rare breed of Victorian industrialist to address the degradation that made them rich.

Titus Salt (later Sir Titus) was one – an enterprising wool-mill owner in the filthy boomtown of Bradford. He shifted production to a huge new purpose-built mill out in the country by the River Aire, set among heather-clad moors. Here, his workers spent their days at his looms in a dramatic, light-filled Italianate building of golden sandstone (larger than St Paul's Cathedral in London), before going home to the spick-and-span model village that Salt built for them next door, complete with imposing church, school, hospital, public baths and parks. There was no pub though – Salt was a religious man and Victorian philanthropy had its limits. Salts Mill and Saltaire village still stand, four miles outside Bradford, and the sheer size of the enterprise never fails to impress. Admittedly, the mill-hands' houses are now desirable bijou residences, and the vast mill itself is stripped of machinery, but in the trim streets named after his eleven children, and in the mill's stone-flagged floors, vaulted ceilings and iron columns you get a real sense of Salt's ambition, paternalism and pride.

The echoing floors of Salts Mill itself are given over to arty retail outlets – contemporary jewellery to writing materials, books to antiques – though its most extraordinary attraction is one that would have surely roused a protest from Sir Titus. You can almost hear the Victorian gent harrumph – a picture gallery, in my mill? In fact, it's a perfect fit, with the light from the open moors illuminating the world's largest collection of works by local boy David Hockney. There, on the mill walls, you can trace Hockney's passions, from the Bradford streets of his youth to the California sunshine, with Salts Mill itself rendered in oil as a celebratory, sun-bathed vision.

Need to know Saltaire and Salts Mill, Shipley, are four miles north of Bradford, West Yorkshire; follow the signs from the motorway or city centre, or take the train from Bradford or Leeds to Saltaire station. Salts Mill ℡ 01274/531163, Ⓦ www.saltsmill. org.uk. Mon–Fri 10am–5.30pm, Sat & Sun 10am–6pm. Free.
Map 3, C9

TOP 5 >>

CONTEMPORARY PUBLIC ART

From the vast men and horses carved into chalk hills, through classic bronzes of heroes of war and large abstracted figures by Henry Moore to the latest contemporary sculptures, installed in the hope of regenerating an area in one quick go, Britain has a very long history of eye-catching public art. It has flourished (with varying levels of success) in the past decade; these five have caught the imagination, caused debate and are worth seeking out in their public homes.

443 The Angel of the North, Gateshead

Quite simply the most famous, iconic and loved of recent public artworks, Antony Gormley's *The Angel of the North* (1998) has done more than any other to spark an interest in public art, and to change the perception of an area. From a small figure in the distance, it looms up as you drive closer, its sheer size – 70ft high, with a 90ft span – is still surprising, however many pictures you've seen. *Map 4, E16*

444 Folkestone

Yes, Folkestone. This seaside town is now home to dozens of imaginative artworks thanks to the inaugural Folkestone Triennial which took place in summer 2008. After the festival ended, several works remained scattered around town in often unexpected places. These include Nathan Coley's *Heaven Is A Place Where Nothing Ever Happens*, a light-up sign of the Talking Heads' lyric, and a tongue-in-cheek comment on sleepy seaside towns; Mark Wallinger's sombre *Folk Stones*, 19,240 numbered pebbles set in the ground near the seafront, commemorating the men who died on the first day of the Battle of the Somme in July 1916 (many would have departed from Folkestone); and Tracy Emin's *Baby Things*, tiny bronzes of abandoned baby clothes dotted around the city (the first is under a bench in the train station) – it would be easy to miss them.

Ⓦ *folkestonetriennial.org.uk. Map 2, F6*

445 Scallop – a celebration of Benjamin Britten, Aldeburgh

An elegant coming together of artwork, location and memorial, Suffolk-born Maggi Hambling's tactile, steel *Scallop* (2003), in a dramatic setting on the beach, is her tribute to the composer Benjamin Britten, who lived in Aldeburgh. "I hear those voices that will not be drowned", a line from his opera *Peter Grimes*, is pierced through the steel, so the sky can be seen beyond. *Map 3, F12*

446 The Fourth Plinth, Trafalgar Square

The most famous public art space in London is more a result of accident than design – an empty plinth in the northwest corner of Trafalgar Square, constructed in 1841 for an equestrian statue that was never built. In 1998 the Royal Society of Arts commissioned the first pieces of temporary art to feature on it, starting with Mark Wallinger's *Ecce Homo: Behold the Man*. Since then there have been seven similar commissions – most famously Antony Gormley's *One and Other*, when he gave the space over to thousands of members of the public for an hour each. More recently Yinka Shonibare's *Nelson's Ship in a Bottle* (2010) reflected playfully on the history of the square. Always controversial, rarely dull, long may they refrain from finding a permanent occupant for the plinth.

Ⓦ *www.london.gov.uk/fourthplinth. Map 1, D3*

447 The Singing, Ringing Tree, Crown Point, near Burnley

One of four artworks commissioned in the Pennines in Lancashire, and collectively called the "Panopticons". Each one is situated at a high point, so that they pinpoint views over the Pennine landscape. Tonkin Liu's *The Singing, Ringing Tree* (2006) resembles a windswept tree made of pipes, but sounds like something altogether more unworldly – as the wind blows through the pipes, a haunting, atmospheric sound is produced.

Ⓦ *www.visitlancashire.com/panopticons. Map 3, C10*

448 The art of enjoyment: the National Gallery

Quietly presiding over the lions and pigeons of Trafalgar Square, the National Gallery is Britain's second most popular visitor attraction, pipped only by the British Museum. This would doubtless please its bewhiskered founders who, back in the 1830s, decided to place a gallery halfway between London's wealthy west and impoverished east, its aim "to give the people an ennobling enjoyment". Today the gallery's power to amaze and educate is undiminished and still, blissfully, free of charge – all the more remarkable when you consider the queues and costs of its continental equivalents.

Perhaps what really sets the National apart, though, is that despite walls heaving with the work of da Vinci, Raphael, Monet and Van Gogh, no single picture dominates in the manner of a *Mona Lisa* with all the iPhone-clicking crush that ensures. Instead, the collection's strength in depth encourages more relaxed contemplation. Yet with over two thousand paintings to choose from, deciding precisely what to contemplate can be a daunting prospect. Wandering aimlessly through the marble corridors can feel like a dutiful school trip and make the in-house café seem more appealing by the minute. The secret is to plan your visit and stick to one era or even one painting at a time.

An excellent place to start is Room 34, perhaps the most "national", or at least the most English part of the gallery, right down to its comfy leather sofas, seemingly lifted straight from a gentleman's club. Here you'll find Turner's mesmerizing seascapes, Stubbs's equine masterpiece *Whistlejacket*, Constable's *Hay Wain* and the rival portraits of Gainsborough and Reynolds, each deserving of a special exhibition in themselves.

If you can attend a free talk given by the gallery's team of experts so much the better. Sprinkled with anecdotes (for example, did you know Gainsborough was often too hungover to paint, leaving his portrait subjects out on the street?), they provide that modern term "infotainment" in spades. As you exit back into the tourist hubbub of the square you'll be left if not ennobled then certainly enlightened.

Need to know National Gallery, Trafalgar Square, London WC2 ☏ 020/7747 2885, Ⓦ www. nationalgallery.org.uk. Daily 10am–6pm, Fri until 9pm. Free except for certain temporary exhibitions. Map 1, D3

449 Strange stones: Rosslyn Chapel

Even if you don't believe the fanciful stories that Rosslyn Chapel conceals Masonic or Templar secrets in its sculpture, or perches on top of secret underground vaults, or is a resting place for the Holy Grail, it's still a very odd place indeed. This weirdness has something to do with the chapel's incongruous location, almost within touching distance of Edinburgh's suburbs. It has something to do with the chapel's bizarre appearance – it looks as if someone began building a miniature cathedral and downed tools halfway (and indeed this is probably precisely what happened: construction work seems to have halted when the chapel's donor, Sir William Sinclair, died in 1484).

The chapel's strangeness, however, is mostly due to its rare and wonderful profusion of stone sculpture. Across arches and architraves, voussoirs and vaults, hardly a stony surface lacks decoration, and the symbolism of some of it is intriguing. There's a bound, upside-down Lucifer, a bagpipe-playing angel, a Dance of Death scene and over a hundred representations of the fertility figure known as the Green Man, some of them stunningly realized. Behind the altar stand the Prentice Pillar (or apprentice pillar), Master Pillar and Journeyman Pillar, all of which have attached legends. The Prentice Pillar, for instance, is supposed to have been carved by an apprentice who so provoked his jealous master that he was murdered. Another theory holds that it is a representation of the World Tree – hence the dragons crawling around its base and the foliage of its capital.

Since 1997, the chapel has been half-buried under a protective canopy but in 2010 this was finally removed, revealing the chapel's flying buttresses in all their glory. For years to come, master stonemasons will be doing restoration work inside and out, but this is not a reason to stay away – far from it. Watching craftsmen using pre-modern techniques firsthand gives a doubly powerful sense of the skill and beauty behind Rosslyn's extraordinary stonework.

Need to know Rosslyn Chapel, Roslin, Midlothian, is seven miles from Edinburgh (Ⓦ www. rosslynchapel.org.uk). April–Sept Mon–Sat 9.30am–5.30pm, Sun noon–4.15pm; Oct–March Mon–Sat 9.30am–4.30pm, Sun noon–4.15pm; £7.50. There are usually buses from Edinburgh (Ⓦ www. lothianbuses.com), or you can get a taxi for about £15.
Map 4, D14

450 The Pitmen Painters

The austere Victorian buildings of the defunct Ashington Coal Company are a ghostly accompaniment to the Woodhorn Mining Museum's modern, strikingly pronged building, its design inspired by the cutting machines of the original coal mine. The site's stillness belies how recently, like hundreds of collieries across Britain, tens of thousands of workers would have descended deep beneath ground to keep Britain's industries powered, its lights on and its hearths warm with coal. Ashington Colliery closed in 1981, and is now a museum with interactive displays and audio histories that vividly illustrate the toughness of the lives of the men and boys who crowded down choking, dark tunnels to the coalface up to three miles away. The dangers, and the owners' intransigence despite the miners' conditions, is heartbreakingly detailed through Ashington's archive of fatalities, such as the January 1862 disaster over at Hartley, when 204 trapped workers suffocated.

Still, from the black stuff grew communities and unions, bound by banners and brass bands, that would form the backbone of the twentieth-century Labour movement. And in Ashington, a unique creative movement also developed when a miners' art appreciation club, founded in 1934, developed into an accomplished group of amateur artists. The Ashington Group, better known as the Pitmen Painters after Lee Hall's play based on its members, produced its own paintings of life above and below ground. During the week, the men of the Ashington Group toiled down the pits; on their days off, they painted scenes from their lives, from the light and warmth of men racing whippets and playing dominoes while women engaged in "progging the mat", to sombre, ruddy-coloured pit scenes. The quality and vivid range of their works, with inspiration from Ruskin, Cézanne and Blake, is what sets this group apart, and many of the paintings were eventually shown across Europe and China. Woodhorn's permanent collection of 74 pictures from the Pitmen Painters depicts half a century of mining community life, all so lovingly portrayed and poignantly lost.

Need to know Woodhorn Mining Museum, just off the A189 coastal route, Ashington, Northumberland Ⓦ www. experiencewoodhorn.com and Ⓦ www.ashingtongroup.co.uk. Wed–Sun: April–Oct 10am–5pm; Nov–March 10am–4pm. Free, parking £2.50.
Map 4, E15

451 The Ship of the Fens: Ely Cathedral

Need to know Ely
Cathedral, Ely, Cambridgeshire
☎ 01353/667735 , Ⓦ www.
elycathedral.org. Summer daily
7am–7pm; winter Mon–Sat
7.30am–6pm, Sun 7.30am–5pm.
£6 including guided tour,
£10 including walking up the
Octagon or West towers as well.
Map 3, E11

Ely Cathedral was created to invoke a sense of awe. Constructed over two hundred years, it's an architectural tour de force, all the more impressive for standing apparently in the middle of nowhere – Ely isn't exactly a big city. Perched atop the "island" of Ely, the cathedral looms over the dykes, drains and rich, black fields of the Fens. Pancake-flat and desolate in winter, this is perhaps the most melancholic landscape in England. Thanks to the Fens, Ely's enormous West Tower can be seen for miles, a castle guarding the shore of a dried-up sea. God-like indeed to the monks that came across the watery marshes to serve here in the Middle Ages – for the folk that lived in wattle-and-daub huts, it must have seemed miraculous.

Not that it seems any less so today. The West Tower rises 215ft, most of it (incredibly) constructed in the twelfth century. Under the tower the great west door is the main entrance to the cathedral, a fine early English Gothic porch built of Barnock stone and Purbeck marble. Aficionados of English architecture are in for a real treat inside, beginning with the nave, surely one of the most inspiring interiors in England. It's the fourth longest of the English cathedrals, but its Norman architecture, with distinctive round arches, is exceptional. Its crowning glory is the Octagon Lantern tower in the centre, which replaced the original tower that collapsed in 1322. Take your time studying this masterpiece of medieval engineering – critics often describe it as one of the most spectacular spaces ever built in an English church. At 74ft wide and 170ft high, it was too big to be built of stone and instead was pieced together in wood and covered in lead, the timber-work done by one William Hurley, the royal carpenter. It took eighteen years to build, and today marks the site of the principal altar in the cathedral.

The current cathedral was started in 1083, but Ely has been a place of Christian worship since at least 673, when Etheldreda, daughter of the king of East Anglia, founded a nunnery there. Back then, Ely really was an island, surrounded by water, and today the cathedral still stands like a beacon, a lightship brightening the way through those flat and featureless Fens.

452 Northern Soul: art at the Lowry

Need to know Lowry,
Pier 8, Salford Quays, Greater
Manchester ☎ 08432 086000,
Ⓦ www.thelowry.com. Lowry
exhibition: Sun–Fri 11am–5pm, Sat
10am–5pm. Free.
Map 3, C10

It seems like a simple attempt at painting. Scores of pin-thin men, women and children, flat caps and tightly wrapped coats, making their way home after a hard day on the mill floor. There's little traffic on the street – a horse-drawn cart – and not much colour. A few red coats and hats brighten the greys and blacks, while the terrace is overshadowed by an increasingly hazy landscape of factories and mills, chimneys belching. Yet in *Coming from the Mill* (1930), the then largely unknown L.S. Lowry managed to capture the essence of working life in Salford, a subject rarely tackled by other painters.

In 1978, when one-hit-wonder Brian & Michael eulogized Lowry with their "Matchstalk Men and Matchstalk Cats and Dogs" (he had died two years earlier), not many people had heard of the northern artist. The song was a bit cheesy, and Lowry was still a bit of a joke (down south at least). Only in recent years is the range and sophistication of his work becoming more fully appreciated.

The Lowry in Salford Quays opened in 2000, a strikingly designed arts centre housing theatres and gallery space. It owns 55 paintings and 278 drawings by the artist – the world's largest collection of his work, many featuring those gritty, industrial scenes of Manchester and Salford. Yet as Lowry aged his fascination with people on the streets focused increasingly on the more bizarre characters. Take *The Funeral Party* (1953), a motley line-up of nine odd-looking individuals, most staring disconcertingly at the viewer in what looks like a British version of *The Addams Family*.

Lowry's oil paintings often reflected this interest, through unflattering and brutally stark portraits. His "horrible head" series includes the haunting *Head of a Man* (1938), whose haggard face and bloodshot eyes seem to stare straight through you. When you finally tear yourself away, there's almost a feeling of embarrassment, as if you've turned your back on a starving man.

Indeed, the key to understanding the Lowry collection is his fascination with people, not industrial decay – Lowry was interested in everyday folk, not just outside mills, but at fairgrounds, football grounds and busy markets. As he said, "You don't need brains to be a painter, just feelings."

453 Banksy's Bristol

Robert Banks or Robin Gunningham? Or neither? Social satirist or deviant vandal? Or both? The street artist known as Banksy, shrouded in mystery despite his fame and dividing opinion because of his art, has spray-painted walls in London, Detroit, Melbourne and, perhaps most controversially, the separation wall built by Israel in the West Bank. It was in the graffiti-hotbed of Bristol, though, that he fostered his talent and developed the stencil style that defines his work.

Much of Banksy's early paintings around the city have been lost, but several key murals remain. Perhaps the most iconic is *The Mild Mild West* (1999), a striking image sprayed across a wall on Stokes Croft. Showing a wobbly white teddy bear pitching a Molotov cocktail at advancing riot police, it was seen by many as a reference to the St Paul's riots of 1980 (which were ignited by a raid on a café in nearby Grosvenor Road), though is actually a reaction to the crackdown on the city's "free parties", a late-twentieth-century Bristol phenomenon where scores of people broke into abandoned warehouses. The piece took three days to paint and even went through a couple of drafts – look closely and you can see that the outlines of the policeman have been slightly adjusted.

There's similar affection for Banksy's image of *Death* (2003) on the waterline of *The Thekla*, a nightclub boat moored in Bristol Harbour. His original tag was removed by the city's harbourmaster (the club wanted to keep it, and subsequently sued for criminal damage), prompting Banksy to return and paint a Grim Reaper figure rowing in the same spot. The stencil is based on *The Silent Highwayman*, an illustration depicting the Great Stink, which appeared in *Punch* in July 1858.

The Banksy that most symbolizes his evolution from scourge of the council to Bristol's favourite son, however, lies a short walk northwest from here, off the bottom of Park Street. Secretly created beneath sheet-covered scaffolding, *The Naked Man* (2006), an adulterous lover hanging from a window (it's painted on the side of a sexual-health clinic), was recently saved thanks to a petition from a Liberal Democrat councillor. The deviant vandal, now boosting the city's coffers with his contribution to tourism, is a social satirist after all.

Need to know See Ⓦ www. bristol-street-art.co.uk/category/ banksy-street-art for the exact locations of *The Mild Mild West*, the image of *Death* and *The Naked Man*, plus Banksy's other surviving murals around the city.
Map 2, C5

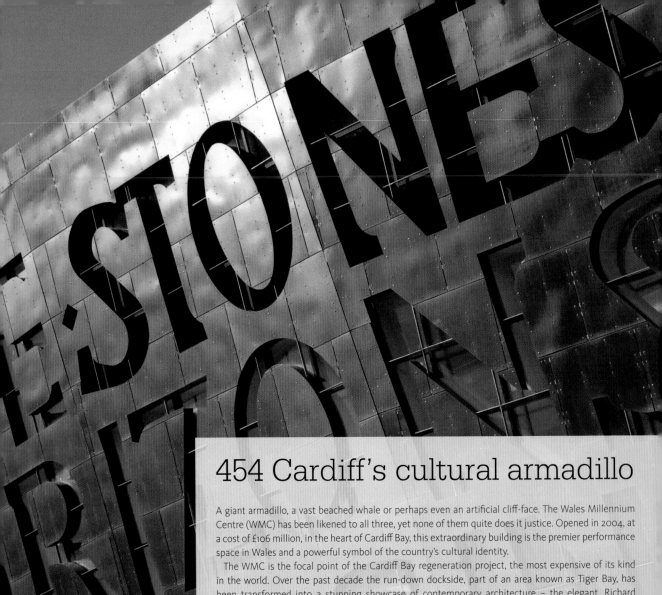

454 Cardiff's cultural armadillo

A giant armadillo, a vast beached whale or perhaps even an artificial cliff-face. The Wales Millennium Centre (WMC) has been likened to all three, yet none of them quite does it justice. Opened in 2004, at a cost of £106 million, in the heart of Cardiff Bay, this extraordinary building is the premier performance space in Wales and a powerful symbol of the country's cultural identity.

The WMC is the focal point of the Cardiff Bay regeneration project, the most expensive of its kind in the world. Over the past decade the run-down dockside, part of an area known as Tiger Bay, has been transformed into a stunning showcase of contemporary architecture – the elegant, Richard Rogers-designed Senedd, home of the National Assembly of Wales, is also here – as well as a lively waterside hub of restaurants, cafés, bars, shops, plazas and pedestrianized areas. To get a scale of the changes, you need only to walk for twenty minutes to the city centre, a journey that takes you through Butetown, one of the most deprived areas in Cardiff.

Home of the Welsh National Opera, dance, drama, music and literary groups, and youth and charitable organizations, the WMC boasts the 1896-seater Donald Gordon Theatre, plus several smaller venues, the excellent *ffresh* restaurant, cafés and bars. Bryn Terfel, the Alvin Ailey American Dance Theater and Jimmy Carr are among the acts to have graced the stages. There are also free daily performances of anything from jazz and hip-hop to poetry and literature.

Architecturally, the centre reflects the country's geographical, cultural and industrial heritage and has been constructed predominantly from Welsh slate, timber, glass and metal, both inside and out. The result is stylish and tactile, creating a warmth and solidity that's a far cry from steel-and-glass minimalism. But its most eye-catching feature is the stainless steel shell, covered in bronze oxide, which has two giant inscribed stanzas, one in Welsh, the other in English, by bilingual poet Gwyneth Lewis: "Creu gwir/ Fel gwydr/O ffwrnais awen" (Creating truth/Like glass/From inspiration's furnace) and "In these stones/Horizons/Sing".

Need to know The Wales Millennium Centre, Bute Place, Cardiff ☎ 029/2063 6464, ⓦ www.wmc.org.uk. Tickets for performances cost £5–42.50; tours of the building cost £5.50.

Map 2, C5

455 Find a hidden piece of India in Neasden

One of London's greatest architectural feats is in a place where you would never expect to find it. Just off the North Circular road, through the unremarkable suburb of Neasden, lies the largest active Hindu temple outside India. Its full name – BAPS Shri Swaminarayan Mandir – will win no awards for catchiness, but its majestic design, both inside and out, is a showstopper. It's almost how Angkor Wat might appear if made of limestone: its seven tiered pinnacles bear similarity with that other great Hindu complex, as do its staircases and elaborate carvings of dancers and deities. Tony Blair, on his first visit, said: "I have never seen such a magnificent work of modern architecture". Richard Branson declared it "one of the wonders of the world".

The miraculous nature of the temple is further enhanced by the manner of its construction. Built in only 27 months (a record for a building of this size), it is made primarily of 2000 tonnes of Indian marble and 3000 tonnes of Bulgarian limestone; uniquely for a modern British building, it contains no iron or steel for support. All that material was shipped to India, where an army of sculptors carved it into 26,300 separate sculpted stones. Those pieces were then transported to Neasden, where the temple was assembled much like an IKEA kit – fittingly, given that there is one of the Swedish megastores only a short walk away.

On the ground floor inside is an assembly hall; a shrine to the eighteenth-century saint Bhagwan Swaminarayan, to whom the temple is dedicated; a small museum that details the origins and principal beliefs of Hinduism; and a shop selling icons, incense, garlands, oil burners and recipe books. But the real reason to come in is to visit the *mandir* upstairs, the central shrine. In this magnificent marble space, filled with intricate carved pillars, are seven *murtis*, or icons of divinities – one underneath each of the seven exterior pinnacles. The air is cool, a near silence prevails, worshippers prostrate themselves. It's here you're reminded that this is a living, breathing temple, and not just a mind-blowing piece of architecture.

Need to know BAPS Shri Swaminarayan Mandir, 105–119 Brentfield Rd, London NW10 ☎020/8965 2651, Ⓦ www. mandir.org. Daily 9am–6.30pm. Free, understanding Hinduism exhibition £2. For directions see the website. The *Shayona* restaurant that adjoins the car park serves Saatvic vegetarian cuisine and is highly recommended. Map 1, E3

456 Reach for the skies at Jupiter Artland

Sitting in a tangle of busy roads in an unattractive semi-rural stretch west of Edinburgh, Jupiter Artland doesn't appear to promise much. But its swirling metal gates are a portal to another world, one of parkland and woodland set around a seventeenth-century mansion, and a series of sight-specific artworks wonderfully woven into the natural environment.

Commissioned by the owners of the house, the works comprise a deeply personal collection, and one that is still evolving. The drive winds past sizeable rocks wedged in the branches of coppiced trees by Andy Goldsworthy, and then opens out to *Life Mounds*, monumental stepped earthworks created by Charles Jencks to evoke and celebrate the cell. There's a brief glimpse of the house before you reach converted stone outbuildings, patrolled by a peacock, where a shiny metal diner car dishes out gourmet sandwiches and coffees – a great refuelling stop before the longish woodland walk ahead.

The walk begins at Shane Waltener's *A World Wide Web*, a scruffy shed in the trees with peepholes of varying heights which reveal a tangle of intricately constructed cobwebs within. Beyond, Anish Kapoor's *Suck* is a disconcerting rusty iron sinkhole in the earth; then a break in the trees reveals Antony Gormley's *Firmament*, a huge crouching figure composed of steel hexagons that frames the view of another iconic metal structure: the rust-red Forth Rail Bridge.

A more intimate work is Laura Ford's *Weeping Girls*, six little downcast bronze figures scattered amongst the trees. Ian Hamilton Finlay's trademark classical Surrealism is evident in the *Xth Muse*, a stately head of Sappho carved from Portland stone, while Andy Goldsworthy gives nature the upper hand in *Stone House*, a seemingly domestic space but with the dark interior dominated by uneven rough-cut stone.

There's a lighter touch to Cornelia Parker's *Landscape with Gun and Tree*, a gigantic shotgun leaning casually against a tree in an echo of Gainsborough's *Mr and Mrs Andrews*. The path circles round to the drive back at *Life Mounds*, which beckon you to climb their terraces to survey the art-filled woodland you have just explored. In a final insouciant touch, Peter Liversidge's fingerpost points skywards, indicating "Jupiter – 893 to 964 million kilometres".

Need to know Jupiter Artland, Wilkieston, West Lothian ☎01506/889900, Ⓦ www. jupiterartland.org. May–Sept daily 10am–4.30pm, though as it's a private house it's wise to check in advance. £8.25. Bus #27 runs to Jupiter Artland from Princes St, and takes around 40min. Map 4, D14

457 Wren's masterpiece: St Paul's Cathedral

In a secular city St Paul's Cathedral continues to reign supreme as the greatest building inherited from a more generous past. Standing high at the top of Ludgate Hill, and with the view of the building from many directions still protected by planning laws, it dominates a large part of the city, and for many Londoners it remains a source of tranquillity and wonder long after the city's other notable sights have become over-familiar.

The new buildings that have sprung up around it can never compete, so great is the esteem in which the cathedral is held. It wasn't always like this. In the eighteenth and nineteenth centuries there were periods when the cathedral's architecture was unfashionable, but its status in the twentieth century was cemented when Churchill gave the order during the Blitz that "the cathedral must be preserved at all costs". The images of the building rising serenely above the smoke and flame of the surrounding destruction stir all the right feelings.

What makes the building so great? There are many answers to this question. One of its triumphs is the marriage of a strong and immediately intelligible form – the dome, the barrel, the great walls turning and folding – with a wealth of beautiful detail. It's also a wonderfully balanced composition: one of Wren's greatest achievements was to give a structure with a dome, rather than a spire or a tower, a truly vertical emphasis. Climb up to the dome's galleries inside and you'll discover its secrets and find out how he managed to raise the dome so high. The dome itself is not a hemisphere: it is taller, egg-shaped – another brilliant touch that adds unmistakeably to the building's impact.

The Millennium Bridge gives a direct approach to the cathedral from across the river. In Tate Modern, on the south bank, it's often the views of St Paul's that really stop people in their tracks as they wander around the gallery. There, beautifully framed in the windows, is a perfect thing that requires no justification or argument.

Need to know St Paul's Cathedral, London EC4. Open for sightseeing Mon–Sat 8.30am–4.30pm, galleries 9.30am–4.15pm; £12.50.

Map 1, E3

458 A walk to the Gallery of Modern Art, Edinburgh

By far the nicest way to reach Edinburgh's Gallery of Modern Art is by walking from the New Town along the Water of Leith, a deep secluded gully lined with mature trees which conceal the tall lines of Georgian terraces. Beyond St Bernard's Well, a folly in the form of a circular temple complete with a stone Classical maiden, you reach Thomas Telford's mighty stone bridge over the river. Then you come to the old mill settlement of Dean village, a cluster of ancient gabled and turreted houses.

Beyond the village and its weir, the water stills and thick foliage edges the path. The imminent presence of the gallery is signalled by a rusting naked male statue by Antony Gormley, standing ankle-deep in the water. Steep steps take you up the riverbank to a hulking green *Reclining Figure* by Henry Moore, and the elegant symmetrical gallery itself, originally built as a school for fatherless children in 1825 and only converted into a gallery in 1984.

The theme of art in the landscape is continued with Charles Jencks's monumental earthwork *Landform* in front of the gallery, comprising spiralling paths and crescent-shaped pools and usually overrun with kids.

Inside, there's a substantial collection by those glamorizers of the Scottish landscape, the Colourists: J.D. Fergusson, Peploe and Cadell, whose Fauvist palette and Post-Impressionist sensibility were a fervent rejection of the Victorian genre painting. Elsewhere, thematic rather than chronological displays juxtapose an early Francis Bacon – an empty coat and hat in a burnt-out landscape – with a late Stanley Spencer nude depicting his second wife. Duane Hanson's life casts of camera-wielding tourists add a light-hearted touch. And the stairwell is inscribed with Douglas Gordon's list of the names of everyone he can remember: both a mind game and a memorial.

Upstairs there are displays on Constructivism, plus a witty Matisse depicting himself painting a young model. And there's a room simply devoted to "White", with Ben Nicholson's card reliefs, a white metal piece by local boy Paolozzi, and Mondrian monochrome squares enlivened by a dash of citrus yellow. Back outside, the sculpture- and flower-filled café garden makes the perfect end to a visit.

Need to know Gallery of Modern Art, Belford Rd, Edinburgh Ⓦ www.nationalgalleries.org. Daily 9am–5pm. Free. The adjacent Dean Gallery (same hours) houses a collection of Surrealist works, temporary exhibitions and the studio of Eduardo Paolozzi.

Map 4, D14

459 Of sheep and sculpture

West Yorkshire might not seem like the most obvious location for a centre of modern art, but step into the glorious grounds of the Yorkshire Sculpture Park and it all suddenly makes a lot of sense. Situated on the Bretton Estate in the village of West Bretton, the 500-acre park encompasses hills, fields, lakes, woodland and formal gardens, which have been continually shaped over the years by the families who lived here. This landscape – striking throughout the year – provides the perfect backdrop for the sculptures it shows, a juxtaposition of the natural and the man-made.

Most fitting of the sculptures are those by Henry Moore, who was born in nearby Castleford; the surrounding countryside inspired his work, so it feels a real privilege to be able to experience it within this context. Alongside Moore, the permanent, revolving, collection also includes work by Antony Gormley, Eduardo Paolozzi and Barbara Hepworth. Each piece has been carefully sited within the park, and there's something about seeing them in the open air, as opposed to the confines of a traditional gallery, which brings them to life. The best way to approach the sculptures is by accident – traipsing through fields of sheep to suddenly discover a larger-than-life reclining figure of a woman, or heading uphill to be greeted by a dramatic modern composition.

In addition to the outdoor exhibitions, there are four indoor galleries, which are worth exploring in their own right. The Project Space is a particular highlight, housing changing exhibitions from the Arts Council Collection, which could include film and photography in addition to sculpture. Once you're done with exploring the extensive grounds and galleries, reward yourself with a cream tea in the visitor centre, from where you can soak up the views over the park – and spot a few more sculptures waiting to be discovered.

Need to know The Yorkshire Sculpture Park, West Bretton, West Yorkshire ☎ 01924/832631, Ⓦ www.ysp.co.uk. Daily: grounds 10am–6pm; indoor galleries 10am–5pm. Free. There's a large car park on site, and buses run from Wakefield bus station, seven miles away (at least hourly Mon–Fri). Map 3, C10

NEW ARCHITECTURE

While this fair isle is world-renowned for the grandeur of Georgian cities such as Edinburgh and Bath, and visitors flock to its historic stately homes and castles, Britain also boasts a wealth of exciting contemporary architecture. From iconic galleries to inspiring cultural centres, public architecture in the UK has undergone something of a renaissance since the millennium. Here are just a few of the highlights:

460 Ashmolean Museum of Art & Archaeology, Oxford

The world's first public museum on its opening in 1683, Oxford's superbly transformed Ashmolean reopened in 2009 after an impressive redesign which has doubled the original display space. Behind the edifice of the surviving Neoclassical Cockerell building, lie 39 spacious new galleries – accessed through a glass-roofed atrium flooded with natural light. Steel and glass bridges connect labyrinthine exhibition spaces packed with treasures of Eastern and Western art.

Ⓦ *www.ashmolean.org. Map 2, D5*

461 Laban Centre, Southeast London

At night the space-age Laban Centre shines like a beacon across Deptford in southeast London, while by day its sharp mirrored surfaces reflect the surrounding grass verges. A stunning slice of coloured polycarbonate and glass, the Laban Centre is a venue for contemporary dance training and performance. The Bonnie Bird Theatre sits at the heart of the complex, while large windows in the dance studios give passers-by tantalizing glimpses of the dancers in rehearsal. Designed by the Swiss architects Herzog & de Meuron, whose portfolio includes Tate Modern, the Laban's remarkable structure states a clear commitment to championing the experimental and progressive.

Ⓦ *www.laban.org. Map 1, F4*

462 Middlesbrough Institute of Modern Art

While Middlesbrough might not be synonymous with the architectural avant-garde, its Institute of Modern Art (or mima) is doing its best to change that. Bang in the centre of town, this substantial glass and limestone gallery is an eye-catching local landmark. Five exhibition spaces, with slate floors sourced from Italy, host the permanent collection of arts and crafts as well as changing shows.

Ⓦ *www.visitmima.com. Map 4, E16*

463 New Art Exchange, Nottingham

As a bold, black box neighbouring a nineteenth-century library, the New Art Exchange cuts a striking architectural pose on Nottingham's Gregory Boulevard. The UK's first regional visual arts centre for Black and Asian arts displays its daring spirit from the outset. Its black bricks contrast dramatically with the traditional red-brick buildings of surrounding streets, and frameless windows of varying sizes are scattered across the edifice – creating a distinctive and unusual gallery space for its changing programme of exhibitions.

Ⓦ *www.thenewartexchange.org.uk. Map 3, D11*

464 The Serpentine Pavilion, London

The roll call of Serpentine Pavilion architects reads like a Who's Who of twenty-first-century architecture. Since its first incarnation in 2000, heavyweights such as Frank Gehry, Zaha Hadid and Oscar Niemeyer have all designed the Serpentine gallery's annually changing summer pavilion. Housing a café and providing a space for the much-loved Serpentine's programme of events, the Pavilion has become one of contemporary architecture's most prestigious and experimental commissions. From Olafur Eliasson and Kjetil Thorsen's timber-clad spinning top, to Rem Koolhaas and Cecil Balmond's futuristic, illuminated egg, it never fails to inspire excitement and debate.

Ⓦ *www.serpentinegallery.org. Map 1, B3*

465 The stained-glass wonders of York Minster

It's hard not be overwhelmed by York Minister. It took around 250 years to complete, is the second largest Gothic cathedral in Europe and one of the most visited sites in northern England, a gorgeous pile of carved limestone with three towers rising to nearly 200ft high. Yet the real genius of York lies in that most underrated of art forms: stained glass.

It should be called "Gothic glass art" instead. For many, "stained glass" conjures up images of cold, dull Sundays in church, or boring museums. York isn't like that at all; the Minster has one of the finest collections of stained glass in England, with 128 windows containing around two million individual pieces of glass. You'd have to be a real aficionado to work your way through every one, but there are some obvious highlights.

The 76ft-high Great East Window is truly monumental, a massive construction comprising an ornate tracery and 117 panels of carefully crafted biblical scenes, everything from the Creation to startling images of the Last Judgement. Easy to believe this is the largest arrangement of medieval glass in the world, but given its age, the brilliance of its painting and colour is outstanding. Unusually, we know the artists name, a glass painter called John Thornton who worked on it between 1405 and 1408.

The Great West Window, completed even earlier in 1338, is known as the "Heart of Yorkshire" thanks to the heart-shape pattern in the tracery. Check out also the Five Sisters Window, a rare composition of "grisaille" glass (of greyish-white colour), completed in 1260, with a vivid mosaic-like effect created by over 100,000 individual pieces of glass.

Finally, the one piece of stained glass almost everyone has heard of. Surrounded by pitch-black darkness, the strangely modern Rose Window glows like a mighty star, its 73 panels of glass emblazoned with white and red roses, symbolic of the union between the houses of York and Lancaster. Completed around 1500, the window commemorates the marriage of Henry VII and Elizabeth of York, effectively ending the Wars of the Roses. It's another whopper, measuring almost 23ft across, but for fans at least, it's just the tip of the iceberg.

Need to know York Minister, York ☎ 08449 390011, Ⓦ www.yorkminster.org. Mon–Sat 9.00am–5.30pm, Nov–March from 9.30am, Sun noon–3.45pm. £8 including guided tour, main tower £5.
Map 3, D9

466 Time for tea: the world's oldest museum café

In the 1980s, London's ailing Victoria and Albert decorative arts museum – the once glorious *grande dame* of South Kensington – was advertising itself as "An ace caff with quite a nice museum attached". Art buffs were scandalized by such philistinism, of course, but café-lovers could also grumble; the V&A "caff" of yore was a stinky subterranean horror. Thirty years later, the tacky adverts are long gone, the museum is thriving again, and the café, well, yes, the café is truly ace.

Anywhere you look in the V&A, your eye lands on beauty – from the world's oldest Persian carpet to the life-size cast of Michelangelo's *David*, from Vivienne Westwood's evening gowns to cypress-carved Japanese *No* masks. And so it is in the original dining rooms, which opened in 1868 – literally the world's first museum café – displaying, like the museum itself, the finest Arts and Crafts to the masses. What you eat here doesn't matter – they serve all the usual modern museum café stuff – but somehow a cream tea seems fitting. Whatever you choose, your food will seem a little tastier, your chitchat a little more significant, than in other museum pit stops.

Cosiest of the three rooms is the hushed warm-hued Morris Room (1866), William Morris's first public commission. An Arts and Crafts haven, bathed in forest-green light from the Burne-Jones stained glass, its embossed wallpaper abounds with fat olive branches while gold panels softly glow with leaves, fruits and ethereal Pre-Raphaelite beauties.

The Gamble room (1865) is chattier, more open and bustly, a High Victorian clatter of gilt and sparkle. Renaissance meets Islamic meets Classical in the moulded Minton ceramic tiles, slathered thick on the walls and columns like luscious icing – so practical, too, with their wipe-clean surfaces. The unlikely giant pompom chandeliers, twinkly modern anomalies, fit perfectly, flashing light across the gloriously creamy ceramic. Light pours in too through the giant arched windows, etched with food-related aphorisms ("Good wine teaches good Latin – Hunger is the best Sauce") running in a slightly crazed stream of consciousness.

You might prefer to sip your tea in Sir Edward Poynter's blue-tiled grill room, designed (in 1876) as a place for the common folk to eat their steak puddings. The exquisitely rendered tiles, swarming with peacocks and fountains and bucolic pastoral scenes, are rustic and rich, quite different from the flashy splendour of Gamble's room.

Need to know Victoria and Albert Museum, Cromwell Rd, London SW7 Ⓦ www.vam.ac.uk. Mon–Thurs, Sat & Sun 10am–5.15pm, Fri 10am–9.30pm. Free. The café closes 15min before the museum.
Map 1, B4

467 Glitz, sparkle and showbiz glamour in rural Wales

After driving along the rolling country lanes of mid-Wales the last thing you'd expect to find upon arrival in the quiet, Tudor-beamed, picture-postcard village of Berriew is an explosion of flamboyance, 1980s decadence and showbiz glamour but that is exactly what lies behind the doors of the Andrew Logan Museum of Sculpture. The building itself is a converted squash court and it was designed by architect, and Logan's partner, Michael Davis, yet despite the blocky exterior, inside it houses a treasure-trove of gaudy, colourful and intriguing artefacts.

Logan's work defies genres and comprises beguiling pieces of sculpture, fashion, fine art and jewellery that manage to mix fantasy and fiction with real-world objects. Much of what appears in the gallery could only be described as site-specific installation art.

The first thing you're confronted with is a giant "cosmic" egg constructed from broken pieces of mirror, coloured glass and jewels. In the back room the walls are lined with cartoon-like portraits of familiar and not-so-familiar faces made from carefully cut pieces of mirror. The star of the show is the life-size effigy of Zandra Rhodes, even more flamboyant (if that's possible) than in real life.

Logan was born in 1945 and trained as an architect before unleashing his flamboyance across the art and theatre worlds in the 1970s, with his work being collected by the late Queen Mother, Viscountess Caroline Windsor and Lord and Lady John Sainsbury, among others. He's a true English eccentric, setting up the Alternative Miss World competition in 1972, a high camp outing open to anyone who rises to the challenge of creating three spectacular, over-the-top outfits. As Ken Russell noted of the 2009 competition "Costumes are more like parade floats than frocks".

This approach stands Logan in good stead for one of his annual pastimes, which is to dress the Miss Berriew float at the annual Berriew Show, the village fête-cum-beauty-pageant that takes place on August bank holiday weekend. As well as the crowning of the beauty queen, you'll find a vast array of traditional village events, with prizes awarded for the longest carrot, the tastiest Welsh cakes, the best plate garden and the most imaginative pipe-cleaner animal among others, plus livestock shows, rural crafts and a whole host of fairground attractions to entertain the kids.

Need to know The Andrew Logan Museum of Sculpture, Berriew, near Welshpool, Powys ☏ 01686/640689, Ⓦ www.andrewlogan.com. June–Sept Sat, Sun & August bank holiday Mon noon–4pm; visits can be arranged at others times by request. For details of the Berriew Show see Ⓦ www.berriew.com.
Map 3, B11

468 The Wallace Collection: ostentatious acquisition, eighteenth-century style

Just north of Oxford Street, past the crowds and chaos, discover a treasure-trove of a house, a paean to another age of acquisition that's a world away from twenty-first-century mass consumerism, but with a similar magpie-like frenzy for all things shiny, gilt and ornate.

The result of five generations of connoisseurship and collecting, the Wallace Collection is housed in the private home of the Hertford family, which was bequeathed to the nation in 1897, and is now a free, public museum jam-packed with art, porcelain, furniture and sculpture in ornate silk-lined and chandeliered rooms, which have been immaculately and lovingly restored.

The Great Gallery, with works by Titian, Rubens, Rembrandt, and the iconic *Laughing Cavalier* by Frans Hals, is the artistic star, but if you go on one of the excellent (free) guided tours, the enthusiastic expert will point out all sorts of other gems, such as pieces of Marie Antoinette's personal furniture, bought after the French Revolution by the canny fourth Marquess of Hertford, portraits of Madame de Pompadour, glitzy Sèvres porcelain, the ornate staircase from Louis XV's bank, with symbols of royalty and mammon cleverly interwoven, and an impressive armoury. The furnishings might not be to everyone's taste, particularly the saccharine paintings by Boucher and lashings of Rococo excess, but when coupled with the fascinating stories and titbits of gossip about the family peppered throughout the tour – such as the story of the third Marquess's wife, the illegitimate daughter of an Italian dancer, who brought great wealth into the family as a result of separate bequests from two men who both believed themselves to be her father – the result is to draw you into the rarefied world of this eccentric family and their unique collections.

Need to know Wallace Collection, Hertford House, Manchester Square, London W1 ☎ 020/7563 9500, Ⓦ www. wallacecollection.org. Daily 10am–5pm. Free. Public tours most days: Wed, Sat & Sun 11:30am & 3pm, also Mon–Fri at 1pm, when there are no other events, check in advance. There's an excellent café and restaurant in the beautiful glass-covered courtyard.
Map 1, C2

469 Beauty and utility at Blackwell

Need to know Blackwell,
The Arts & Crafts House,
Bowness-on-Windermere,
Cumbria ☎ 015394/46139,
Ⓦ www.blackwell.org.uk. Daily
10.30am–5pm, Nov–March till
4pm. £6.50.

Map 3, B9

From the outside, Blackwell doesn't give much away – it's a fairly plain, lime-washed country house with an elevated position above Windermere. But its architect M.H. Baillie Scott, like his contemporary Charles Rennie Mackintosh, designed from the inside out. He started with the requirements of the owner before addressing the exterior, and thus incorporated William Morris's maxim about beauty and utility being of equal importance. Stepping inside Blackwell – one of the most complete Arts and Crafts houses open to the public – into the magnificent main hall, you encounter an artistic vision to rival that of Mackintosh.

The high-ceilinged hall gives a respectful bow to the past, with half-timbered walls, a huge fireplace and a musician's gallery, while the simplicity of its lines and the harmonious use of oak panelling ensures the space doesn't fall victim to twee medievalism. It just looks like a beautiful space for a party, though the industrialist owner Sir Edward Holt, who commissioned Blackwell as a holiday home, didn't use it much after the death of his son in World War I.

Elsewhere at Blackwell, shining oak corridors open out into high-ceilinged rooms featuring stained glass with stylized elongated floral and animal motifs. Leaf-shaped door handles continue the natural theme, as does the carved foliage in the main hall. Beyond the hall, the white drawing room is more elegant but equally dramatic. It has some slender pieces of furniture from the period and the fireplace features vibrant blue tiles, but otherwise the room is restrained, with centre stage given to sweeping panoramas of Windermere.

Appropriately, given the Arts and Crafts ethos of supporting and developing the work of artisans, Blackwell is emphatically not a museum piece. There are imaginative temporary displays of ceramics, glass and metalwork – both contemporary and from Arts and Crafts designers – in the Gallery Rooms upstairs, while the shop showcases contemporary crafts. The hand-crafted theme is reflected in the light-flooded café, where artworks line the walls and home-made lemonade, teabread, scones and cakes are served up. You can eat outside on the garden terrace, surrounded by herbaceous terraces laid out by Thomas Mawson to capitalize on the views, and watch ferries nip across the waters of Windermere.

470 Art in St Ives

Stand in the rotunda of Tate St Ives and listen to the echo of the waves. Gaze out from the roof terrace to dramatic views of Porthmeor Beach and the wild Cornish coast. This magnificent building on the site of a former gasworks is more than just an art gallery: Tate St Ives is an experience of modern and contemporary art which reflects and highlights the natural environment that inspired much of the artwork on display.

While artists have been drawn to St Ives and its famous quality of light since the early nineteenth century, the gallery's main collection celebrates a succession of painters and sculptors whose work is firmly rooted in modernist traditions, a tribute to the seaside town's unique connection with many renowned twentieth-century artists. The gallery's permanent collection includes some of Cornwall's big names, with displays changed around frequently to showcase the works, while the gallery also features temporary exhibitions of current international stars and a programme of artists in residence to encourage the creation of new work relating to St Ives and its surrounds. Inside, the architecture and art beautifully fuses with the scenery and light, and the seaside location works a treat in the top-floor café from where you can feast your eyes on the vista as you tuck into delectable Cornish produce.

Need to know Tate St
Ives, Porthmeor Beach and
Barbara Hepworth Museum &
Sculpture Garden, Barnoon Hill
☎ 01736/796226, Ⓦ www.tate.org.
uk/stives. Daily 10am–5.20pm,
Nov–Feb closes 4.20pm. Joint
ticket £8.75. Back Road Trail
information available from the
tourist office (☎ 01736/796297);
for guided art tours see Ⓦ www.
guidedtoursofstives.co.uk.

Map 2, A7

Also managed by Tate is the nearby Barbara Hepworth Museum and Sculpture Garden, once home to one of Britain's most significant twentieth-century artists. The centre of attention is the magical sub-tropical garden featuring Hepworth's monumental stone and bronze sculptures where she designed them to stand. You can peep into the garden studio where the artist worked and take a journey through her life via archive materials on display.

While these two galleries are the biggest crowd-pleasers in town, they are by no means the only noteworthy ones, as the town's artistic tradition endures. Meet local artists on the Back Road Trail of galleries (pick up a map at the tourist office) or take a guided art tour.

471 A weekend of snooping and sky-high views: Open House London

Open House London – two days in September when hundreds of buildings are open to the public – is Londoners' annual opportunity to sneak a peek into some of the buildings they walk past every day, from the big, the imposing and iconic to private houses and offices.

And, whatever Prince Charles may think, many Londoners love the most experimental and the most dramatic. Early on Saturday morning the queue snakes around the block of Richard Rogers' Lloyd's Building, a perennial favourite. One of the city's boldest twentieth-century buildings, it's a stunning temple to concrete and commerce. The vast escalators, Willy Wonka-style glass elevators and magnificent views through the external metal pipes are well worth the wait.

For every building with a queue, or a lottery of a pre-booking system, there are dozens more that you can just turn up at and look around, often with architects on hand to guide you. Spend a day visiting a few, and the result is the ultimate whistle-stop tour of the mishmash of architectural styles that makes up London: from the barely finished office blocks of Broadgate to ancient guildhalls, via Arts and Crafts Bloomsbury buildings, eco-residences in the Elephant & Castle and designers' studios made from disused Tube carriages in Old Street.

But there's one thing everyone wants to do: ascend to the top. London's skyline is spiked by a small – and growing number – of very tall towers indeed, and the chance to visit one always ranks among the weekend's highlights. In 2010, the golden ticket was one of the 460 places to go up the BT Tower (30,000 applied), the towering 1960s relic, closed to the public since 1971. It's no longer the city's tallest building, but its location north of Oxford Street makes for stupendous views; its residual air of mystery – it was originally classified as an official secret and only appeared on Ordnance Survey maps in the 1990s – and the retro-splendour of the viewing deck's revolving floor (sadly no longer decked out as the 1970s *Butlins* restaurant it once was) just adds to the appeal.

The list of buildings changes each year, so maybe, just maybe, one of the magnificent new towers – The Shard, The Heron, or whatever Londoners choose to call these architectural carbuncles – will open their doors next year. Fingers crossed.

Need to know London Open House, Sat & Sun, usually end of Sept; entrance to all buildings is free. The programme is published about six weeks before (printed guide £6.50; Ⓦ www.londonopenhouse.org). Some require pre-booking around a month in advance.

Map 1, E3

TAKE THE HIGH ROAD

great journeys

We might have an A66 rather than a Route 66, but Britain yields to no nation in the breadth and drama of its great journeys. From the times of the very earliest cross-country tracks, carrying settlers, armies, traders and pilgrims, these routes were made for walking – along river and coast and over moorland, mountain and plain. In more recent times, journeys may have speeded up as technology has devoured the miles (and there may not be much drama in the easyJet flight from Luton to Aberdeen) but nothing touched the age-old British spirit of adventure and exploration. One celebrated route in particular – 900 miles south to north, from Land's End to John O'Groats – still stands as a kind of national shorthand for seeing the entire country, end to end, an enduring challenge for hikers, cyclists, and charity fundraisers dressed as giant rabbits. This aside, there are nineteen official long-distance routes or National Trails across England, Wales and Scotland, including what's claimed to be Britain's oldest road – the 87-mile-long Ridgeway, an ancient chalk-ridge route once tramped by prehistoric man. The coming of the canals, and later, the railways – a British invention, let's not forget – brought more dramatic journeys, from the spectacular narrowboat ride over the breathtaking Pontcysyllte Aqueduct in Wales to the fabulously engineered Settle to Carlisle railway line (dubbed, with no hint of exaggeration, England's most scenic railway). Other iconic British trips and journeys might not have the same natural majesty but hold plenty of nostalgic charm, whether it's the annual run of veteran cars down to Brighton, the short ferry 'cross the Mersey (we defy you not to sing that song) or the paddle up the River Thames (central to *The Wind in the Willows* and *Three Men in a Boat*). Elsewhere, there are surviving steam railways galore, helicopter rides over the dramatic Cornish coastline, the perilous walk across the shifting sands of Morecambe Bay, tall-ship voyages, long-distance horseback rides, and the world's only rotating boat lift. So, on with your boots, out with the bike, all aboard and saddle up – Britain's greatest journeys await.

472 London to Brighton in vintage style

"How about this old crock? Think it will make it to Brighton?" Decked out in period goggles and a cape, a driver and his Edwardian-dressed wife putter over Westminster Bridge at a modest bicycle speed in an open-topped 1898 Benz. The couple are travelling in an eye-opening procession of hundreds of gleamingly preserved museum pieces taking part in the annual London to Brighton Veteran Car Run, a joyous public celebration of still-functioning ancient vehicles, which chugs, steams and stutters its way through a Sunday in early November. The venerable event starts at Hyde Park and ends on Madeira Drive, within sight of Brighton's Palace Pier, the sixty-mile route lined by an enraptured crowd of up to a million. Repairs and mechanical failures on the way are facts of life – some machines have been known to burst into flames before crossing the finishing line. Speeding (that's a top speed of more than 20mph) is discouraged, and the rules state that the run is not a race (more of a test of endurance) but those that arrive by 4.30pm get a medal. For a few glorious hours, the Brighton seafront transforms itself into an impromptu free museum of Victorian and Edwardian automobiles.

Made famous worldwide by the classic 1953 British comedy caper *Genevieve*, the London to Brighton dates from 1896 when the so-called Emancipation Run was held to celebrate a new law allowing "locomotives of the highway" to attain heady speeds of up to 14mph; even more excitingly, vehicles were no longer required to be preceded by a red-flag-bearing attendant. The motoring editor of the *Daily Sketch* instigated a revival of the run in 1927, establishing rules that are still enforced today: vehicles must be three- or four-wheeled and, most importantly, must have been built before January 1, 1905. Yet, remarkably, more than a hundred years later, the organizers are still bombarded with entries, with keen participants from twenty countries – the full quota of 550 vehicles registered in 2010. But best to get form-filling early: fail to register your 1901 Wolseley tonneau or your 1899 Léon Bollée voiturette six months in advance, and you might just find yourself waiting on the sidelines.

Need to know The London to Brighton Veteran Car Run starts at sunrise in Hyde Park on a Sunday in early November, and takes in Westminster Bridge, Croydon, Redhill, Horley, Crawley (the official coffee-break stop), Cuckfield and Burgess Hill, en route to Brighton. Maps showing the best vantage points can be downloaded from Ⓦ www.lbvcr.com.
Map 1, B3–Map 2, E6

473 Snowdon: the mountain, the train and the new summit café

A haunting whistle cries out across the wild Snowdonia valleys as *Wyddfa*, one of the original 1895 steam locos, leaves the Halfway station bound for the summit of Snowdon – the highest mountain in Wales. Ever since the Victorians finished building the rack-and-pinion railway, plucky little engines have been chugging their way to the summit, halted each year by winter snows and with services frequently restricted by high winds. Many locos are diesel these days, but on busy summer days bridges and embankments will be thick with camera-toting rail fanatics getting shots of puffing steam engines pushing ancient red-and-white-liveried carriages up the one-in-eight gradient.

But not everyone is a fan of the train. Bearded Gore-Tex mountain types hate slogging their way to the top only to find a trainload of inappropriately dressed tourists packing out the café and spoiling the serenity taking smartphone photos of their friends. Stalwarts won't even enter state-of-the-art new *Hafod Eryri*, even though £8.3 million has been spent on replacing the ugly old café that Prince Charles once referred to as the "highest slum in Wales" with this. They'd rather sit outside with a cheese sandwich in a blizzard than deign to grace the modern Welsh-oak interior for a hearty Welsh pasty and a pint. Copa'r Wyddfa – the summit of Snowdon – is certainly more cosmopolitan than most Welsh mountaintops.

Those same hikers find little at fault with the mountain itself, however, or the exhilarating routes to the top – there are seven in all. The gentlest approach, the Llanberis Track roughly follows the train tracks and is the route taken by the annual Snowdon Race, which sees the winners up to the summit and back in, astonishingly enough, little more than an hour. Alternatively, if you want to save yourself 800 feet of ascent, start at Pen-y-Pass, a col from which three popular routes begin: the relatively easy Miners' Track, which passes the remains of a crushing mill from the old copper mines, while the more rugged Pig Track climbs Bwlch y Moch (the Pass of the Pigs). Those with a head for heights meanwhile tackle the knife-edge ridge of Crib Gogh, part of the wondrous Snowdon Horseshoe route.

Whichever route you choose, or mode of transport, it's an honour to reach the top – and with luck you'll see more than just the inside of a cloud.

Need to know The Snowdon Mountain Railway starts from Llanberis, Gwynedd ☎08444 938120, Ⓦ www.snowdonrailway. co.uk. Trains run from late March to the end of October (6–25 services per day). The adult summit return fare is £25.

Map 3, B11

474 A tall story on the high seas:

Few experiences can be more invigorating than sailing out in the open seas. The speed you can obtain gliding through the waves is truly uplifting. But trying the experience on a 180ft long, 368-tonne tall ship with eighteen sails is something else – and if you're over 16, you can do just that, even if you've never set foot on a boat before.

Based in Southampton, the Jubilee Sailing Trust (JST) is a charity that operates two tall ships specially built to be sailed by novices, including those with disabilities. Called the *Lord Nelson* and *Tenacious*, these magnificent vessels regularly set off on voyages which range from day-trips to month-long expeditions overseas.

It's somewhat daunting boarding ship for the first time. Confronted by a spaghetti of ropes, you're expected to help set the sails and even take the helm. But that's really the point: as the workings of a tall ship are alien to virtually every new participant, everyone boards as an equal, whether you're physically able or otherwise. Teamwork becomes the key word, and the permanent crew of experienced professional sailors soon spot people's strengths, assigning them appropriate tasks.

Working with people with disabilities is a major part of the experience: it's amazing how quickly you bond with your team-mates. And it's not all hard work, either. First-class meals are provided on board, and you also get "smoko", twice-daily rations of freshly baked biscuits, scones and flapjacks.

Many of the trips, such as that to Jersey, are overnighters – the cabins are spacious and spotless (everyone mucks in for "happy hour" – aka cleaning duty) and the gentle motion of the sea usually helps you to sleep, though you may find the beanbags in the bar a tempting alternative.

When the wind billows over 10,000 square feet of sail, the ships can hit an impressive ten knots. Equally awesome is the knowledge that, thanks to a few design tweaks and the right equipment, anyone can sail these wondrous vessels, whatever their physical ability.

Need to know Jubilee Sailing Trust, 12 Hazel Rd, Woolston, Southampton ☎ 023/8044 9108 ⓦ www.jst.org.uk. The two-day voyage from Southampton to Jersey costs £150, while day sails from Southampton costs £135. Anyone over the age of 16 can apply.
Map 2, D6

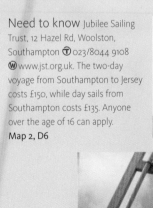

475 Row, row, row your boat: simply skiffing on the Thames

It's not the destination that matters – it's all about the journey. A traveller's platitude maybe, but it certainly holds true when the journey in question is a lazy boat trip along the Thames, immortalized in Jerome K. Jerome's bestselling 1889 yarn *Three Men in a Boat*. As the book's hapless heroes discover, the riverside towns – while full of charm – could never be as much fun as messing about on the river.

Boating was a highly fashionable activity in the late nineteenth century, when dapper gents in stripy blazers and their parasol-twirling sweethearts took to the Thames in all manner of pleasure craft. The Victorian camping skiff favoured by Jerome's trio of adventurers is a rare sight nowadays, but eight of these beautiful, hand-hewn specimens are still waterborne, thanks to Thames Skiff Hire. They come complete with attachable metal hoops, over which you sling a canvas roof to transform your boat into a cosy nest if you decide to forego the easy but less authentic option of a riverside B&B. The most popular route is from Oxford to Henley, a leisurely four-day trip in the opposite direction from that taken in the book, saving you the arm-ache of rowing upstream. You could cover the whole 132 miles of navigable river from Lechlade to Richmond in a week.

Apart from the boaters and blazers and the penchant for pipe-smoking, there's little to distinguish Jerome and pals from twenty-first-century lads on holiday, grumbling, bantering, snoozing and boozing their way down the river. You might try and avoid the worst of their scrapes – getting attacked by swans, capsizing, etc – but you could have fun getting lost in Hampton Court maze, hobnobbing with the toffs at Henley, or exploring the world's oldest inhabited castle at Windsor. The idyllic island campsites of Hurley and Cookham are highlights in themselves, while the friendly folk at *Amerden Lodge* in Taplow will deliver your full English to your boat in the morning.

But the real point of a skiffing holiday is its simple pleasures: in the absence of big-city noise, you can enjoy the gentle sloshing of oars in water or bacon sizzling in a pan, and revel in the nostalgia of lock-keepers' cottages and cream teas. Long stretches of countryside are interrupted only by colourful cottage gardens, or by ranks of stately mansions, their sweeping lawns framed by weeping willows – not to mention the inviting riverside pubs. To miss out on all this, in the words of Jerome himself, would just be bally foolishness.

Need to know Thames Skiff Hire (☎ 01932/232433, Ⓦ www.skiffhire.com) is based in Walton-on-Thames, Surrey, though trips can be arranged anywhere along the river. Prices for three people start at £320 for four days. See Ⓦ www.visitthames.co.uk for accommodation and sights along the river.
Map 1, E4

476 Horsing around on the Jack Mytton Way

If you want to discover the definition of "rural", turn off any A-road in Shropshire and head into the countryside. Once on the small country lanes, all road signs magically disappear, villages drift by unannounced, and you're just as likely to encounter a posse of horsey sorts out for a hack as you are another car. It's ideal territory for saddling up and exploring on four legs – though you could equally do it on two legs or two wheels.

The Jack Mytton Way travels across almost a hundred miles of rural Shropshire, combining bridleways and quiet country lanes with open countryside that offers glorious views across to Wales. Named after local landowning bad boy John "Mad Jack" Mytton, who boozed, gambled and generally partied his way through his fortune in the early nineteenth century, it's ironic that a man known for his Byron-esque debauchery should give his name to a route associated with all that is hale and hearty.

The Way begins in the tiny village of Cleobury Mortimer and heads north across rolling farmland up to handsome Much Wenlock, from which it follows the thickly wooded limestone escarpment of Wenlock Edge before descending to picturesque Church Stretton. From here it climbs the upland heath of Long Mynd, passes through the chocolate-box-pretty village of Clun, follows the course of Offa's Dyke for a while, and eventually finishes up on the Welsh border. On horseback, it takes around five to seven days to ride from end to end, depending on experience, but there is an option for a circular ride at the eastern end of the Way, which begins and ends in Cleobury Mortimer. The "southern loop" can be completed in two to three days and offers the chance to really explore some of the most unspoilt parts of the county.

Local stables can organize guided treks, with overnights in local pubs and B&Bs, or shorter weekend rides. Alternatively, it's easy to just book a day or a morning's hack or a day trek and get a taste of what the Way has to offer. Peace, tranquillity, silence, beauty – everything Jack spent his life trying to avoid.

Need to know A leaflet of the route, with maps and directions, can be downloaded from Ⓦ www.shropshire.gov.uk. Country Treks (☎ 01746/718436, Ⓦ www.horsetreks.co.uk) organize day-long, weekend and week-long treks on the Way.
Map 3, C12

477 Take the famous ferry 'cross the Mersey

The service may date back to the twelfth century but as you step onto the *Snowdrop* ferry (one of the three that still service this route) there's no mistaking which era you're being transported to. Hackneyed it may be, but it almost goes without saying that the tannoy is only going to be playing one tune.

"Life goes on day after day/Hearts torn in every way", sings Gerry Marsden as the 1965 hit he recorded with his band The Pacemakers cranks into life for the millionth time. Liverpool's golden age of music may now be half a century old, but the charm of taking a ferry across the River Mersey from Liverpool to the Wirral Peninsula to this soundtrack still hasn't diminished.

The ferry provides the best view of the iconic Three Graces –the collective name given to Liverpool's celebrated trio of monumental dockside buildings. The most famous is the Royal Liver Building, complete with its two clocktowers – both larger than Big Ben, topped with the famous Liver Bird statues, a pair of cormorants that have become the city's symbol. Opened in 1911 and still home to Royal Liver Assurance, it was one of the first reinforced concrete buildings in the world.

The Italianate Cunard Building, home to the shipping firm of the same name, and the Port of Liverpool Building, awash with Baroque excess, don't get quite the same plaudits but they're both equally impressive. The sculptures of Britannia and Neptune that decorate the outside of the former building are delightful, as is the huge central dome atop the latter.

On board ship, unless the weather is truly atrocious, it's worth sitting out on deck where, once Gerry's singing ceases, you'll hear a decent audio commentary telling you much about the city and the long history of the ferry service, which was operated by monks from Birkenhead Priory until the monastery's dissolution in 1536. Today's typically irreverent Scouse boat skippers don't appear to share quite the same fervour – but there are plenty of Liverpudlians out there who'll tell you that taking this famous ferry is nothing short of a religious experience.

Need to know Mersey Ferries (☎ 0151/330 1444, Ⓦ merseyferries.co.uk) operate up to thirteen times a day from Pier Head in Liverpool to Woodside (for Birkenhead) and Seacombe (Wallasey). A round trip takes 50 minutes; tickets cost £2.45 return for adults.
Map 3, B10

478 Hike the Welsh Marches: Offa's Dyke Path

Need to know for more information consult the National Trail website (Ⓦwww.nationaltrail.co.uk/offasdyke), and contact the Offa's Dyke Association, who manage the Offa's Dyke Centre, West St, Knighton, Powys (Ⓣ01547/528753, Ⓦwww.offasdyke.demon.co.uk).

Map 2, C5–Map 3, B10

Sitting on a gravel beach trying to put hiking socks over cold, wet feet might not seem like an auspicious finish to one of Britain's oldest long-distance trails, but this is the classic finale to Offa's Dyke Path. Purists wade at least ankle deep into the Irish Sea at the path's northern terminus, Prestatyn on the north Welsh coast – a repeat of the performance twelve days or so earlier at Sedbury Cliffs, near Chepstow on the Severn Estuary, where (minus blisters) they began. In between, hikers negotiate 177 miles of some of the finest and most varied landscape that the Welsh Marches has to offer, from gentle green valleys to wild moors and ancient woodland by way of historic towns and hidden hamlets. The route hugs close to the Welsh–English border all the way, crossing it twenty times in all.

The path is named after Offa's Dyke, a massive earthwork (ditch and rampart) up to twenty feet high and sixty feet wide built in the eighth century by Offa, King of Mercia, to separate his territory from rival kingdoms – whether to keep out the Welsh or to keep out the English, opinion divides. The path broadly follows the course of the rampart, though while it was being developed in the 1960s the route planners made a few judicious improvements: rather than follow the dyke through Wrexham and other industrially marred areas they diverted it through the Wye Valley, over the Black Mountain in Brecon Beacons National Park and along the Clwydian Range with its long views over north Wales to Snowdonia. The result is one of Britain's finest national trails – never too crowded and never monotonous.

The path comes within striking distance of half a dozen train stations and numerous bus routes, so organizing a day walk along the dyke is no problem, but the classic enterprise is coast to coast in a single push. A network of hostels, B&Bs, bunkhouses and campsites close to the path make finding accommodation fairly easy, though you'll need to plan ahead to get exactly what you want. Some places even organize bag transfer each day so that you can just walk with a day sack. Set aside a couple of weeks and be sure to follow the acorn signs.

479 Scenic survivor: the Settle to Carlisle railway

Often dubbed "England's most scenic railway", the Settle to Carlisle line, which runs from the Yorkshire Dales almost to the Irish Sea, is a joy from end to end. Yet as walkers, families, railway buffs and locals board at pretty-as-a-picture Settle station, all flowers and wraparound friendliness, few realize just how privileged they are to be able to ride it. For it's a miracle that this engineering masterpiece, almost stillborn in the nineteenth century, and close to violent death in the twentieth, exists at all.

It's invariably a holiday atmosphere – happy, excited, expectant – as the train climbs northwards out of Settle through the beautiful Dales countryside. Yorkshire's famous Three Peaks rock past – Sphinx-like Pen-y-ghent to the right, Ingleborough and Whernside to the left. Sheep and farmhouses dot bleak uplands rising to limestone scars, rough pasture is edged by dry-stone walls. Out onto the great Ribblehead Viaduct, you'll feel like you're flying. Far below, rivers and roads meander, and people stand by their cars taking pictures as you cross. After the viaduct, the train dives into Blea Moor Tunnel, said to be haunted. From Ais Gill, the railway's 1169-foot zenith, the line drops down the idyllic Eden Valley through lush fields and prosperous villages, finally fetching up, brakes squealing, at the fine sandstone city of Carlisle.

As you enjoy the shining beauty of the countryside, however, spare a thought for the history of this remarkable railway. The line – 73 miles across some of the most inhospitable country in England, with eleven stations, nineteen viaducts and fourteen tunnels – was built by a tough and unruly army of six thousand navvies, mainly Irish, over a seven-year period from 1869. Using only horse-drawn winches, wheelbarrows, picks, shovels, dynamite and their own brute strength, they dug cuttings, built embankments and, with only candles for light, excavated tunnels. They lived with their wives and children in squalid temporary camps (or even in the tunnels themselves); many were felled by accident, disease or exposure, and were buried along the route in unmarked graves. A plaque in the church at Chapel-le-Dale bears testament to their efforts.

A century later several attempts were made by penny-pinching governments to close the whole thing down – all those viaducts and tunnels were expensive to maintain – but ferocious opposition bore fruit, and in time tourist interest picked up and ensured its future. So it survives, thanks to the enthusiasts and the visionaries, the engineers and the working men.

Need to know Ⓦwww.settle-carlisle.co.uk. A day return from Settle to Carlisle costs £20, and can be booked via National Rail (Ⓦwww.nationalrail.co.uk).

Map 3, C9–Map 4, D16

480 Rolling along the Ridgeway

The Ridgeway really is as old as the hills – well, almost. For over 5000 years, travellers, farmers, soldiers and, more recently, cyclists have followed this 87-mile-long trackway between Avebury in Wiltshire and Ivinghoe Beacon in Buckinghamshire – part of an ancient trading route that once stretched from the Dorset coast all the way to Norfolk. The chalky downland ridge that comprises the Ridgeway's western half is open to cyclists all year round, and provides a moderately challenging 42-mile ride.

Starting out from Overton Hill, near Avebury, it's worth checking out the mystical 4000-year-old stone circle to draw inspiration from the mind-boggling amount of human effort that was required to haul over a hundred stones, weighing up to fifty tonnes each, into this massive enclosure. The initial climb instantly provides some fine vistas across the rolling valleys, which on a clear winter morning often fill with swirling mist, veiling the somewhat more unsightly views of the M4 and Swindon beyond.

There's no shortage of visual reminders to tell you just how old this trail is either: Barbury Castle, Liddington Castle and Uffington Castle all display the classic, hilltop-fort attributes that make 10-year-olds (and grown-ups alike) run around with improvised swords, defending the honour of any fair maiden that might be in need of a passing white knight. Uffington also has a uniquely stylized white horse dug out of the chalk hillside, best viewed from the flat-topped Dragon Hill, itself steeped in the legend of St George.

And no trip along the Ridgeway would be complete without mounting Scutchamer Knob – a place of magic where apparently the men of Berkshire used as a meeting place. After that, the open trail encourages sporadic surges in speed, with the odd tough hill providing opportunities for heroic climbs. From the trig point at Hill Barn near Sparsholt, it's predominantly downhill all the way to the river at Streatley – so lots of freewheeling joy all the way to the pub

All along the Ridgeway, it is almost impossible not to be engulfed by a sense of timelessness. Knowing that you are riding where feet have trod, hoofs have galloped and carts have trundled for thousands and thousands of years really helps to make you feel a part of something ancient and never-ending. A final word of warning though – be prepared for punctures. The flint stone found in most chalk hillsides can cut rubber tyres in to ribbons.

Need to know See Ⓦ www. nationaltrail.co.uk/ridgeway for more details. The Ridgeway is an exposed ride, so layer up and be sure to keep warm during the obligatory picnic stop.
Map D5–E5

481 Bridge with a view: narrowboating on the Llangollen Canal

Mallards scud across the dark, glossy water. Walkers and cyclists offer cheery nods and smiles from the sun-dappled towpath. The engine of your narrowboat chugs softly as you nose your way along, with stately progress. There are few more peaceful ways to enjoy North Wales than this.

Llangollen lies near the western extreme of one of the most beautiful and popular canal journeys in Wales; some would argue it's the best in Britain. The town itself is thoroughly appealing, its small, historic centre energized by the rushing waters of the River Dee and the shrill whistles of steam trains, chuffing their way out of the picturebook station. Every summer, this cheerful place resounds with song: singers and dancers converge on Llangollen for the International Musical Eisteddfod and it celebrates the occasion by decking its streets out with banners, bunting and bright hanging baskets.

Llangollen's famous canal, a masterwork of the Industrial Revolution, was created by the great Scottish civil engineer Thomas Telford. The first surprise is its location: high above the town, on the Dee Valley's steep slope. The second is that there are so few locks to negotiate, despite the hilly terrain: in the thirty-mile run to Whitchurch in Shropshire, there are only two. So if your idea of a blissful few days' boating is to snooze on deck while somebody else mans the tiller, Llangollen is an excellent choice.

Heading east, the canal winds its way through the lush Denbighshire countryside, crossing into England at Chirk and continuing through the open pastures of rural Shropshire and Cheshire. Before you cross the border, you exchange the calm serenity of wooded banks for heady drama as you steer your way onto a masterwork within a masterwork: the breathtaking Pontcysyllte Aqueduct. Soaring over 38m above the wide Dee valley, it's the longest and highest aqueduct in Britain, and at the time of its completion, 1805, it was revolutionary. At the heart of the design is a long cast-iron trough of water, just wide enough to carry one narrowboat at a time, supported by graceful arches set on hollow masonry pillars. Dare to look out over the sheer drop on the west side and you can enjoy dizzying panoramas of verdant pasture and the lively churning below.

Need to know Narrowboats can be hired from Marine Cruises (☎ 01244/373911, Ⓦ www. marinecruises.co.uk) in Chirk and UK Boat Hire (☎ 01905/734168, Ⓦ www.waterwaysholidays.com) in Whitchurch from around £560 per week. At Llangollen Wharf in Llangollen, Aqueduct Cruises (☎ 01978/860702, Ⓦ www. horsedrawnboats.co.uk) offer short trips along the canal and across the aqueduct in a horse-drawn or motorized barge.
Map 3, B11

482 On the buses: down memory lane in a Routemaster

In 2010, London mayor Boris Johnson unveiled the city's new Routemaster bus, a gleaming, asymmetrical bullet, part-designed by Aston Martin. The revamped double-decker may have kept the old buses' beloved (if controversial) open platform and its scarlet exterior, but to most Londoners this was a Johnny-come-lately upstart with none of the heart, soul or style of its stately predecessor.

The original Routemaster, designed in the 1950s especially for the capital, is not only a style icon, with its simple, classic lines, but also a shiny red emblem of London pride, its famed hop-on-hop-off platform encapsulating the city's rakish sense of spontanaiety, urbanity and rebellious lack of respect for queues. Today just two "heritage routes" remain, designed not only for tourists but also to appease the crowds who blocked the roads in protest during the last buses' final run in 2005. The Routemaster of old may be on its last legs – but tell that to the postcard-vendors, to the tourists who leap into traffic to snap a shot as the heritage bus rumbles by, or to those nostalgic souls who long to take one last ride, to hear that quintessential "ding-ding" bell one last time.

Despite passing a string of tourist hotspots, riding a Routemaster today has little to do with the destinations – that hotchpotch of roadworks and chain stores, monuments and traffic jams can be seen from any London bus. No, this journey is a game of Remember When. If you want to "drive the bus" like when you were a kid, rush up top and sit at the front, grab the railing and go. If you want to enjoy the interplay between conductor (clippie) and driver, or hear the clippie's familiar "Only five standing inside, please!", then settle down below. Jettison your Oyster card and buy a ticket – it may not be spat out of a clickety, hand-cranked machine, but being handed a real ticket by a real person is a rare experience, one that most Londoners miss more than they know. One quick tug on the wire bell strung from the ceiling, one final "ding-ding", a bold leap from the open deck, and your trip down memory lane is done.

Need to know There are two Routemaster heritage routes (daily 9.30am–6.30pm; single fares £2): the #9 (between Aldwych and the Royal Albert Hall) and the #15 (between Trafalgar Square and Tower Hill).
Map 1, D3

483 Roll on, Caledonia: take the sleeper train to the Highlands

Normally, waking up in the middle of a place as desolate as Rannoch Moor might be a cause for concern. But not this morning, oh no. This morning, with a soft Scottish Highland light streaming through your window and the gentle rock and quiet rattle of the train carriage nudging you awake, your worries and stresses have melted away.

Being ensconced in a comfortable bunk with a duvet wrapped snugly around you helps, of course. But what's even better is this: the awe-inspiring view, and the returning memory that so much of the sheer joy of travel lies not in reaching your destination, but in the journey itself. And what a journey this is.

The Caledonian Sleeper rolls along a ribbon of iron for 500-odd miles between London and Fort William, one of only two overnight routes in Britain (the other is London to Penzance). Taking you through some of the most stunning scenery in the country, it's a wonderful, leisurely alternative to the often soul-destroying experience that flying has become, connecting you more intimately to the great British landscape.

From zipping through London's twinkling urban majesty during an evening departure, to rolling past the quiet countryside of England's rural northwest, the length and breadth of Britain unfolds right in front of you. By the time you reach Scotland you'll more than likely be fast asleep – perhaps with a little help from the dram or three of single malt you had earlier in the lounge car (which also sells hot meals, including haggis, neeps and tatties).

By 7am, you're skirting the shores of Loch Lomond, awake just in time for the best scenery. Like the hard C sounds of the passing station names – Crianlarich, Bridge of Orchy, Rannoch, Currour, Tulloch – the Highland landscape can be harsh, but not without its own lasting appeal. Among the green, ochre and dun-coloured crags, you'll catch a quicksilver flash of a stream or loch, the occasional burst of yellow gorse, the unmistakeable patch of purple thistle and even the fiery-orange coats of Highland cattle, not to mention the odd deer bounding away as the train passes.

So roll on, Caledonia, because the closest you'll get to any of this beauty at 30,000 feet is in the pages of the in-flight magazine.

Need to know The Highland Caledonian Sleeper leaves London six nights a week (Sun–Fri), splitting at Edinburgh and dividing into three portions – one bound for Inverness, one for Aberdeen and one for Fort William. Cabins are equipped with single or double bunks, plus hot- and cold-water washbasin. Tickets from £19, including a light breakfast. See Ⓦ www.scotrail.co.uk for more information.
Map 1, C2–Map 4, B13

484 Helicopter to the Isles of Scilly: a short descent to paradise

It's easy to tell as soon as you board who is a regular and who is a novice. Some are nonchalant, others are nervous, but it's the earplugs that really give it away. For as the engine fires up and the blades begin to rotate, the noise inside the Sikorsky S-61 truly is deafening.

Leaving St Michael's Mount behind it feels like you are skimming the western tip of Cornwall. An undulating patchwork of fields stretches out to the horizon, while right beneath you the coastline is peppered with secluded coves and sheer clifftop drops. In moments, you're flying over enchanting Mousehole, its compact huddle of cottages encircling its tiny harbour. Soon after, your eye makes out the magnificent Minack Theatre, and it strikes you how inspirational it would be to watch Shakespeare with spectacular Porthcurno Bay as a backdrop. As north and south coasts converge a few minutes later, you pass over Land's End, and with it just the endless expanse of shimmering blue sea. As you leave the mainland behind you the helicopter drops to just 1500ft above sea level allowing you to keep an eye out for dolphins and porpoises in the ocean below.

While you have your nose pressed against the window, some of your fellow passengers – the old-timers – are getting stuck into a book. You all, however, share a sense of smugness as you pass over the *Scillonian*, the boat that left Penzance for St Mary's an hour ago and will arrive nearly an hour and a quarter after you: a very rocky journey of almost three hours, it's not one for seasickness sufferers.

But the best part of this journey has to be the descent to St Mary's, and the realization that you're about to embark on your island adventure. Flying in with the gorgeous white-sand beaches of St Martin's on your right, you'd be forgiven for thinking you were about to set foot in the Caribbean. But no – you're just 25 minutes from the Cornish coast. Just five inhabited islands (and a hundred other uninhabited strips of land), with subtropical gardens, opportunities for seal- and puffin-watching, diving and kayaking, plus fabulous seafood and as much sunshine in March as London in June – truly this little archipelago is a piece of paradise.

Need to know British International (Ⓦ www. islesofscillyhelicopter.com) run flights from Penzance to St Mary's throughout the year; an adult open return costs £175, though cheaper day returns are available. See Ⓦ www.simplyscilly.co.uk for more on the Isles of Scilly.
Map 2, A7–A8

485 Crossing the quicksands: Britain's most dangerous walk

Backed by the Lakeland fells and famed for its spectacular sunsets, Morecambe Bay may look dramatically beautiful, but with its shifting sands and fast-moving tides this vast expanse of tidal mud flats is one of the most dangerous stretches of coast in Britain. In medieval times, though – and right up until the coming of the railways in the mid-nineteenth century – crossing the sands by foot was one of the principal routes between Lancashire and Cumbria.

To attempt to ford this treacherous terrain by yourself would be sheer folly. There are quicksands, hidden channels and swirling currents, and when the tide roars in, its speed is said to be faster than any horse can gallop – as testified by the countless stories of disappearances (not least the tragic tale of the Chinese cockle pickers in 2004) over the years. Once upon a time, monks from Cartmel Priory conducted travellers safely across the bay. But following a petition in the 1530s, the sands were deemed so dangerous that an official guide was appointed by royal command – a tradition that continues today. Step forward Cedric Robinson, 25th Queen's Guide to the Sands.

For almost half a century, Cedric has earned his keep – a modest £15 salary per annum, plus cottage – by his intimate knowledge of the ever-changing terrain; he claims he can read the sands in the way that others read newspapers. He plants laurel branches to mark the route – when rain and fog descend it's the only way to trace a path back to safety.

Once a fortnight between May and September, Cedric takes groups out at low tide on the eight-mile walk, usually from Hest Bank or Arnside to Grange-over-Sands or Flookburgh Point. It's an exhilarating hike in the strangest, most ethereal of landscapes. Cedric leads the way, followed by a tractor and trailer and up to 150 hikers, many of whom attempt the walk for charity. Having spent his childhood cockling the bay, he often sets his nets at high tide to catch the tasty flounder ("flukes" as they're known locally) feeding on the cockles.

Cedric is well into his seventies now, but he's in no mood to retire just yet. "Always follow the tide out rather than wait for the turn" is his advice. Yet only the most reckless hiker would ever attempt to cross these perilous sands without Cedric and his laurel branches to guide and protect them.

Need to know Numbers are limited, so you should register for the walk with Cedric at least two weeks in advance on ☎ 015395/32165. The schedule can be checked with Grange-over-Sands tourist office (☎ 015395/34026, Ⓦ www.grange-over-sands.com).
Map 3, B9

TOP 5 >>

STEAM RAILWAYS

Is it the fact that the British invented them? Or that children know Thomas and Percy better than their own parents? Or that peaked caps, billowing steam and *The Railway Children* bring a strange quiver to grown men's hearts? Whatever the reason, there's something about the British and their steam railway heritage that only a ride down the line can start to explain. All aboard our pick of the steam.

486 Ffestiniog Railway

The world's oldest independent railway company (founded 1832) is surely the place to spark a love for steam, and the thirteen-mile journey through the spectacular North Wales countryside pulls out all the engineering stops, from full-circle loops to mountain tunnels. What's more, with the completion of the link to the Welsh Highland Railway from Caernarfon, through Snowdonia National Park, Wales has a "Great Railway Journey" all of its own – forty magnificent miles of narrow-gauge steam.

☎ 01765/516000, Ⓦ www.festrail.co.uk. Map 3, B11

487 Isle of Man Steam Railway

First indication that you're not in Kansas any more? Probably the request halt that connects Ronaldsway Airport to Douglas on the Isle of Man. If you can get over the fact that you can go from baggage reclaim to island capital by steam train, ponder – as you rattle along fifteen miles of narrow-gauge countryside line – that this is still government-owned and run, no less, with trains and carriages that have hardly changed a jot since 1874.

Ⓦ www.visitisleofman.com; timetables on Ⓦ www.iombusandrail.info. Map 3, A9

488 North York Moors Railway

There's railway heritage packed into the very DNA of the NYMR – it's one of the oldest lines in the country, built in 1835 by railway pioneer George Stephenson of *Locomotion* fame. It connects Pickering in the heart of the North York Moors to the coast at Whitby, puffing through a dramatic high moorland backdrop and stopping at time-warp village stations for cream teas and hearty walks. It's pretty wizard all round, so no surprise to see Goathland station double as Hogsmeade in the Harry Potter films.

☎ 01751/472508, Ⓦ www.nymr.co.uk. Map 3, D9

489 West Somerset Railway

Ten stations in twenty miles, not to mention the rolling Somerset countryside, brings the steam buffs out in raptures. It's all about tradition and nostalgia on this resurrected branch line of the old Great Western Railway, and what names to conjure with as the stations flit past – Crowcombe, Stogumber, Doniford Halt and Blue Anchor – each with a tale to tell.

☎ 01643/704996, Ⓦ www.west-somerset-railway.co.uk. Map 2, C6

490 Bluebell Railway

Every steam railway worth its salt runs Christmas Santa specials and days out with Thomas the Tank Engine, but the fifty-year-old Bluebell is a hard act to beat with its annual calendar of platform Punch and Judy shows, Victorian picnics, brass bands and food festivals. An observation carriage from 1913 is hauled into service for the changing colours of the Sussex autumn, while out comes the best china in First Class for a traditional afternoon tea served in the burnished lounge car.

☎ 01825/720800, Ⓦ www.bluebell-railway.com. Map 2, E6

491 A capital walk

Need to know Each section of the walk is detailed on Ⓦ www.tfl.gov.uk; maps are available at Ⓦ www.walklondon.org.uk. *The Capital Ring*, written by Colin Saunders and published by Aurum Press, is a highly recommended guide.

Map 1, F4

London is not a destination frequently extolled by ramblers, for obvious reasons. Tranquillity, space and wildlife habitats are thought to be in short supply – but only by those who haven't heard of the Capital Ring, an under-publicized 75-mile trail that begins and ends in Woolwich, and loops through Lewisham, Richmond, Greenford, Highgate and Hackney en route. It's neatly divided into fifteen sections, each of which can all be walked in an afternoon.

The route passes some recognized highlights of London, including the Thames Barrier and Wimbledon Common, but the fun lies in discovering areas you'd never otherwise visit, and getting a sense of the rich social history of the hinterland. Be honest: have you ever heard of Severndroog Castle, a Gothic tower on Shooters Hill built to remember a man who defeated a pirate king named Angrier? Or did you know that the Great North Wood, which once stretched from Camberwell to Croydon, lives on in patches such as Biggin Wood? You'll pass both of these as you trundle along the trail.

Although urban at times, most of the Capital Ring sticks closely to London's parks, fields and waterways. Along the way you'll follow the Grand Union Canal and the rivers Brent, Ravensbourne and Quaggy; you'll pass Walthamstow marshes, where the rare marsh warbler resides, and the nature reserve at Perivale Wood, home to over five hundred species of moth. Sometimes, the Ring throws up some delightful surprises: on the Highgate to Stoke Newington stretch, you've barely emerged from the underground station before you turn onto the 4.5-mile-long Parkland Walk, a disused railway line abandoned since 1970 and allowed to stay overgrown. Popular with walkers and cyclists, it's a magical place: a pathway left to nature in the middle of an ever-developing metropolis.

Navigation is never much of an issue on the Capital Ring as handy green signs point you along the way, and the designers even had the foresight to divert the path past cafés and pubs (for a quick coffee or pint) and toilets (for the inevitable consequence of said refreshments). The writer Cyril Connolly said: "No city should be too large for a man to walk out of in a morning." The good news is that thanks to the Capital Ring, you don't need to walk outside of London's boundaries for a true slice of escapism.

492 Heights and hairpins on the Hardknott Pass

Need to know From Ambleside, head towards the Langdale Valley to reach the Wrynose Pass. You might want to start your journey at the historic *Three Shires Inn*, a traditional staging post on the way to the high passes.

Map 4, D16

Tackling the almost impossible angles of the Hardknott Pass in the Lake District, you'll lock eyes with other drivers as you squeeze past each other on the zigzag single-lane track. Hands clenched to steering wheels, people tend to look a little wild-eyed at the prospect of the stony heights ahead, and the dizzying fell views below, with steep mountainsides dropping down to the deep and verdant valley bottom.

The first challenge is the Wrynose Pass, which climbs sharply from the long glacial Langdale Valley, leaving behind the snaking lines of stone dykes and stands of mature trees to enter more desolate and windswept terrain. The only vegetation is of the low and hardy variety, and rugged boulders edge the narrow road as it makes its dogged climb up the mountain wall. There's a brief respite before the next stage – the Hardknott Pass itself, which rears up at a gradient of one in three, making it a contender for the title of steepest road in England.

Although it's certainly not a good idea to be trapped on these precipitous roads in the dark, late afternoon is a wonderful time to make the drive: as you top the pass and begin to descend a series of perfect hairpin bends, the epic western fells which slope down to the Cumbrian coast are softened by the evening light. To the right on the descent, keep your eyes peeled for the Hardknott Roman Fort, whose still sturdy and imposing walls cut across the boggy hillside, providing a windbreak for Herdwick sheep.

Though the walls don't rise much above head height, with a bit of imagination and a hillside bird's-eye view it's just about possible to make out the shapes of the baths, parade ground, granaries and the once-grand commandant's house, built around 120 BC during the reign of Hadrian to protect the road from invasion from the north.

Take a moment to stand in Roman shoes in a place as wild and impressive – and almost as isolated – as it was two thousand years ago.

493 Coasting along the Atlantic Highway

Whether on four wheels or two, the grandly named Atlantic Highway provides a magnificent entry into Cornwall. Essentially, it's the more prosaically titled A39, one of the county's two arteries connecting it with the rest of the world, and bringing you within reach of fabulous coastline and some of the West Country's most enticing beaches.

The Atlantic Highway actually starts its journey on the empty, cliffy coast of Bideford Bay in Devon before plunging due south over the county line. Though the road rarely approaches the shore, the sea is usually within sight, a blue-grey ribbon of ocean that lends the journey its sense of excitement and anticipation. In fact the Highway comes as close to the sea as it ever will at Bude, the first town into Cornwall, which, while not particularly Cornish in character, possesses the two crucial characteristics of this whole coast: great beaches and pounding surf.

Below Bude, minor roads wander off to the more typically Cornish harbour village of Boscastle and the grim ruins of Tintagel Castle. It's difficult to ignore the Arthurian associations here (it's supposed to be the Once and Future King's birthplace), but you don't need to swallow the myth to appreciate the site's desolate splendour. West lies Padstow, hub of Rick Stein's food empire, and worth a stop for a slap-up fish supper. More A-star beaches lie all around, the kind favoured by certain heirs to the throne and in recent years the likes of the Right Hon. David Cameron, PM.

From Padstow it's a short hop to Newquay, capital of the surf scene and home to Cornwall's hottest nightlife. The A39 joins up with the A30 just west of here, but you could continue exploring the northern seaboard by carrying on down the A30 through the heart of Cornwall's mining country, the granite landscape dotted with ruined stacks and engine houses. Soon after, the road sweeps past the golden sands of Hayle Bay, beyond which lies St Ives, that quirky, almost Mediterranean-style resort that can't make up its mind whether to be a full-on beach town for the bucket-and-spade brigade or a centre for the arts, but does quite well at being both. The peninsula runs out just west of here at Land's End, the mainland's westernmost point. So turn about, and start back along the southern coast for a whole other experience.

Need to know Access the A39 Atlantic Highway from Barnstaple in Devon, reachable from the M5 via the A361. See ⓦ www.atlantic-highway.co.uk and ⓦ www.atlantic-heritage-coast. co.uk for more information.
Map 2, B6

494 Taking a spin on the Falkirk Wheel

The first thing you'll notice about the Falkirk Wheel is that it's not overly wheel-like in shape. Dominating the postindustrial landscape around the town of Falkirk, it looks more like a huge silvery claw, a visual echo of the mighty structures that turned the area into a powerhouse of the Industrial Revolution: Falkirk and its surrounds were once famous for the Carron Company, one of the largest ironworks in nineteenth-century Europe.

Opened in 2002, the wheel was designed to solve the problem of the 115-foot gap between the Union and Forth & Clyde canals. Back in the 1930s, before the canals went to rack and ruin, barges had to spend a tedious day passing though eleven locks. The resurgence of the canals as a playground for boaters brought the problem back into focus. The solution? A brilliantly engineered giant lift, which scoops a boat in one claw and an equal weight of water in the other. The simple process of rotating the perfectly weighted claws and depositing the boat in the other canal is said to use only the same energy that it takes to boil eight kettles.

And you can see this ingenuity close at hand on an hour-long trip that takes you in a specially designed boat for the sweeping ride from the basin outside the excellent visitor centre and up into the wheel. Your boat ascends in what's termed a gondola to join the Union Canal above, where you're deposited for a trip along an aqueduct and past the remains of the second-century Antonine Wall, built by the Romans as the northern frontier of their empire. From here, you make the return trip in the gondola to the basin.

A spin on the Falkirk Wheel may be the antithesis of a fairground ride – its progress is nothing if not stately – but it's surprisingly engaging for kids, and for anyone likely to enjoy seeing the Archimedean principal executed in steel on a truly impressive and elegant scale.

Need to know Boat trips (daily: April–Oct every 30min 9.30am–4.30pm; Nov–March hourly 10am–3pm; £7.95) can be booked online or at the Falkirk Wheel Visitor Centre (ⓣ 01324/619888, ⓦ www.thefalkirkwheel.co.uk; daily 9.30am–6pm.
Map 4, C14

495 In the footsteps of Chaucer: follow the Pilgrim's Way to Canterbury

Need to know The Chilham to Canterbury stretch of the Pilgrim's Way follows the North Downs Way (Ⓦ www. nationaltrail.co.uk/northdowns). In Chilham, stay in the *Woolpack Inn*'s converted stable block (Ⓣ 01227/730351, Ⓦ www. woolpackinnchilham.co.uk; doubles from £80), which is also the place to go for dinner.

Map 2, F6

The Garden of England is a tourist-board cliché, but one that does perfectly describe the lush country explored on the Pilgrim's Way. The landscape is domesticated but beautiful, with rolling vistas, apple and pear orchards and the odd scattering of tile-hung or half-timbered cottages. And you are following in some very ancient footsteps: this was an Iron Age trading route, acquiring its pilgrimage status only after the murder of Thomas Becket in 1170. The original Pilgrim's Way was an amalgam of country roads and paths leading from Winchester and serving pilgrims from south and west England and continental Europe (via Southampton). At Harbledown, just outside Canterbury, this route merged with Watling Street, the route for the main body of pilgrims from London and the north. All were bent on seeing Becket's gold- and jewel-encrusted tomb, buying indulgences and a badge as a token of their pilgrimage and, as Chaucer's *Canterbury Tales* testifies, having a bit of fun along the way.

This abundant countryside is especially appealing in April – when Chaucer set his tales and when the fruit trees are covered in blossom – or in late summer and early autumn, when they're heavy with fruit. You can make a selective two-day pilgrimage yourself, exploring a particularly bucolic stretch of the route, and arriving at the pilgrims' goal – magnificent Canterbury Cathedral. The walk begins at Charing in Kent, leading through woods and farmland to Boughton Lees, home to the *Flying Horse* pub which has been serving pilgrims for hundreds of years. From here you continue to idyllic Chilham where you can stay overnight at the friendly *Woolpack Inn* before hiking across fields and through dense woodland to Canterbury.

From a distance the city's cathedral rises quite ethereally from its medieval surrounds, but as you draw closer and your pilgrimage reaches its goal, what impresses is its colossal physical presence. The building totally dominates the otherwise slightly tatty townscape, and it's fascinating to speculate how miraculous the stately nave and soaring bell tower would have appeared to medieval visitors trekking in from the remote countryside.

There's little mention of the topography of the walk in the *Canterbury Tales*, so it hardly serves as a travelogue, but nonetheless it's quite fun to take the book with you on this walk. If you're put off by the (for most people) incomprehensible Middle English monty, pick up a copy of Nevill Coghill's rhythmic and vigorous modern verse offering – that should save you stumbling over too many wympuls and lordynges.

496 Up, up and away…and down, down deep in the ground at Matlock Bath

All dressed up in their tweeds and hobnail boots, the Victorian gentlemen who headed off to Matlock Bath by the trainload were prone to call this part of Derbyshire our "Little Switzerland" on account of its rearing hills, dense woods and the churning waters of the River Derwent. There may have been some exaggeration here perhaps, but as if in fulfilment of its early nickname, Matlock Bath now has its own cable car, whose six-seater glass and metal pods take a little more than five minutes to scuttle over the Derwent River Valley, pausing halfway along to swing gently in the breeze as passengers take in the panoramic view. It's all good fun, and you can expect an excited squeal from the kids long before the cable cars reach their destination, the Heights of Abraham, grandly named after a famous British military victory over the French in Canada.

From the cable car's top station, it's the briefest of strolls to several attractions, including the Explorers' Challenge, a first-rate adventure playground, and the stone Prospect Tower, from which there are fine views over the surrounding countryside. There's also a fossil shop where you can buy some of the semi-precious stones for which the area is famous, but the best thing about the Heights is the guided trip underground down to the dark, dank and dripping Great Masson Cavern. Lead has been mined here at Masson Hill – as the Heights were originally known – for hundreds of years, but in the early 1800s the miners hit water, flooding their best seams and putting themselves out of work. Yet, what might have been a disaster was soon turned to the miners' advantage: one bright spark or another decided to pioneer an early sort of adventure tourism, lowering visitors down into the old lead workings by rope and even installing a crude chandelier to help light the way.

Need to know The Heights of Abraham, Matlock Bath, Derbyshire Ⓣ 01629/582365, Ⓦ www.heightsofabraham.com. Open daily Feb half-term, late March to Oct 10am–4.30pm; £11.50. It's an easy five-minute walk to the cable car's lower station from Matlock Bath train station.

Map 3, C10

497 Single track inclined: Wester Ross by road

Granted, the prospect of a British road trip mightn't evoke the infinite horizons of its American cousin, yet it's all a question of perspective. What this island lacks in expanse it often makes up in its ever wuthering heights, not least in the wilds of Wester Ross.

Driving down the A890 from the Ross-shire gateway village of Achnasheen to pretty, whitewashed Lochcarron, you may well wonder how they managed to build roads here at all, never mind the parallel Kyle of Lochalsh railway line. Many years ago, Michael Palin passed this way filming his *Great Railway Journeys of the World*, though Glen Carron's contrasting flanks and its pockets of pine, birch and broom are perhaps more viscerally experienced at the wheel, on tarmac, in the slightly queasy knowledge that you're driving along a geological fault line.

Even this pales, though, in comparison to the Bealach-na-Bà (Pass of the Cattle). At over two thousand feet, it's one of the highest road summits in Britain, the dramatic legacy of an old drove road that sheers off the A896 – itself a continuation of the A890 – just north of Kishorn. You won't see any trains here, just the sphinx-like mountains and glacial valleys of the Applecross Peninsula. It's a breathlessly remote and beautiful drive with all the random uncertainty of a single-track road, plus relentless hairpins and gradients that'll test the limits of your gearbox – not, as a rather stern sign makes clear, one for the L-plates. However confident you are behind the wheel, the adrenaline and the awe will likely still be coursing through your system by the time you descend an hour or so later into Applecross itself, a perfect place to catch your breath and a bite to eat.

From here a far less daunting single-track road clings to the coast for the entirety of the peninsula's northern perimeter, skirting the depths of the Inner Sound and the shores of Loch Torridon before rejoining the A896 near Shieldaig. Hebridean horizon gives way to primeval rockscape as the road swings northeast under the ramparts of the Torridon range, past Kinlochewe and back to Achnasheen, nigh-on a hundred of the most dizzying miles you'll ever clock up.

Need to know Achnasheen is located approximately fifty miles northwest of Inverness. See Ⓦ www.celticfringe.org.uk, Ⓦ www.applecross.info, Ⓦ www. lochcarron.org.uk and Ⓦ www. visittorridon.co.uk for details of the places passed along the route.
Map 5, C19

498 Flying into Barra and beyond

BE6855 is perhaps the oddest scheduled domestic flight in Britain. It is a twenty-seater propeller plane that takes off daily from Glasgow and lands an hour later directly on the beach at the island of Barra. There is no airstrip, nor are there even any lights on the sand, and the flight times shift to fit in with the tide tables, because at high tide the runway is submerged. It's probably also the only flight in the UK on which the person who demonstrates the safety procedures then turns around, gets into the cockpit and flies the plane.

Even if Barra were a dreary destination, the flight would be worth taking simply for the views it gives of Scotland's beautiful west coast and the islands of Mull, Skye, Rum and Eigg. But take some time to explore Barra itself, just eight miles long by four miles wide. Visually, the island is a stunner, with white-sand beaches, backed by machair, and barren rocky mountains which offer superb walking; and Barra's history is writ large on the landscape, with an atmospheric medieval island-fortress, Bronze Age burial site and a remarkable hamlet of Iron Age roundhouses exposed during a storm in 2005.

Barra is the southernmost island of the hundred-mile-long archipelago of the Western Isles, the only part of Britain – and one of only a few in the world – where you can experience a truly stunning landscape in solitude; there are a million exquisitely beautiful acres here, with a population that would leave Old Trafford stadium two-thirds empty. Give yourself a week to drive slowly up through the island chain, from Barra to Eriskay, site of the famous "Whisky Galore" shipwreck (both the real and the fictional one), then South Uist to Benbecula, to North Uist, and finally to Harris and Lewis. Some islands are linked by causeways (all of which have "Beware: Otters Crossing" traffic signs), others by car ferries. Stop if you can at *Scarista House*, a gourmet paradise set alongside a vast, perpetually empty white sandy beach in the midst of a walker's Eden.

Need to know Flights can be booked on Ⓦ www.flybe.com. See Ⓦ www.isleofbarra.com for more about Barra and Ⓦ www.scaristahouse.com for info on *Scarista House*.

Map5, A20

499 Hiking the Pennine Way

After two weeks' walking through rain and shine (and with moods to match), the final day of the Pennine Way, Britain's oldest and longest long-distance footpath, is upon you: a 27-mile marathon over the desolate Cheviot Hills. It's a challenging finale but the narcotic effects of mounting euphoria ought to numb your multiple aches. Anyway, if you're one of the few who've made it this far, you'll not give up now.

The Pennine Way begins at the village of Edale in the Peak District and meanders 270 miles north to Kirk Yetholm beneath the Cheviots, a mile across the Scottish border. Along its course, it leads through some of England's most beautiful and least crowded countryside. In the early stages, it passes the birthplace of the Industrial Revolution – today, stone slabs from the derelict mills and factories have been recycled into winding causeways over the once notorious moorland peat bogs. This is Brontë country, too, grim on a dank, misty day but bleakly inspiring when the cloud lifts.

The mires subside to become the rolling green pastures and dry-stone walls of the Yorkshire Dales that rise up to striking peaks like the 2278ft-high Pen-y-ghent – the "Mountain of the Winds".

The limestone Dales in turn become the wilder northern Pennines, where no one forgets stumbling onto the astounding glaciated abyss of High Cup Nick. The Way's final phase begins with an invigorating stage along Hadrian's Wall before ending with the calf-wrenching climax over the Cheviots.

Walking the wilds is exhilarating but staying in pretty villages along the way is also a highlight. Again and again you'll find yourself transported back to a bygone rural idyll of village shops, church bells and, of course, pubs. Memories of mud and glory will pass before your eyes as you stagger the last few yards onto Kirk Yetholm's village green, stuff your reviled backpack in the bin and turn towards the inviting bar at the *Border Hotel*.

Need to know See ⓦ www.nationaltrail.co.uk/pennineway for more information. Most people walk the Way in two to three weeks, covering twelve to twenty miles per day.
Map 3, C10–Map 4, E15

500 End to End: Land's End to John O'Groats

People have used their feet (both running and walking), cars, motorbikes, public transport, bicycles, tricycles, unicycles, skateboards, wheelchairs and even a motorized bathtub. Some do it in fancy dress and at least one courageous fellow – "the naked rambler" – has done it in nothing more than a hat and pair of walking boots. It's attracted everyone from schoolchildren to celebs. Most do it for charity, some for competition, others simply to say they've done it.

It is, of course, Land's End to John O'Groats, Britain's most epic journey. By road, it's something like 900 miles, while off-road walkers will cover upwards of 1200. It generally takes cyclists around two weeks to complete (though astonishingly the record stands at little over 44 hours); for walkers, it's more like two or three months – and a lot of blisters.

The earliest records of people attempting the route – or more accurately routes, as there are plenty of different ways to attack it – date from the 1800s, and since then it's been completed by tens of thousands. Which is not to say that it is not a challenge: the Scottish leg of the journey involves an overall ascent of almost 27,000ft, the equivalent of Mount Everest.

Gruelling it may be – and the sense of achievement you feel when you arrive is immense – but if you arrive at John O'Groats and feel slightly underwhelmed by its souvenir shops and coach parties, you wouldn't be the first. So a word to the wise: press on east beyond the crowds to Duncansby Head, the real end of the road, which with its lighthouse, spectacular cliffs and sea stacks is a much more fitting end to your odyssey.

All that remains, then, is to plan the return trip. If you're a glutton for punishment, then dramatic Cape Wrath or Durness Head, in the northwest, down to Dover (the D2D, as opposed to the E2E) is the only one to consider. And of course from Dover you can hop across the Channel for another expedition. But then that's a different book altogether...

Need to know The Land's End–John O'Groats Association (ⓦ www.landsend-johnogroats -assoc.com) and the Land's End–John O'Groats Club (ⓦ www.endtoenders.co.uk) both offer advice and support for people who want to make the journey.
Map 2, A7–Map 5, D18

MAPS

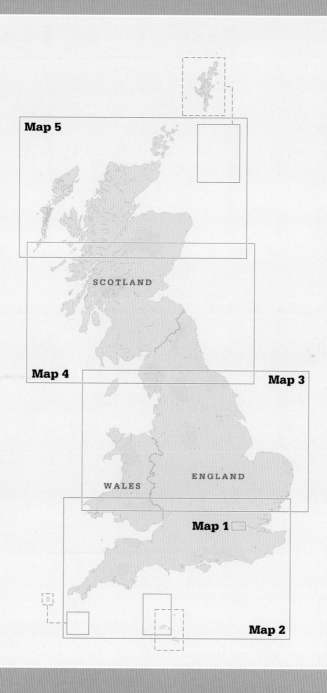

Key

Map 1

A | B | C

Fishguard

St David's

PEMBROKESHIRE

Pembrokeshire Coast National Park

Haverfordwest

Milford Haven

Pembroke

Tenby

CARMARTHENSHIRE

Carmarthen

Laugharne

Llanelli

Pontardawe

Swansea

Neath

Port Talbot

Pontypridd

Porthcawl

Bridgend

Llandovery

Llandeilo

POWYS

Brecon

Brecon Beacons National Park

Crickhowell

Merthyr Tydfil

Ebbw Vale

Caerphilly

Pontypool

Newport

Barry

Cardiff

Portishead

Clevedon

Avonmouth

Weston-super-Mare

Burnham-on-Sea

Shepton Mallet

Bridgwater

Glastonbury

Taunton

Wellington

Chard

SOMERSET

Yeovil

Sherborne

HEREFORDSHIRE

Ross-on-Wye

Glouc

GLOUCESTER

Abergavenny

Monmouth

Chepstow

Bristol

217

242

161

222

292

244

344

315

353

306

185

365

035

056

346

433

146

478

079

357

389

454

427

429

489

241

148

432

094

205

127

410

134

453

025

032

112

401

Channel Islands

Alderney

Guernsey

St. Peter Port

Le Manoir

Sark

302

Jersey

131

279

St Helier

249

263 Ilfracombe

305

247 328

493

Barnstaple

Bideford

Dulverton

Exmoor National Park

Lynton

177

Minehead

Bridgwater

238

Tiverton

289

Cullompton

Honiton

Wellington

DEVON

Bude

Okehampton

Exeter

Lyme Regis

157 Burton Bradstock

Dorchester

335

Weymouth

171

282

345

123

Sidmouth

Exmouth

Dawlish

Teignmouth

Newton Abbot

Dartmoor National Park

Moretonhampstead

087

215

425

304

299

291

Wadebridge

Padstow

Bodmin

309

190

198

Newquay

CORNWALL

St Austell

034

422

382 Truro

Redruth

470

St Ives

153

484

184

Penzance

Helston

500

313

354

The Lizard

098

168

163

Falmouth

258

054

Liskeard

Saltash

Launceston

Tavistock

Buckfastleigh

Plymouth

318

Torquay

Paignton

Brixham

364

Isles of Scilly

St Martin's

Bryher

Tresco

314

201 484 330

St Mary's

St Agnes

A | B | C

Map 2

Map 3

Key

001 Cycling Manchester Velodrome
010 Shopping in Manchester
011 Cycling the Black Country's canals
012 Sheffield Ski Village
015 Punting on the Cam
017 Lincoln's Christmas market
018 Historic Chester
019 Williamson Tunnels
024 Harrogate Turkish baths
028 Imperial War Museum North
039 Warwick Castle
041 Rushton Triangular Lodge
043 Wainhouse Tower, Halifax
049 Snowshill Manor
051 Birmingham's Back-to-Backs
052 Stowe
053 Plas Mawr
057 Castell Dinas Brân
058 Penrhyn Castle
059 Caernarfon Castle
060 Chatsworth
061 Stokesay Castle
062 The National Memorial Arboretum
063 Cheshire's gardens of distinction
064 Fountains Abbey
074 Fat Rascals at Bettys
076 British Asparagus Festival
078 Pontefract Liquorice Festival
080 Aldeburgh Food & Drink Festival
085 Ludlow: Slow Food capital
088 Leeds Corn Exchange
090 Ye Old Trip to Jerusalem
091 Wensleydale Creamery
092 Pudding Club, Mickleton
093 Dockers' pubs in Liverpool
100 Britain's smallest pub: The Nutshell
101 Herefordshire cider, Much Marcle
103 Stilton cheese
104 Yorkshire's Rhubarb Triangle
105 Hand-crafting a pork pie
106 Foraging in Wales
107 A pint in the Dyffryn Arms

109 The Balti Triangle
111 Lancashire's perfect chippies
116 Sutton Hoo
122 Imperial War Museum Duxford
125 Peter Rabbit: Hill Top
126 The Mini Festival, Gaydon
130 Seaside fun at Bridlington
132 Portmeirion
135 Soar-y-Mynydd Chapel
136 Tewkesbury Medieval Festival
139 Ironbridge
142 Wartime Weekend in Ramsbottom
143 Tudor re-creations at Kentwell Hall
150 Bressingham Steam and Gardens
151 The Pendle Witches Trail
154 Caving around Castleton
155 Husky rides, Thetford Forest
158 Swimming in the River Waveney
159 Swimming at Llyn Idwal
164 Gliding at Sutton Bank
172 Tryfan
175 Stanage Edge
176 Mountain biking in Coed-y-Brenin
178 Canoeing on the River Wye
180 Boating on the Norfolk Broads
186 Whitewater rafting in Bala
187 Paddleboarding in The Fens
191 Fforestcamp, Cardigan
193 Underleigh House, Hope
196 Appleton Water Tower
209 Cley Windmill, Holt
209 Devonshire Arms, Bolton Abbey
210 Under the Thatch
211 Langar Hall
212 Pen-y-Dyffryn Country Hotel
216 Lavenham Priory
221 Hipping Hall, Kirkby Lonsdale
225 The Temple, Badger
226 Seals at Blakeney Point
230 Orford Ness Nature Reserve
234 Malham Cove
235 Geology in the Peak District
239 Widdale Red Squirrel Reserve

246 Minsmere RSPB Reserve
248 Norfolk Lavender
252 The Calf of Man
253 Dolphin-spotting in Cardigan Bay
254 Wwoofing in Norfolk
255 Centre for Alternative Technology
257 Spotting daffodils, Woodland Trust
259 Pistyll Rhaeadr waterfall
262 Jorvik Viking Centre
270 Manchester Art Gallery
272 Magna
274 Thomas at Kirklees Light Railway
276 The Forbidden Corner
277 Africa Alive!
278 The Deep
284 Eureka!
285 Preseli Venture
286 Jimmy's Farm
287 Bewilderwood
288 Shambala Festival
290 Oblivion at Alton Towers
293 Tatton Park
295 North Norfolk Coastal Path
298 Pembrokeshire Coast Path
301 Exploring Southwold
303 Sauce-free seaside at Filey
311 Shingle Street
312 Cliché-free Blackpool
320 Holkham beach
321 Crosby beach
325 Llandudno's Great Orme
327 Bardsey Island
333 Tŷ Coch Inn, Port Dinllaen
338 York Mystery Plays
341 The Railway Children, Haworth
350 Comedy at The Frog and Bucket
352 Birmingham Royal Ballet
359 The Electric Cinema
360 Kinema in the Woods
367 Shakespeare's Stratford
369 Fab Four folklore in Liverpool
374 Point-to-point at Hornby Castle
375 The Cotswold Olimpicks

379 Archery in Sherwood Forest
388 Shrovetide football, Ashbourne
390 Grand National, Aintree
392 Isle of Man TT Races
393 Race the train, Talyllyn Railway
394 Racing around Silverstone
400 World Coal Carrying Championships
404 Bog-snorkelling, Llanwrtyd Wells
406 Gravy-wrestling, Stacksteads
409 Black Pudding Throwing, Ramsbottom
413 The Great Yorkshire Show
414 Llangollen International Eisteddfod
415 Diwali in Leicester
417 Hay Festival
418 Aldeburgh Festival
419 Robin Hood Festival
426 Chinese New Year, Liverpool
430 Cambridge Folk Festival
431 Download Festival
434 Secret Garden Party
438 The Sainsbury Centre, UEA
442 Hockney at Salts Mill
445 The Scallop, Aldeburgh
447 The Singing, Ringing Tree, Burnley
451 The Ship of the Fens: Ely Cathedral
452 The Lowry, Salford
459 Yorkshire Sculpture Park
463 New Art Exchange
465 The stained glass of York Minster
467 Andrew Logan Museum of Sculpture
469 Blackwell, The Arts & Crafts House
473 Snowdon Mountain Railway
476 Jack Mytton Way
477 Ferry 'cross the Mersey
478 Offa's Dyke Path
479 Settle to Carlisle Railway
481 Narrowboating Llangollen Canal
485 Walking across Morecambe Bay
486 Ffestiniog Railway
487 Isle of Man Steam Railway
496 North York Moors Railway
496 Heights of Abraham cable car
499 The Pennine Way

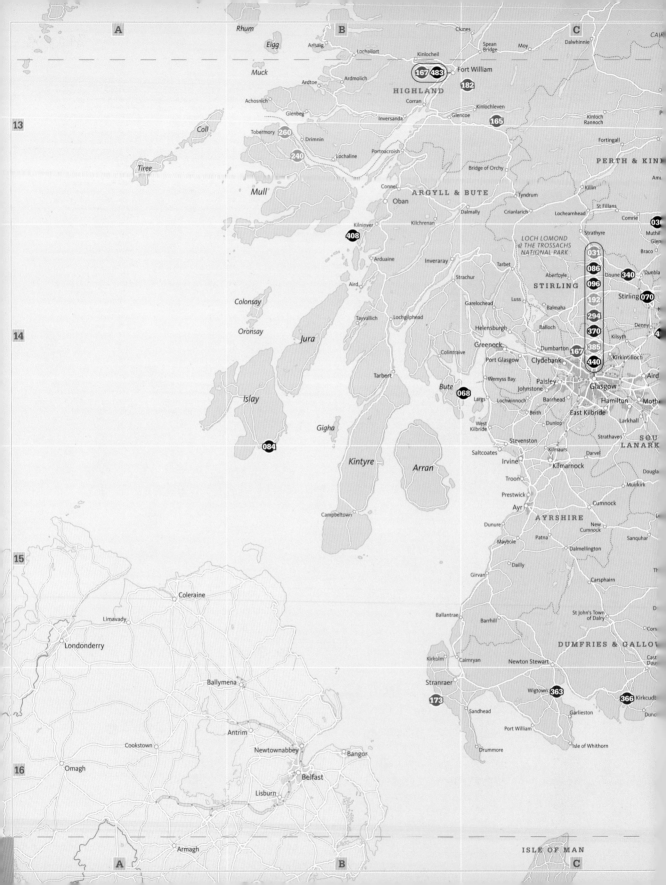

Map 4

Key

003 Out on the Toon	188 Tubing in Pitlochry	363 Wigtown: Scotland's book town
014 Arthur's Seat	189 Honister Slate Mine's Via Ferrata	366 Wicker Man country
029 Ghost tours in Auld Reekie	192 Hotel du Vin	368 Evensong at Durham Cathedral
031 Glasgow's club scene	195 La Rosa, Whitby	370 Sharmanka Kinetic Theatre
036 Drummond Castle Gardens	208 The Old School B&B	372 The Great North Run
044 The National Monument, Calton Hill	213 Staying at Durham Castle	376 Playing golf at St Andrews
048 Traquair House	218 The Balmoral	385 The Old Firm derby: Celtic vs Rangers
065 Alnwick Poison Garden	222 Augill Castle, Kirkby Stephen	395 Cumberland and Westmorland wrestling
068 Mount Stuart	228 The Devil's Beef Tub	407 Gurning championships, Egremont
069 Dawyck Botanic Garden	236 Lake District Osprey Project	408 Stone-skimming, Easdale
070 Stirling Castle	237 Salmon Viewing Centre, Ettrick Weir	411 Hogmanay
072 Cragside	240 Mull Eagle Watch	412 Appleby Horse Fair
084 Islay's whisky distilleries	243 Chillingham Wild Cattle Park	421 Whitby Gothic Weekends
086 Glasgow's ice-cream parlours	256 Dry-stone walling in Northumberland	423 The Common Ridings
096 Deep-fried heaven in Glasgow	260 Whale watching in Mull	424 Edinburgh Fringe
102 Arbroath Smokie	266 Linlithgow Palace	435 T in the Park
110 Tibbie Shiels Inn	267 Seven Stories	437 Art on the Tyne: Baltic
117 The Bond Museum, Keswick	271 Our Dynamic Earth	440 Glasgow School of Art
128 Vindolanda	294 Pantomime in Glasgow	443 The Angel of the North
129 Fife's Secret Bunker	300 Fife Coastal Path	449 Rosslyn Chapel
141 Beamish	307 Surfing at Saltburn-by-the-Sea	450 The Pitmen Painters
145 Hartlepool's Maritime Experience	316 Bamburgh beach	456 Jupiter Artland
160 Swimming in Crummock Water	332 Northumberland's castle coast	458 Gallery of Modern Art
162 Cycling the Four Abbeys Route	337 Wordsworth country	462 Middlesborough Institute of Modern Art
165 Scotland's ski resorts	340 Monty Python, Doune Castle	479 Settle to Carlisle Railway
166 Hadrian's Wall Path	347 Harry Potter, Alnwick Castle	483 Sleeper train to the Highlands
167 West Highland Way	348 Withnail & I, Sleddale Hall	492 Hardknott Pass
170 Helvellyn	361 Tyneside Cinema	494 The Falkirk Wheel
173 Southern Upland Way		499 The Pennine Way
182 Ice climbing Ben Nevis		

Map 5

Key

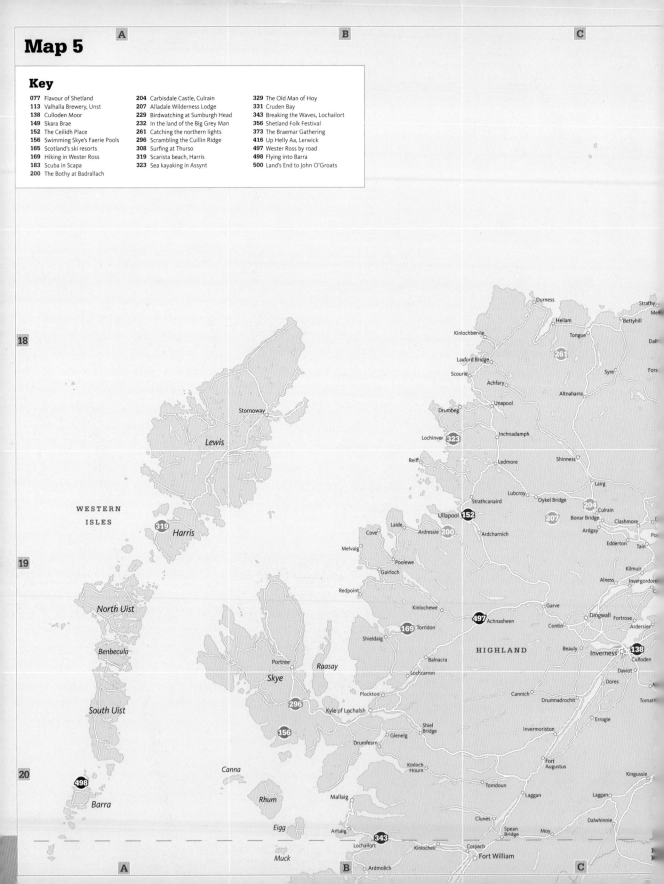

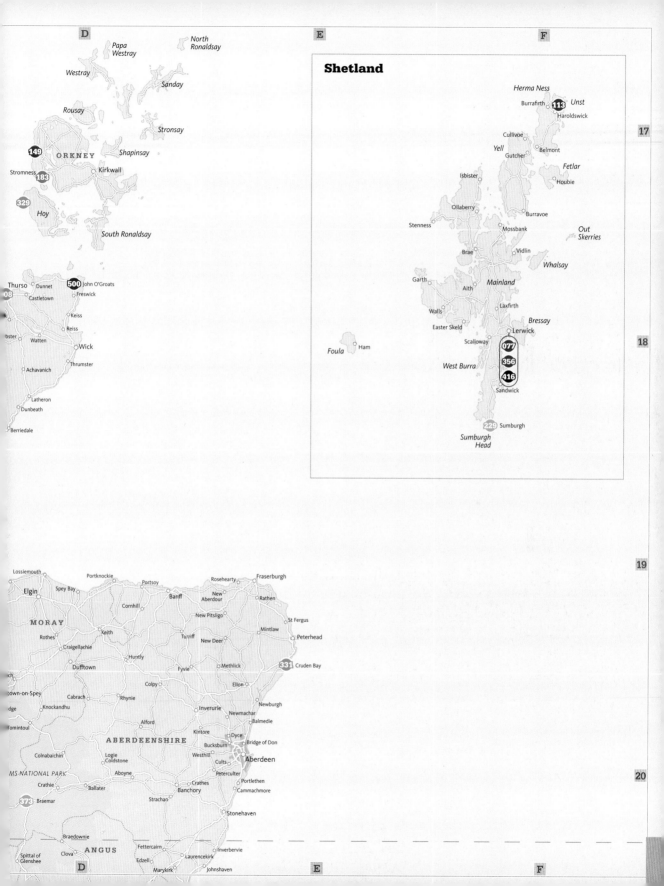

AUTHOR CREDITS

1. Escape to the city

1. Ann-Marie Shaw
2. Samantha Cook
3. Lucy White
4. Matthew Hancock
5. Lara Kavanagh
6. Lara Kavanagh
7. Lara Kavanagh
8. Lara Kavanagh
9. Lara Kavanagh
10. Ann-Marie Shaw
11. Phil Lee
12. Jos Simon
13. Nicholas Jones
14. Brendon Griffin
15. Emma Gregg
16. Phil Lee
17. Rob Crossan
18. Rob Crossan
19. James McConnachie
20. James McConnachie
21. James McConnachie
22. James McConnachie
23. James McConnachie
24. James McConnachie
25. James McConnachie
26. Joanna Kirby
27. Lucy Cowie
28. Stephen Keeling
29. Shafik Meghji
30. Samantha Cook
31. Jay Richardson
32. Keith Drew

2. To the manor born

33. Edward Aves
34. James Rice
35. Emma Gregg
36. Helena Smith
37. Emma Gregg
38. Samantha Cook
39. Shafik Meghji
40. James McConnachie
41. James McConnachie
42. James McConnachie
43. James McConnachie
44. James McConnachie
45. James McConnachie
46. Andy Turner
47. Alice Park
48. Helena Smith
49. Robert Andrews
50. Emma Gibbs
51. Phil Lee
52. Gavin Thomas
53. Shafik Meghji
54. James Rice
55. Paul Whitfield
56. Paul Whitfield
57. Paul Whitfield
58. Paul Whitfield
59. Paul Whitfield
60. Jules Brown

61. Helena Smith
62. Annabelle Thorpe
63. Rob Crossan
64. Jules Brown
65. Robin Tudge
66. James McConnachie
67. Keith Drew
68. Helena Smith
69. Brendon Griffin
70. Stephen Keeling
71. Emma Gregg
72. Jules Brown

3. Eat, drink and be merry

73. Steven Vickers
74. Lucy White
75. Edward Aves
76. Jules Brown
77. Jules Brown
78. Jules Brown
79. Jules Brown
80. Jules Brown
81. Rob Crossan
82. James Rice
83. Andy Turner
84. Brendon Griffin
85. Rob Crossan
86. Brendon Griffin
87. Hayley Spurway
88. Jos Simon
89. Monica Woods
90. Shafik Meghji
91. Lucy White
92. Keith Drew
93. Rob Crossan
94. Keith Drew
95. James McConnachie
96. Jay Richardson
97. Lara Kavanagh
98. James Rice
99. Lucy White
100. Phil Lee
101. Matthew Hancock
102. Matthew Hancock
103. Matthew Hancock
104. Matthew Hancock
105. Matthew Hancock
106. Alison Roberts
107. Paul Whitfield
108. Andrew Humphries
109. Shafik Meghji
110. Brendon Griffin
111. Rob Crossan
112. Lucy Cowie
113. Rob Crossan

4. The good old days

114. Gavin Thomas
115. Lara Kavanagh
116. Stephen Keeling
117. Steven Vickers
118. Steven Vickers

119. Steven Vickers
120. Steven Vickers
121. Steven Vickers
122. Steven Vickers
123. Steven Vickers
124. Steven Vickers
125. Steven Vickers
126. Steven Vickers
127. Diana Jarvis
128. Keith Drew
129. Brendon Griffin
130. Jules Brown
131. Emma Gregg
132. Paul Whitfield
133. Lara Kavanagh
134. Emma Gregg
135. Paul Whitfield
136. Shafik Meghji
137. Matthew Hancock
138. Brendon Griffin
139. Annabelle Thorpe
140. Emma Beatson
141. Jules Brown
142. Jules Brown
143. Jules Brown
144. Jules Brown
145. Jules Brown
146. Paul Whitfield
147. Emma Gregg
148. Keith Drew
149. Helena Smith
150. Edward Aves
151. Edward Aves
152. Helena Smith

5. Thrills and spills

153. Hayley Spurway
154. Luke Waterson
155. Martin Dunford
156. James Stewart
157. James Stewart
158. James Stewart
159. James Stewart
160. James Stewart
161. Alf Alderson
162. Brendon Griffin
163. Hayley Spurway
164. Alf Alderson
165. Brendon Griffin
166. Brendon Griffin
167. Brendon Griffin
168. Brendon Griffin
169. Brendon Griffin
170. Brendon Griffin
171. Brendon Griffin
172. Brendon Griffin
173. Brendon Griffin
174. Brendon Griffin
175. Brendon Griffin
176. Hayley Spurway
177. Rob Andrews
178. Helena Smith
179. James Stewart
180. Martin Dunford

181. Emma Gregg
182. Alf Alderson
183. Sorrel Cosens
184. Lucy White
185. James Stewart
186. James Stewart
187. James Stewart
188. Jay Richardson
189. Jules Brown

6. Forty winks

190. Hayley Spurway
191. James Stewart
192. Helena Smith
193. Annabelle Thorpe
194. Steven Vickers
195. Steven Vickers
196. Steven Vickers
197. Steven Vickers
198. Steven Vickers
199. Steven Vickers
200. Steven Vickers
201. Steven Vickers
202. Steven Vickers
203. Steven Vickers
204. Helena Smith
205. Keith Drew
206. Claire Saunders
207. Helena Smith
208. Lucy White
209. Jules Brown
210. Emma Gregg
211. Charlotte Melville
212. Annabelle Thorpe
213. Lucy White
214. Natasha Foges
215. Hayley Spurway
216. Steven Vickers
217. Natasha Foges
218. Natasha Foges
219. Natasha Foges
220. Natasha Foges
221. Natasha Foges
222. Jules Brown
223. Steven Vickers
224. James Stewart
225. Annabelle Thorpe

7. The birds and the bees

226. Stephen Keeling
227. Róisín Cameron
228. Brendon Griffin
229. Jay Richardson
230. Edward Aves
231. Róisín Cameron
232. Brendon Griffin
233. Emma Gregg
234. Jules Brown
235. Alf Alderson
236. Jules Brown
237. Matthew Hancock
238. Matthew Hancock

239. Matthew Hancock
240. Matthew Hancock
241. Matthew Hancock
242. Edward Aves
243. Matthew Hancock
244. Matthew Hancock
245. Matthew Hancock
246. Edward Aves
247. Rob Andrews
248. Stephen Keeling
249. Hayley Spurway
250. James McConnachie
251. Brendon Griffin
252. Jules Brown
253. Alf Alderson
254. Melanie Kramers
255. Melanie Kramers
256. Melanie Kramers
257. Melanie Kramers
258. Melanie Kramers
259. James Stewart
260. Alison Roberts
261. Brendon Griffin

8. Are we nearly there yet?

262. Jules Brown
263. Hayley Spurway
264. Lara Kavanagh
265. Andy Turner
266. Helena Smith
267. Lucy White
268. Hayley Spurway
269. Hayley Spurway
270. Hayley Spurway
271. Hayley Spurway
272. Hayley Spurway
273. Emma Gibbs
274. Jos Simon
275. Hayley Spurway
276. Jules Brown
277. Hayley Spurway
278. Hayley Spurway
279. Hayley Spurway
280. Hayley Spurway
281. Hayley Spurway
282. Emma Gregg
283. Kathryn Lane
284. Jos Simon
285. Hayley Spurway
286. Kathryn Lane
287. Martin Dunford
288. Kathryn Lane
289. Hayley Spurway
290. Steven Vickers
291. Hayley Spurway
292. Emma Gregg
293. Ann-Marie Shaw
294. Helena Smith

9. The Sea, the Sea

295. Helena Smith
296. Alf Alderson

PICTURE CREDITS

Front cover Sandcastle and beach huts, Southwold © Polka Dot Images/Photolibrary **Back cover** Up Helly Aa, Shetland © Doug Houghton/Alamy. Hiker at Stanage Edge, Peak District © Ben Osborne/Getty. Wales Millennium Centre, Cardiff © UK City Images/Alamy. Mountain biking at Cwmcarn, Newport © Seb Rogers/Alamy **Outside front flap** New Year swim, Edinburgh © Jeff J Mitchell/Getty Images. St Non's Head, Pembrokeshire © Rough Guides/Diana Jarvis. Ingleborough, Yorkshire Dales © Ian Cumming/Axiom. Puppets © Little Angel Puppet Theatre **Inside back cover** Bournemouth beach © Rough Guides/Diana Jarvis. British Museum © Rough Guides/Mark Thomas. Salts Mill © Rough Guides/Diana Jarvis. Bonfire Night in Lewes © Rough Guides/Mark Thomas. Cricket at Bamburgh Castle © Rough Guides/Tim Draper. Seals at Blakeney Point © Alan Spencer Norfolk/Alamy. Notting Hill Carnival © Rough Guides/Demetrio Carrasco. Glencoe © Peter Chisholm/Alamy. Ice cream © Rough Guides/Diana Jarvis. Surfing at Rhossili beach © Rough Guides/Scott Stickland. Bridlington harbour © Rough Guides/Diana Jarvis. York Minster © Rough Guides/Diana Jarvis. Puffins © Christina Bollen/Getty/Photolibrary. Bettys Tearooms, Harrogate © Rough Guides/Diana Jarvis

Introduction

Picnicking on the South Downs © Irek/4Corners Images. Notting Hill Carnival © Timothy Allen/Axiom. Derwent Water © Latitudestock/Getty Images. Clowns, Edinburgh © Scott Barbour/Getty Images. Perran Bay, Newquay © John Harper/Corbis

1. Escape to the city

Introduction View from St Paul's Cathedral © Mark Thomas **001** National Cycling Centre, Manchester © Anthony Collins/Alamy **004** Spinnaker Tower © Rough Guides/Diana Jarvis **005** Teacher and blackboard © The Ragged School Museum **008** Bethnal Green Working Men's Club © Tom Medwell **009** 40 Winks interior © Aliona Adrianova **010** Trafford Centre, Manchester © Ashley Cooper/Alamy **013** Isle of Dogs © Scott Robin Barbour/Getty Images **014** Arthur's Seat © Dan Tucker/Alamy **015** Punting on the Cam © Rough Guides/Tim Draper **017** Lincoln Christmas market © Roy Childs/Alamy **018** Chester © Colin Palmer/Alamy **021** Oxford colleges © Rough Guides/Chloe Roberts **023** Exterior of Trumper's © Trumper's **026** Martini © Dukes Bar **027** Dubstep in London © Jamie Baker/Everynight **028** Imperial War Museum North © Rough Guides/Tim Draper **030** The British Museum © Rough Guides/Mark Thomas **032** Aerial view over Bath © David Williams/Getty Images

2. To the manor born

Introduction Bodiam Castle © Tim Gartside/Alamy **033** Bedroom at Dennis Severs' House

© Tim Gartside/Dennis Severs' House **036** Drummond Castle Gardens © Nagele Stock/Alamy **037** Royal Pavilion, Brighton © Rough Guides/Tim Draper **038** Dining Room, Sir John Soane's Museum © The Sir John Soane's Museum **044** The National Monument, Edinburgh © David Robertson/Alamy **045** Rose garden, Mottisfont Abbey © Craig Roberts/Photolibrary **046** Bodiam Castle © Jon Arnold Images/Photolibrary **049** Snowshill Manor © Rob Andrews **050** Hampton Court Palace © Rough Guides/Mark Thomas **051** Hurst Street, Birmingham Back-to-Backs © Trinity Mirror/Alamy **053** Plas Mawr © Rough Guides/Paul Whitfield **054** The Maze, Glendurgan Gardens © Magnus/Alamy **056** Carreg Cennen Castle (thumbnail) © Rough Guides/Diana Jarvis **059** Caernarfon Castle (main picture) © Rough Guides/Diana Jarvis **060** Chatsworth House and grounds © Raymond Boswell/Alamy **061** Stokesay Castle © TLL Images/Alamy **062** The National Memorial Arboretum © Rosemary Roberts/Alamy **064** Fountains Abbey © Michael Rose/Alamy **065** The Poison Garden © Alnwick Castle **069** Dawyck Botanic Garden © Dawyck Gardens **070** Stirling Castle © David Robertson/Alamy

3. Eat, drink and be merry

Introduction Full English breakfast © Tim Hall/Getty Images **074** Bettys Tearooms © Rough Guides/Diana Jarvis **075** Borough Market © Justin Lightley/Getty Images **079** Great British Cheese Festival, Cardiff © Jeff Morgan/Alamy **082** Great British Beer Festival © Jonathan Goldberg/Alamy **083** Seafood list, Whitstable © Rough Guides/Diana Jarvis; oysters, Whitstable © Rough Guides/Diana Jarvis; boat, Whitstable © Rough Guides/Diana Jarvis **084** Whisky © Andrew McCandish/Alamy **087** The Seafood Restaurant, Padstow © Rough Guides/Tim Draper **088** Leeds Corn Exchange © Rough Guides/Diana Jarvis **089** Billingsgate Market © Adrian Arbib/Alamy **091** *A Grand Day Out with Wallace and Gromit* © NFTS 1989 **092** Puddings © The Pudding Club **095** Watercress © Rough Guides/Diana Jarvis **097** E Pellicci © Eleanor Farmer **098** Cornish pasties © Rough Guides/Tim Draper **099** Kent winery © Jon Wyand/Photolibrary **100** The Nutshell pub, Bury St Edmunds © Edward Aves **105** Pork pies © Jon Arnold Images/Alamy **106** Wild garlic © Chris Howes/Alamy **107** Bessie and Dyffryn Arms interior © Rough Guides/Paul Whitfield **108** Quail jelly, truffle toast and oak film strip © A. Palmer Watts/The Fat Duck **110** Tibbie Shiels Inn © David Kilpatrick/Alamy **111** Fish and chips © Rough Guides/Tim Draper

4. The good old days

Introduction Sutton Hoo mask © Brian Harris/Alamy **114** Bekonscot Model Village © Biblio Photography/Alamy **115** Chap © The Chap Olympiad **117** Sean Connery as James Bond © Bettman/Corbis **118** Royal Ascot © Adrian Dennis/Getty Images **122** Spitfire © Linda Kennedy/Alamy **123** Cup of tea © ICP/Alamy **126** Jean Shrimpton in a Mini © Duffy/Getty Images **127** Cerne

Abbas giant © Rough Guides/Diana Jarvis **130** Bridlington rock; Bridlington Harbour; Bridlington donkeys © Rough Guides/Diana Jarvis **132** Portmeirion © Rough Guides/Diana Jarvis **133** The Museum of Brands, Packaging and Advertising © Eleanor Farmer **134** SS Great Britain © SS Great Britain **136** Battle re-enactment © Tim Gainey/Alamy **138** Culloden Moor © Epicscotlan **139** Blists Hill Victorian Town, Ironbridge © TravelibUK/Alamy; Iron Bridge © Paul Thompson/Getty Images **140** Summer Solstice, Stonehenge © Rough Guides/Tim Draper **141** Beamish © Paul Thompson Images/Alamy **142** Tea dance © Nick Hanna/Alamy **146** Big Pit National Coal Museum © Chris Howes/Alamy **148** Glastonbury Tor © Guy Edwards/Getty Images **149** Skara Brae © Patrick Dieudonne/Corbis

5. Thrills and spills

Introduction Climbing in Snowdonia © David Pickford/Getty Images **153** Bosigran Ridge © Baxter Bradford/Photolibrary **154** Husky © Martin Dunford **156** Faerie Pools of Skye © Edward Aves **161** Surfing the Seven Bore © Philip Mugridge/Alamy **164** Gliding at Sutton Bank © Mike Kipling/Alamy **165** Skiing, Nevis Range © Scottish Viewpoint/Alamy **166** Hiking Hadrian's Wall Path © Ian Cumming/Axiom **176** Mountain biking in Wales © Wig Worland/Alamy **177** Canoeing © Diana Jarvis **179** Zorbing in Dorset © Jack Sulivan/Alamy **180** Sailing in The Broads © Tim Graham/Getty Images **183** Wreck of SMS Dresden, Scapa Flow © Simon Brown/Photolibrary **185** Bushcraft in the Gower © Dryad Bushcraft **186** Whitewater rafting, Wales © Paul Thompson Images/Alamy **189** Honister Slate Mine © Ashley Cooper/Alamy

6. Forty winks

Introduction The Mod Room, Hotel Pelirocco © Hotel Pelirocco **190** Terrace at The Scarlet Hotel © The Scarlet Hotel **191** Geodesic dome and Nomad tunnel-tent, fforestcamp © fforestcamp **193** Breakfast room at Underleigh House © Underleigh House **195** La Rosa caravan (top right) © Alf Alderson **199** Cley Windmill © Tom Mackie/Alamy **200** Balladrach Bothy (bottom right) © Balladrach Bothy **202** The Play Room, Hotel Pelirocco (middle) © Hotel Pelirocco **206** Belle Toute Lighthouse © Tim Gartside/Alamy **207** Wildlife and lodge © Allerdale Wilderness Lodge **209** Devonshire Arms © Devonshire Arms **210** Thatched cottage and caravan © Under the Thatch **211** Langar Hall © Langar Hall **213** Bishop's Suite, Durham Castle © Durham Castle **214** Beaufort Bar and afternoon tea, The Savoy © The Savoy Hotel **215** Dining Room, Woodlands Country House © Woodlands Country House **219** Lucknam Park © Lucknam Park **222** The Piano Room © Augill Castle **225** The Sitting Room, The Temple © The Temple

7. The birds and the bees

Introduction Puffin © Steve Allen/Getty Images **226** Grey seal © Ernie Jones/Alamy **229** Razorbill © Tul De Roy/Getty Images **230** Orford Ness

Nature Reserve © David Chapman/Alamy **231** Epping Forest © Photoshot Holdings/Alamy **233** New Forest ponies © Rough Guides/Diana Jarvis **234** Malham Cove © Alan Curt/Alamy **235** View from Stanage Edge © Rough Guides/Tim Draper **238** Badger © Andrew Parkinson/Getty Images **246** Avocets © David Tipling/Alamy **247** Otter © Mike Powles/Getty Images **249** Lundy © Last Refuge/Getty Images **250** Bluebell wood © David Clapp/Alamy **251** Bumblebee © Chris Gomersall/Alamy **253** Bottlenose dolphin © Terry Whittaker/Alamy **255** Centre for Alternative Technology © Keith Morris/Alamy **257** Daffodils © Darryl Gill/Alamy **259** Pistyll Rhaeadr waterfall © Rough Guides/Paul Whitfield **261** Northern lights over Scotland © Wildlife GmbH/Alamy

8. Are we nearly there yet?
Introduction Oblivion, Alton Towers © Andrew Fox/Alamy **264** Puppets © Little Angel Puppet Theatre **265** Pooh Sticks at Poohsticks Bridge © Jim Holden/Alamy **266** Linlithgow Palace © Neiliann Tait/Alamy **267** Seven Stories © Doug Hall **272** Magna © Rough Guides/Diana Jarvis **273** Xstrata Treetop Walkway, Kew Gardens © Maurice Crooks/Alamy **275** Legoland © Howard Davies **276** The Forbidden Corner © Christine Whitehead/Alamy **281** Rodders and Ash at Monkey World © Monkey World **282** Fossils, Lyme Regis © Rough Guides/Diana Jarvis **284** Eureka! © Eureka! **285** Coasteering © Camera Lucida Lifestyle/Alamy **287** Bewilderwood © Martin Dunford **288** Shambala Festival © Fergus Coyle/Shambala Festival **291** Camel Trail © Images Europe/Alamy **292** Rockpooling, Marloes Sands © Camera Lucida/Alamy **293** Deer stag © Ian Hainsworth/Alamy

9. The Sea, the Sea
Introduction Beachy Head © Rough Guides/Tim Draper **297** Margate Shell Grotto © Edward Aves **298** Pembrokeshire coast © CW Images/Alamy **301** Southwold beach © Richard Surman/Photolibrary; Lighthouse, Southwold © Diana Jarvis **302** Saints Bay, Guernsey © Hemis/Alamy **303** Filey beach © John Devlin/Alamy **309** Watergate Bay © Charlie Surbey/Photolibrary **310** Durdle Door © Diana Jarvis **312** South Shore Promenade, Blackpool © Gordon Sinclair/Alamy **321** Another Place, Crosby Beach © Richard Freestone/Alamy **323** Sea kayaking in the Highlands © Robert Harding/Alamy **324** White Cliffs of Dover © Rough Guides/Tim Draper **326** Kitesurfing © PCL/Alamy **329** The Old Man of Hoy © Nick Carraway/Alamy **332** Bamburgh Castle and beach © Lee Frost/Getty Images **333** Porth Dinllaen © The Photolibrary Wales/Alamy

10. All the world's a stage
Introduction Birmingham Royal Ballet © Alternative Shotz/Alamy **334** Globe Theatre © Linda Nylind/Shakespeare's Globe Image Library **335** Thomas Hardy's Cottage © Rough Guides/Diana Jarvis **338** York Mystery Plays © Purple Marbles/Alamy **340** Still from *Monty Python and the Holy Grail* © Moviestore Collection

344 Filming *Robin Hood* at Freshwater West © CW Images/Alamy **348** Still from *Withnail and I* © Moviestore Collection **349** Keith Harding's World of Mechanical Music © Rob Andrews **351** Gig at The Union Chapel © Rosie Reed Gold **354** Performance at dusk © Minack Theatre **355** Ballet at Sadler's Wells © Jane Hobson/Alamy **356** Shetland Folk Festival © Dave Donaldson/Alamy **356** Chapter Arts Centre © Neil Setchfield **359** Electric Cinema © Electric Cinema **362** Charleston Farmhouse © Arcaid/Alamy **364** Greenway Quay and the River Dart © Stephen Bond/Alamy **365** Welsh Male voice choir © Rough Guides/Paul Whitfield **366** Still from *The Wicker Man* © British Lion/The Kobal Collection **367** Shakespeare statue © Colin Underhill/Alamy **370** Sharmanka © Sharmanka Kinetic Theatre **371** Bookslam © Nick Cunard

11. A question of sport
Introduction Test Match at Lord's © Anthony Eva/Getty Images **372** The Great North Run © Ian Walton/Getty Images **373** Highland Games © Rough Guides/Helena Smith **375** Wheelbarrow race, Cotswold Olimpicks © Mark Boulton/Alamy **376** Golf at St Andrews © Phil Inglis/Getty Images **378** World Darts Championships, Lakeside © Christopher Lee/Getty Images **383** Beach volleyball, Yellowave © Elliot Nichol/Alamy **384** Jack Wills Varsity Polo day © Andy Turner **386** Cowes Week © Kos Picture Source/Getty Images **387** Boxing at York Hall © Dean Mouhtaropoulos/Getty Images **388** Shrovetide Football, Ashbourne © Peter Macdiarmid/Getty Images **390** Grand National © Glyn Kirk/Getty Images **391** Andy Murray at Wimbledon © Bob Martin/Getty Images **392** Isle of Man TT races © Dan Kitwood/Getty Images **395** Cumberland and Westmorland wrestling © David Reed/Alamy

12. High days and holidays
Introduction Bestival © Tabatha Fireman/Getty Images **396** Notting Hill Carnival © Oli Scarff/Getty Images **397** Lewes Bonfire Society parade © Rough Guides/Mark Thomas **399** Last Night of the Proms © Ben Stanstall/Getty Images **404** Bog snorkelling © Rough Guides/Diana Jarvis **405** Bognor Birdman © Matt Griggs/Alamy **410** Bristol International Balloon Fiesta © Diana Jarvis **411** Hogmanay © Rough Guides/Michele Grant **413** The Great Yorkshire Show © Wayne Hutchinson/Alamy **414** Llangollen International Musical Eisteddfod © Rough Guides/Diana Jarvis **415** Diwali © Stringer/Getty Images **416** Up Helly Aa © Doug Houghton/Alamy **417** Hay Festival of Literature and the Arts © Diana Jarvis **419** Robin Hood Festival © Greg Evans/Alamy **420** Pride, Brighton © Edward Simons/Alamy **421** Whitby Gothic Weekend © Tommy Louth/Alamy **423** Common Ridings © P. Tomkins/Visit Scotland **425** Obby Oss, Padstow © Roger Cracknell/Alamy **426** Chinese New Year © Chris Kewish/Alamy **428** Bestival © Tabatha Fireman/Getty Images **432** Glastonbury Festival © Timothy Allen/Axiom **436** WOMAD © C. Brandon/Getty Images

13. Grand designs
Introduction The Angel of the North © Brian Lawrence/Getty Images **437** Baltic Centre for Contemporary Art © Roger Coulam/Alamy **439** De la Warr Pavilion © Roger Bamber/Alamy **440** Glasgow School of Art © Rough Guides/Helena Smith **441** The Weather Project, Tate Modern © Guy Bell/Alamy **447** The Singing, Ringing Tree © Alan Novelli **448** Gallery interior © The National Gallery, London **449** Green Man carving, Rosslyn Chapel © John Heseltine/Alamy **450** Jimmy Floyd, Trapping My First Job, 1959 © Ashington Group Trustees **451** Ely Cathedral © Rod Edwards/Alamy **453** Banksy street art, Bristol © Matt Cardy/Getty Images **454** Wales Millennium Centre, Cardiff © Rough Guides/Diana Jarvis **455** BAPS Shri Swaminarayan Mandir © Rough Guides/Mark Thomas **456** Jupiter Artland © Helena Smith **457** St Paul's Cathedral © Mark Thomas **459** Yorkshire Sculpture Park © Rough Guides/Diana Jarvis **462** Middlesbrough Institute of Modern Art © Mike Kipling/Alamy **465** Rose Window, York Minster © Rough Guides/Diana Jarvis **467** The Andrew Logan Museum of Sculpture © Rough Guides/Diana Jarvis **468** Wallace Collection © Alex Segre/Alamy **470** Barbara Hepworth Museum and Sculpture Garden © Diana Jarvis **471** Lloyd's Building, Open House Weekend © Andrew Holt/Alamy

14. Take the high road
Introduction Road across Rannoch Moor © Gary Cook/Alamy **472** London to Brighton Veteran Car Run © Eleanor Bentall **473** Snowdon Mountain Railway © Grasstrax/Alamy **474** Tall ship, Jubilee Sailing Trust © James Marshall Pilgrim **476** Jack Mytton Way © itdarbs/Alamy **477** Mersey Ferry and Liverpool waterfront © McCoy Wynne/Alamy **478** Offa's Dyke Path sign **479** Ribblehead Viaduct © Rolf Richardson/Alamy **480** Mountain biking on the Ridgeway © Wig Worland/Alamy **481** Pontcysyllte Aqueduct © Alan Novelli **482** Routemaster bus © Peter Macdiarmid/Getty Images **484** Isles of Scilly © Skyscan Photography/Alamy **485** Walk across the sands, Morecambe Bay © Philip Dunn/Alamy **490** Bluebell Railway © Bob Mazzer/Alamy **491** Parkland Walk, north London © Off The Roll/Alamy **494** Falkirk Wheel © Keith Hunter/Alamy **496** Heights of Abraham cable car © Robert Morris/Alamy **497** Alpine road, Loch Torridon © Jonathan Andrew/Corbis **498** Barra Airfield, Traigh Mhòr © David Robertson/Alamy **499** Swaledale, Yorkshire Dales © Joe Cornish/Photolibrary **500** Land's End sign © Bailey Cooper/Alamy

INDEX BY COUNTY

INDEX BY THEME

A–Z INDEX